GREAT BARS OF NEW YORK CITY

JAMES T. & KARLA L. MURRAY

WORDS BY DAN Q. DAO

GREAT BARS OF NEW YORK CITY

30 OF MANHATTAN'S FAVORITE STORIED DRINKING ESTABLISHMENTS

PRESTEL

MUNICH · LONDON · NEW YORK

CONTENTS

"IF YOU WANT TO KNOW ABOUT A CULTURE, SPEND A NIGHT IN ITS BARS."

ERNEST HEMINGWAY

After the publication of our latest book, *Store Front NYC: Photographs of the City's Independent Shops, Past and Present*, we were pleased that our ongoing work documenting the city's beloved neighborhood store fronts was again met with acclaim and critical praise. There is a physical beauty to these small shops that native New Yorkers, visitors, and even those who have never been to New York can instantly see. Yet we realized there was more for us to tell, and we knew what direction our story must take: we were going to concentrate on what many consider to be the heart of New York City's culture and neighborhoods—its bars. We also wanted to showcase our interior photography, something we have never featured in any of our previous books.

Bars have always been melting pots; they're places where people from all backgrounds and cultures can mingle and share stories while enjoying a drink, and where relationships often start. Above all, in New York City, where millions of people are crowded into a relatively small amount of land but often live in isolating apartments, the bar serves as a home away from home, an antidote to loneliness, or even a workspace.

When selecting the thirty locations to feature in this publication, we decided to concentrate on only the borough of Manhattan. We've chosen to showcase many historic establishments, often elegant in appearance, which evoke stepping back into a grander time. These include the Campbell, designed as a thirteenth-century Florentine palace for railroad tycoon John W. Campbell, King Cole Bar, which is credited as the birthplace of the Bloody Mary cocktail, and Old Town Bar and Restaurant, known as a gathering place for many literary greats (as well as for its iconic shoulder-height ceramic urinals).

We've also included many former speakeasies that sold illegal alcoholic beverages during the Prohibition era—from 1920 to 1933—including Holiday Cocktail Lounge in the East Village and Pete's Tavern in Gramercy Park. (Pete's was the only bar that legally remained open during Prohibition due to its proximity to Tammany Hall, the city's political machine at that time—the bar's main room was even disguised as a flower shop so that politicians could enter under the pretense of looking for flowers).

We additionally feature many lesser-known dive bars, including some that open at 8 a.m., a rarity in New York. These include Milano's Bar, Spring Lounge, and Rudy's Bar & Grill, one of the city's last affordable "working man" bars, where you can still get a beer and a whiskey and not break the bank while eating a free hot dog.

Most of the photography included in this book was completed in 2023, as we wanted to concentrate on bars currently in business. However, there are a number of establishments that we photographed in the past and would have loved to highlight—including the renowned Lenox Lounge in Harlem, Mars Bar in the East Village, and Chumley's in the West Village—which unfortunately all fell victim to economic pressures, increasing rents, and rapidly changing demographics.

We invite you to pay attention to the often-overlooked details inside the bars we've photographed. A few notable examples are the two human leg bones hanging from the ceiling at P. J. Clarke's that are known as an Irish American good luck charm; the stained-glass windows and backbar insets made by the world-famous Tiffany & Co. at Peter McManus Cafe; the original sign that hangs in the entrance of the Stonewall Inn indicating that the establishment was a raided premises by the New York Police Department in 1969; the turkey wishbones hanging at McSorley's Old Ale House, put there during World War I by doughboys projecting hopes for a safe return from the war; the oil paintings found above the wood paneling at Minetta Tavern depicting scenes of Greenwich Village, painted by Holden D. Wetherbee in 1953; and the saloon licenses dating back to the 1800s hanging at Fanelli Cafe.

We hope our book encourages you to visit one of your neighborhood bars so that they stay in business for many more generations to come. And just as the sign posted inside Jimmy's Corner advises its patrons, "Let's not discuss politics here," and instead have a friendly conversation while sitting over a drink and escaping the noise and stress of urban life.

JAMES T. & KARLA L. MURRAY

McSORLEY'S OLD ALE HOUSE

15 EAST 7TH STREET, EAST VILLAGE

In a city once brimming with Irish pubs, McSorley's Old Ale House stands out not only as one of the oldest still in operation but also one of the most iconic and beloved. It has remained standing through numerous moments of social upheaval in America, from the years before the Civil War to Prohibition, during which it continued to secretly serve alcohol by advertising it as "near beer."

For much of its history, the bar enforced a strict no-women policy, gaining notoriety for its slogan, "Good ale, raw onions, and no ladies." However, in 1970 women filed a lawsuit against the bar, *Seidenberg v. McSorleys' Old Ale House*, which ultimately resulted in McSorley's law, prohibiting sex discrimination in bars, hotels, restaurants, airplanes, golf clubs, and other public accommodations.

Now, McSorley's has earned the distinction of being one of the longest continuously operating bars in America. And despite its great age, it has remained remarkably unchanged: one of its most noted features is its perpetually sawdust-covered floors, a holdover from a time in which sawdust was used to soak up moisture from the muddy, damp shoes of workers coming in from blue-collar jobs.

McSorley's is most frequently said to have been opened in 1854, by Irish immigrant John McSorley. First called the Old House at Home, the bar catered largely to his fellow countrymen, many of whom worked labor-intensive jobs at factories and breweries. It also served as a space for political mobilization within the Irish diaspora. By the late nineteenth century, when it was owned by McSorley's son, Bill, it had become a meeting place for the Ancient Order of Hibernians, an Ireland-based organization that provided aid and assistance to Irish Americans. It was also a favored rendezvous for members of the Democratic political machine Tammany Hall.

While these everyman origins are part of the bar's timeless appeal, it's also noted for its long roster of A-list patrons, which have included US presidents going back to Teddy Roosevelt and beyond, including Abraham Lincoln—who in 1860 allegedly ran to McSorley's after delivering the Cooper Union address that's often cited as helping him win his party's presidential nomination.

McSorley's was considered to be notable starting in the early twentieth century, having been central to the Ashcan School of art, a movement that included artists like George Bellows, John Sloan, and Robert Henri, who focused on illustrating quotidian life in working-class neighborhoods. By its heyday in the mid-1900s, McSorley's patronage had come to encompass a who's who of literary and cultural luminaries from various decades, including Harry Houdini, F. Scott Fitzgerald, E. E. Cummings, and *New Yorker* writer Joseph Mitchell. In the latter half of the century, it's believed Hunter S. Thompson and John Lennon were among those who had visited.

The ownership of McSorley's has always remained close to its original community. It was kept in the family for nearly a century until 1936, when descendant Bill McSorley sold it to longtime employee Daniel O'Connell. His daughter, Dorothy O'Connell Kirwan, took it over next—initially resisting demands to allow women to enter. In 1977, Dorothy's son Danny Kirwan sold it to longtime bartender and night manager Matthew Maher, who, like original owner John McSorley, was an Irish immigrant. Upon Maher's passing in 2020, his daughter Teresa Maher de la Haba took over, maintaining and upholding its traditions. She is, notably, the first woman to work behind the bar.

Today, you can pull up a seat at the bar to enjoy its two styles of house beer: the flagship McSorley's Ale, an Irish-style malted ale, and the McSorley's Dark, a heavier variety. It's recommended that you bring at least one friend, since the bar has a tradition of serving beer in a pair of small mugs, called schooners, as opposed to a single pint.

While you're there, seek out the many items that tell of the bar's past—from a real wanted poster offering a reward for the capture of Lincoln's assassin, John Wilkes Booth, to a bust memorializing a visit from John F. Kennedy before he became president. Last but not least are the turkey wishbones hanging from an old gas lamp. "Many of the turkey wishbones were hung up by doughboys during World War I as wishful symbols of a safe return from the war," Maher de la Haba explains. "When they returned, they would remove the wishbone they had placed there. The bones left dangling represent those who never came back."

Relics like these speak to McSorley's lasting significance and emotional connection to those who've visited. "Some things customers left at the bar just because they wanted to add to our collection," Maher de la Haba adds. "We have a good number of old fireman hats, and the orange one is from a fireman who was at the World Trade Center on 9/11."

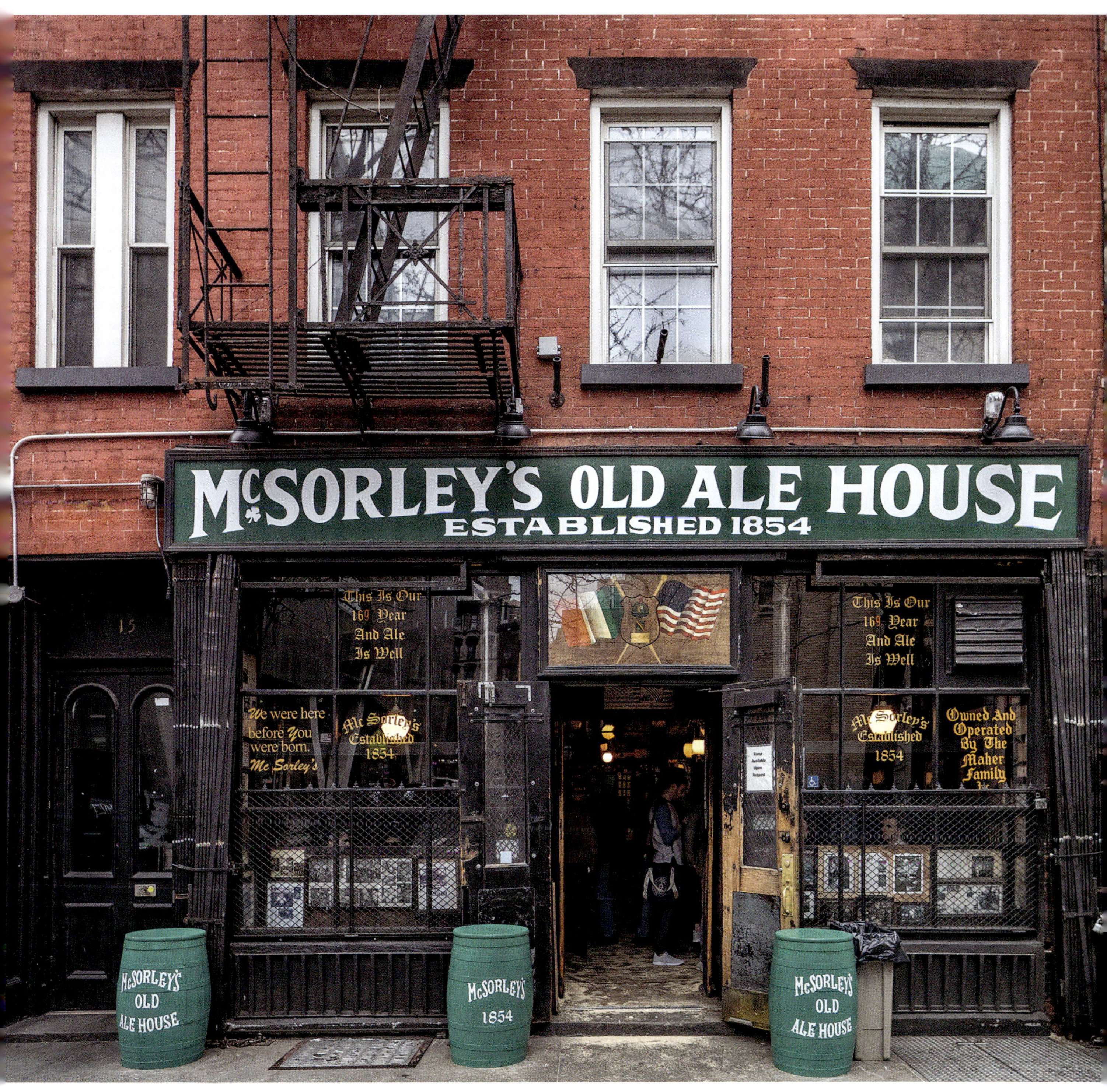

ABOVE   *McSorley's was originally an all-male establishment, known by its slogan, "Good ale, raw onions, and no ladies."*

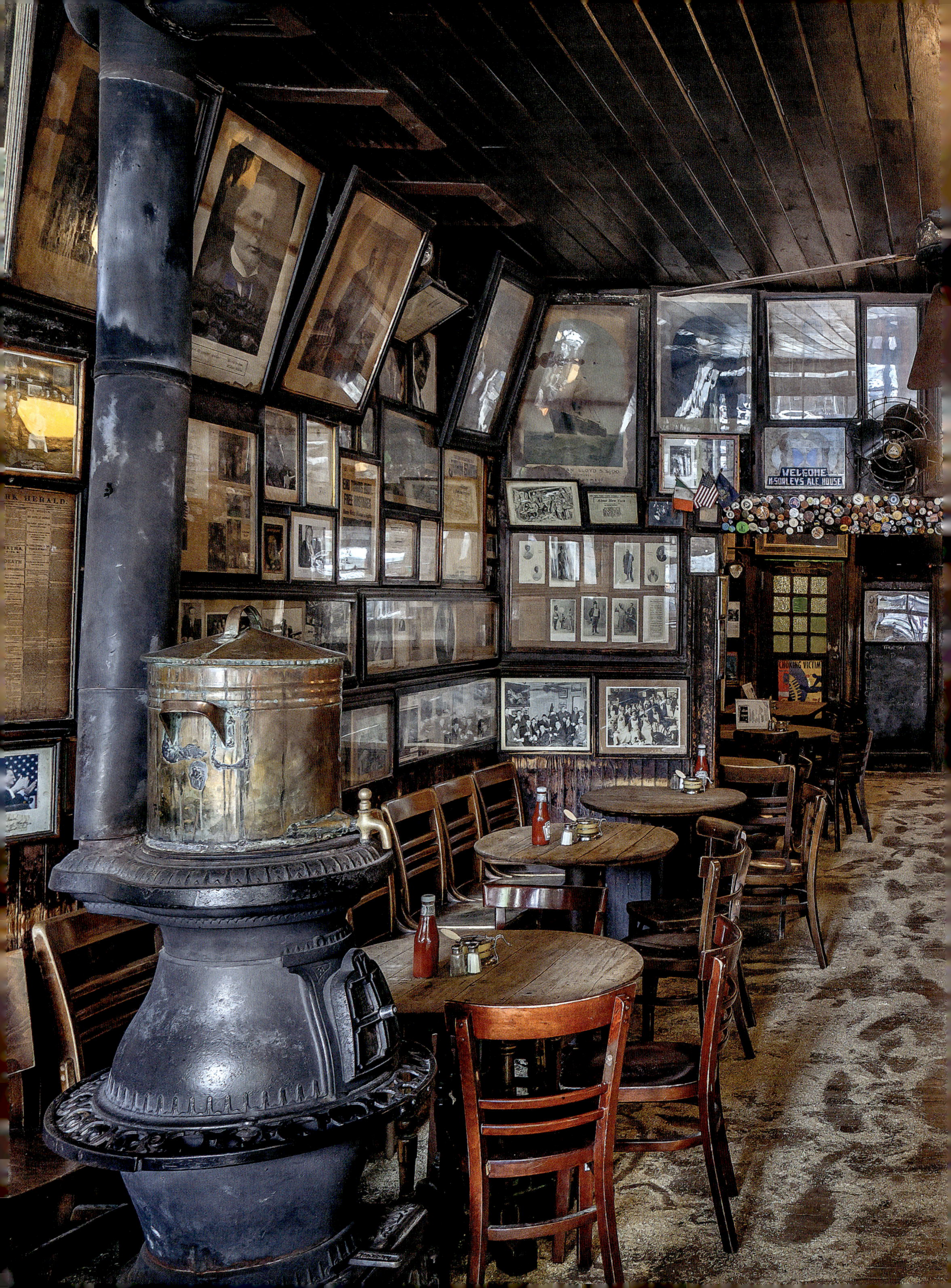

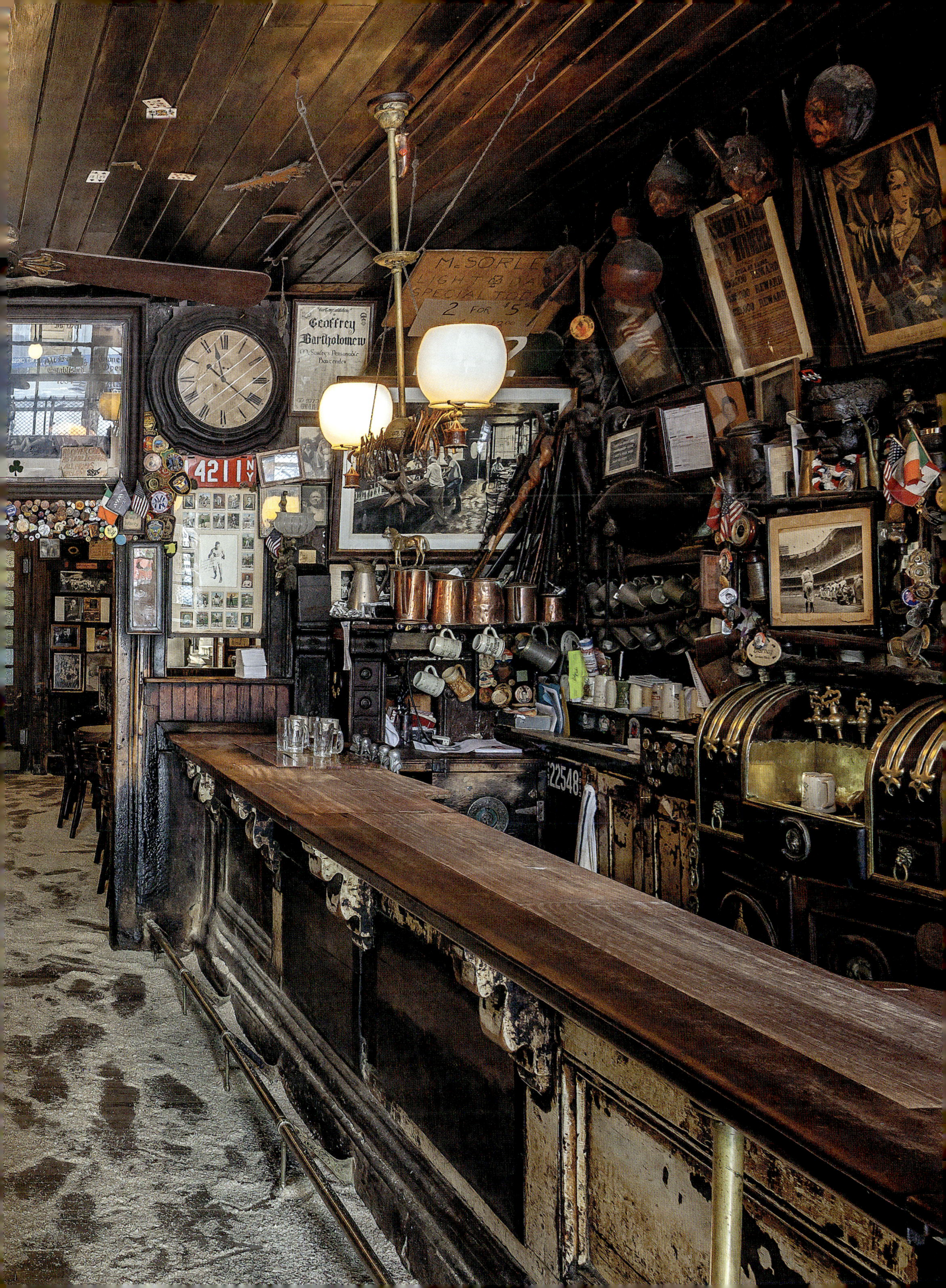

McSORLEY'S
LIGHT & DARK
SPECIAL TODAY
2 FOR $5
Geoffrey Bartholomew
McSorley's Personable Bartender
4211 NY
22548

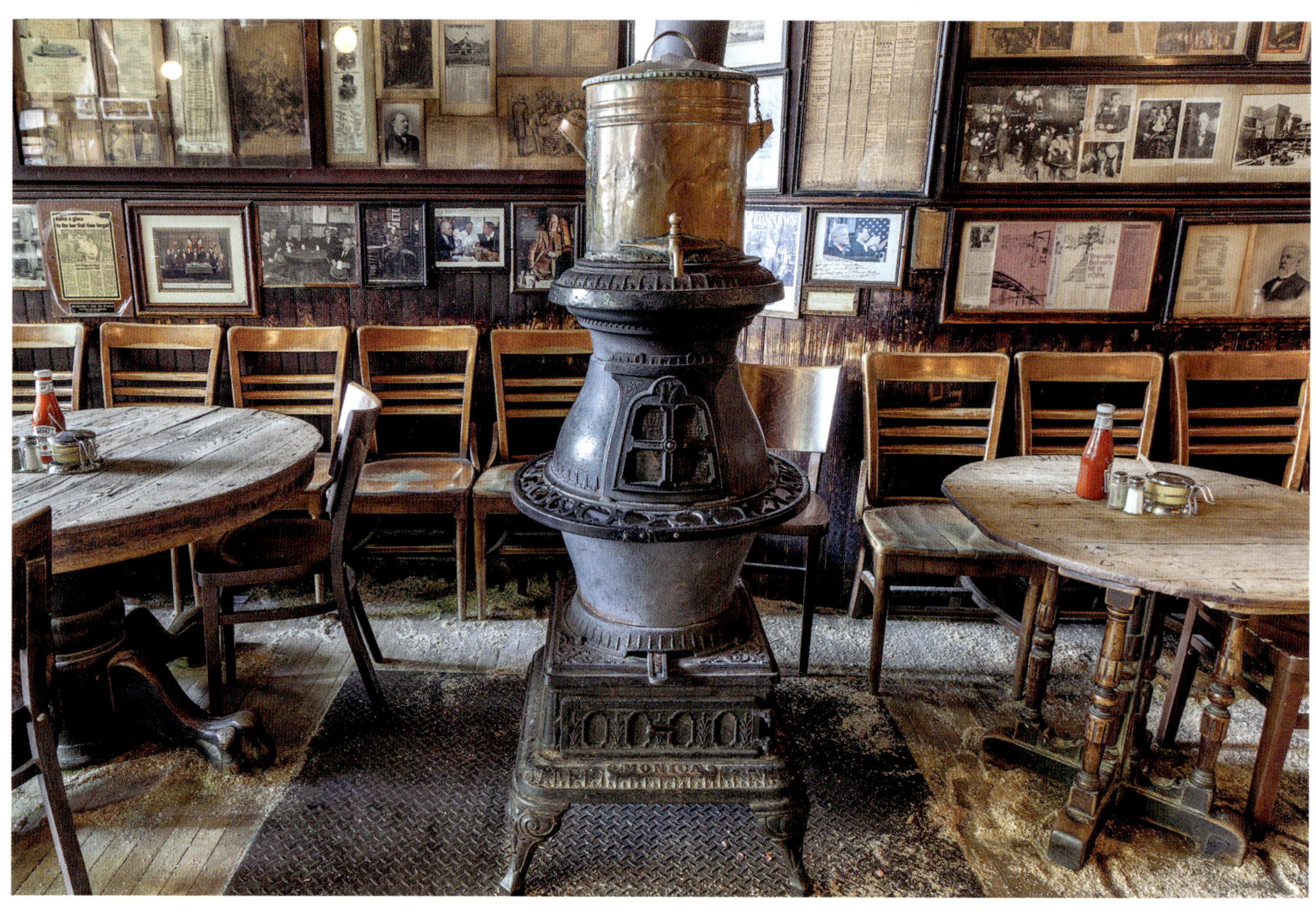

MONROE

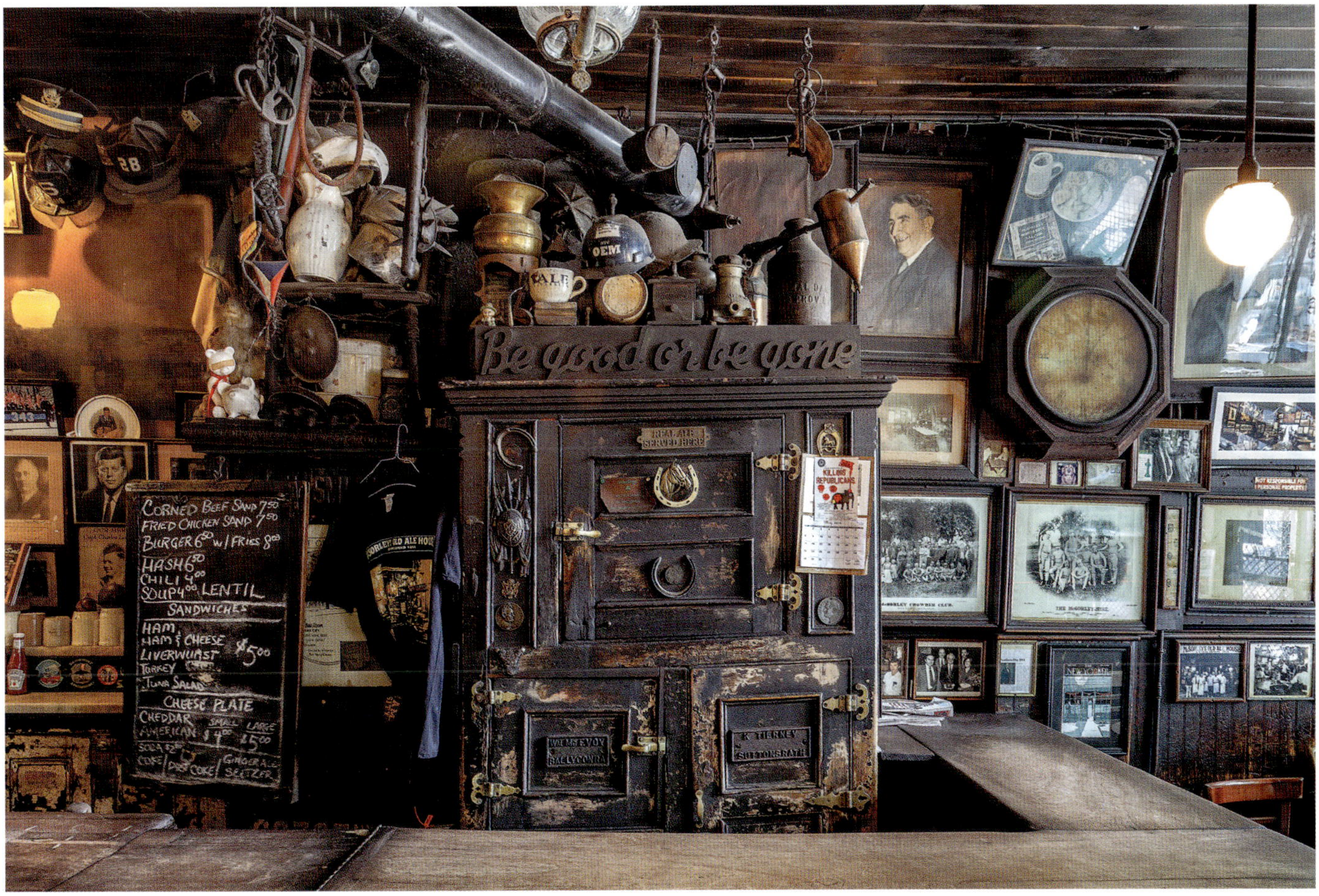

Be good or be gone
REAL ALE
SERVED HERE
CORNED BEEF SAND 7.50
FRIED CHICKEN SAND 7.50
BURGER 6.50 w/ FRIES 8.00
HASH 6.50
CHILI 4.00
SOUP 4.00 LENTIL
SANDWICHES
HAM
HAM & CHEESE
LIVERWURST $5.00
TURKEY
TUNA SALAD
CHEESE PLATE
CHEDDAR SMALL LARGE
AMERICAN $4.00 $5.00
SODA $2
COKE / DIET COKE / GINGER ALE SELTZER
W. McEVOY BALLYCORRA
K. TIERNEY SHELTONBRATH

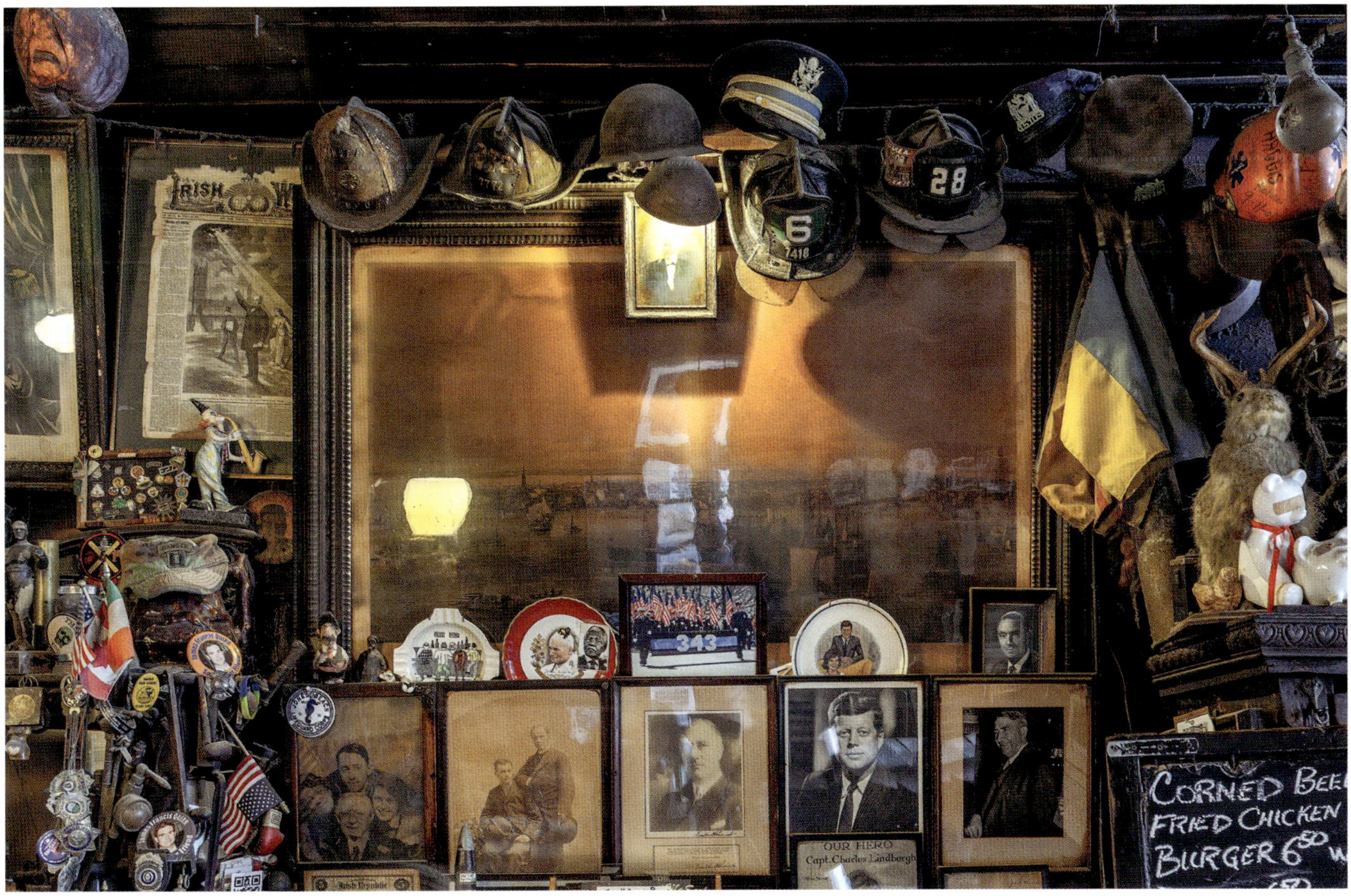

IRISH COW
6
4418
28
343
OUR HERO
Capt. Charles Lindbergh
CORNED BEEF
FRIED CHICKEN
BURGER 6.50 w

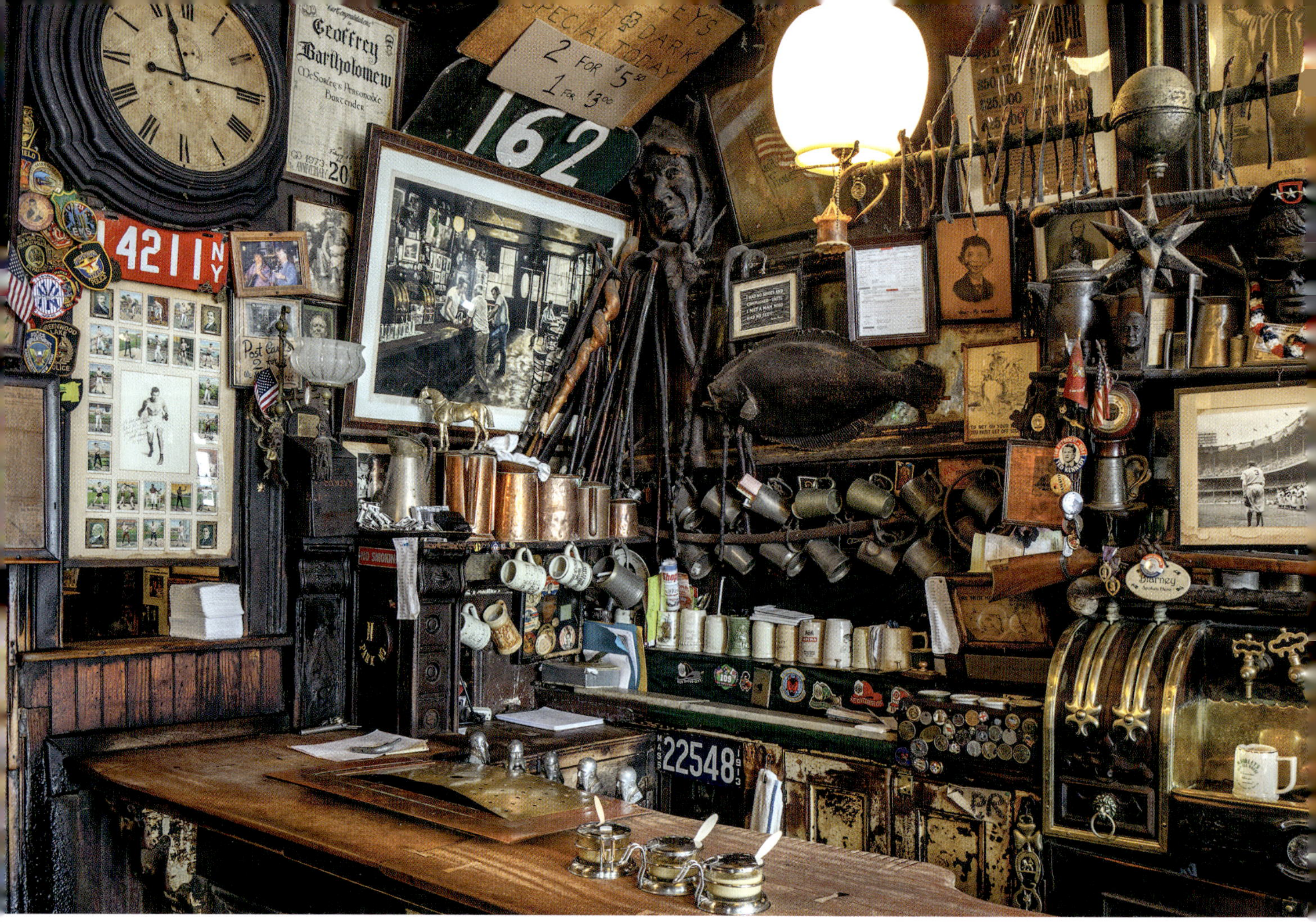

Geoffrey Bartholomew
McSorley's Personable Bartender
1973-20

SPECIAL TODAY
2 FOR $5
1 FOR $3.00

162

42 11 NY

22548 1913

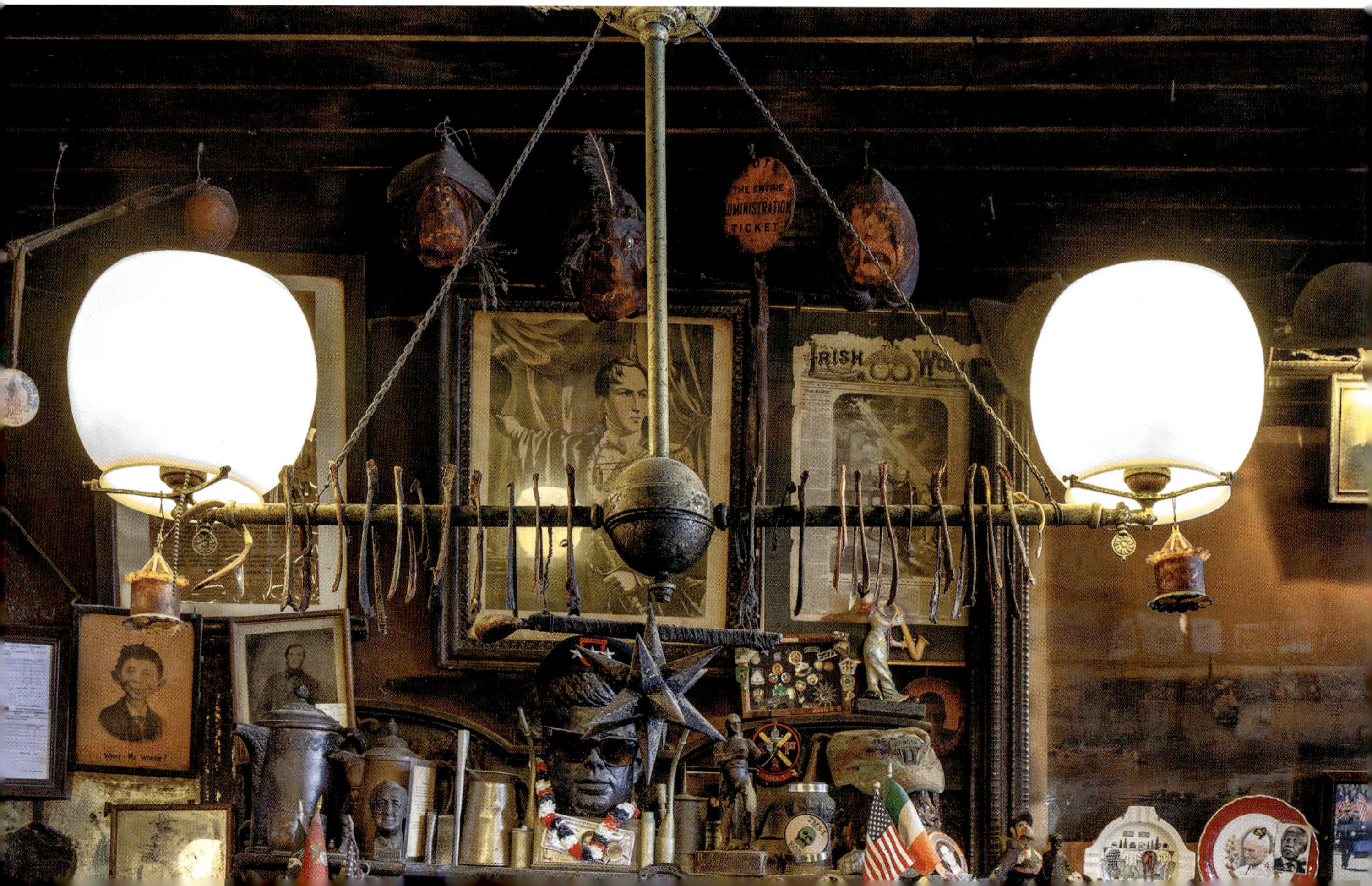

VOTE
THE ENTIRE
ADMINISTRATION
TICKET

IRISH WORLD

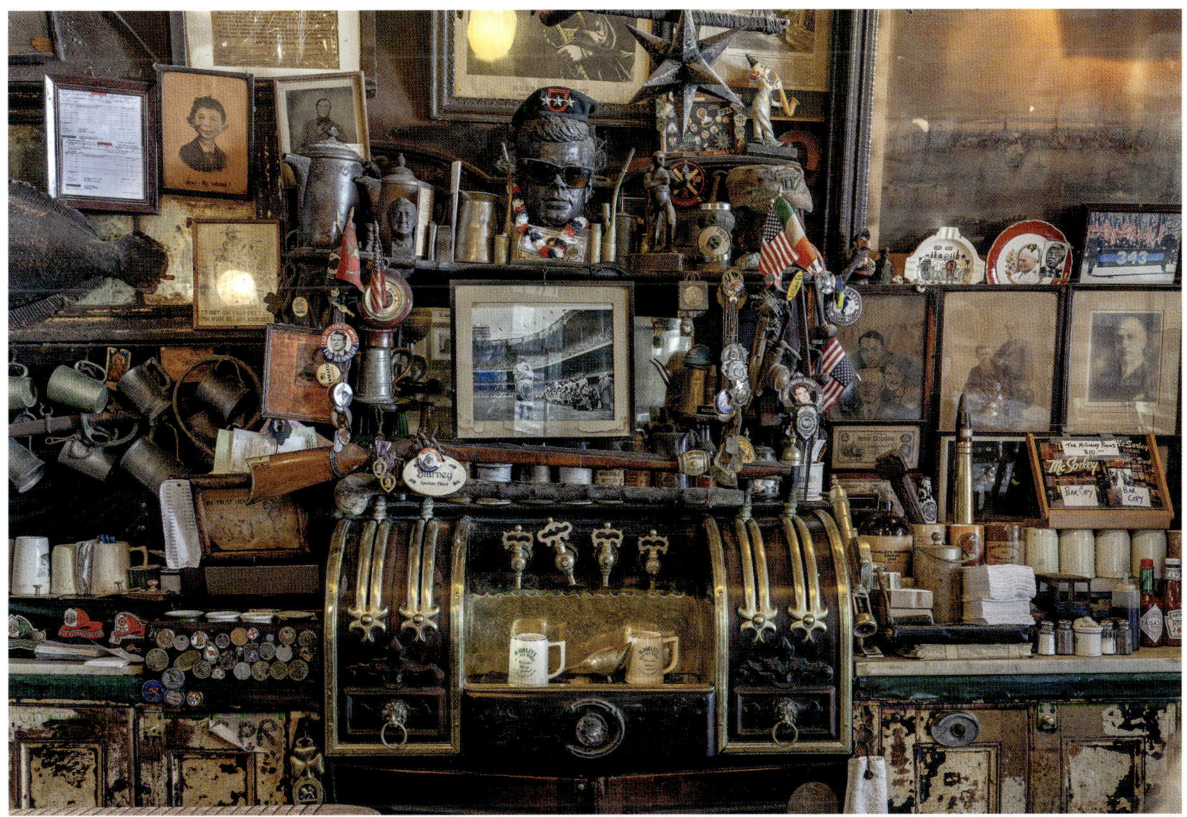

OPPOSITE BOTTOM *The turkey wishbones on the vintage gas lamp were hung by doughboys hoping for a safe return from World War I. When they came back, they would remove the bone they had placed. The ones left dangling represent those who never returned.*

ABOVE *McSorley's still has its original bar taps, wooden bar, and the pot-bellied stove from when it opened in 1854.*

THE CAMPBELL

GRAND CENTRAL TERMINAL,
15 VANDERBILT AVENUE, MIDTOWN EAST

Although the Campbell has only been operating as a swanky cocktail bar since 1999, it's been a famed room for far longer. Set clandestinely within Midtown East's Grand Central Terminal, the space, also referred to as the Campbell Apartment, was once used as the offices—and man cave—of a mysterious Jazz Age financier named John W. Campbell.

Campbell first acquired the lease for the 25-by-60-foot (8-by-18 meter) corner office in 1923 from none other than his friend and contemporary scion William Vanderbilt, who was then chair of the board of the New York City Railroad. Equipped with a kitchen, balcony, and 25-foot (8-meter) high ceilings, it was the perfect location for the tycoon, who lived with his wife nearby on Park Avenue.

The legendary design was undertaken by Augustus N. Allen—an architect known for masterminding grand Long Island estates and Manhattan townhouses—who took inspiration from a thirteenth-century Florentine palazzo (a reflection of the decadent tastes of the era). Located above the terminal's main concourse, it boasted leaded glass windows and a hand-painted ceiling.

Some of the Campbell Apartment's original furnishings included an oversized stone fireplace featuring Campbell's family coat of arms, as well as one of the world's largest hand-knotted Persian rugs that is estimated to cost over $5 million at the time of writing this book. After installing a grand piano and pipe organ, which would be used for performances by famous guests, Campbell regularly held decadent receptions for up to sixty people. He also employed a butler named Stackhouse.

The high-society revelry would go on until Campbell passed away in 1957. Over the years, the Campbell Apartment fell into disuse, and the furniture mysteriously vanished. In the following decades, the space was unceremoniously converted into a signalman's room before becoming an MTA police station and later a gun storage area. A small jail even sat where the bar sits today.

In 1999 Mark Grossich, CEO of Hospitality Holdings, Inc. (which also owns Midtown West's Carnegie Club), took ownership of the lease of the dilapidated Campbell Apartment. "There was water damage, wires hanging down, all the colors had faded, every piece of furniture was gone," Grossich told the *New York Post* of the space's condition at the time he took over. Through a painstaking $1.5 million renovation, he reincarnated the bar to its bygone splendor, filling it with dark wood trimmings and hiring painters to restore the colorful designs of the faux-wood ceiling beams. Modernizing the bar in the mixology-centric era of the early aughts, he also introduced premium liquors and classic cocktails that were enjoyed in the moody, dimly lit atmosphere.

In 2007, feeling that the bar was showing signs of age, Grossich tapped London-based interior designer Nina Campbell (no relation to the original owner) to execute a second renovation costing $350,000. Not wanting to close even for a night, Grossich asked the team to complete the entire process—which included laying carpet and installing new banquettes—in just twelve hours.

Early in its twenty-first-century reincarnation, the Campbell Apartment enjoyed—and continues to enjoy—a status as one of New York City's most beloved special occasion bars. Over the years, countless celebrities, politicians, and business owners would visit. These included former president Bill Clinton and actors like George Clooney and Scarlett Johansson. During this time, the bar was famously known for enforcing a no-sneakers dress code that sometimes drew bemusement for its old-school attitude.

After seventeen years running the bar, Grossich gave up the lease in 2016 to Scott Gerber and the Gerber Group, proprietors of trendy bars and clubs, who performed additional renovations and restorations to bring the bar back to its original glory. Today you can enter through a staircase from the terminal's balcony level to enjoy not only cocktails but trussed-up bar bites, like a charcuterie plate and fancy grilled cheese. Though the new owners have since adapted to modern times by doing away with the dress code and including the occasional pop song with the usual jazz tunes, the Campbell still offers a sense of grandeur that harkens back to an earlier time.

OPPOSITE   *The Campbell is tucked away in a discreet corner of Grand Central Terminal, at Forty-Second Street and Vanderbilt Avenue.*

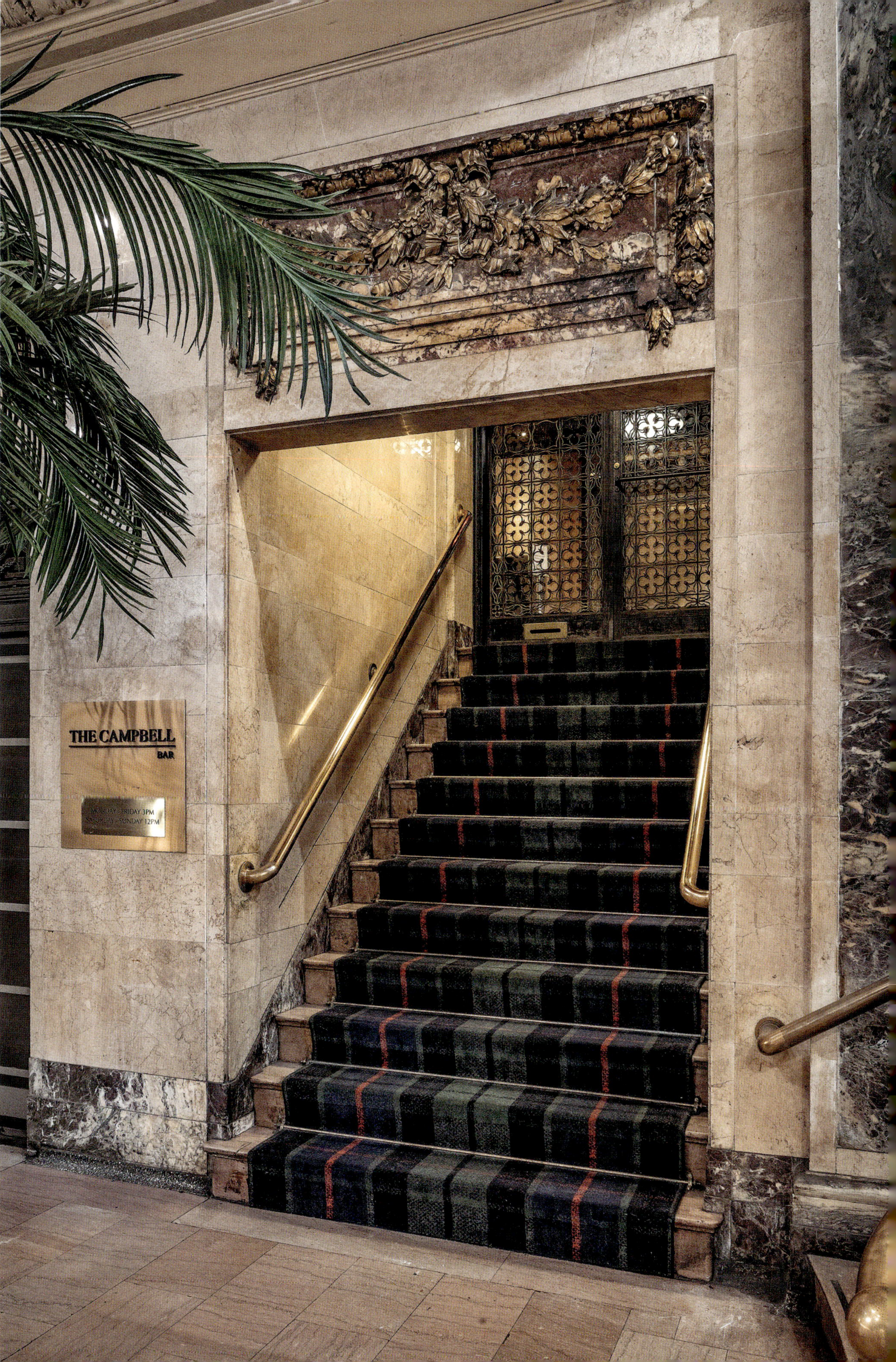

THE CAMPBELL
BAR
MONDAY - FRIDAY 3PM
SATURDAY - SUNDAY 12PM

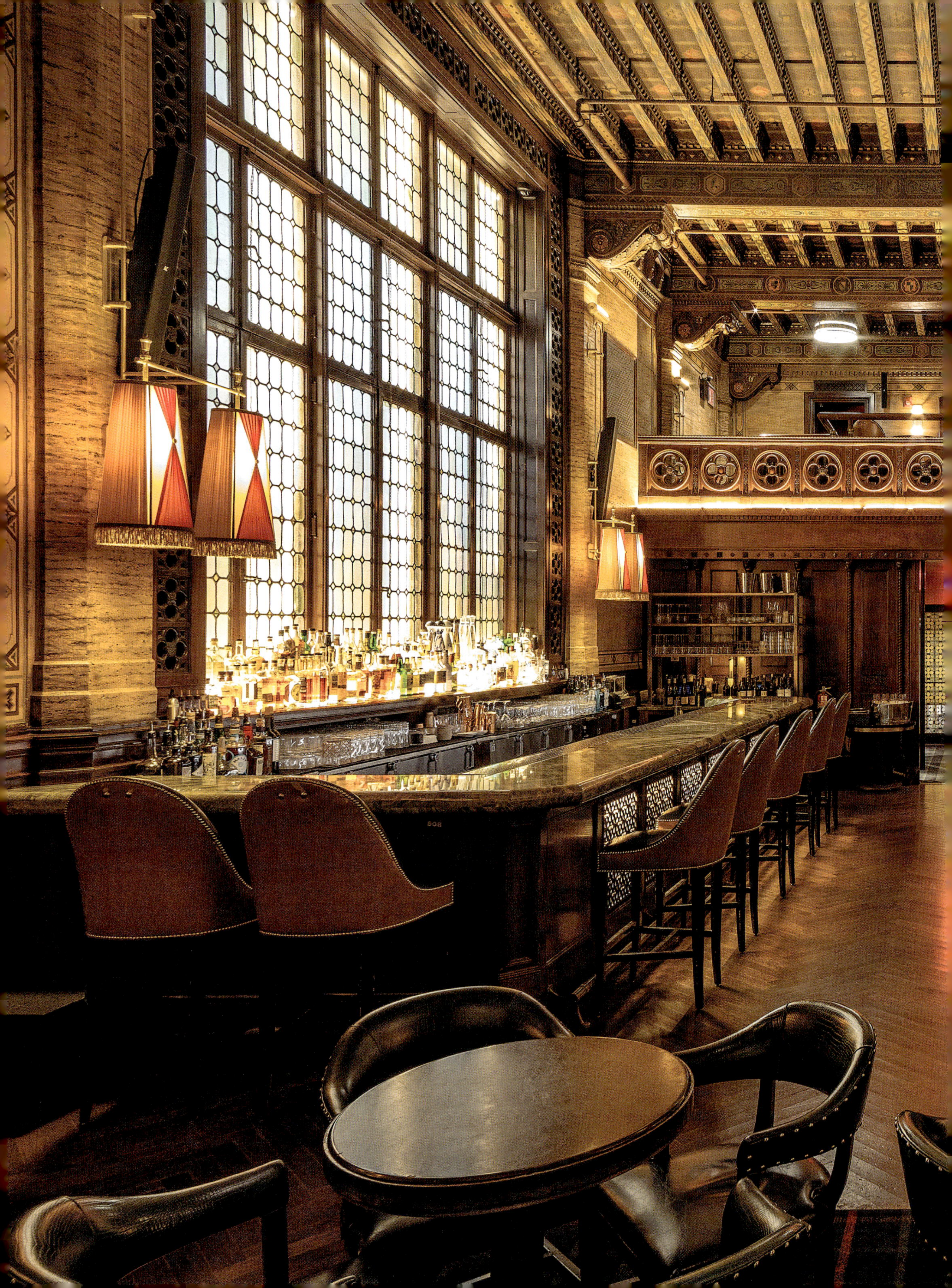

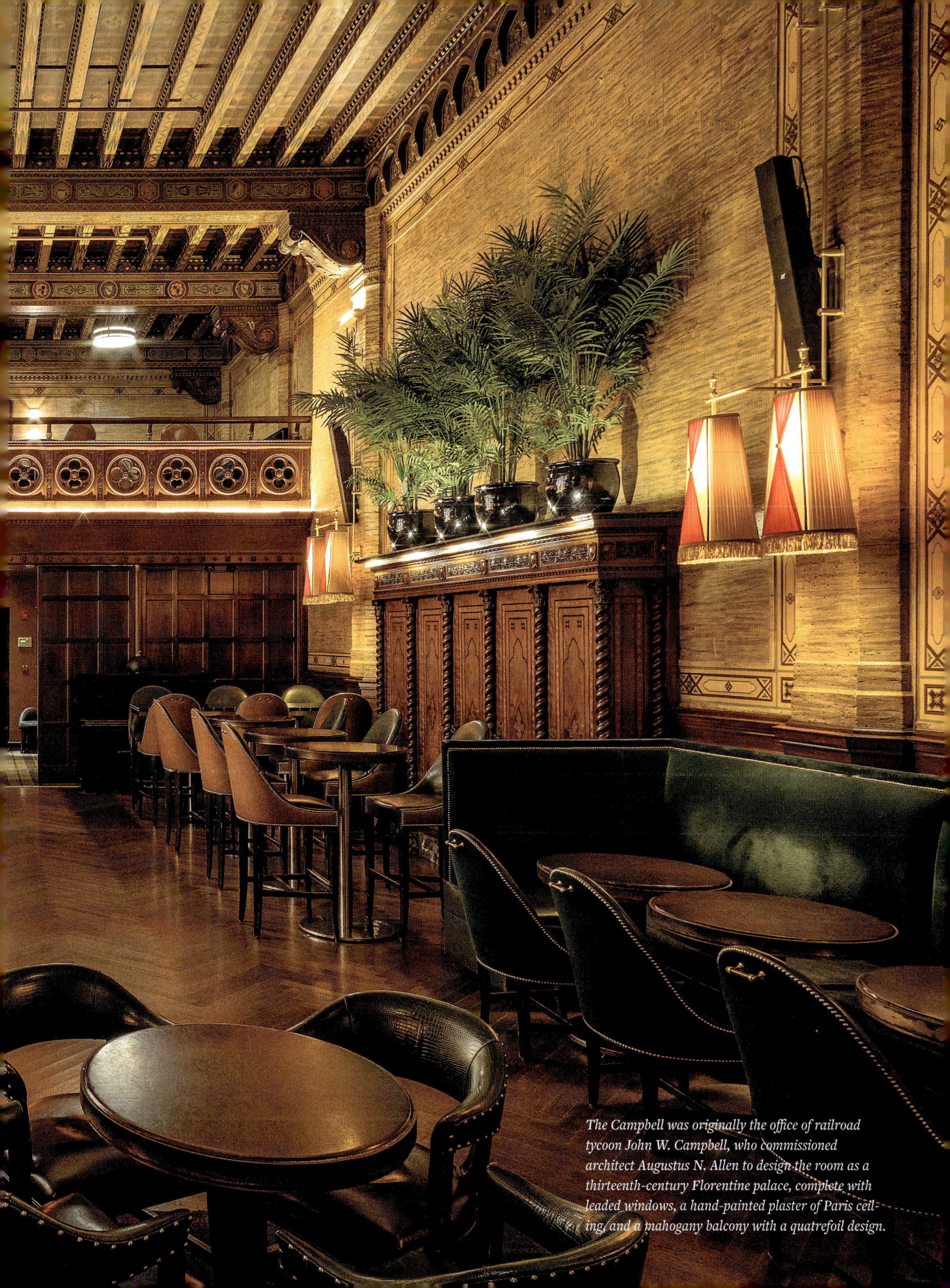

The Campbell was originally the office of railroad tycoon John W. Campbell, who commissioned architect Augustus N. Allen to design the room as a thirteenth-century Florentine palace, complete with leaded windows, a hand-painted plaster of Paris ceiling, and a mahogany balcony with a quatrefoil design.

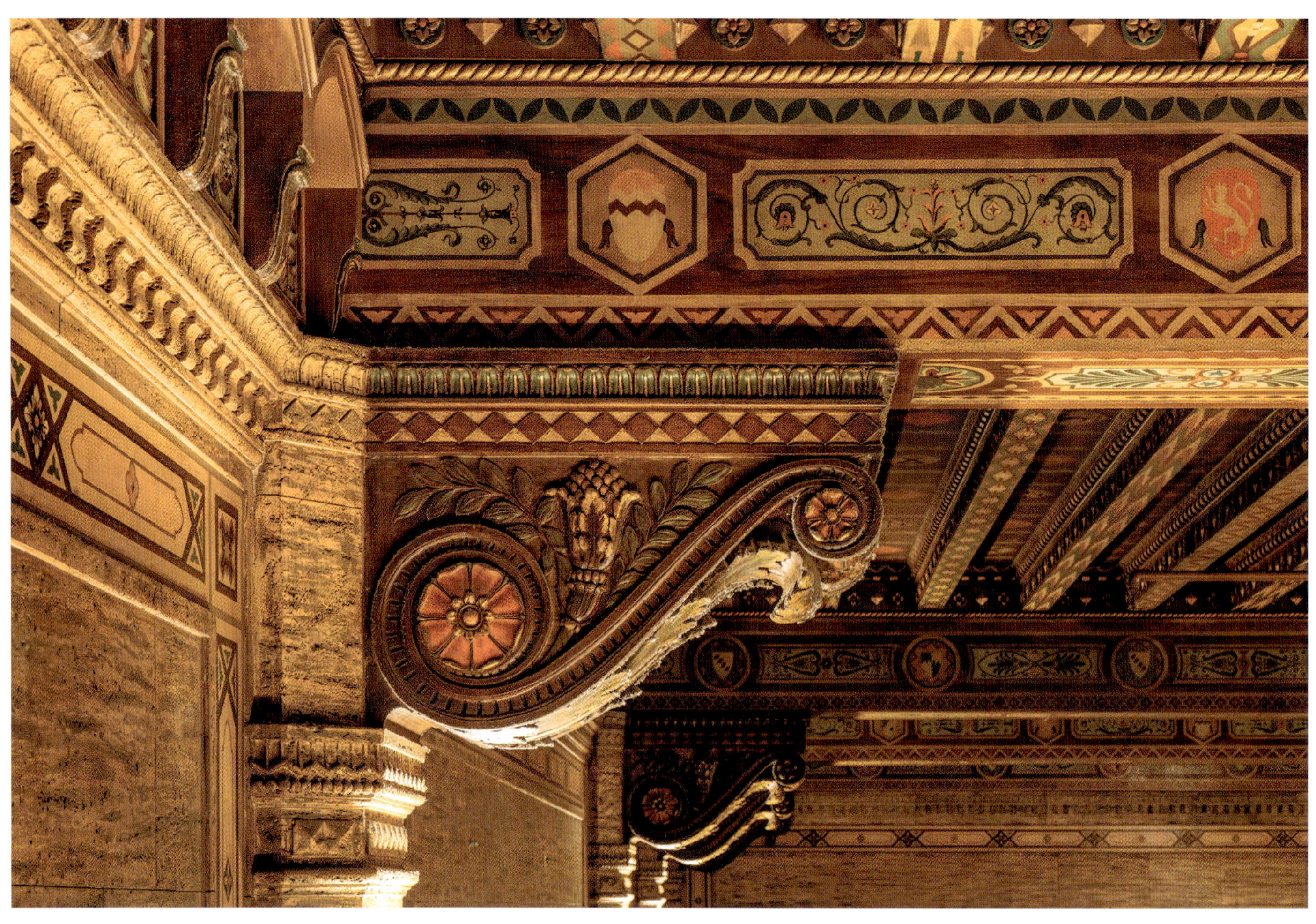

OPPOSITE BOTTOM   *The original steel safe, once hidden behind a wall, now sits in the massive faux fireplace as a reminder of Campbell's wealth.*

OVERLEAF   *Following Campbell's death in 1957, the space fell into disrepair. After extensive restoration and renovation work at a cost of over $1.5 million, it was transformed into a cocktail lounge, complete with a new bar.*

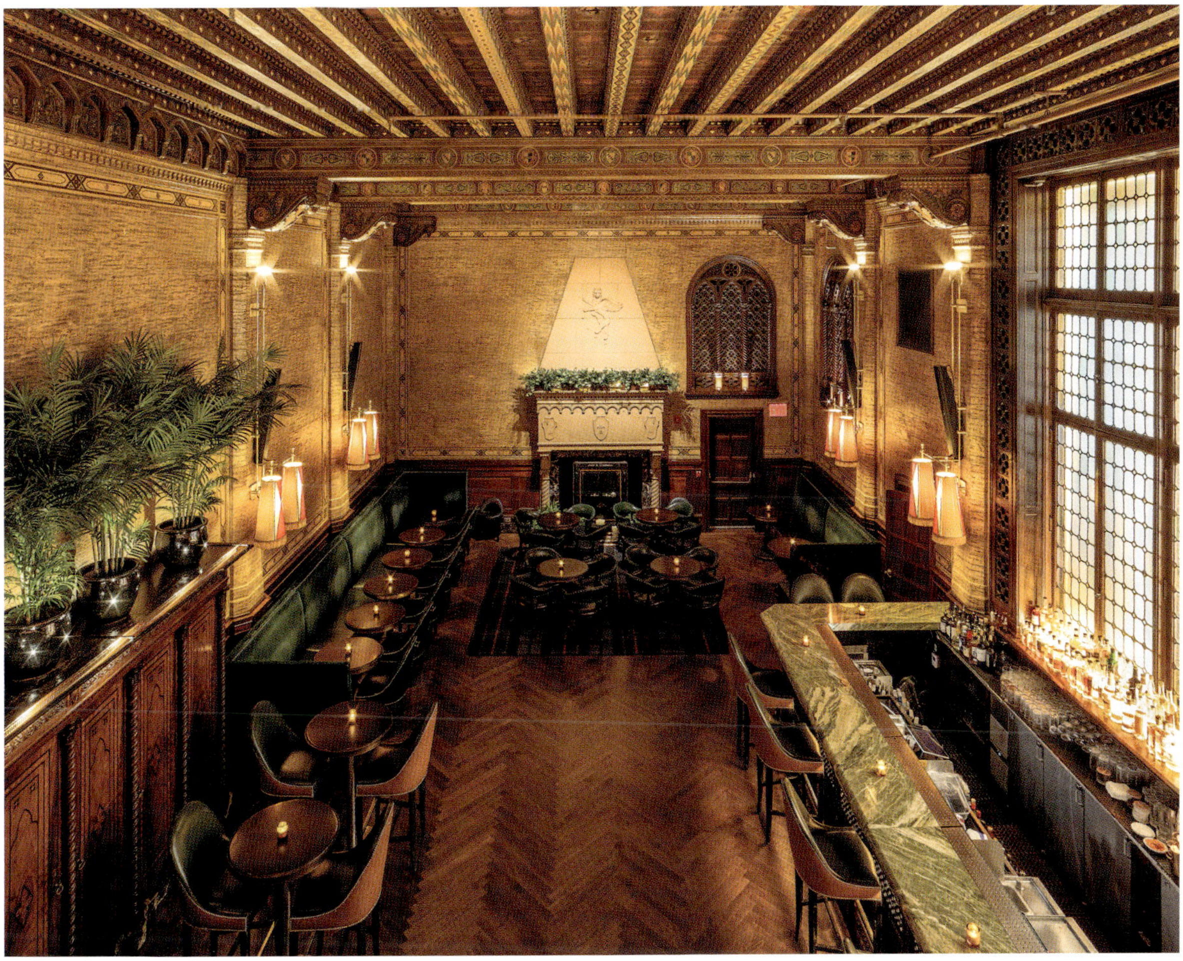

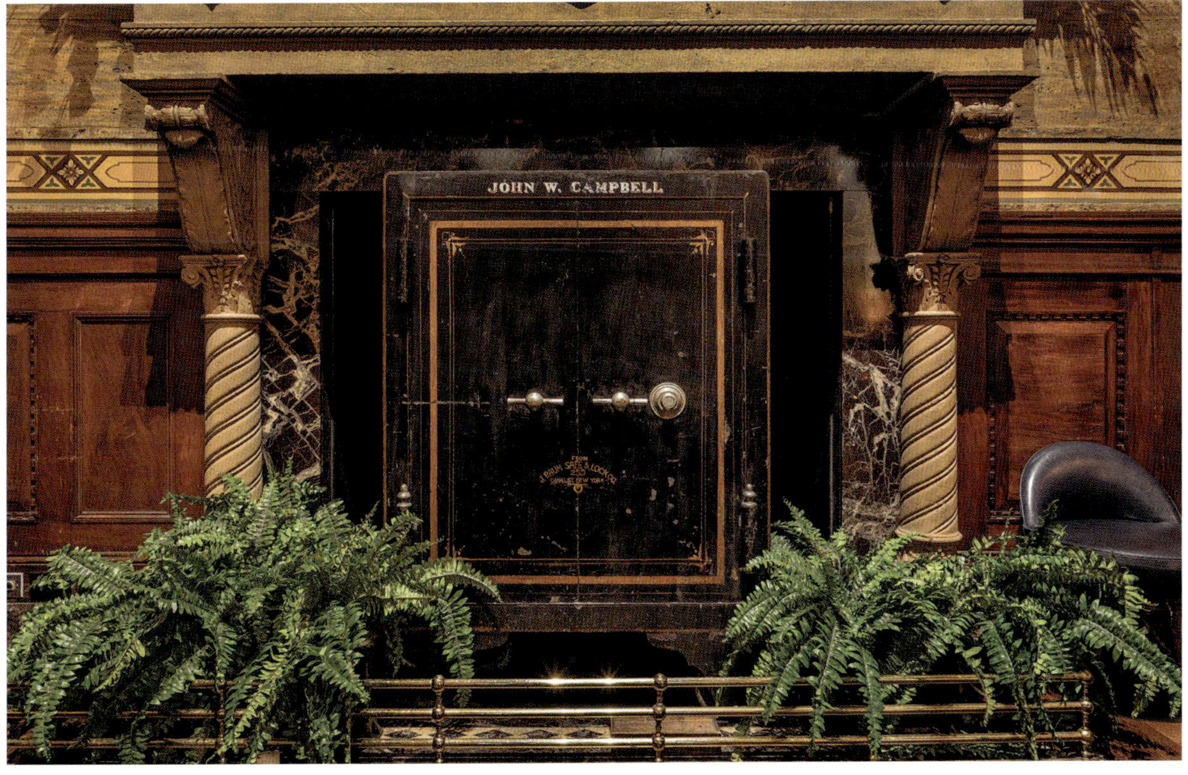

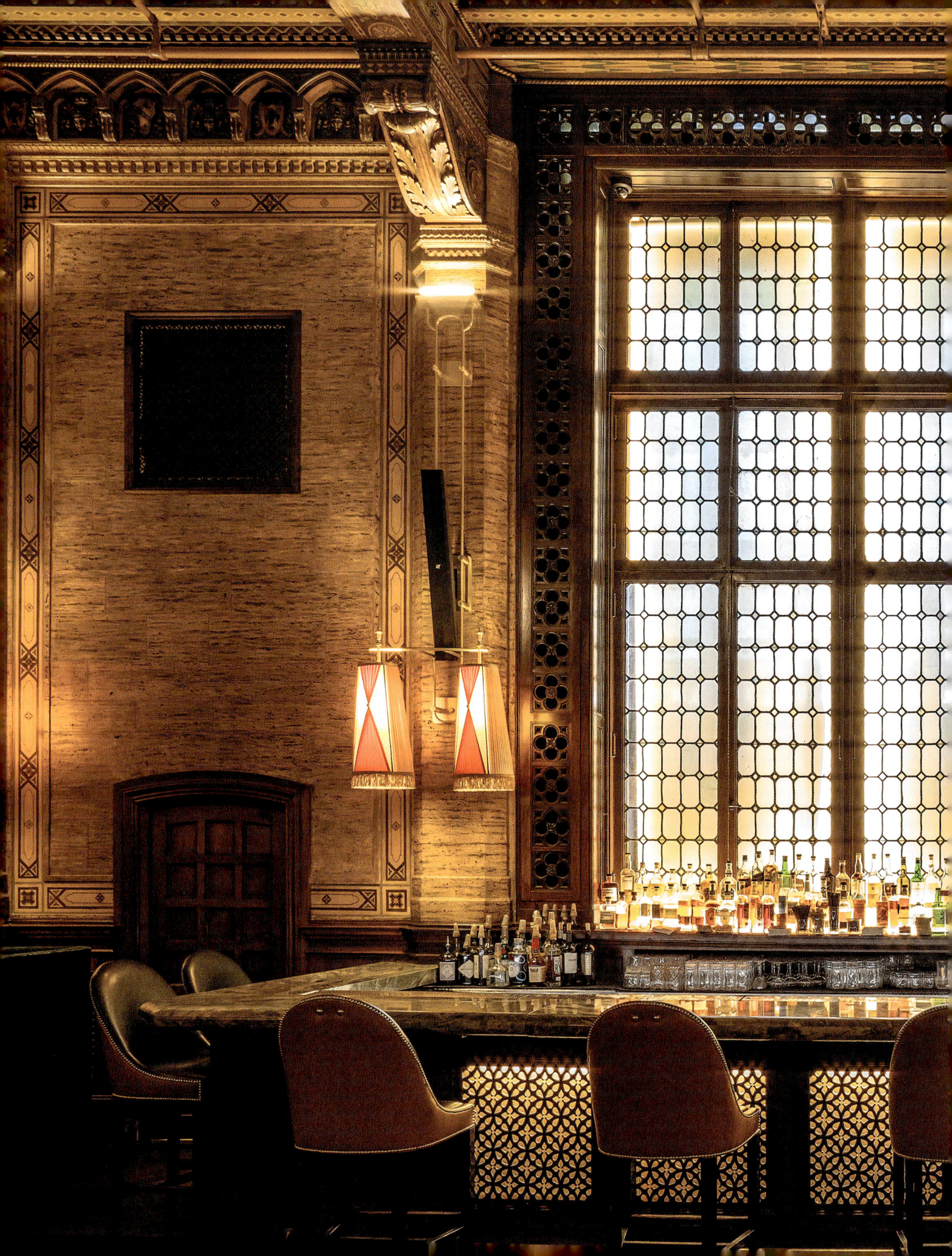

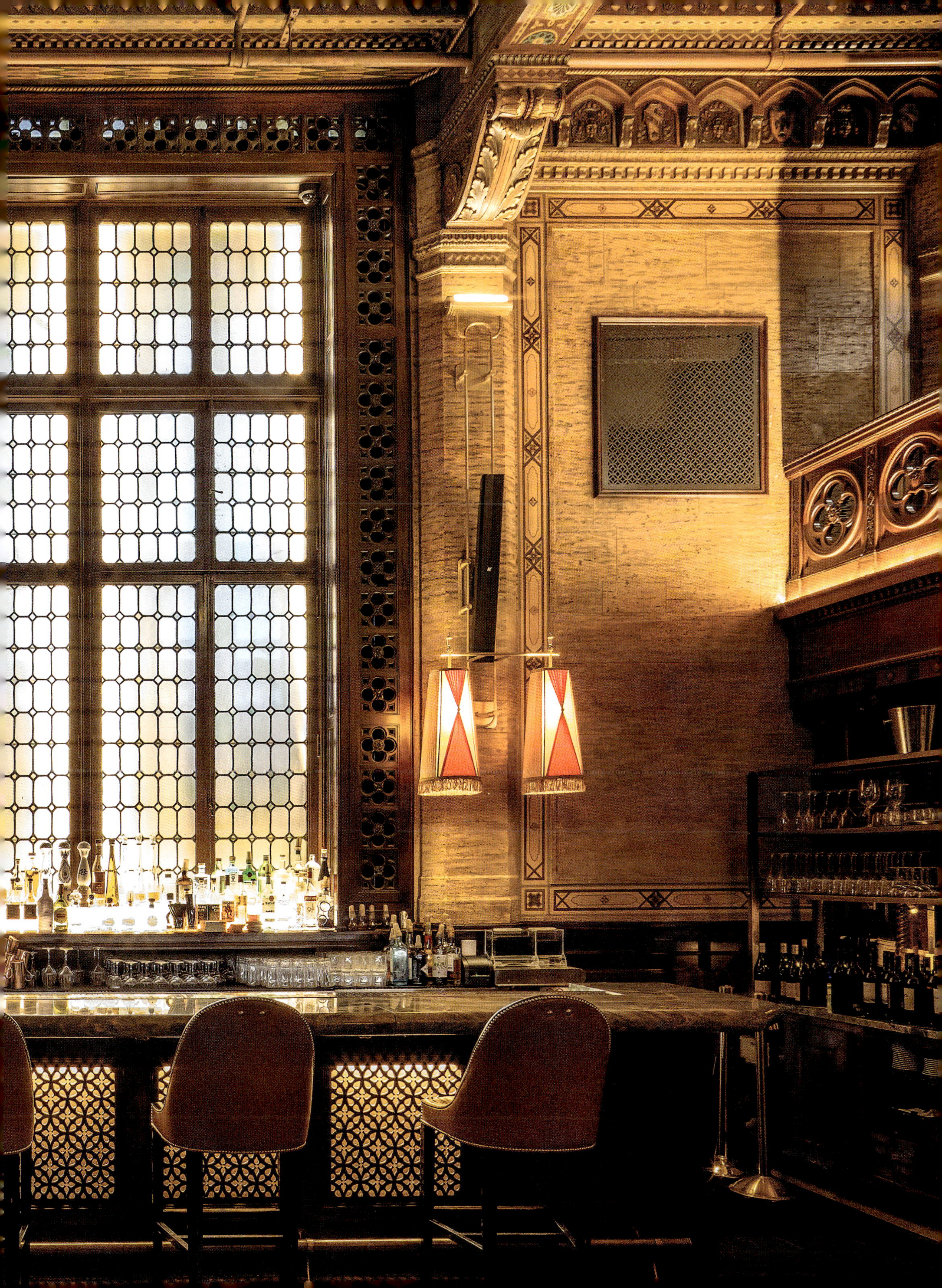

FRAUNCES TAVERN

54 PEARL STREET, FINANCIAL DISTRICT

There are few New York City buildings as central to America's origin story as Fraunces Tavern. If walls could talk, then these might tell centuries-old tales of revolution, statesmanship, and the birth of a nation.

The history of this National Historic Landmark site goes back to the colonial era. It was initially established in 1671 as the home of New York City's first native-born mayor, Stephanus van Cortlandt, who then passed it on to his son-in-law, Étienne de Lancey. The latter would build the current structure as a home in 1719; it's a reconstruction of this eighteenth-century building that stands on Pearl Street today.

Now a Revolutionary War museum and full-service restaurant, Fraunces Tavern was once one of the city's most important taverns. The current name comes from Samuel Fraunces, who purchased the building from the de Lancey family in 1762 and established it as the Queen's Head Tavern in 1765. Fraunces, believed to be a mixed-race man from the West Indies, is known for befriending George Washington and later serving as a steward for the president's house.

In this period of history, taverns notably weren't just places to enjoy a pint. They were hubs of commerce, arenas for discourse, and spaces for mobilization. Before the war, the bar was a gathering place for the Sons of Liberty, an underground organization largely known for its role in the Boston Tea Party.

In 1775, Fraunces Tavern was damaged when a British ship, the *HMS Asia*, sent a cannonball through its roof. By 1776, it had become Washington's official operating headquarters, serving as the de facto war room of the Continental Army.

One of Fraunces Tavern's most storied moments took place after the war ended in September 1783. That December, Washington gathered his officers in the bar's Long Room to dine together for a final goodbye. The event is depicted in Alonzo Chappel's 1865 oil painting *Washington's Farewell to His Officers*, with the president embracing one soldier while another tearfully rests his head in his hand. According to the Fraunces Tavern Museum, the on-site organization dedicated to preserving the space's history, Washington said, "With a heart full of love and gratitude I now take leave of you. I most devoutly wish that your latter days may be as prosperous and happy as your former ones have been glorious and honorable."

Washington wouldn't be the last political icon to eat and drink at Fraunces Tavern. Others would include his successors John Adams and Thomas Jefferson, as well as the nation's first secretary of the treasury, Alexander Hamilton. During Hamilton's tenure, the building housed the very first offices for the Departments of Foreign Affairs, War, and Treasury.

Sadly, Fraunces Tavern would fall victim to numerous fires throughout the nineteenth century. So extensive and numerous were these incidents that it's unclear how many times its exterior has been redone. What's known is that, following a particularly devastating fire in 1852, two stories were added to the building, making it five stories total.

In the early twentieth century, Fraunces Tavern was set to be demolished to make room for a parking lot. These plans were, fortunately, thwarted by the Sons of the Revolution, a patriotic organization that acquired the building and remains its owner today. Notably, this was made possible by the bequest of one Frank Samuel Tallmadge, grandson of Washington's director of military intelligence, Benjamin Tallmadge. The Tallmadge Dining Room honors his memory.

Following this purchase, a reconstruction of the building, resulting in its current appearance including an on-site museum, was completed in 1907. It was supervised by historical preservationist William Mersereau, who based his design around a few remaining walls and other typical buildings of the time.

One of New York's oldest buildings, Fraunces Tavern today stands as a proud reminder of America's quest for independence. Beyond being a restaurant serving transatlantic classics—from Scotch eggs to burgers—the key draw is the museum, which boasts numerous artifacts, from documents and paintings to Revolutionary War memorabilia. Notable among these are the tent that served as George Washington's headquarters, Alexander Hamilton's writing desk, and war-era flags.

The bar's current owners, Eddie Travers and Dervilla Bowler, who are from Ireland, purchased it in 2011 and performed a major renovation to expose the original walls, floors, and ceilings. They also brought with them furniture from Ireland, including church pews from County Wexford and a bowling alley from Dublin, which now makes up the tables in the main bar.

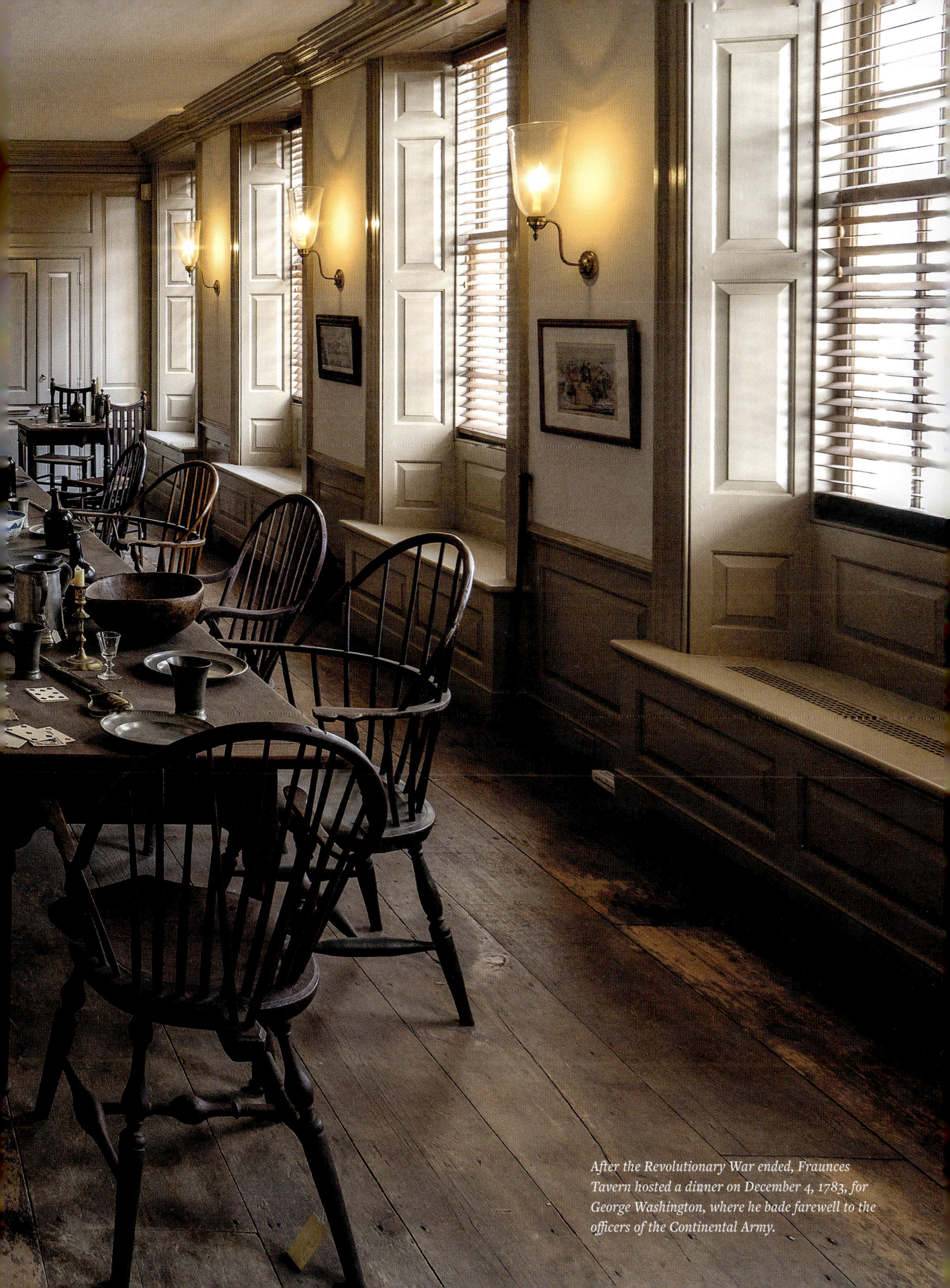

After the Revolutionary War ended, Fraunces Tavern hosted a dinner on December 4, 1783, for George Washington, where he bade farewell to the officers of the Continental Army.

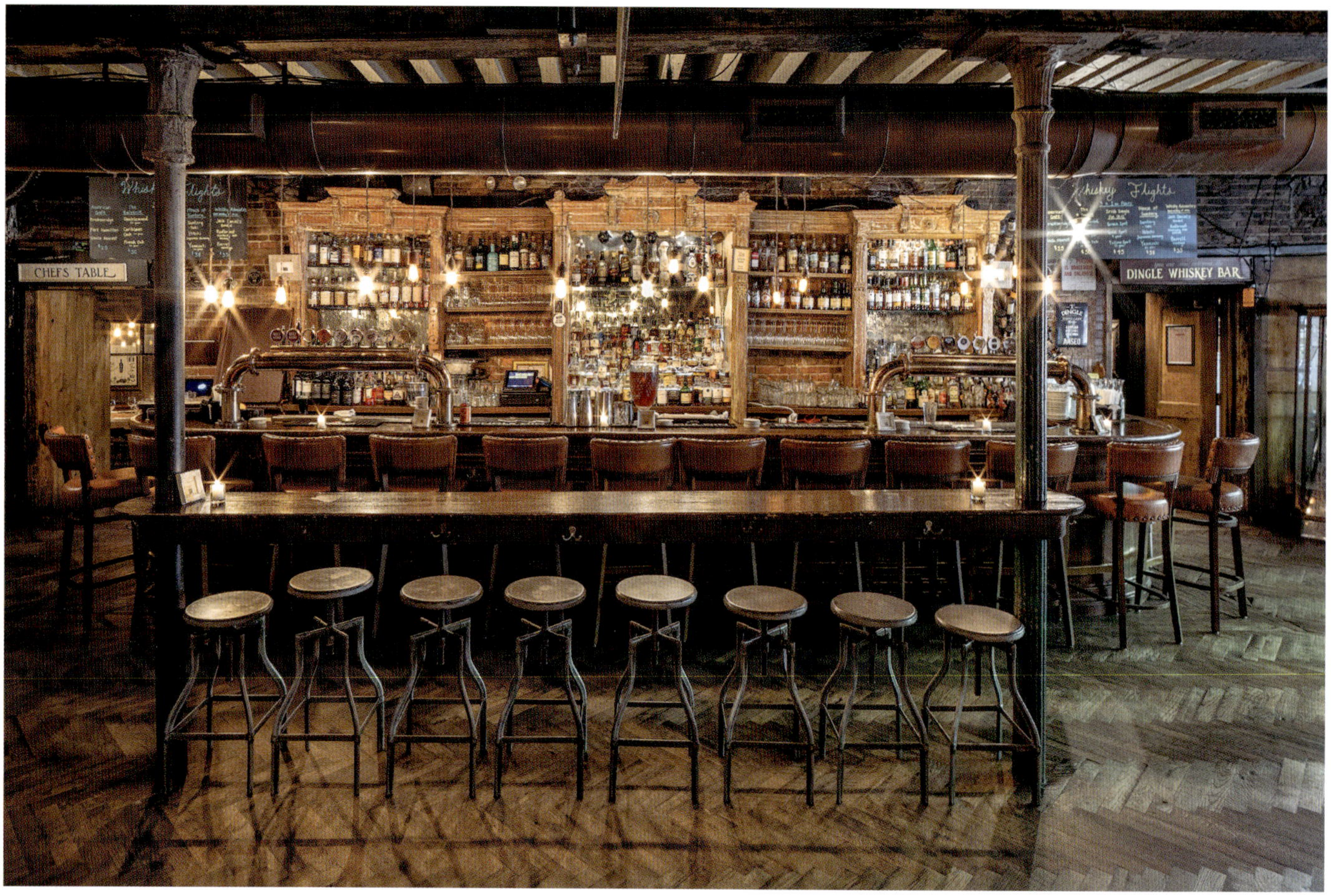
CHEFS TABLE
Whiskey Flights
DINGLE WHISKEY BAR

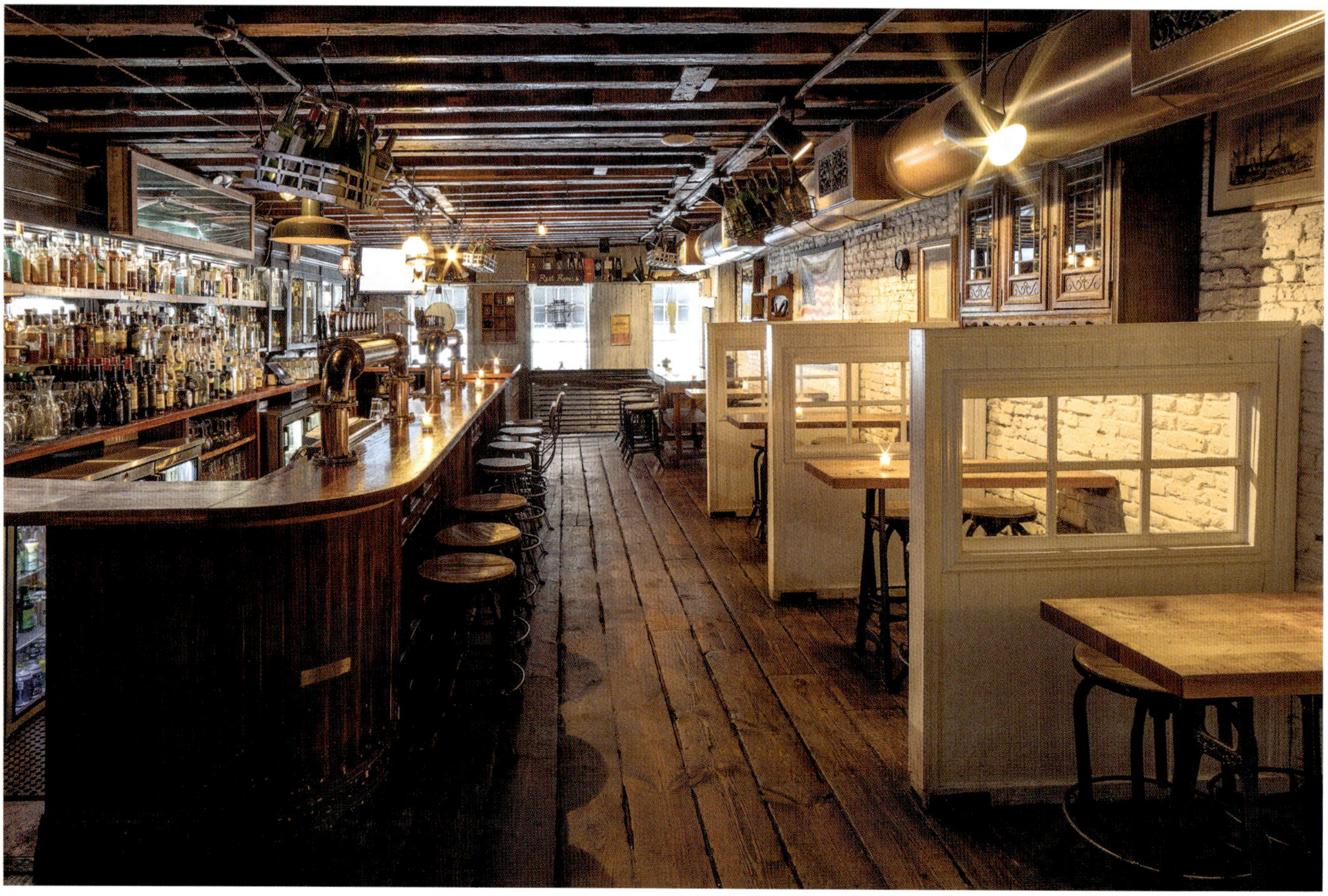

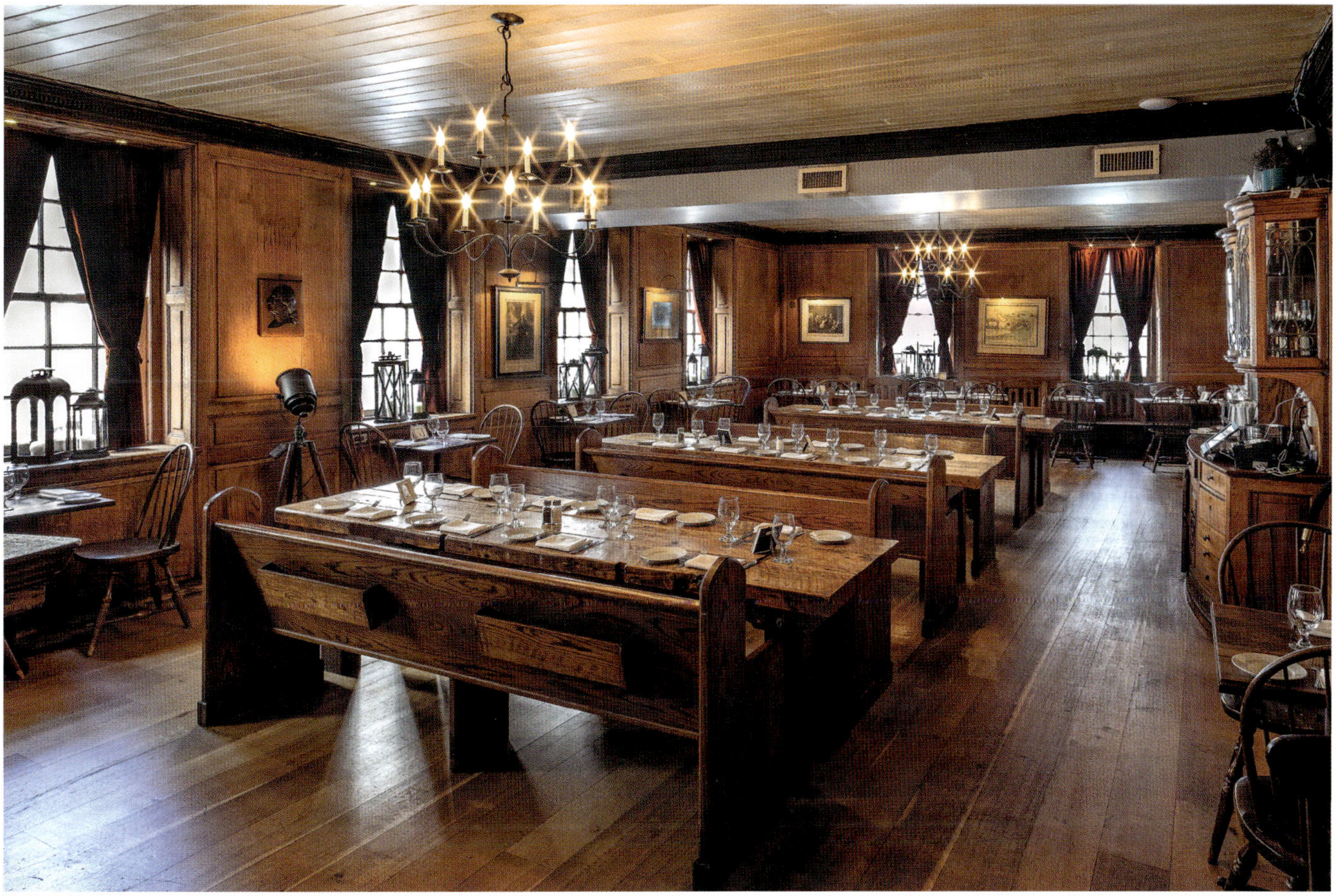

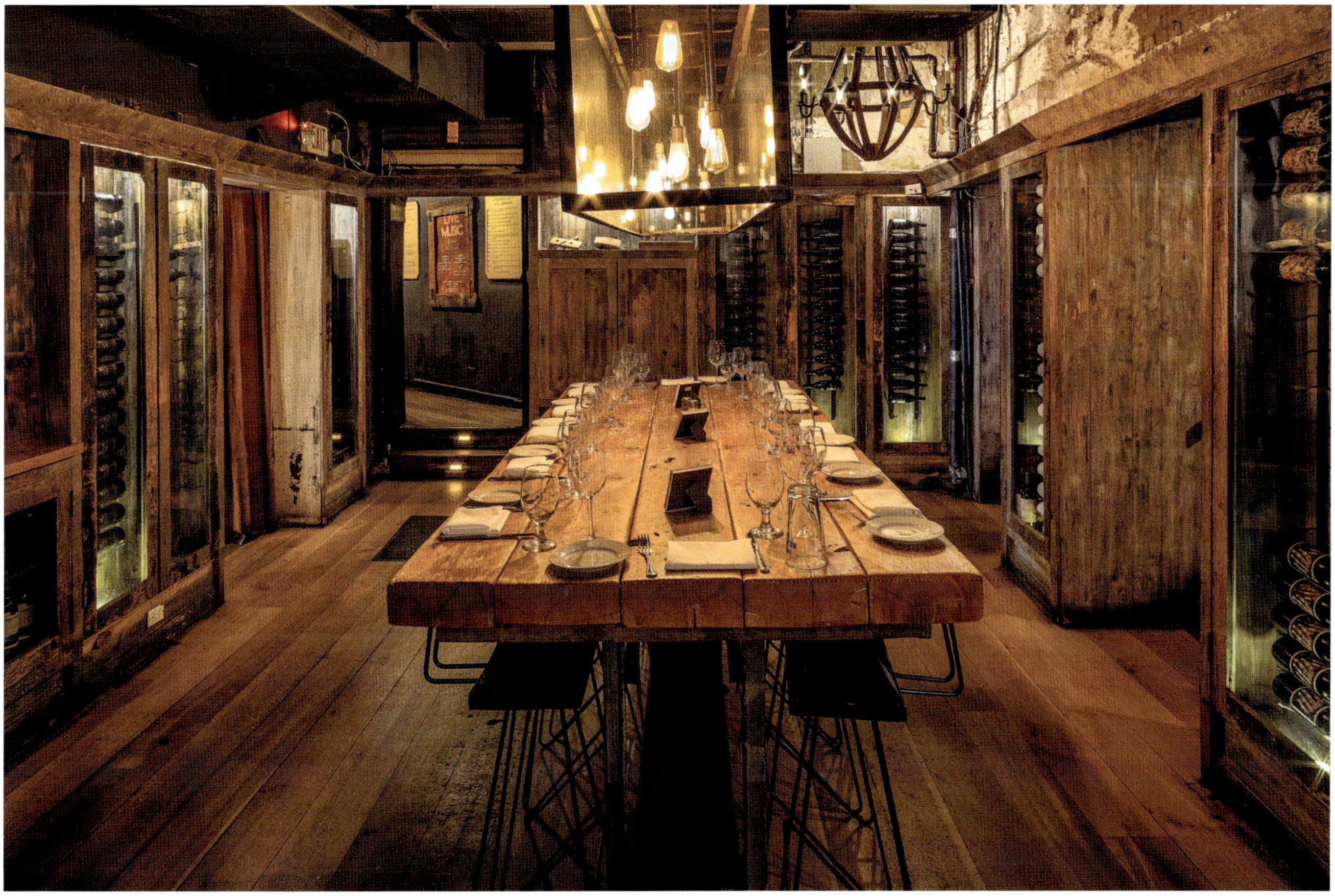

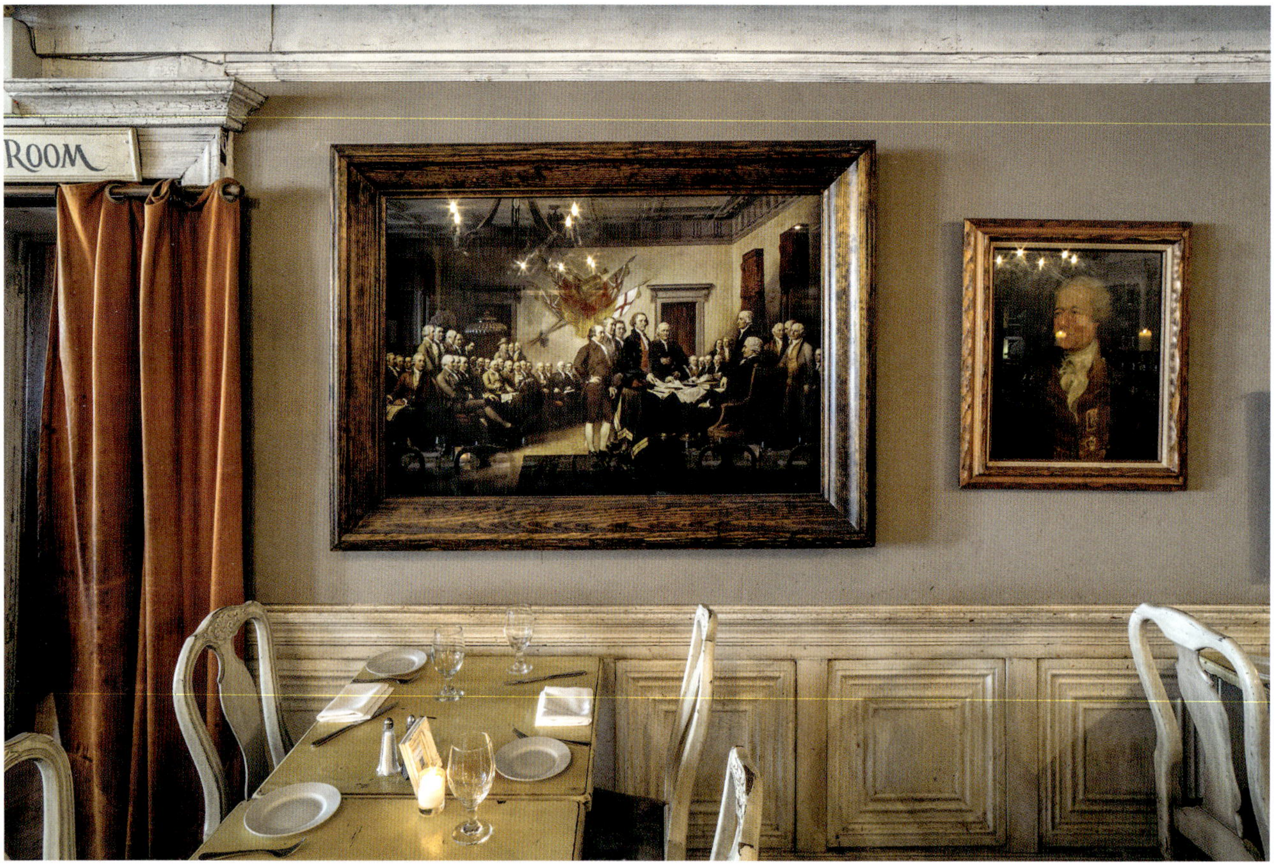

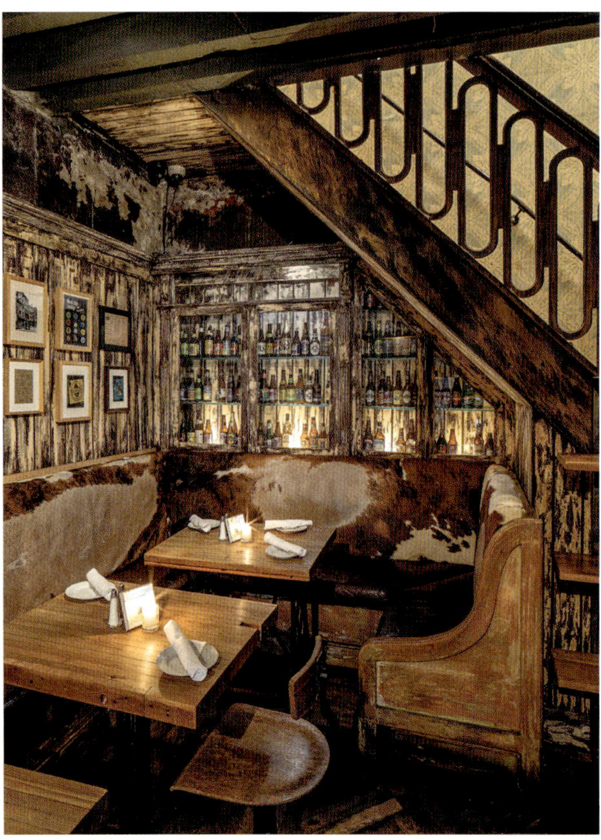

GREAT BARS OF NEW YORK CITY

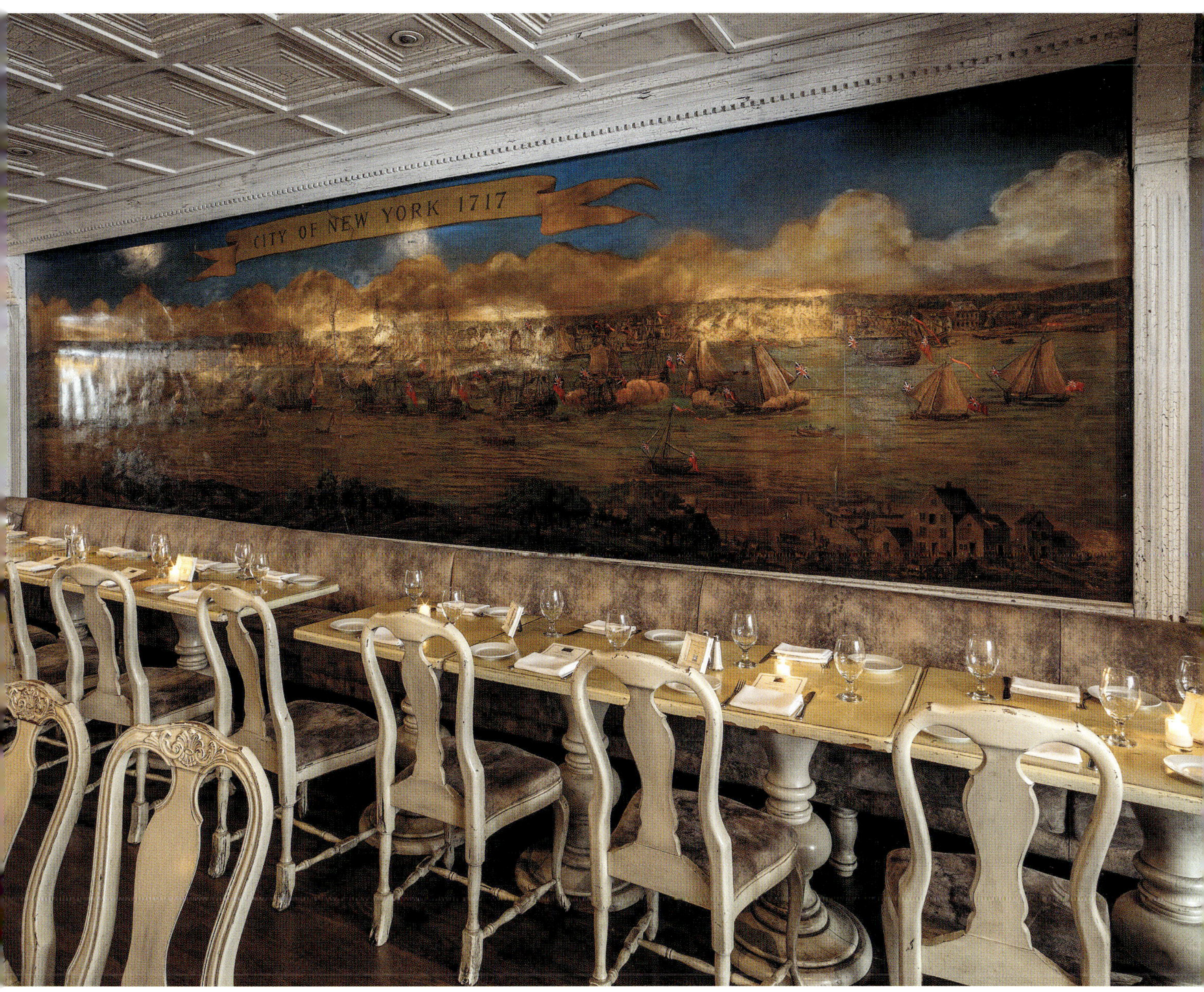

PREVIOUS SPREAD TOP RIGHT

*The Tallmadge Dining Room is named in honor of
Frederick Samuel Tallmadge, whose bequest allowed
the Sons of the Revolution to purchase Fraunces
Tavern in 1904, saving it from demolition.*

ABOVE   *The Bissell Dining Room is named in
honor of the ancestors of Revolutionary War private
Isaac Bissell and is dominated by a mural of New
York in 1717.*

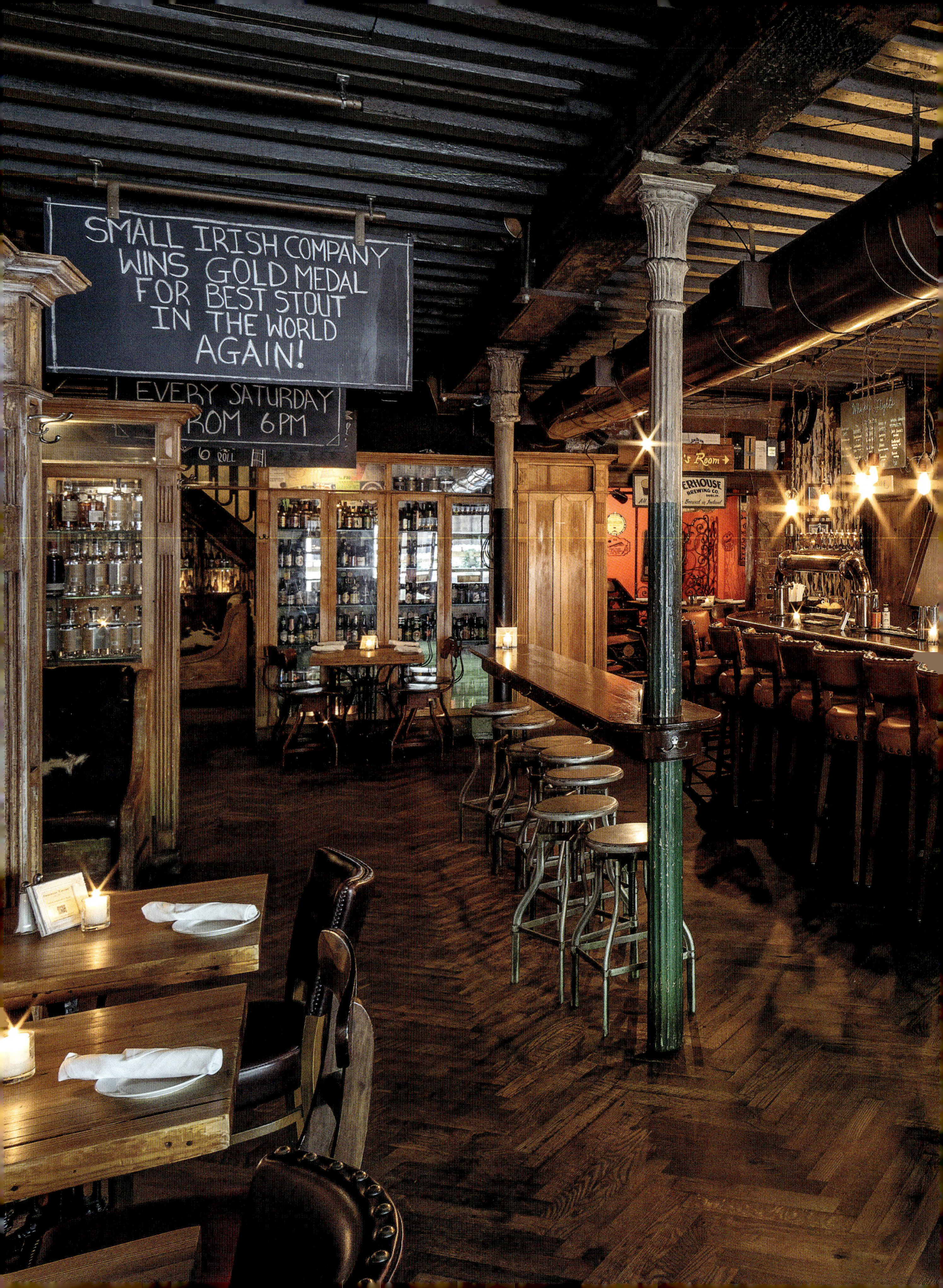

SMALL IRISH COMPANY WINS GOLD MEDAL FOR BEST STOUT IN THE WORLD AGAIN!
EVERY SATURDAY FROM 6 PM

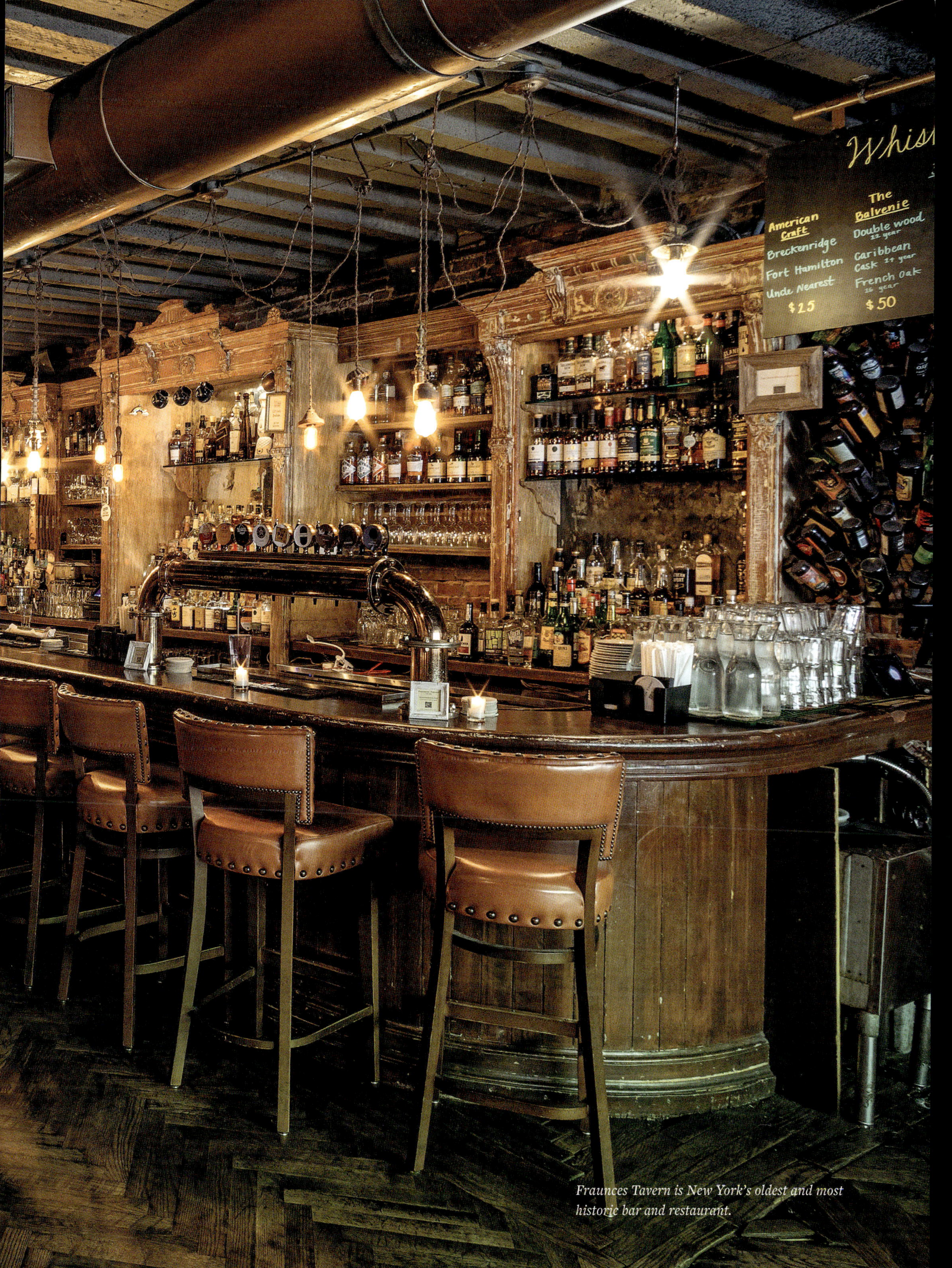

Fraunces Tavern is New York's oldest and most historic bar and restaurant.

DANTE

Having served coffee in Greenwich Village for over a century, Dante is a testament to the neighborhood's rich history, evolving from a tightly knit Italian immigrant enclave in the early 20th century to a Bohemian area decades later. After changing hands many times across generations to reach its modern form—a trendy cafe, cocktail bar, and eatery—Dante is perhaps best known today for earning the coveted top spot at the annual peer-voted World's 50 Best Bars event back in 2019.

Its story starts amid the height of immigration from Italy to New York. Between 1900 and 1915, some two million people, largely from Sicily and Campania, would arrive in the city, many settling downtown in a section that was then known as South Village, in the area south of Washington Square Park. Streets like Carmine and Sullivan were lined with Italian businesses, grocers, and more. Catholic churches sprung up nearby.

In 1915 Caffe Dante, an Italian coffeehouse, opened on MacDougal Street. With all records lost to time, the original owners of the venue are mysteriously unknown. Whoever they were, Caffe Dante quickly became a hub for Italian immigrants to meet, sip an espresso, and catch up on events back in the homeland.

In 1971 it was purchased by Mario Flotta. Over the years, the cafe's prime downtown Manhattan location would draw in A-list clientele spanning decades, from writers like Anaïs Nin and Ernest Hemingway to musicians including Patti Smith and Bob Dylan, who became a regular (it's easy to imagine: after all, Caffe Dante's sidewalk seating faced the door to the latter's apartment). Yet despite these celebrity patrons, extending today to Al Pacino and Whoopi Goldberg, it remained, for decades, a simple neighborhood establishment.

It wasn't until 2015 that Caffe Dante would undergo a modern transformation to become Dante, the world-renowned business that it is today. The current iteration is the brainchild of Sydney, Australia–born husband-and-wife team Linden Pride and Nathalie Hudson, who married and moved to New York City in 2013. Enamored with the space, the duo persuaded Flotta to sell. Naturally, with such a cherished institution at stake, the couple was met with apprehension from locals at first. Now it's worth pointing out that under their stewardship, Dante has won unprecedented global attention—all while preserving a great deal of its timeless charm.

The bar's renovation remained faithful in spirit to the source material while making some design-forward modernizations. Pride and Hudson installed pressed-tin ceilings, chosen for a pattern meant to evoke the original. They curated and framed old photographs of Caffe Dante, including one of Flotta. An original sign still hangs in its place on MacDougal Street, above the cafe's signature green awning.

On the food front, the all-day, any-occasion menu includes reliable takes on cured meat plates, pastas, and a standout chicken parmigiana. Meanwhile, the white wooden bar shelves brim with brightly-colored bottles of herbal and citrusy *aperitivo* liqueurs popular in Italy. In fitting Italian fashion, the drinks menu—much of it created by former creative director Naren Young—includes selections of creative Negronis and spritzes, along with an acclaimed take on the classic Italian Garibaldi, a two-ingredient concoction of "fluffy" shaken orange juice and Campari.

Reconciling the couple's Australian background with the bar's Italian ethos, Pride told *T: The New York Times Style Magazine* in 2020 that he'd grown up around Italian coffee culture due to the influx of immigrants who came to Australia following World War II. "Caffe Dante reminded us of the old coffee houses we grew up with—it was the connection to community, the daily rituals that were so important," he said.

In 2019 Dante's bar program was named the world's best by a panel of over 500 independent experts from around the globe. And by 2020 Pride and Hudson were opening their second act, Dante West Village, at 551 Hudson Street. In 2023, they opened the first outpost outside of New York City: Dante Beverly Hills.

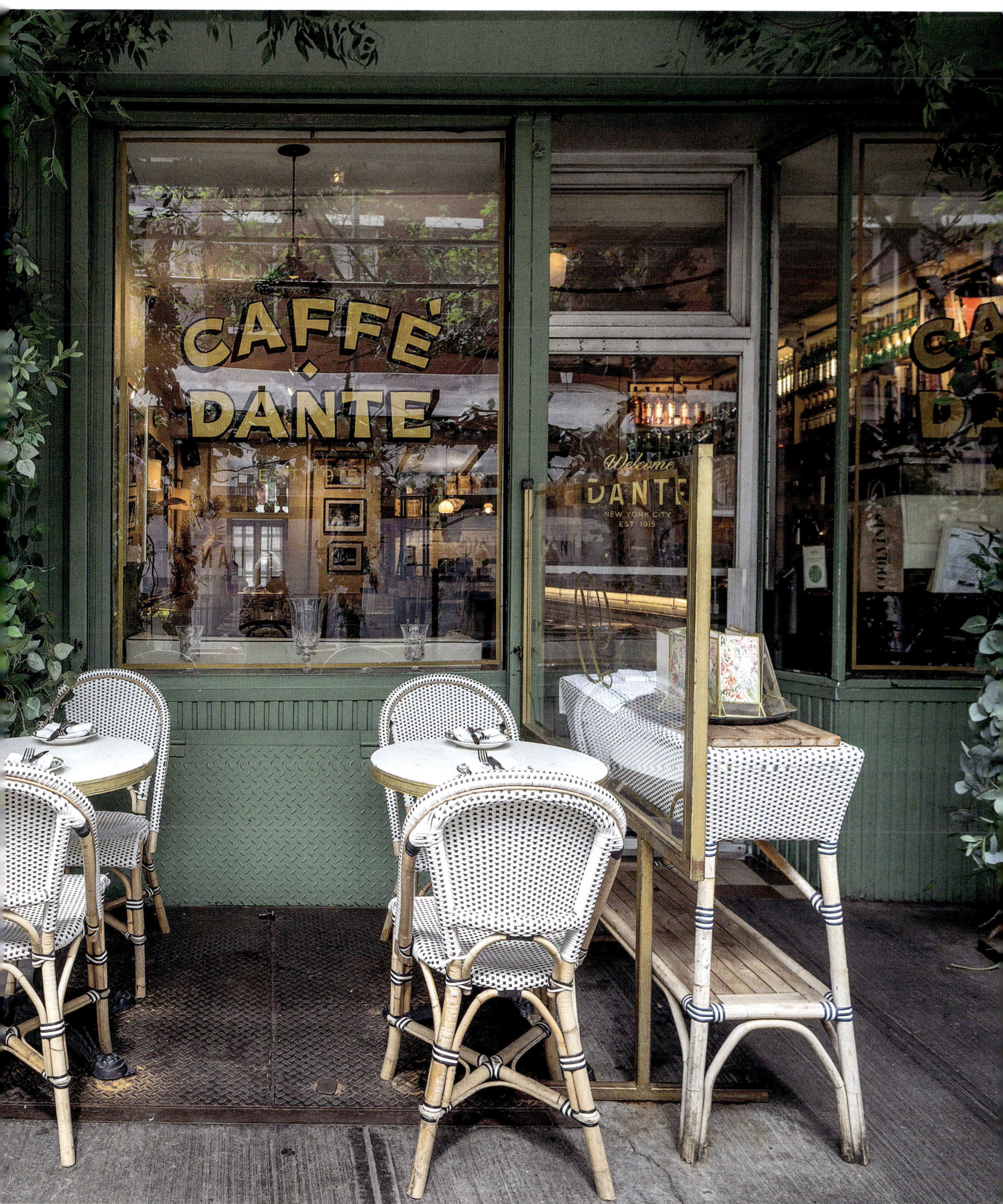

CAFFÉ
DANTE
Welcome
DANTE
NEW YORK CITY
EST 1915

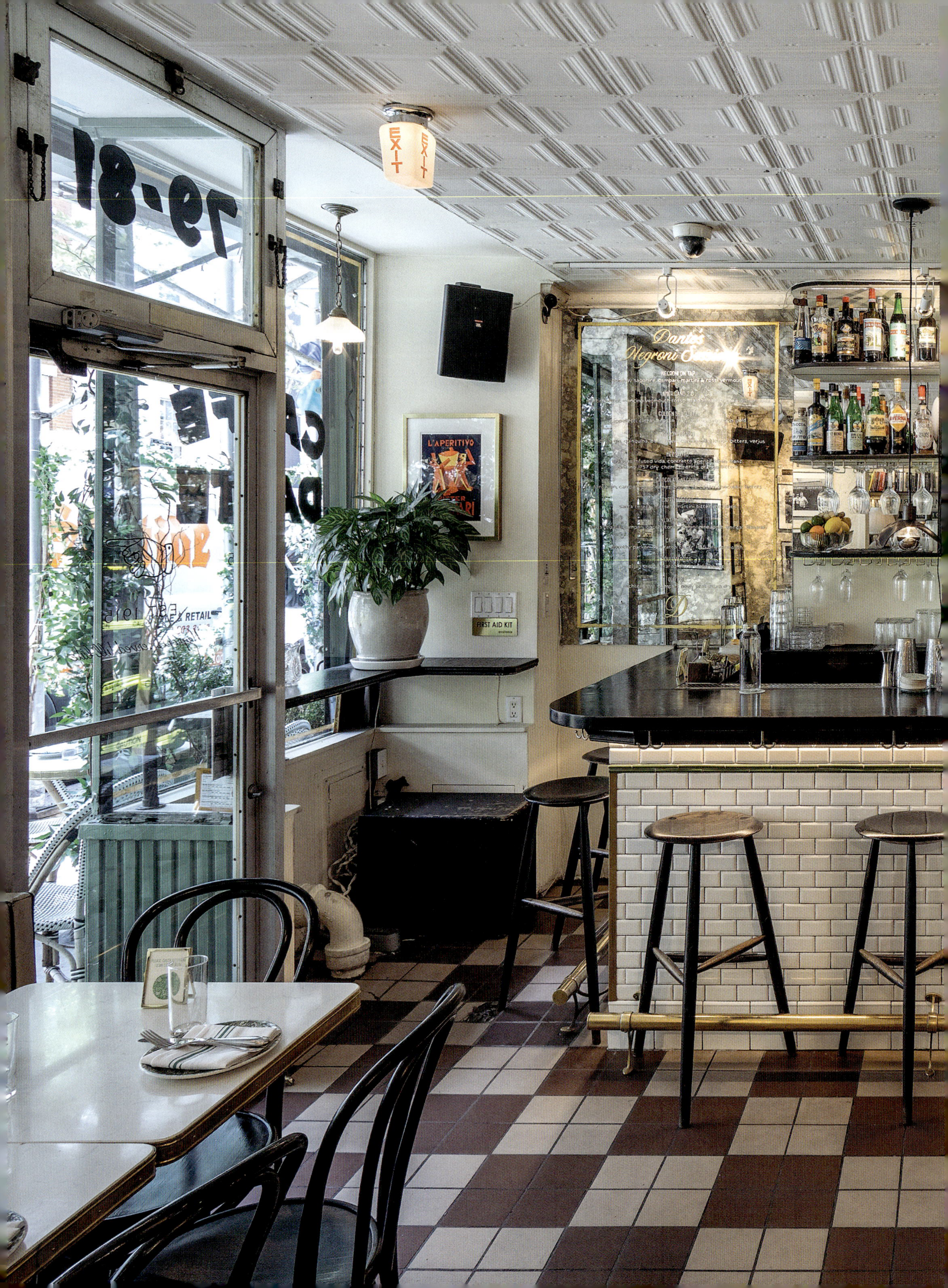
79-81
EXIT
L'APERITIVO
FIRST AID KIT
Dante's
Negroni Season

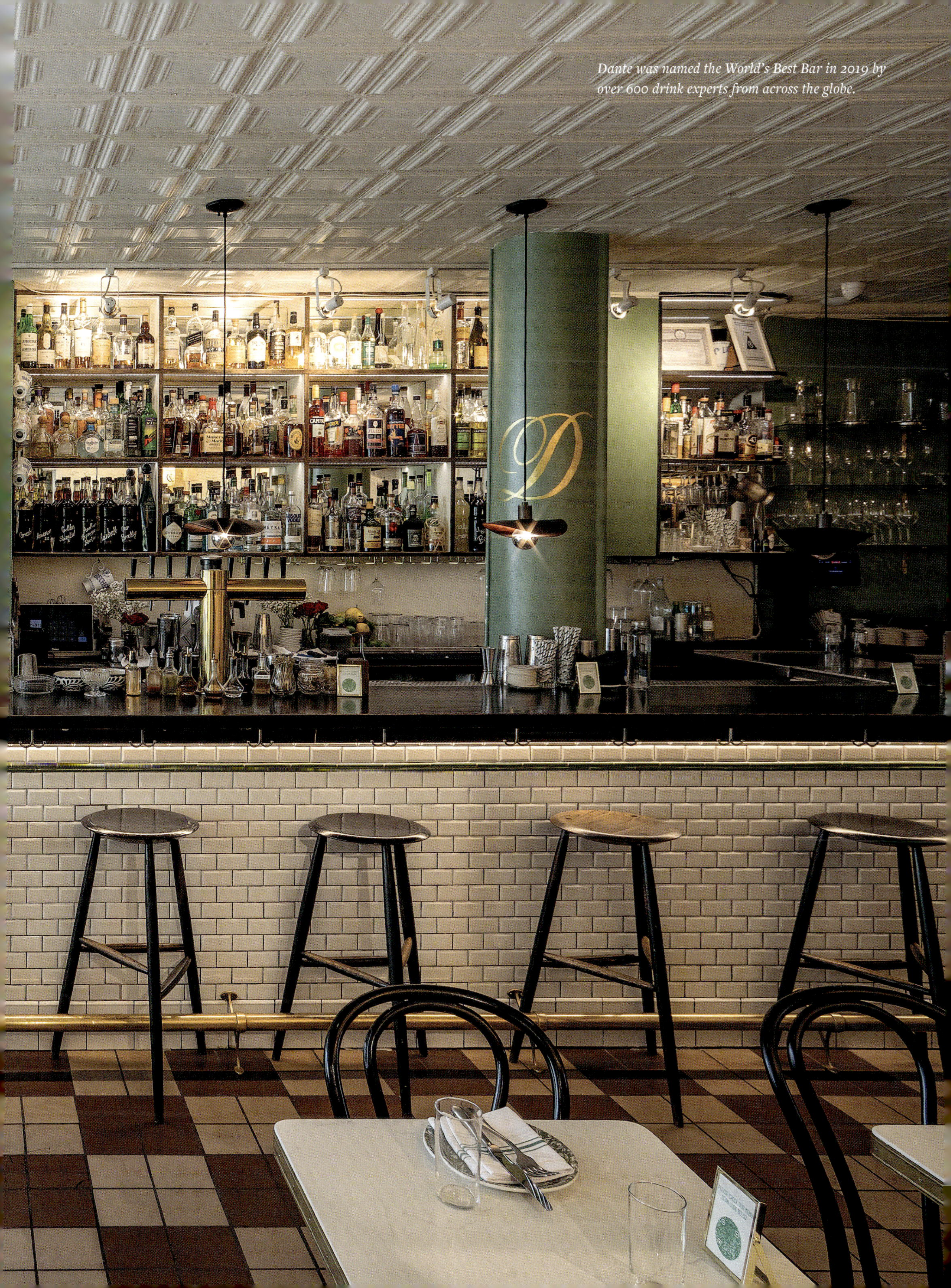

Dante was named the World's Best Bar in 2019 by over 600 drink experts from across the globe.

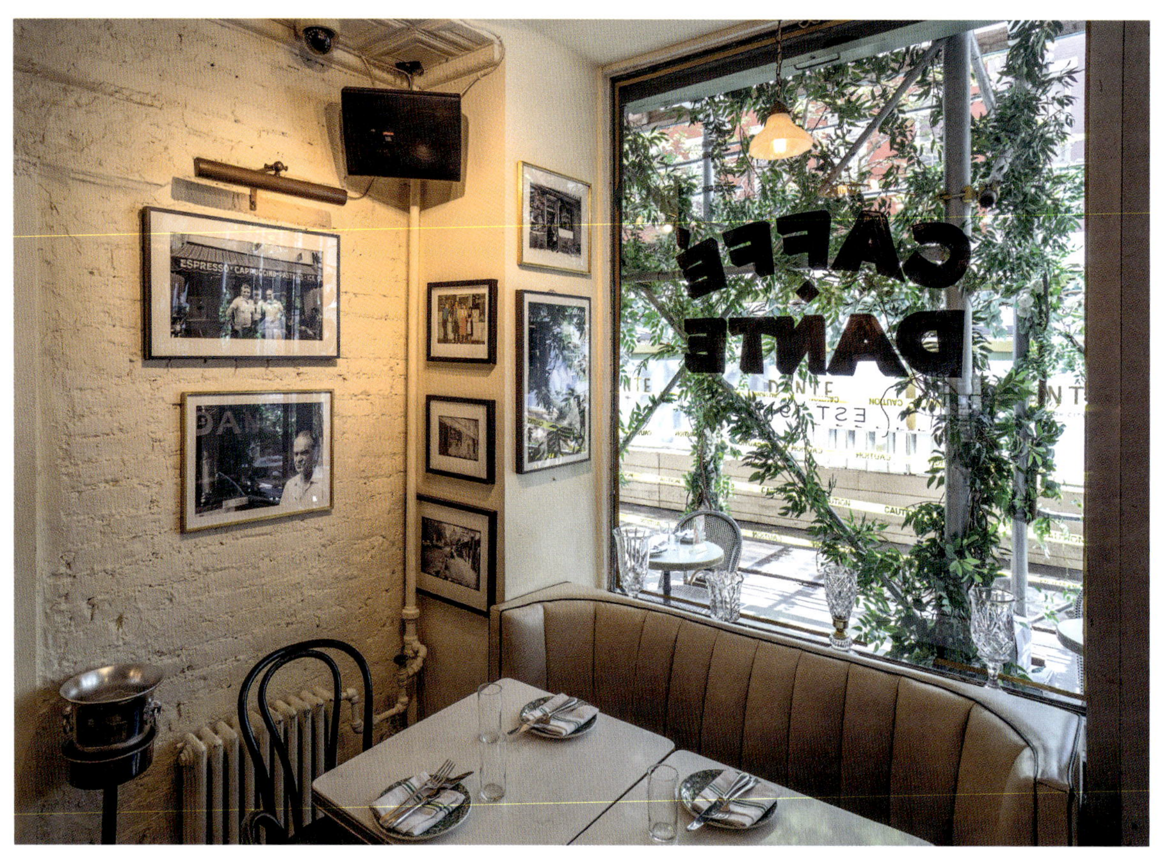

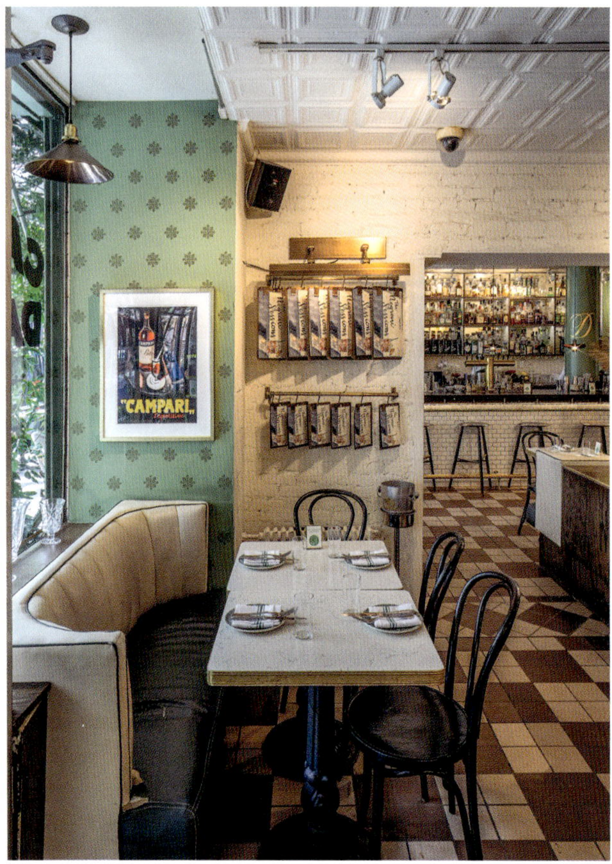

OVERLEAF *The original Caffe Dante opened its doors in 1915 as an Italian meeting place serving espresso.*

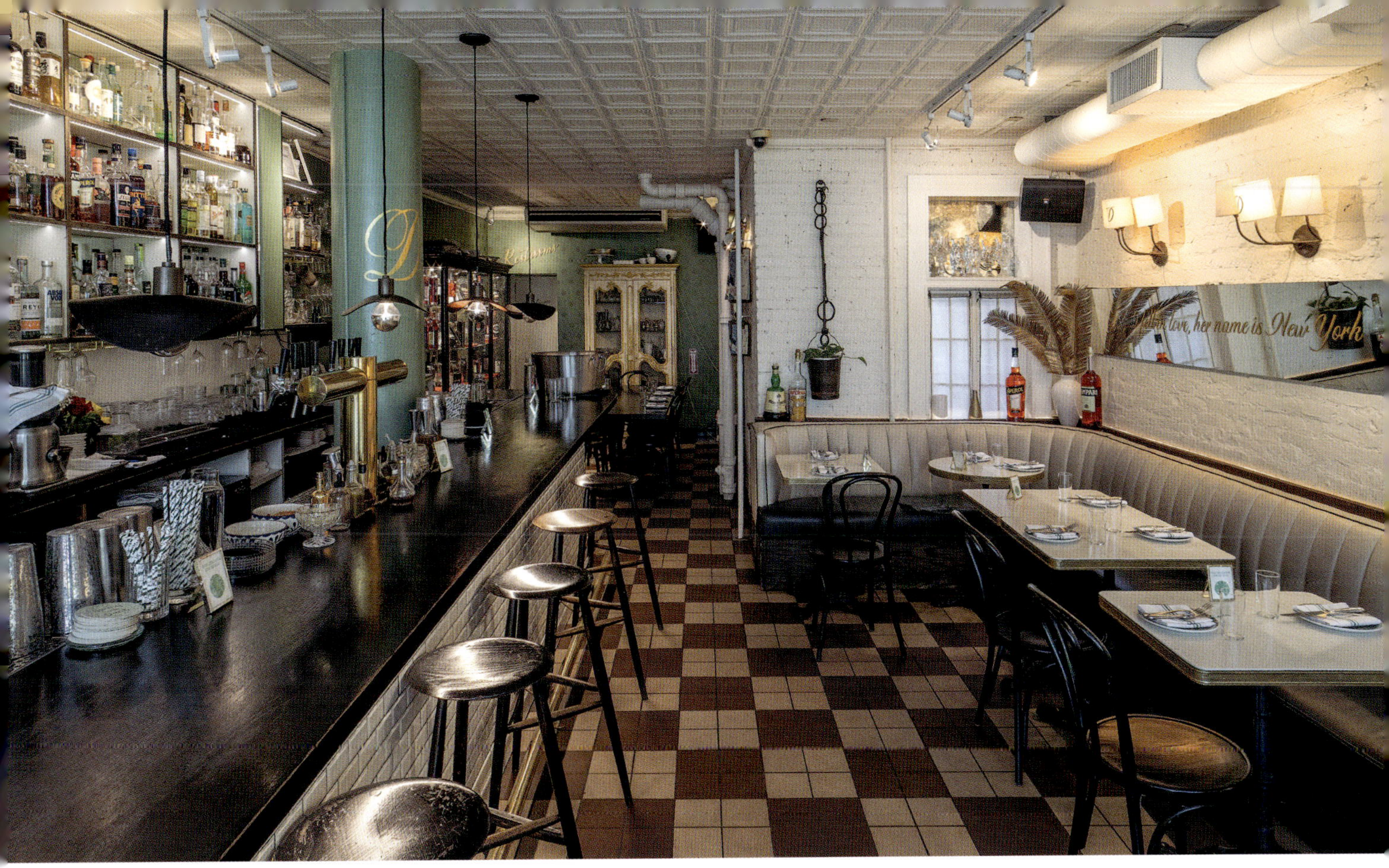

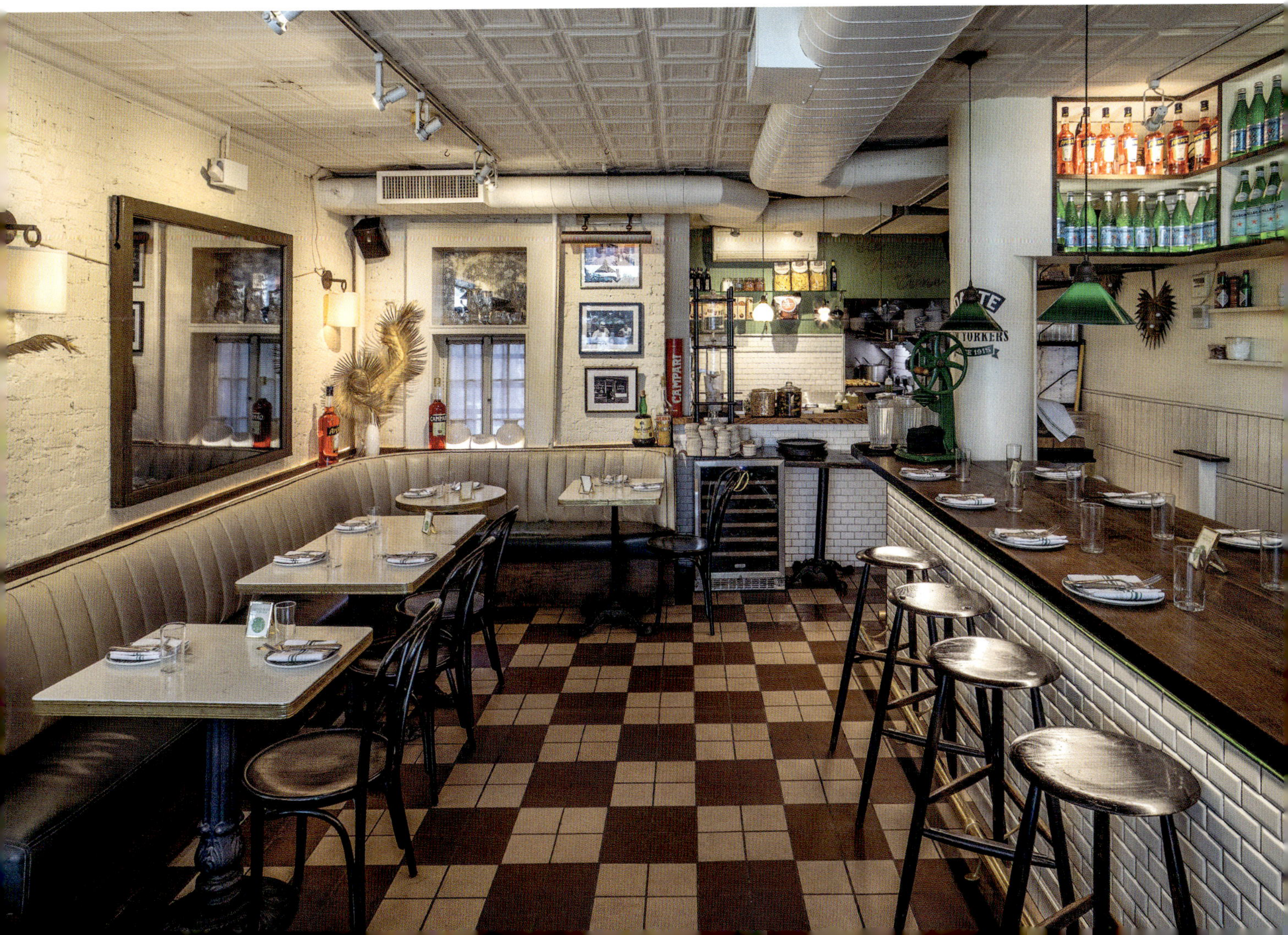

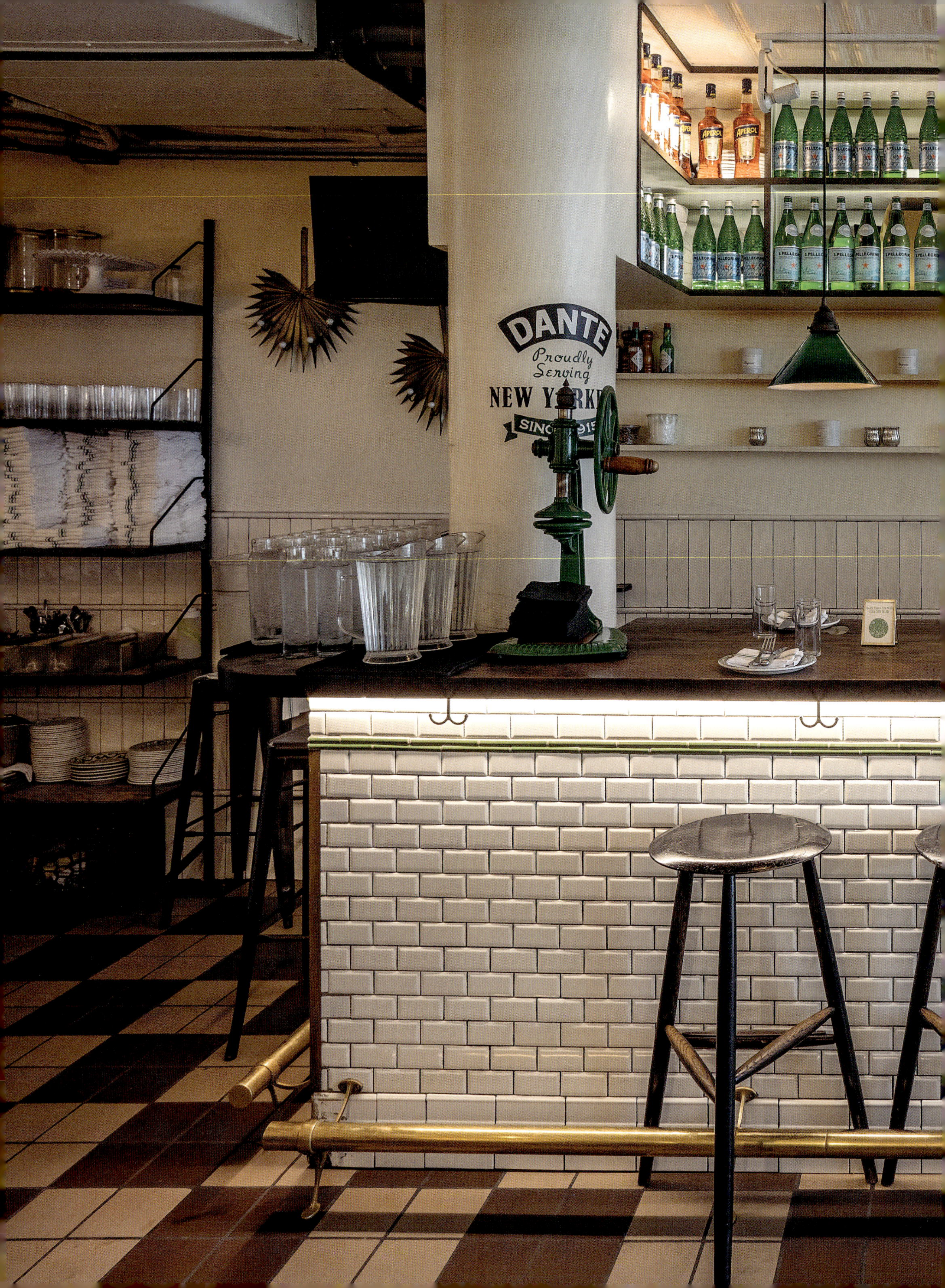

DANTE
Proudly Serving
NEW YORK
SINCE 1915

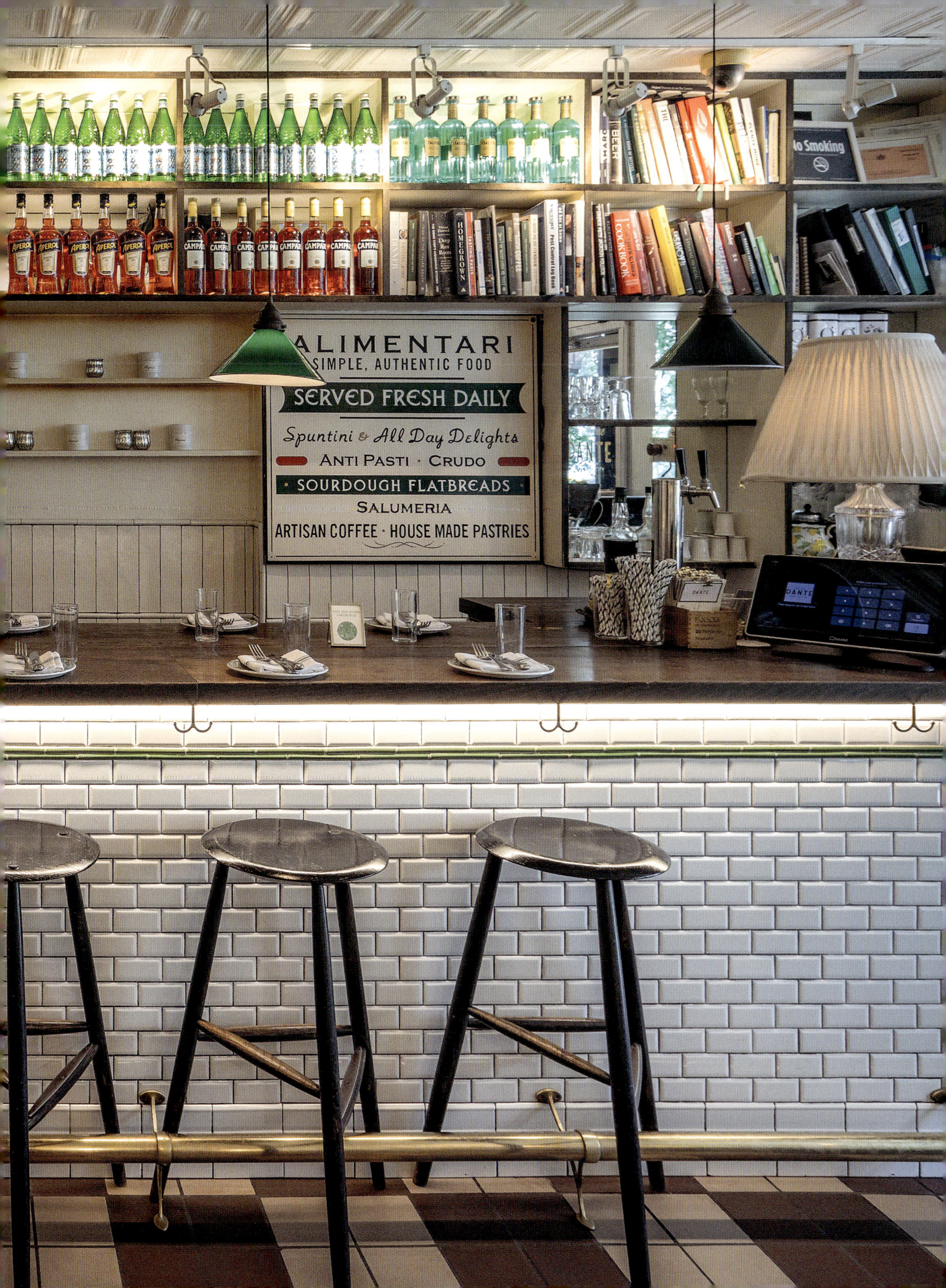
No Smoking
ALIMENTARI
SIMPLE, AUTHENTIC FOOD
SERVED FRESH DAILY
Spuntini & All Day Delights
ANTI PASTI · CRUDO
SOURDOUGH FLATBREADS
SALUMERIA
ARTISAN COFFEE · HOUSE MADE PASTRIES
APEROL
CAMPARI
DANTE

7B HORSESHOE BAR

108 AVENUE B, EAST VILLAGE

The first thing to know about the 1930s-era corner dive at 108 Avenue B in the East Village is that it goes by three different names. Depending on which longtimer you're talking to, it could be Horseshoe Bar, Vazacs, or simply 7B—referring to its intersecting streets. Complicated nomenclature notwithstanding, 7B is the gold standard for an understated neighborhood saloon, catering to punk audiences, young locals, and undergrads in equal measure as the neighborhood around it transforms over the decades.

The nondescript red-brick building that houses 7B dates back to 1935, when it was first erected as a catering hall. At the time, the area was home to a sizable Eastern European population, with thriving businesses and churches established over several waves of large-scale migration. Until it was recently painted over, the building's facade was still emblazoned with bold but faded signage reading Vazac Hall, along with the business's original phone number: OR4-2568.

In 1962 American writer Dawn Powell mentioned a Vasyk's Avenue A bar in her novel *The Golden Spur*, using it to mark what was then considered the "eastern edge" of New York City. 7B sits directly across from Tompkins Square Park, which opened in 1834 but was redesigned in 1936, one year after the bar opened. Prior to this, the park was known as a site for social unrest and demonstration, and the 1936 renovation served the gathering crowds.

Today, from the park, it's easy to spot the bar's arched, castle-like doors and colored, multipaned Tudor windows. Inside, a giant U-shaped bar—hence the Horseshoe Bar moniker—is rigged with thirty-one beer taps. At some point several decades ago, apartments were added to the building's upper floors. The bar's back staircase now leads to nowhere and has been converted into a storage space.

Perhaps as a testament to its timeless appeal, 7B has also gone by dozens of fictional names in films and television shows across the better half of a century. In 1974, it was the scene of a Mafia hit in *The Godfather: Part II*, and in 1986's *Crocodile Dundee*, the Australian protagonist meets a sex worker there. Also notable was 2005's film adaptation of the musical *Rent*; 7B served as the exterior for the movie version of Life Cafe, which functions as the main characters' neighborhood haunt.

In more recent times, 7B has been featured prominently in top-billing Netflix series like Natasha Lyonne's *Russian Doll*—whose time-traveling plot is set across decades—where it was retrofitted as a mysterious bar named the Black Gumball. In Marvel's *Jessica Jones*, it's called Luke's and is owned by the character Luke Cage. Meanwhile, the cameo that brings in the most young folks? The 2013 romcom *Begin Again* starring Mark Ruffalo and Keira Knightley.

7B is a family business: today, it's managed by Nicole Hudson, who took over in 2002 from her father Steve, who likewise took over from his father, who passed in 1984. As Hudson recalls: "When I first started, the Strokes lived two doors down and were regulars for some time. One night, they brought in Beck, the White Stripes, Macaulay Culkin, Drew Barrymore, and more. It was so much fun! Every time [Culkin] turned his back, all of our regulars would put both hands on their faces to recreate the signature *Home Alone* face."

For celebrities and regular patrons alike, the main draw to 7B is its good old-fashioned fun vibe, from arcade games to a photo booth. And yet despite being a famous movie location and hosting some A-listers over the years, it's remarkably unpretentious.

True to its relaxed nature, the bar has never even tried to eliminate the name confusion; it's just embraced them all. A little over a decade ago, a bartender designed a logo, adding a small "7B" inside of a horseshoe. And for years, the bar resisted adding any signage, only acquiescing once they received a fine from the police because there was no number on the exterior.

OPPOSITE *Until recently, the facade of the building that houses 7B was emblazoned with bold but faded "ghost signage" reading Vazac Hall, a nod to its past as a catering hall.*

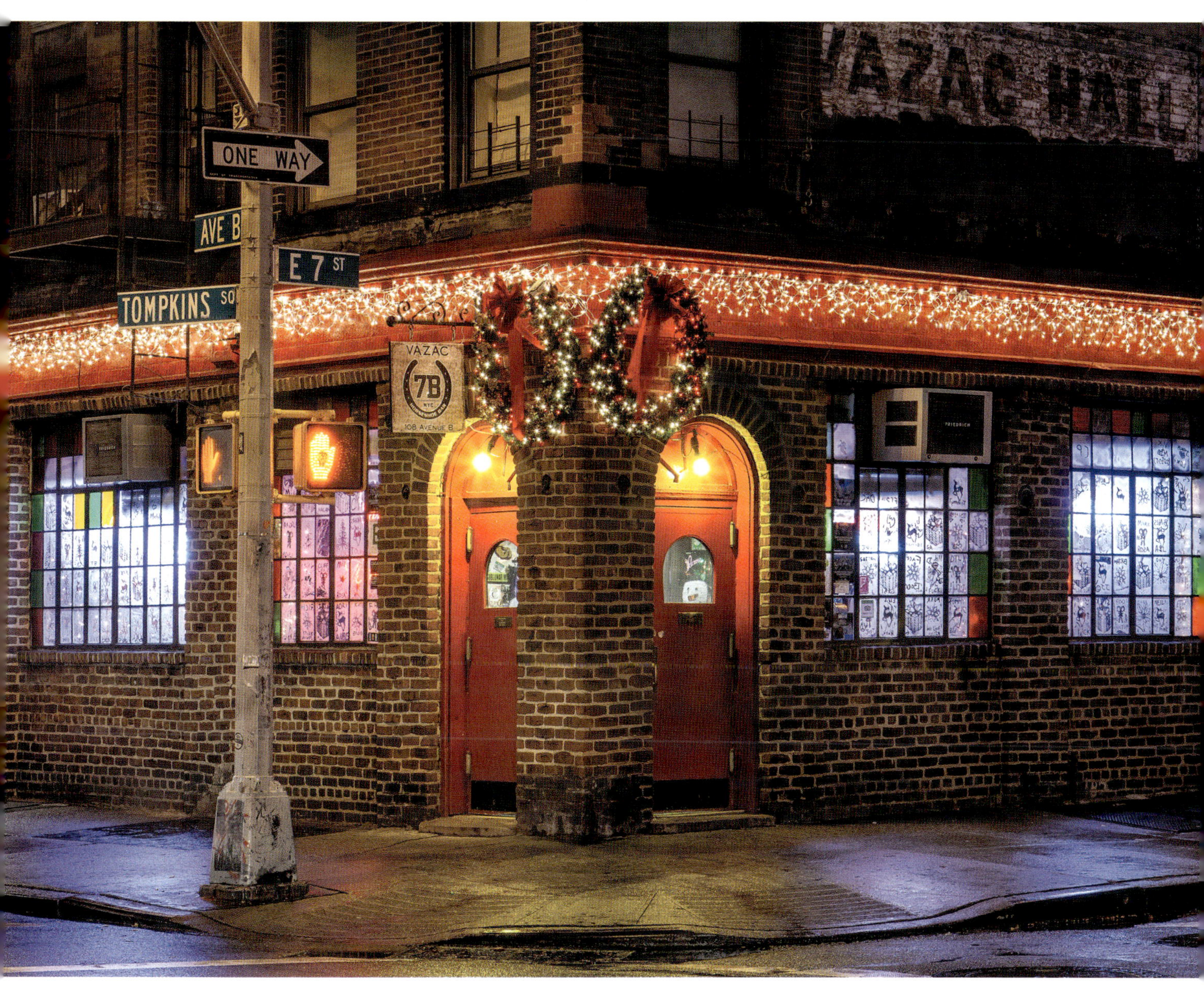

7B HORSESHOE BAR

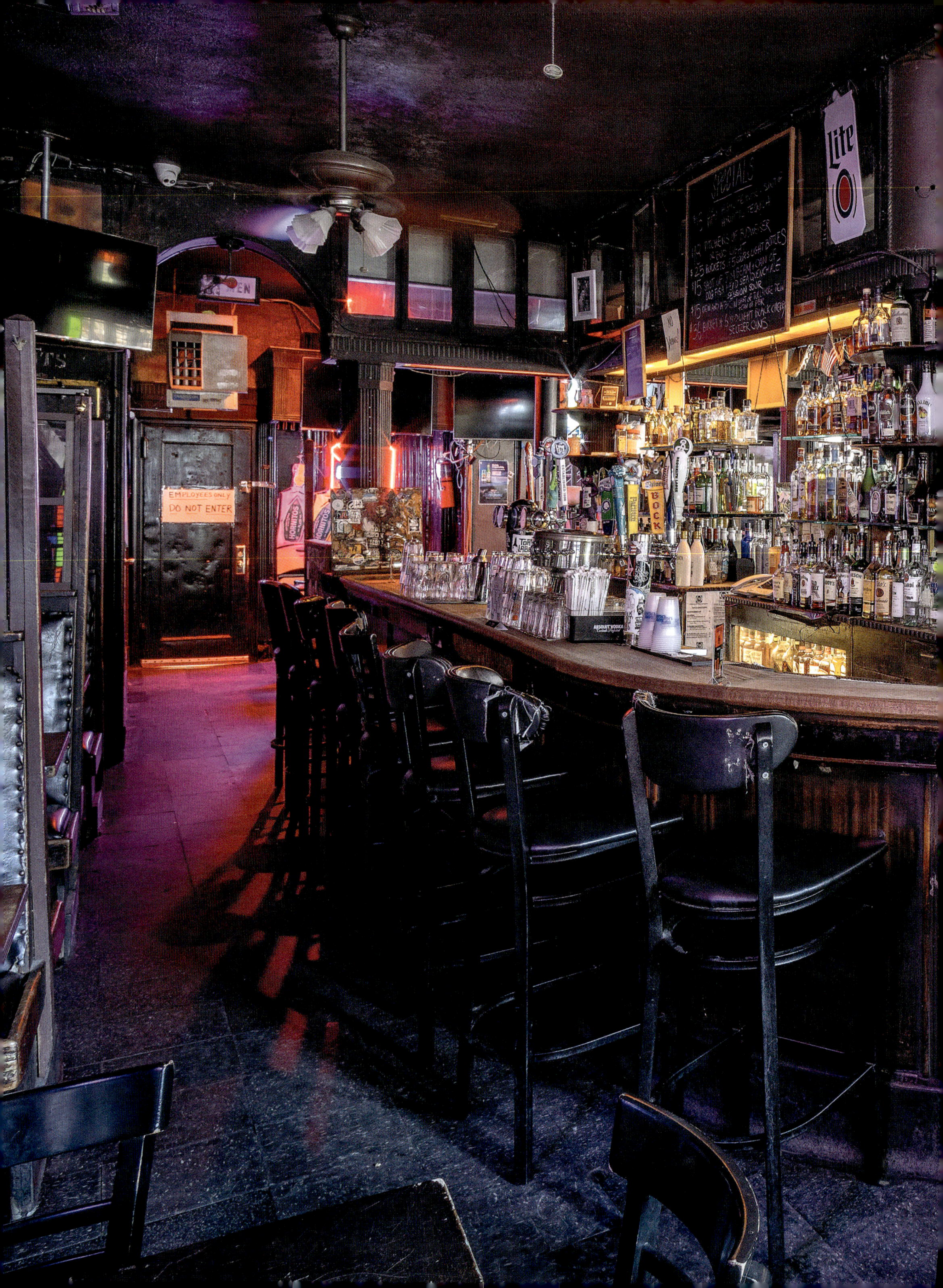

Lite
SPECIALS
EMPLOYEES ONLY
DO NOT ENTER
BOCK

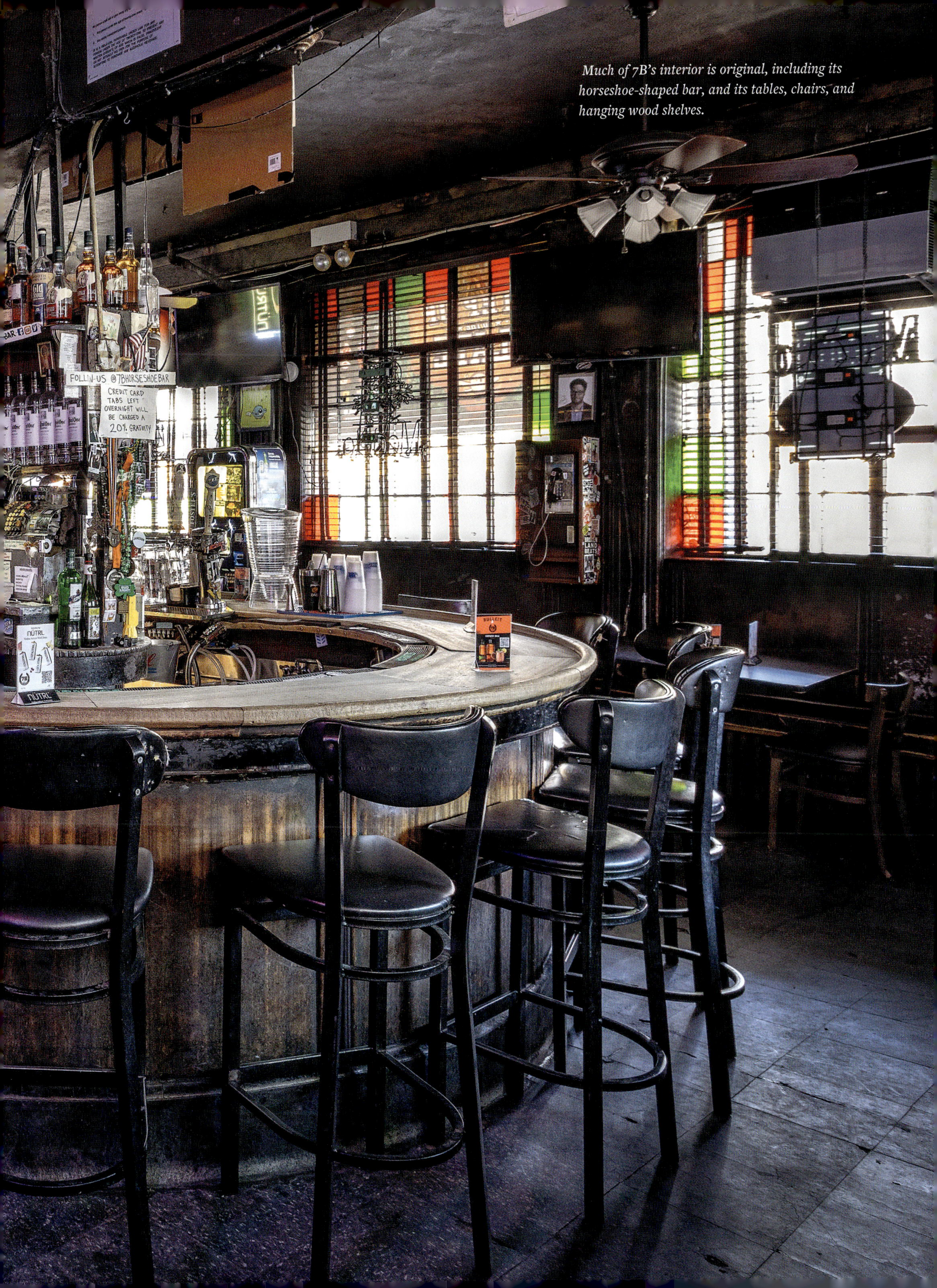

Much of 7B's interior is original, including its horseshoe-shaped bar, and its tables, chairs, and hanging wood shelves.

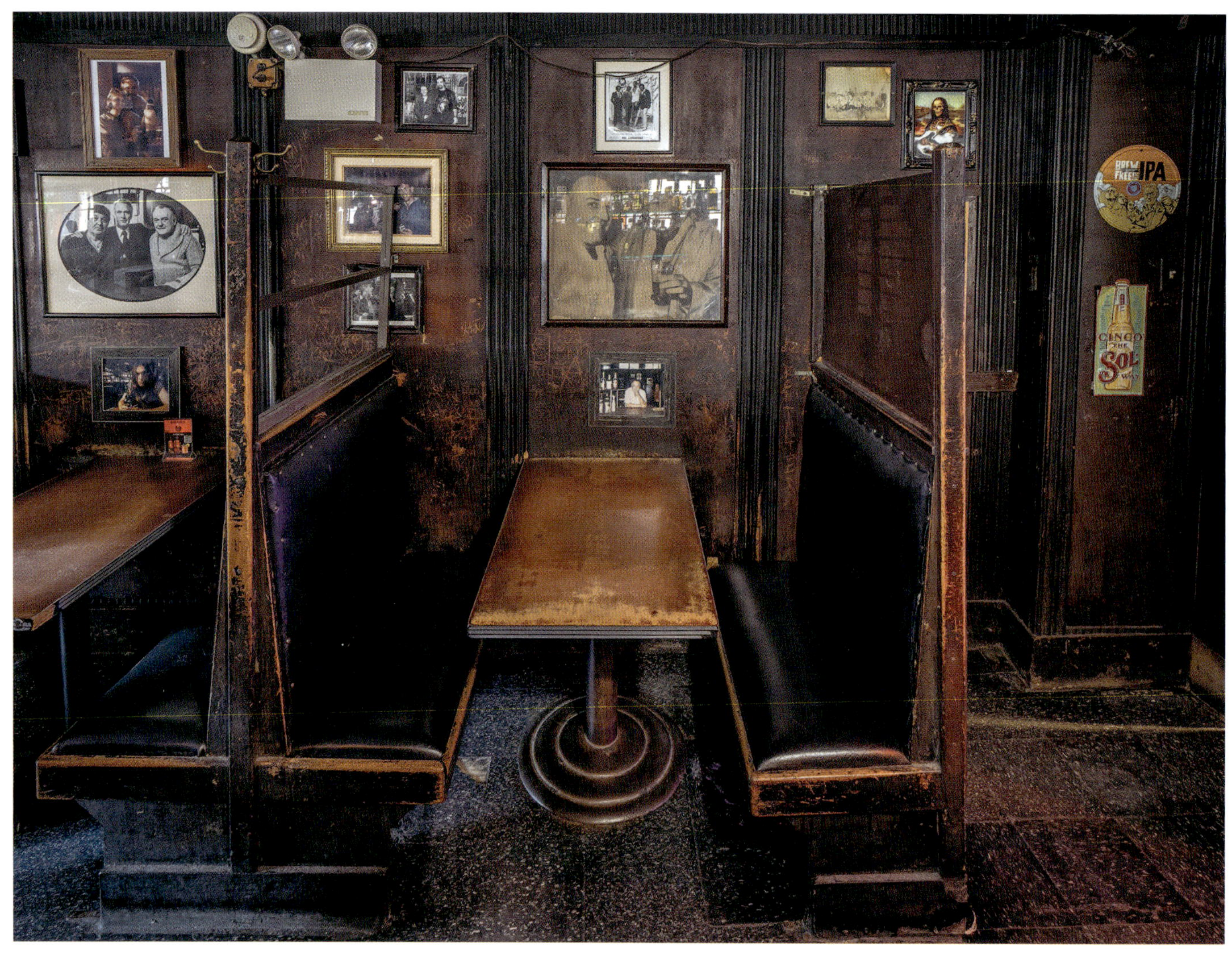

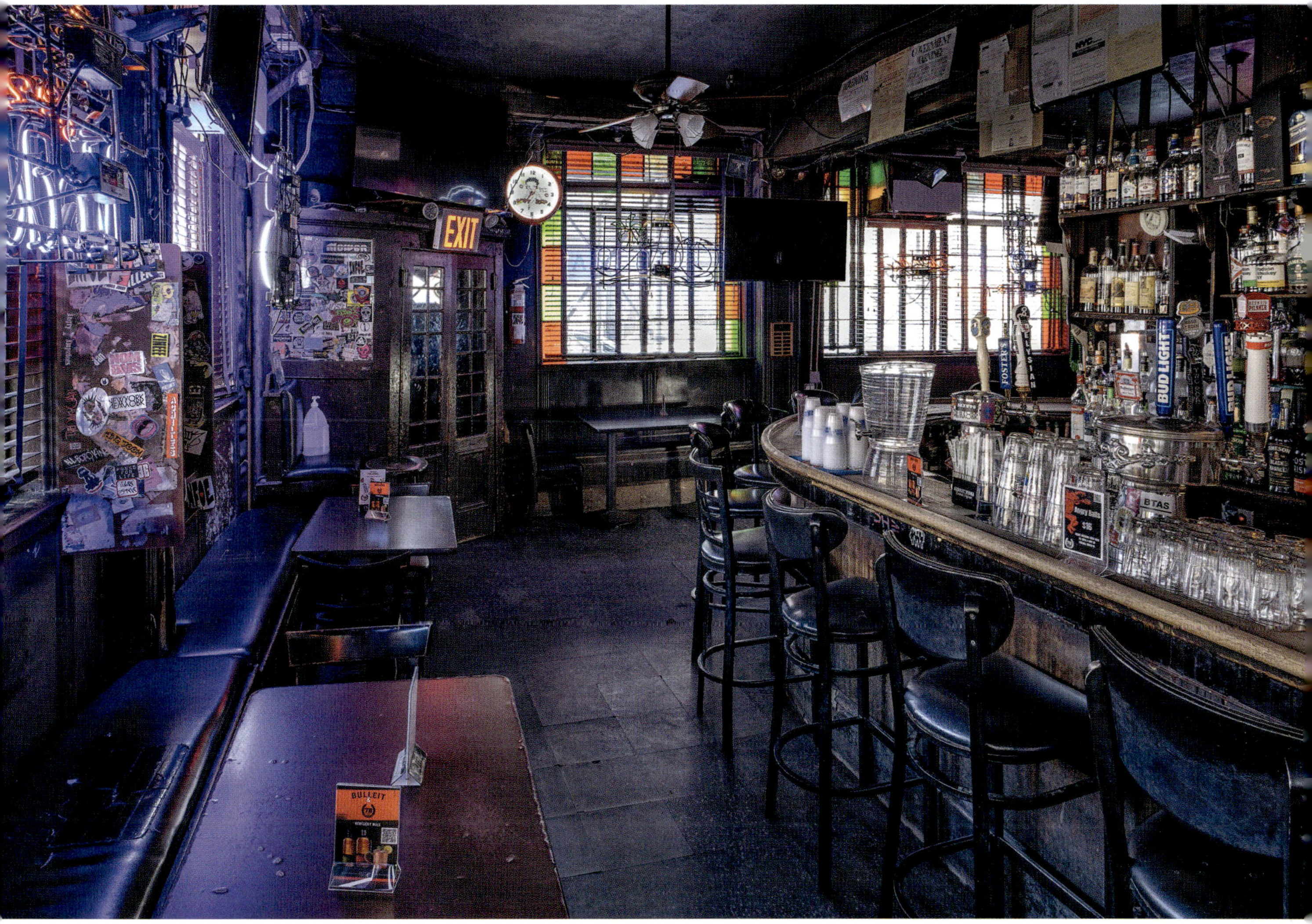

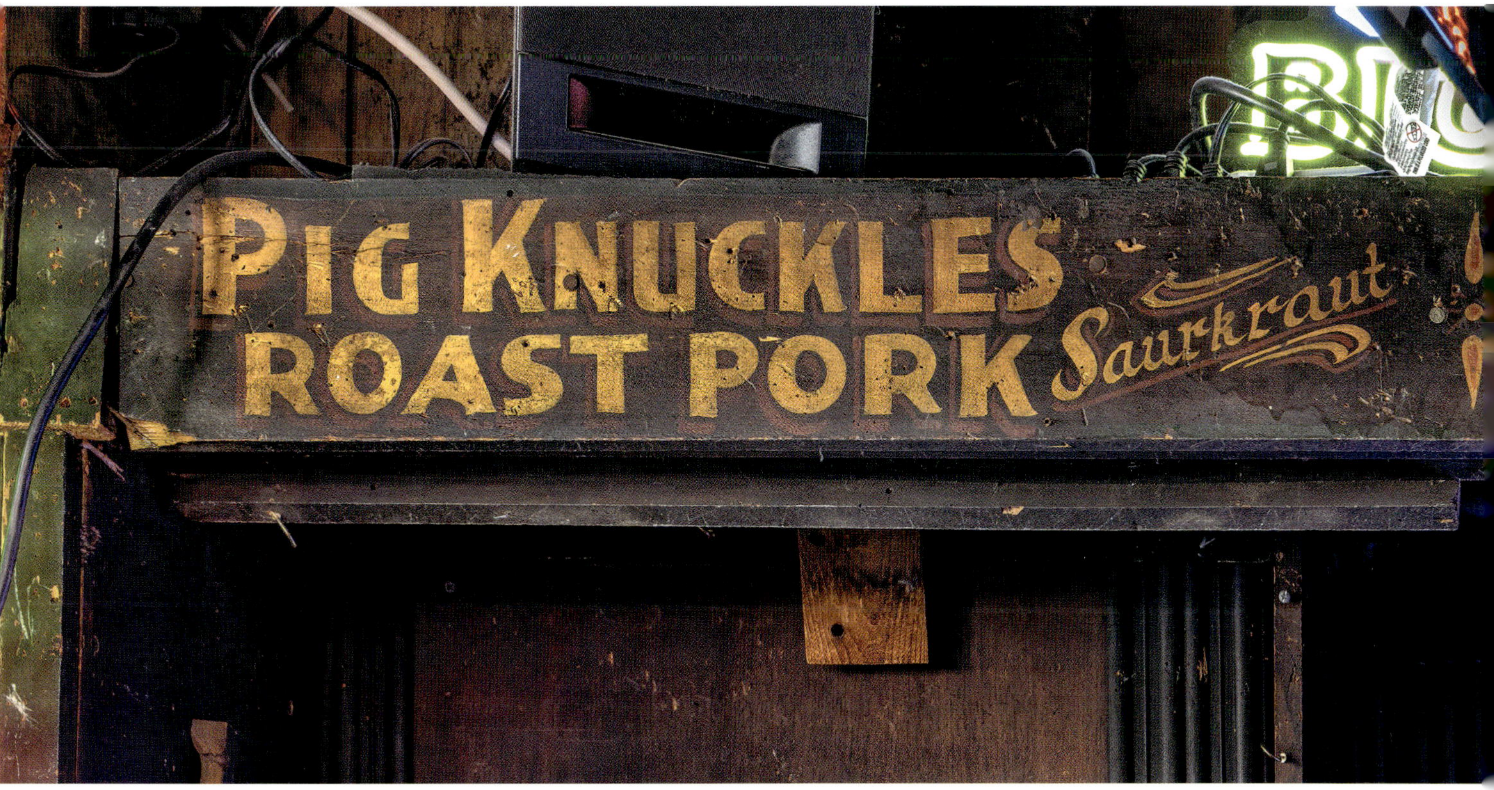

PIG KNUCKLES
ROAST PORK Saurkraut

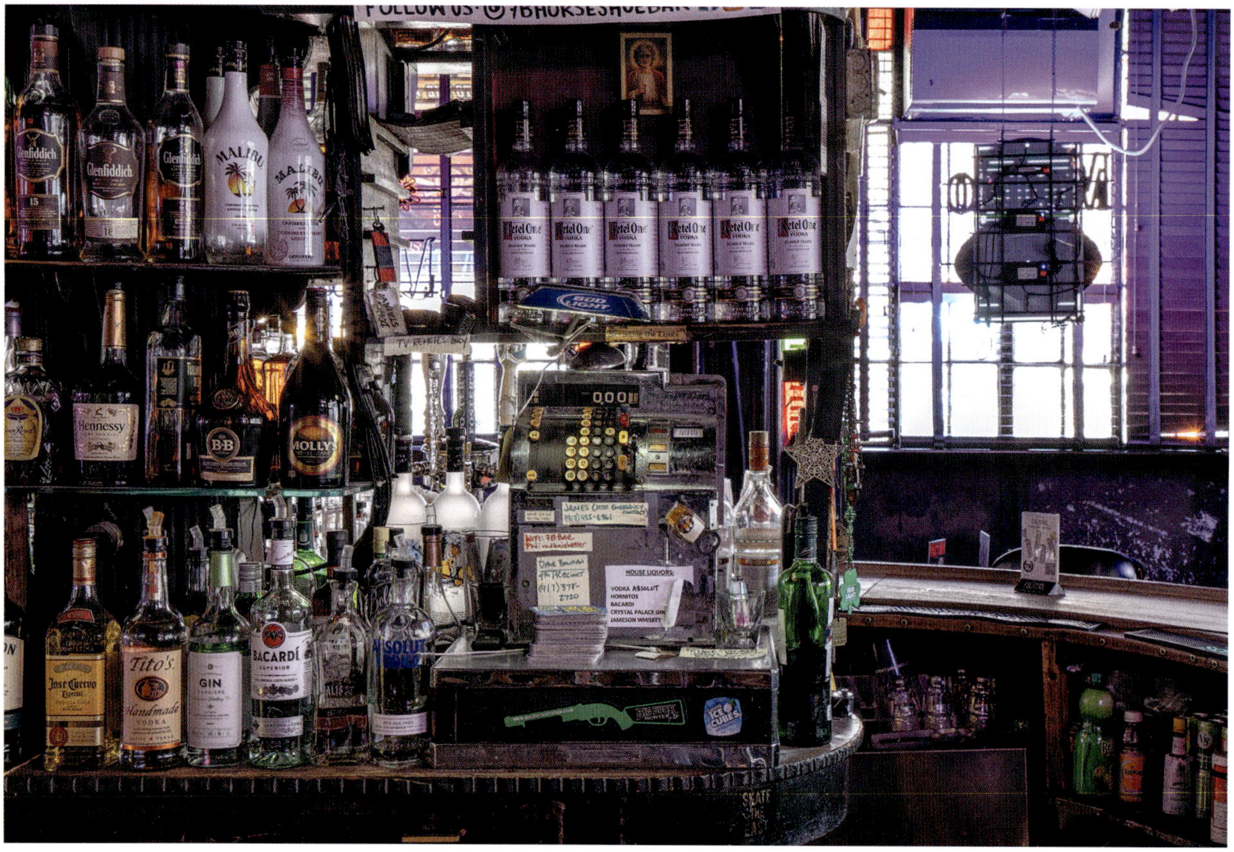

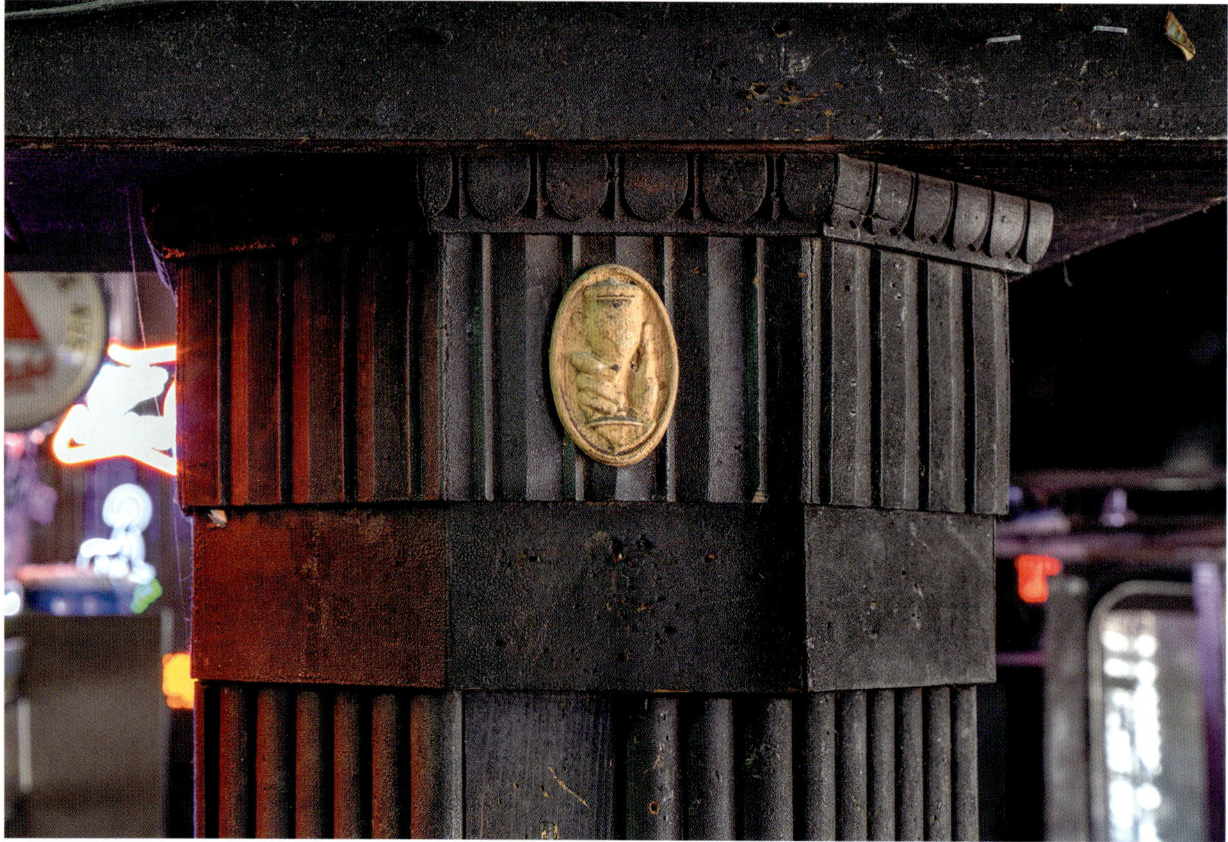

GREAT BARS OF NEW YORK CITY

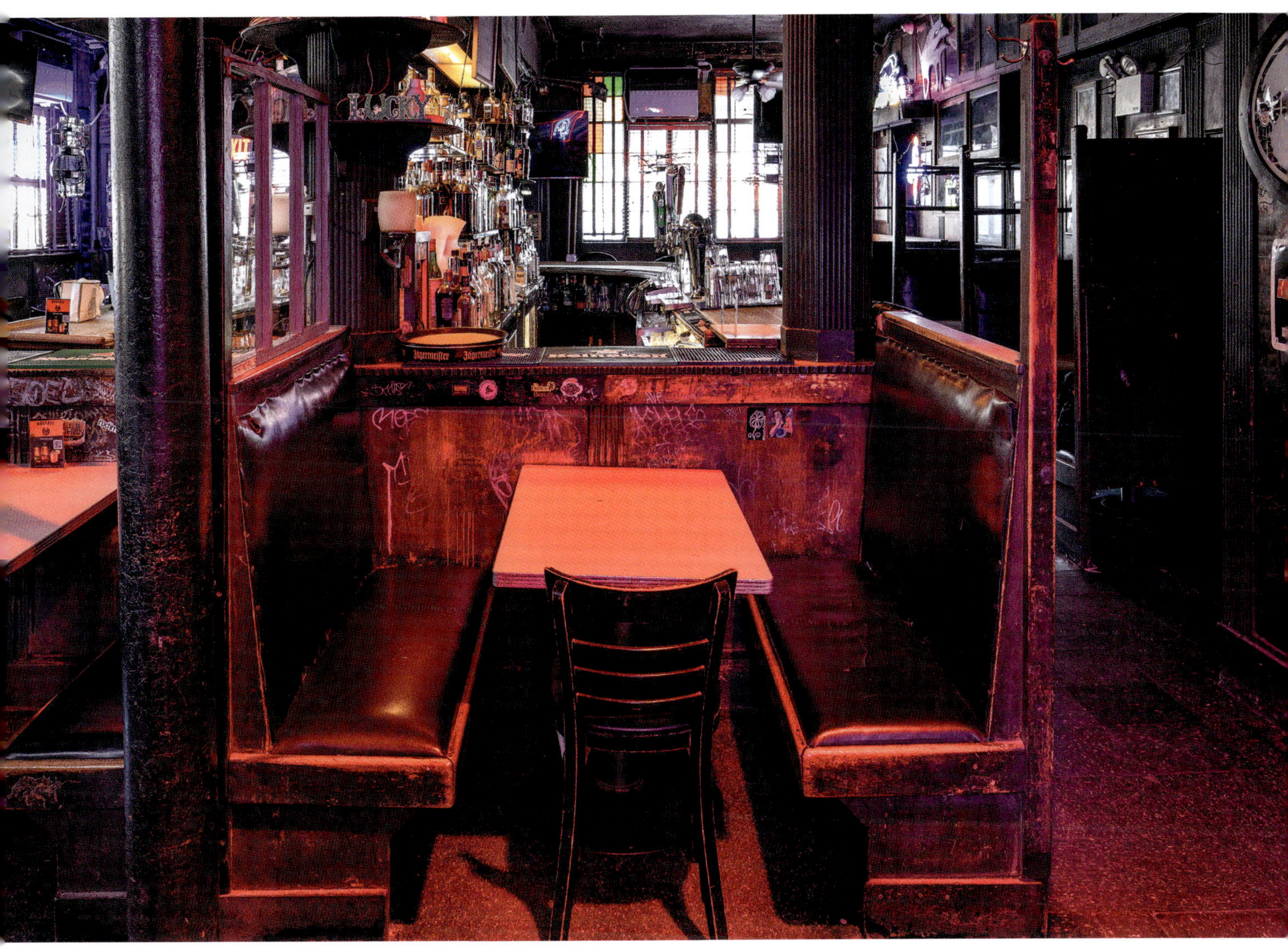

OPPOSITE TOP   *The bar also has the oldest liquor license in the East Village, dating back to 1948.*

ABOVE   *7B was originally opened in 1935 as a neighborhood catering spot known as Vazac Catering Hall.*

MINETTA TAVERN

113 MACDOUGAL STREET, GREENWICH VILLAGE

Surviving in one of Manhattan's now priciest neighborhoods for nearly a century, Minetta Tavern has aged gracefully from clandestine pub, to literary haunt frequented by the likes of Ernest Hemingway, to the chic West Village steakhouse it is today.

It's believed to have opened as a speakeasy called the Black Rabbit during Prohibition on the corner of MacDougal Street and Minetta Lane—a small street that, at the time, had a big reputation for crime and prostitution. The bar's official stance is that it was opened in 1937 by owner Eddie Sieveri, who the food website Eater says was "a fan of boxers, wrestlers, and starlets."

The theory behind the space's name is that it came from the Minetta Brook, a now nonexistent, 2-mile (6-kilometers) long water stream that ran from Twenty-Third Street to the Hudson River. Some neighborhood residents say it still flows under their apartments.

In its early days, the tavern's affordable prices attracted a wide array of local writers. According to legend, *Reader's Digest* magazine was founded in its basement. In addition to Hemingway, writers who held court at Minetta Tavern included Ezra Pound, E. E. Cummings, Eugene O'Neill, Dylan Thomas, John Dos Passos, and Beat Generation artists along with poets known as the Ravens. There was also F. Scott Fitzgerald who, along with his wife Zelda, was emblematic of Greenwich Village's laidback culture at the time (they were once photographed jumping into the fountain at Washington Square Park).

But perhaps the most loyal devotee was Joe Gould, the legendary bohemian writer and poet also known as Professor Seagull. So frequently was he at the Minetta Tavern—acting as a sort of philosopher-in-residence—that he was said to receive his mail there. Often homeless, he would trade a poem for two Martinis.

Later in the 1950s it was a hangout for William S. Burroughs and his friends Allen Ginsberg, Lucien Carr, and Jack Kerouac—some of whom remembered writing graffiti on the bathroom walls. In 1951 Minetta Tavern was the site of a fight between poet Gregory Corso and another patron over sculptor Marisol Escobar, who the former was dating at the time.

By the late 2000s Minetta Tavern was owned by Taka Becovic, originally from Montenegro, who had started working there as a busboy. He had purchased the bar thirteen years earlier but kept most of it completely intact, including the Northern Italian fare. The original owner, Eddie Sieveri, still came in to eat on his birthday. But as rents went up in the neighborhood, Becovic, as well as the Sieveri family (who tried to make an offer), would be priced out.

In 2008 it was announced that restaurateur Keith McNally of Balthazar and Pastis fame would be taking over Minetta Tavern, in partnership with his chefs Riad Nasr and Lee Hanson, with plans to reenvision it as a European bistro with a New York–dive spirit. In the deal, McNally purchased the space and its contents, from the wooden bar with leaded glass barback cabinetry dating back to 1937, to some of the artwork and photographs of erstwhile patrons. Above the wood-paneled walls in the main dining area, you'll find oil paintings depicting scenes of Greenwich Village, painted in 1953 by Texan silhouette artist Holden D. Wetherbee.

After a year of renovation, McNally unveiled the new Minetta Tavern, retrofitted to its 1930s splendor. The opening was hotly covered by New York food media, including Eater, which provided by-the-minute updates on the restoration, calling it the "MinettaWire."

The year it reopened, a *New York Times* restaurant critic gave the Minetta Tavern a three-star review. However, today, it is perhaps thought of more as a serious restaurant than a rowdy clubhouse for writers. Indeed, it now boasts a Michelin star and is known for serving one of the city's best burgers, a Black Label burger made with a special patty from renowned butcher Pat LaFrieda—a blend of New York strip, skirt steak, brisket, and dry-aged rib eye.

"Over the years, the faces have changed along with the times," says Erin Wendt, director of operations for McNally Restaurants. "If you are wandering through the neighborhood and want to stop in for a drink, a perfect Manhattan, a warm conversation with the bar staff, and a three-star dining menu are waiting for you. Minetta Tavern's bar is an escape from the present and the past in the comfort of timeless hospitality."

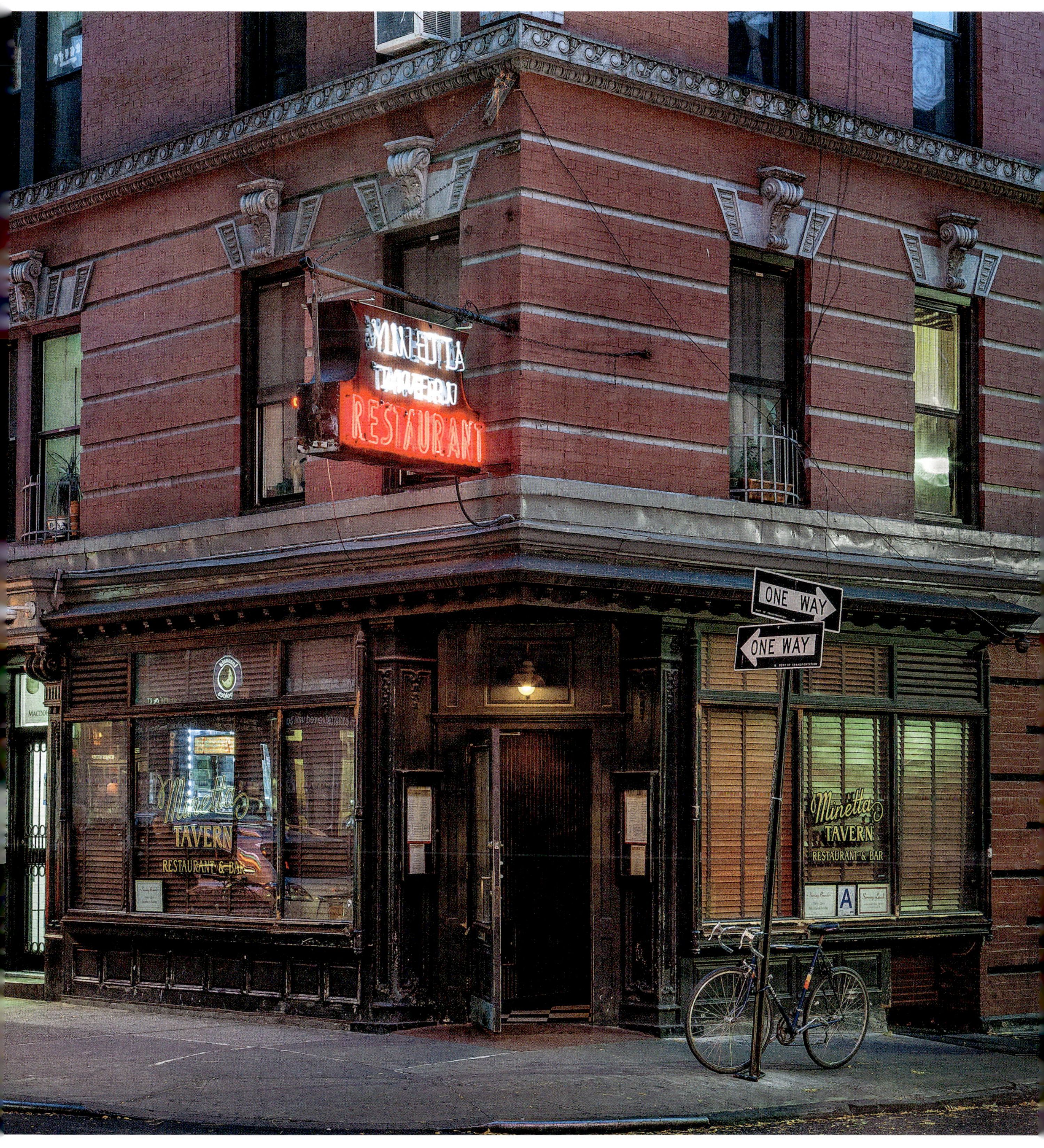
MINETTA
TAVERN
RESTAURANT
ONE WAY
ONE WAY
Minetta
TAVERN
RESTAURANT & BAR
Minetta
TAVERN
RESTAURANT & BAR
A

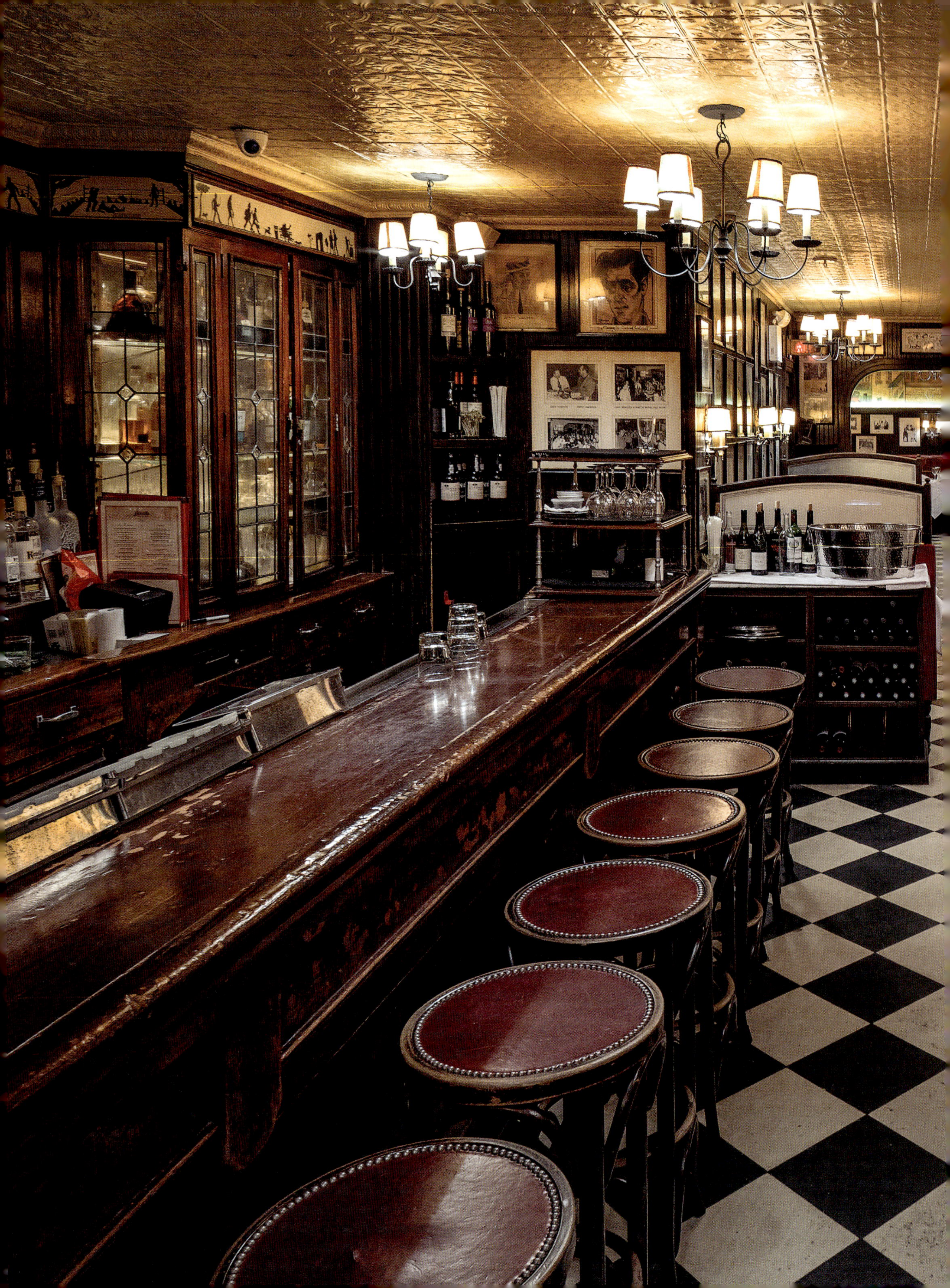

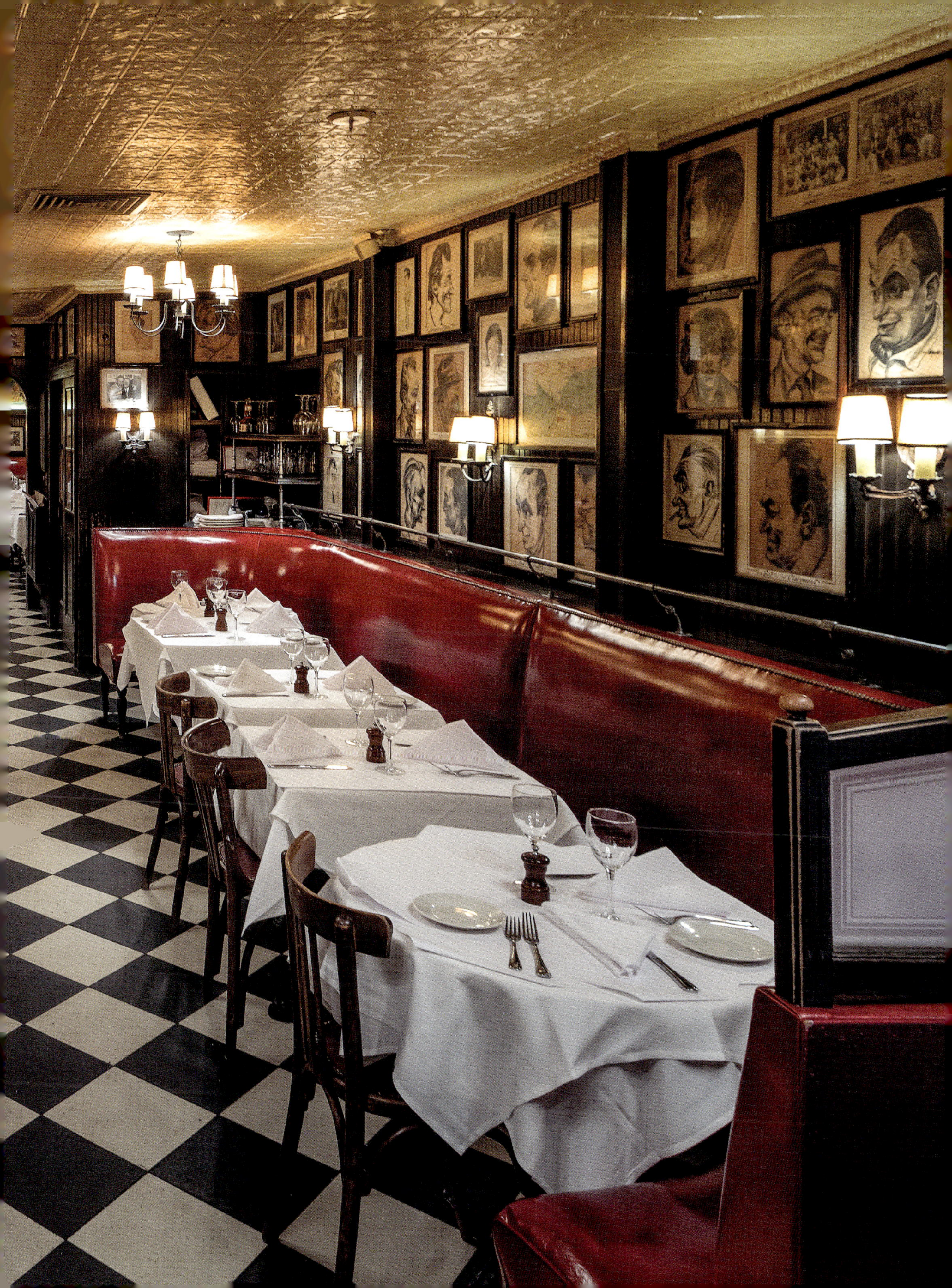

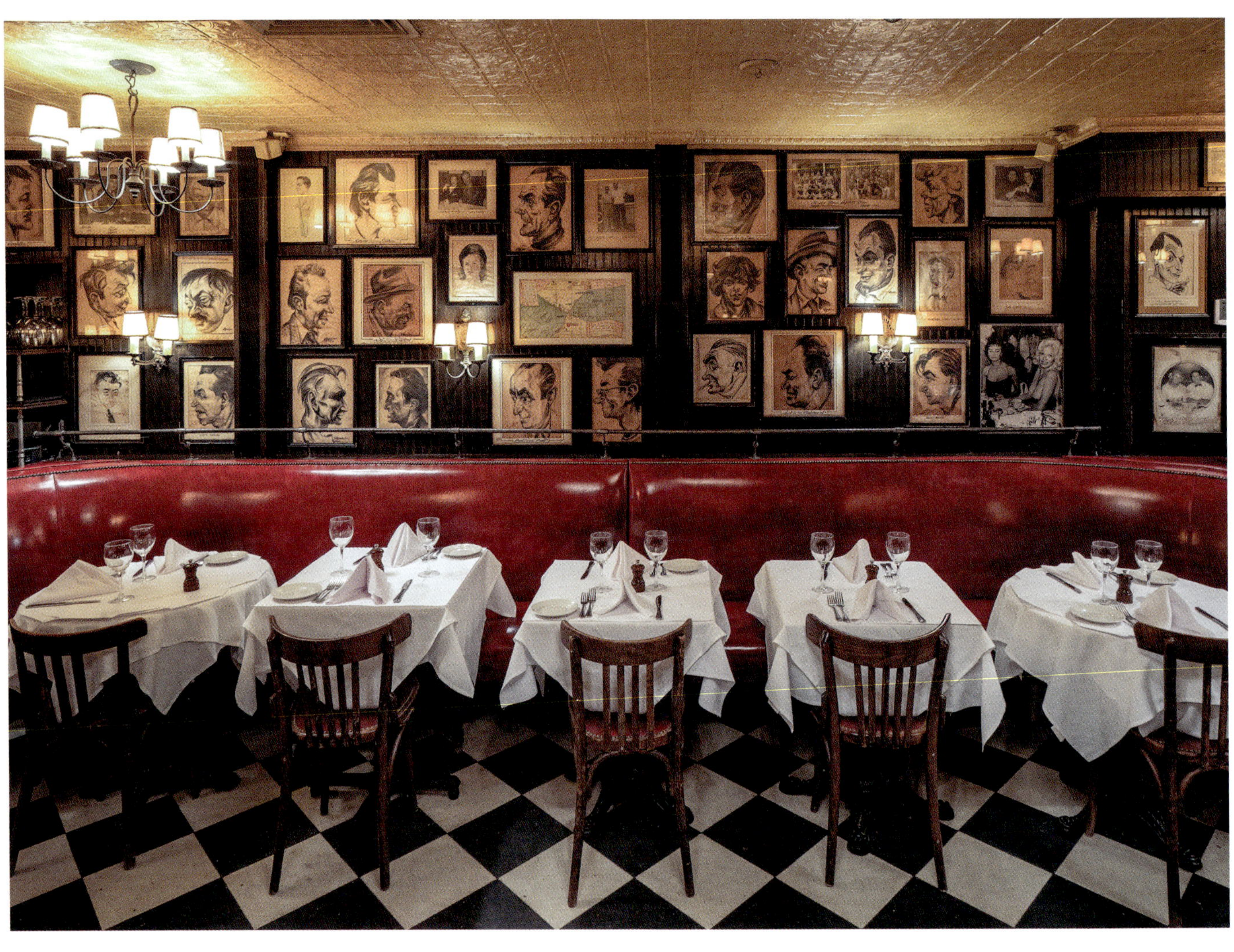

   GREAT BARS OF NEW YORK CITY

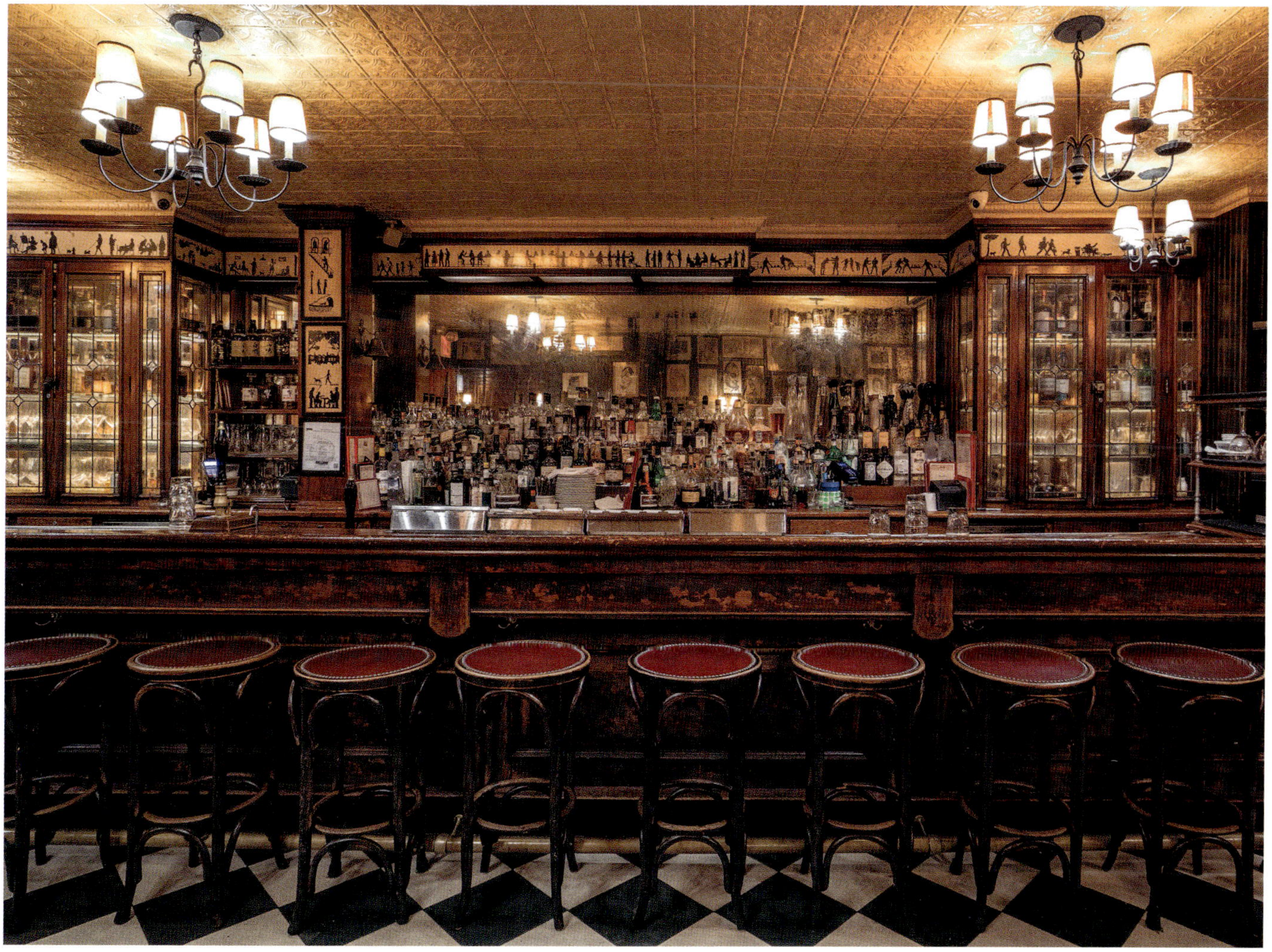

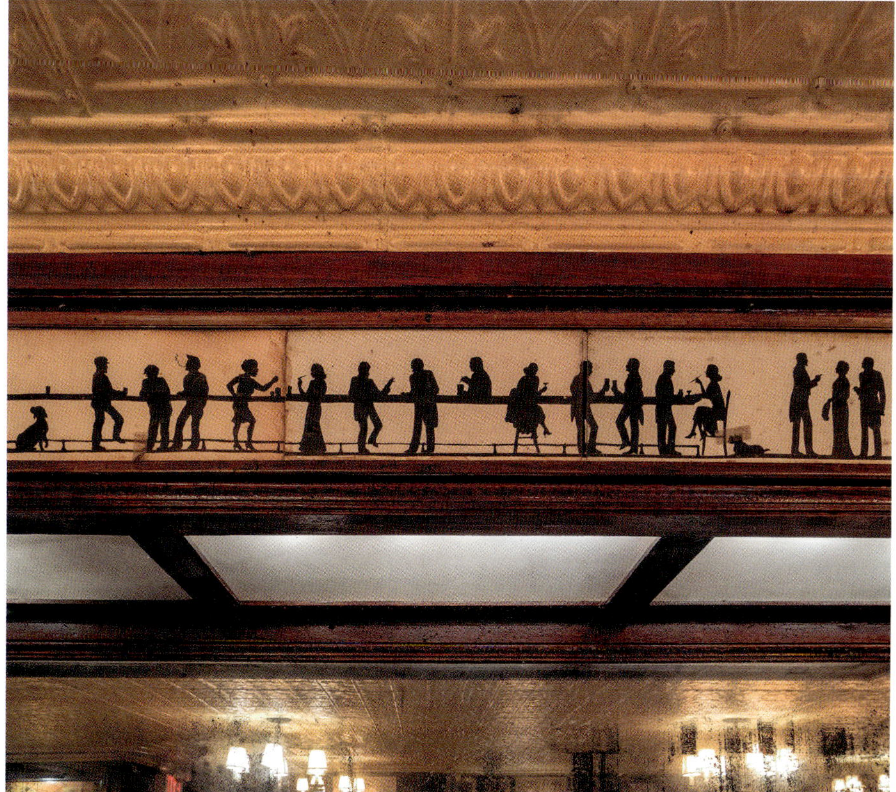

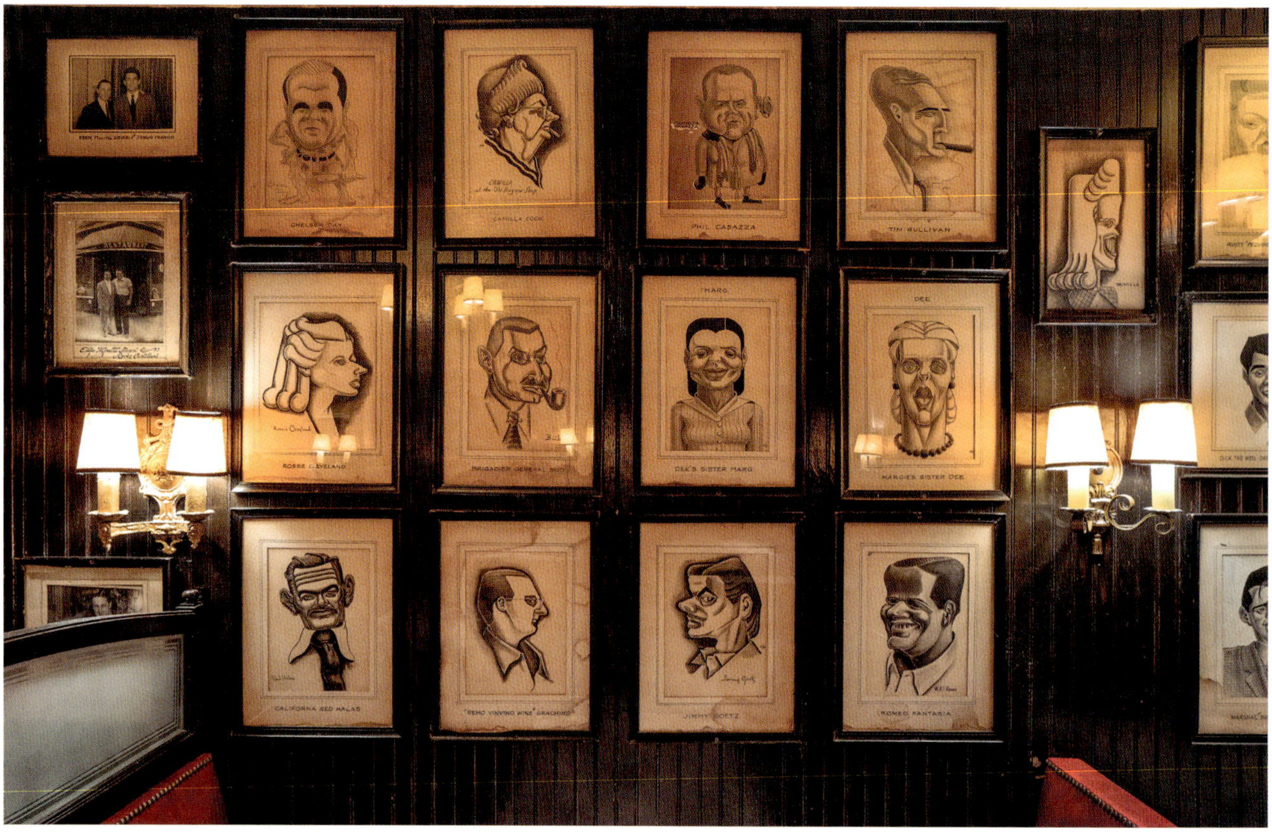
CAMILLA COOK
PHIL CASAZZA
TIM SULLIVAN
MARG
DEE
ROSSIE CLEVELAND
DEE'S SISTER MARG
MARGIES SISTER DEE
CALIFORNA RED HALAS
"REMO VINVINO WINE" GRACHINO
JIMMY GOETZ
ROMEO FANTASIA

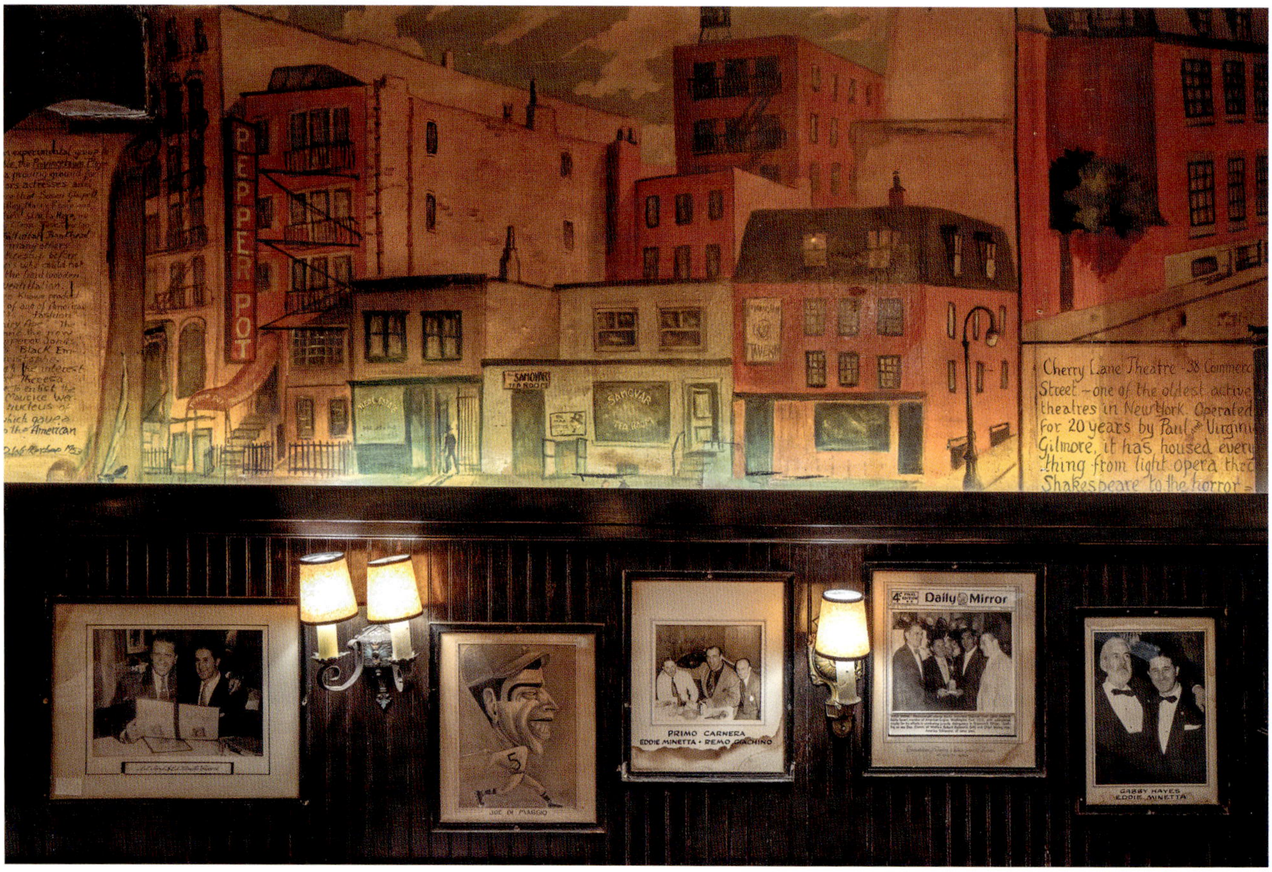
PEPPER POT
SAMOVAR
Cherry Lane Theatre - 38 Commerc
Street - one of the oldest active
theatres in New York. Operated
for 20 years by Paul & Virgini
Gilmore, it has housed every
thing from light opera thro
Shakespeare to the horror -
Daily Mirror
PRIMO CARNERA
EDDIE MINETTA + REMO GRACHINO
JOE DI MAGGIO
GABBY HAYES
EDDIE MINETTA

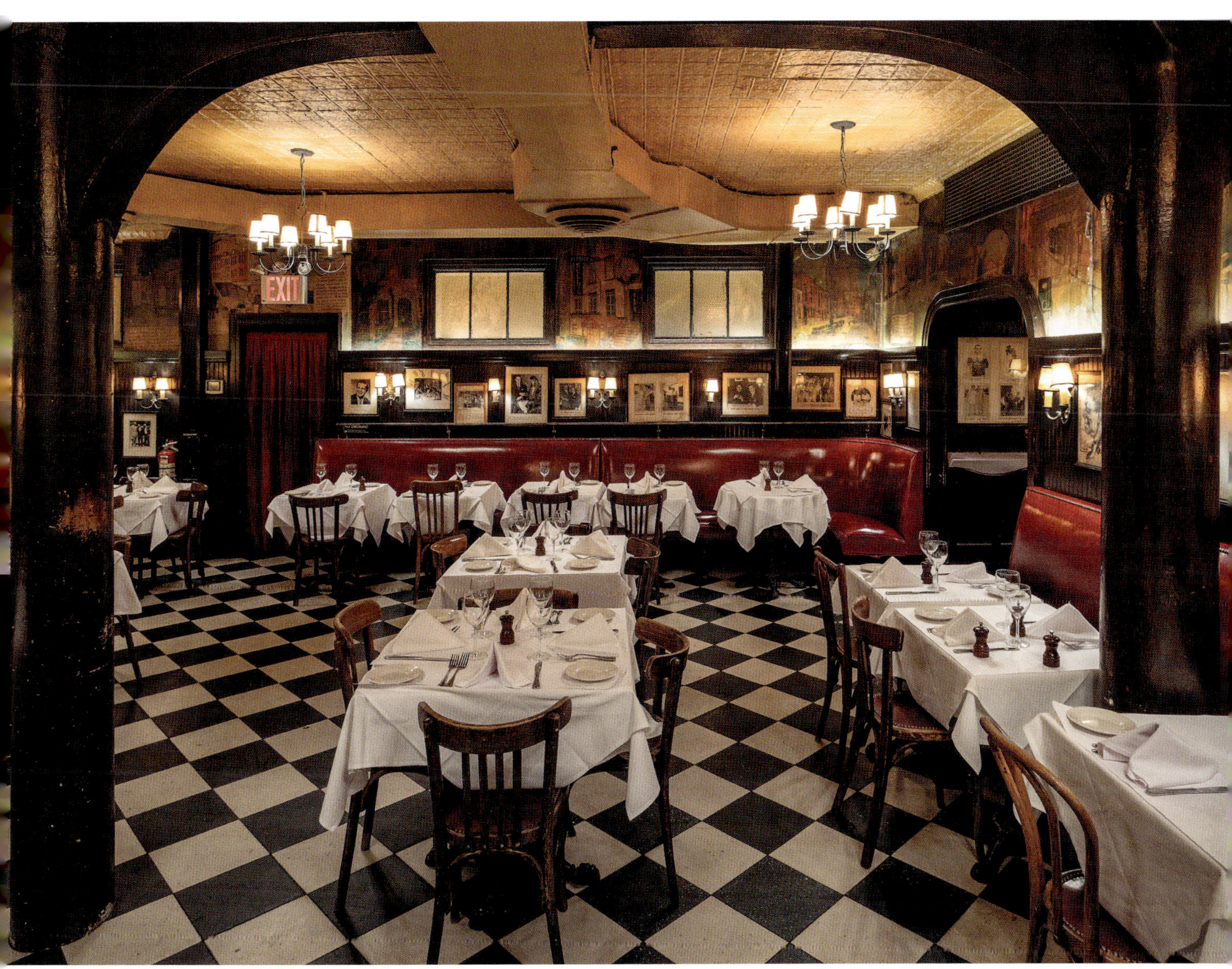

OPPOSITE TOP   *Framed caricatures of many of the bar's patrons, including struggling artists, bohemians, and eccentric writers, line the walls.*

OPPOSITE BOTTOM   *Above the wood paneling are gorgeous oil paintings depicting scenes of Greenwich Village painted by Holden D. Wetherbee in 1953.*

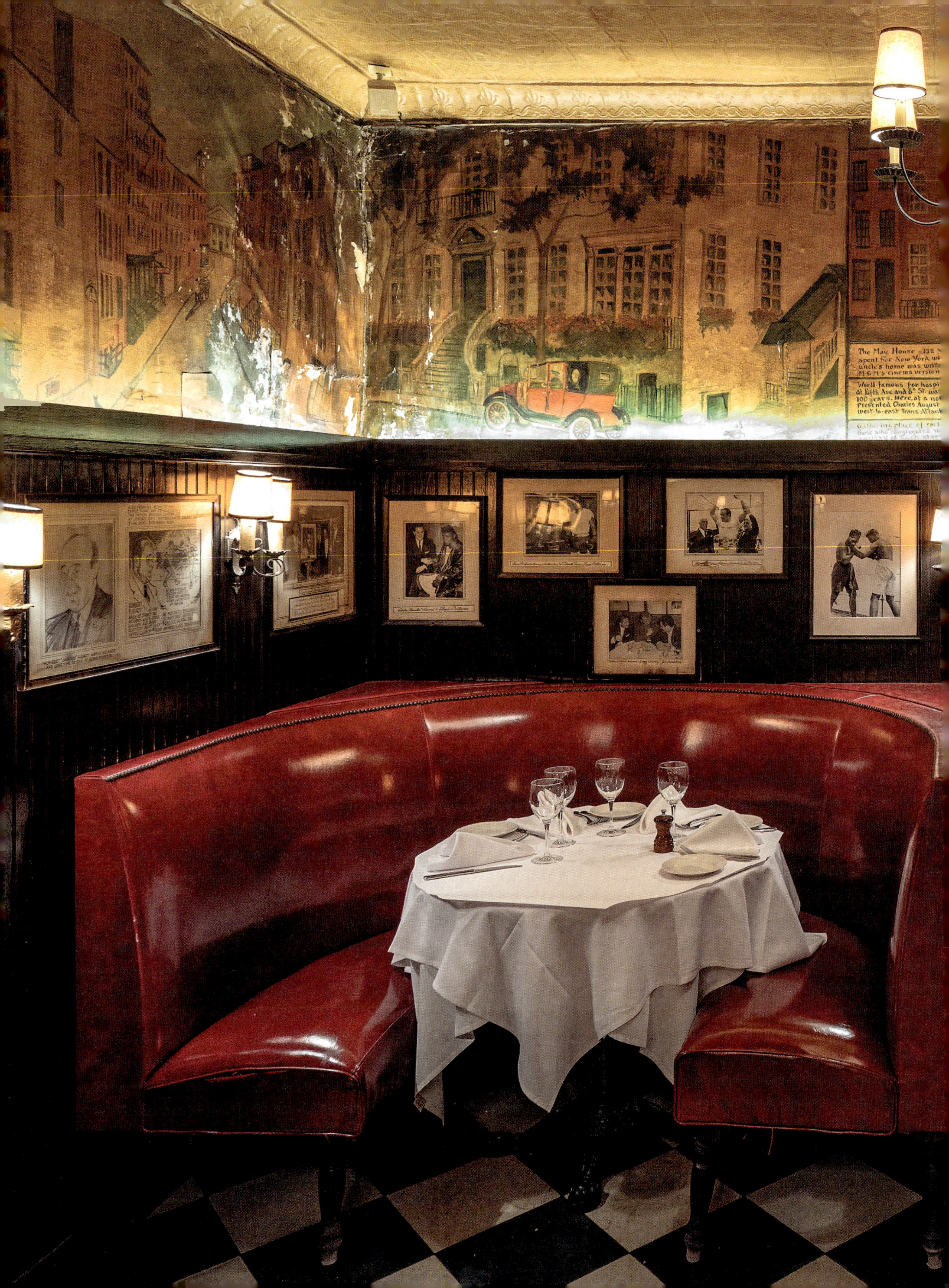
The May House - 132 N
spent her New York wi
uncle's home was writte
M-G-M's cinema version
World famous for hospi
at Fifth Ave. and 8th St. was
100 years. Here, at a no
presented Charles August
west-to-east trans-Atlant

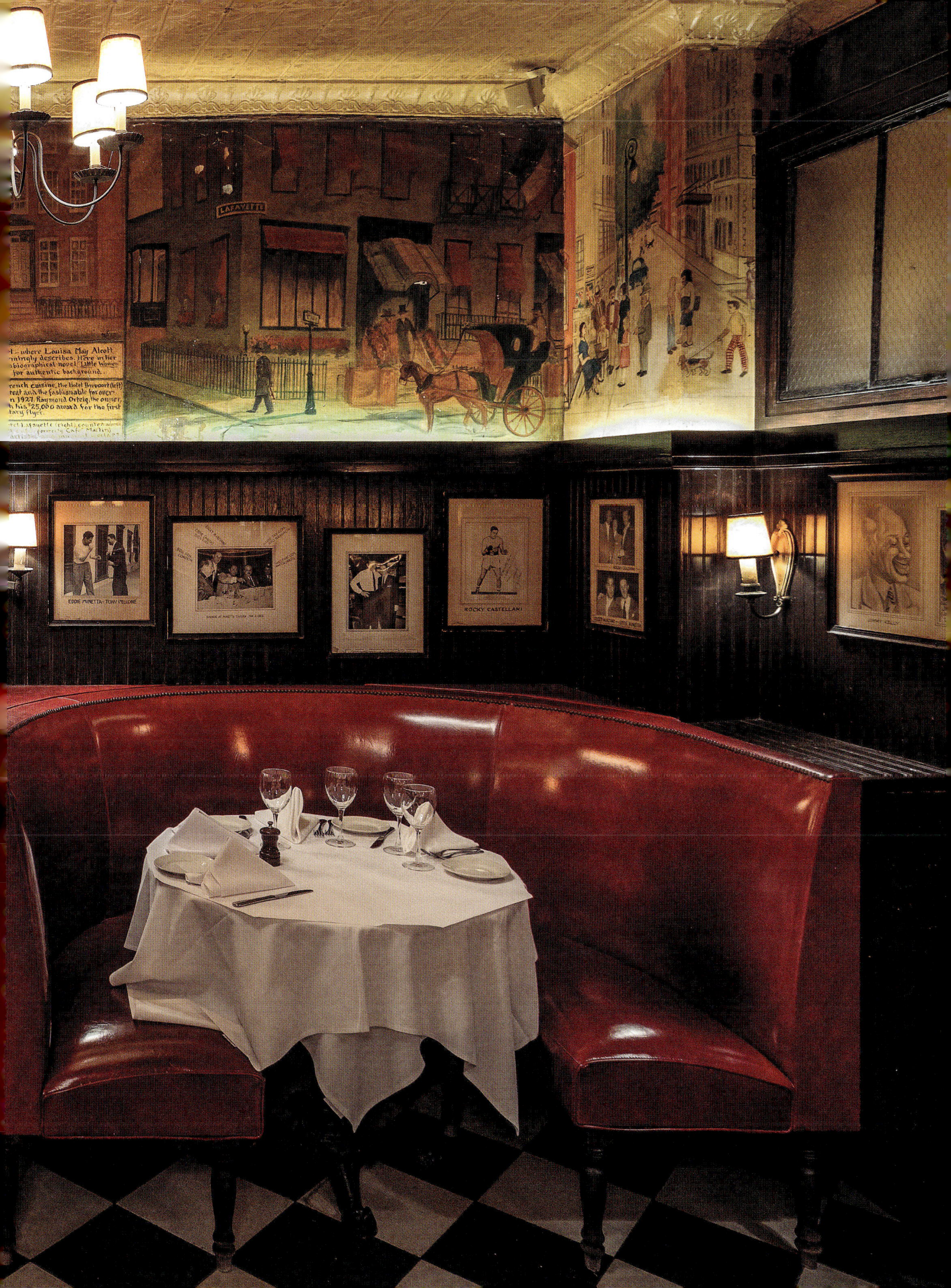

LAFAYETTE
— where Louisa May Alcott
...mingly describes. Here in her
...biographical novel "Little Women"
...for authentic background.
...rench cuisine, the Hotel Brevoort (left)
...reat and the fashionable for over
...1927, Raymond Orteig, the owner,
...h his $25,000 award for the first
...tary flyer.
...tel Lafayette (right) counter...
...(formerly Café Martin)
EDDIE MINETTA — TONY MELLONE
ROCKY CASTELLANI

JIMMY'S CORNER

140 WEST 44TH STREET,
TIMES SQUARE

With its illuminated billboards and crowds of tourists, Times Square is no longer the gritty slice of old New York City it once was. However, in the world-famous neighborhood that has undergone tremendous change within the last half century—from a seedy entertainment district to a sanitized corporate hub—one beloved bar has withstood the test of time.

Tucked away on Forty-Fourth Street between Sixth and Seventh Avenues, Jimmy's Corner is one of the city's remaining legendary dives that today serves as a time capsule to yesteryear. After all, it opened in 1971, a period during which Times Square was filled with go-go bars and adult movie theaters. Crime was rampant and would remain so until a commercial building boom in the 1980s that brought in offices and hotels, followed by a drastic drop in unemployment in the '90s.

Throughout its history, the bar has been synonymous, both in name and spirit, with its late owner Jimmy Glenn—a former fighter, professional boxing trainer, and cutman/manager for Floyd Patterson. Glenn, the grandson of a South Carolina sharecropper, who had moved to Harlem as a teenager, opened his bar during the same year Joe Frazier went up against Muhammad Ali at nearby Madison Square Garden. To keep sex workers and pimps out, he posted two signs: "No unescorted women" and "No hats allowed."

Glenn, who passed away in 2020, was known to work six nights a week at the bar (on the seventh, he worked with boxers). Due to his relationships in the sport, Jimmy's would quickly become known as a destination for fans of boxing as well as those in the boxing community. Glenn cheekily nailed a ringside bell from Madison Square Garden to the wall, tempting those who might ring it, thus having to buy a round for the whole bar.

Several years after opening Jimmy's, he also opened the Times Square Boxing Club on Forty-Second Street. Among those who sparred at the gym was Muhammad Ali. Photos of Glenn and Ali blanket the walls, and the bar still shows fights on its multiple TVs.

Beyond boxers, Jimmy's served numerous A-list customers, from Sammy Davis Jr. to Frank Sinatra and Michael Jordan. It also captured the attention of Martin Scorsese, who shot the closing scenes of his 1980 biographical sports drama *Raging Bull*, about boxing champion Jake LaMotta, here. A still of Robert DeNiro as LaMotta still hangs near the cash register.

Today, Jimmy's still attracts loyal boxing fans, but also theatergoers attending Broadway shows, as well as countless visitors from around the world who step into its narrow, dimly lit space filled with memorabilia, vintage fight posters, and autographed photographs of iconic boxers. It exudes an aura of old-school charm thanks to its well-preserved features, including a vintage jukebox that turns out soulful tunes from the likes of Etta James and Sam Cooke, and a sign hanging behind the bar advising patrons: "Let's not discuss politics here."

When the *New Yorker* revisited Jimmy's in 2018, it called the bar's survival an underdog story, noting that Glenn was still working behind the bar and adding, "Even the price of booze—draft beers for three dollars, mixed drinks from the rail for fifty cents more—remains stubbornly out of step with inflation."

Since Glenn's passing, his son Adam has taken over the reins, keeping the bar within the family. The younger Glenn had grown up in the space: at the age of seven, he was already starting to take cash deposits from the bar to the bank. And despite graduating from Harvard Law School and working at a prestigious firm nearby, he still moonlighted as a bartender. By 2015 he traded his life as a lawyer to follow in his father's footsteps, running the bar and managing boxers.

Nowadays, if you find yourself in Times Square, stop by Jimmy's and sidle up to the wooden counter for an ice-cold beer, or the house cocktail, the Jimmy's Hurricane, which blends spiced rum, amaretto, and juice for a heady kick.

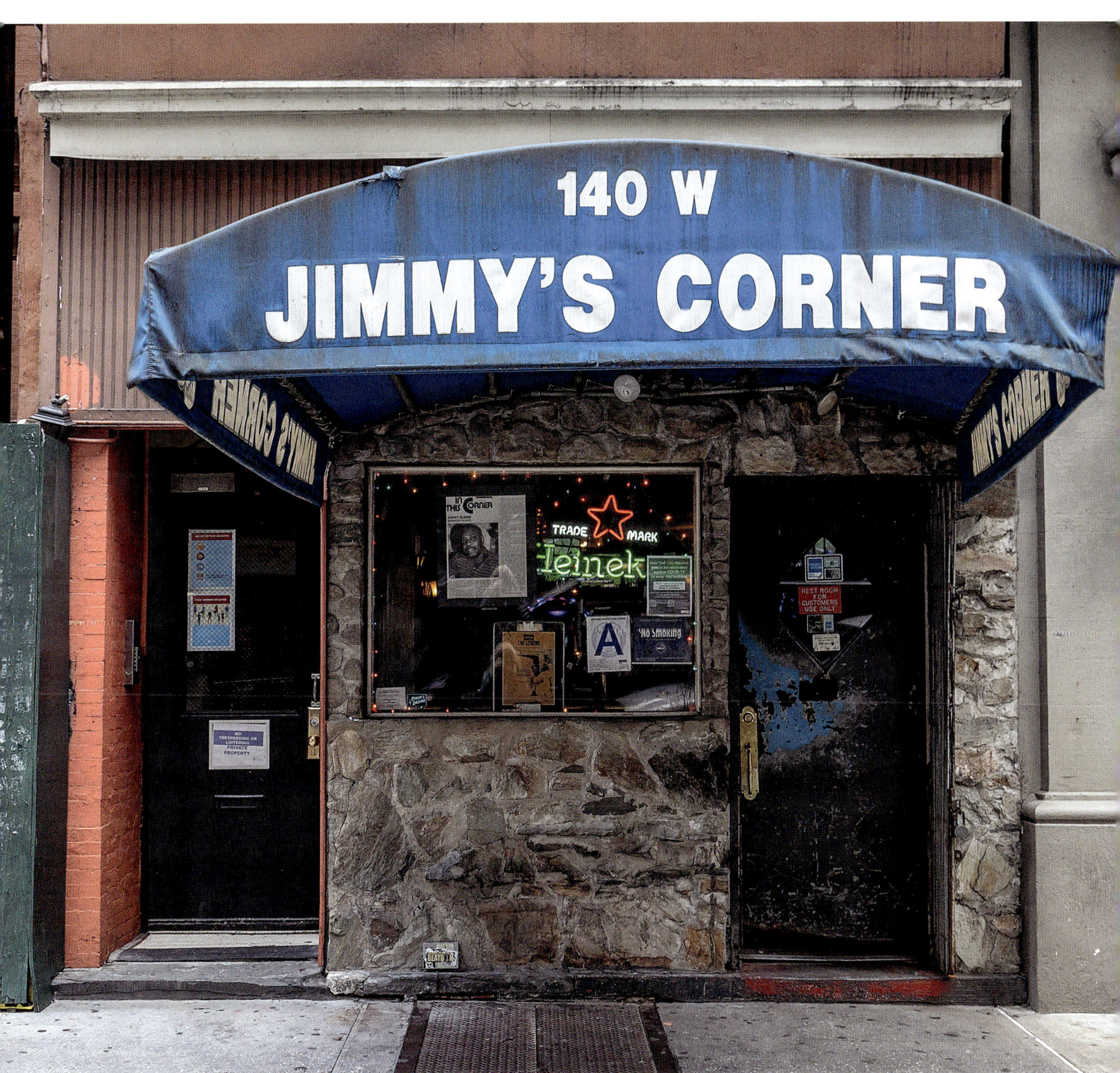

140 W
JIMMY'S CORNER

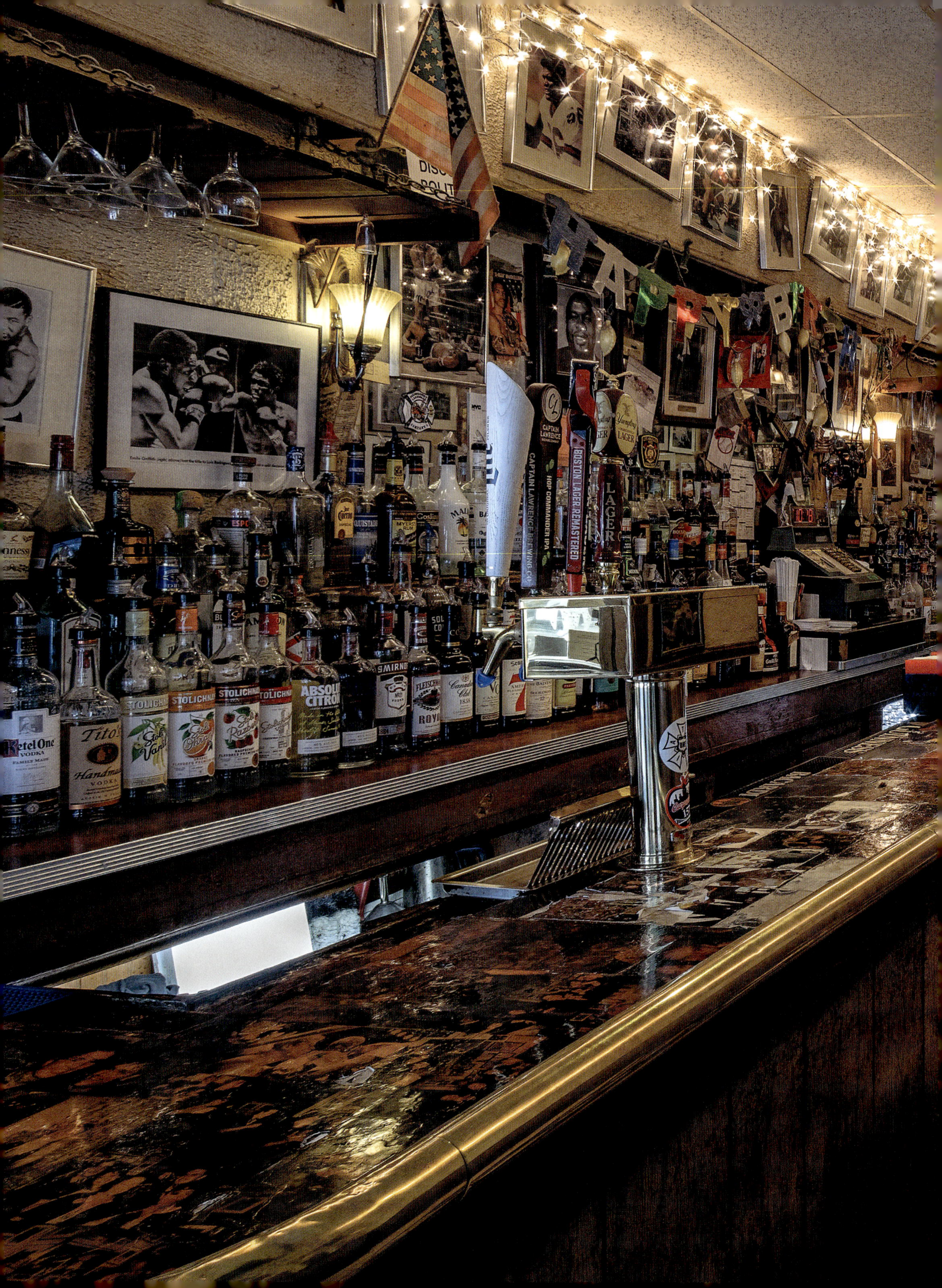

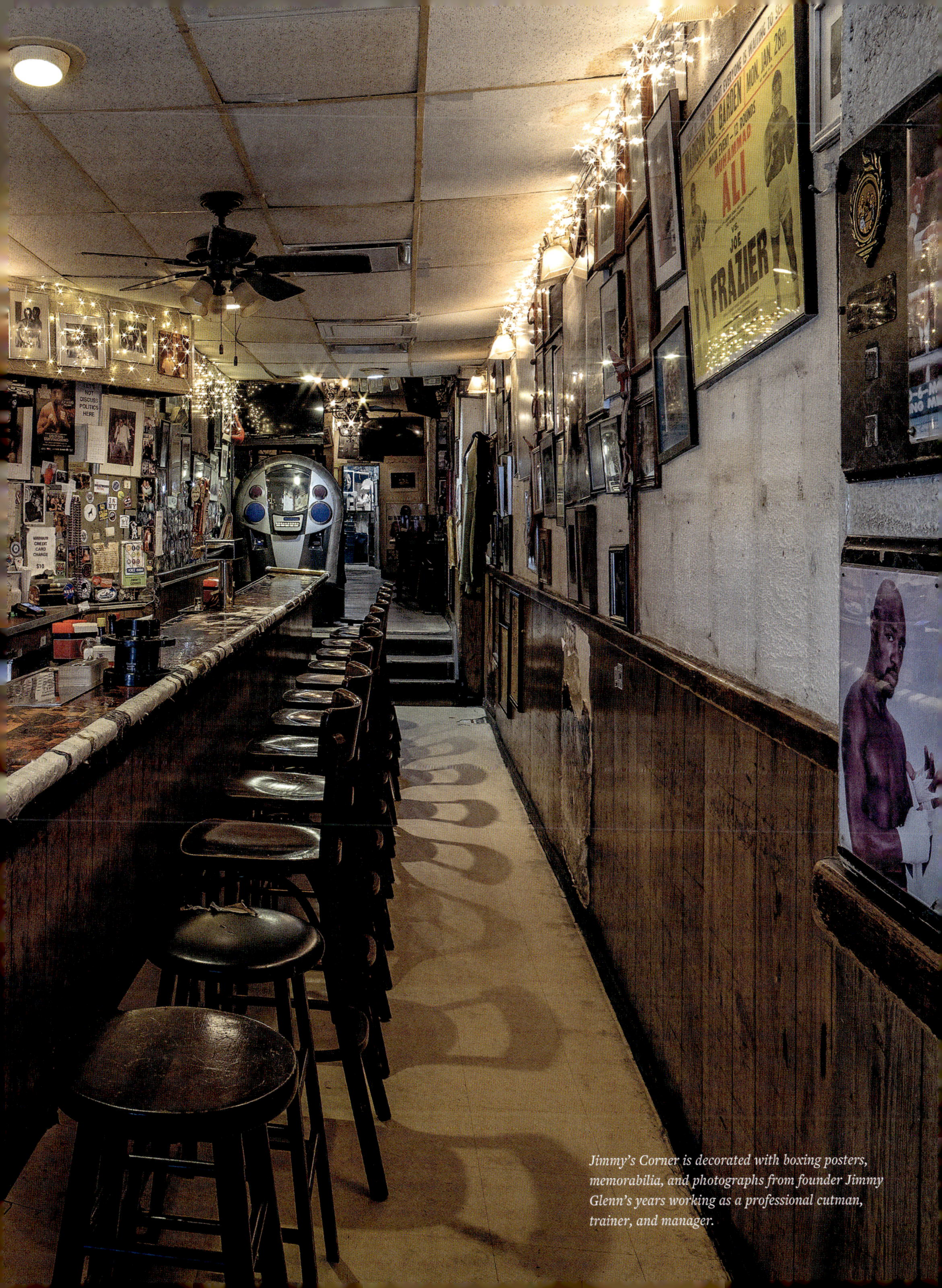

Jimmy's Corner is decorated with boxing posters, memorabilia, and photographs from founder Jimmy Glenn's years working as a professional cutman, trainer, and manager.

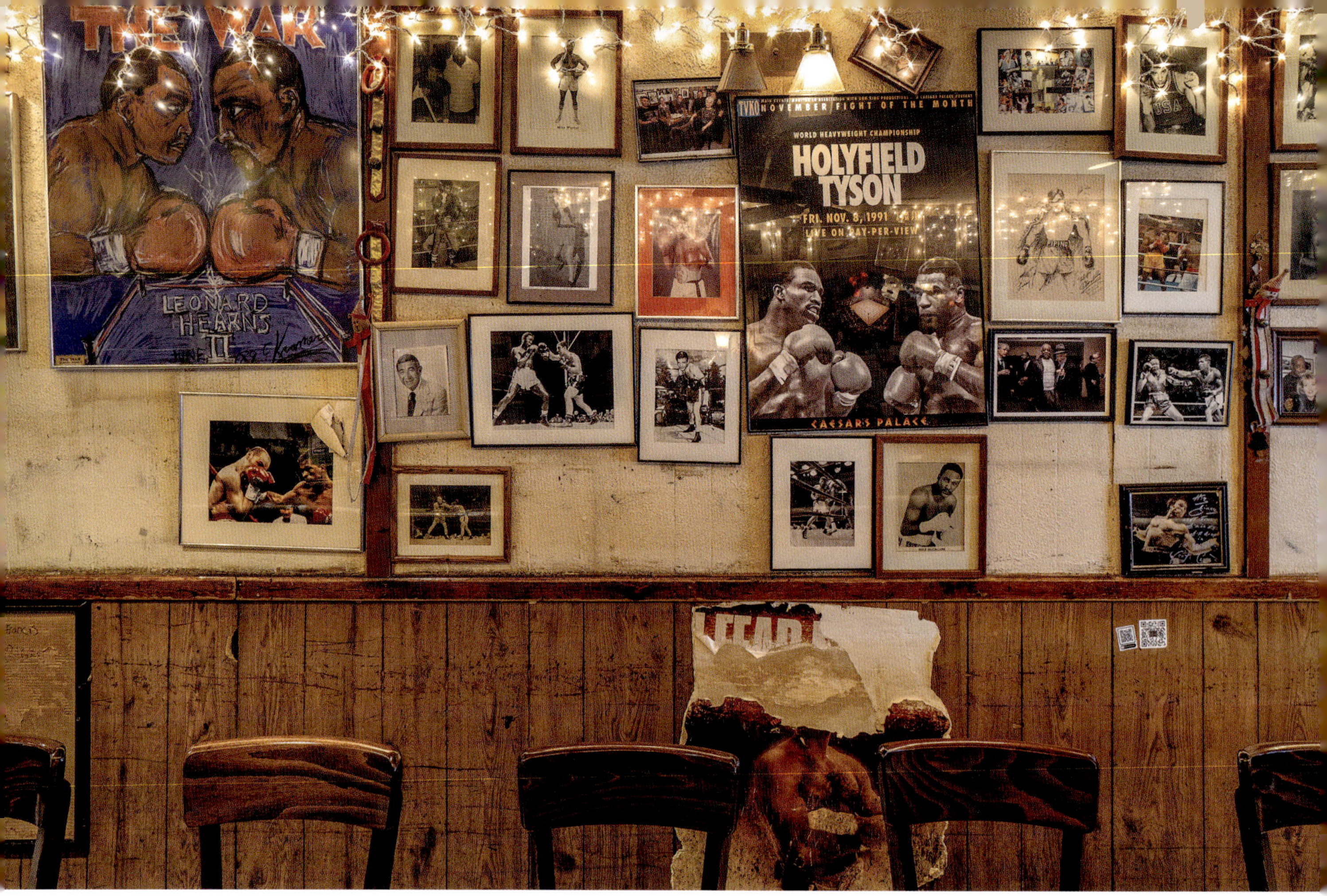

THE WAR
LEONARD
HEARNS
II
JUNE 12 '89
TVKO NOVEMBER FIGHT OF THE MONTH
WORLD HEAVYWEIGHT CHAMPIONSHIP
HOLYFIELD
TYSON
FRI. NOV. 8, 1991
LIVE ON PAY-PER-VIEW
CAESARS PALACE
MUHAMMAD ALI
PROCLAMATION

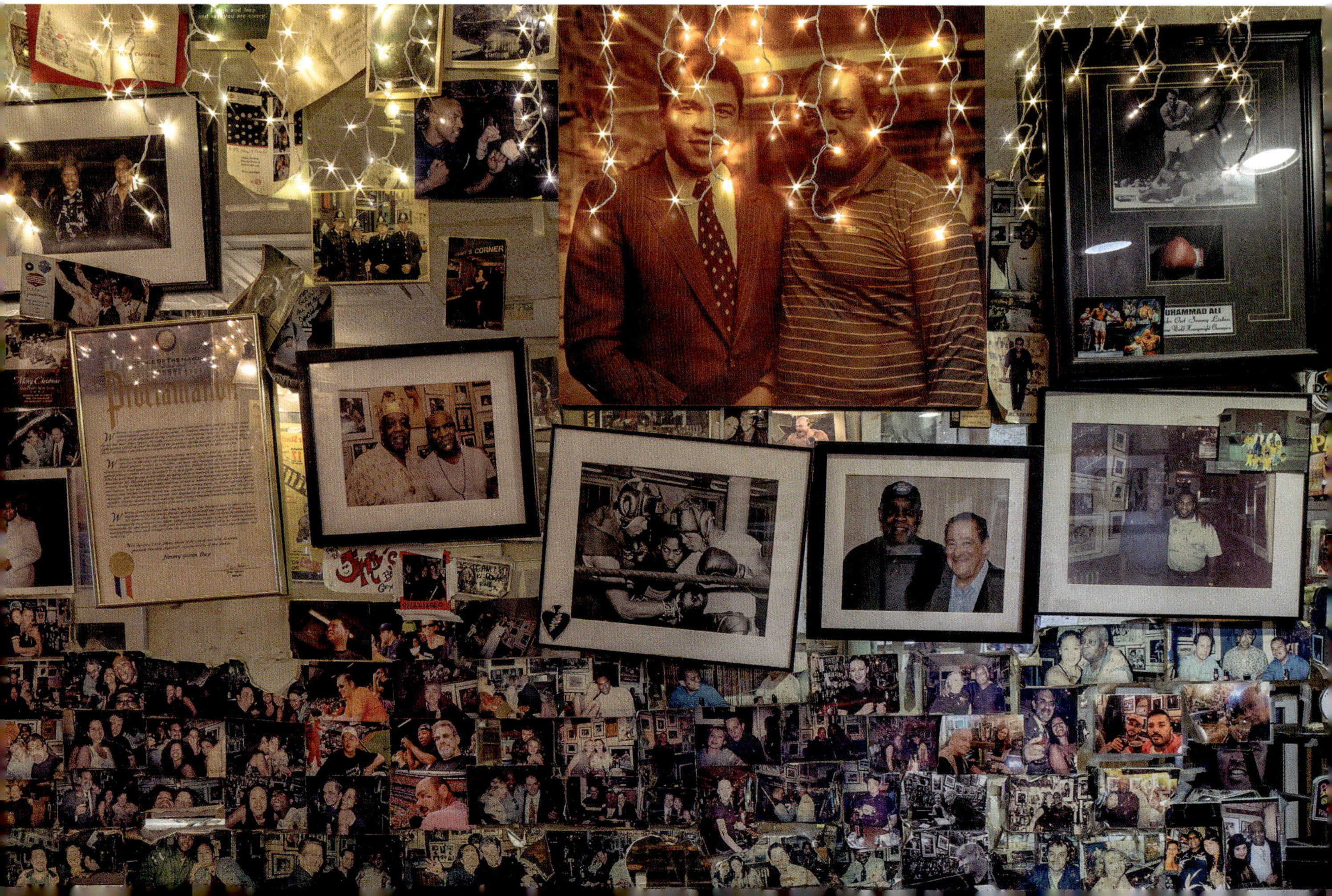

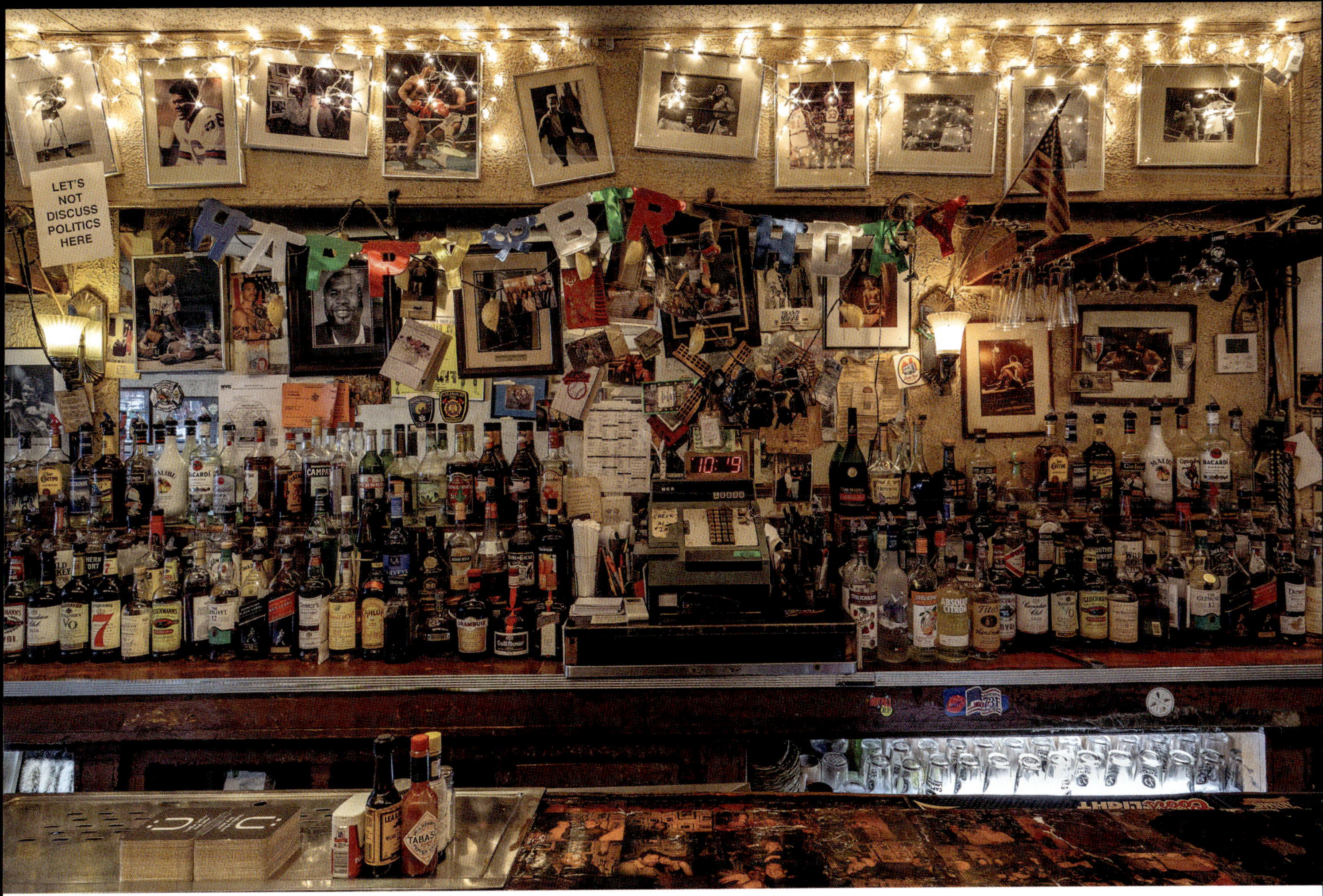

LET'S
NOT
DISCUSS
POLITICS
HERE
HAPPY BIRTHDAY

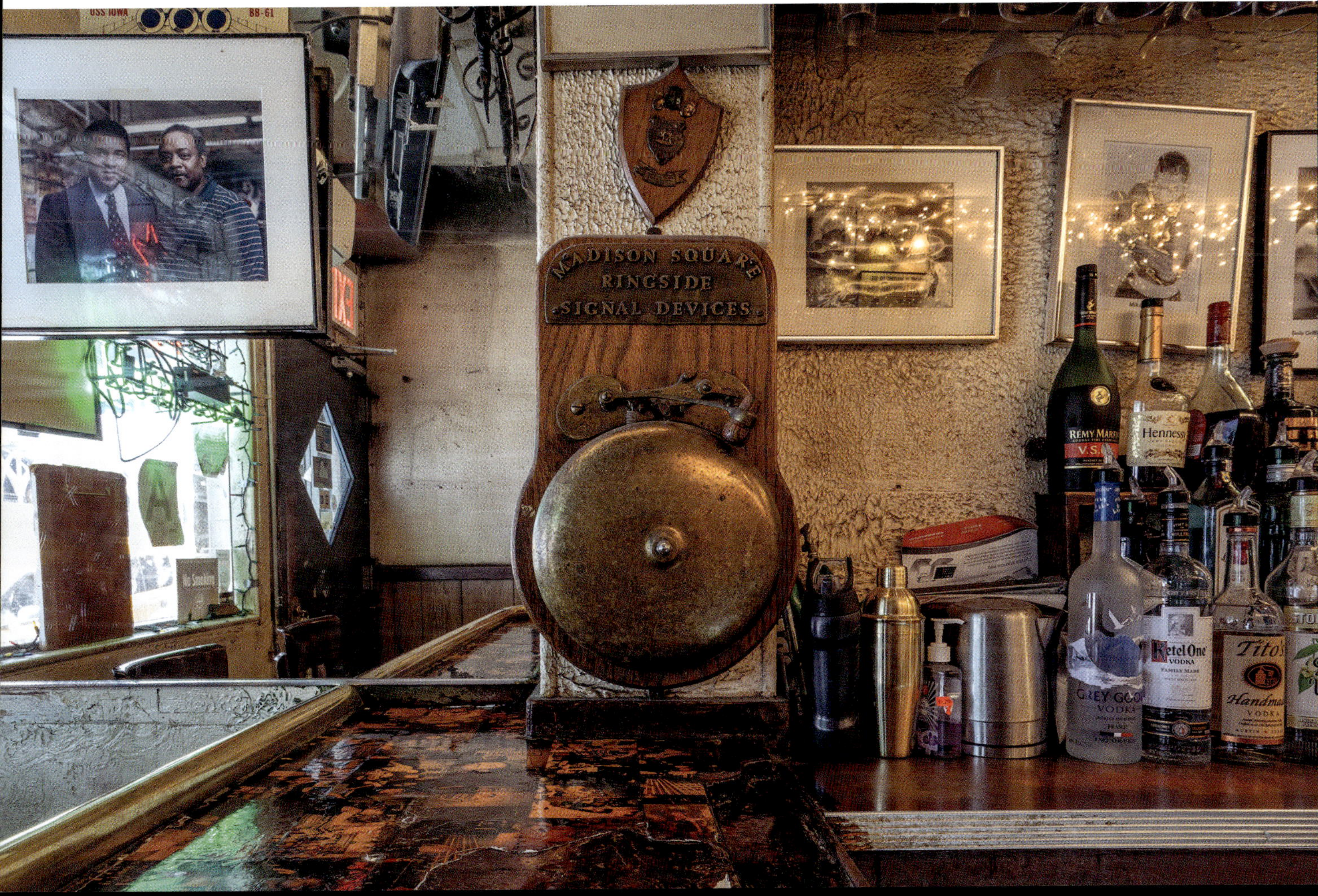

MADISON SQUARE
RINGSIDE
SIGNAL DEVICES
USS IOWA BB-61
REMY MARTIN
V.S.O.P.
Hennessy
GREY GOOSE
VODKA
KETEL ONE
VODKA
Tito's
Handmade
VODKA

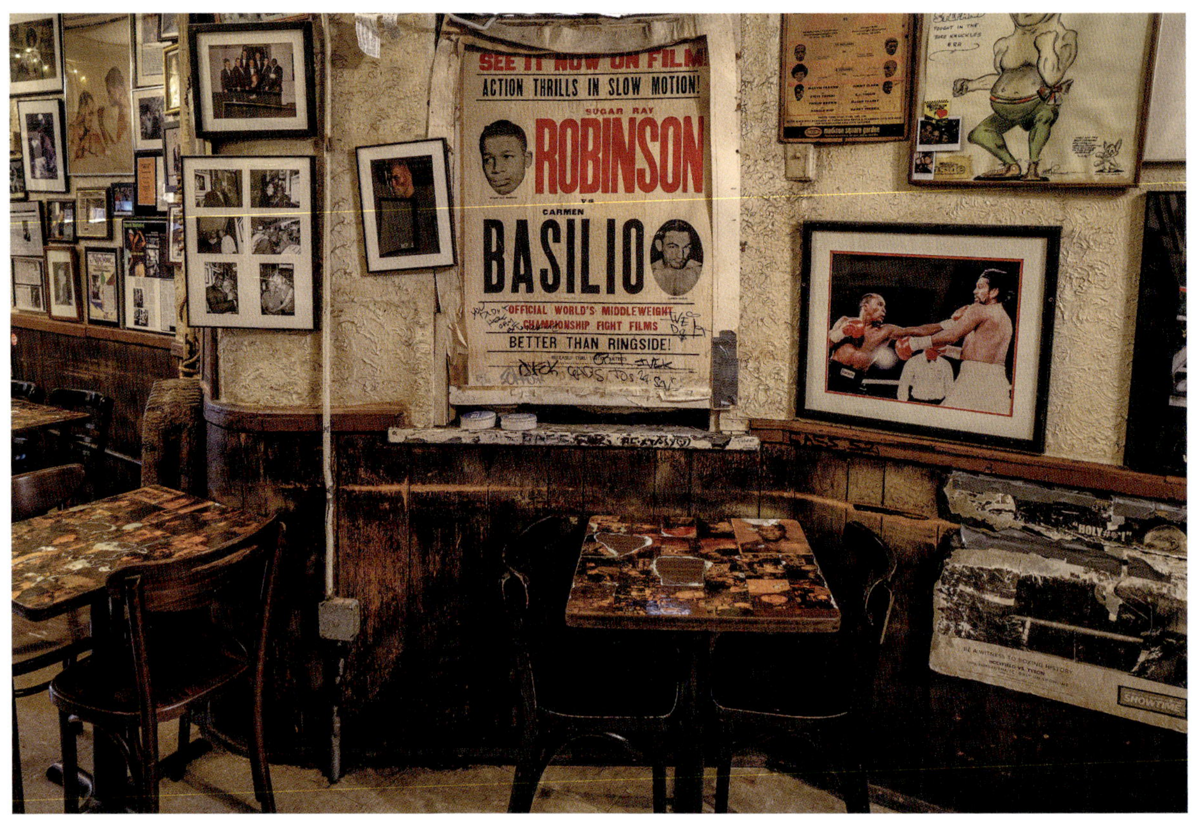
SEE IT NOW ON FILM
ACTION THRILLS IN SLOW MOTION!
SUGAR RAY
ROBINSON
vs
CARMEN
BASILIO
OFFICIAL WORLD'S MIDDLEWEIGHT
CHAMPIONSHIP FIGHT FILMS
BETTER THAN RINGSIDE!
"HOLY #!"

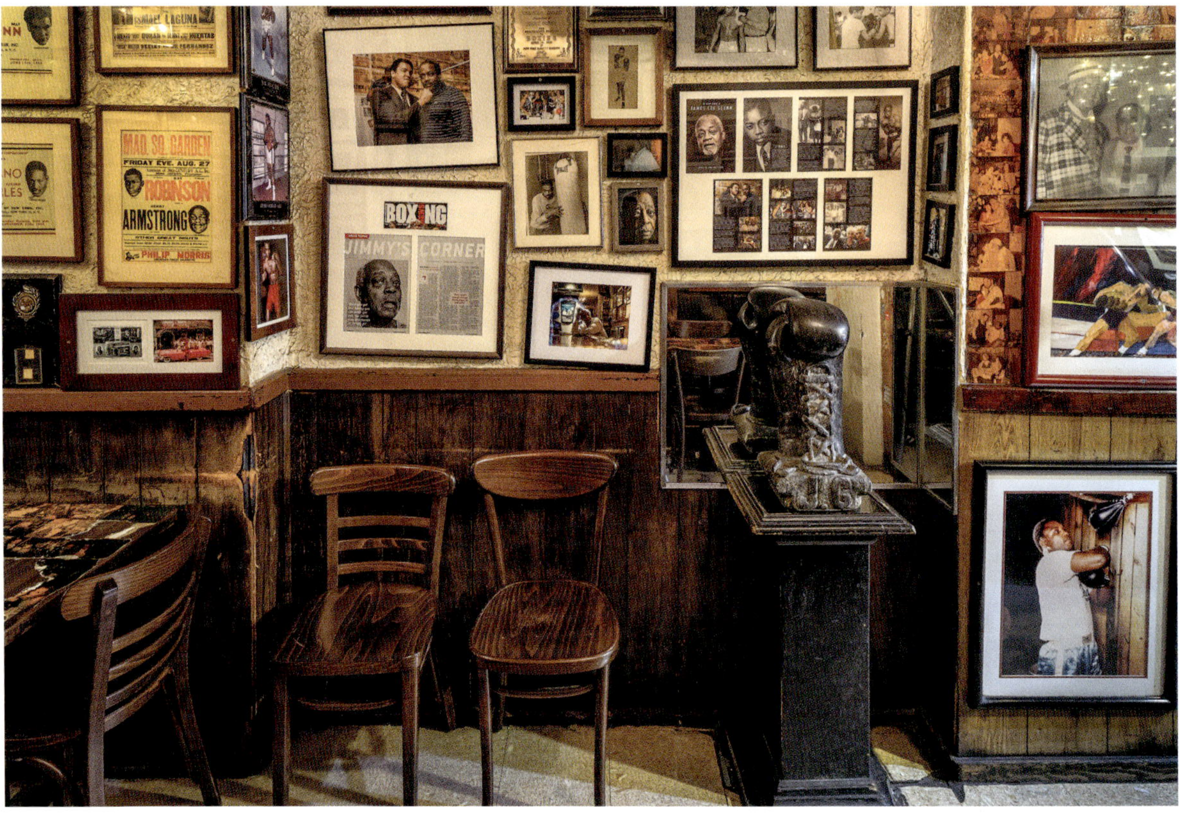
MAD. SQ. GARDEN
FRIDAY EVE. AUG. 27
ROBINSON
vs
HENRY
ARMSTRONG
PHILIP MORRIS
BOXING
JIMMY'S CORNER

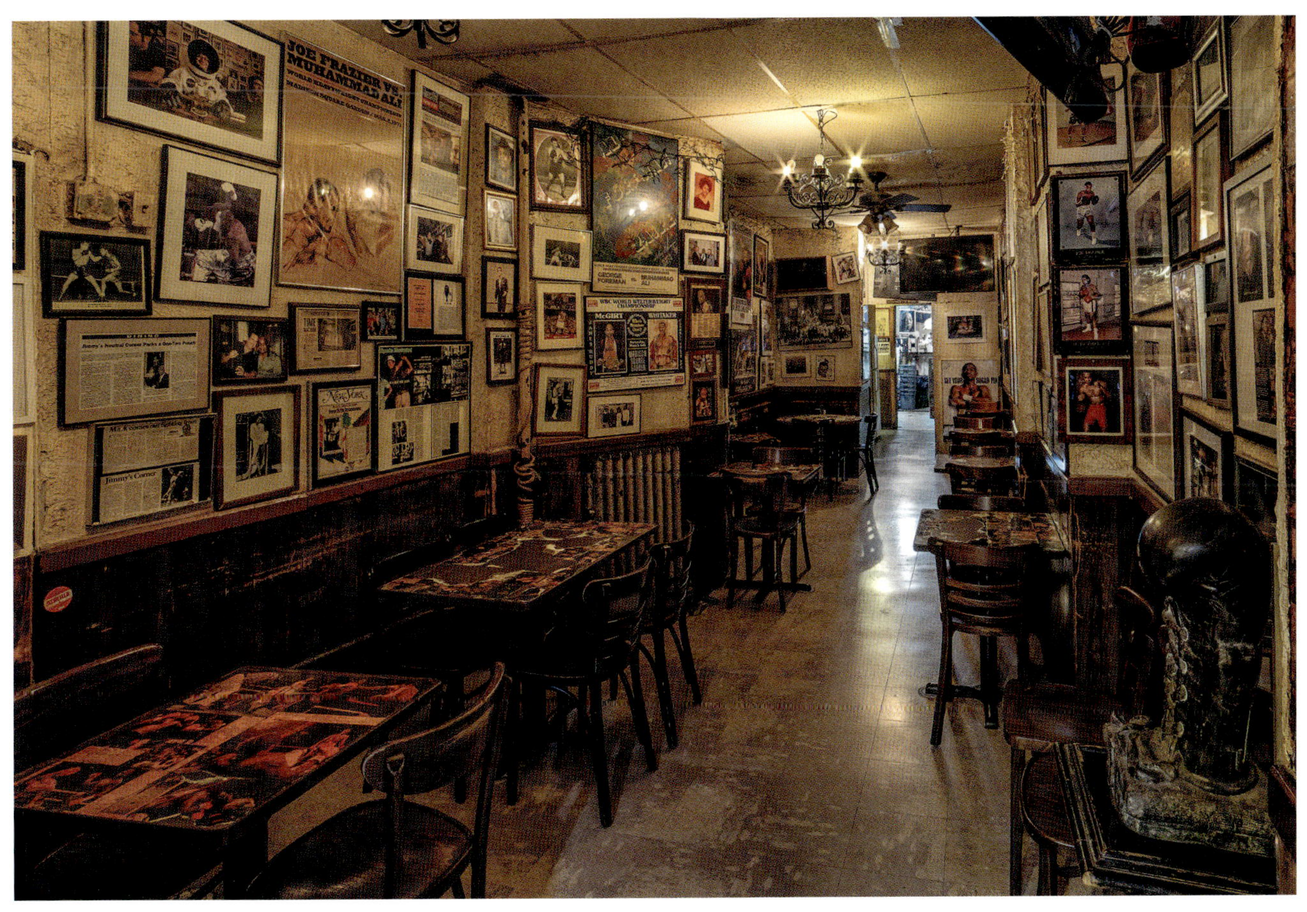

PETE'S TAVERN

129 EAST 18TH STREET, GRAMERCY PARK

Opened during the presidency of Abraham Lincoln, Pete's Tavern is perhaps best known as one of the oldest continuously operating bar-restaurants in all of New York City. Though it's gone by several different names throughout the course of its history, the venue has always served booze—and was the city's only bar that was legally permitted to remain in operation during the Prohibition era.

The building that Pete's Tavern occupies has a long history that dates back even further, to 1851. The first business it housed was a local grocery and grog, or liquor store, and it only became a tavern in 1864. At the time, taverns were not just bars—they were also often inns offering lodging and equipped with stables for horses. Food and drink was also served.

In 1899 Tom and John Healy purchased the bar, and it was then known as Healy's Cafe. As Healy's, it was the favorite watering hole of short-story writer O. Henry, whose real name was William Sydney Porter. The author, who lived in a nearby boarding house on Irving Place, often dined in the first booth. Healy's appears in his short story "The Lost Blend," under the name Kenealy's.

It's also believed that O. Henry wrote his more famous "The Gift of the Magi" in a booth at Pete's Tavern in 1905, and that the bar's atmosphere may have inspired the setting of the story (a plaque on the wall commemorates this event). Other notable works that were supposedly penned here include *Madeline*, a 1939 children's book that was allegedly started by Ludwig Bemelmans on the back of one of the bar's menus.

It wasn't until the 1920s, during Prohibition, that Peter D'Belles took over the tavern, renaming it Pete's. The logo of the bar was hand-painted by a local artist and colored with gold leaf; the sign still hangs from the corner of the facade today.

Because of the bar's proximity to what was then Tammany Hall, the building at 44 Union Square, it was allowed to remain open through Prohibition. After all, Tammany Hall was one of the city's major political machines, and these politicians needed a place to eat and drink. To keep the revelry discreet, Pete's Tavern covered its windows and transformed the entry space into a flower shop; drinkers would enter through a canopied entrance on Eighteenth Street. Humorously, when *New York* magazine interviewed then-owner John Reynolds in 2000, he noted

that the disguise was apparently not too effective: "They didn't kill themselves changing the facade—I almost laugh when I look at the pictures."

In more recent years, Pete's Tavern catered to the likes of John F. Kennedy Jr., who became fond of the bar after noticing a photo of his parents on the wall. Indeed, the family had long-standing ties to the bar, and it was its patriarch, old Joe Kennedy, who supplied Pete's with liquor during Prohibition.

Visitors to the bar today can slide into one of its well-preserved high-backed booths and take in countless other original elements of the storied space. These include tin ceilings, tile floors, and wooden liquor cabinets, as well as the beveled glass and mirror behind the bar. The original lighting fixtures, which were once lit with candles and gas-powered lamps before the widespread use of electricity, are also intact. However, the 40-foot (12-meter) curved bar is perhaps the most notable original feature. Made of sturdy rosewood, it used to contain a cutout for storing cold plates of cured meats and sandwiches on sale for a penny or two.

Nowadays Pete's Tavern operates as a full-service bar and restaurant. The prices aren't quite what they used to be—although the burgers continue to be modestly-priced—but you can still tap into the past by ordering an O. Henry Negroni. Inside, you'll find images of numerous celebrities who have dined there, including Cher, James Cagney, Ben Stiller, Bruce Willis, James Gandolfini, Tom Cruise, and Natalie Portman.

The bar is now overseen by longtime manager Gary Egan, who entered a partnership deal with the building's landlord, and who was responsible for faithfully restoring its interior when it closed during the pandemic. Egan personally handles its extensive holiday decorations, from baubles to hanging lights.

Because of its iconic status in New York City history, Pete's Tavern has been featured as a set location in numerous NYC-based films, like 1981's *Ragtime* and 1962's *Two for the Seesaw*, as well as TV shows like *Law & Order*, *Seinfeld*, and *Sex and the City*—in an episode where Miranda Hobbes proposes to her longtime boyfriend Steve Brady.

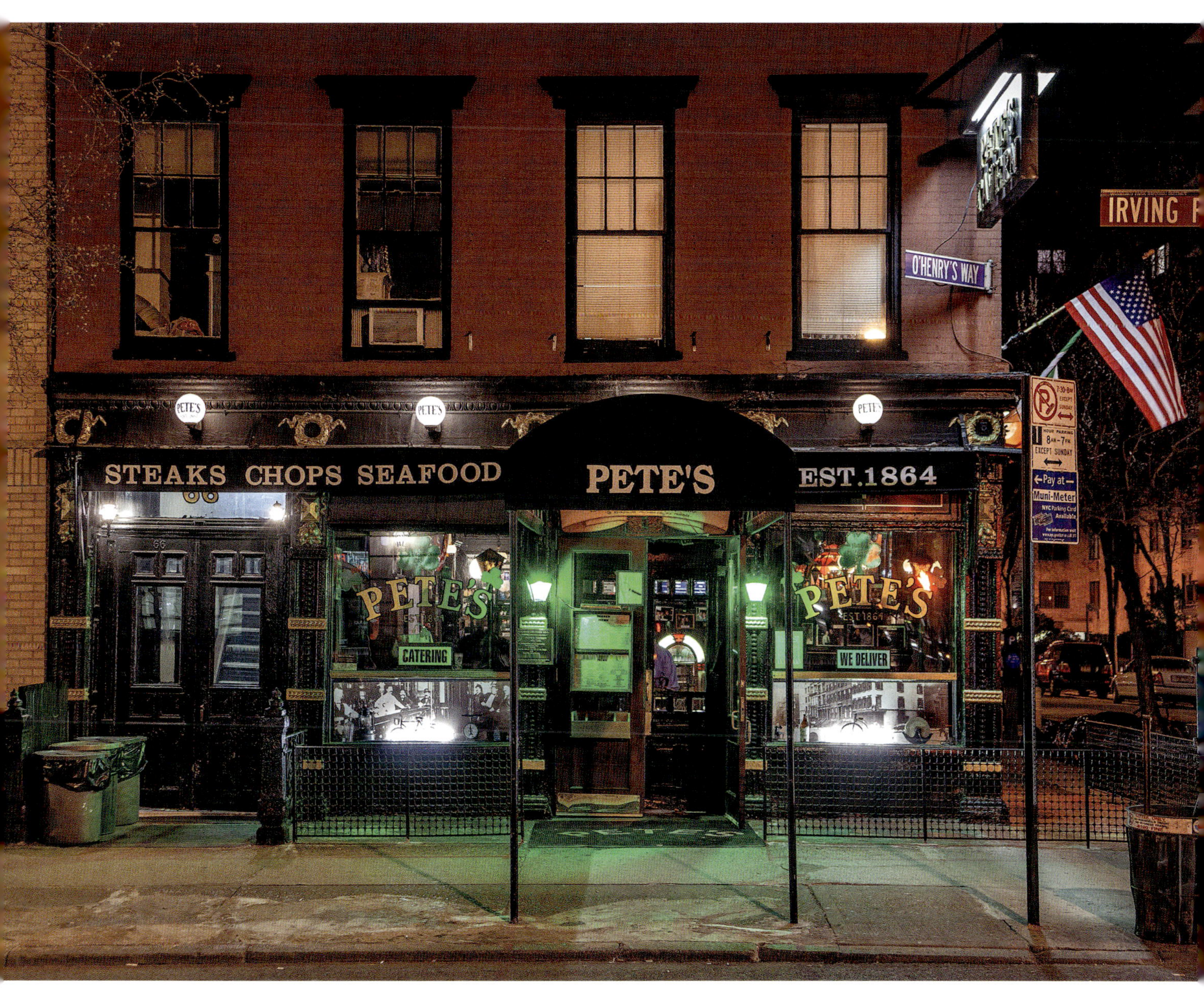

STEAKS CHOPS SEAFOOD
PETE'S
EST.1864
PETE'S
CATERING
PETE'S
WE DELIVER
O'HENRY'S WAY
IRVING P

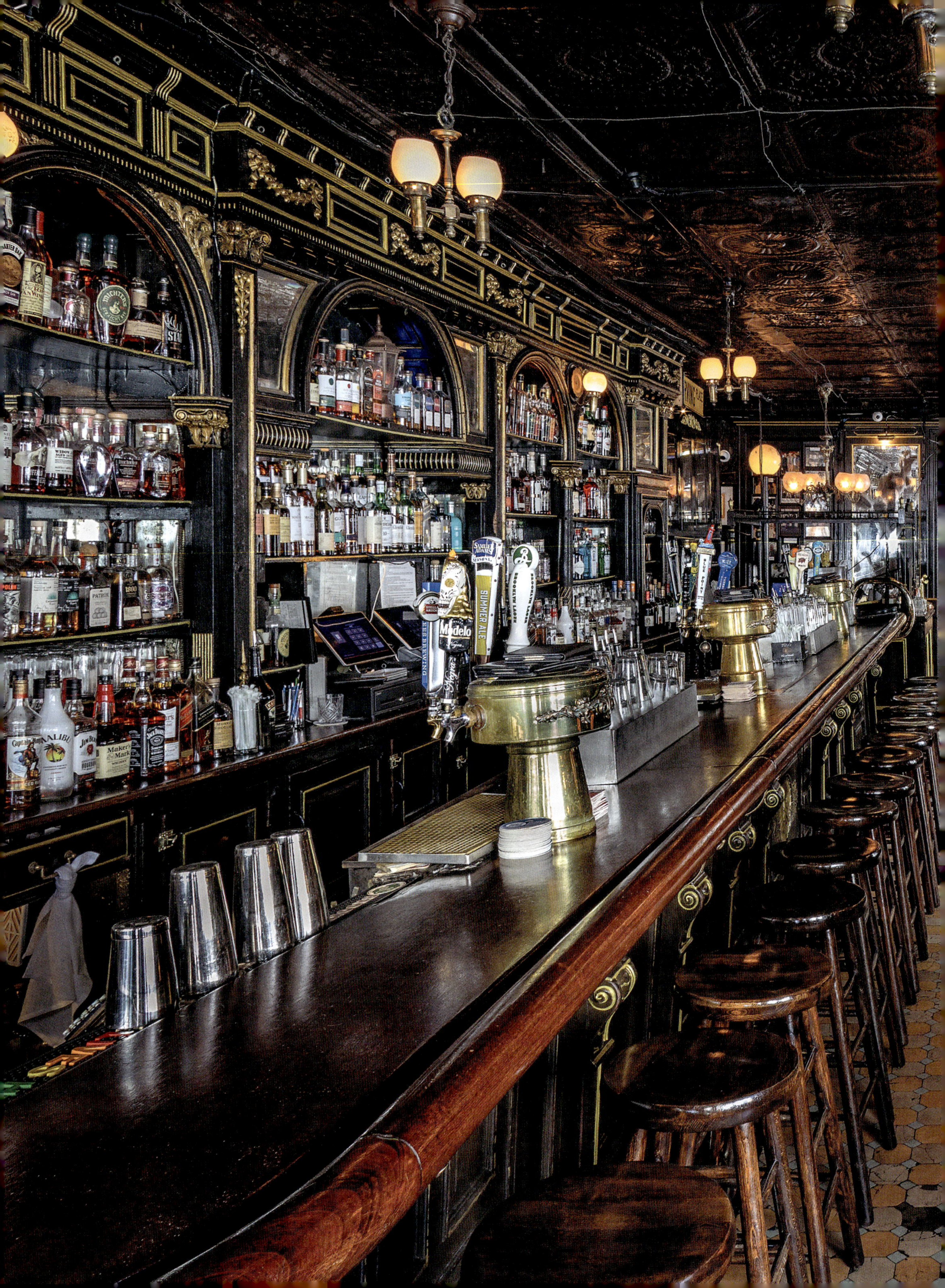

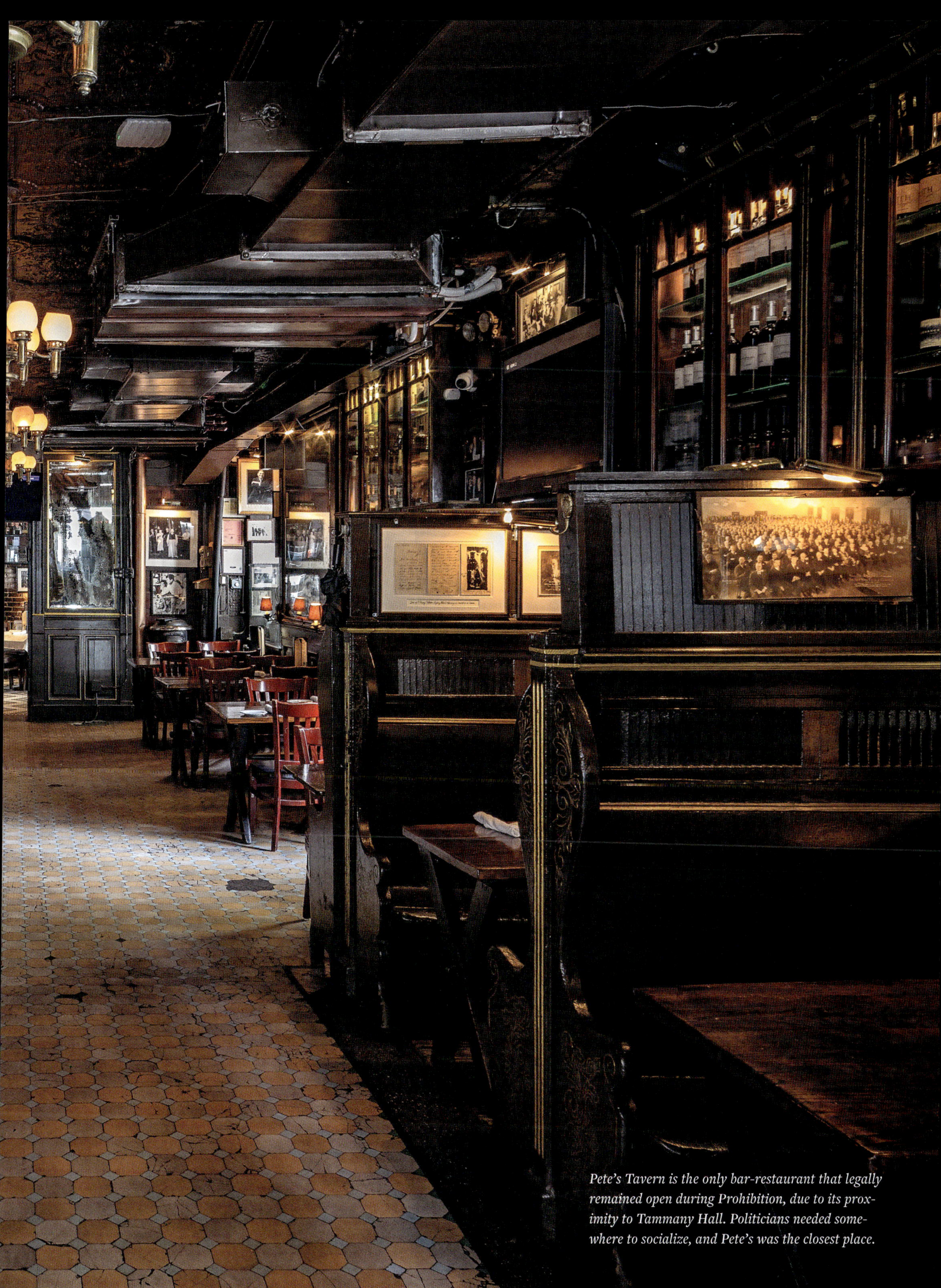

Pete's Tavern is the only bar-restaurant that legally remained open during Prohibition, due to its proximity to Tammany Hall. Politicians needed somewhere to socialize, and Pete's was the closest place.

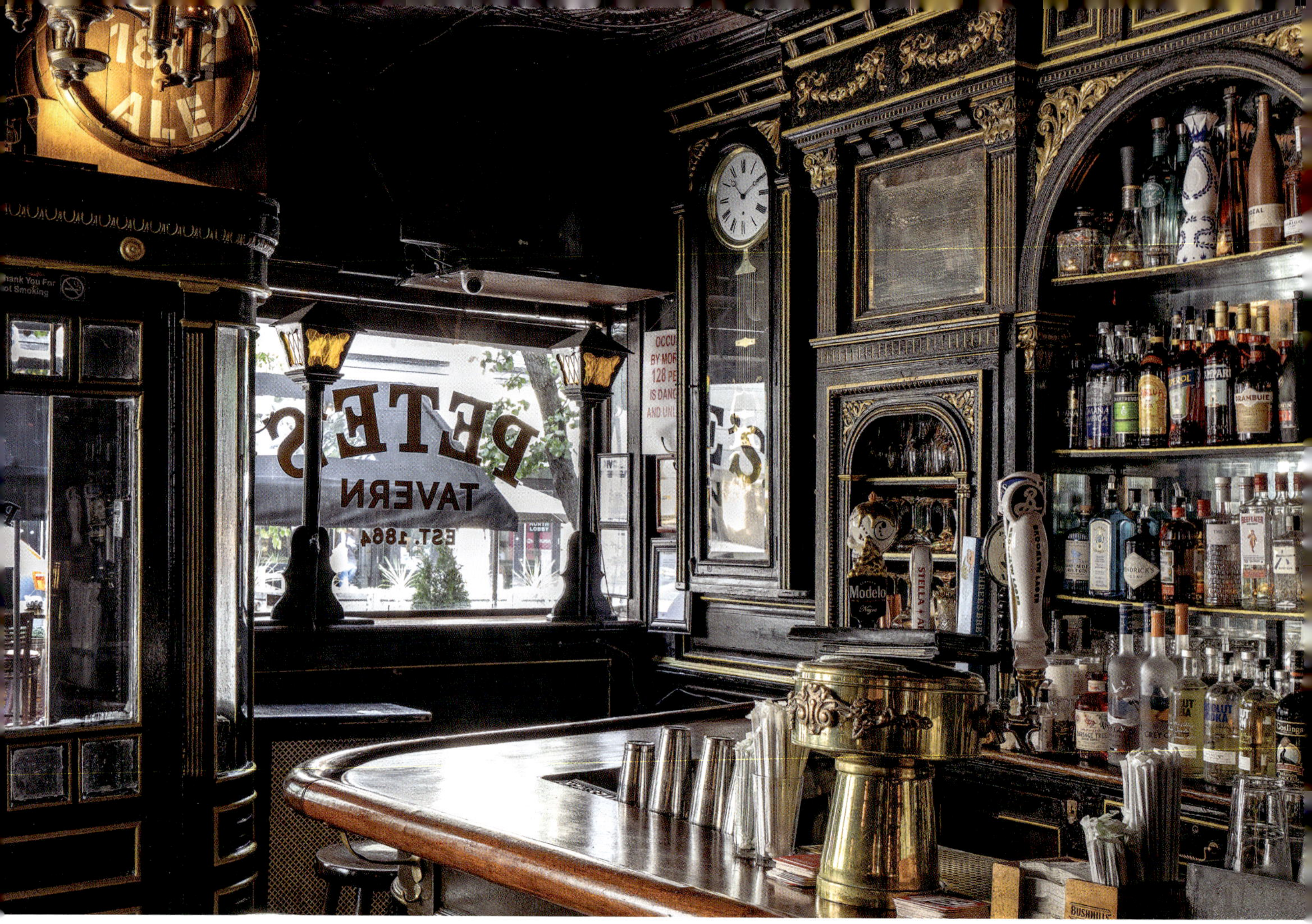
PETE'S
TAVERN
EST. 1864
Modelo
BUSHMILLS

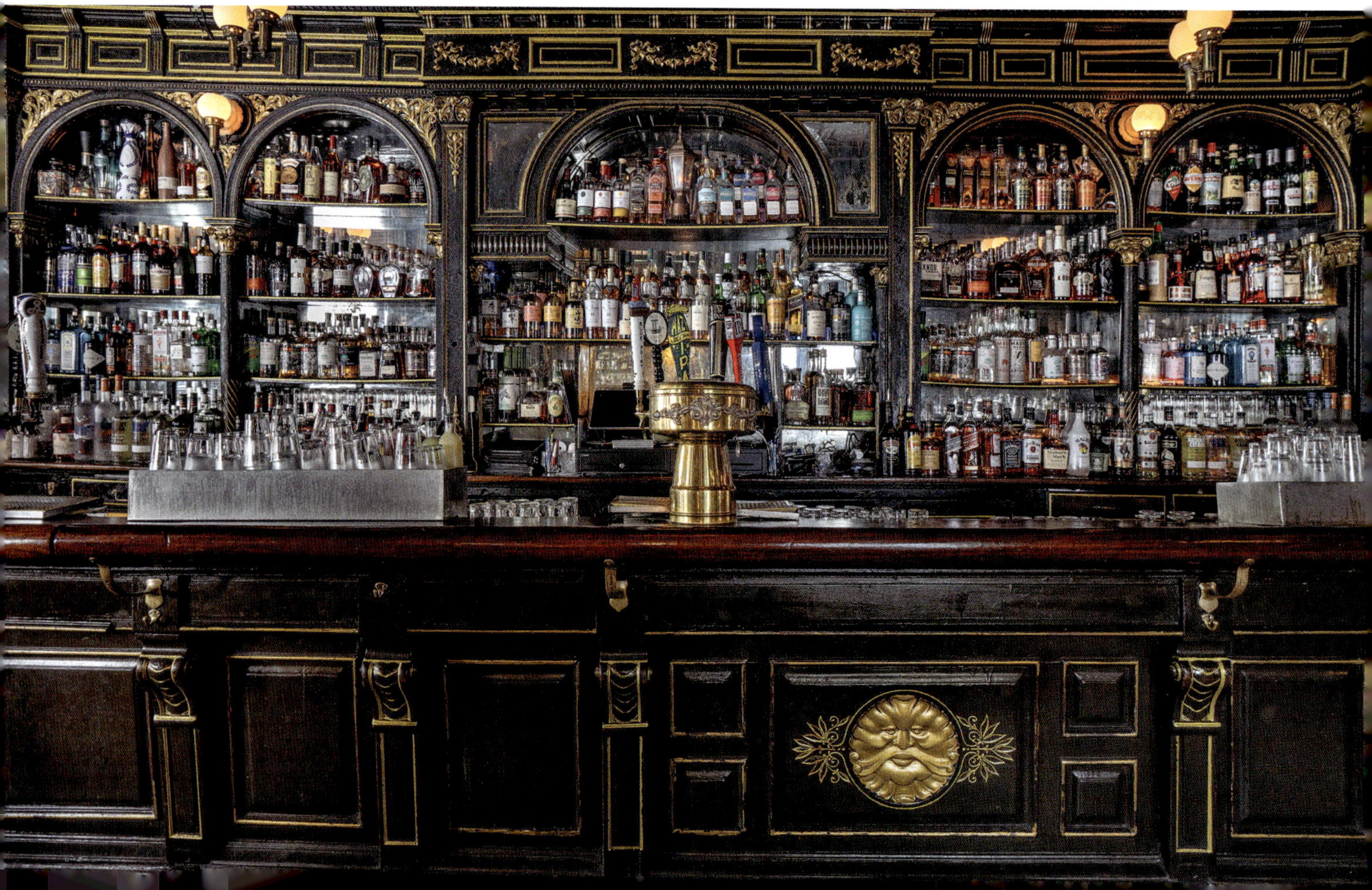

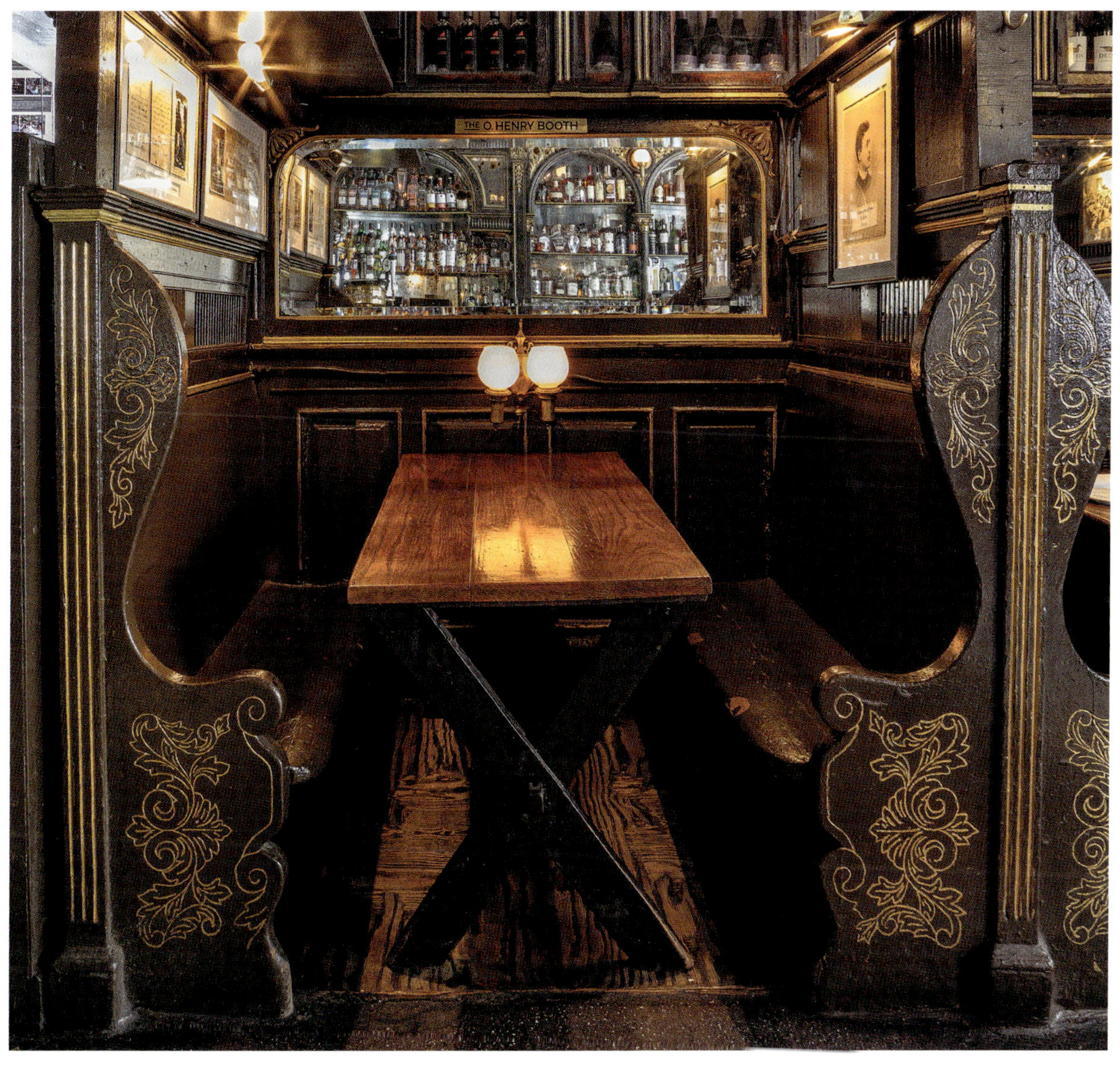

THE O. HENRY BOOTH

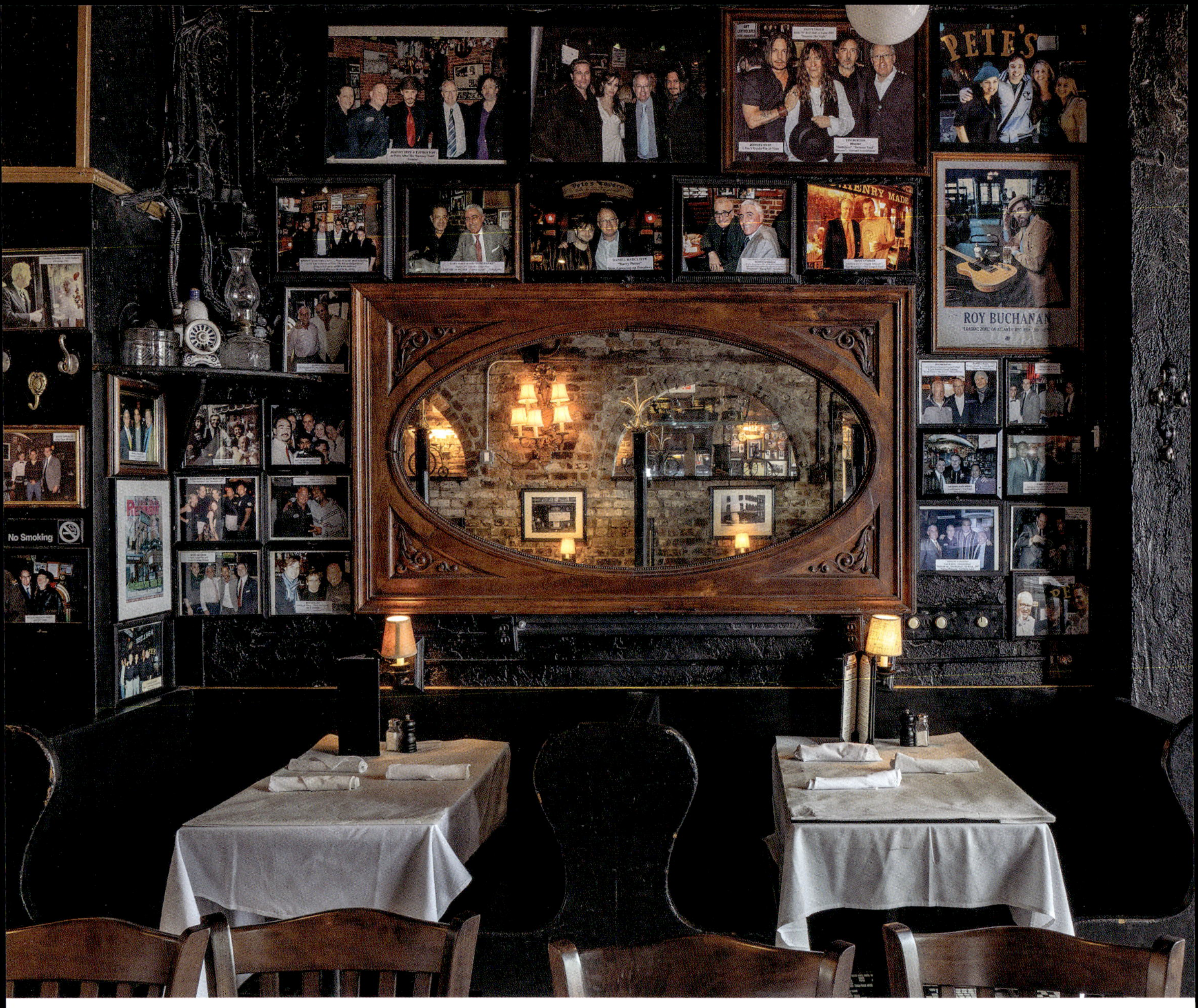

OPPOSITE BOTTOM *O. Henry is said to have written the classic short Christmas story "The Gift of the Magi" at Pete's in 1905.*

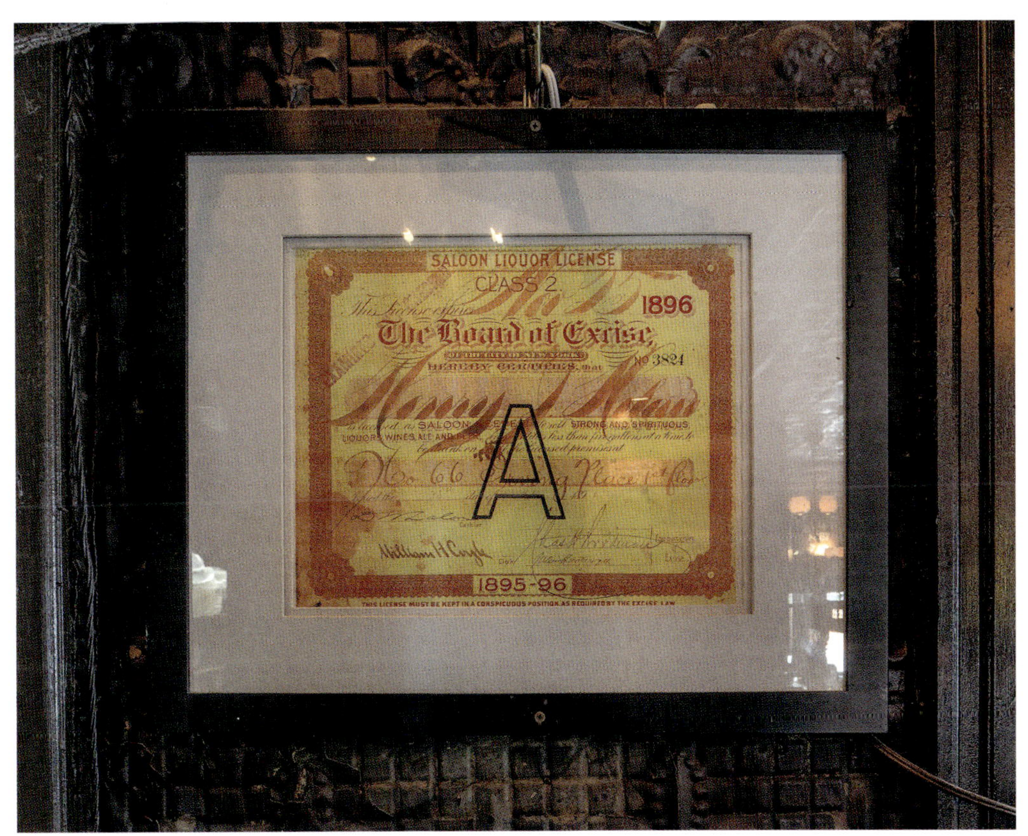

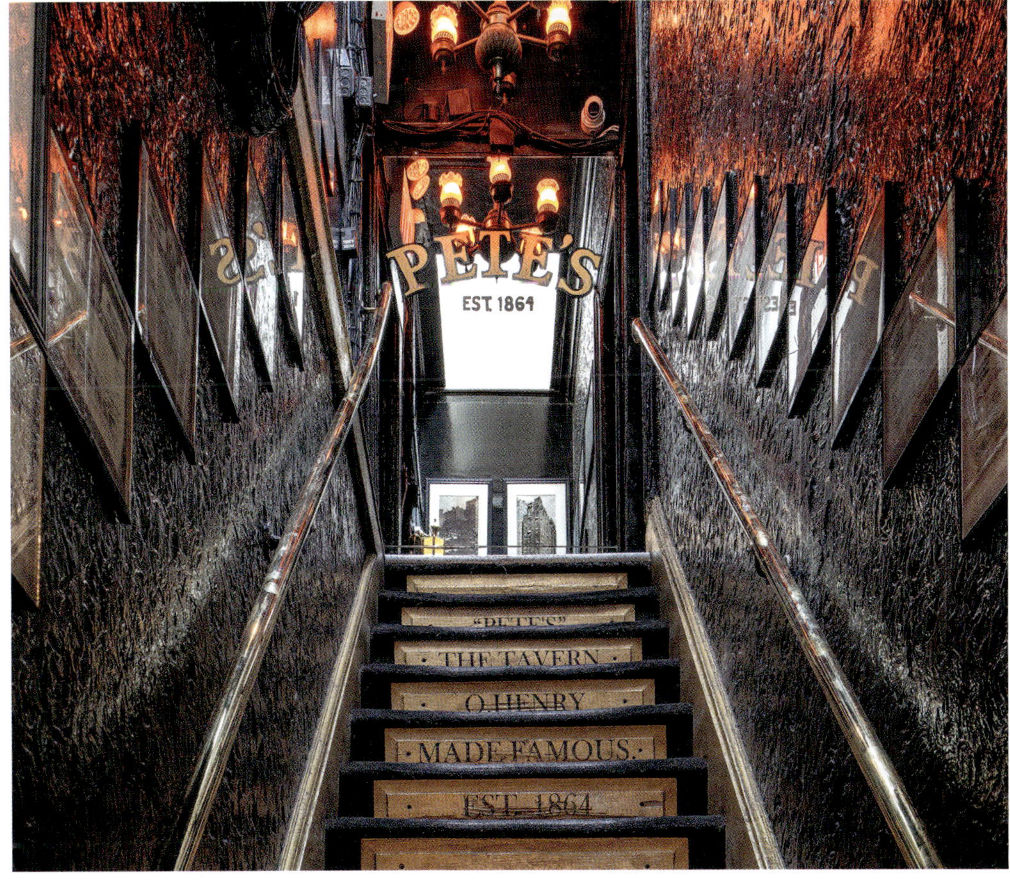

PETE'S
EST 1864
"PETE'S"
THE TAVERN
O. HENRY
MADE FAMOUS.
EST. 1864

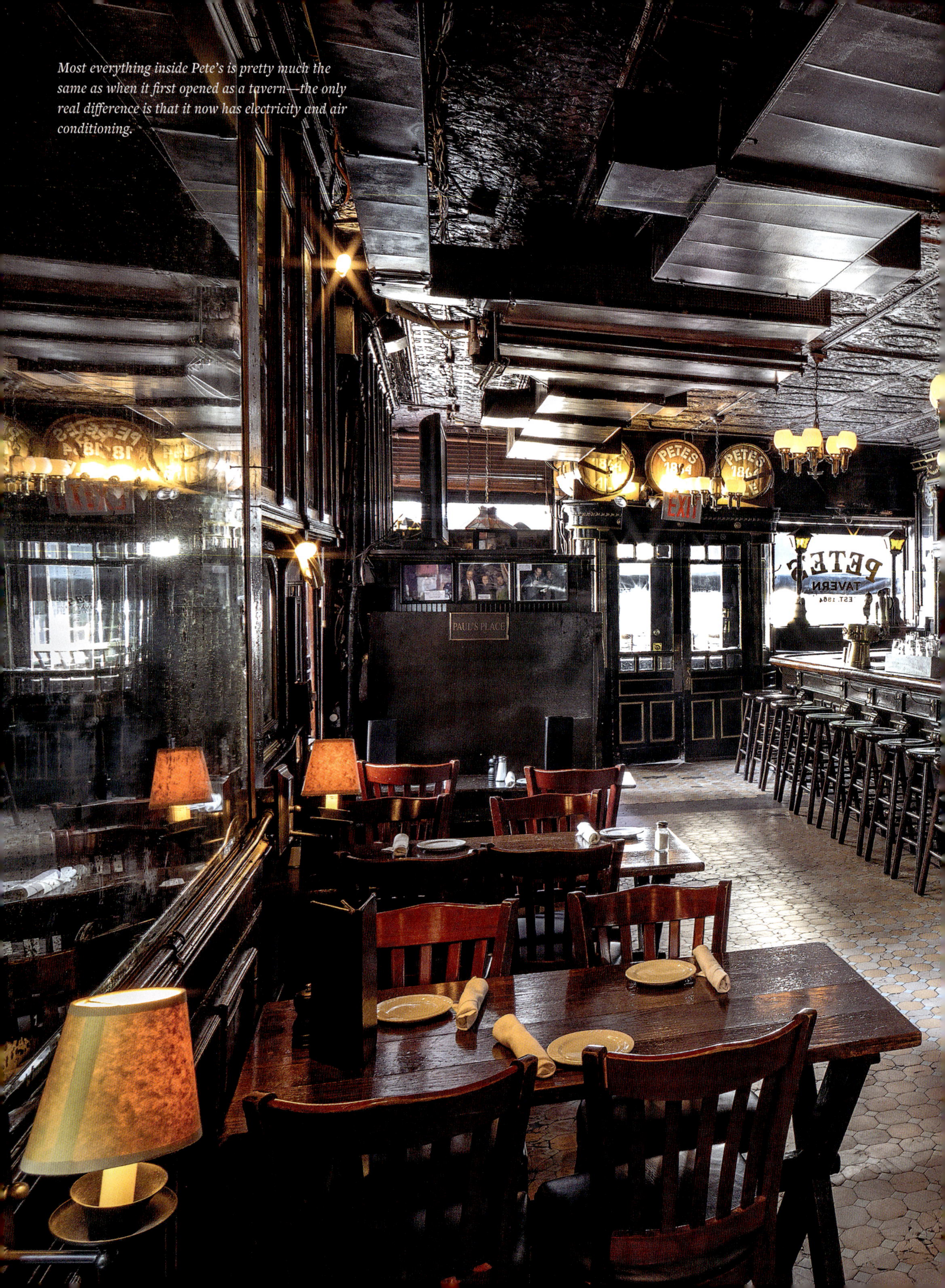

Most everything inside Pete's is pretty much the same as when it first opened as a tavern—the only real difference is that it now has electricity and air conditioning.

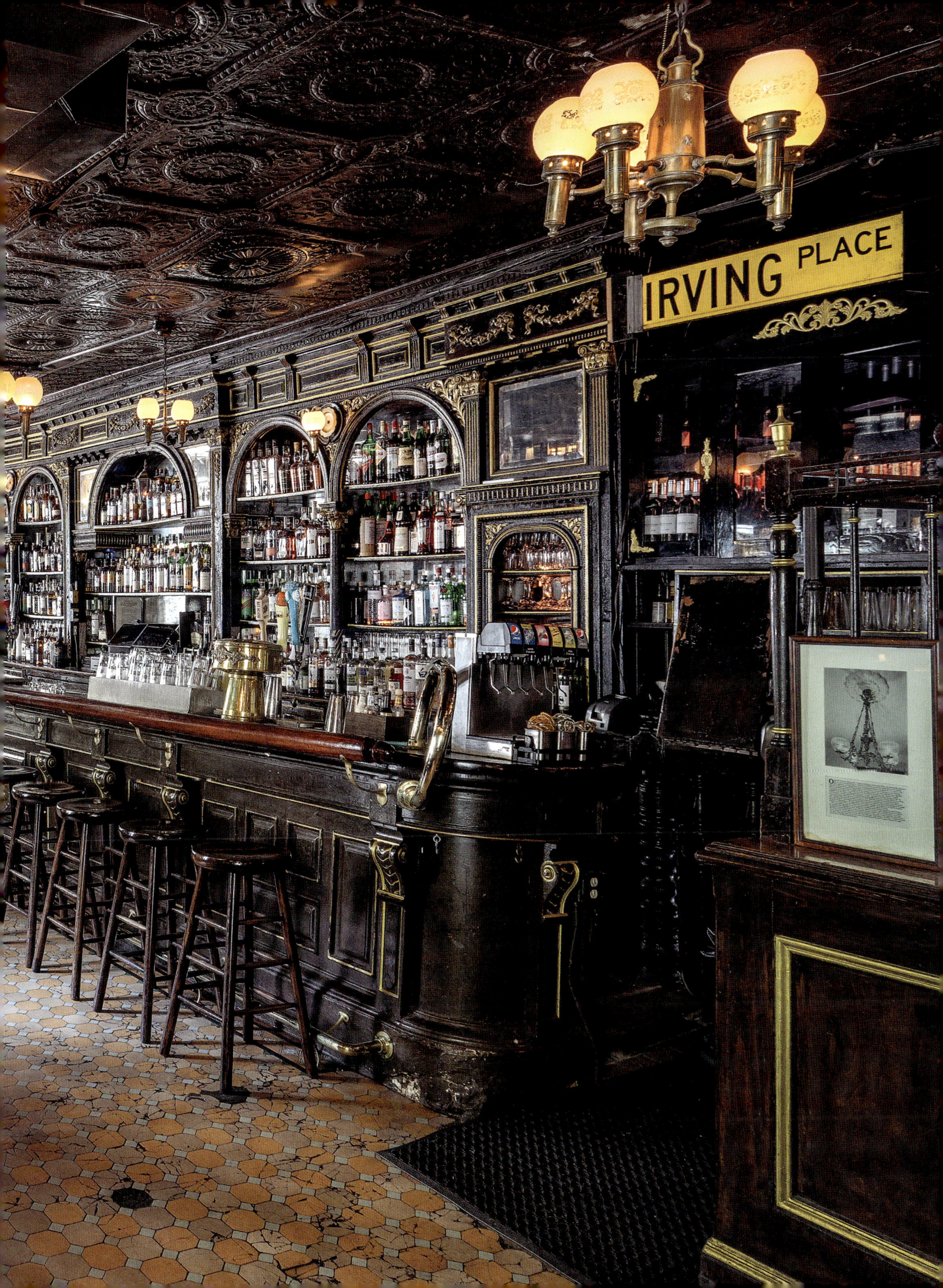

IRVING PLACE

THE STONEWALL INN

53 CHRISTOPHER STREET,
WEST VILLAGE

A fixture of the West Village, the Stonewall Inn is certainly the most hallowed bar for New York City's LGBTQ+ community as the site of the famed Stonewall uprising of 1969. Indeed, while Julius' (see p. 128) is the oldest gay bar in the city, Stonewall is considered the true birthplace of the modern equality movement in the United States.

The first Stonewall Inn was opened at 91 Seventh Avenue in 1930, when it was also known as Bonnie's Stonewall Inn—a name believed to have come from the original proprietor, a local businessman named Vincent Bonavia. Initially billed as a bakery and tearoom, it was in actuality a speakeasy and was raided by the police in December of that year.

In 1934, after the end of Prohibition, Bonavia relocated to Christopher Street and officially opened Stonewall as a legal bar and restaurant. It became a popular neighborhood haunt, operating until 1964, when a fire destroyed the interior.

By this time homosexuality was legal in New York City, but the New York State Liquor Authority (SLA) considered establishments serving gay people to be, by default, "disorderly houses." The SLA refused to grant new licenses to these bars, and even older ones had licenses revoked for "indecent conduct." Bartenders were wary of serving "suspected homosexuals," as it was common practice for the police to raid gay establishments and harass people. Recognizing the opportunity to profit from such circumstances, the New York Mafia began getting involved in gay bars as early as the '30s. And in 1967 Stonewall was reopened with investment from several Mafia members.

In order to circumvent the need for a liquor license, they operated as a "private" gay club with bottle service. To enter, guests would need to pay a cover fee of $1 on weekdays and $3 on weekends. They'd also need to sign a register, which most chose to do using pseudonyms of famous divas and cartoon characters. (On a darker note, the owners of Stonewall were also involved in highly profitable extortion schemes, specifically targeting and blackmailing wealthy patrons who were known to be closeted).

By 1969 tension in the neighborhood was high. Everything would come to a swift halt in the early morning hours of a fateful Saturday, June 28, at Stonewall. Unbeknownst to those inside, a police unit was camped out across the street, waiting for the go-ahead to conduct a routine raid. It would be the second raid there in less than a week.

Officers entered the venue in the early morning hours and began to line patrons up to be taken to the police station, as was standard procedure. By this time, a growing crowd of onlookers had started to form outside. After a woman resisting arrest was struck by an officer, the crowd—now in the hundreds—erupted into a full-blown riot. While the police barricaded themselves in the bar, the crowd outside hurled bricks, cobblestones, and glass bottles at the venue. A parking meter was taken out and used as a battering ram. The doors were set ablaze. The protest lasted through the night, and continued for a second night, with skirmishes between thousands of citizens against multiple precincts of police officers.

The Stonewall uprising is now considered to have been the starting point of the modern fight for LGBTQ+ rights in the United States. In the decades immediately following, however, Stonewall fell into disrepair, with various businesses taking over, including a bagel shop, Chinese restaurant, and shoe store. By the '90s it was once again a gay nightclub, having undergone some renovation. But it wasn't until 2007 that Stacy Lentz, a lesbian queer rights activist, reopened the bar with help from outside investors, reinvoking its rich history. Along with co-owner Kurt Kelly, Lentz is the co-founder of the Stonewall Inn Gives Back Initiative.

Since then, Stonewall has been the subject of numerous films and books about the riots. It has also hosted many celebrity visitors, from Neil Patrick Harris and Alicia Keys to Lady Gaga. Notably, in the first moments of the new year in 2019, Madonna gave a surprise performance there.

In 2016 President Obama designated the bar and its surrounding area as the Stonewall National Monument, the first-ever US National Park Service site dedicated to LGBTQ+ history. And in 2020, during the Covid-19 pandemic, Stonewall was saved from closure through crowdfunding as well as a $250,000 donation from the Gill Foundation.

Today you can stop in for a pint or to catch various events, including drag shows, trivia nights, and cabaret performances. In honor of the culmination of Pride Month and to commemorate the Stonewall riots of 1969, New York City holds a pride march annually, which includes a much-celebrated stop along the parade route in front of Stonewall.

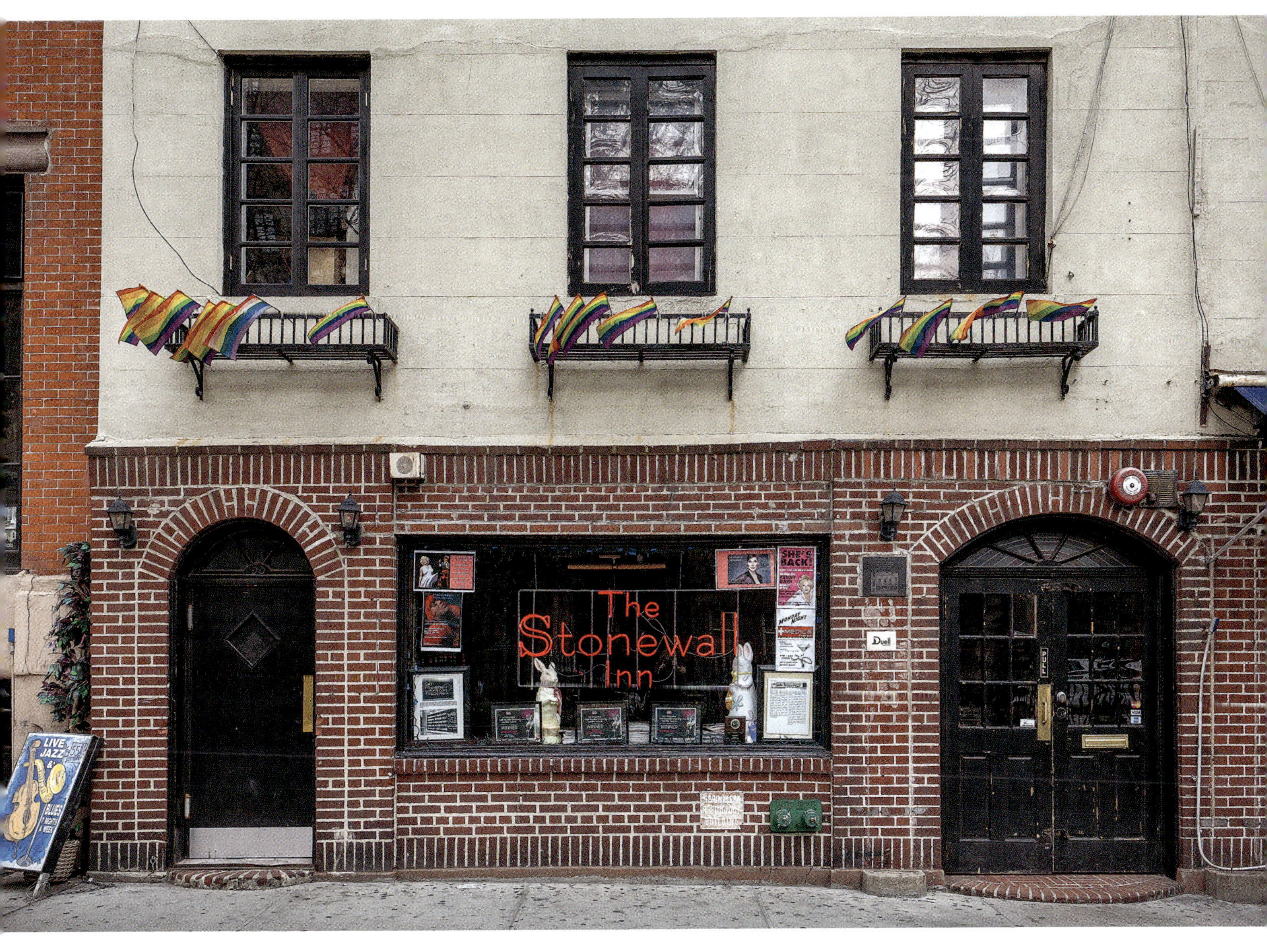

ABOVE *The Stonewall Inn is a NYC and National Historic Landmark because of its cultural significance to queer history.*

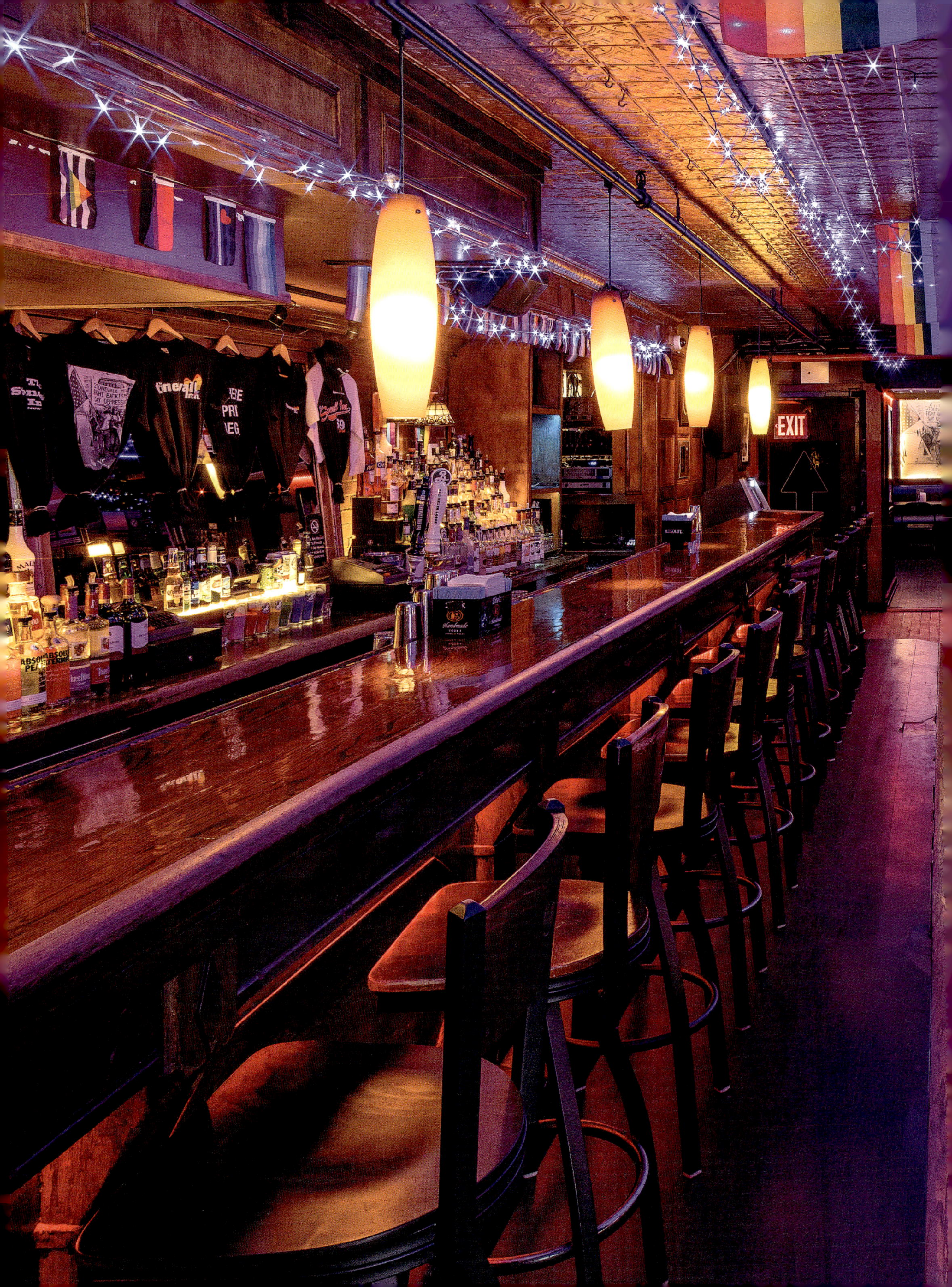

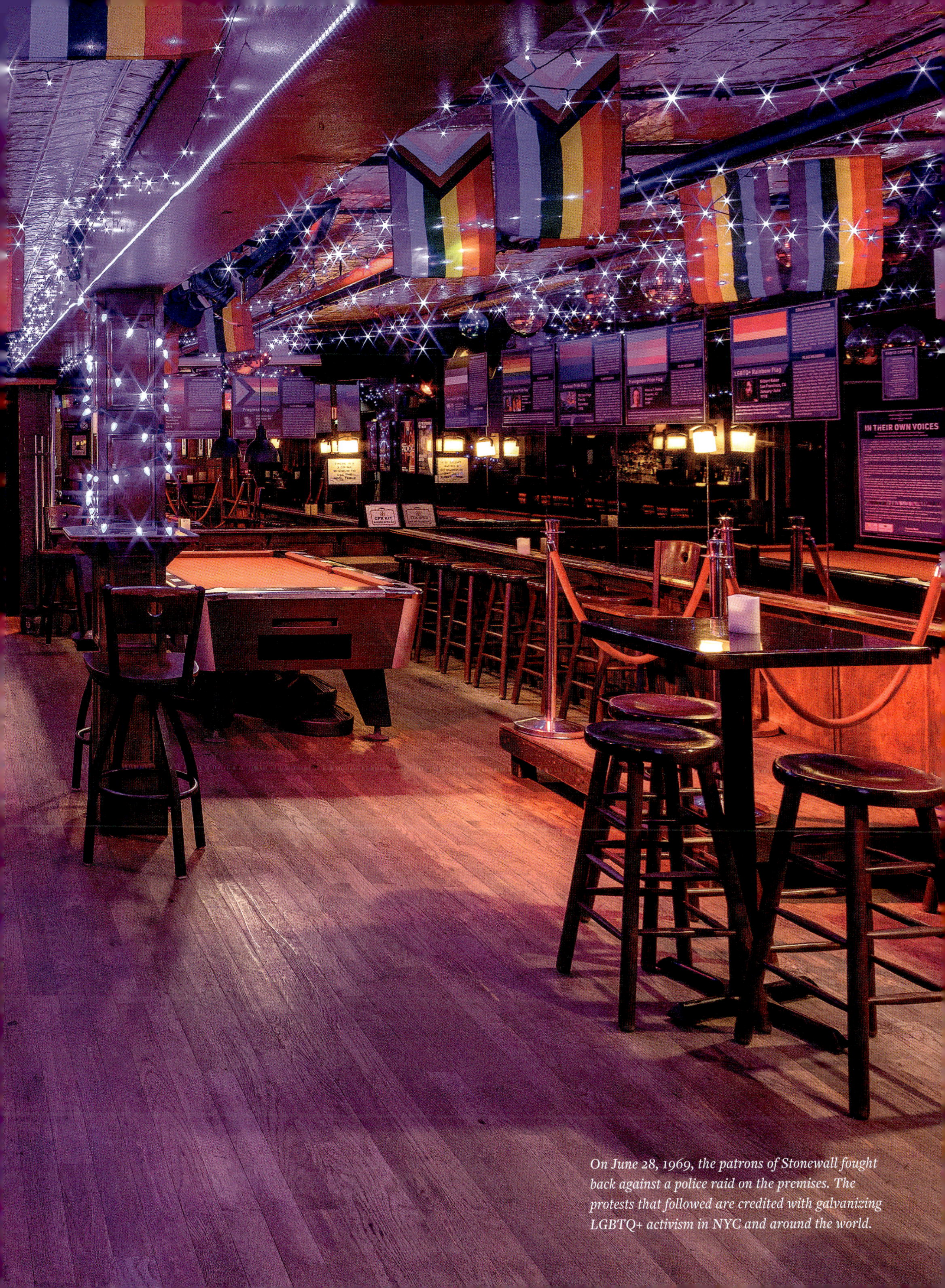

On June 28, 1969, the patrons of Stonewall fought back against a police raid on the premises. The protests that followed are credited with galvanizing LGBTQ+ activism in NYC and around the world.

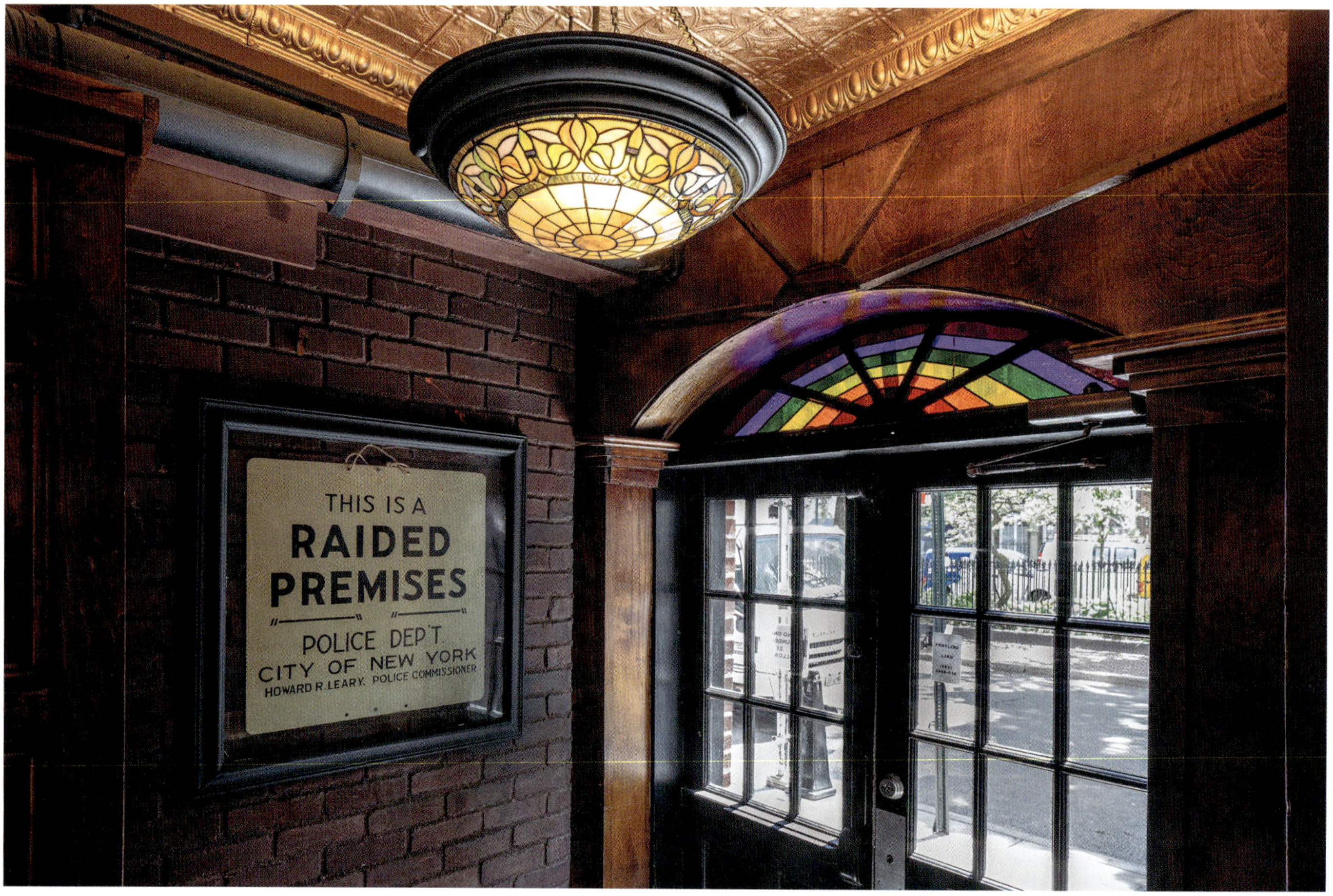

THIS IS A
RAIDED
PREMISES
POLICE DEP'T.
CITY OF NEW YORK
HOWARD R. LEARY, POLICE COMMISSIONER

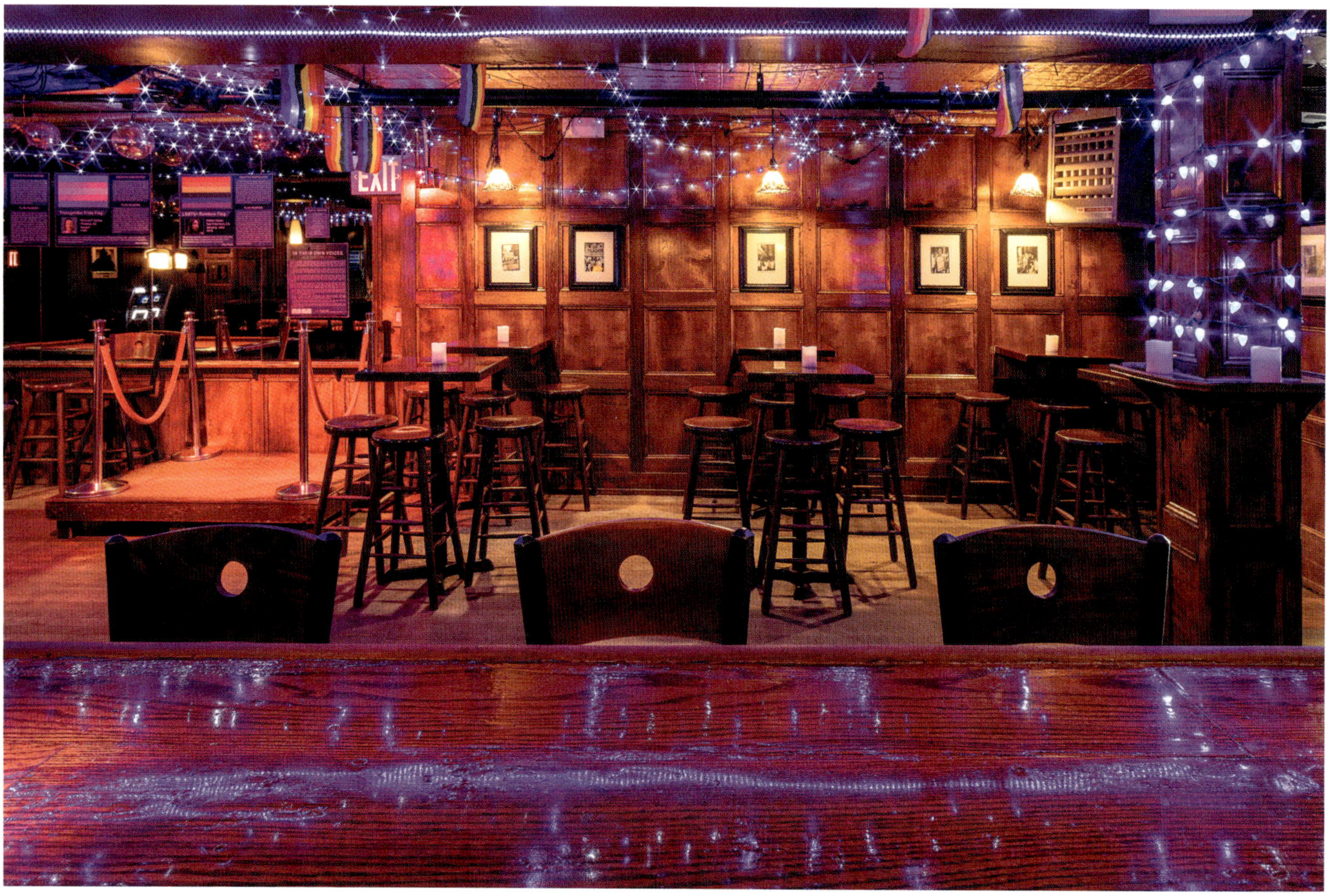

EXIT

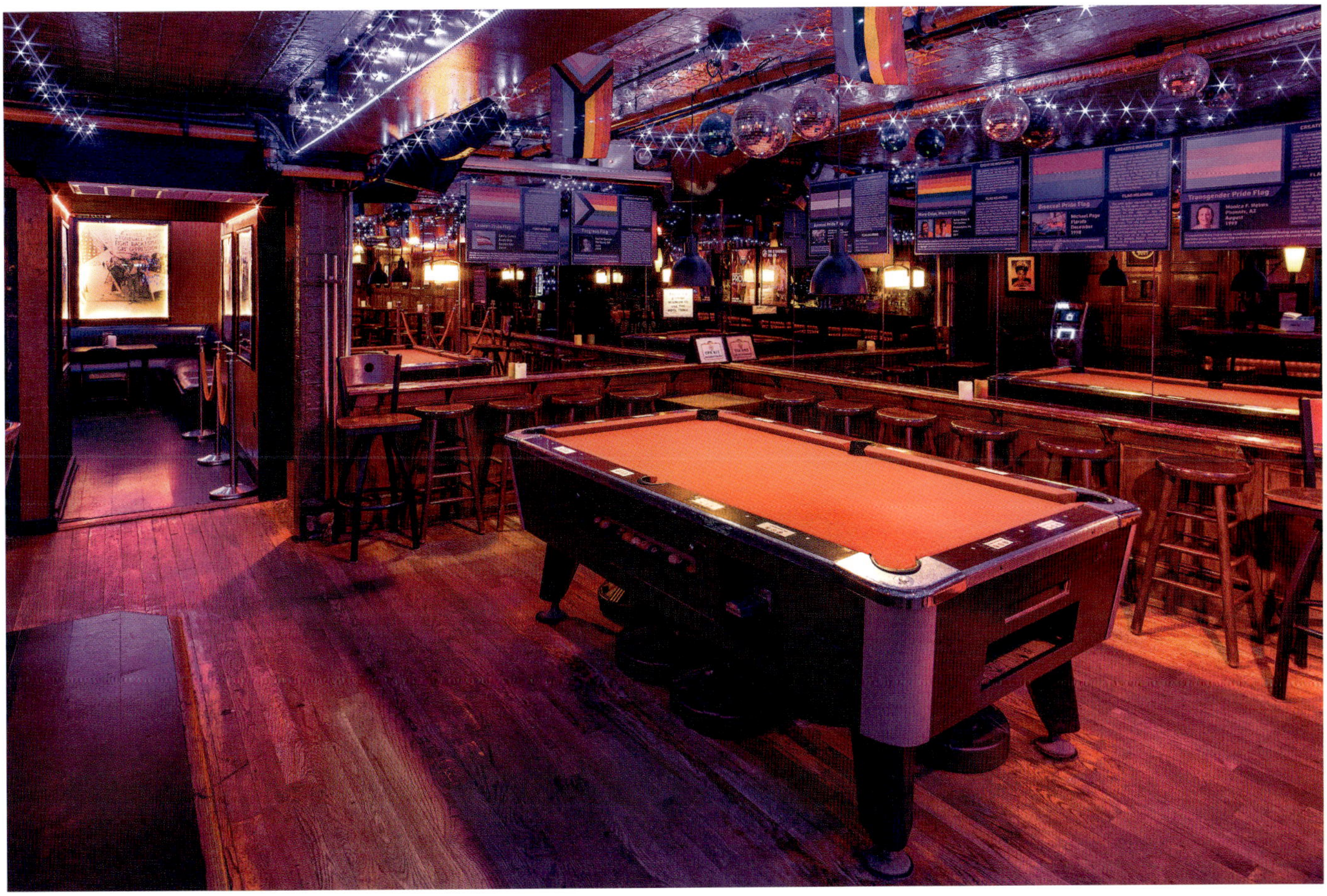

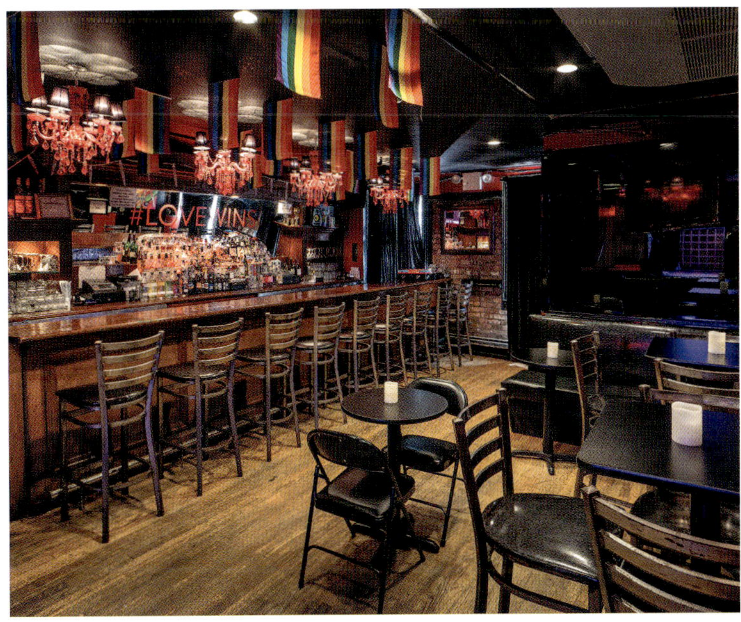

OPPOSITE TOP   *The original sign that was posted by the New York City Police Department, indicating that the establishment was a raided premises, was later returned to the present owners of Stonewall and now hangs framed in the entrance.*

ABOVE   *In 2020 Stonewall was saved from closure through crowdfunding as well as a $250,000 donation from the Gill Foundation. The back room has been dedicated as the Tim Gill and Scott Miller Room to honor the generous support of the foundation's co-chairs.*

SOPHIE'S

507 EAST 5TH STREET, EAST VILLAGE

For a pregentrification holdout set smack in the middle of the highly coveted East Village, there is surprisingly little known about the dive bar called Sophie's. But at first glance, its bare trimmings—a pool table, a jukebox, a few old barstools—and well-worn interiors suggest a long history, dating back to the area's time as a working-class Eastern European neighborhood and artists' enclave.

The oldest-known owner of the bar was the titular Sophie Polny, a once-hardscrabble Ukrainian immigrant described by *New York* magazine in 2008 as a "worldly wise *babushka*." Polny had previously run another venue, called Polny Restaurant Corp., in the neighborhood since 1914. In its early days, it catered to older Ukrainians, who would line up at 10 a.m. every morning, waiting for doors to open.

Polny moved her operation to its current location at Fifth Street between Avenues A and B around 1986, taking over another bar, named Chic Choc, that had previously existed at that address (you can still see the words "Chic Choc" in the metal threshold of the doorway). Being frugal, she chose to bring her entire oak wood bar with her when she changed locations. It's still there today, with its shingled cottage-roof motif and cabinet doors featuring stained-glass dormer windows. The jukebox was also acquired during Polny's era, though she often used it as a chair.

Bob Corton bought the bar from Polny that same year, having worked for her as a manager first. Corton chose not to renovate or change the name of the bar, saying it seemed lucky. In 2008 he decided to put it up for sale, citing health reasons. But, wanting to keep it in the family, he ultimately transferred ownership of the bar to his brother, Rich Corton, and Kirk Marcoe that year. The duo also owns the similarly mononymous, long-standing watering holes Mona's and Josie's.

Speaking to the website VinePair, Marcoe said they wanted to preserve the bar's authenticity while making it safer, since the location was not a particularly pleasant place. First on his list? Kicking out the drug dealers and cleaning the bathrooms.

Throughout its history, several generations of East Village residents have warmed the barstools at Sophie's. These have on occasion included local celebrities, like actors Jeff Bridges and Alexander Skarsgård. Most notable among these, however, was the late, great Anthony Bourdain, who visited the bar in 2009 for a "Disappearing Manhattan" episode of his show *No Reservations*. It was perhaps Bourdain who encapsulated the staying power of Sophie's best. "I don't want no wide screens, high-fiving white guys, no fauxhawks or gel heads or hot chicks with douchebags," he said. "I don't want anything on the jukebox that will distract an old gentleman such as myself from drinking the heart right out of the afternoon if I should choose to do so. Where can a guy get a drink when the last gin mill closes down, when there's nothing left but the fern bar or the lounge, when the barkeep has been replaced by a mixologist?"

While the crowds at Sophie's have changed dramatically, even since 2009, there's still something familiar that happens when you stumble on the right mix of neighborhood longtimers, artists, and students. And, if nothing else, the beers are still inexpensive.

OPPOSITE *Sophie's was founded over a hundred years ago. It has remained an unassuming neighborhood dive bar, despite many changes in ownership and the gentrification that has taken place in the East Village.*

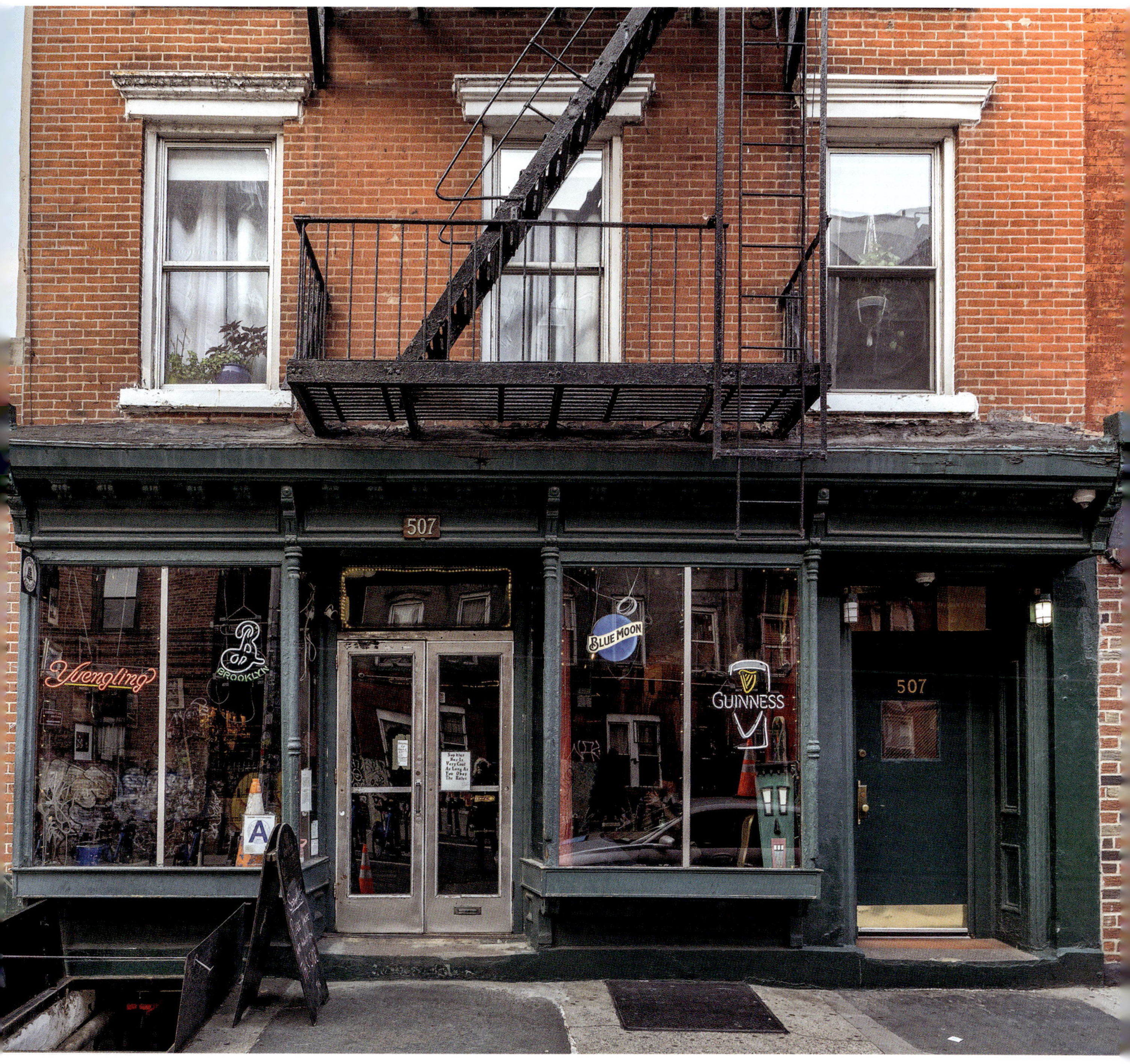

507
Yuengling
BROOKLYN
BLUE MOON
GUINNESS
507
A

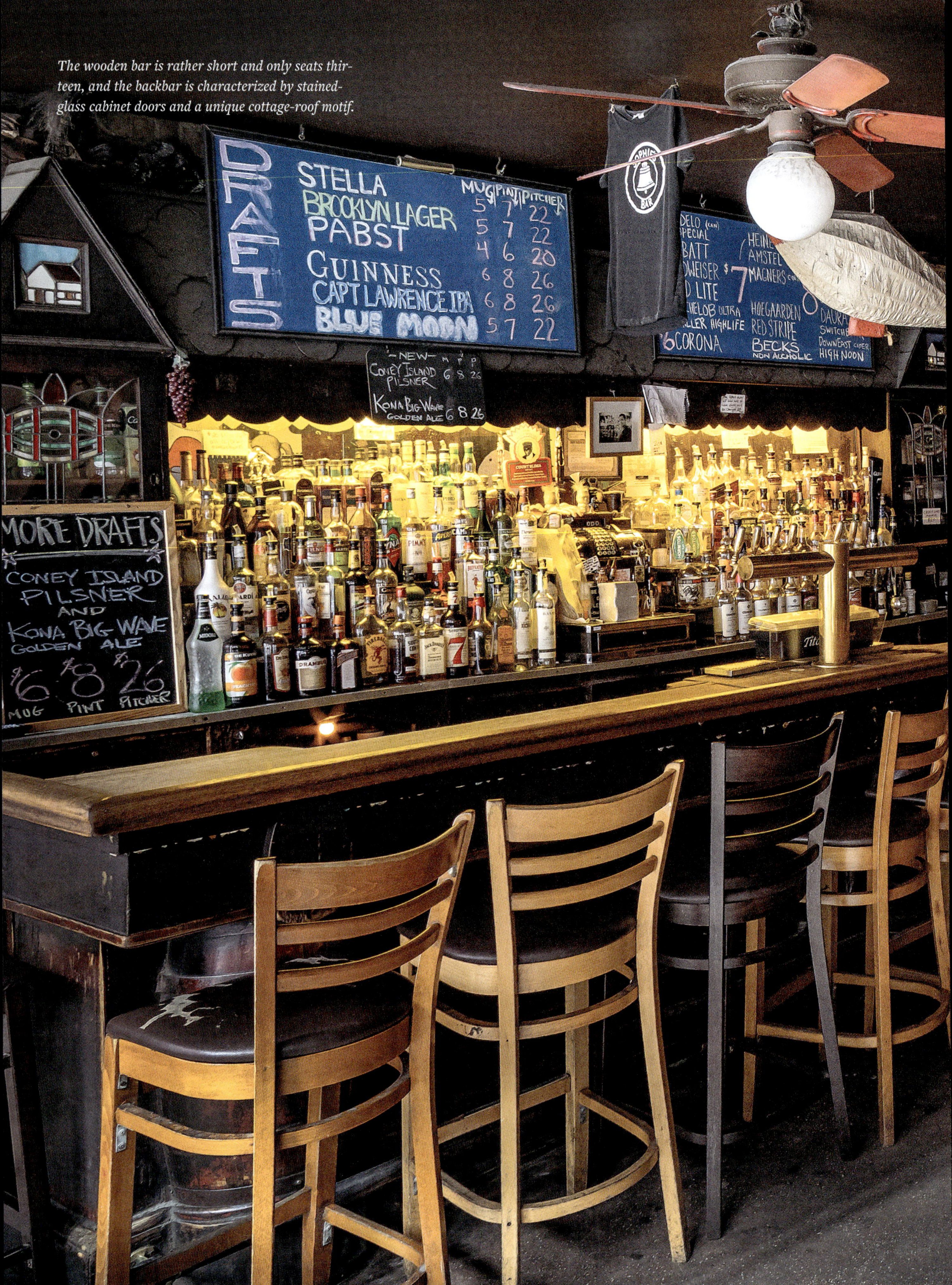

The wooden bar is rather short and only seats thirteen, and the backbar is characterized by stained-glass cabinet doors and a unique cottage-roof motif.

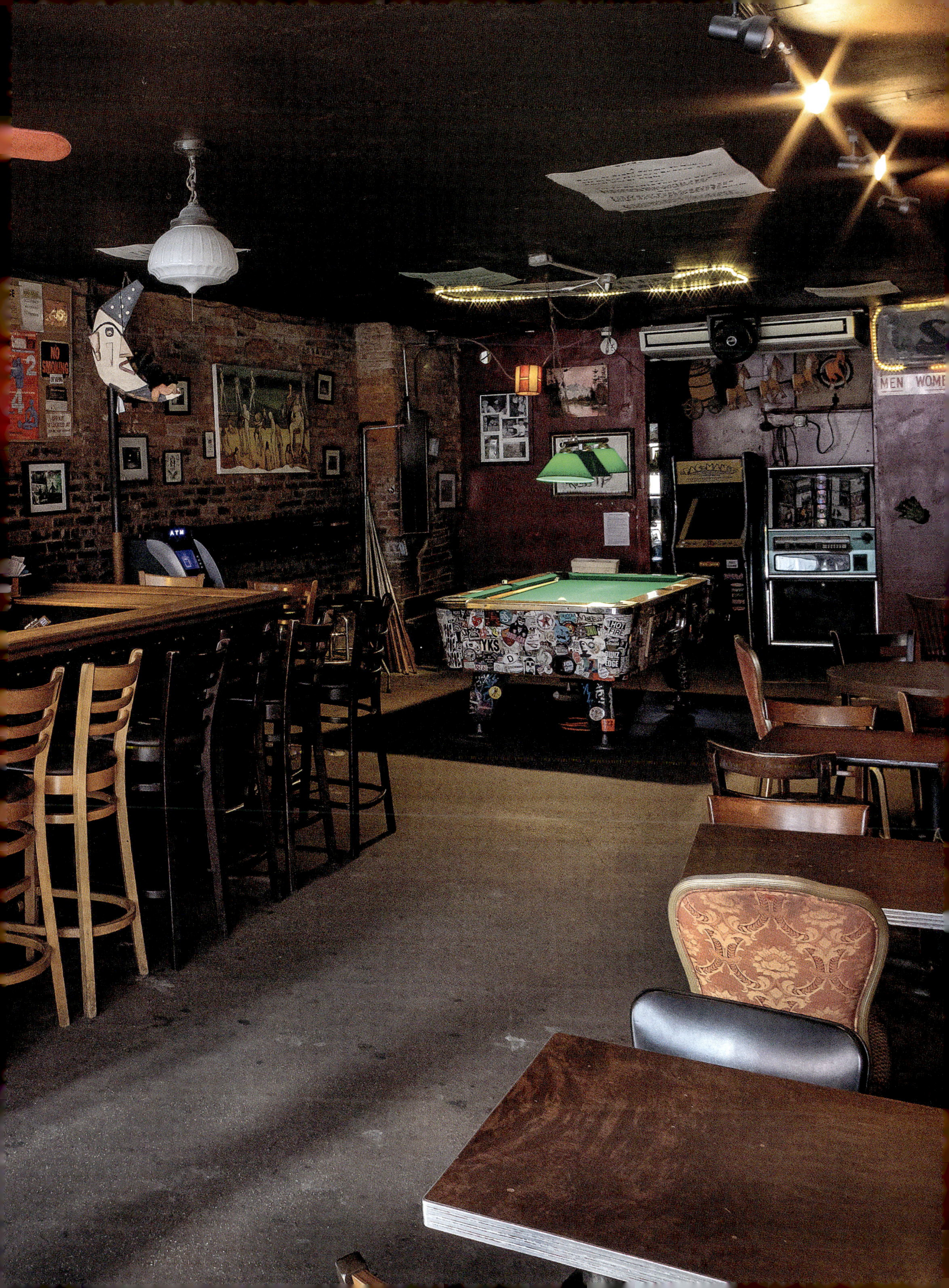

NO SMOKING
ATM
MEN WOME

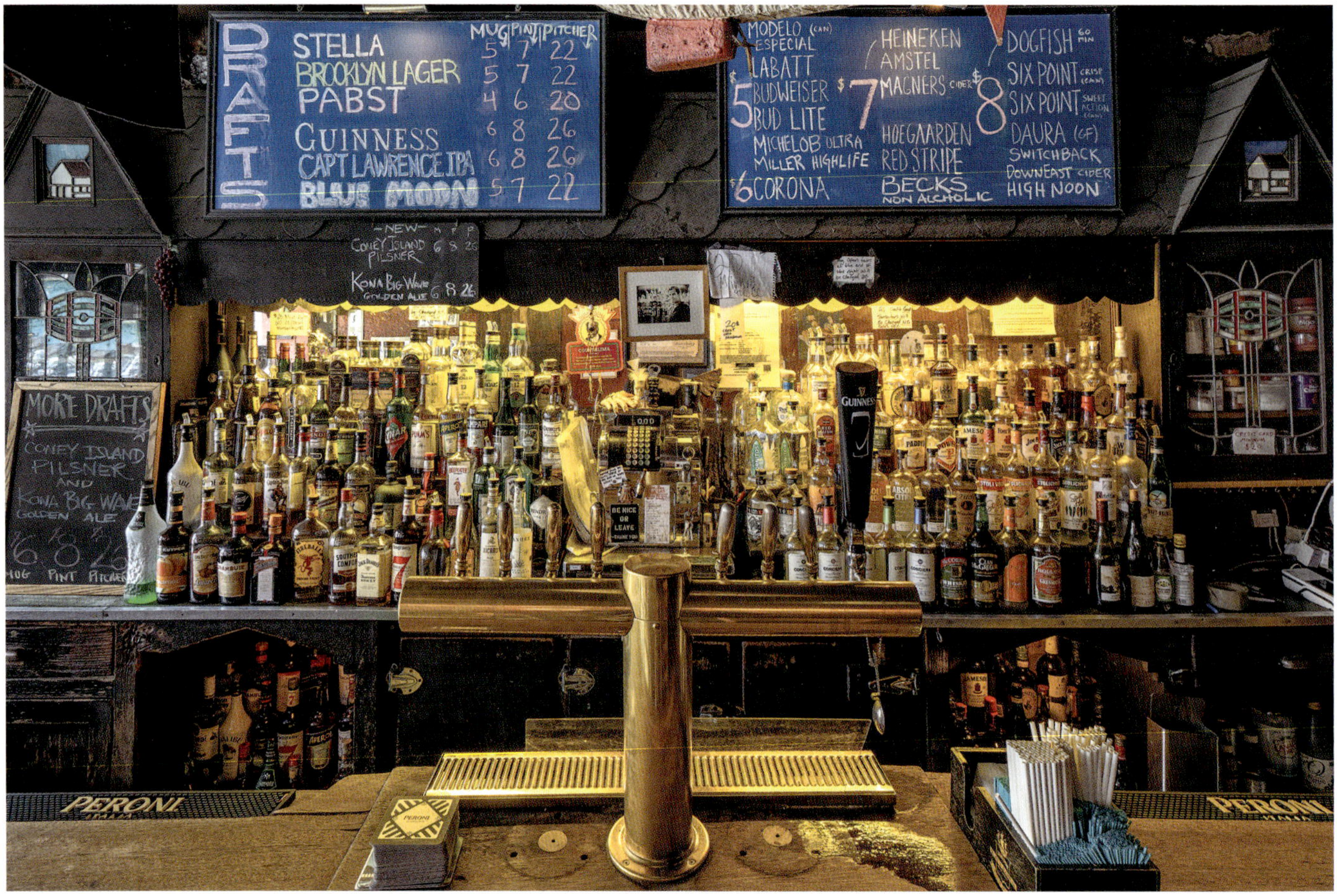

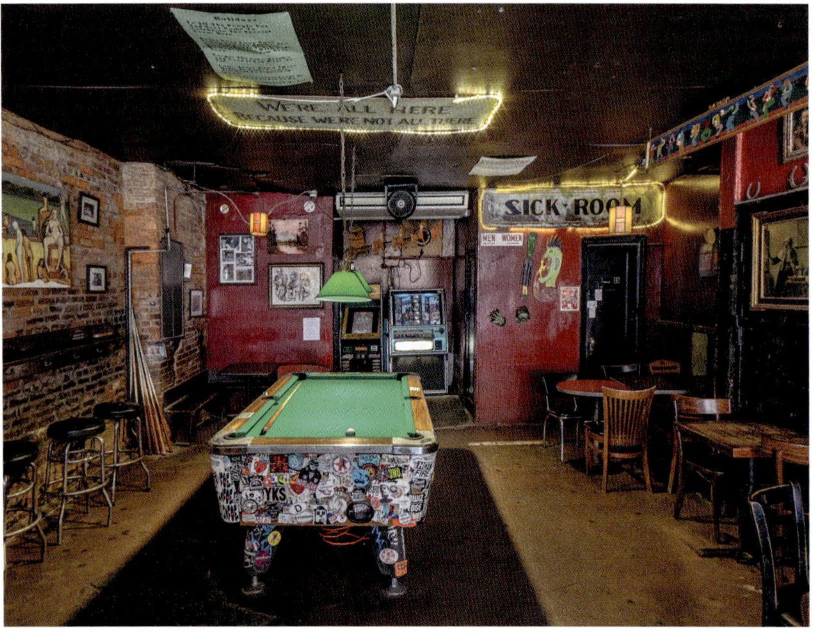

ABOVE *Chalkboards over the bar proudly display its simple offerings. There are no mixologists tending bar at Sophie's.*

LEFT *The bar has seen its share of celebrity patrons, including the late Anthony Bourdain, who visited in 2009 for his television show No Reservations.*

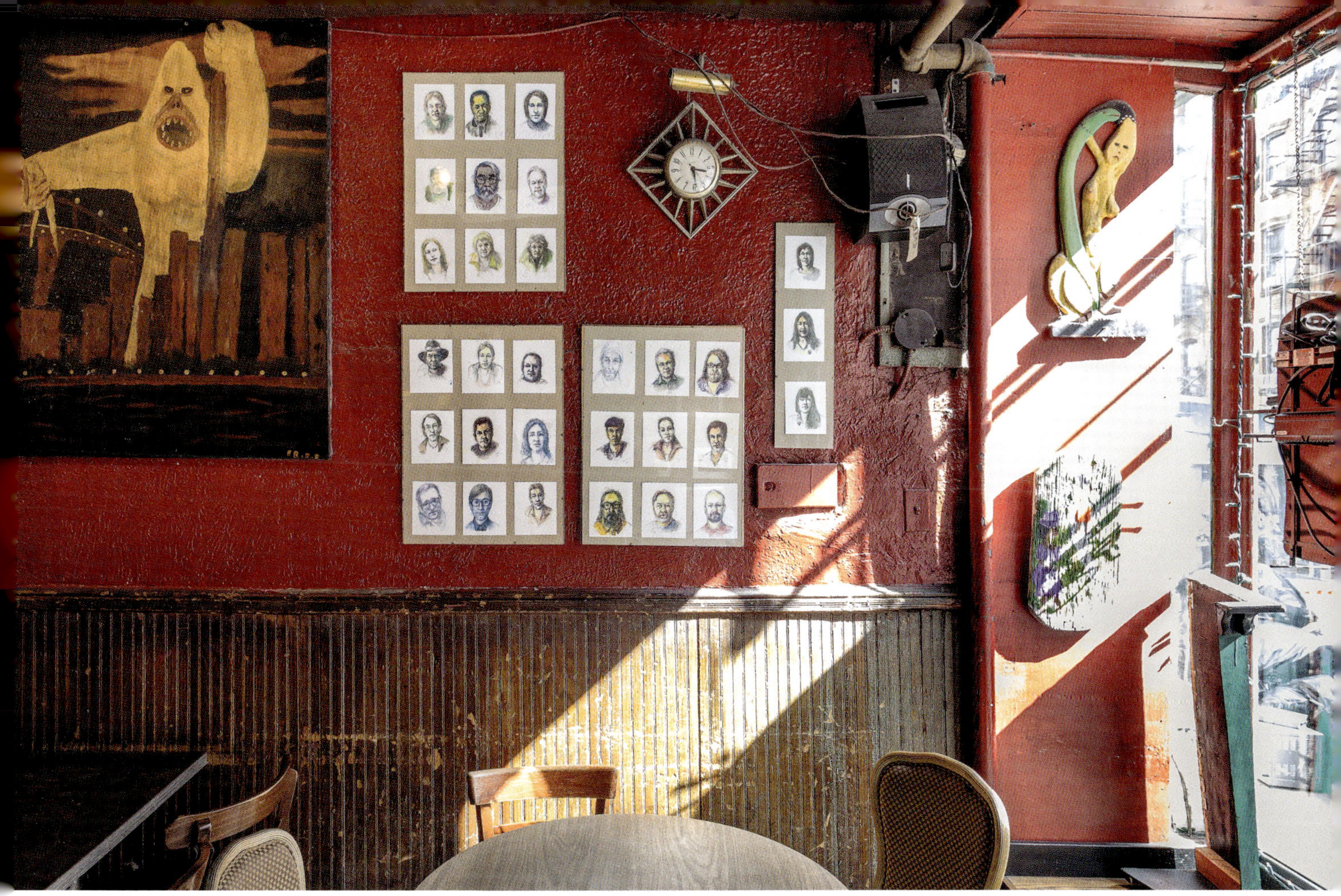

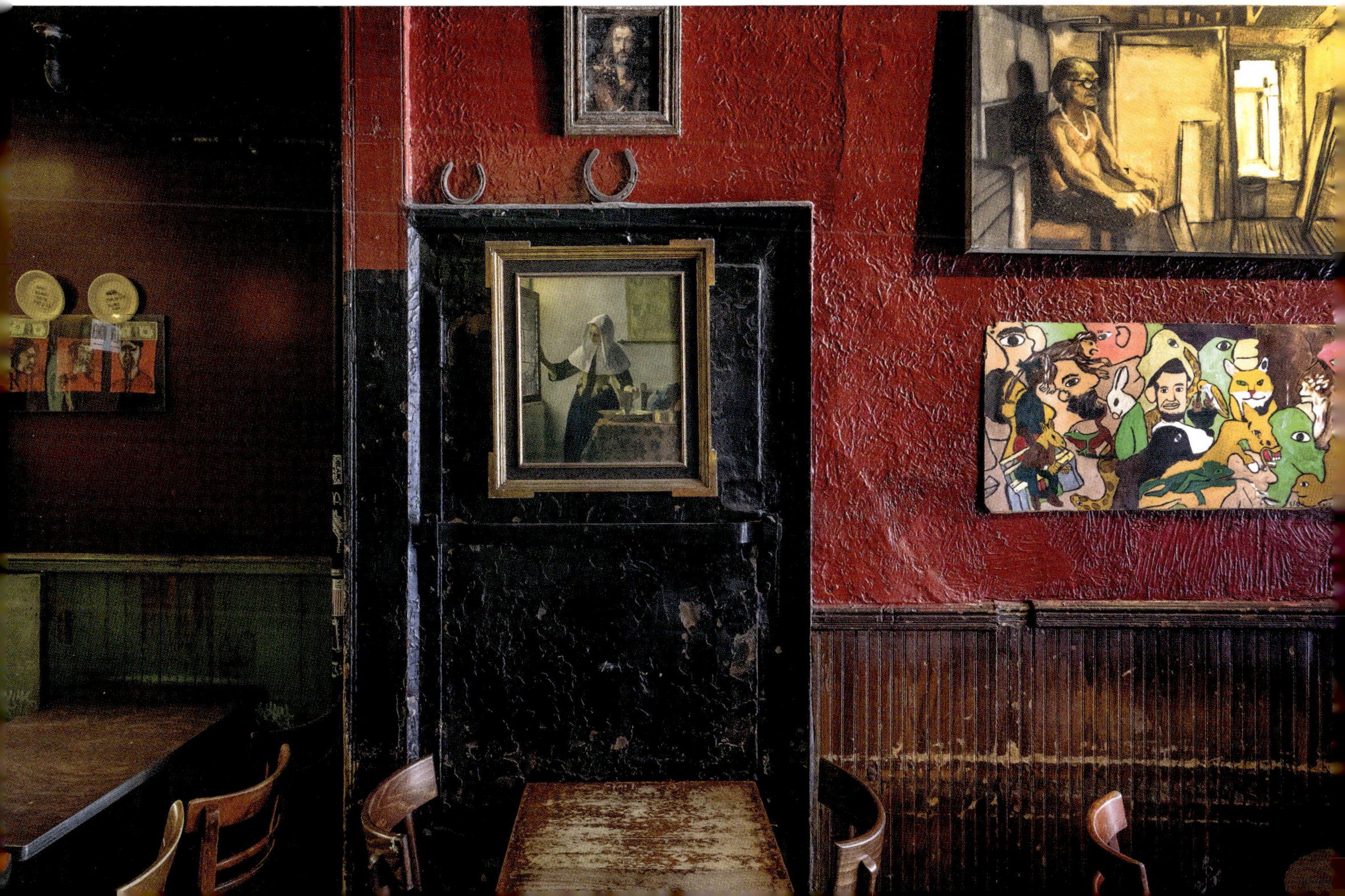

OLD TOWN BAR AND RESTAURANT

45 EAST 18TH STREET, UNION SQUARE

Walking down a nondescript block of East Eighteenth Street, it's hard to miss the splendid, reddish-brown wood facade of Old Town Bar. And even if you've never been to New York, you may recognize its well-trodden interiors from the show *Sex and the City*, a Madonna music video, or the opening credits montage of *Late Night with David Letterman*.

The bar has remained in continuous operation since it was opened in 1892 by Jacob Berckel. Located near an old German stronghold in Union Square, it was called Viemeisters in the early twentieth century, and was a known meeting place for members of the Tammany Hall political machine.

Old Town would go by yet another name during the Prohibition era, Craig's Restaurant, when it started offering food, masquerading as an eating establishment to help conceal its booze-selling speakeasy operations. After the repeal of the Volstead Act, it was purchased by the Lohdens, a German American family, who would own it through the mid-1900s.

Despite surviving Prohibition, the bar fell into a state of disrepair in the 1950s. This was partially due to the closing of the nearby Eighteenth Street subway station in 1948, which caused an increase in crime in the neighborhood. But it may also be attributed to the fact that, by the end of World War II in 1945, German bars were less popular in the US than they were before.

In the 1970s, Larry Meagher, an Irish immigrant, took the reins of the bar as its manager, working for then-owner Henry Lohden, who was having trouble maintaining the business. Meagher became a fixture, breathing life back into the space and, notably, making it progressive for its time. Speaking to the *New York Observer* in 2007 after his father's passing, Meagher's son, Gerard "Gerry" Meagher, recounted the scene there when Larry first took over: "The only people here were truckers and Andy Warhol's crowd from his Factory around the corner." Under Larry's guidance, the bar properly welcomed women, who had once only been allowed upstairs; it was also known to be gay-friendly. According to the *Irish Echo*, he personally protected Warhol, a regular, from the taunts of homophobic clientele.

Larry also brought food back to the menu, allegedly because a construction foreman working a project nearby told him that his workers were getting drunk at lunch. When Lohden passed away in the mid 1980s, he left the bar—and its building—to Larry and his wife, who in turn left it to Gerry.

It's worth mentioning that Warhol was among the first of many creatives and intellectuals to have frequented the Old Town Bar. Particularly in the modern era, countless writers, actors, and musicians have held court in its booths, among them the Rolling Stones and Liam Clancy of the Clancy Brothers. It's also been known as a gathering place for literary greats: novelists like Pete Hamill, Nick Hornby, and Frank McCourt were decades-long patrons.

Beyond its A-list clientele, Old Town has also been featured as a setting in numerous films, like *The Devil's Own*, *State of Grace*, *Last Days of Disco*, and *Bullets Over Broadway*, and was a setting in the television show *Gossip Girl*. The interior of the bar can be seen in the music video for Madonna's 1993 song "Bad Girl," which features a bartender lighting the singer's cigarette.

Today, Gerry oversees the bar his father preserved, with long-standing old-time features like the original tile floors, pressed-steel ceilings, New York's oldest dumbwaiter, and a 55-foot (17-meter) mahogany bar that was first built in the nineteenth century.

One of Old Town's most fascinating features, however, is tucked away in the men's room: the shoulder-height ceramic urinals dating back to 1910 are the last working Hinsdale urinals on the whole of the East Coast. Arguably the most famous urinals in New York City, they received a centennial celebration in 2010 that attracted history buffs from far and wide. "I love all the old urinals of Manhattan—the ones at Old Town are probably the best," *New York Times* restaurant critic Pete Wells told *Bon Appetit* magazine in 2017. "They're so grand they turn the act of urinating into something sacramental. I'm fascinated by the way the top edge scoops in—I'm not sure if it's so you can see what's going on in there, or if it was meant to accommodate the jutting stomachs of Tammany Hall officials who ate steak three times a day."

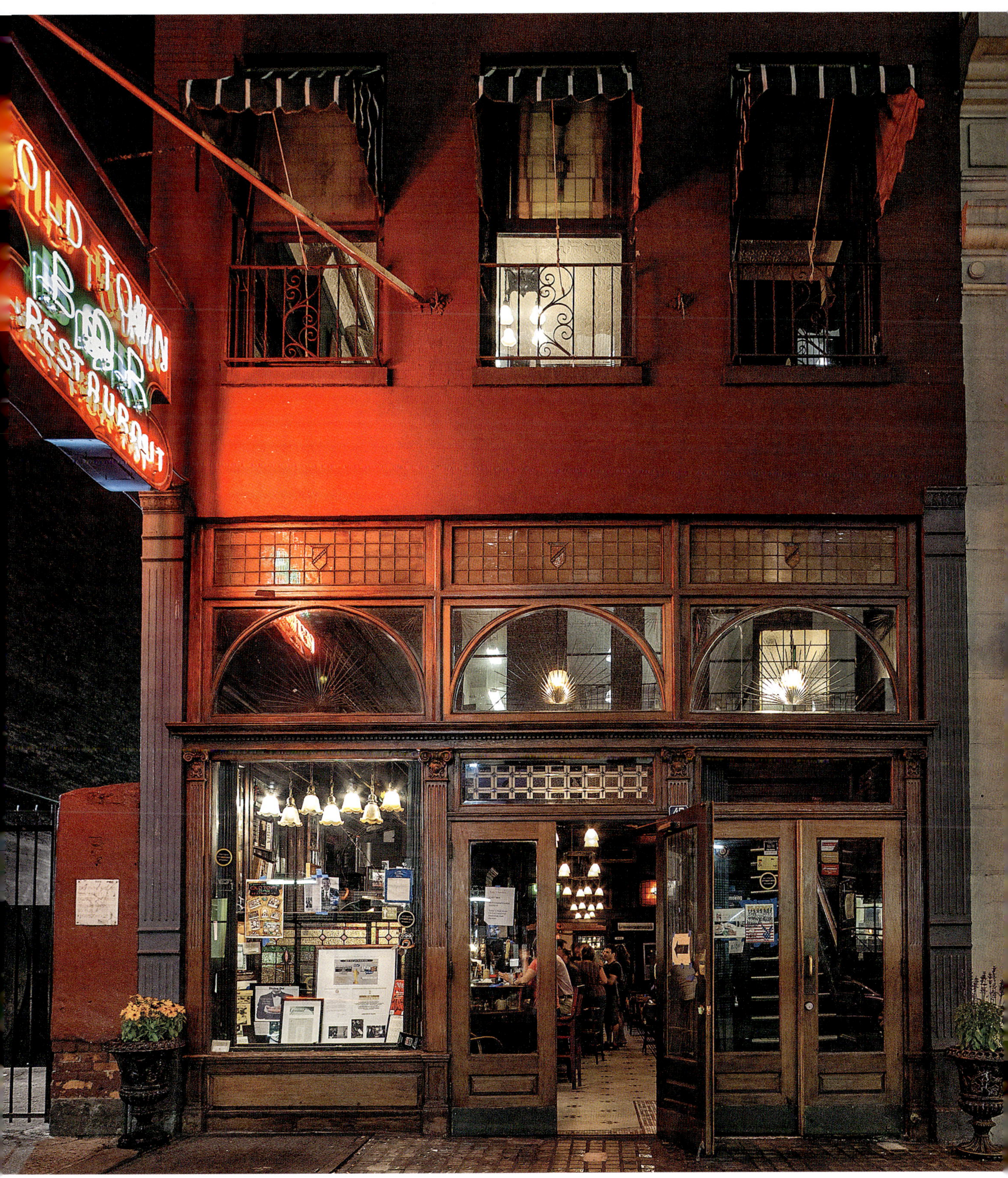

OLD TOWN BAR AND RESTAURANT

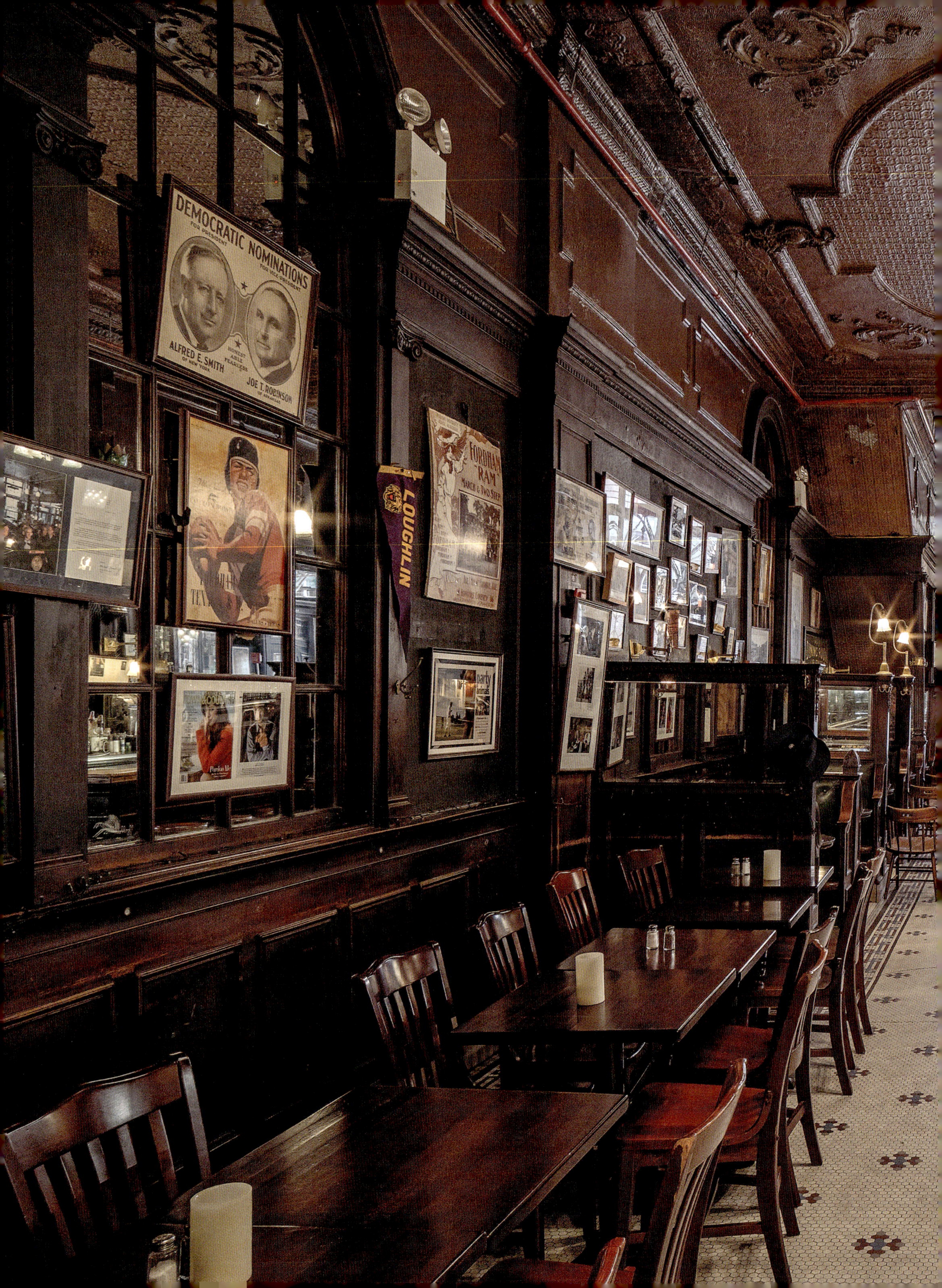
DEMOCRATIC NOMINATIONS
ALFRED E. SMITH
JOE T. ROBINSON
LOUGHLIN
FORDHAM RAM
MARCH & TWO-STEP

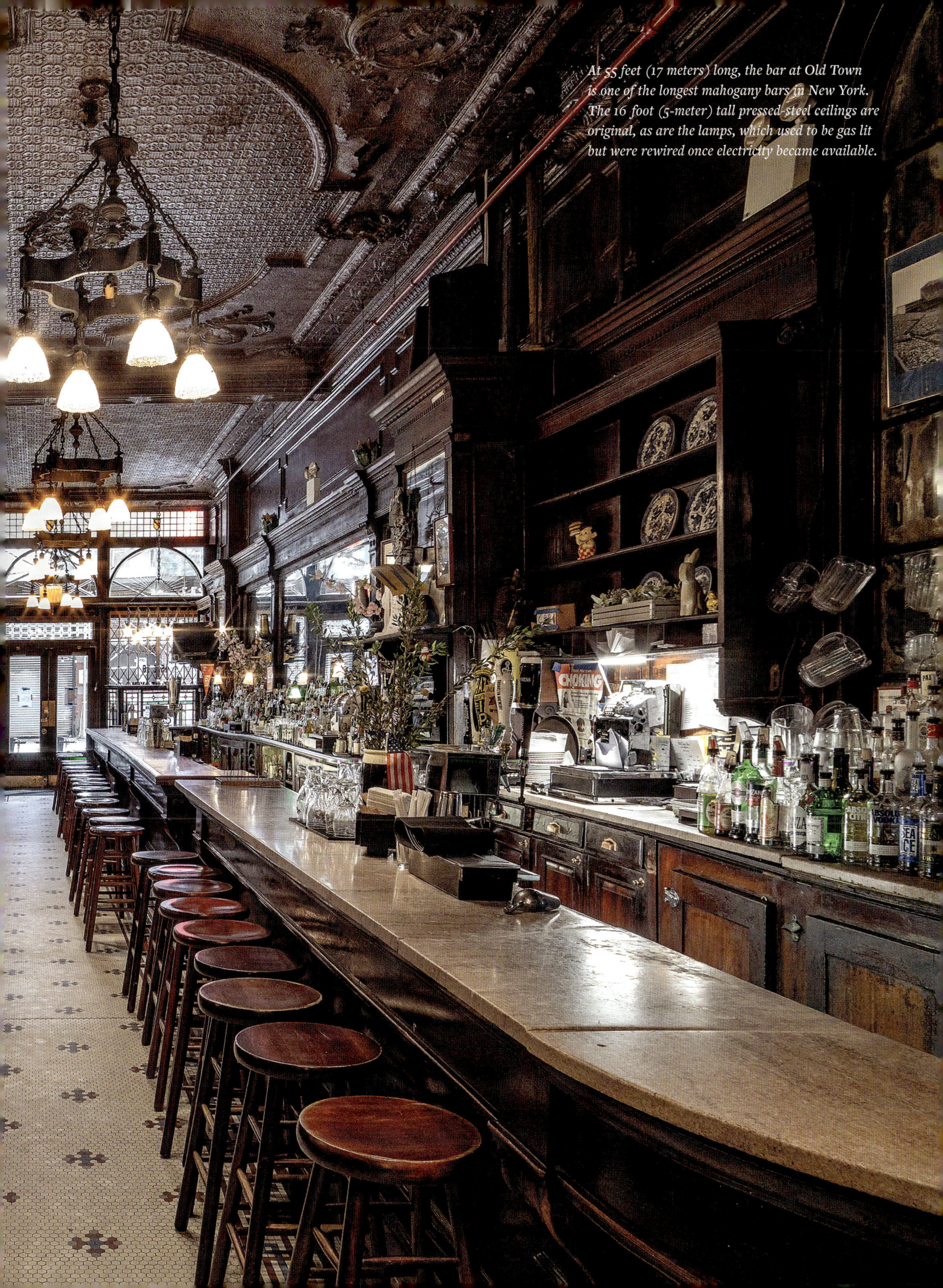

At 55 feet (17 meters) long, the bar at Old Town is one of the longest mahogany bars in New York. The 16 foot (5-meter) tall pressed-steel ceilings are original, as are the lamps, which used to be gas lit but were rewired once electricity became available.

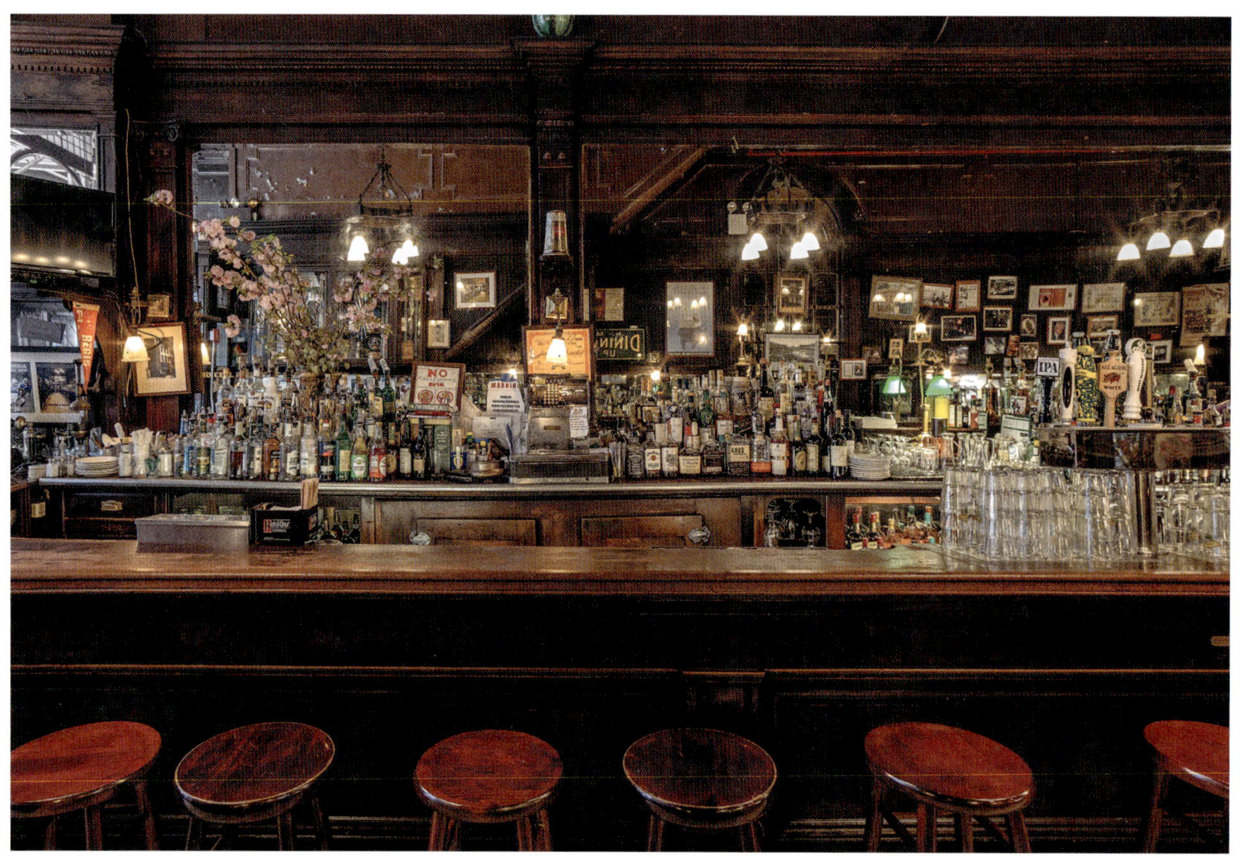

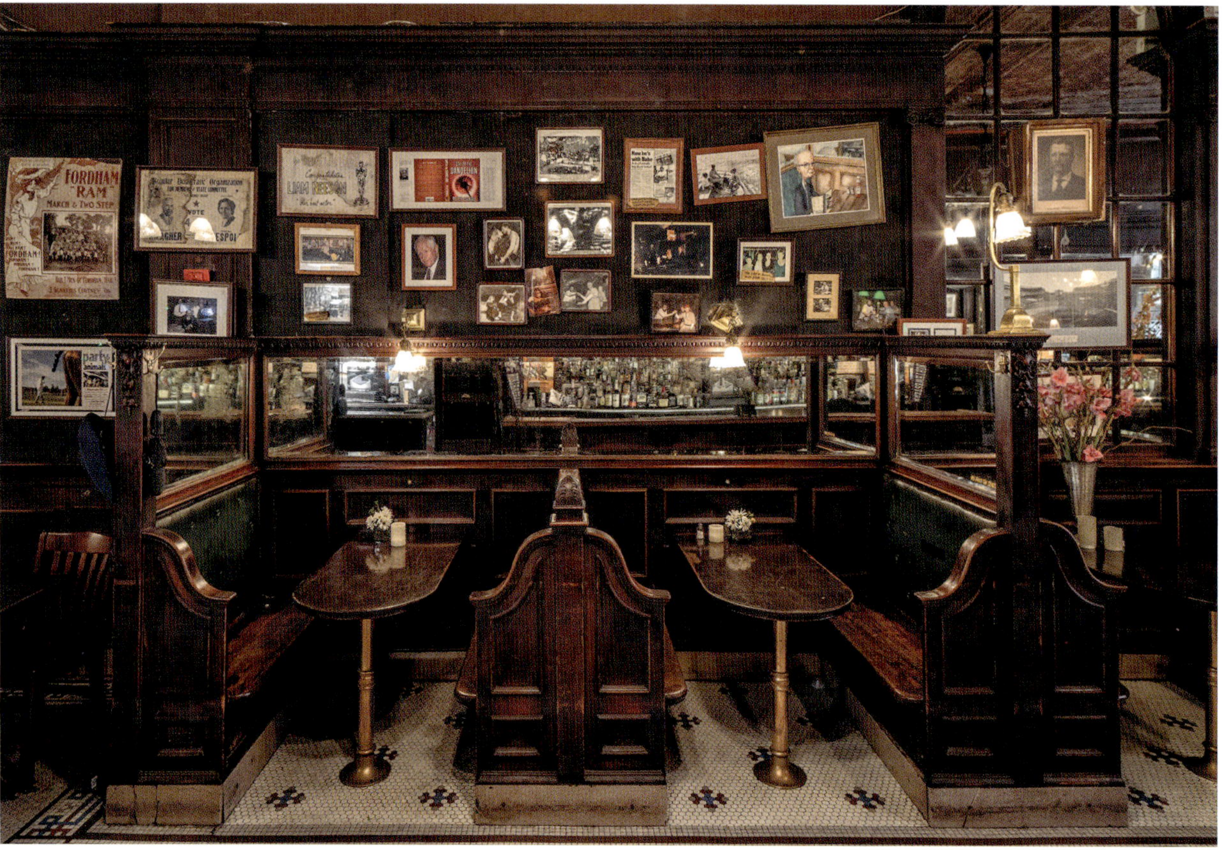

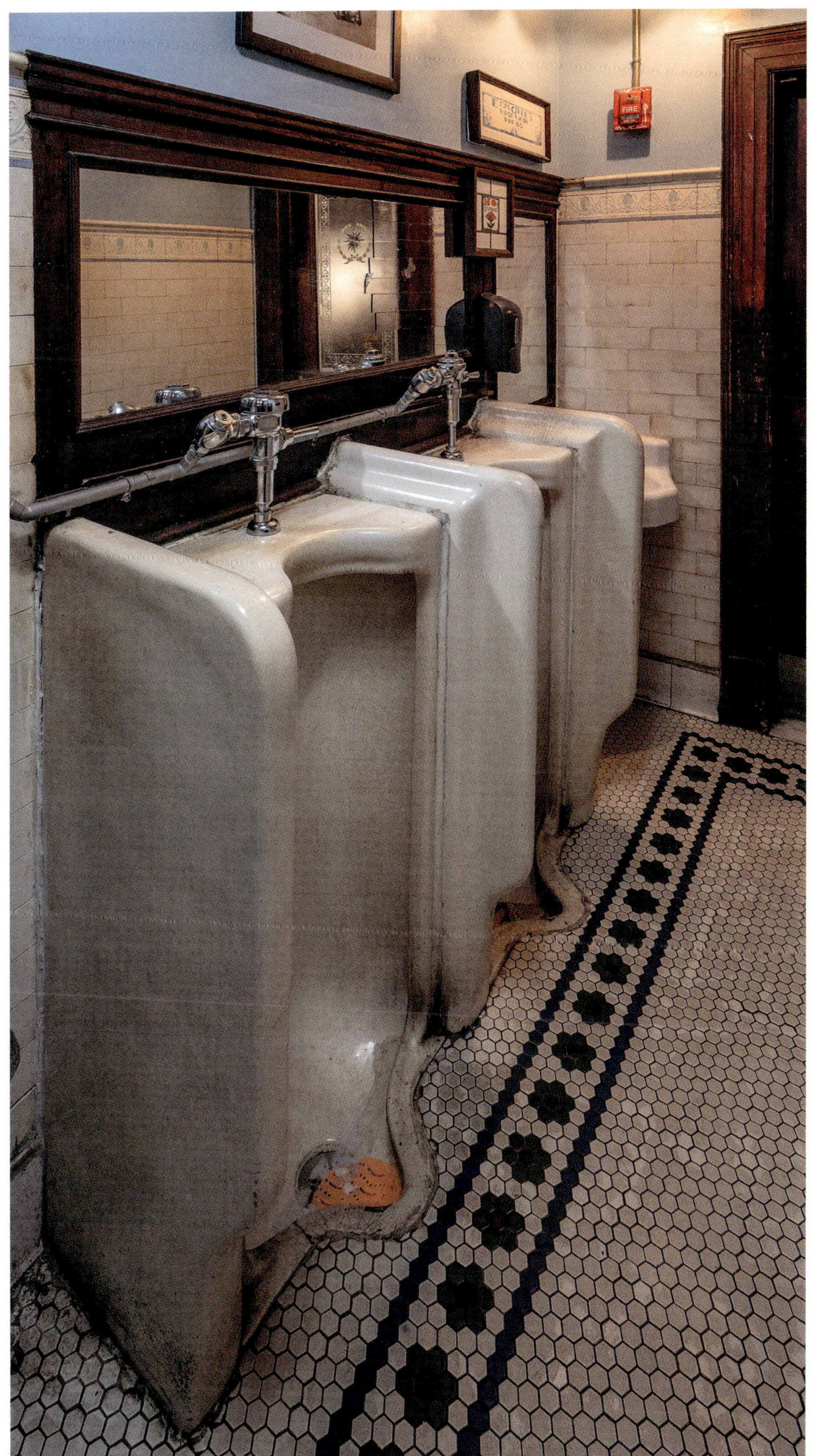

OPPOSITE TOP   *The backbar features 258 square feet (24 square meters) of bevel-edged plate mirrors.*

OPPOSITE BOTTOM   *Many literary and political figures have frequented the bar, and their photos and books line its walls.*

RIGHT   *The famous shoulder-height porcelain urinals in the men's bathroom were made by Hinsdale in 1910.*

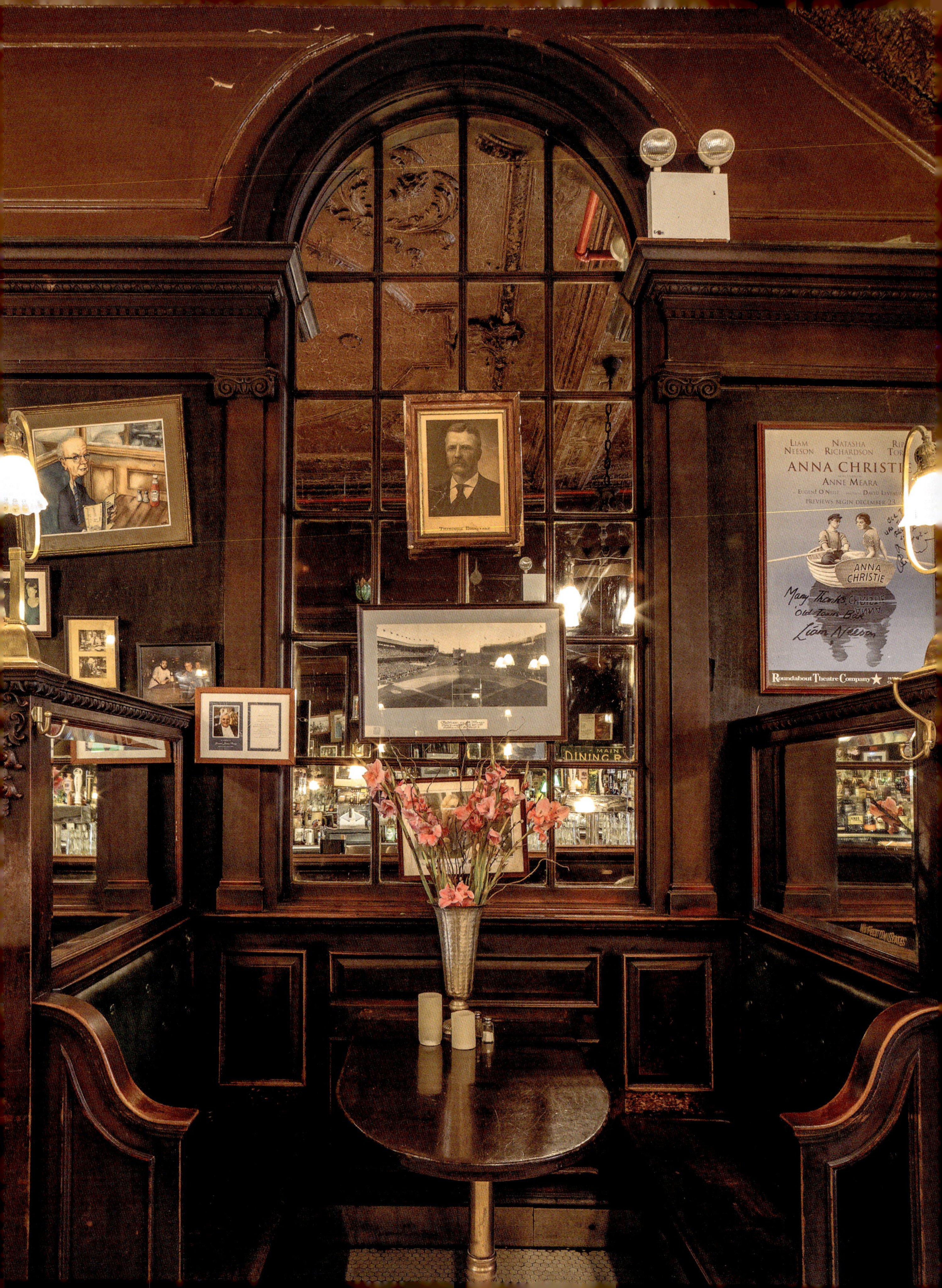

LIAM NEESON NATASHA RICHARDSON RIP TORN
ANNA CHRISTIE
ANNE MEARA
EUGENE O'NEILL DAVID LEVEAUX
PREVIEWS BEGIN DECEMBER 23
ANNA CHRISTIE
Mary Thanks
Old Town Bar
Liam Neeson
Roundabout Theatre Company

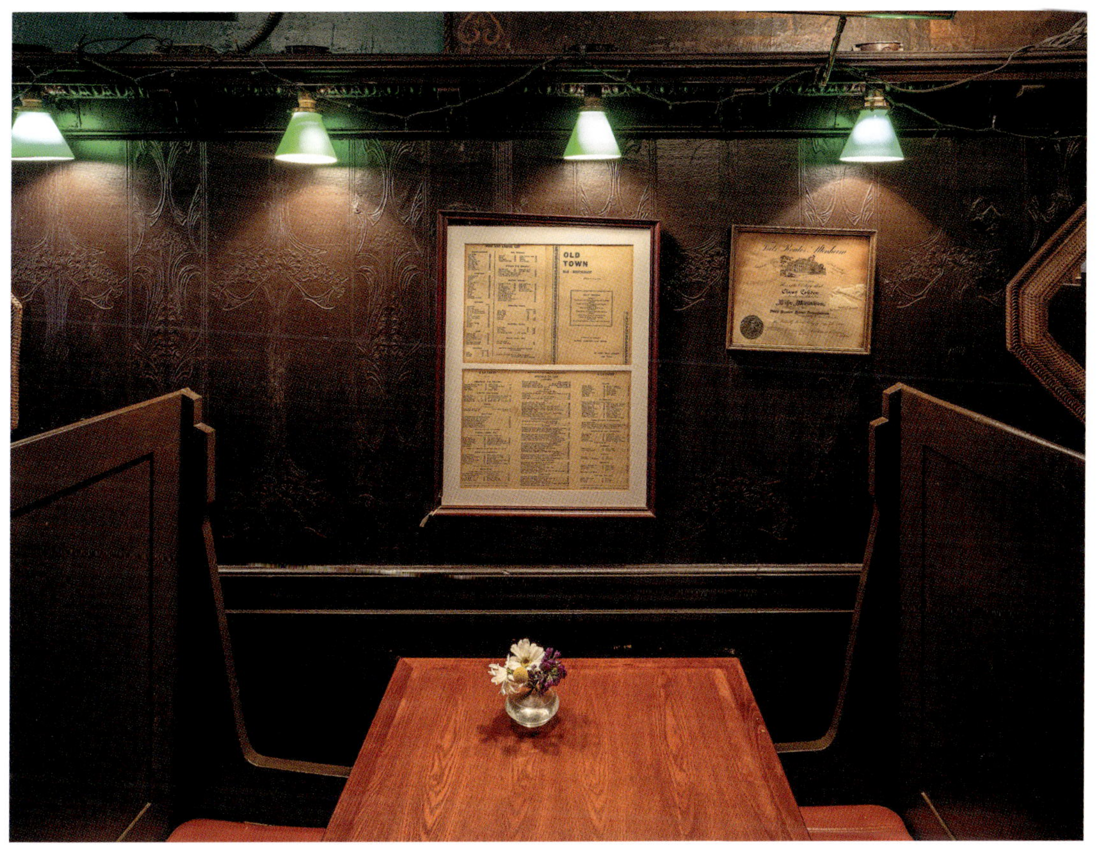

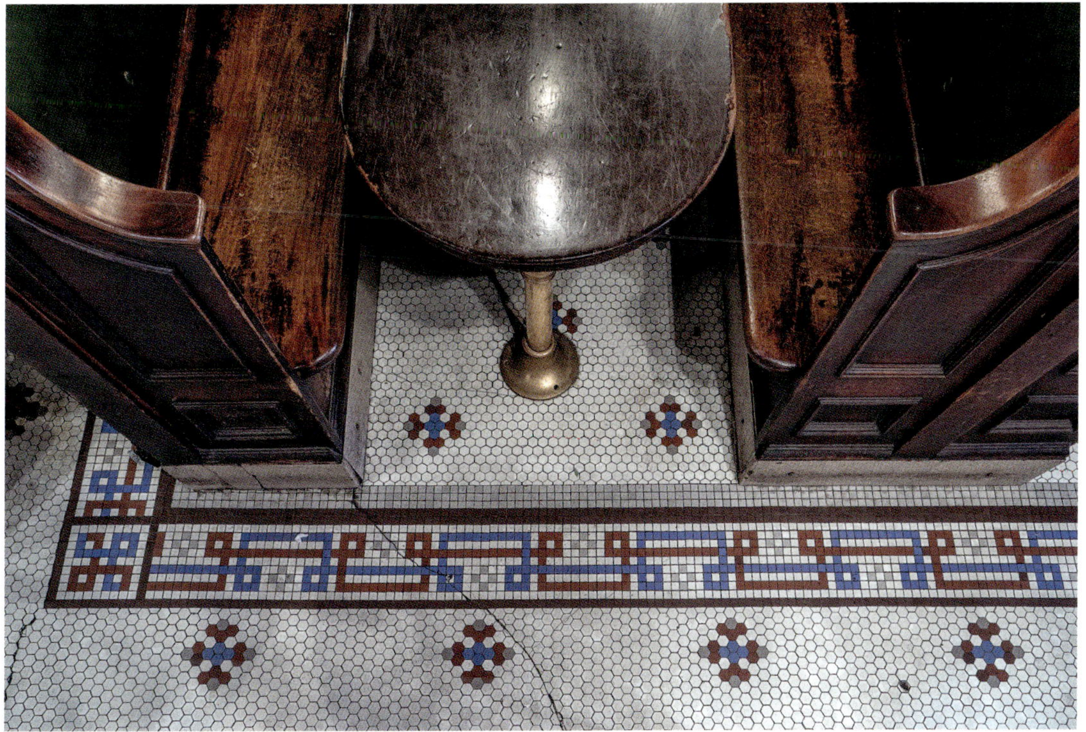

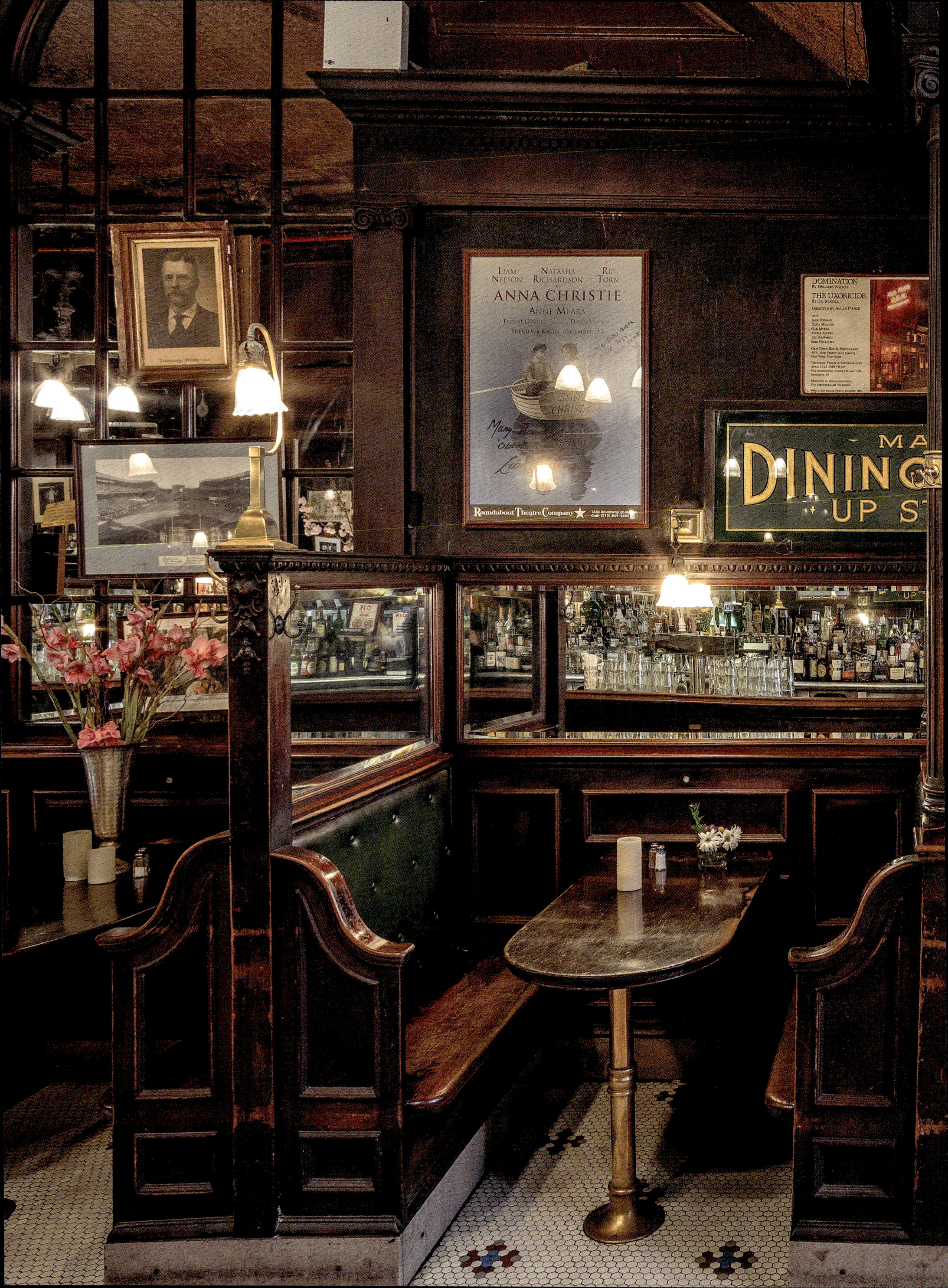

LIAM NEESON
NATASHA RICHARDSON
RIP TORN
ANNA CHRISTIE
ANNE MEARA
EUGENE O'NEILL
DAVID LEVEAUX
PREVIEWS BEGIN DECEMBER 23
ANNA CHRISTIE
Roundabout Theatre Company
1530 Broadway at 45th St.
Call (212) 869-8400

DOMINATION
BY DOLORES WILSON
THE UXORICIDE
BY GIL REAVILL
DIRECTED BY ALLAN PIERCE
WITH
JACK FORMAN
DANA MORTON
GAR MYERS
MARIA MYERS
JILL RAFFERTY
ERIC WILLIAMS
OLD TOWN BAR & RESTAURANT
45 E. 18TH STREET (2ND FLOOR)
NEW YORK, NEW YORK
THURSDAY, FRIDAY & SATURDAY EVES.
APRIL 11-27 1985 · 8 PM.
FOR RESERVATIONS, PHONE 718-622-1534
ADMISSION: $8
PRODUCED IN ASSOCIATION WITH
THE STRUCTURALIST WORKSHOP

MAIN
DINING
UP STAIRS

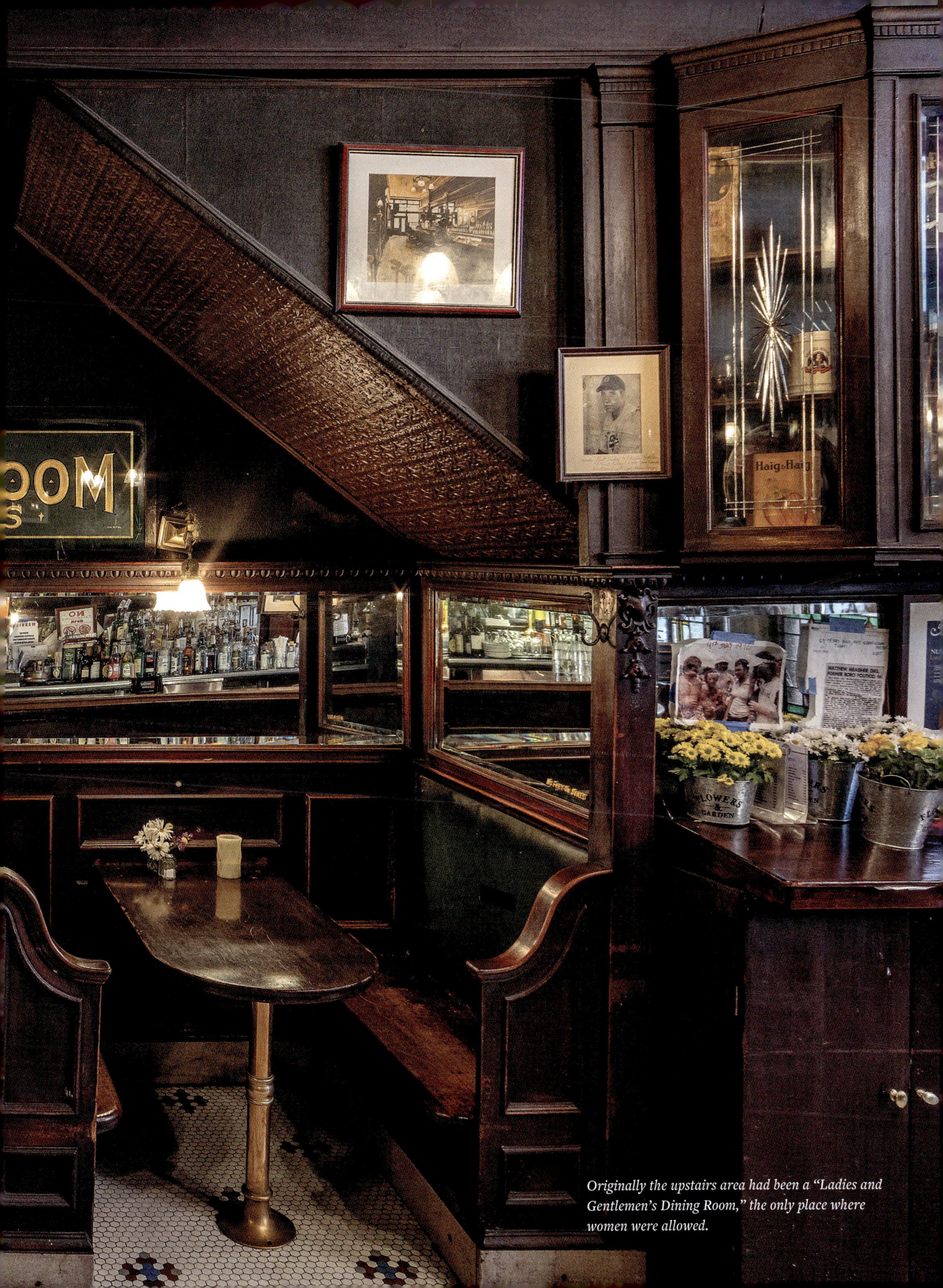

Originally the upstairs area had been a "Ladies and Gentlemen's Dining Room," the only place where women were allowed.

SPRING LOUNGE

48 SPRING STREET, NOLITA

Spring Lounge is the fourth name of the bar located at the corner of Spring and Mulberry Streets in what is now NoLIta (for "north of Little Italy"). Set across from a children's park and playground, the simply decorated, wood-trimmed bar has survived here for around a century as the neighborhood around it has evolved into a fashionable shopping and dining district.

The bar at 48 Spring Street first came into the world in the 1920s as an unnamed illegal to-go shop, filling buckets of beer for takeout during the Prohibition era. In the 1940s it took the name Chappy's, and in the 1960s it was a craps hall known as Wilson's 10:30, alluding to the start time of the nightly game in the basement. (According to the bar's website, a craps table was unearthed during later renovations.)

It wasn't until the 1970s that it became known as Spring Lounge. When the *New York Times* visited in 1978, it mentioned that youngsters in the tenement-filled area would congregate there to "keep a secure eye on the neighborhood."

For many years, the bar has also been colloquially known as the Shark Bar, thanks to a shark mural and a number of stuffed and taxidermied sharks adorning its walls. They were all caught by a previous owner, Pat Caserta, and include among them a now-endangered species of golden dusky shark caught on Miami Beach in 1976.

The current owner, Bryan Delaney, purchased the bar in 1996. He paid for at least a portion of it with bills in a paper bag, since the previous owner, a woman he believes was married to a Mafia member, had asked for cash. These days, decor held over from previous proprietors is mixed with photographs from Delaney's family: his mom's wedding photo; his brother's military portrait; a few old baby photos scattered on the walls. In 2019, he told the website Thrillist he was moved to buy the bar because of its history, saying, "These kinds of old places were rare…they're even rarer now."

Despite its unvarnished appearance and homey feel, Spring Lounge has had its share of star visitors in the modern era. Singer John Mayer was a longtime regular, often holding court with friends, including Katy Perry. Eric Roberts and Mickey Rourke shot a scene from 1984's *The Pope of Greenwich Village* at the bar, and actresses Kate Hudson and Ginnifer Goodwin stop in during a scene in the 2011 romantic comedy film *Something Borrowed*.

Today, Spring Lounge still opens at 8 a.m. six days a week (on Sunday, it's 10 a.m.) and closes at 4 a.m. As you might have guessed, there are people lining up at the door to get in right when business hours commence.

"We have these big giant windows that look out on the corner of Spring and Mulberry Streets, and it is the best people watching you'll ever see," says general manager Jen Maslanka, who's worked at Spring Lounge for twenty years. "All walks of life pass by our corner on a daily basis, and most of them stop in for a drink at some point. Whether they were a morning person or a Saturday-night warrior, almost everyone in NYC has had a time in their lives that they spent with us."

OPPOSITE *Spring Lounge opens at 8 a.m. six days a week and at 10 a.m. on Sundays, a rarity in the neighborhood.*

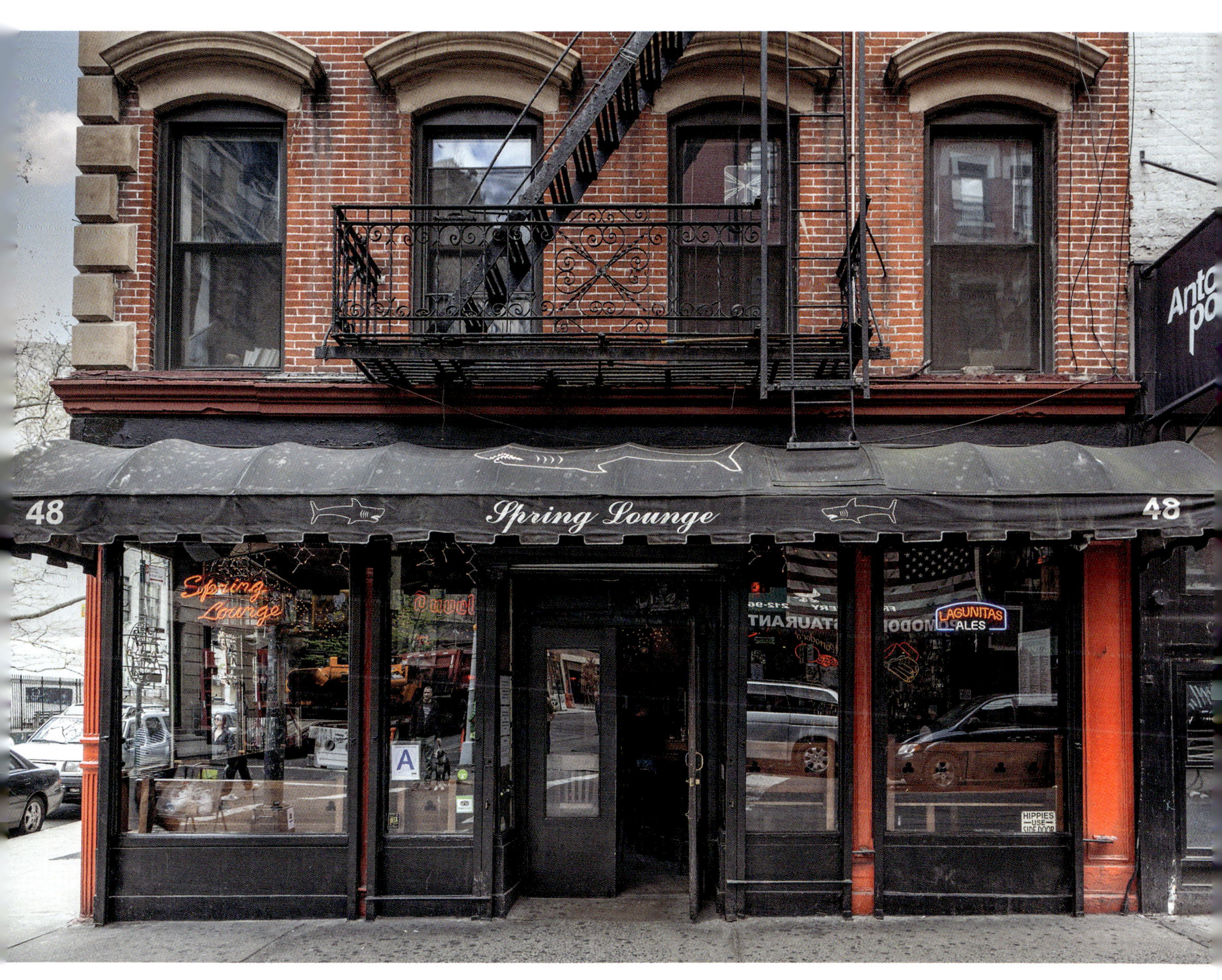

SPRING LOUNGE

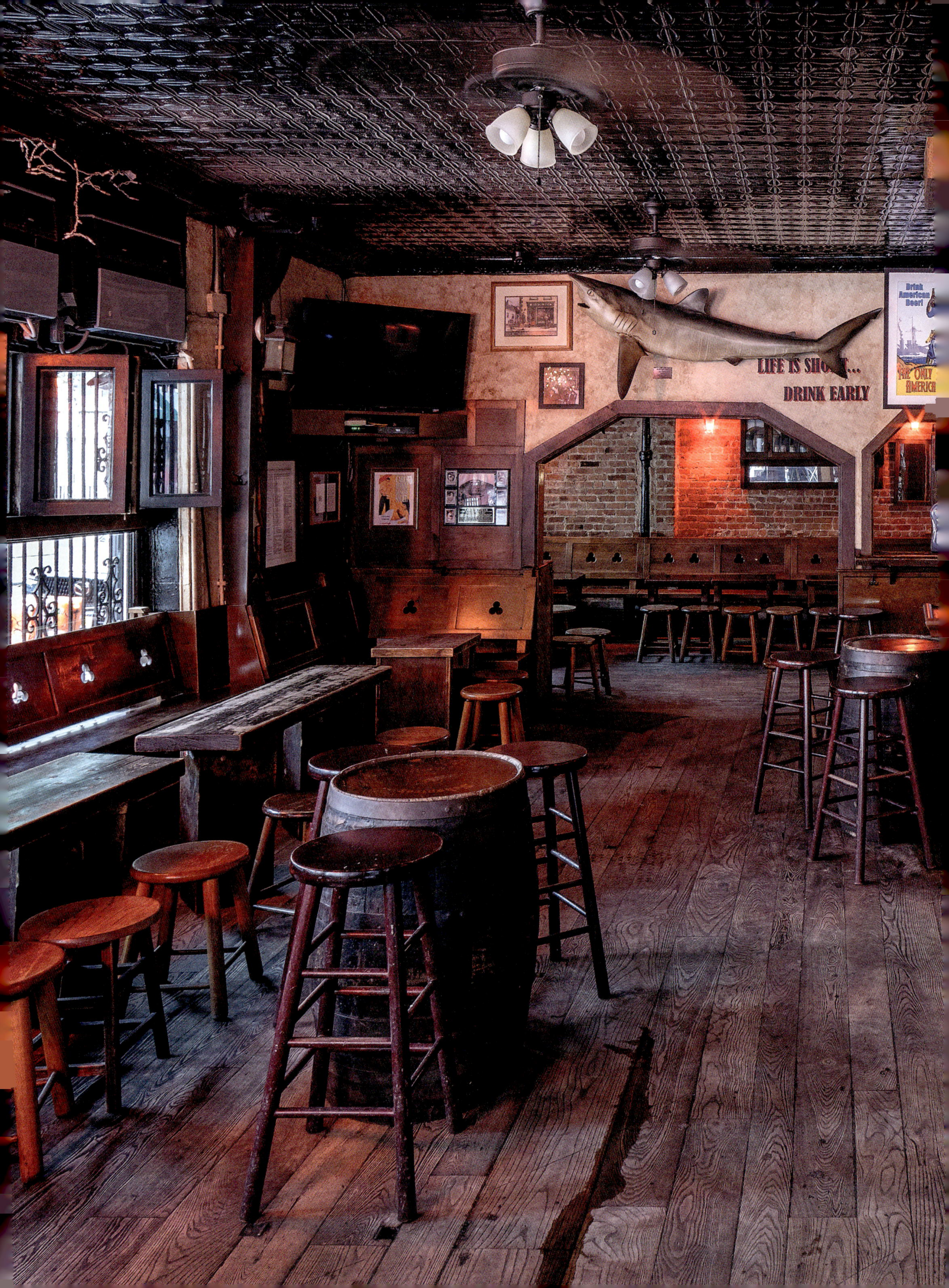

LIFE IS SHORT...
DRINK EARLY
Drink American Beer!
THE ONLY AMERICA

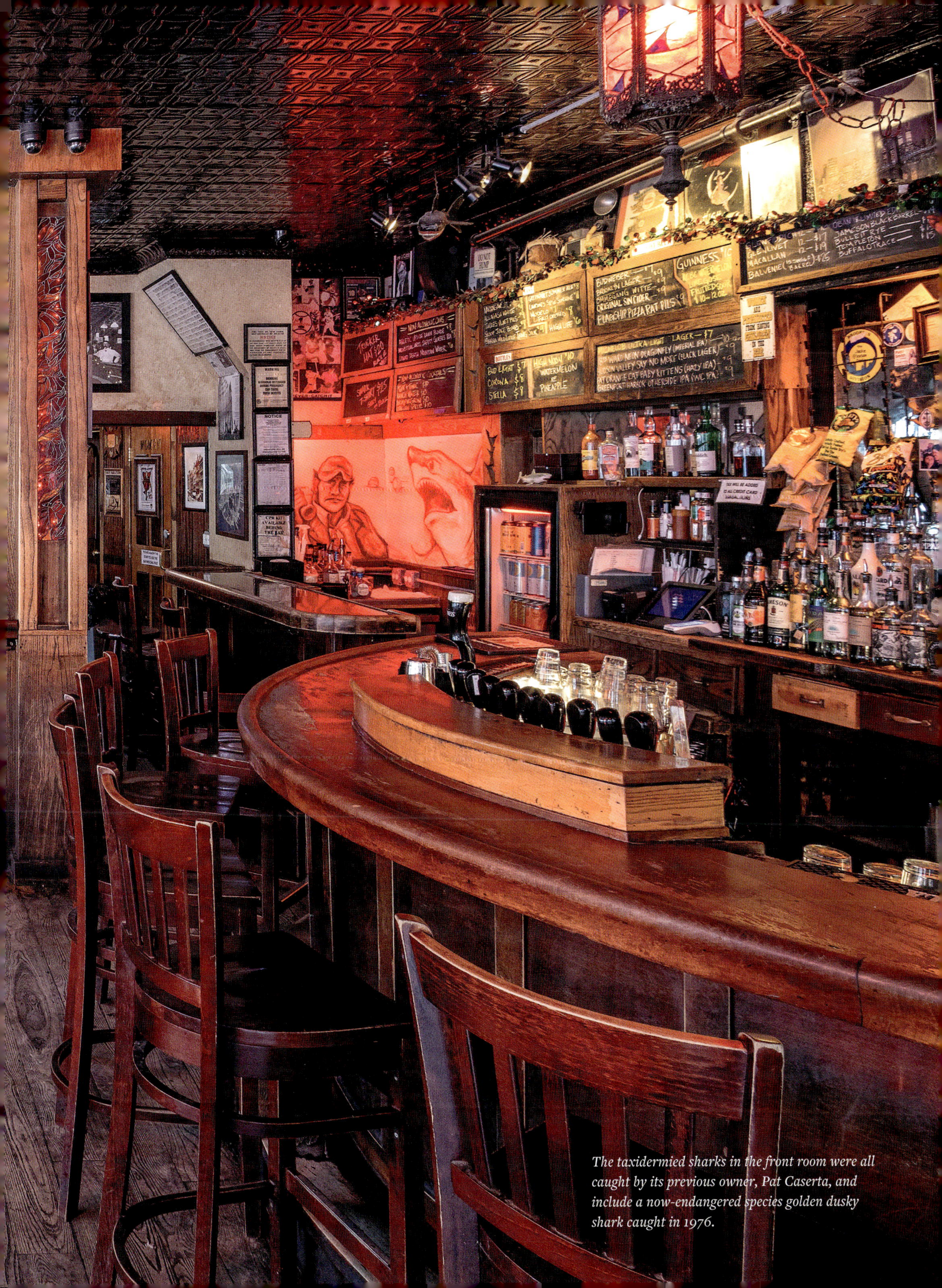

The taxidermied sharks in the front room were all caught by its previous owner, Pat Caserta, and include a now-endangered species golden dusky shark caught in 1976.

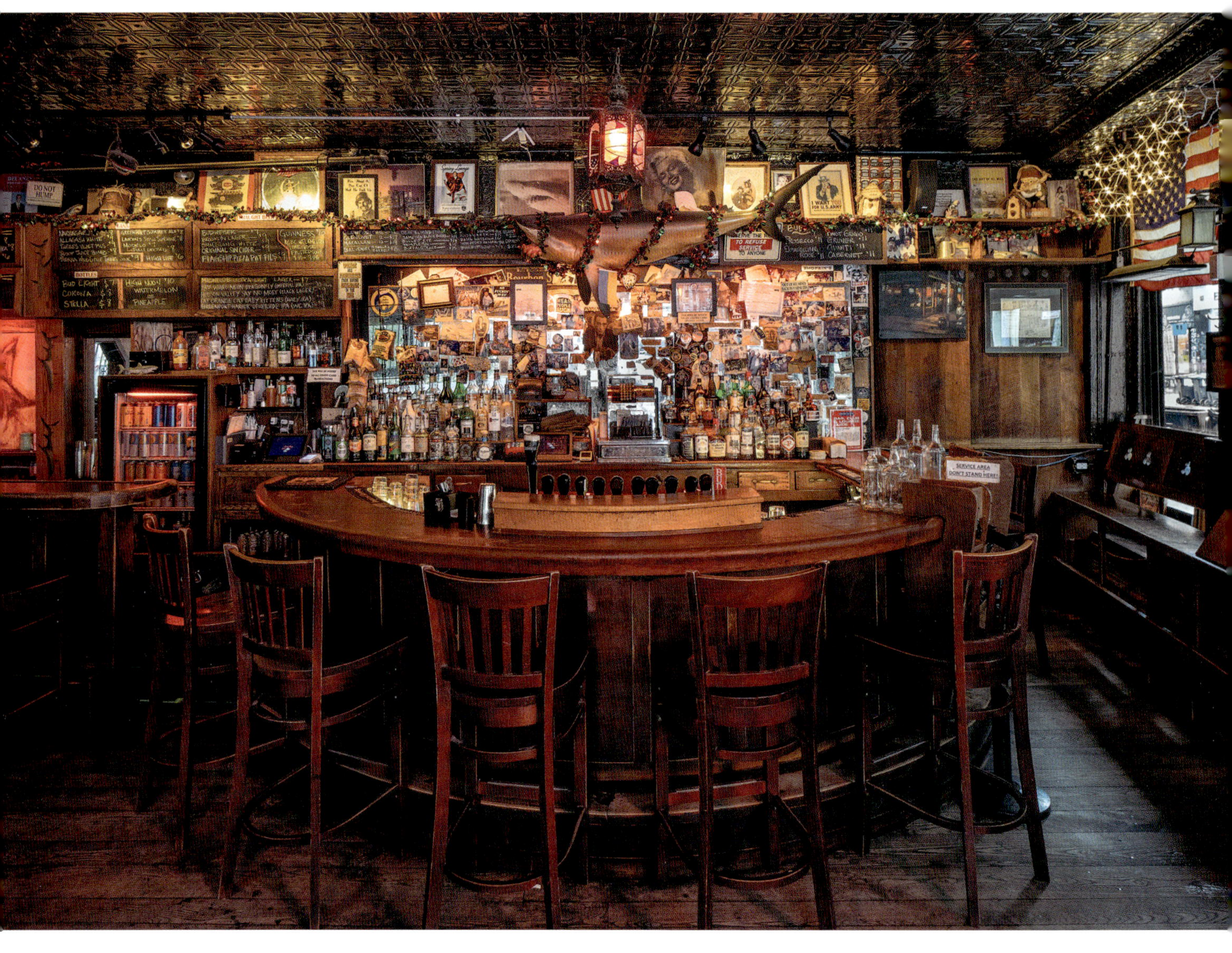

ABOVE *The original horseshoe-shaped bar only seats five people.*

OPPOSITE TOP *The custom seating found throughout the bar, with its unique shamrock cut-outs, was added by owner Bryan Delaney.*

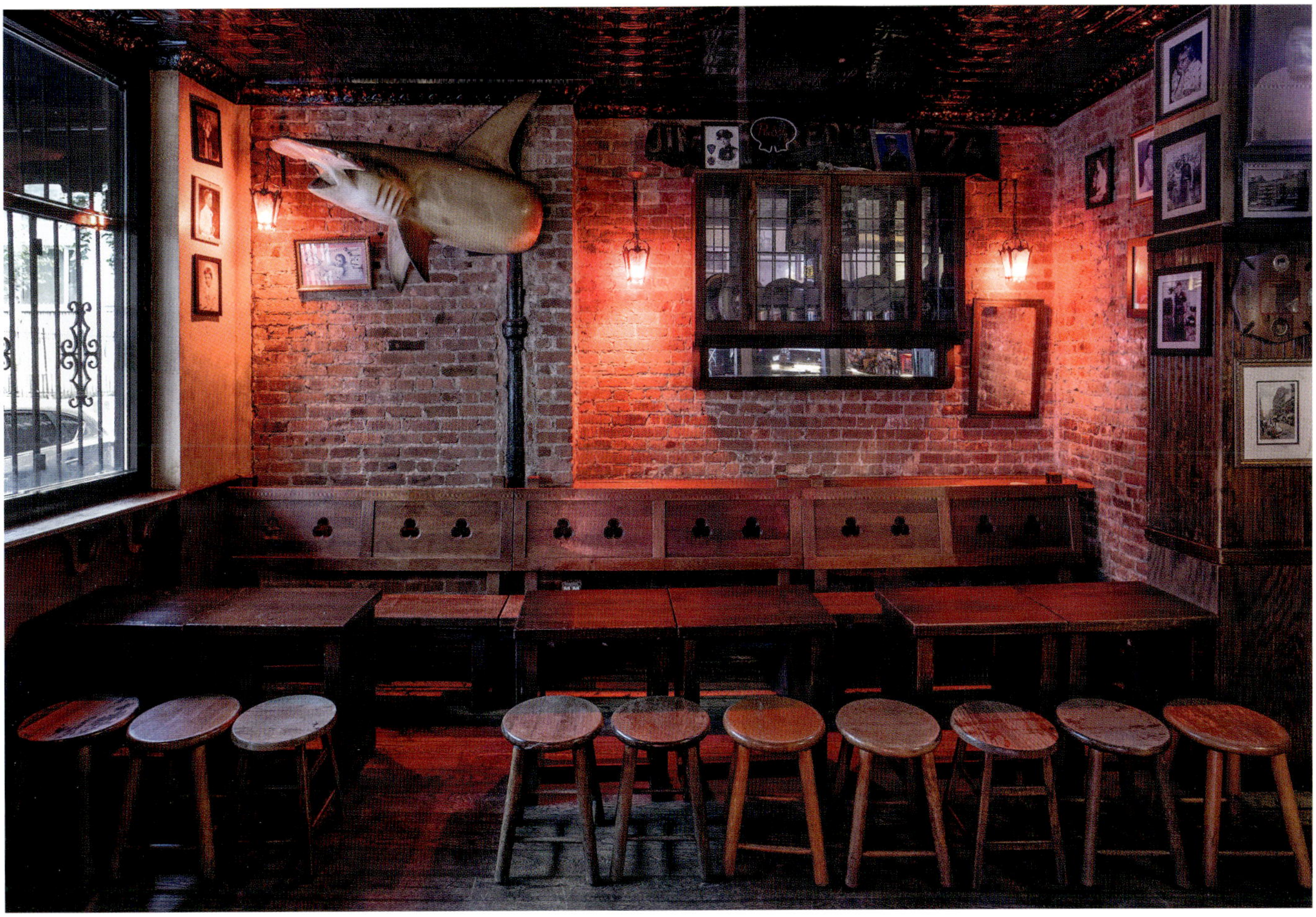

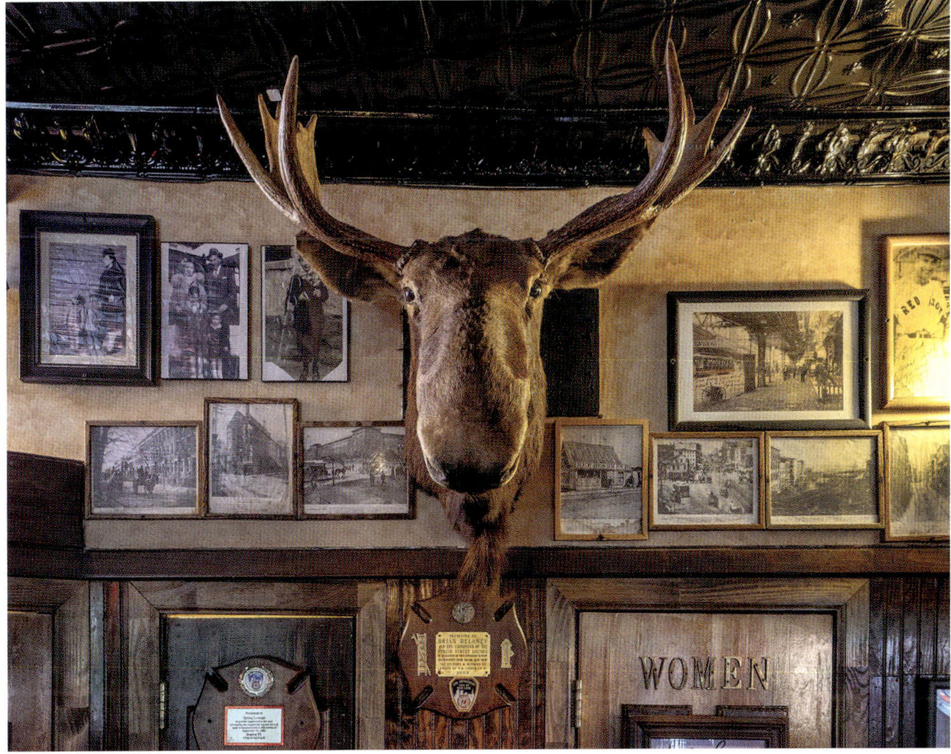

WOMEN

FANELLI CAFE

94 PRINCE STREET, SOHO

Though young people today might know Fanelli Cafe as one of New York's most trendy, see-and-be-seen restaurants, it has a much longer, more illustrious history as the city's second-longest continuously operating drinking establishment (Fraunces Tavern is the first; see p. 24). Indeed, before it attracted models and downtown influencers, the iconic corner cafe played host to the likes of Bob Dylan and the Beat poets.

Naturally, the place has changed hands many times, and lived numerous lives over the years. Constructed in 1847 as a wooden structure, the building was first leased by German immigrant Herman Gerken, who operated it as a grocery. In 1857 he rebuilt it as the five-story brick building it is today. It wasn't turned into a tavern until 1863, when the top floors were rented as apartments.

Through the late nineteenth century, the surrounding area on Prince Street was a rough-and-tumble neighborhood, packed densely with brothels. Indeed, according to the Fanelli Cafe website, even the adjoining back building at 135 Mercer Street—which now contains the bar's kitchen—is suspected to have been used as a brothel.

In 1922 Michael Fanelli bought the place, changing its name from Prince Cafe to Fanelli Cafe (however, regulars just call it Fanelli's). A one-time prizefighter, Fanelli hung up black-and-white photos of boxing greats like Joe Louis and Rocky Marciano, which remain on the walls today. From 1920 to 1933 Fanelli's resisted Prohibition by operating as a speakeasy, slinging whiskey and basement-brewed beer in secret. (Its website also notes that even the 1925 city directory referred to the locale as a saloon.)

By the '50s, as SoHo began to transform, creative types started to replace the existing working-class crowd, foreshadowing the neighborhood's future as a global nexus of the modern and contemporary art world. At this time, Fanelli's was believed to have been a regular haunt of writers from the Beat Generation literary movement.

In the '70s and '80s, galleries and artists moved into the area in earnest, and the neighborhood truly took on its current name: SoHo, for "south of Houston Street." Through the late twentieth century, Fanelli's catered to the likes of singer Bob Dylan and numerous visual artists, including sculptors like Christopher Wilmarth and Lynda Benglis, as well as painters, like Lynn Umlauf and David Diao—many of whom were drawn to the location by the nearby Paula Cooper Gallery.

Following sixty years as custodians of 94 Prince Street, the Fanelli family sold the business in 1982 to Hans Noe, an architect and artist from present-day Ukraine. Speaking to the *New York Times* in 2018, Noe revealed he had only intended to purchase the building but "found out that Fanelli's came with it." Still, he stuck around and ran the place for nearly two decades. During his tenure as a restaurateur, the bar notably employed Bob Bozic, a beloved New York legend and former professional boxer, as a bartender until 2016.

Since the early 2000s, Fanelli's has been helmed by Noe's son, Sasha, an artist who still resides in the neighborhood with his family. Though he's gotten numerous offers on the space, he's still holding out and keeping this slice of old New York alive. And while the area's galleries have long since been replaced by retail stores, Fanelli's largely maintains the same atmosphere it has since its early days, with its long mahogany bar, retro furnishings, and old-timey lighting. Original features of the space include tin ceilings, three-globe chandeliers, and a tile floor. In addition to vintage photos, there are liquor licenses from the late nineteenth century, when the bar was owned by a man named Nicholas Gerdes, framed in the back dining room.

In the early 2020s, Fanelli's saw a resurgence in popularity, due in part to young New Yorkers' interest in a grittier, less manicured side of the city. Nowadays you'll find a mix of Gen Z influencers, fashionable downtowners, and curious tourists packing into the back room. These new audiences have helped popularize the Dirty Shirley, an adult (read: booze-spiked) version of the grenadine-and-maraschino-cherry drink. Videos of the cocktail garnered millions of views on the social media platform TikTok.

After over a century in operation, Fanelli's is now known as a reliable SoHo mainstay not only for its past but also its food. Indeed, it's got the best burger in the neighborhood, along with standout sides like chicken vegetable soup and Moroccan lamb stew—both a must when sitting outside in the winter. Next time you're in the area, pull up one of the tables (which are covered in cute red-and-white tablecloths) to enjoy a bite and a drink with a side of SoHo history.

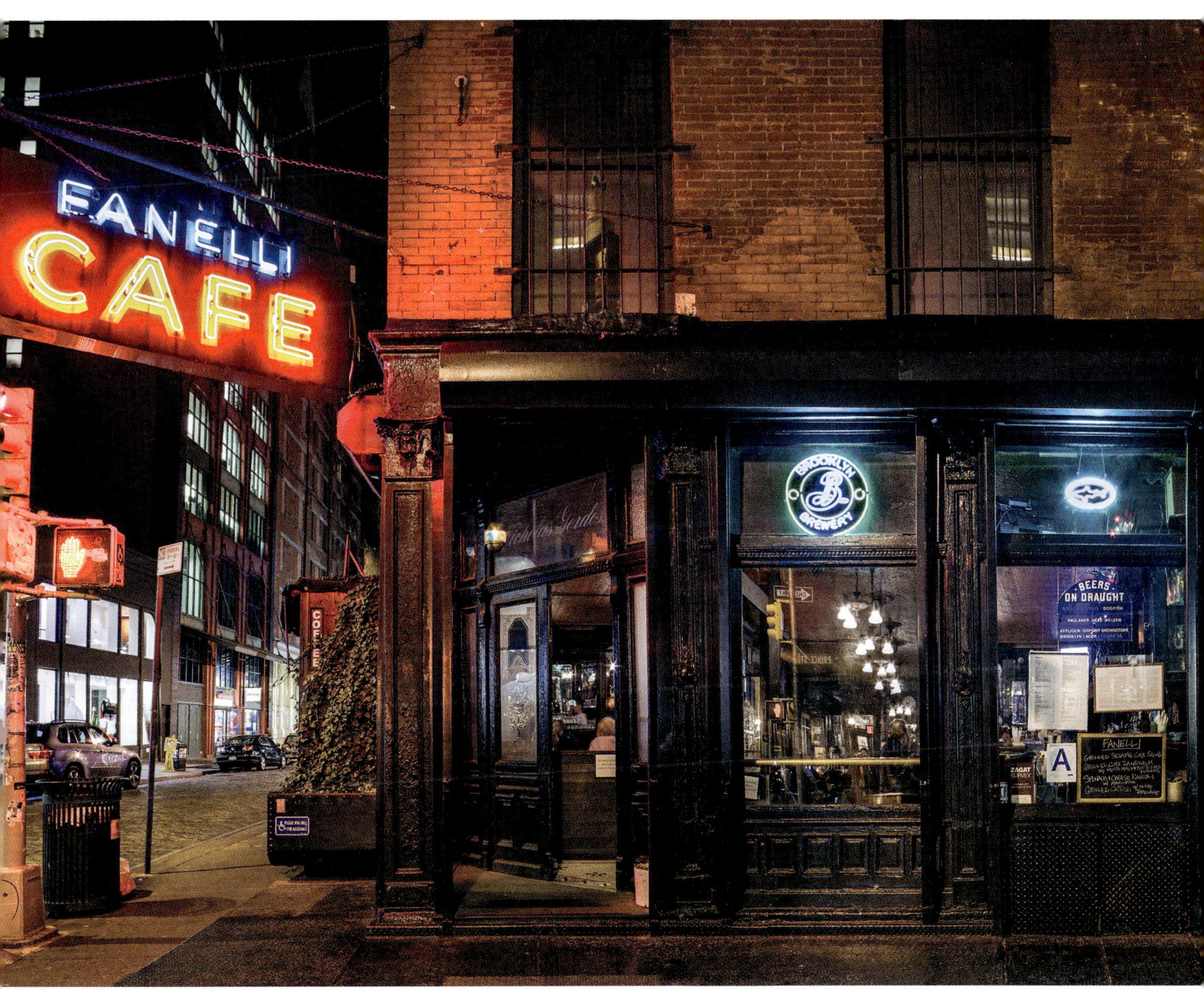

FANELLI CAFE

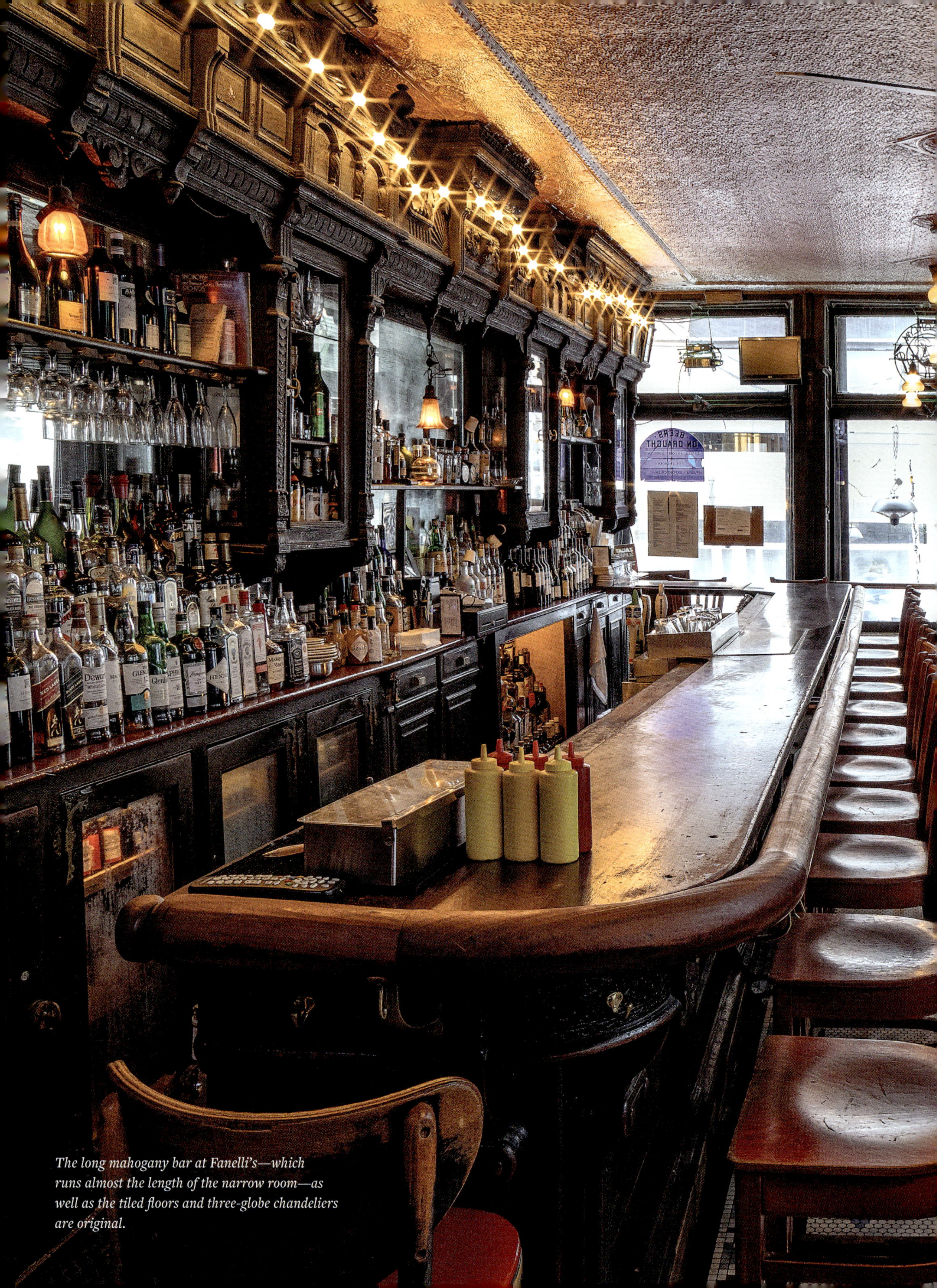

The long mahogany bar at Fanelli's—which runs almost the length of the narrow room—as well as the tiled floors and three-globe chandeliers are original.

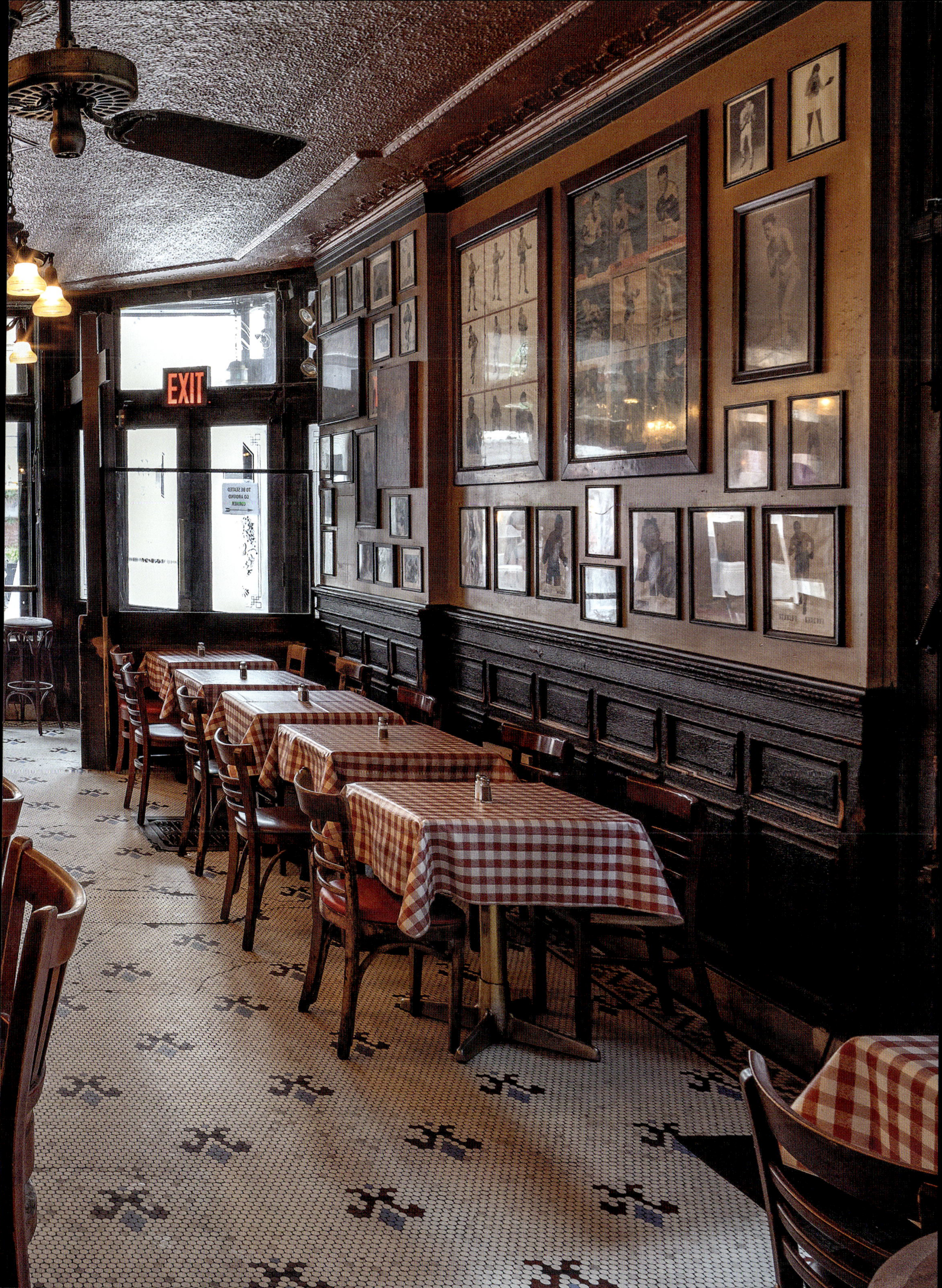
EXIT

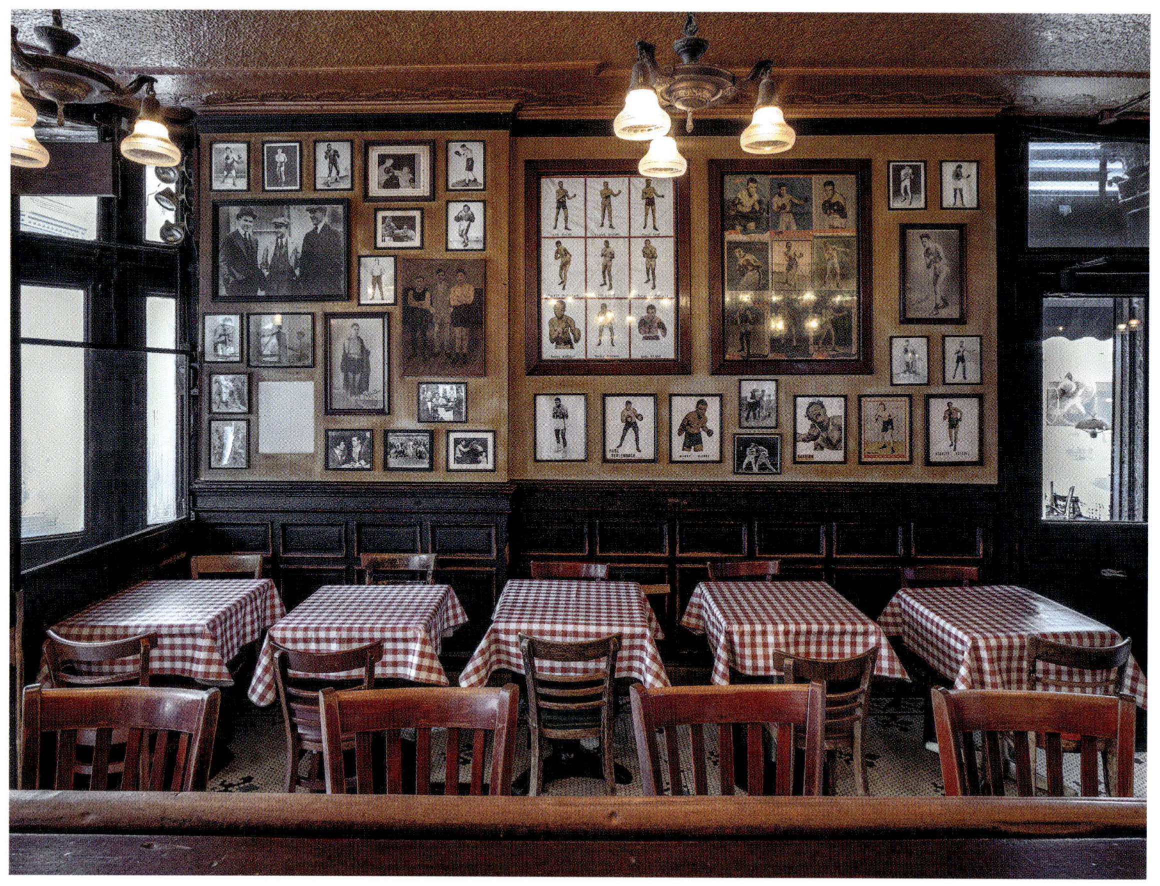

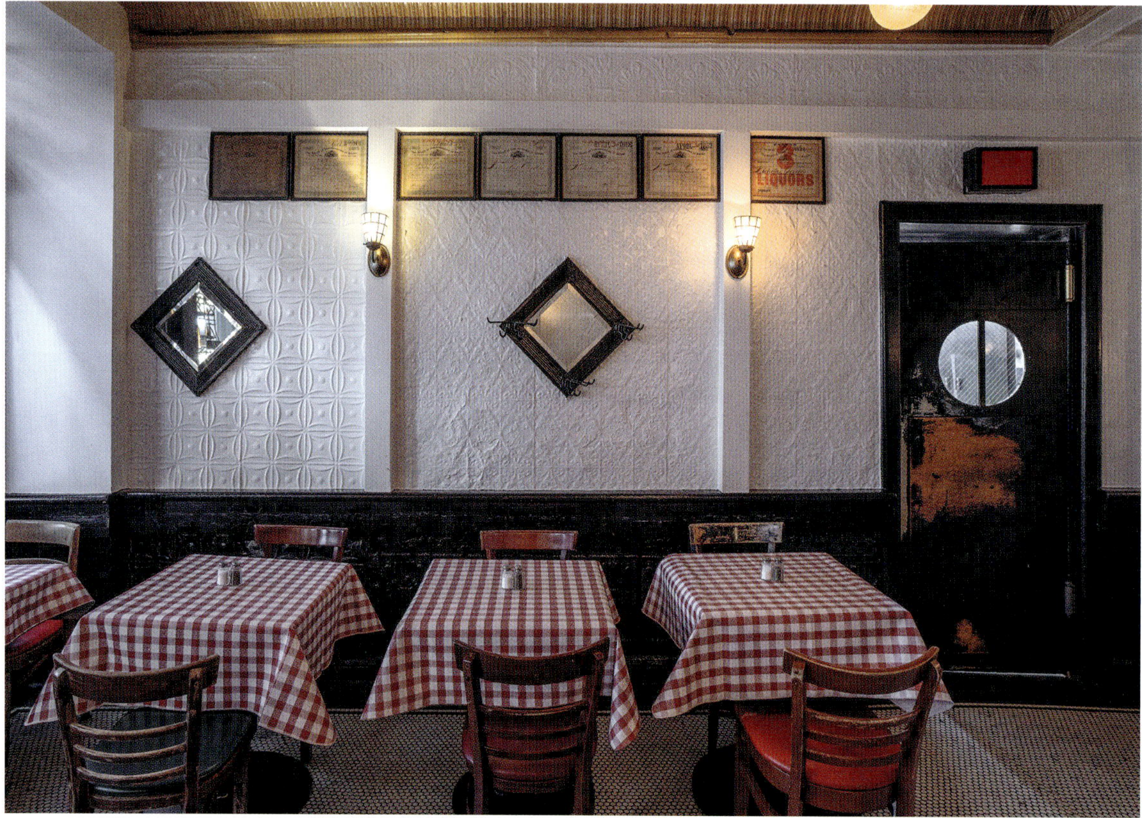

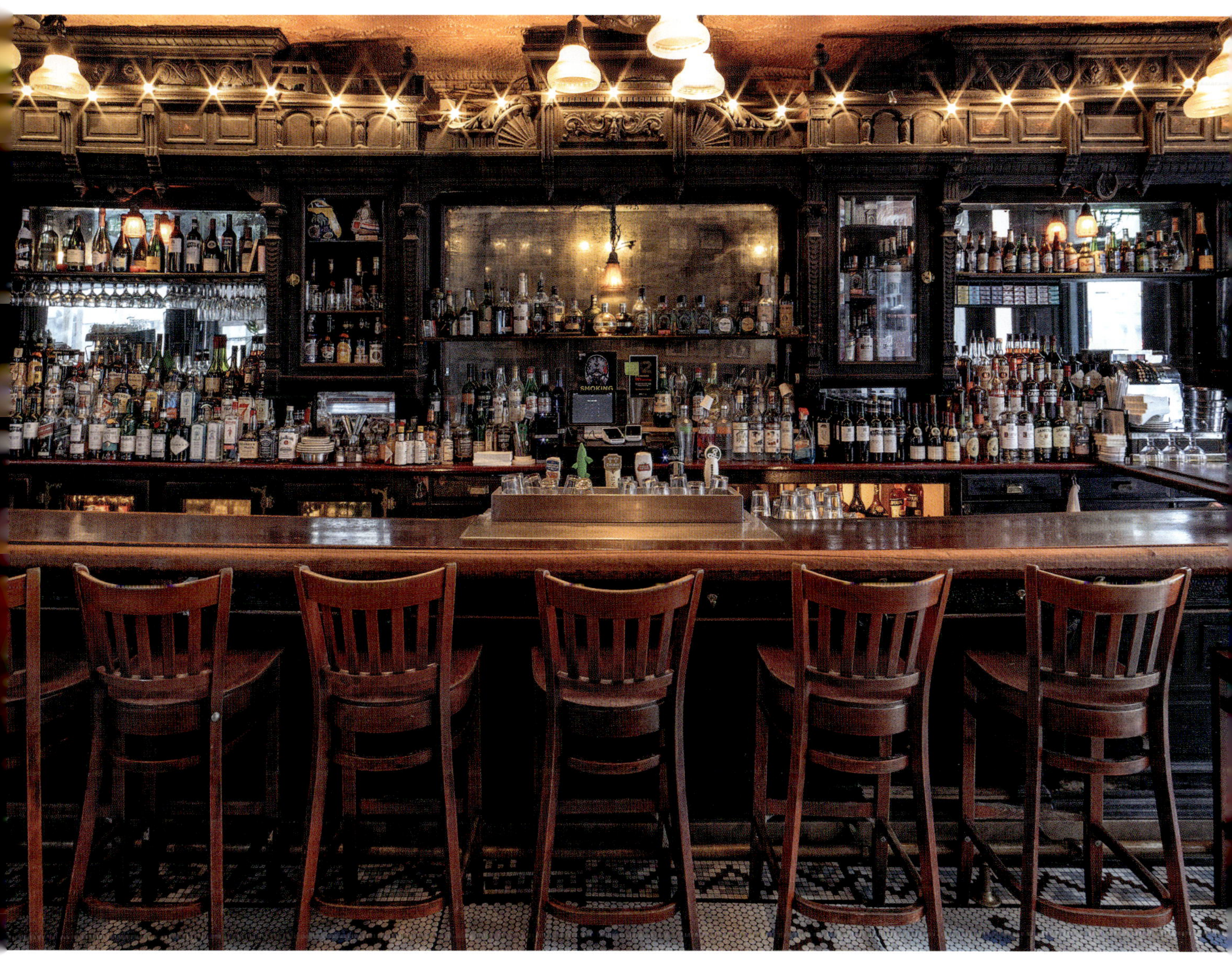

OPPOSITE TOP *Lining the wall opposite the bar are vintage photos of boxers. Michael Fanelli, who purchased the bar in 1922, was a fighter himself.*

OPPOSITE BOTTOM *Framed saloon licenses from the late 1800s, when the bar was owned by Nicholas Gerdes, decorate the back dining room.*

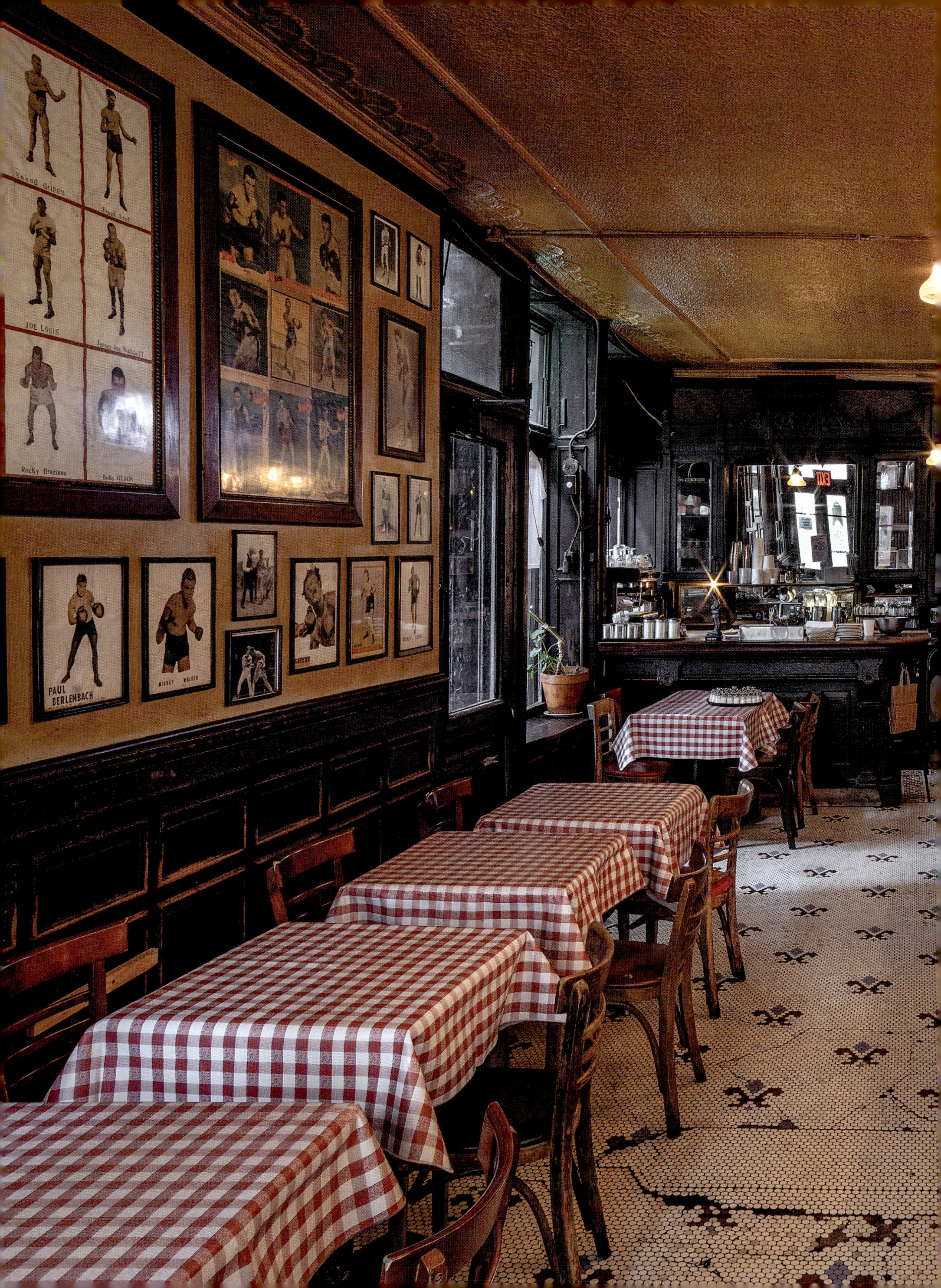

Young Griffo
Frank Erne
Joe Louis
Jersey Joe Walcott
Rocky Graziano
Bobo Olson
Paul Berlenbach
Mickey Walker

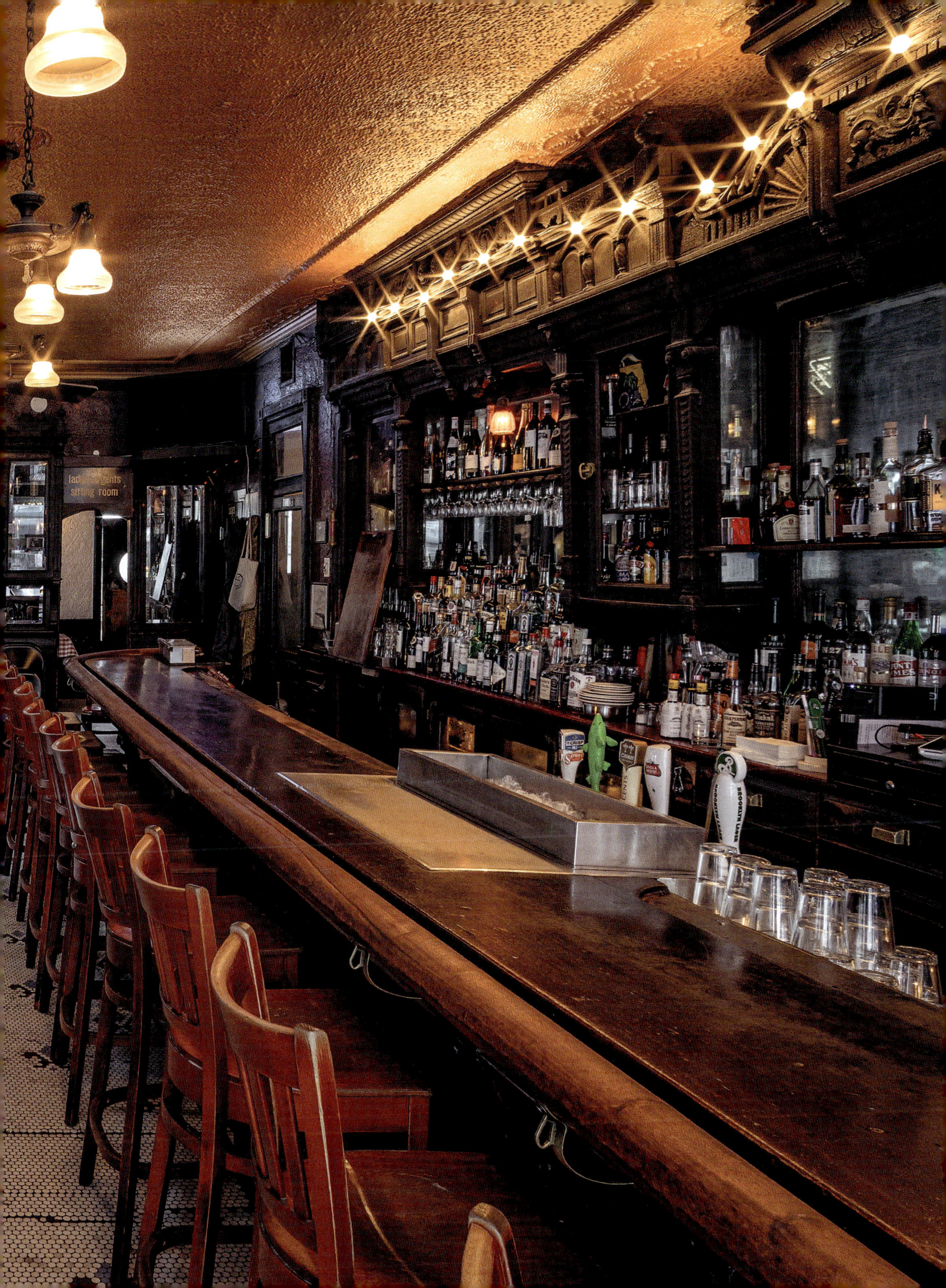

MILANO'S BAR

51 EAST HOUSTON STREET,
NOLITA

Taking up a skinny sliver of space at 51 East Houston Street, Milano's Bar should be commended for holding out on one of New York City's busiest major throughways. Indeed, the bar far predates the relatively recent designation of the trendy NoLIta neighborhood that it sits in today.

Though the original name is unknown, it's believed that a liquor-selling operation first launched at this address as early as 1880. At the time, Nikola Tesla's lab was directly across the street when he was inventing the radio. During the time of World War II, the bar was known as Peter Milano—as seen in a ceiling prices list on the wall, which reveals the costs of common goods like coffee (5 cents), lamb stew (35 cents), and spaghetti and meatballs (35 cents). And by the late twentieth century, the bar was known as Tommy Milano's before simply becoming Milano's.

Throughout its history, Milano's only shuttered briefly in the 1920s when Prohibition criminalized alcohol city-wide. In 1923, it reopened as an Italian cafe and later a bar, becoming an important gathering place for those living and working along the Bowery, which intersected Houston Street a couple blocks over. At the time, the Bowery was known as a rougher part of town, consisting primarily of flophouses, social welfare missions, and drinking establishments. Milano's became a place for men to socialize, learn about work opportunities, and cash checks. Despite the well-documented epidemic of alcoholism at the time, Milano's welcomed all in search of a drink.

Until the '70s, the area was known as the "Skid Row" of New York City. This reputation would change slowly, driven by rapid gentrification of the Lower East Side in the 1990s. By 2007 the New Museum of Contemporary Art had opened on the Bowery, and by 2008 there was a Whole Foods Market a stone's throw away from Milano's.

Nearly 150 years after the first drops of booze were poured here, the bar's original tin ceilings remain, and the space is dotted with tchotchkes and relics from earlier days—like beer advertisements spanning five decades and a drum with a photo of Frank Sinatra attached to it. Sports memorabilia at the bar includes a Louisville Slugger baseball bat, team photos of the 1949 Brooklyn Dodgers and Yankees, as well as a signed photo from radio sports sponsor Billy Taub, which also includes Babe Ruth, Jack Dempsey, and Johnny Dundee.

Meanwhile, on the back wall hangs a unique stone sculpture by the artist Ken Hiratsuka, who included his friend and fellow Rivington School member Geoff "Gizmo" Gilmore's name in the intricate carving.

Revisiting Milano's in 2010, Eater's Robert Simonson noted that one can find copies of Richard Avedon's 1993 *New Yorker* photo study of surviving members of the Kennedy administration all around the bar. Even more modern additions, like always-on Christmas lights, offer a dated sense of place.

In 2016, the *New York Times* profiled the jazz scene emerging at Milano's, led by local musicians who had started with impromptu performances during the day. "The effect is that of a speakeasy, known only to daytime drinkers, restaurant and night-shift workers, and other musicians who drop in to listen," the paper wrote.

Today, Milano's still caters to a loyal customer base, many of whom moved to the area in the '80s and '90s, along with newcomers and tourists curious to revisit one of the neighborhood's most historic dives. Patrons can always count on cold beer and enjoy live music on some days and a jukebox blasting decades-old tunes on others. Amazingly, the bar opens at 8 a.m.—a rarity in New York City. Recently, a morning-shift bartender confirmed that many regulars still come in to drink early in the morning.

OPPOSITE *The storefront housing Milano's Bar is believed to have been selling liquor since 1880.*

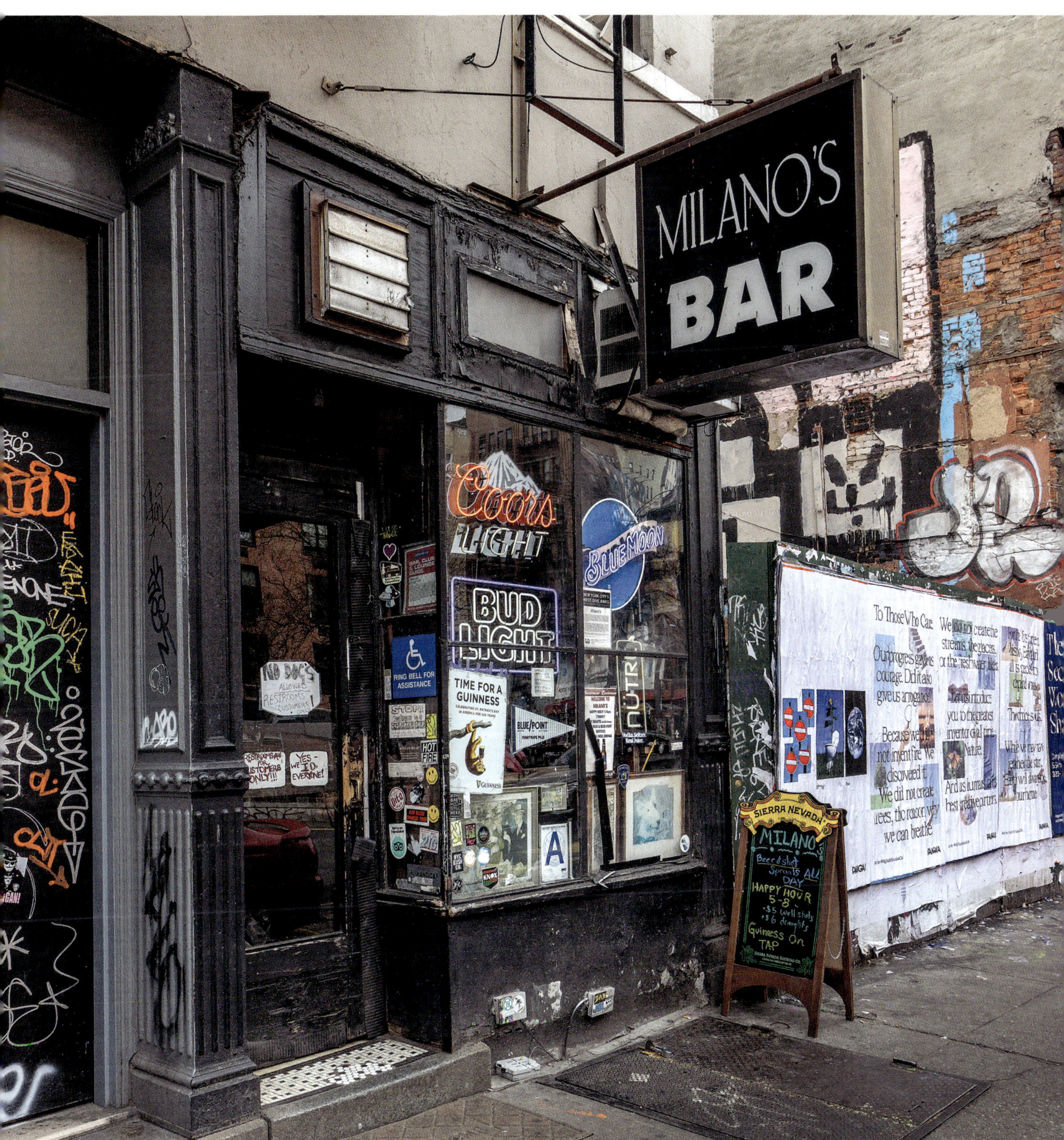

MILANO'S
BAR
Coors LIGHT
BLUE MOON
BUD LIGHT
TIME FOR A GUINNESS
NO DOGS
RING BELL FOR ASSISTANCE
SIERRA NEVADA
MILANO
HAPPY HOUR
5-8
GUINNESS ON TAP

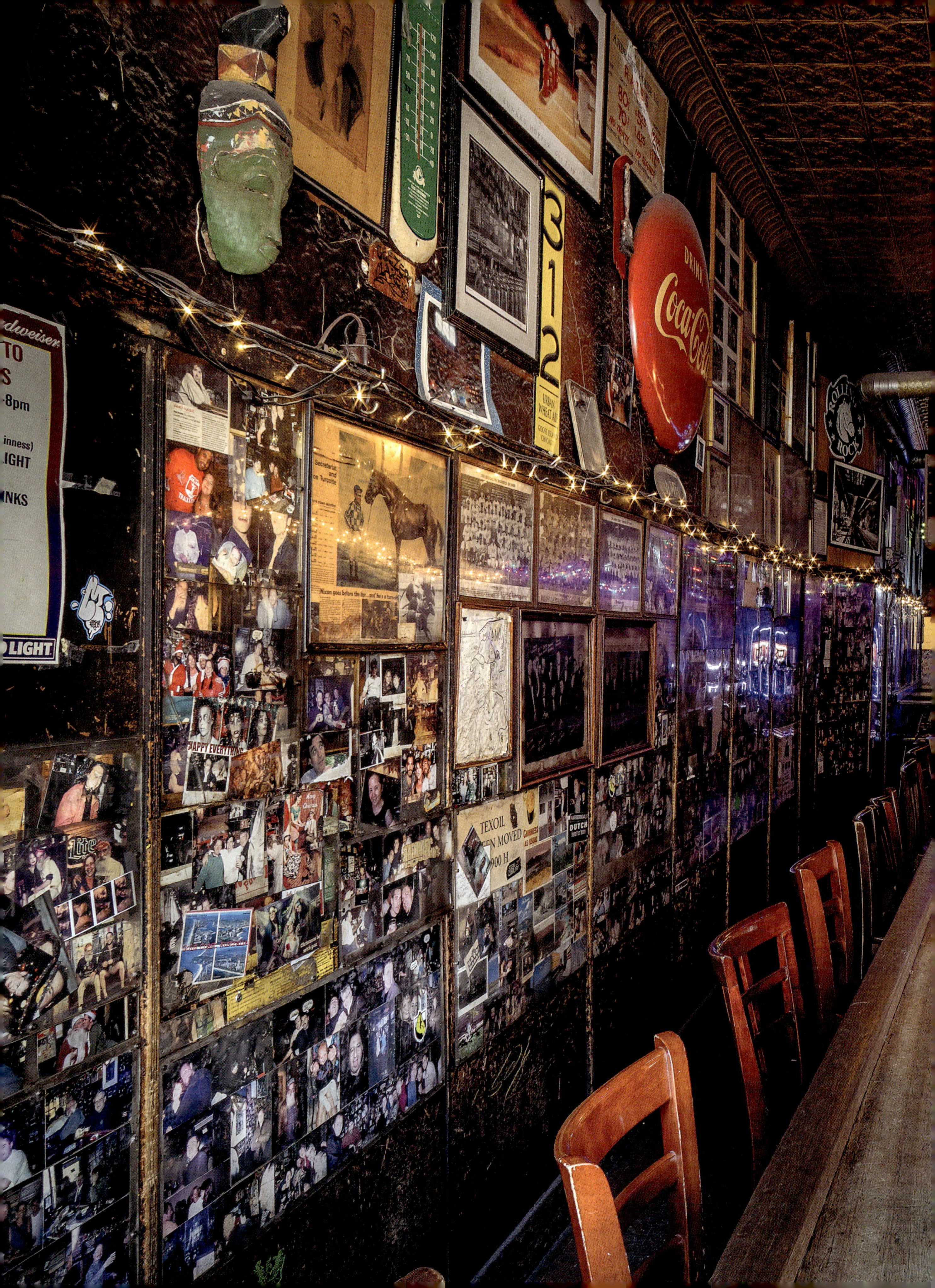

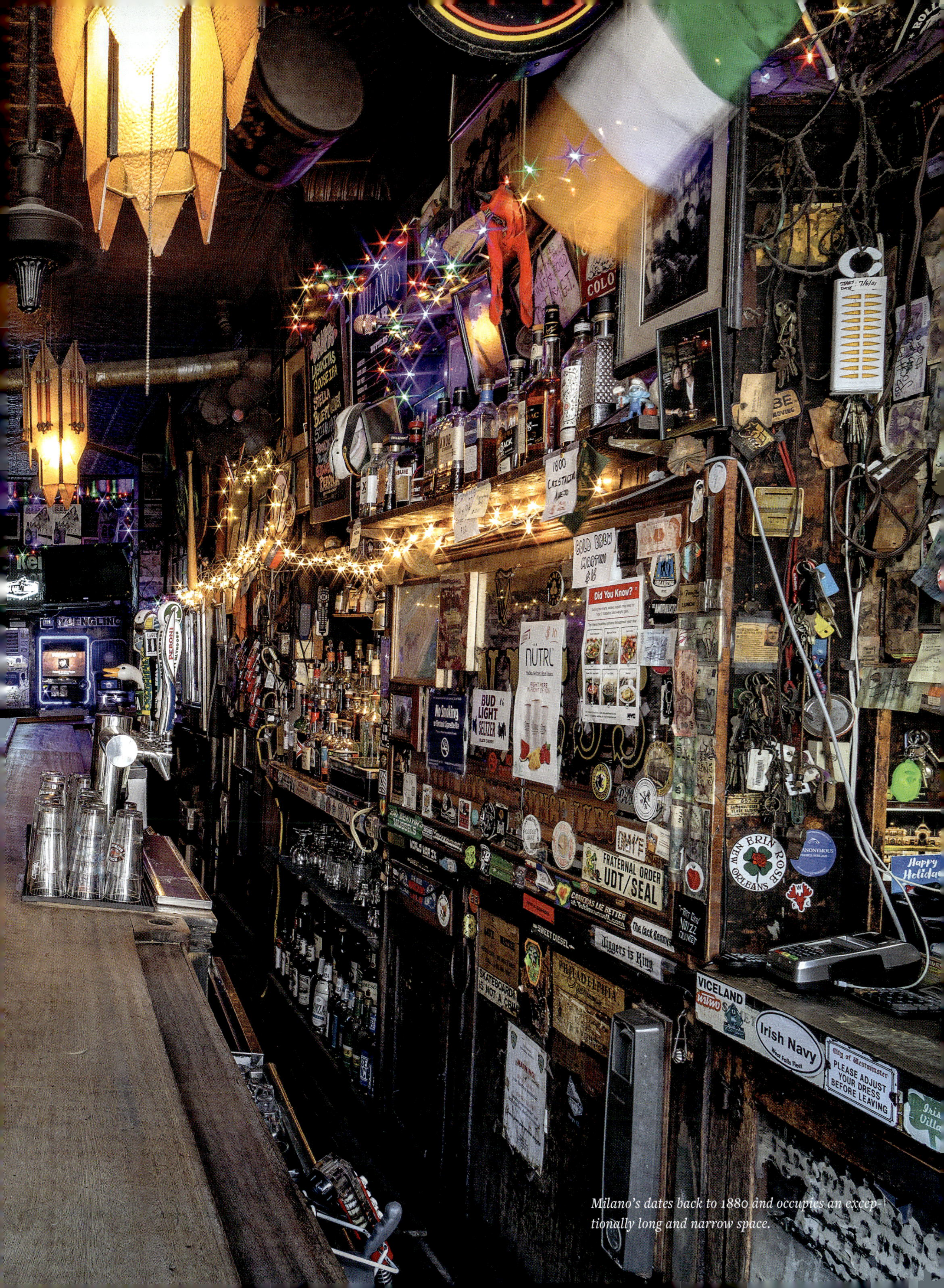

Milano's dates back to 1880 and occupies an exceptionally long and narrow space.

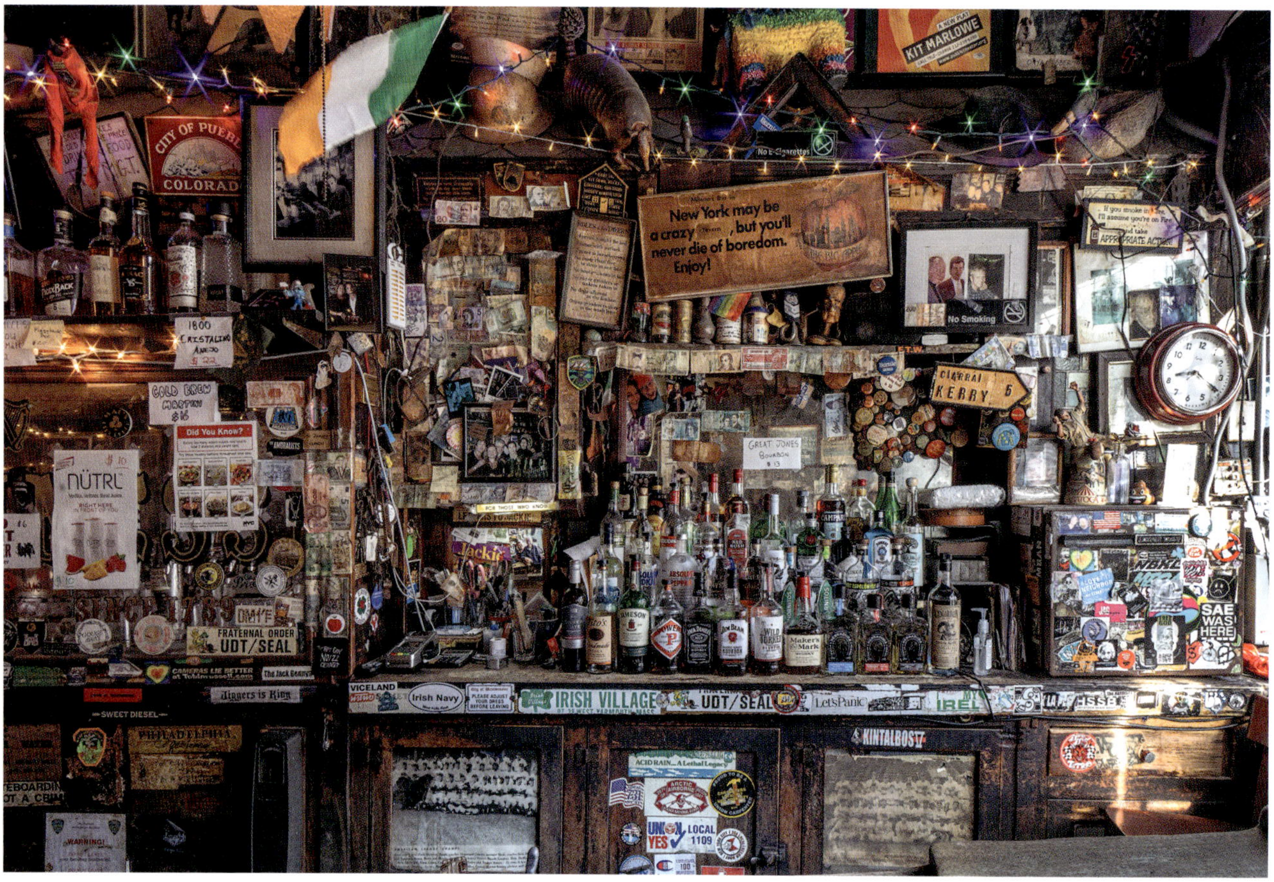

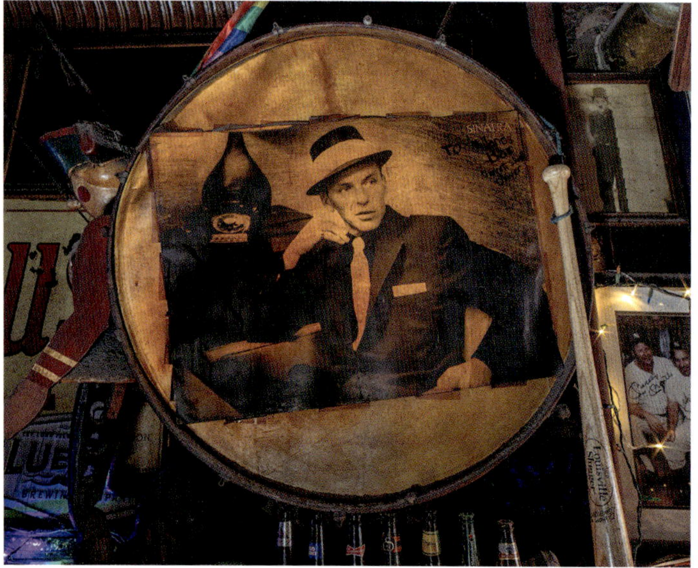

ABOVE The bar's walls are covered with photos of patrons both old and new, as well as beer advertisements and other memorabilia.

LEFT A drum with a photo of Frank Sinatra attached to it hangs above the bar, alongside a Louisville Slugger baseball bat.

OPPOSITE TOP On the back wall hangs a unique stone sculpture by the artist Ken Hiratsuka of the Rivington School.

OPPOSITE BOTTOM Sports memorabilia, including team photos of the 1949 Brooklyn Dodgers and Yankees, hangs on the wall, as well as a signed photo from radio sports sponsor Billy Taub, which also includes Babe Ruth, Jack Dempsey, and Johnny Dundee.

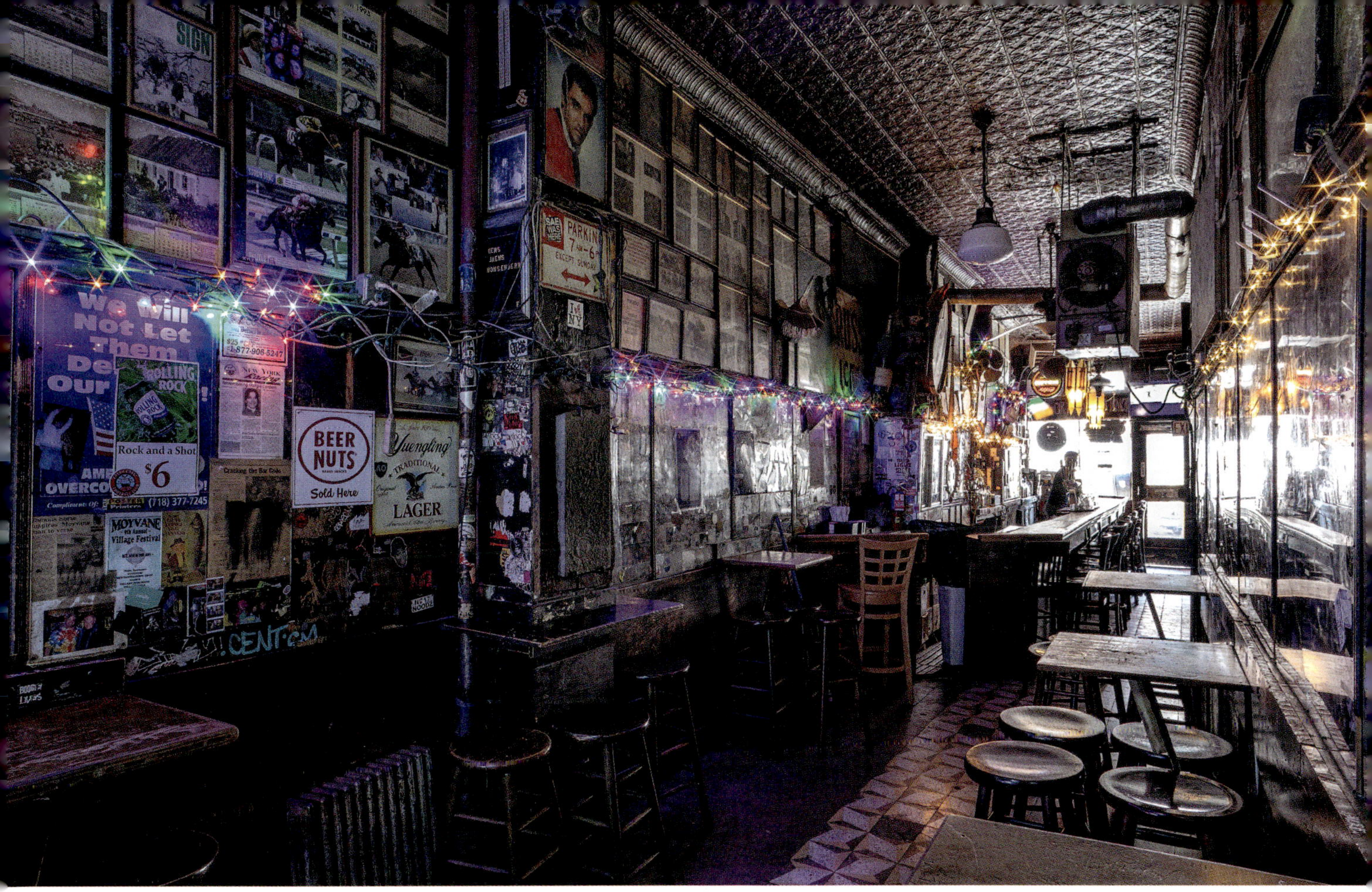
BEER NUTS
Sold Here
Yuengling
Traditional
LAGER
Rock and a Shot
$6

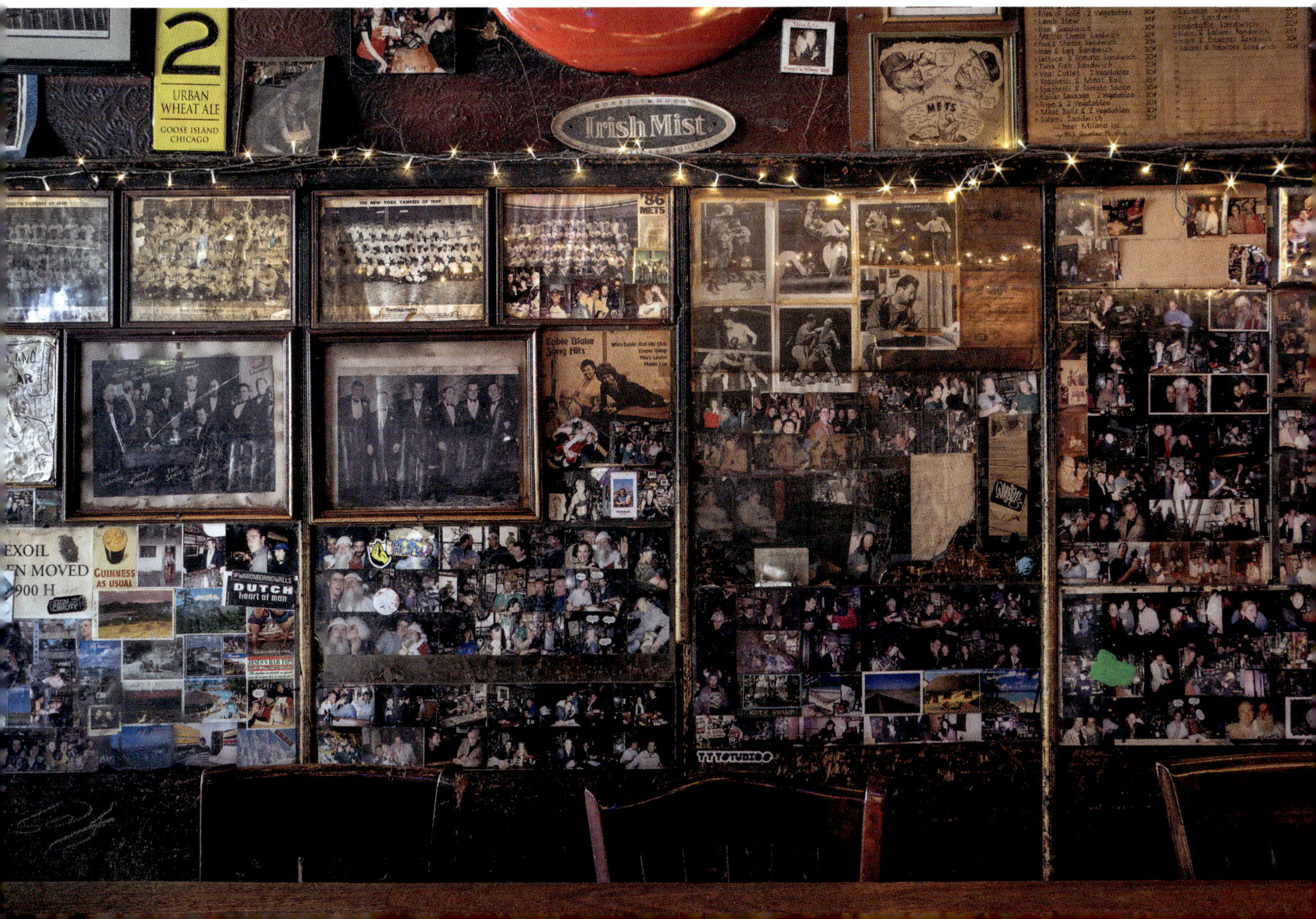
2
URBAN
WHEAT ALE
GOOSE ISLAND
CHICAGO
Irish Mist
METS
GUINNESS
AS USUAL

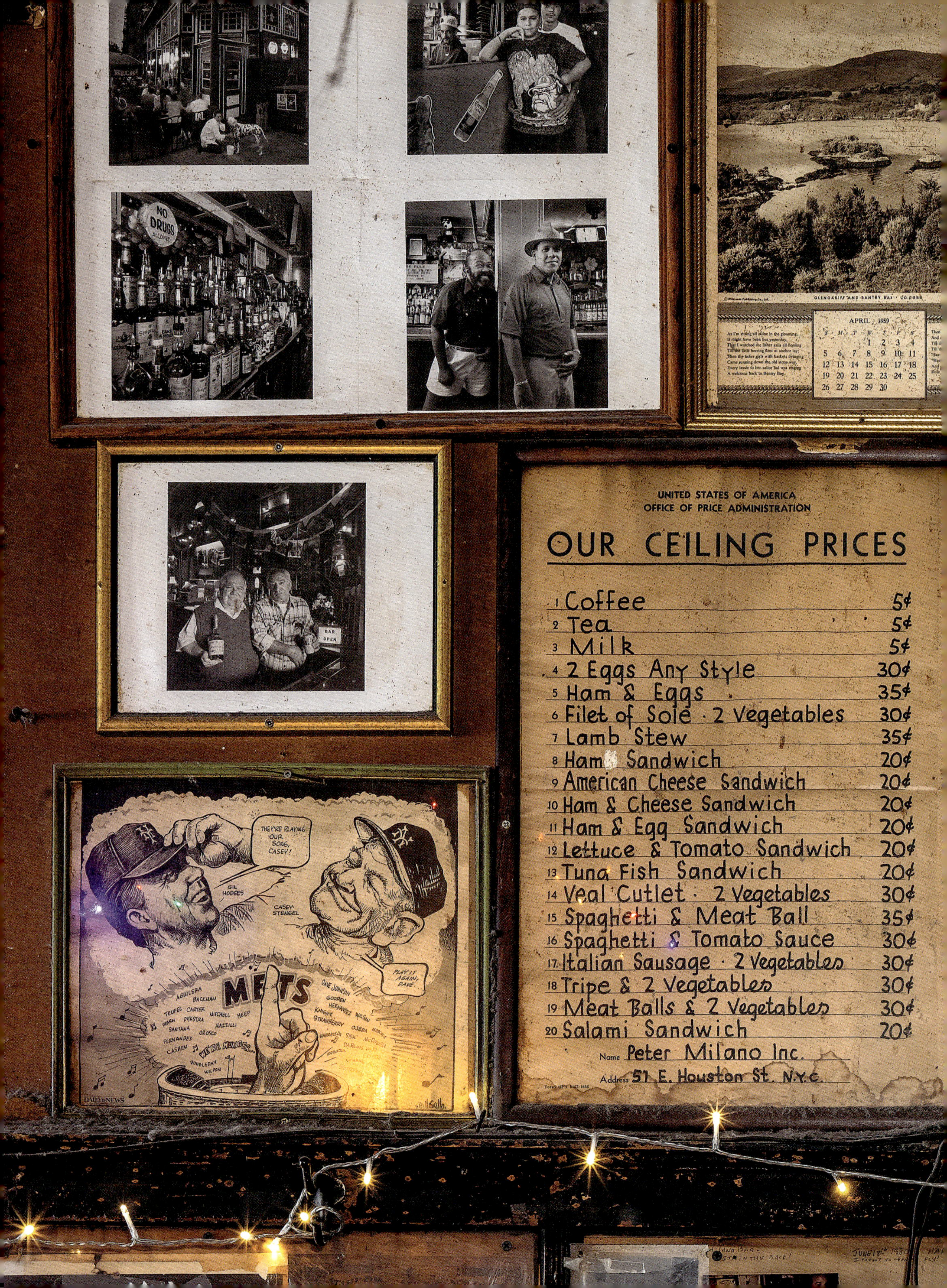
UNITED STATES OF AMERICA
OFFICE OF PRICE ADMINISTRATION
OUR CEILING PRICES
1 Coffee   5¢
2 Tea   5¢
3 Milk   5¢
4 2 Eggs Any Style   30¢
5 Ham & Eggs   35¢
6 Filet of Sole · 2 Vegetables   30¢
7 Lamb Stew   35¢
8 Ham Sandwich   20¢
9 American Cheese Sandwich   20¢
10 Ham & Cheese Sandwich   20¢
11 Ham & Egg Sandwich   20¢
12 Lettuce & Tomato Sandwich   20¢
13 Tuna Fish Sandwich   20¢
14 Veal Cutlet · 2 Vegetables   30¢
15 Spaghetti & Meat Ball   35¢
16 Spaghetti & Tomato Sauce   30¢
17 Italian Sausage · 2 Vegetables   30¢
18 Tripe & 2 Vegetables   30¢
19 Meat Balls & 2 Vegetables   30¢
20 Salami Sandwich   20¢
Name   Peter Milano Inc.
Address 51 E. Houston St. N.Y.C.
APRIL 1989
NO DRUGS ALLOWED
BAR OPEN
THEY'RE PLAYING OUR SONG, CASEY!
GIL HODGES
CASEY STENGEL
PLAY IS AGAIN, BABE
METS
DAILY NEWS

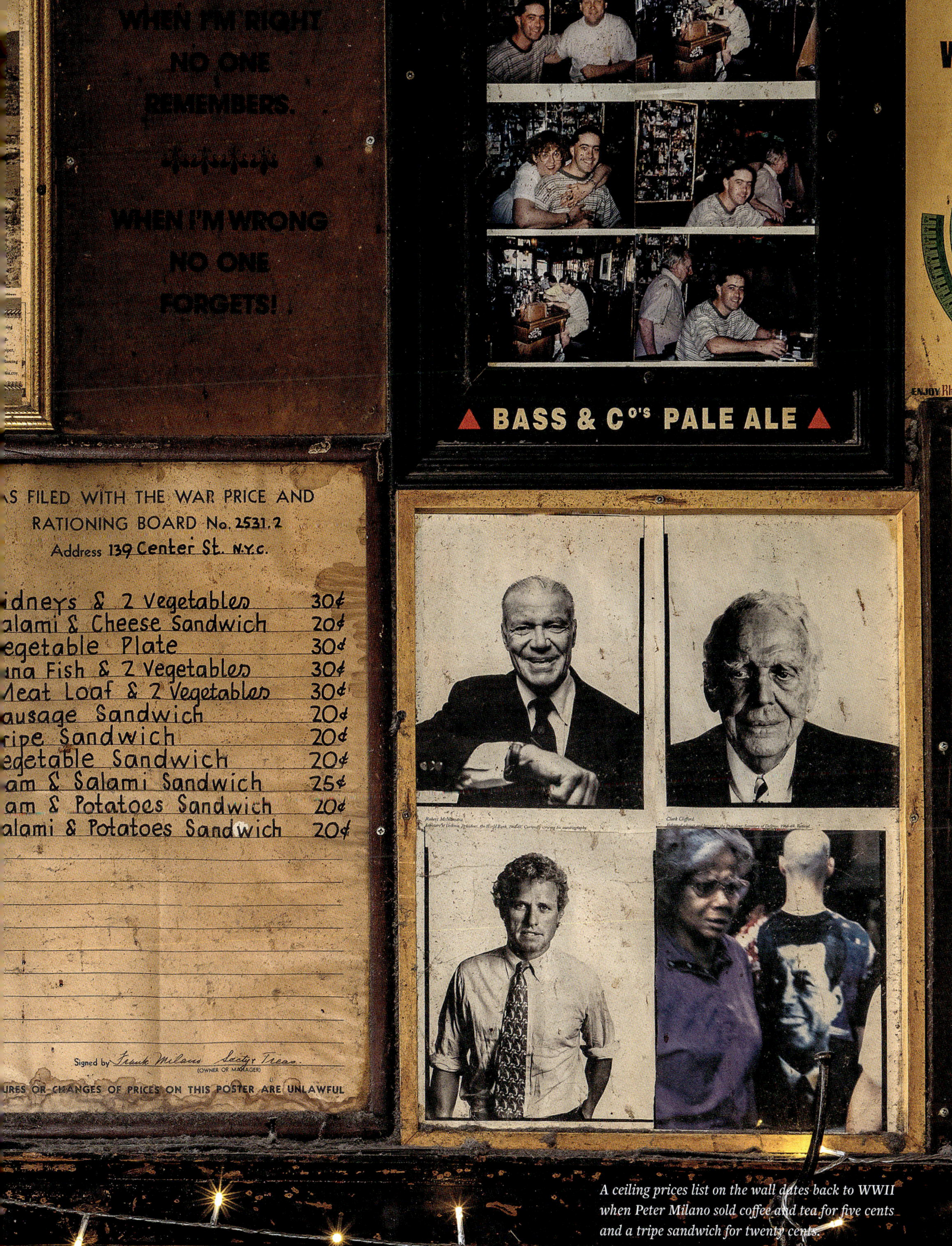

A ceiling prices list on the wall dates back to WWII when Peter Milano sold coffee and tea for five cents and a tripe sandwich for twenty cents.

THE PARIS CAFE

There aren't many bars that can claim both Thomas Edison and Bob Dylan as past guests. And yet, the Paris Cafe in the South Street Seaport district has played host to both—and many more—over the course of its history.

Located at 119 South Street, the landmarked double-brick edifice that houses the Paris Cafe was initially built in 1873 as the Harriet Onderdonk Building. Designed by prominent New York architect John B. Snook for a woman named Harriet Onderdonk, the first floor housed a corner store while the second to fifth floors contained loft space.

In 1883 Onderdonk sold the building to a liquor merchant named Henry L. Meyer, who quickly converted the corner store into a bar, adding to his growing collection: he already owned two others in the area, on Front and Pearl Streets. The ornate German Victorian carved bar he installed still stands today as living witness to the bar's legendary past.

By 1903 Meyer had rearranged the upper stories to fit offices on the second floor, and forty-one hotel rooms on the remaining three. He called it Meyer's Hotel, and in its early days it was for men only. (Fun fact: until it was converted into apartments in the modern era, there were hoistways available to lift inventory up into the lofts). The bar operation would expand into a full-service eatery called Meyer's Restaurant.

It was during this pivotal moment, around the turn of the century, that Meyer would host famous guests from the West, including shooters Annie Oakley and Buffalo Bill Cody, as well as outlaws Butch Cassidy and the Sundance Kid. On the other end of the spectrum, Meyer's Hotel was visited by then-police chief Teddy Roosevelt and inventor Thomas Edison, who used it as a second office.

Up until this period the seaport had catered predominantly to sailors, dockworkers, captains, and even mobsters involved in maritime business. Many would spend time resting and drinking in the area before heading off on long trips to Europe or South America. The Fulton Fish Market, the most important wholesale seafood operation on the East Coast, was located just across the street from the bar (nowadays it's up in the Bronx). But by the 1930s, when the seaport began to see a decline in passenger ships—which preferred the more spacious Chelsea Piers—the Mafia took over, and the hotel experienced a brief period of disrepair. Joseph "Sockz" Lanza, a Genovese crime family member and professional racketeer who controlled the fish market, headquartered some of his operation in the hotel. (Lanza was apparently so effective in this role that the US Navy approached him to help them use fishing boats to spy on German submarines).

According to the website Forgotten NY, the estate of Henrietta Meyer sold the building in 1951 to South Front Realty Corp. owner Silvio "Steve" Schiaffino, who renovated both the hotel and the bar-restaurant. It was Schiaffino who named it the Paris Bar and Restaurant, after another restaurant he owned that had been taken by the City of New York under eminent domain.

In later years the bar would see the likes of actress Lauren Bacall and Bob Dylan among its many patrons. The Schiaffino family came to oversee the final days of the hotel as a residence, when it was home to many retired seamen. In 1980, the family sold the building, and it was converted into twenty-eight apartments.

During Hurricane Sandy in 2012, the bar shuttered after being flooded by more than 11 feet (3 meters) of salt water, leaving its interior completely destroyed. Thankfully, the centerpiece Victorian bar, with its polished wood and intricately adorned arched mirrors, was lovingly restored when it reopened in 2013. The bar would close again in 2020 due to Covid-19. The mural hanging over the dining area, meanwhile, was uncovered behind a wall and brought back to life when it reopened in late 2021.

In 2023 the Paris Cafe reopened yet again under the ownership of Chris Reda and Eytan Sugarman (who also owns the White Horse Tavern; see p. 178). In keeping with changing times, they serve modern brasserie fare like onion soup, burgers, and chicken paillard until 10 p.m., after which the space becomes a lounge until the wee hours.

OPPOSITE *The landmarked brick building the Paris Cafe is housed in is located in the historic South Street Seaport district and was originally frequented by longshoremen, captains, and mobsters.*

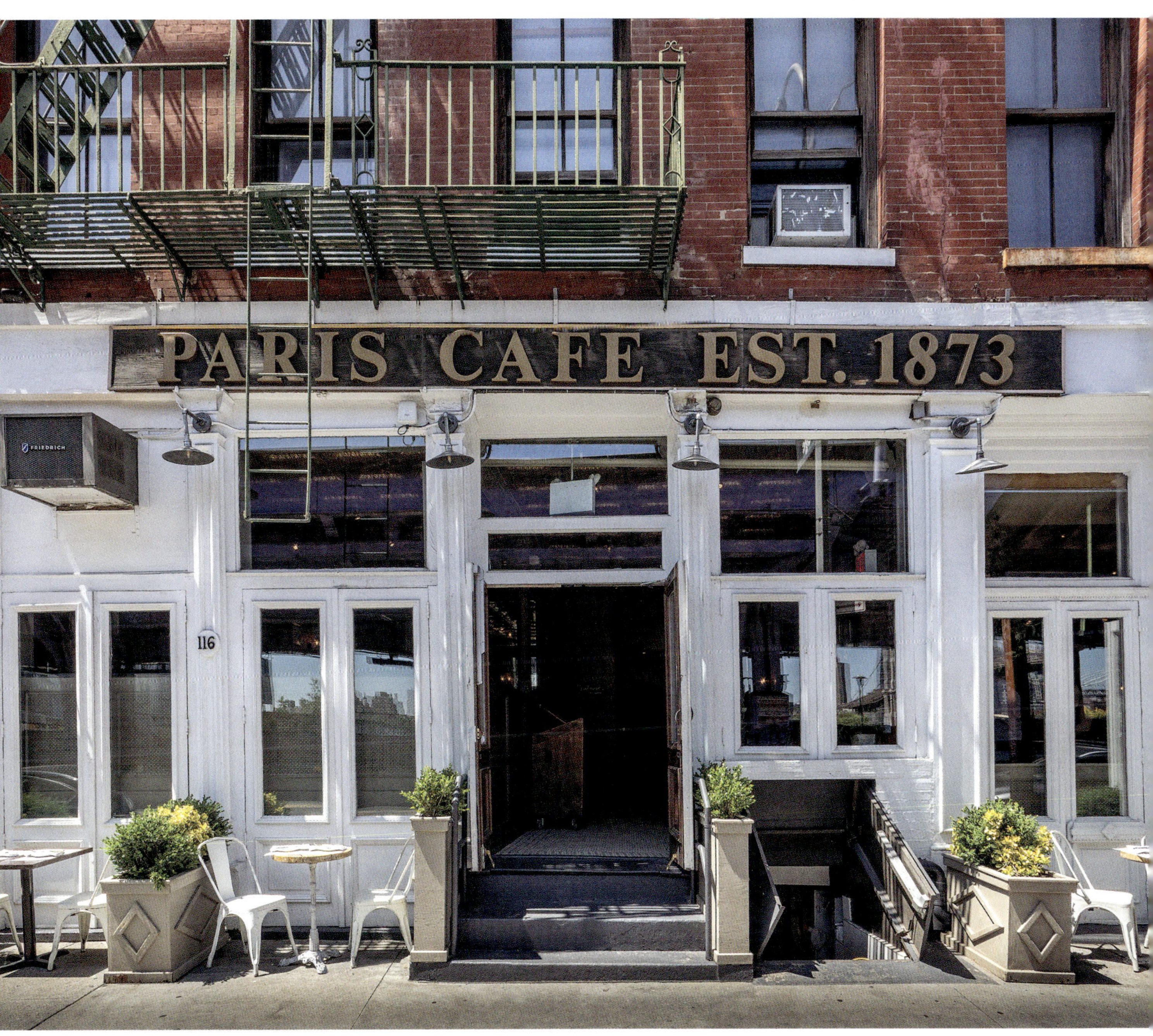

THE PARIS CAFE

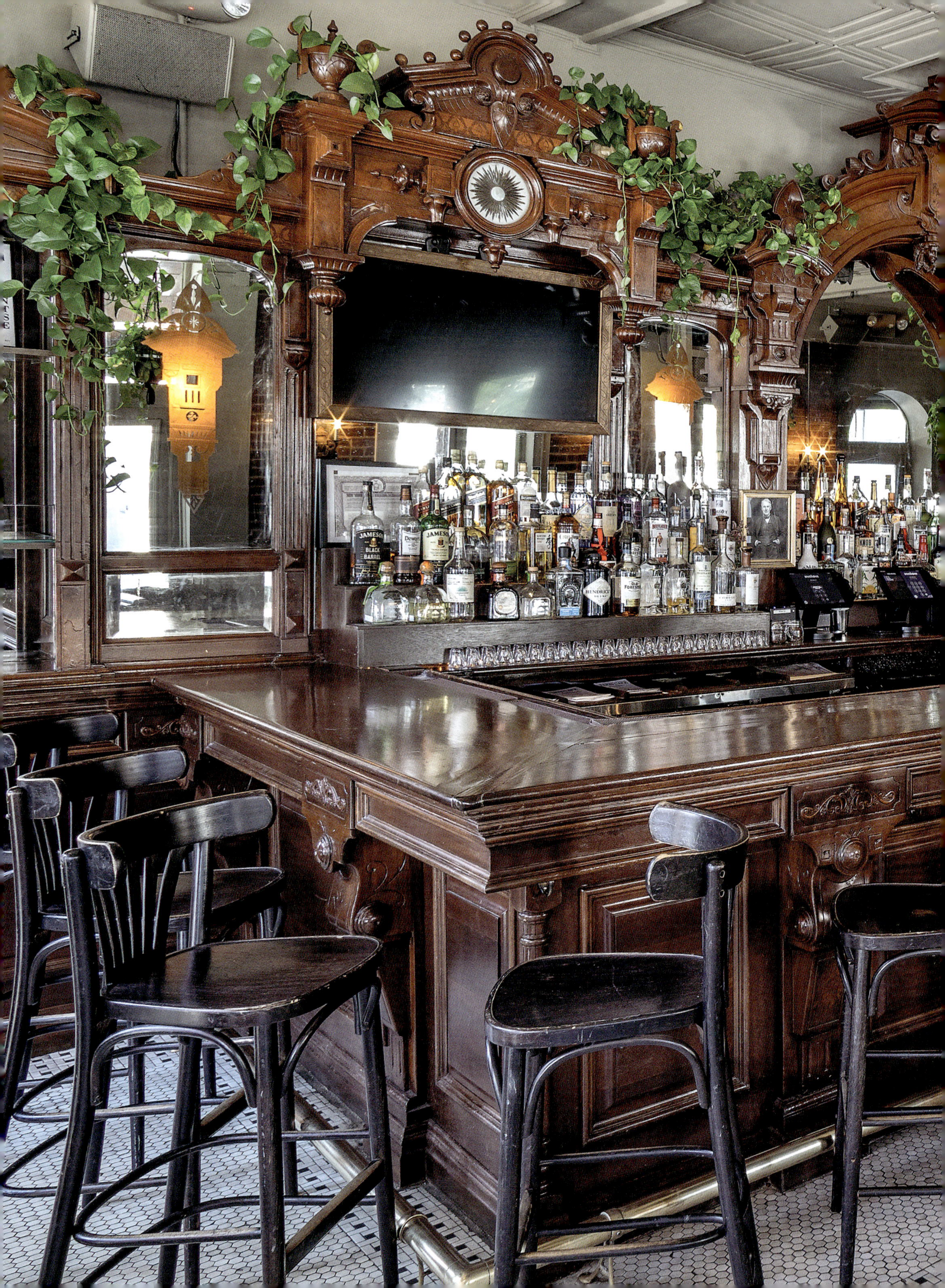

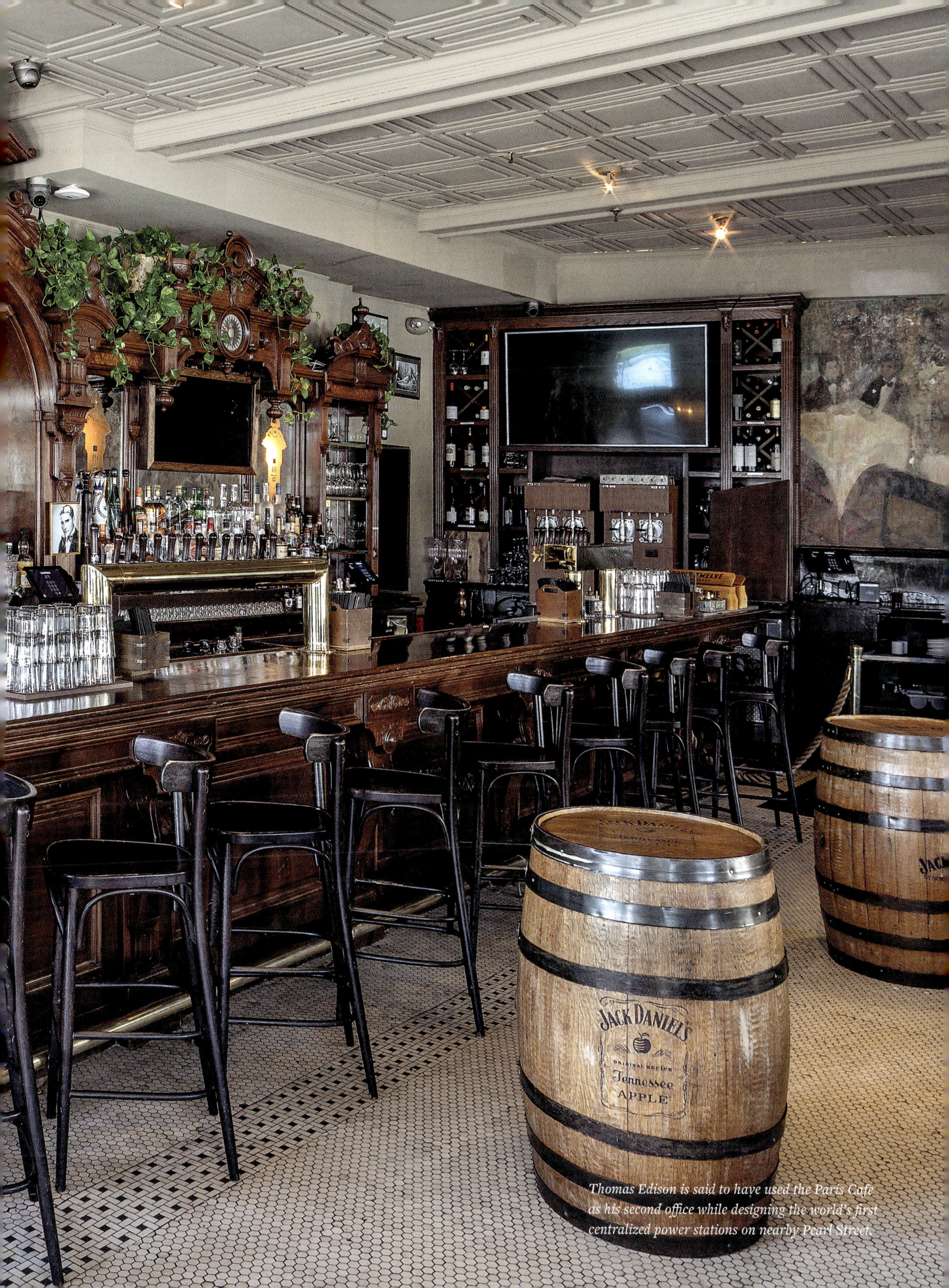

*Thomas Edison is said to have used the Paris Cafe
as his second office while designing the world's first
centralized power stations on nearby Pearl Street.*

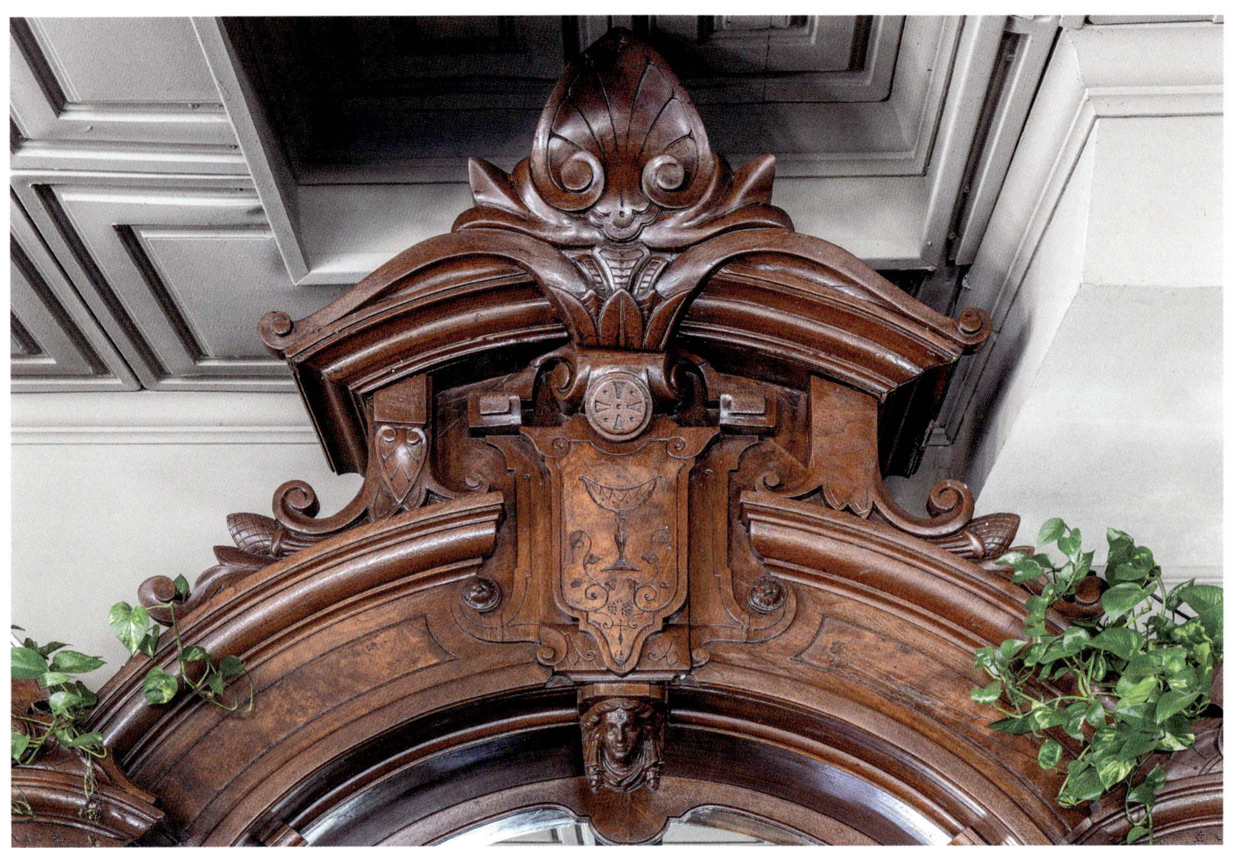

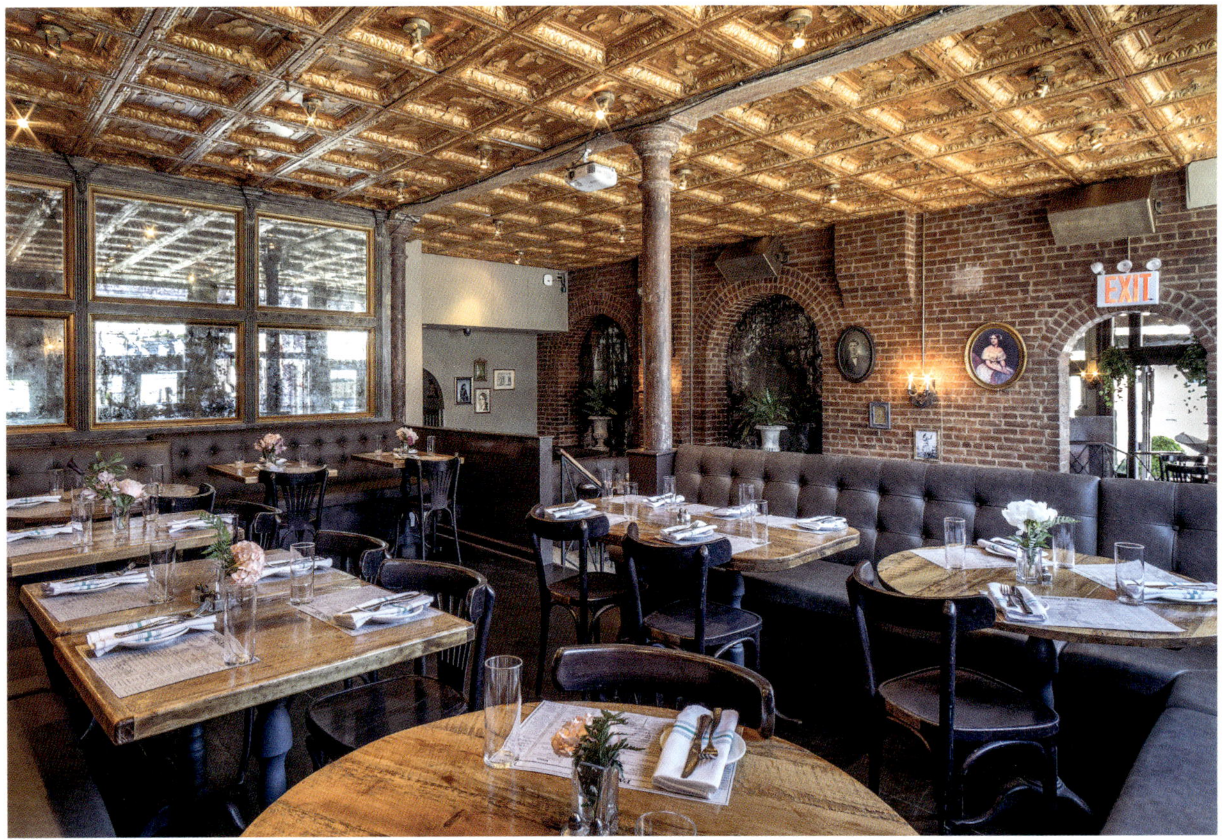

GREAT BARS OF NEW YORK CITY

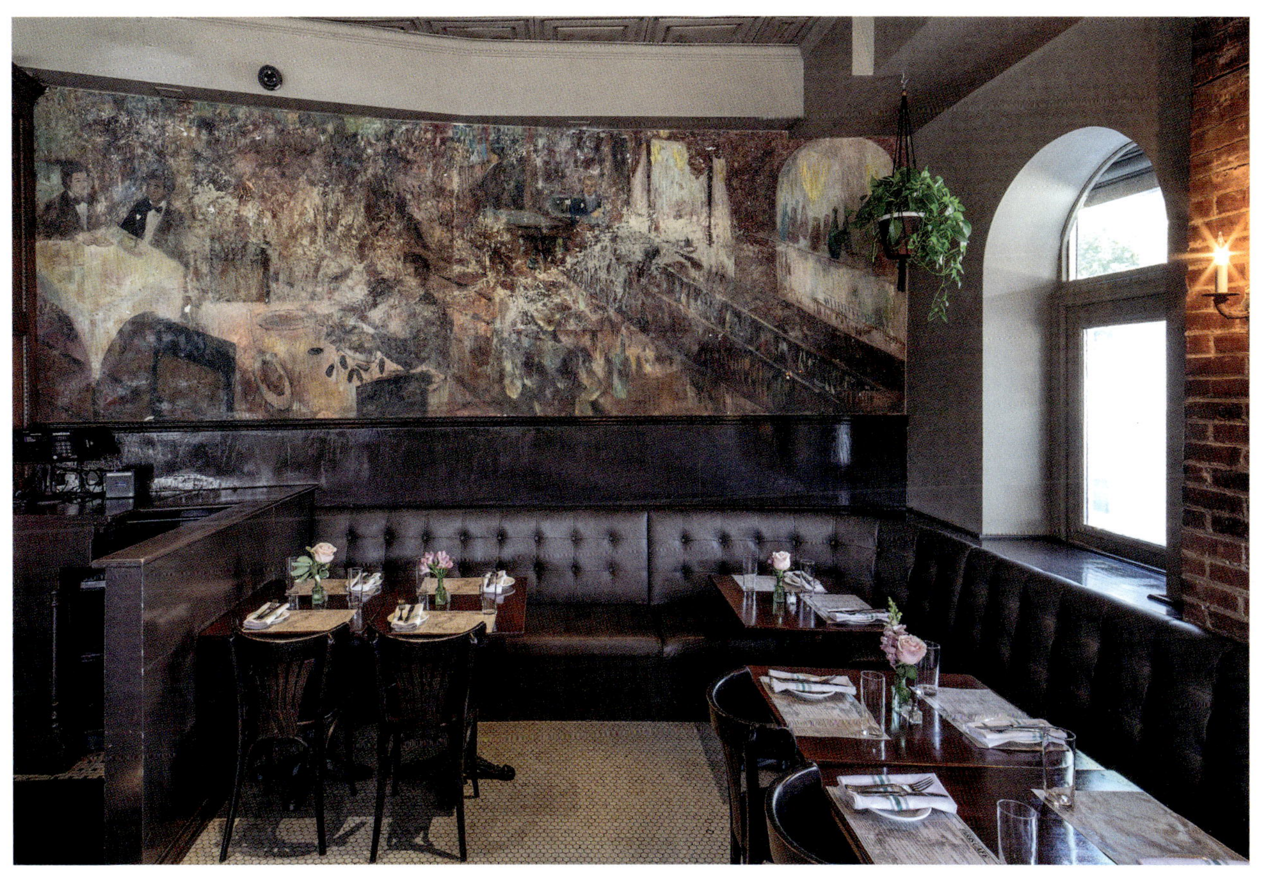

OPPOSITE TOP   *The bar was flooded by more than 11 feet (3 meters) of saltwater during Hurricane Sandy in 2012, leaving its interior completely destroyed. Luckily, its centerpiece German Victorian bar, with its polished wood and mirrors, was lovingly restored.*

ABOVE   *The mural hanging over the dining area was uncovered behind a wall and was meticulously restored when the bar reopened in late 2021.*

JULIUS'

159 WEST 10TH STREET, WEST VILLAGE

Though the Stonewall Inn (see p. 78) might be New York's best-known historic gay bar, the city's oldest one is actually Julius', located nearby. But Julius' wasn't always a destination for queer people. Erected in 1826 at the corner of present-day West Tenth Street and Waverly Place, the building has been welcoming patrons since 1840 when it was a grocery store selling dry goods.

Later, in 1864, it became a bar, and in the 1930s it was allegedly named Julius' because the original owner's dog was a Basset Hound named Julius (which would also explain the Basset Hound footrests once found at the base of the bar). In the early 1900s the bar catered to writers, artists, and performers, including celebrity press photographer Weegee and singer Billie Holiday, who allegedly performed there.

Julius' only started attracting a queer clientele in the 1950s—and even then, it was technically illegal to serve "suspected homosexuals" in bars on account of perceived disorderly conduct. As such, the management at the time was unwelcoming toward its gay patrons, including luminaries like playwright Tennessee Williams, novelist Truman Capote, and ballet dancer Rudolf Nureyev.

On April 21, 1966, three years before the first brick was thrown at Stonewall, a gay rights group called the Mattachine Society organized what would become known as the "Sip-In." Led by activists Dick Leitsch, Craig Rodwell, and John Timmons, the protesters ordered a drink at Julius' and announced themselves as homosexuals. Since the bar had recently been raided, the bartender, who had started making a drink, placed his hand over the glass to deny them service—a moment that was photographed and led to a *New York Times* article proclaiming "3 Deviates Invite Exclusion by Bars."

The activists challenged the New York State Liquor Authority's rule in court, which led to a decision that they had the right to peaceful assembly, paving the way for legal gay bars to open. To this day, scholars consider this moment a catalyst of the broader queer liberation movement. In 2015, Julius' was listed on the New York State Register of Historic Places, and in 2022, the building housing the bar was given landmark status by the New York City Landmarks Preservation Commission.

Beyond being a shrine to the struggle for gay liberation, Julius' is a time capsule to the city's past, having witnessed nearly two centuries of history. Decades before it became a hush-hush rendezvous for the queer community, it was a Prohibition-era speakeasy that circumvented police raids by allowing guests to come in and out of alternate doors. Tunnels under the bar, which were installed in the 1800s for coal delivery between neighboring businesses, were used as escape routes both during Prohibition crackdowns and gay raids.

Etched with the names of customers who have visited throughout the years, the long wooden bar, which is believed to predate Prohibition, is propped up by vintage beer barrels. Meanwhile, smaller barrels from the Jacob Ruppert Brewery (established in 1867) have been repurposed as seating. Julius' also still uses its original wagon wheel light fixtures, which came from the old ice wagons that delivered ice to the business. Originally gas powered, they are now electric.

The bar has been featured prominently on-screen, including in the 1970 film *The Boys in the Band* and 1976's *Next Stop, Greenwich Village*. More recently, it was a shooting location for comedian Melissa McCarthy's 2018 movie *Can You Ever Forgive Me?* and served as the Boy Lounge in the FX drama *POSE*, about New York City's ballroom culture. Today's celebrity customers have included Julia Roberts, Sarah Jessica Parker, and Lady Gaga—who came in alone once, according to longtime bartenders. It has also hosted the Mattachine dance party, thrown by Broadway star John Cameron Mitchell.

Throughout the years, the bar has changed hands numerous times, with each owner adding new photographs and mementos all over the walls. During one of these eras, for example, Julius' catered to bookies, which explains the many photographs of derby-winning horses. Today the bar is owned by Helen Buford, who purchased it with her husband in 1999. She's been running it since his passing in 2009. "The LGBTQ history is the most important," she says of Julius' staying power. "The bar is very welcoming to all, and our burgers are amazing. I'm happy I created a welcoming place for everyone. This is how you strengthen your community. Together we are stronger."

If you come in today, grab a burger and a pint to toast to "good health"—which is hand-painted in many languages across the top of the wooden barback.

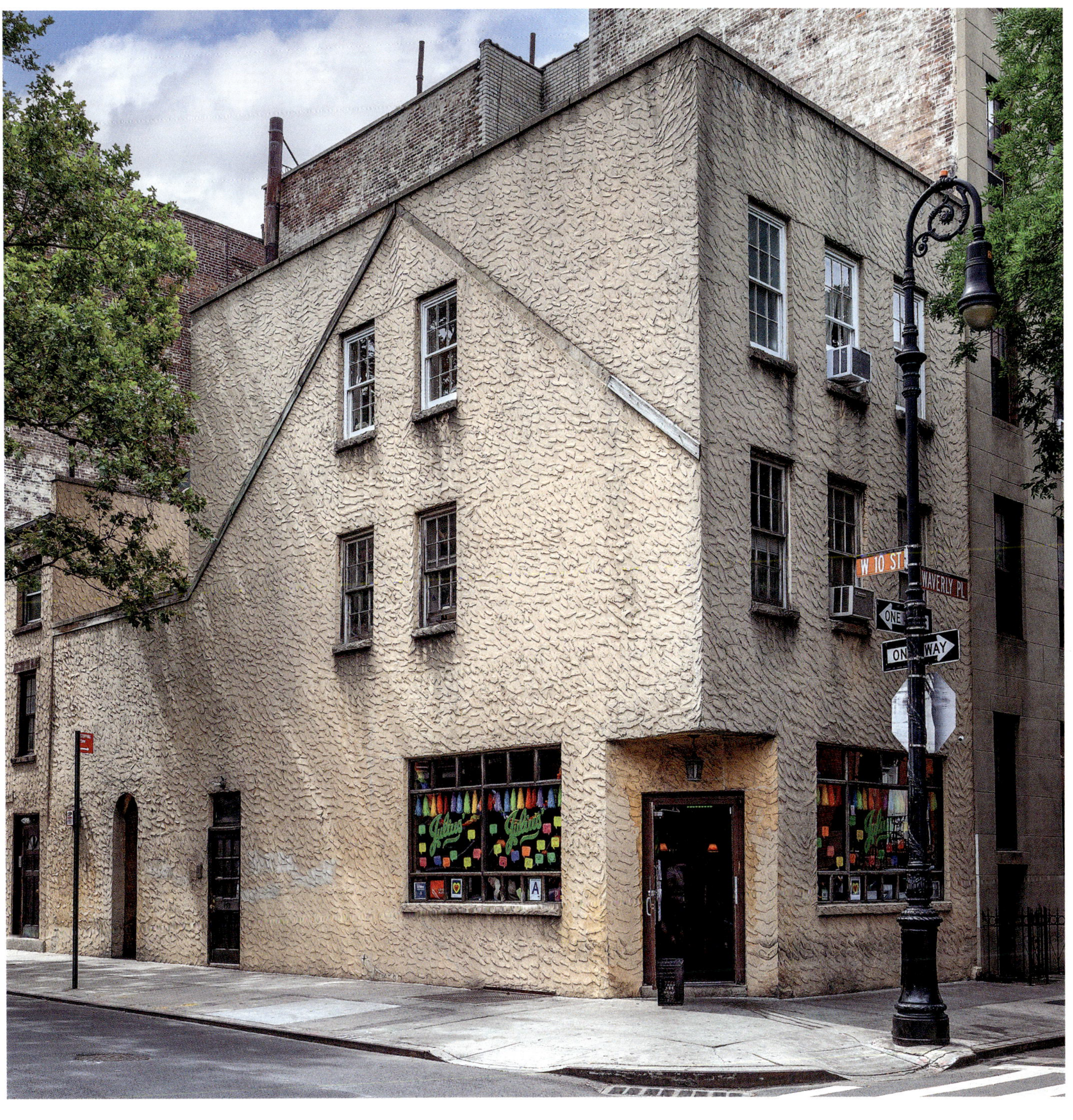

ABOVE *The landmarked building that houses Julius' dates back to the 1840s, when it originally operated as a dry goods store.*

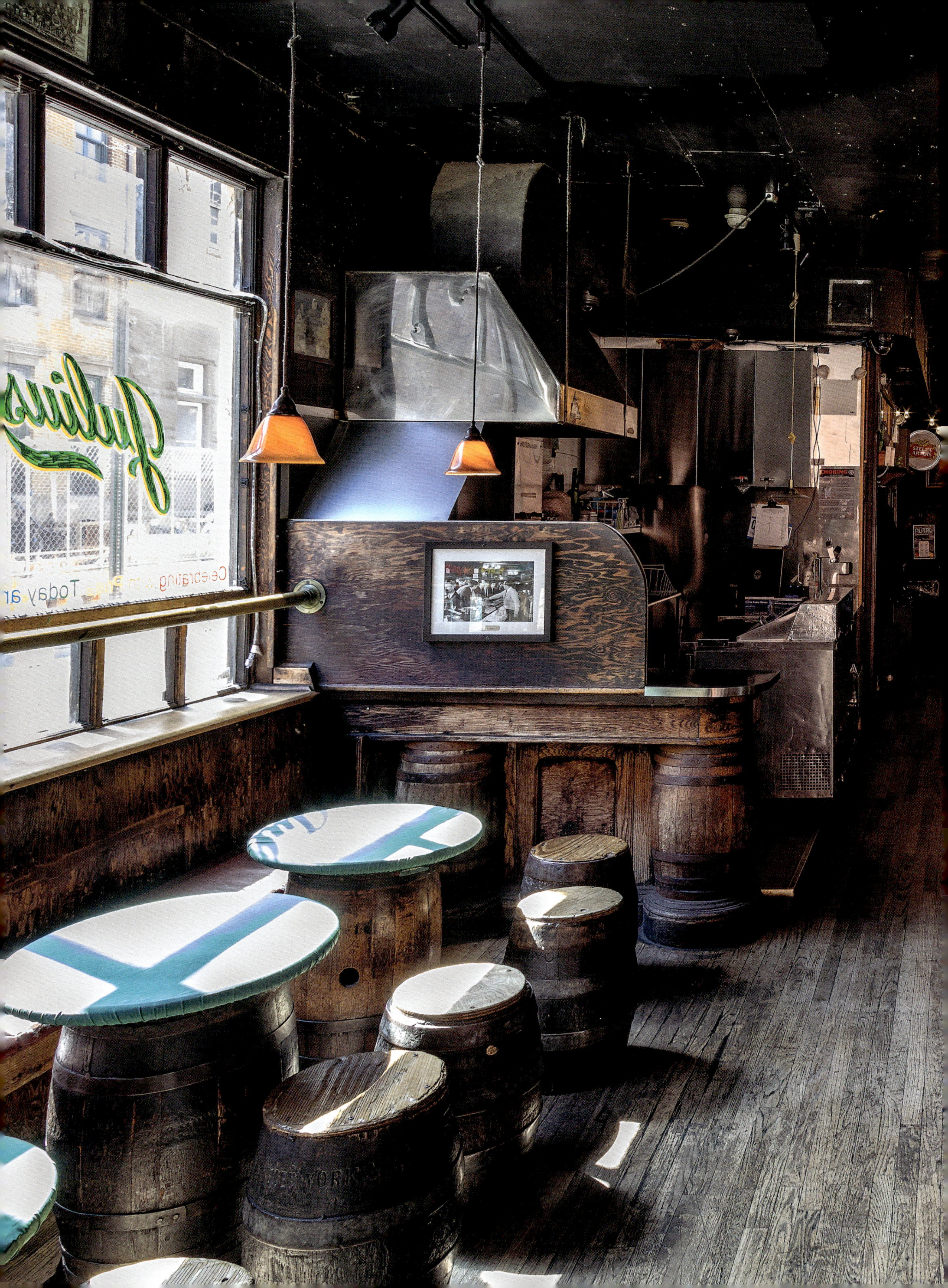

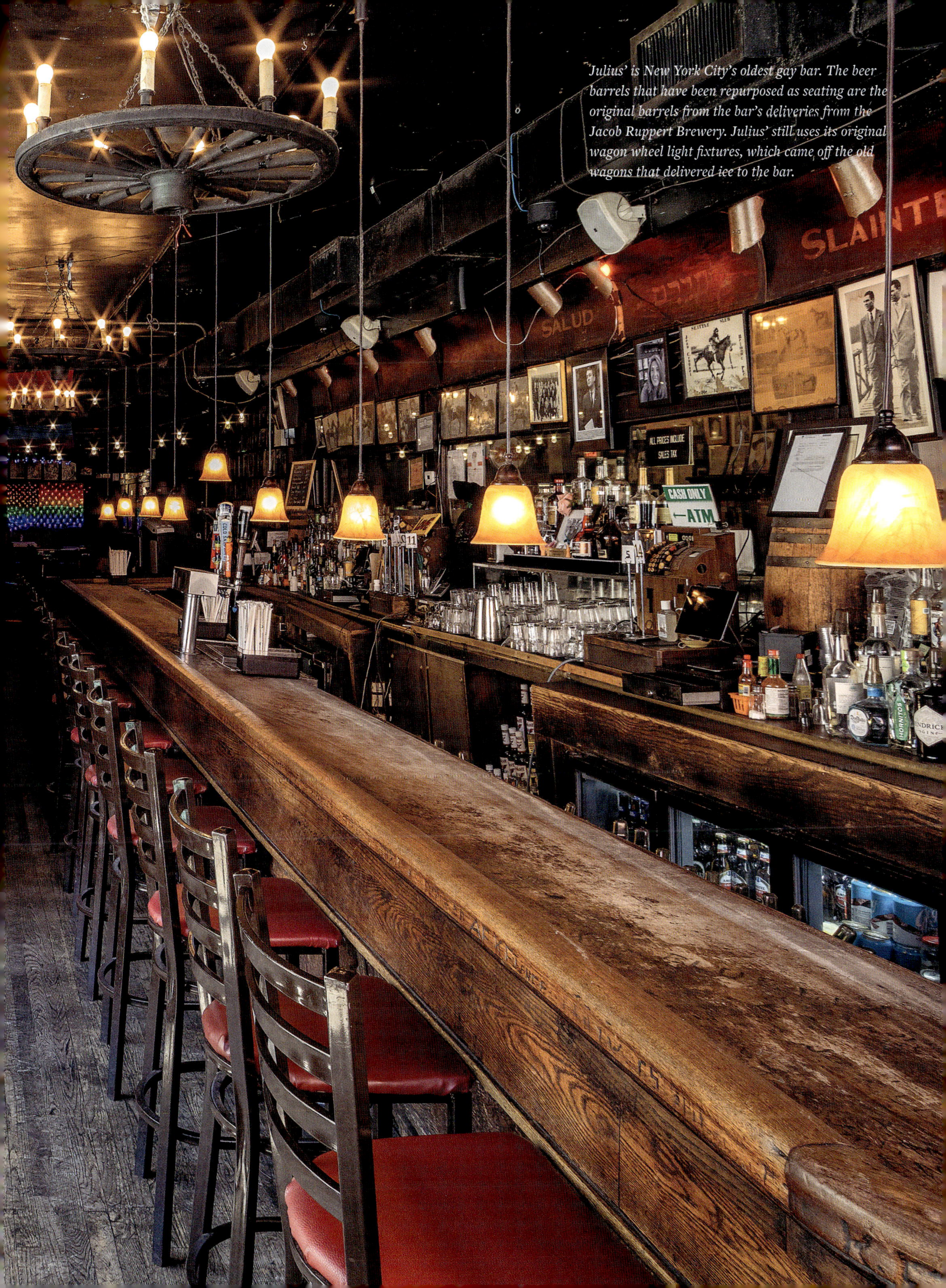

Julius' is New York City's oldest gay bar. The beer barrels that have been repurposed as seating are the original barrels from the bar's deliveries from the Jacob Ruppert Brewery. Julius' still uses its original wagon wheel light fixtures, which came off the old wagons that delivered ice to the bar.

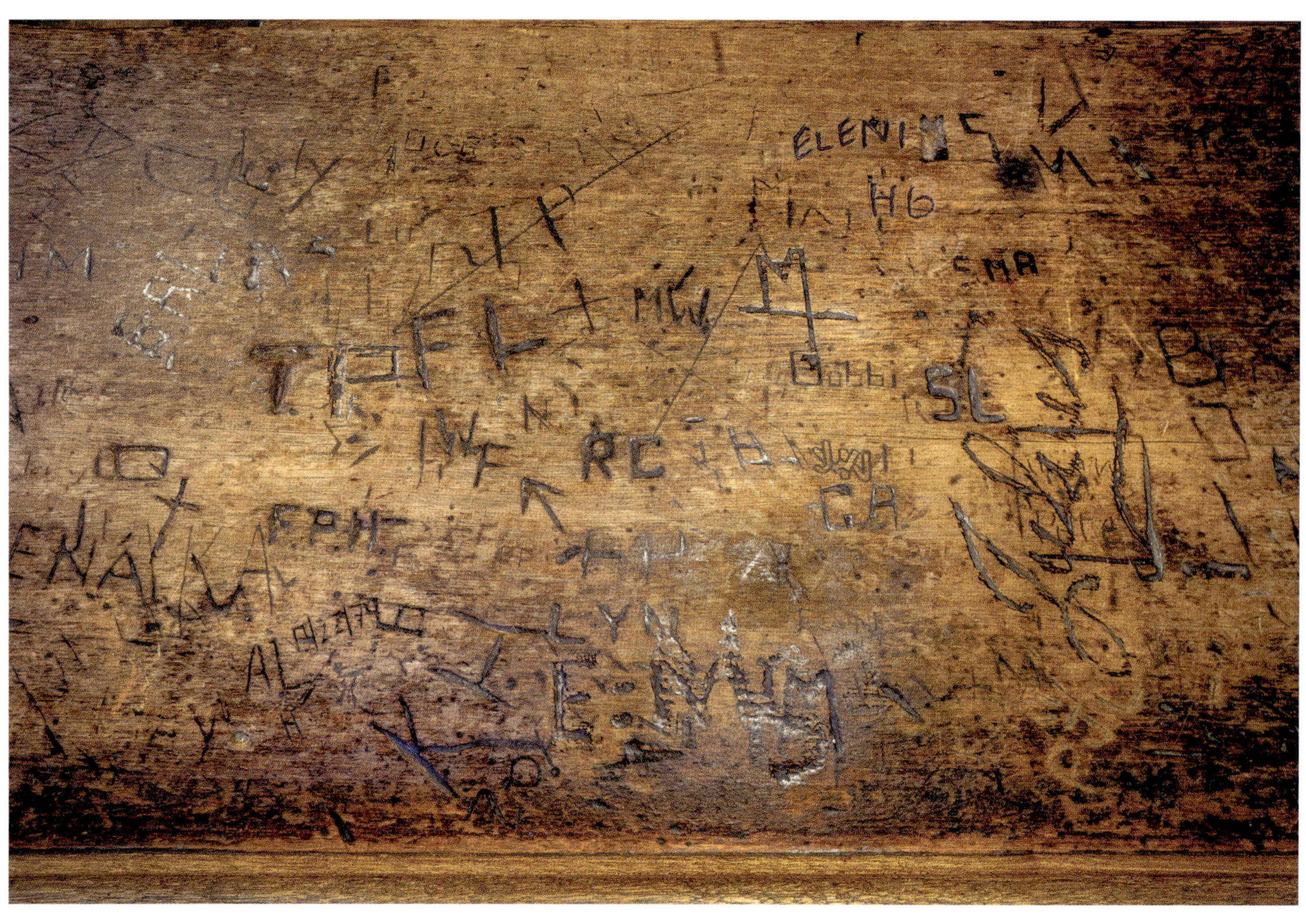

ABOVE   *The names and dates of people who have visited Julius' over the decades are carved in the bar.*

OPPOSITE TOP   *The antique wood bar is itself propped up by vintage beer barrels.*

OPPOSITE BOTTOM   *Julius' is known for its historic "Sip-In" on April 21, 1966, when members of the Mattachine Society protested a state law that prohibited bars from serving "suspected gay men or lesbians."*

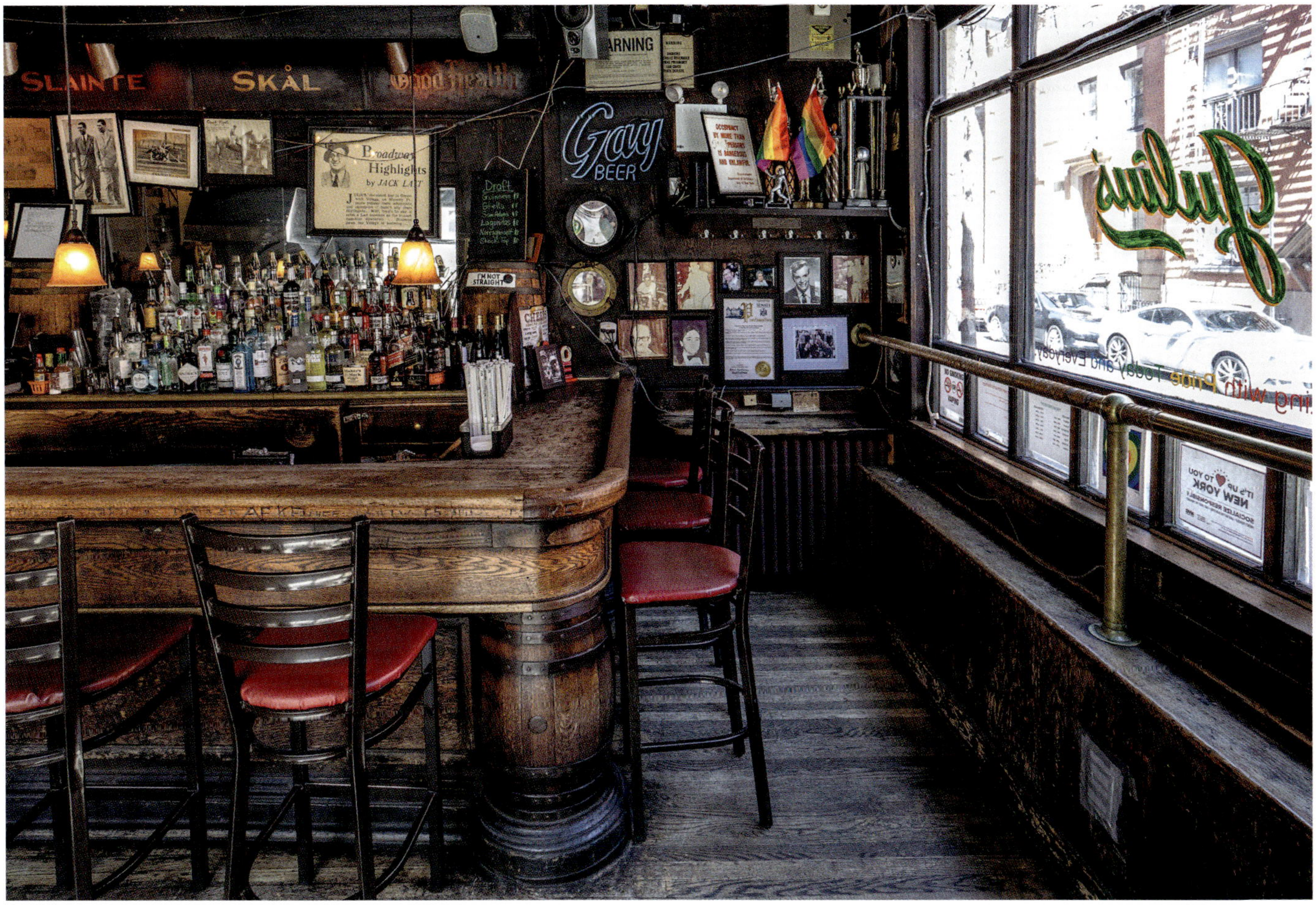

Mattachine Society members at Julius' bar during the "sip-in," New York, April 21, 1966. Left to right: John Timmins (coat over shoulder), Dick Leitsch, Craig Rodwell, and Randy Wicker.
© FRED W. McDARRAH

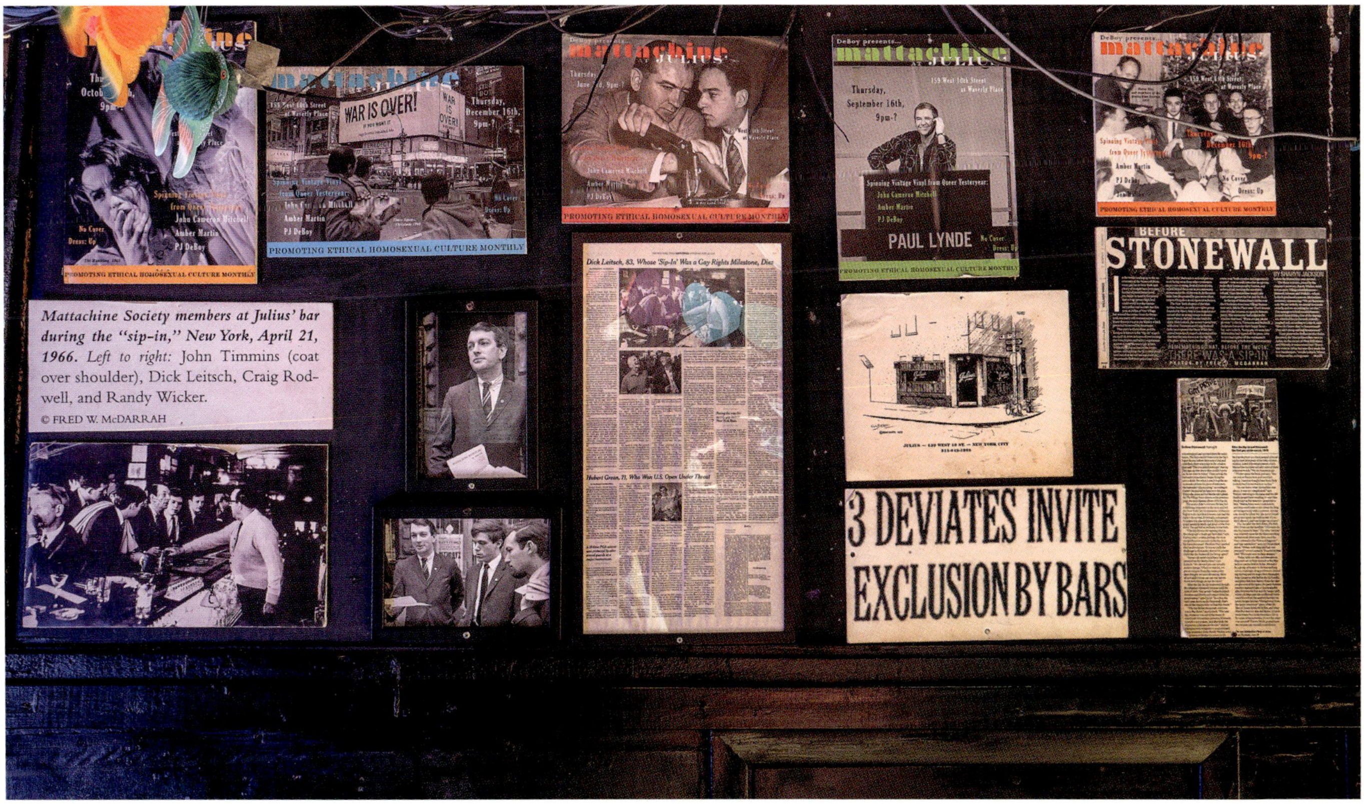

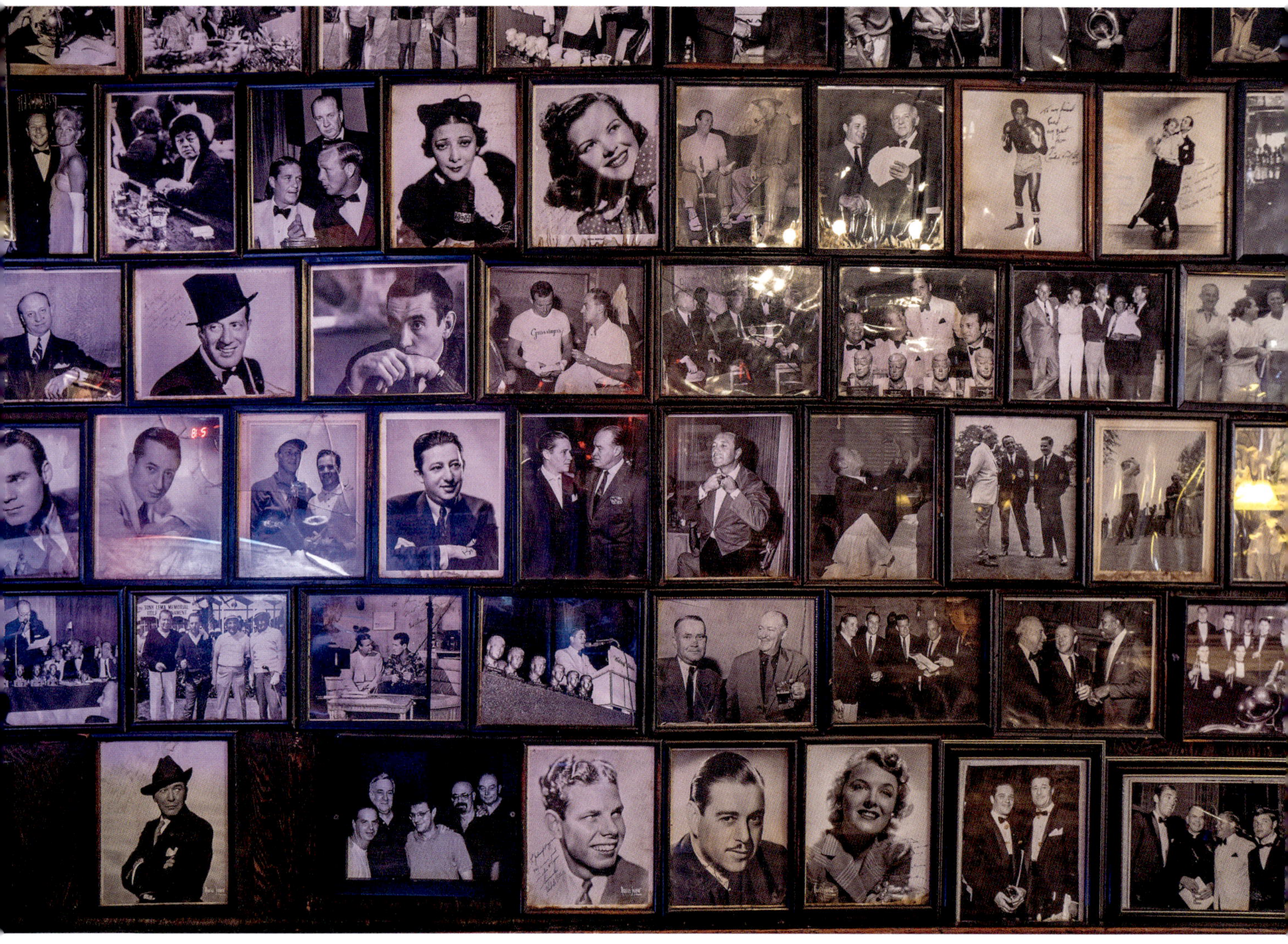

ABOVE   *There have been quite a few different owners of Julius' over the years, and each one has added photographs of famous patrons and memorabilia to the walls.*

OPPOSITE TOP   *Julius' was once a pony bar where bookies would hang out drinking, which is why there are many photographs of derby-winning horses over the bar.*

OPPOSITE BOTTOM   *Toasts to "good health" in many languages have been hand-painted across the top of the wooden barback.*

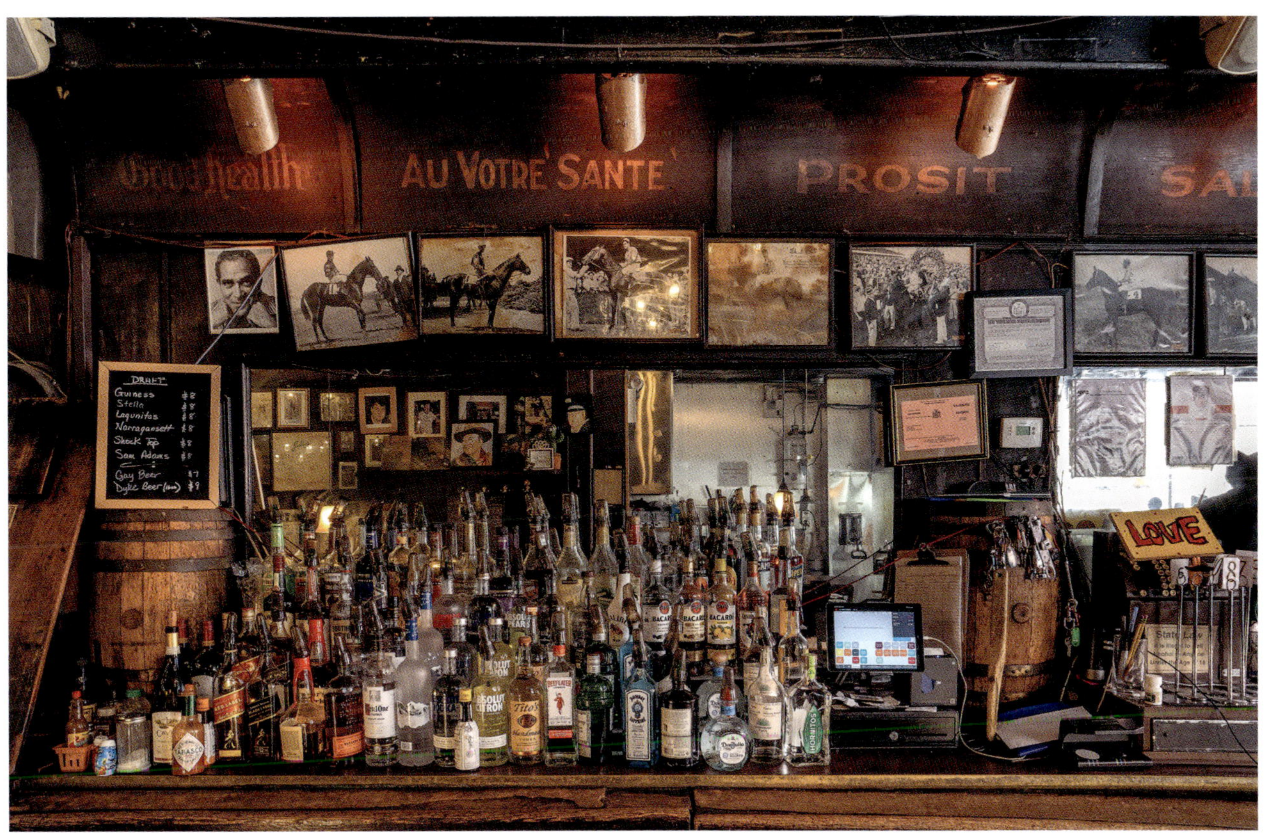
Good Health
AU VOTRE SANTE
PROSIT
SANTE

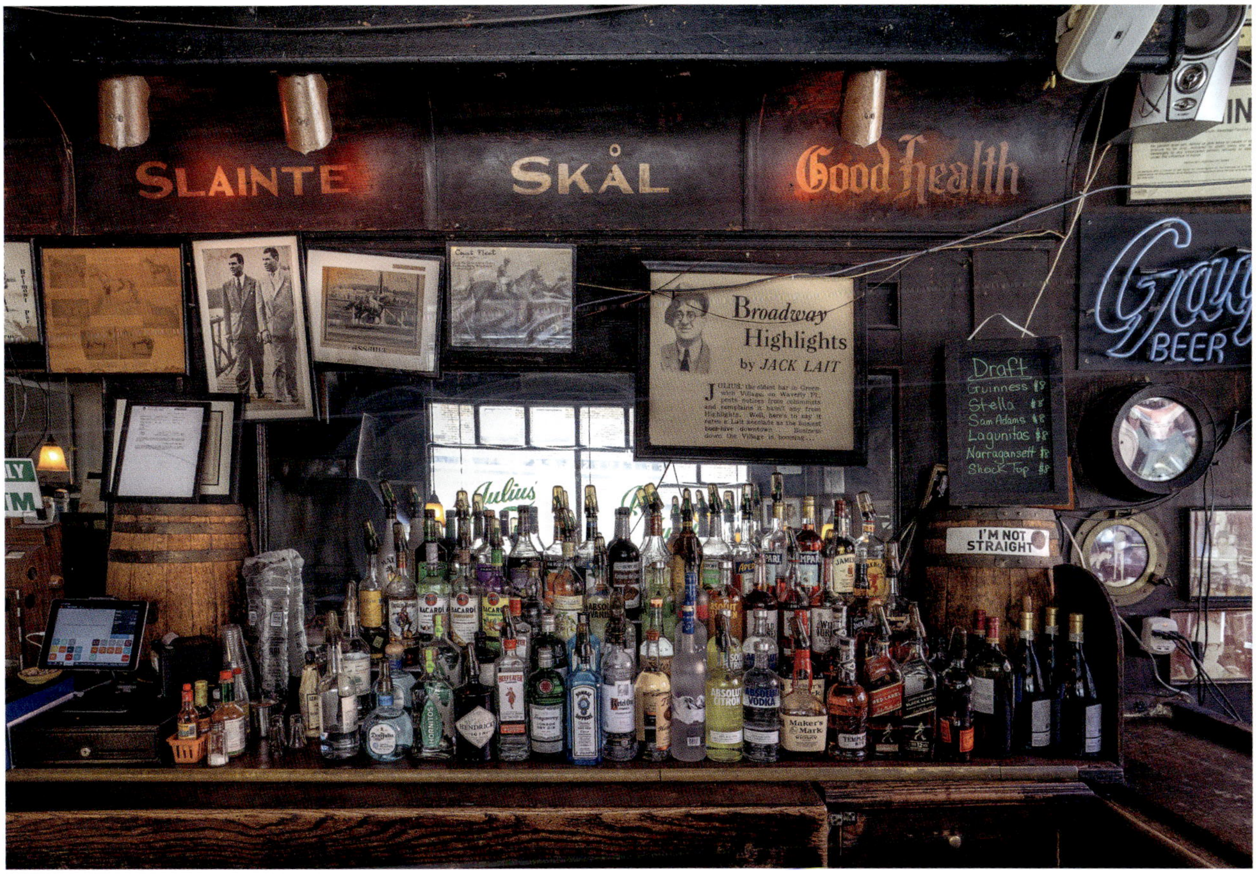

SLAINTE
SKÅL
Good Health
Gay BEER
Broadway Highlights
by JACK LAIT
Draft
Guinness
Stella
Sam Adams
Lagunitas
Narragansett
Shock Top
I'M NOT STRAIGHT

RUDY'S BAR & GRILL

627 NINTH AVENUE,
HELL'S KITCHEN

Rudy's Bar & Grill is a New York City dive in its purest form. A one-time gritty Hell's Kitchen speakeasy frequented by the likes of mobster Al Capone, it's mentioned in a Steely Dan song and has been a safe haven for stars—including Frank Sinatra and Ava Gardner before they went public as a couple—looking to keep a low profile while enjoying a drink.

It's unclear when exactly Rudy's opened; some believe that it was originally born as a speakeasy in 1919. Whatever the case, it was one of the first bars to receive a liquor license in 1933 after Prohibition ended. The first owners of Rudy's were the eponymous Rudy family, of German heritage. One of the women in the family, Helen Rudy, was known to keep two German Shepherds at the bar to help maintain order.

In the 1950s one of the owners' sons, Ewald Rudy, took over. According to a blog called Bored and Thirsty, though he was hard-working, he was also cheap, and allegedly somewhat disliked by staff. The bar struggled during this time.

In the '60s and '70s, Hell's Kitchen was a crime-ridden no man's land run by gangs, including the Irish American Westies. In 1977, American rock band Steely Dan mentioned Rudy's in the song "Black Cow," singing, *I saw you in Rudy's / you were very high.*

In the mid 1980s, Rudy's and the building it's housed in were sold to Jack Ertl, who was amassing a portfolio of neighborhood dives that also included Holland Bar and Full Moon Saloon. However, attempts to "clean up" the bar during this time didn't stick: people apparently liked it the way it was.

The '90s ushered in a period of change and the neighborhood began to show signs of gentrification, with younger residents moving in for affordable prices. While managers at Rudy's remember many newcomers being wary of the dive, it eventually started to win over this fresh audience.

Manager Ernie Schroeder, who started working at Rudy's in 1989, commissioned its three wall mosaics of Ella Fitzgerald, Count Basie, and a 12-foot (4-meter) long saxophone. Also introduced in the past few decades is the 6-foot (2-meter) tall pig statue outside the bar, named Baron von Swine. He has been stolen twice in the past, but he is now bolted down and can be found wearing custom outfits around the holidays. The matching Baron von Swine taps at the bar were made by a longtime customer.

Through all these changes, Schroeder sought to keep Rudy's looking generally well-worn, adding duct tape to its red leather banquettes. But, most importantly, he kept drink prices low—firmly believing beers should never cost more than $2—and introduced free hot dogs, a tradition that continues to this day under the eye of his successor, Danny DePamphilis.

Today, Rudy's is known for having one of New York's best jukeboxes—playing sounds from the likes of Billie Holiday and the Rat Pack—as well as being the city's ultimate cheap beer and free hot dog destination. That reputation even earned it the attention of Anthony Bourdain, who featured the bar on a 2003 episode of his show *A Cook's Tour*. "A free hot dog?" Bourdain quipped, continuing, "After a couple beers, it seems like a very good idea."

Throughout its long history, Rudy's has hosted countless stars, including Halle Berry, Paul McCartney, John F. Kennedy Jr., Slash of Guns N' Roses, James Gandolfini, Ethan Hawke, Lauryn Hill, and many Mets players. According to the bar's website, Drew Barrymore used to slip in as a regular—until newspapers revealed she was only twenty. "The saddest night I ever had in this bar was when I had to tell Drew Barrymore she couldn't come back 'til she was legal," DePamphilis said.

Nowadays the house blond ale at Rudy's will still only set you back a few dollars. So sidle up to the original mahogany bar—custom-made for $300 on the Bowery—to order a cold one and a hot dog that can be enjoyed in the stone-paved backyard, which has been the site of a wedding on more than one occasion.

OPPOSITE *The 6-foot (2-meter) tall pig statue outside Rudy's Bar & Grill is named Baron von Swine. He has been stolen twice in the nearly three decades he has stood vigil, but he's now bolted down.*

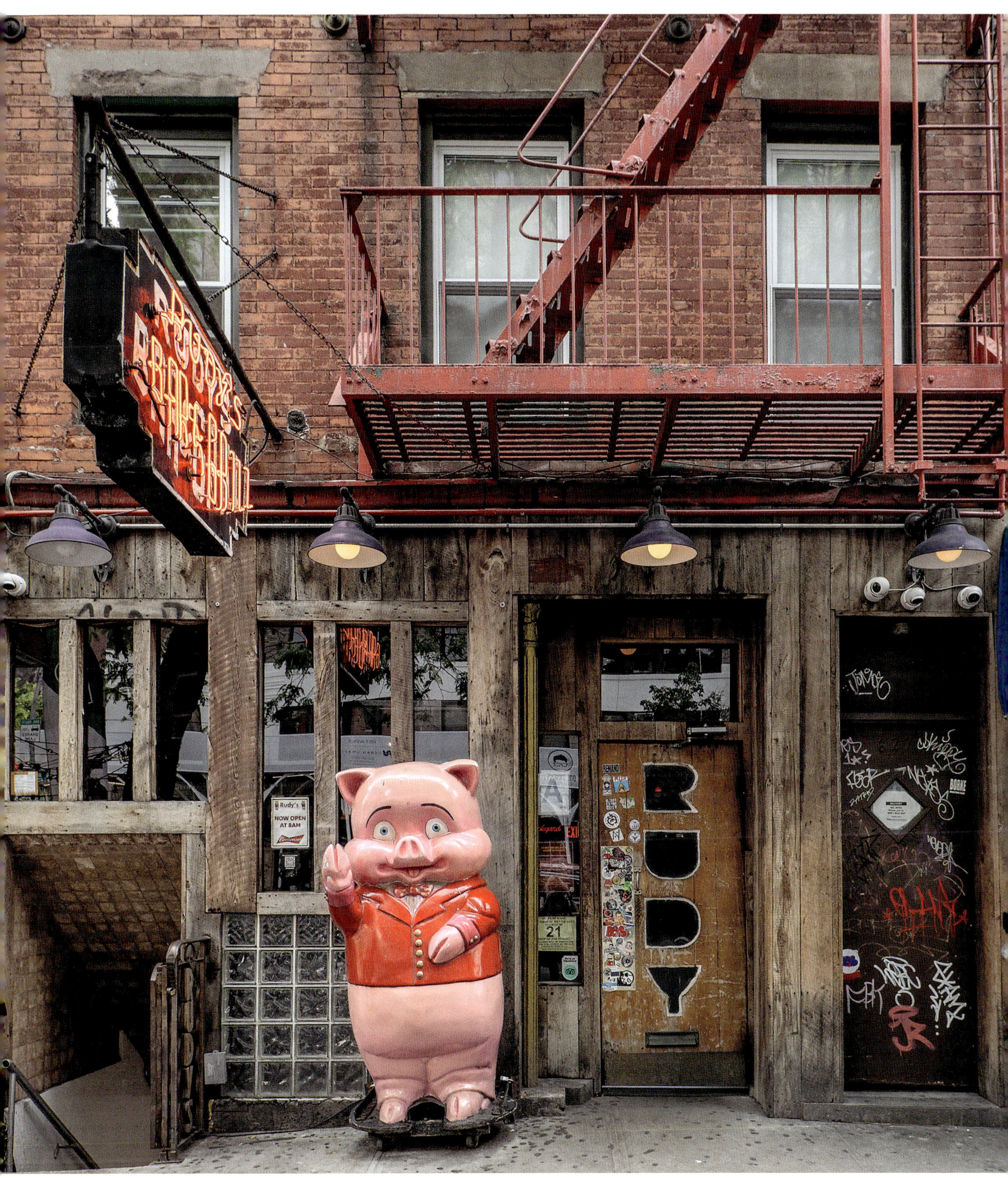

RUDY'S BAR & GRILL

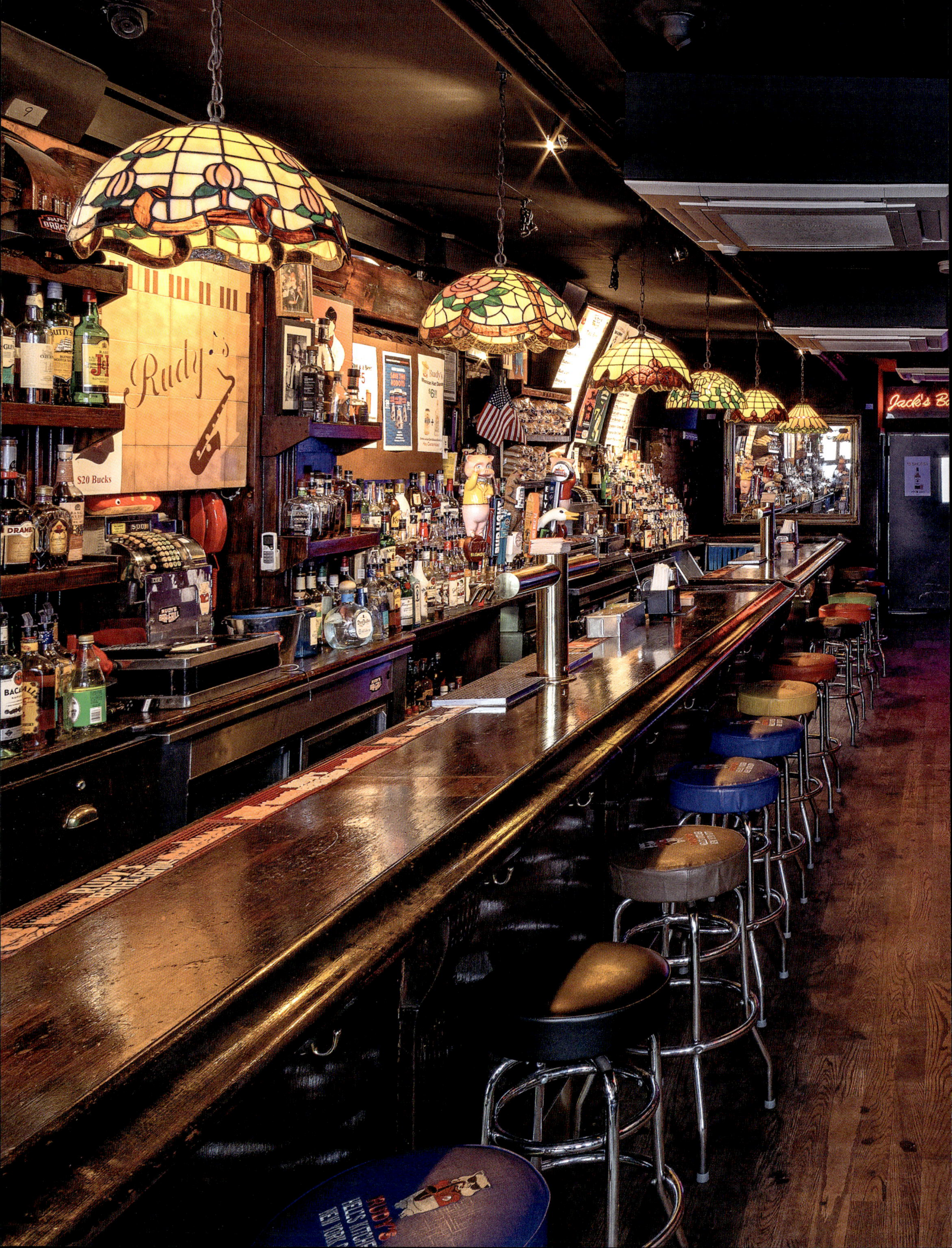

Rudy's
$20 Bucks
Jack's B

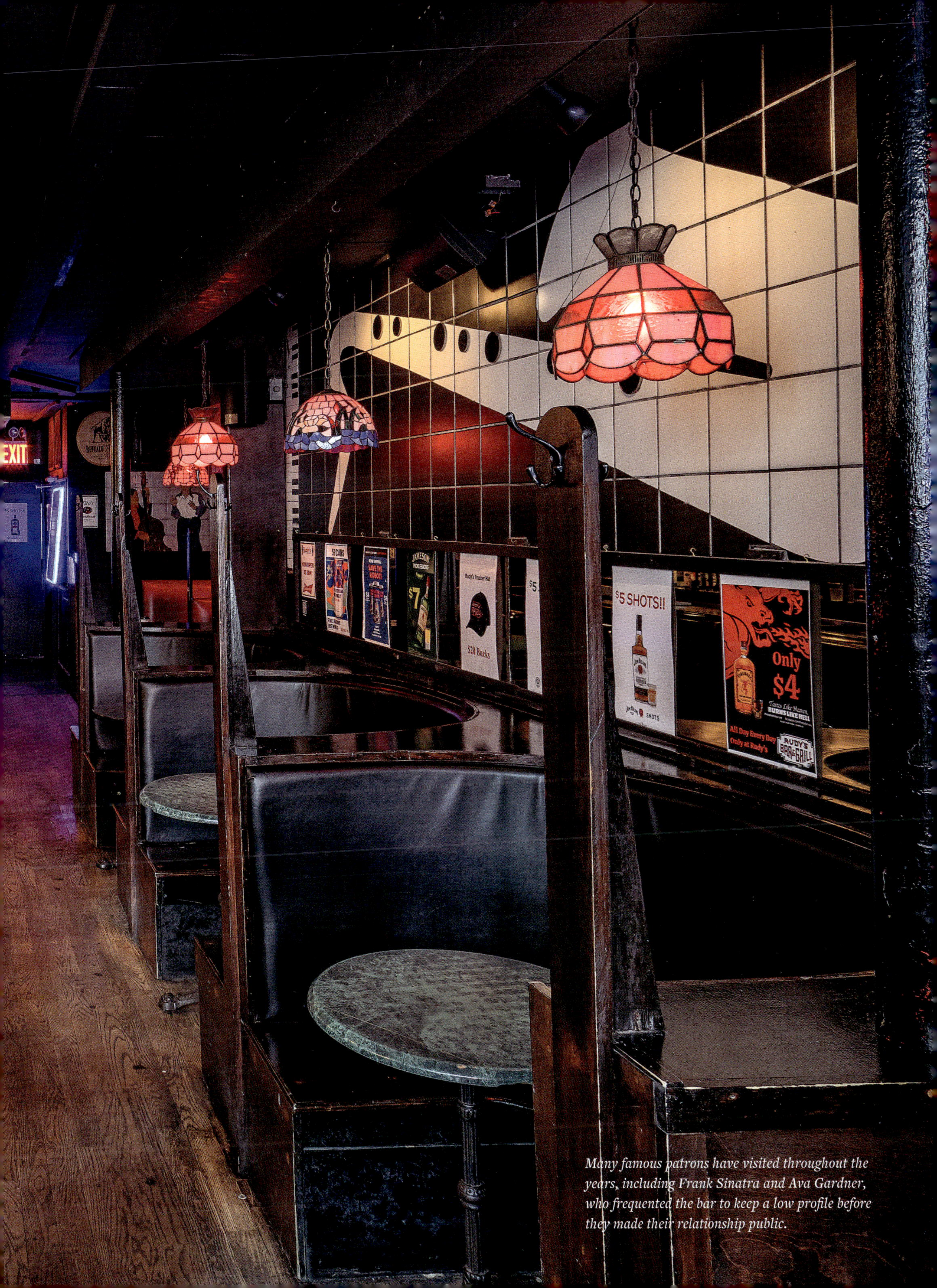

Many famous patrons have visited throughout the years, including Frank Sinatra and Ava Gardner, who frequented the bar to keep a low profile before they made their relationship public.

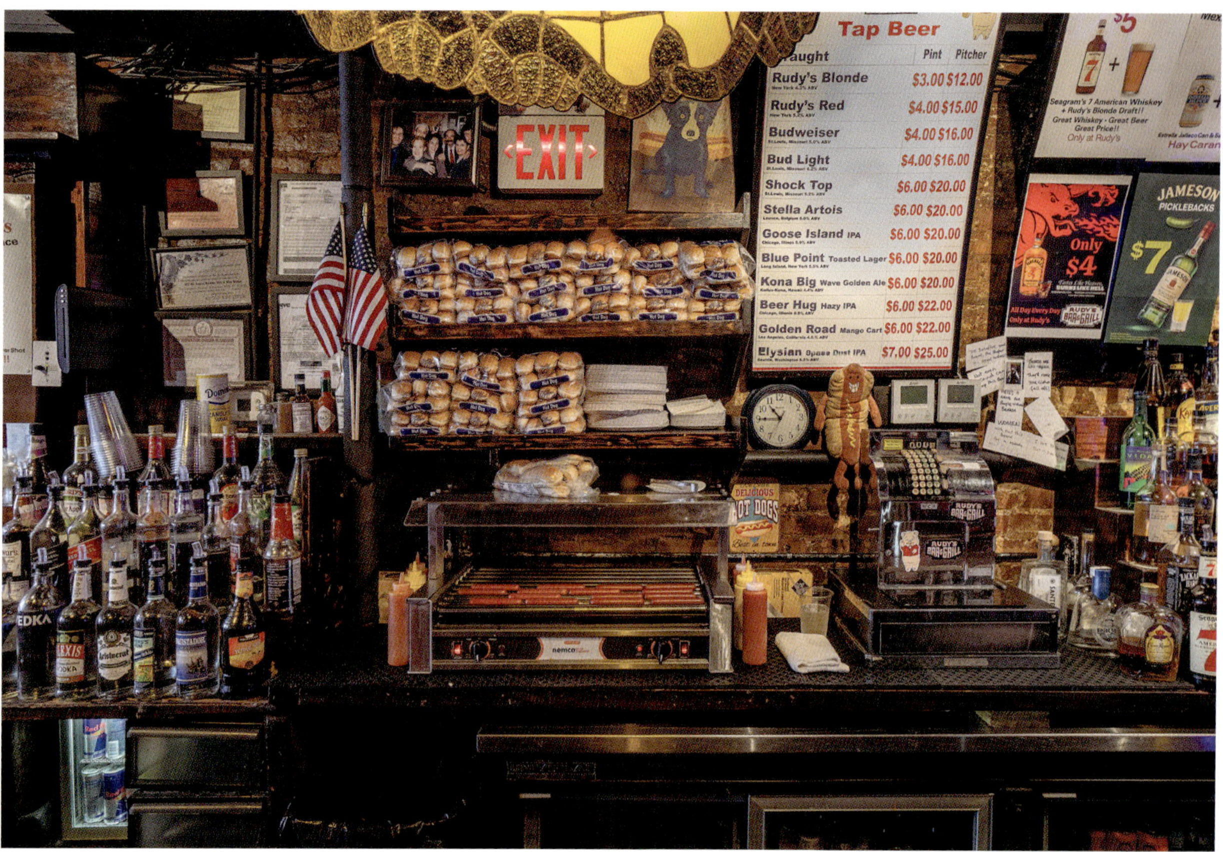

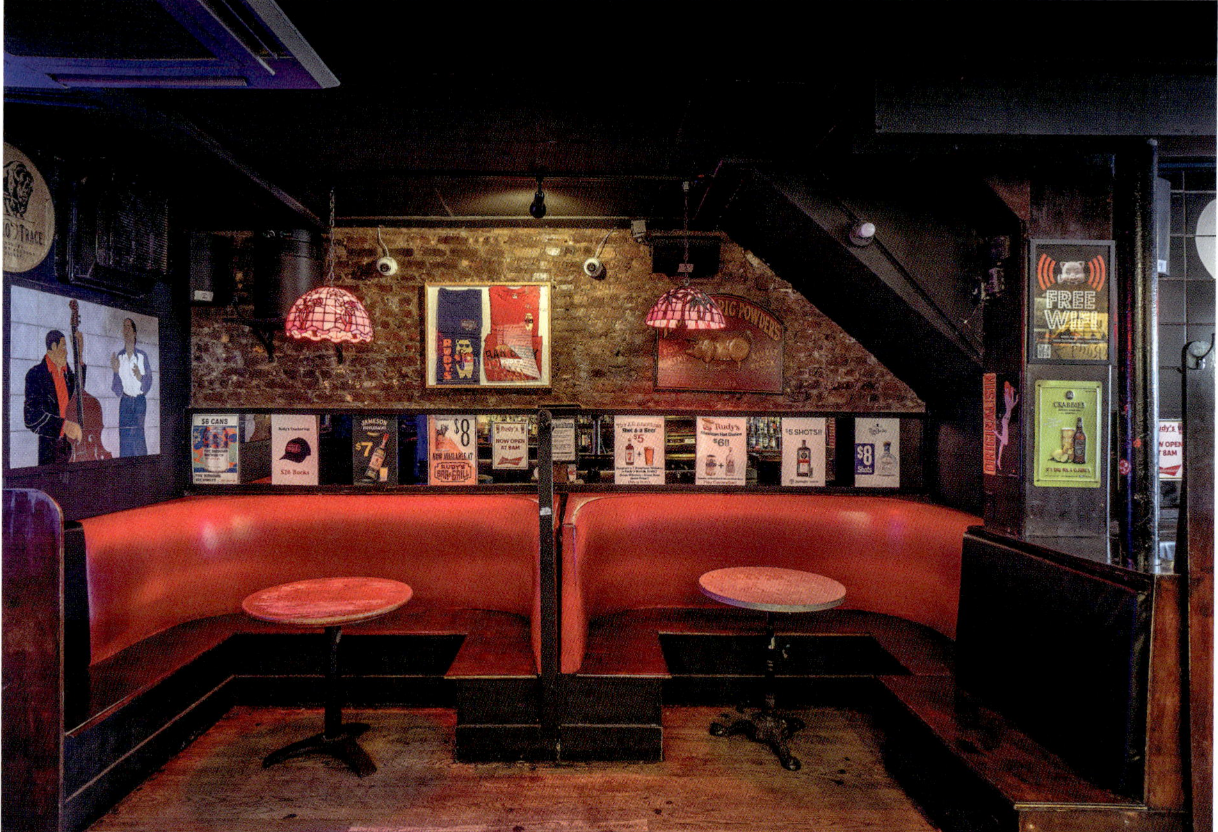

GREAT BARS OF NEW YORK CITY

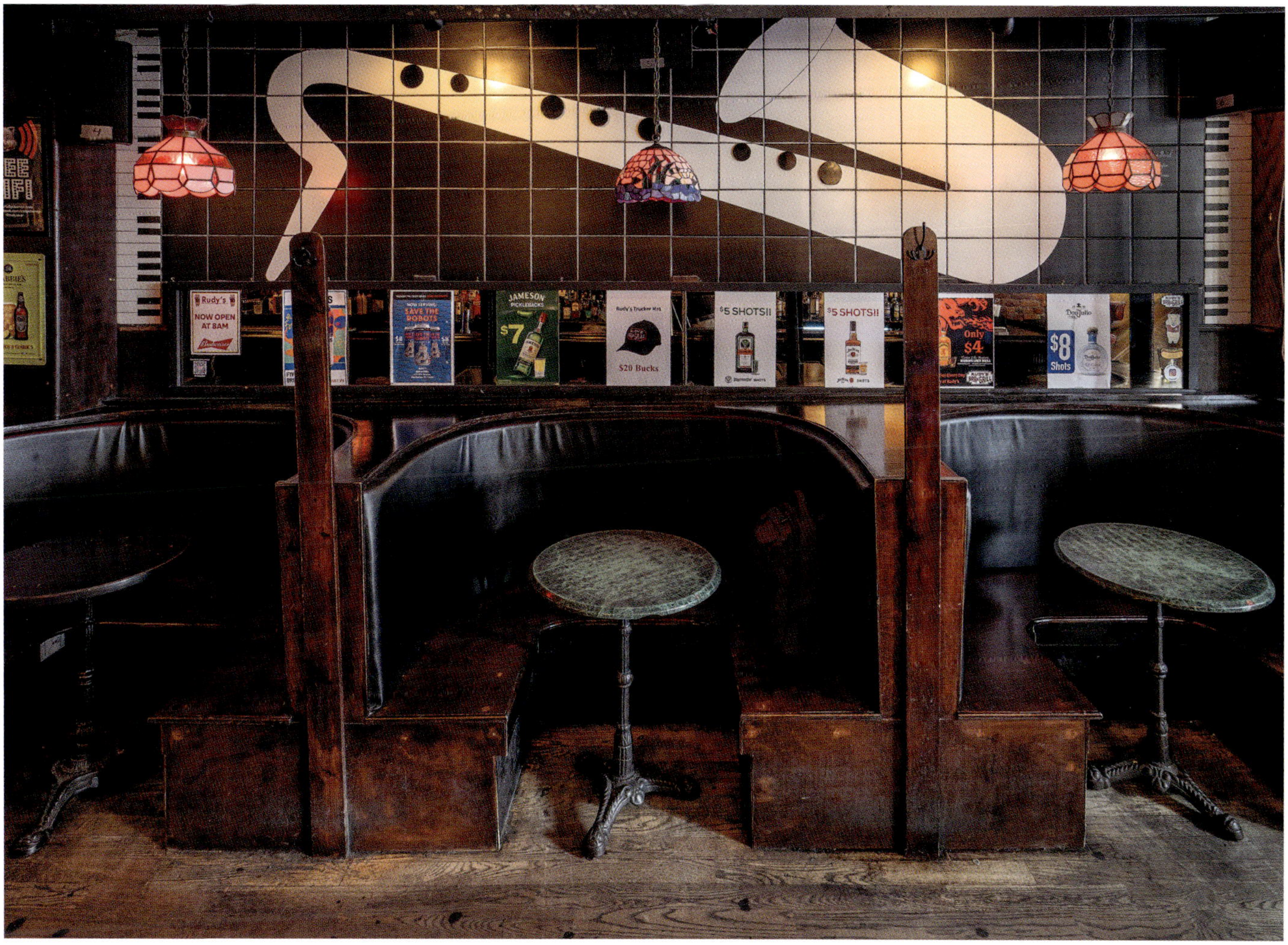

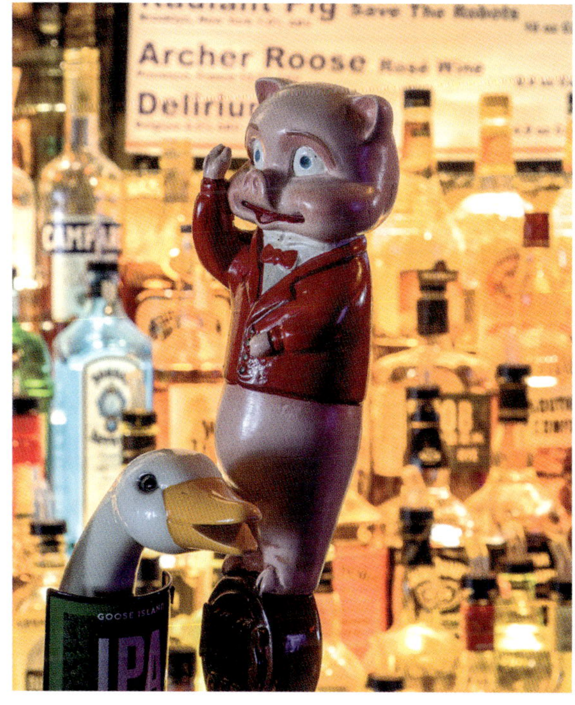
Radiant Pig Save The Robots
Archer Roose Rosé Wine
Deliriu
CAMPA
GOOSE ISLAND
IPA

KING COLE BAR

You may know the King Cole Bar from its iconic 1906 Maxfield Parrish mural painting, which makes cameos in the films *The First Wives Club* and *The Devil Wears Prada*, as well as the original *Gossip Girl* TV show. Or perhaps you've been to the St. Regis Hotel, where the stately saloon first opened in the 1930s. But even if you've never heard of any of these things, you've likely tried the cocktail that was allegedly invented at the King Cole: the Bloody Mary.

Though the St. Regis was unveiled in 1904 by John Jacob Astor IV, one of New York City's then-wealthiest men, there are many conflicting reports about when the King Cole Bar itself first came to be. The *New York Times* reported on the opening of a King Cole Room several times throughout history; however, this may be because it underwent a number of name changes in its early days. Further confusing matters is that a King Cole venue has existed in various parts of the hotel, sometimes as a bar and sometimes as a restaurant. And for a brief moment, the King Cole Bar was renamed the Iridium Room and used as an event space.

In any case, most reports point to 1932 as the true start of the hotel's booze-slinging activities. It's fitting, as this was also the year that Parrish's 30-foot (9-meter) painting arrived there. Depicting the nursery rhyme character Old King Cole on his throne, surrounded by attendants, the piece had originally been commissioned by Astor for the Knickerbocker Hotel. As legend tells it, Astor had his own visage painted as the face of King Cole. But what's more: perhaps as part of a dare or a satirical competition between artists of his era, Parrish painted Astor's facial expression in the midst of a fart.

One could talk at length about the relationship between Astor and Parrish—a connection that mirrors many had between a financier and an artist. Coming from a conservative Quaker family, Parrish was initially reluctant to take the job, even for an extremely generous-for-the-era $5,000, and his cheeky approach to the subject may have been somewhat pointed. And thus, his mural ended up on Millionaires' Alley, as Fifty-Fifth Street was known at the time.

Another one of the bar's claims to fame is the Bloody Mary cocktail, which is generally credited to French bartender Fernand "Pete" Petiot in 1934. As early as 1921 the barman had been experimenting with vodka-and-tomato-juice prototypes of the drink while working at the New York Bar in Paris; it was originally called a Bucket of Blood. After moving stateside, Petiot claimed to have codified the modern version of the drink—now containing salt, black pepper, cayenne pepper, Worcestershire sauce, and a dash of lemon juice—in 1934 at the King Cole. Attempts to name it Red Snapper clearly never caught on with the drinking public. By the 1960s, the St. Regis was serving over a hundred Bloody Marys a day in the King Cole Room and its other on-site restaurants.

The bar has lived many lives, having played host to New York's elite for decades. Notable patrons over the years have included Salvador Dalí, Marilyn Monroe, John Lennon, and Joe DiMaggio. It has also changed hands numerous times. When the King Cole's original owner perished onboard the Titanic, his son Vincent Astor initially sold it before reacquiring it and running it until his death in 1959. By 1966 it was part of the Sheraton Hotels's portfolio, and in 2016 it joined the Marriott chain.

Along with the rest of the Beaux Arts hotel it's housed in, the King Cole Bar has undergone many renovations and changes. In 2007, as part of a $400,000 makeover, its famous mural was taken off the wall for the first time since the '50s to remove dents, grime, nicotine residue, and a couple of accidental bartender misfires. In 2013 a multimillion-dollar renovation breathed new life into the bar, opening up the space, lowering chandeliers, and freshening up the Parrish mural.

Today you can still sidle your way up to the bar and order an original Red Snapper—or one of the four other distinct variations of the beloved Bloody Mary.

OPPOSITE *King Cole Bar is located inside the St. Regis Hotel. It has been frequented by the likes of Salvador Dalí, Marilyn Monroe, John Lennon, and Joe DiMaggio.*

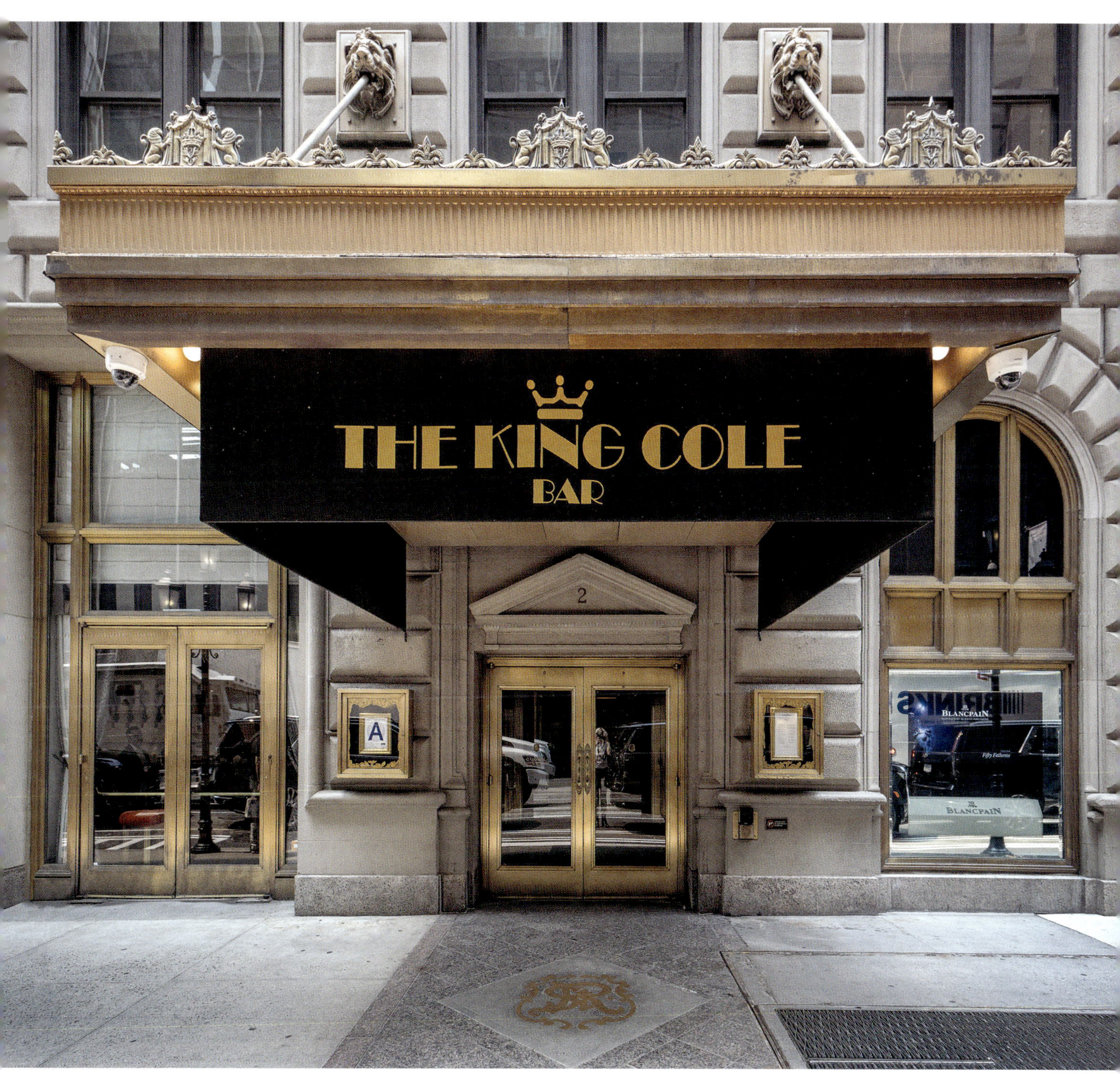

THE KING COLE
BAR
2
A

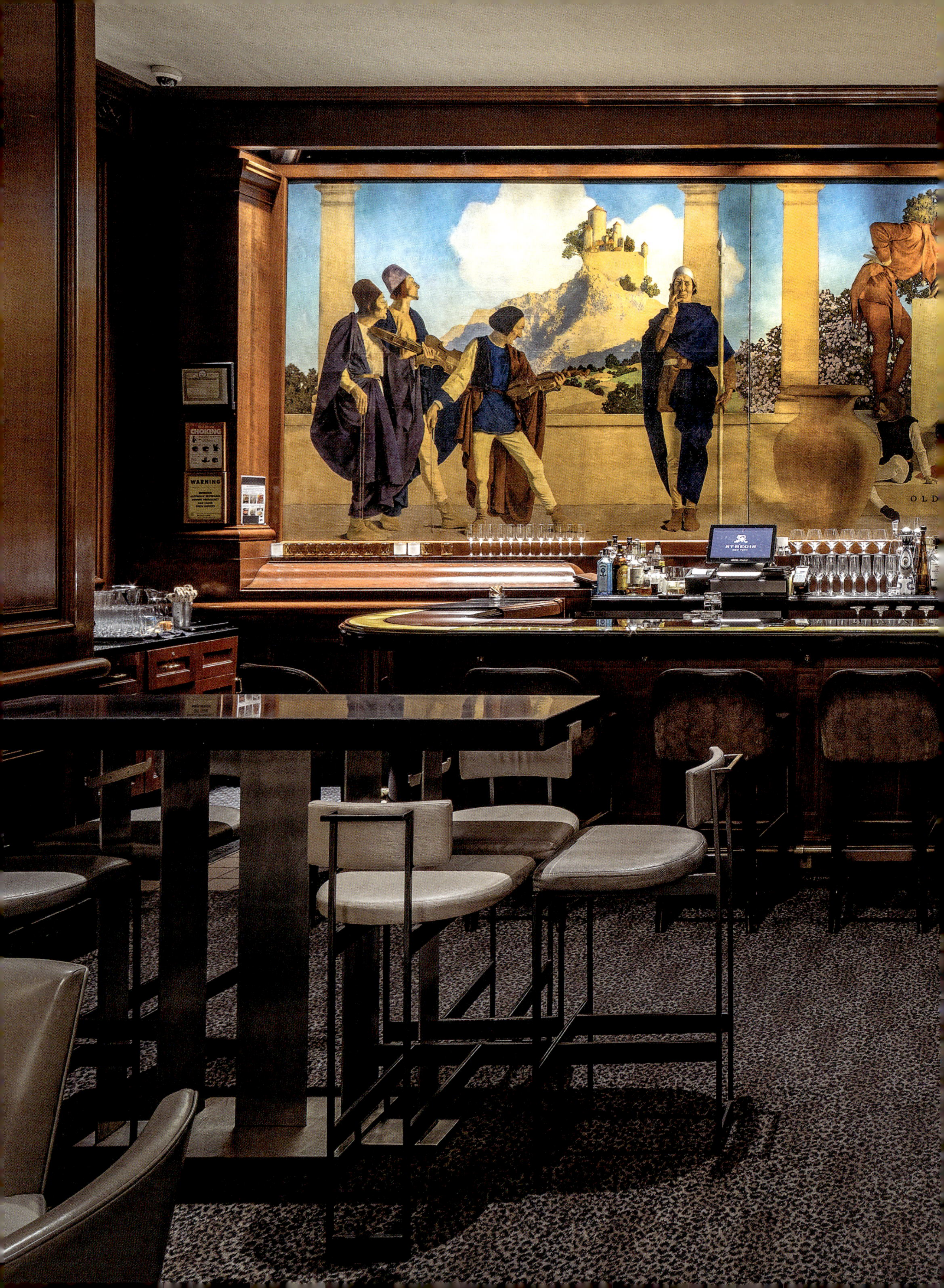

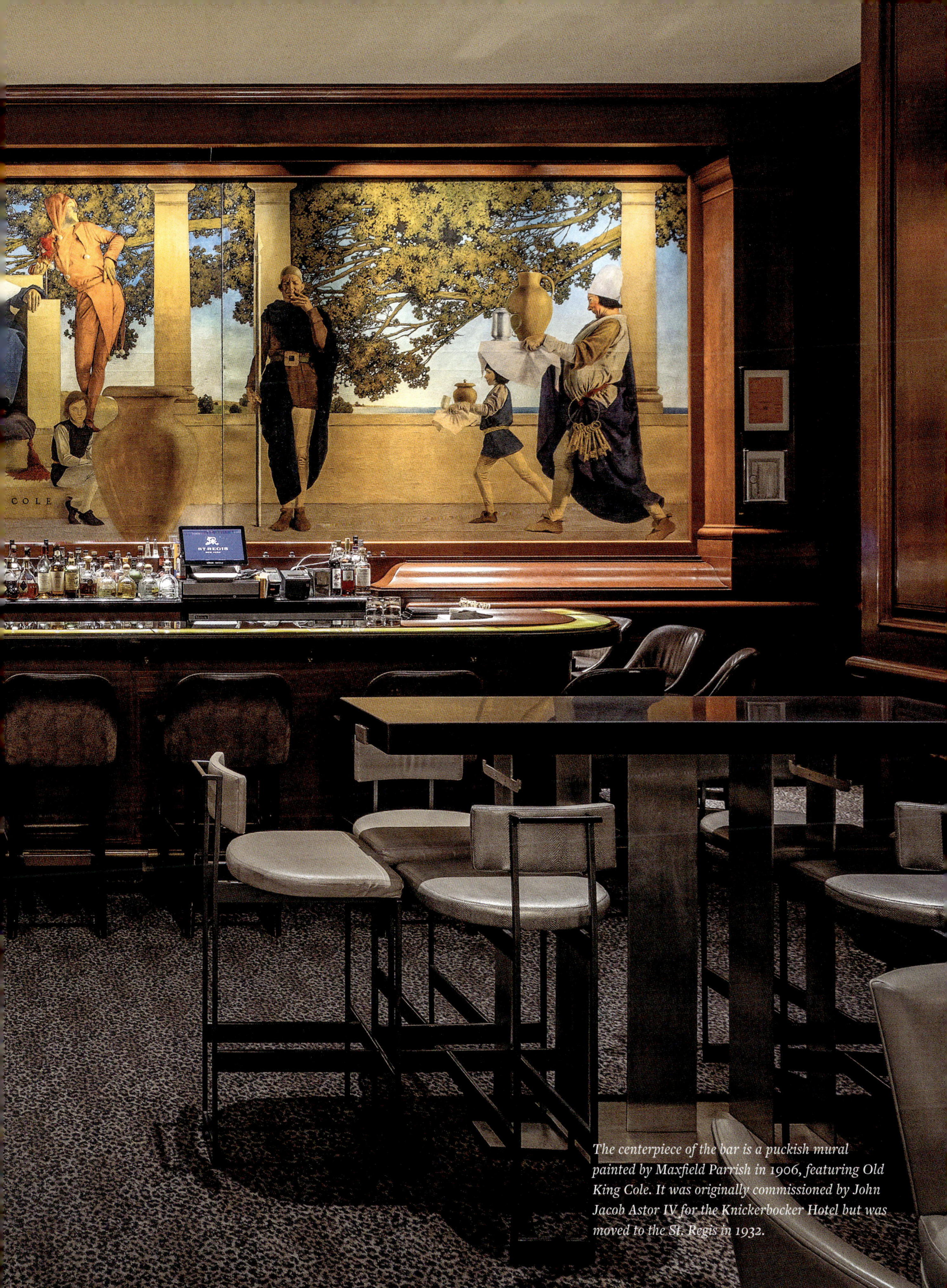

The centerpiece of the bar is a puckish mural painted by Maxfield Parrish in 1906, featuring Old King Cole. It was originally commissioned by John Jacob Astor IV for the Knickerbocker Hotel but was moved to the St. Regis in 1932.

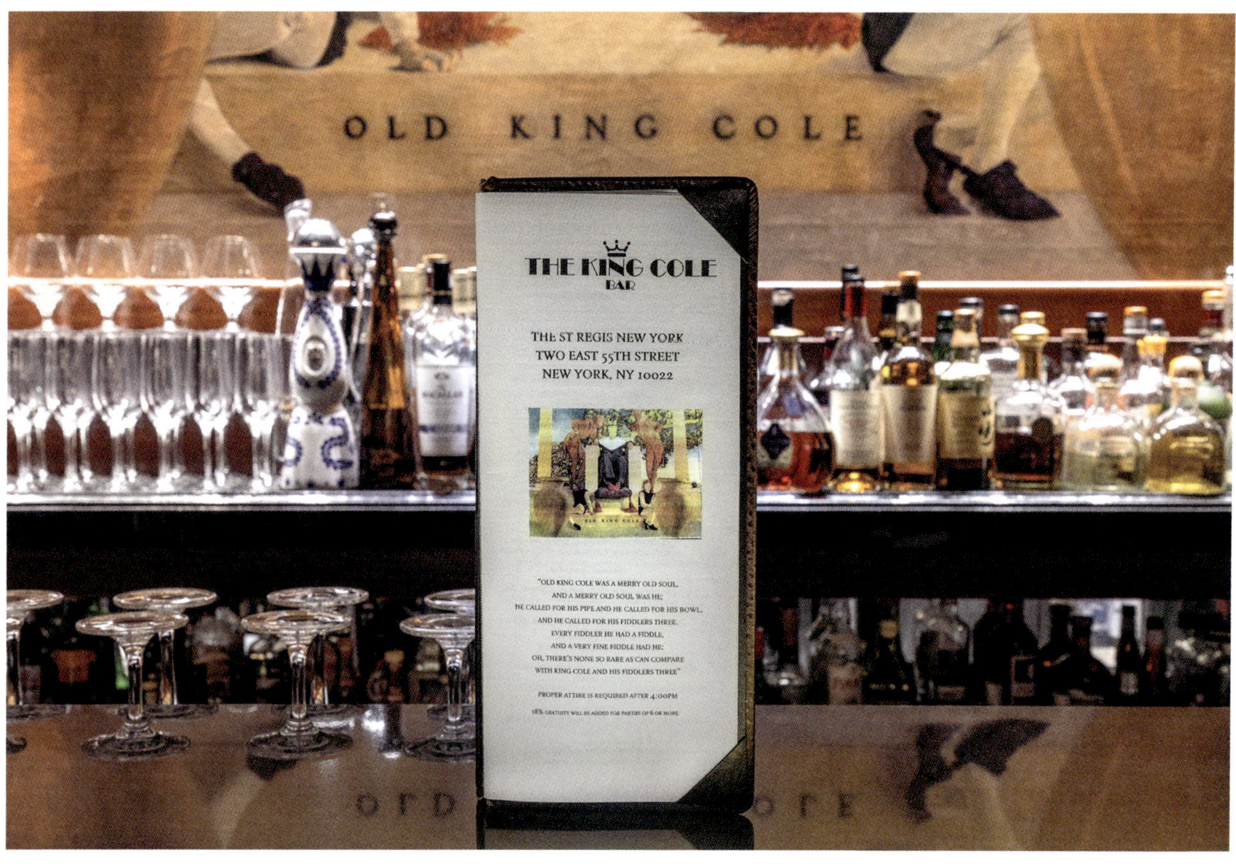

ABOVE   *The Bloody Mary is not only the signature cocktail of the King Cole Bar but is said to have been invented there. In 1934 bartender Fernand "Pete" Petiot perfected the recipe, which he called the Red Snapper, as Bloody Mary was deemed too vulgar for the hotel's elegant patrons.*

OPPOSITE TOP   *Astor had himself painted as the face of King Cole. However, on a dare, Maxfield Parrish depicted him in the midst of a fart.*

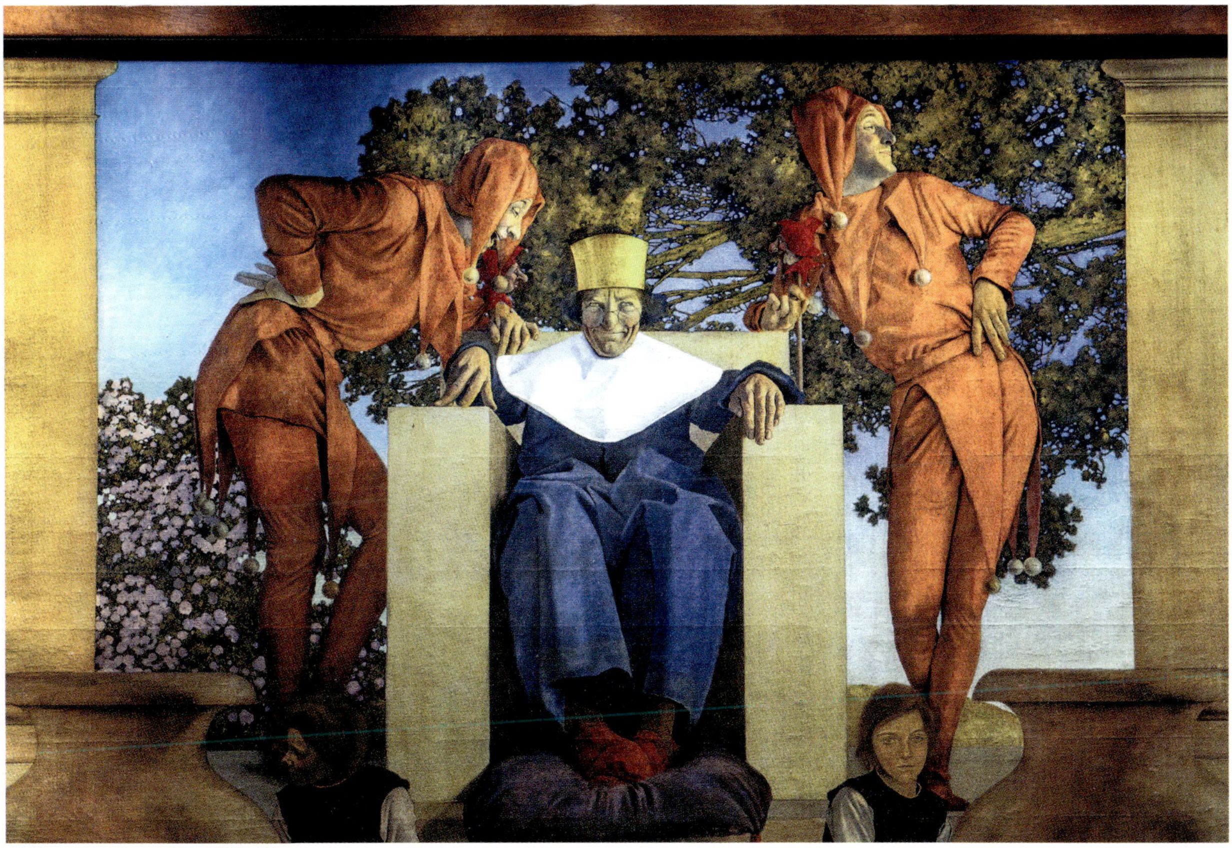

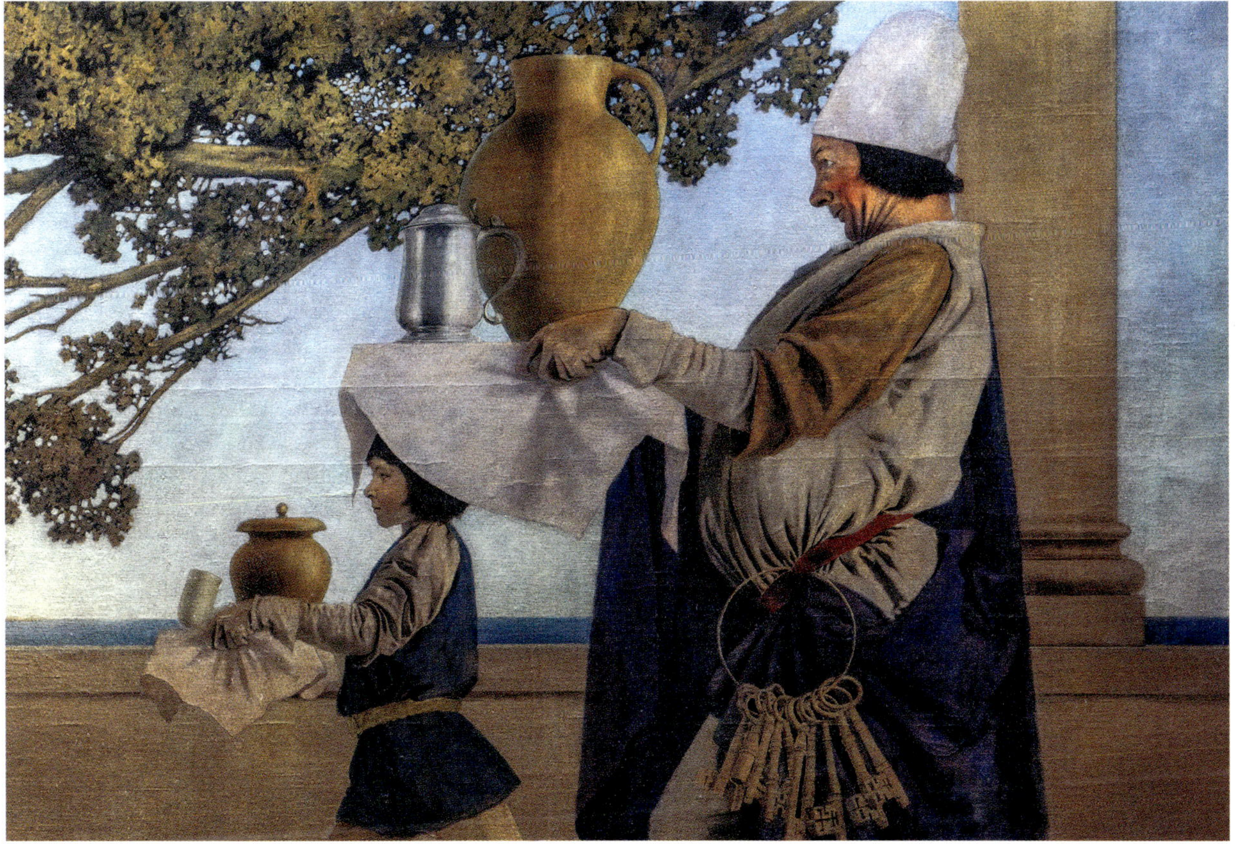

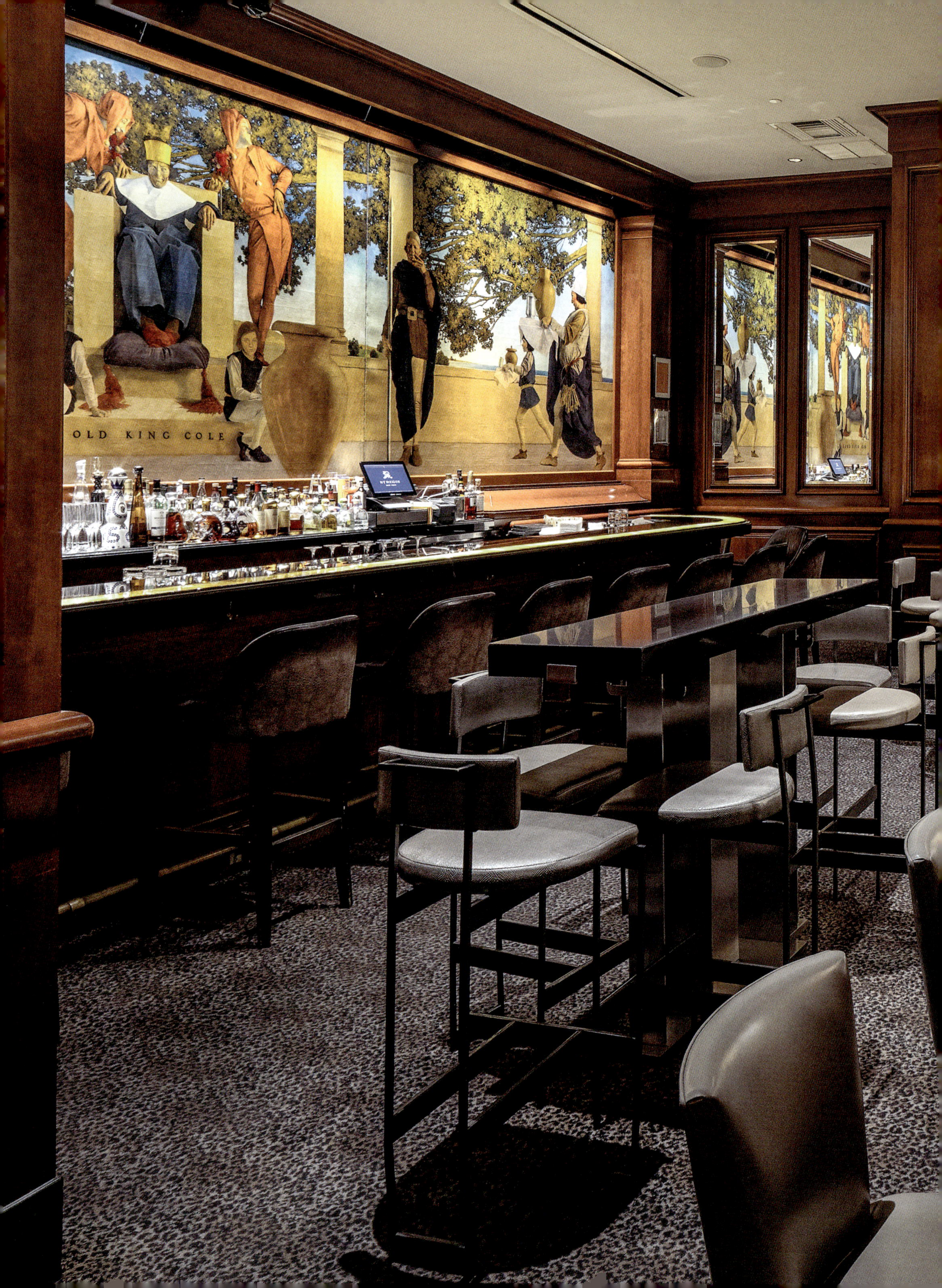
OLD KING COLE

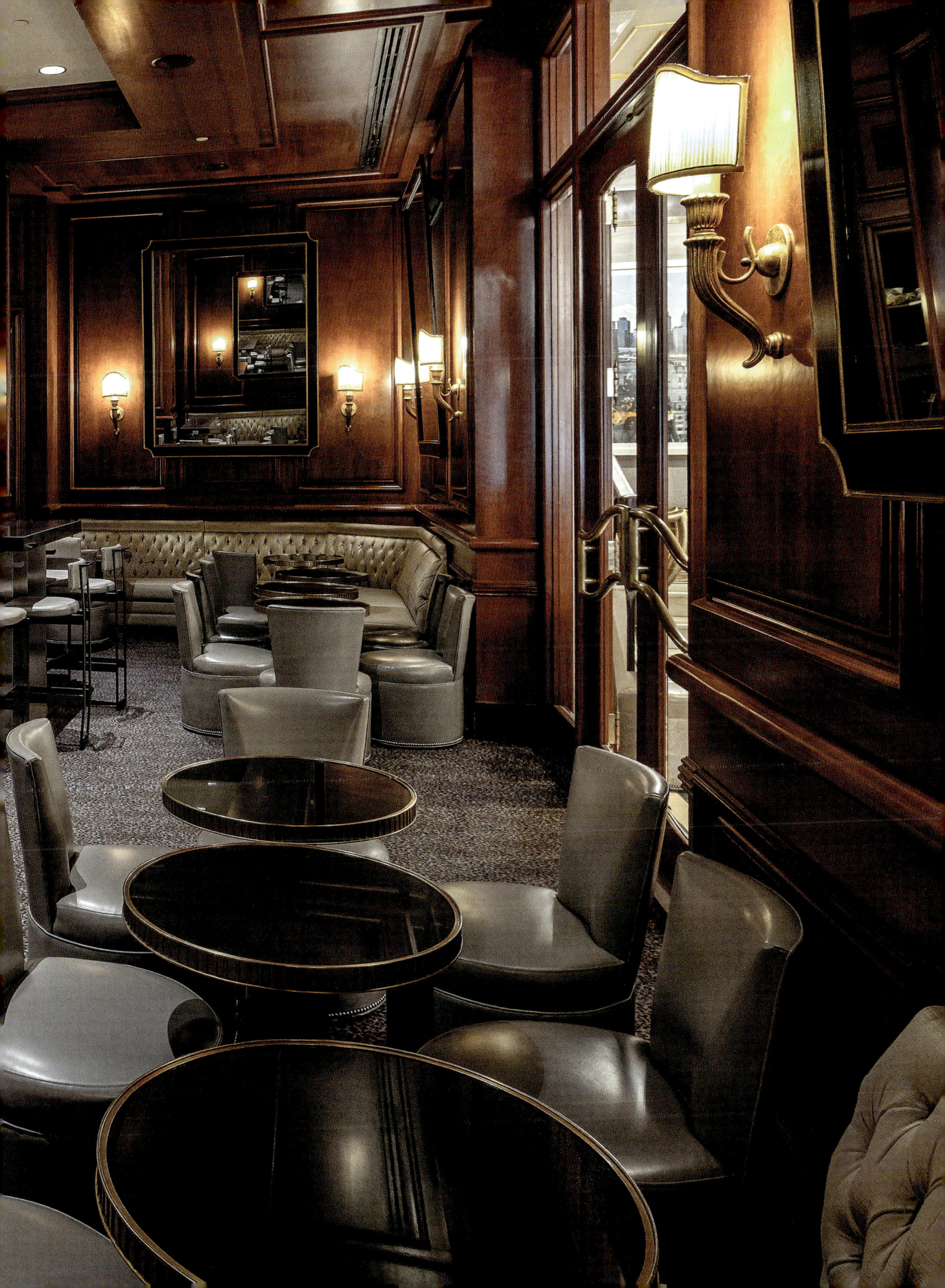

PETER McMANUS CAFE

152 SEVENTH AVENUE, CHELSEA

The history of Peter McManus Cafe is one for the books: it's the self-proclaimed oldest family-run bar in New York. Made famous as a setting in dozens of quintessential films and television shows set in the city, the saloon was first opened by Irish immigrant brothers James and Peter McManus in 1936. It has stayed in the family for four generations and is today faithfully run by Peter's great-grandson, Justin McManus.

Located at 152 Seventh Avenue in Manhattan's Chelsea neighborhood, the McManus of today wasn't James and Peter's first bar. In 1911, they opened McManus as a watering hole for longshoremen working the loading docks at the nearby river on West Fifty-Fifth Street. That first bar "closed because of a stupid thing called Prohibition," Justin revealed to the food magazine *Edible Manhattan* in 2017.

As the city cracked down on booze in the 1920s, the brothers pivoted the space into a general store, funneling their liquor business into hush-hush speakeasies. Their success inspired them to move into larger digs downtown on Seventh Avenue, a few years after the Volstead Act was repealed.

The Peter McManus Cafe opened during a period of rapid transformation in Chelsea. During the early twentieth century, the neighborhood had been a hotspot for the pre–World War I film industry. It became an industrial hub in the 1930s with the construction of the West Side Freight Line and West Side Highway. The London Terrace—at the time one of the world's largest apartment blocks—had opened just six years before the bar.

Now, even as the surrounding neighborhood has transformed into a high-end cultural and residential area, the bar has preserved its charm and simplicity throughout the decades. A 2001 *New York Times* obituary for James J. McManus Sr.—son of Peter—recalled a time that the paper's restaurant critic, Bryan Miller, visited the barkeep to learn his secret to the perfect Rob Roy cocktail: "Don't bruise the vermouth."

Current owner Justin grew up in the bar, and told *Edible Manhattan* that he even remembers pouring a couple of beers here and there as a young child. After studying at Cornell and working at Danny Meyer's buzzy Union Square Hospitality Group, he returned to the family business. Although he's done some modernizing—like adding credit cards and updating draft lines—he's kept the spirit of McManus largely intact.

As a testament to keeping things in the family, the bar is remarkably well-preserved, from the hand-carved woodwork and crown molding to the rare terrazzo floors that can no longer be produced. But perhaps the most notable design feature is the original stained-glass windows made by Tiffany in New York City, which can be found in the front facade as well as behind the 75-foot (23-meter) long bar, which is custom-made from seven different types of wood.

Mementos and cultural ephemera around McManus also speak to its rich history. A vintage ceiling price list from the early days hangs on the walls. It's one of the few bars with two original phone booths. The neighborhood spot's decor includes red-and-green-upholstered chairs (the booths in the back room are covered in Kelly green, a color named after the common Irish surname and reminiscent of the isle's lush landscape).

It's this memorable decor that's served as a beloved shooting location for numerous films. Over the years the bar has welcomed stars ranging from Sean Connery in the 1986 fantasy action flick *Highlander* to Edward Norton, who used it in his 2000 rom-com *Keeping the Faith*. In more recent history, it's been seen on shows like *Saturday Night Live* and the irreverent comedy *Broad City*. Off-screen, it's been known as a haunt for the Upright Citizens Brigade since the days that the improv group was started by Amy Poehler and other comedians.

In 2015 the fate of the bar became uncertain after a developer purchased the building. But in a symbolic victory for family-owned holdouts across the city, Justin was able to negotiate a continuation of the lease. In the wake of that little scare, you can thankfully still stop in to McManus for a pint whenever you like.

And the next time you're looking for somewhere to celebrate St. Patrick's Day, why not head to this quintessential Irish drinking den? It's the busiest day of the year at McManus, which opens for business at 8 a.m. and typically serves some seven hundred pounds of their famous house-brined corned beef.

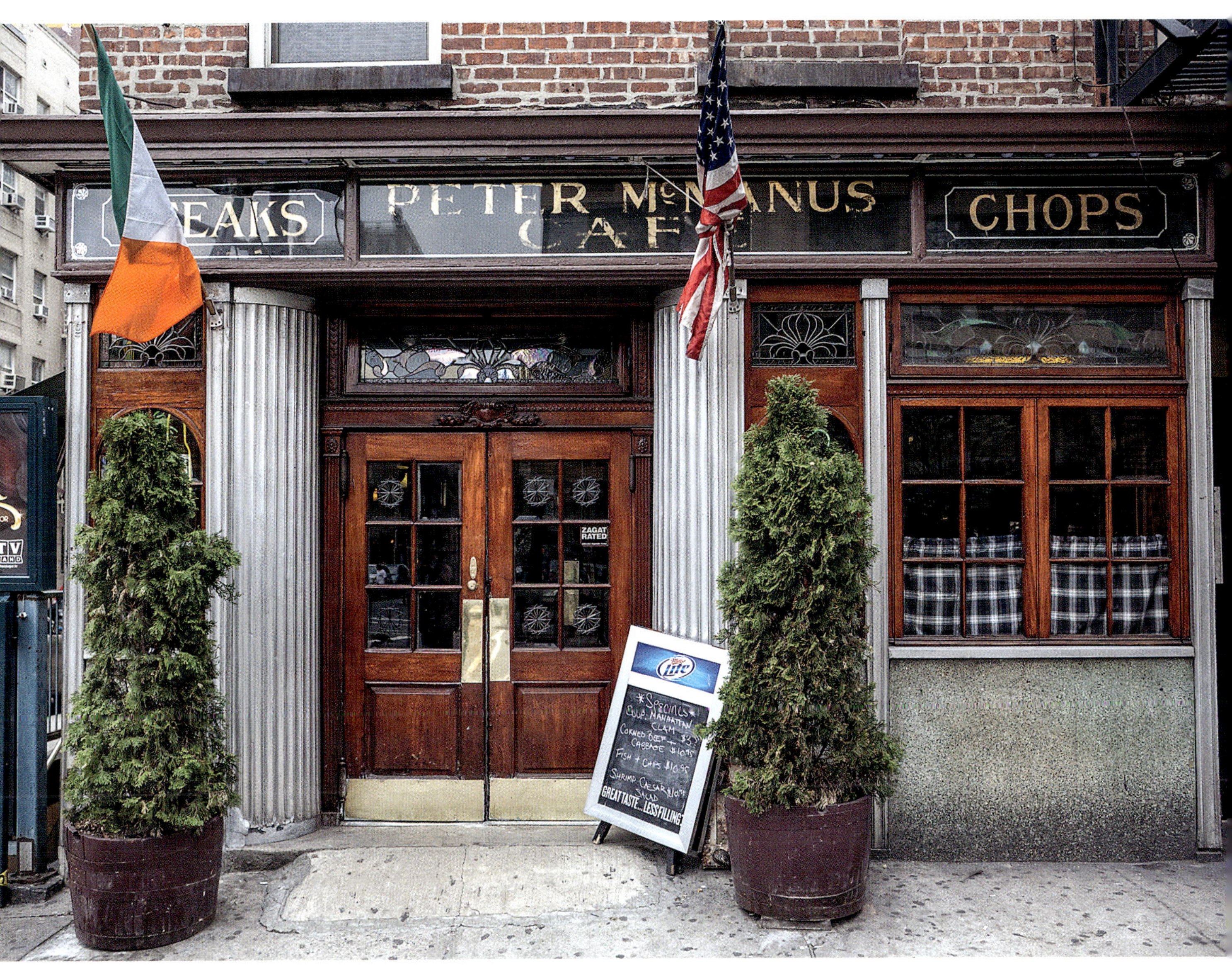

EAKS
PETER McMANUS
CAFE
CHOPS
ZAGAT
RATED
Miller Lite
SPECIALS
COLE MANHATTAN
CLAM $3.?
CORNED BEEF $?
CABBAGE $10.95
FISH + CHIPS $10.95
SHRIMP CAESAR $10.95
SALAD
GREAT TASTE...LESS FILLING

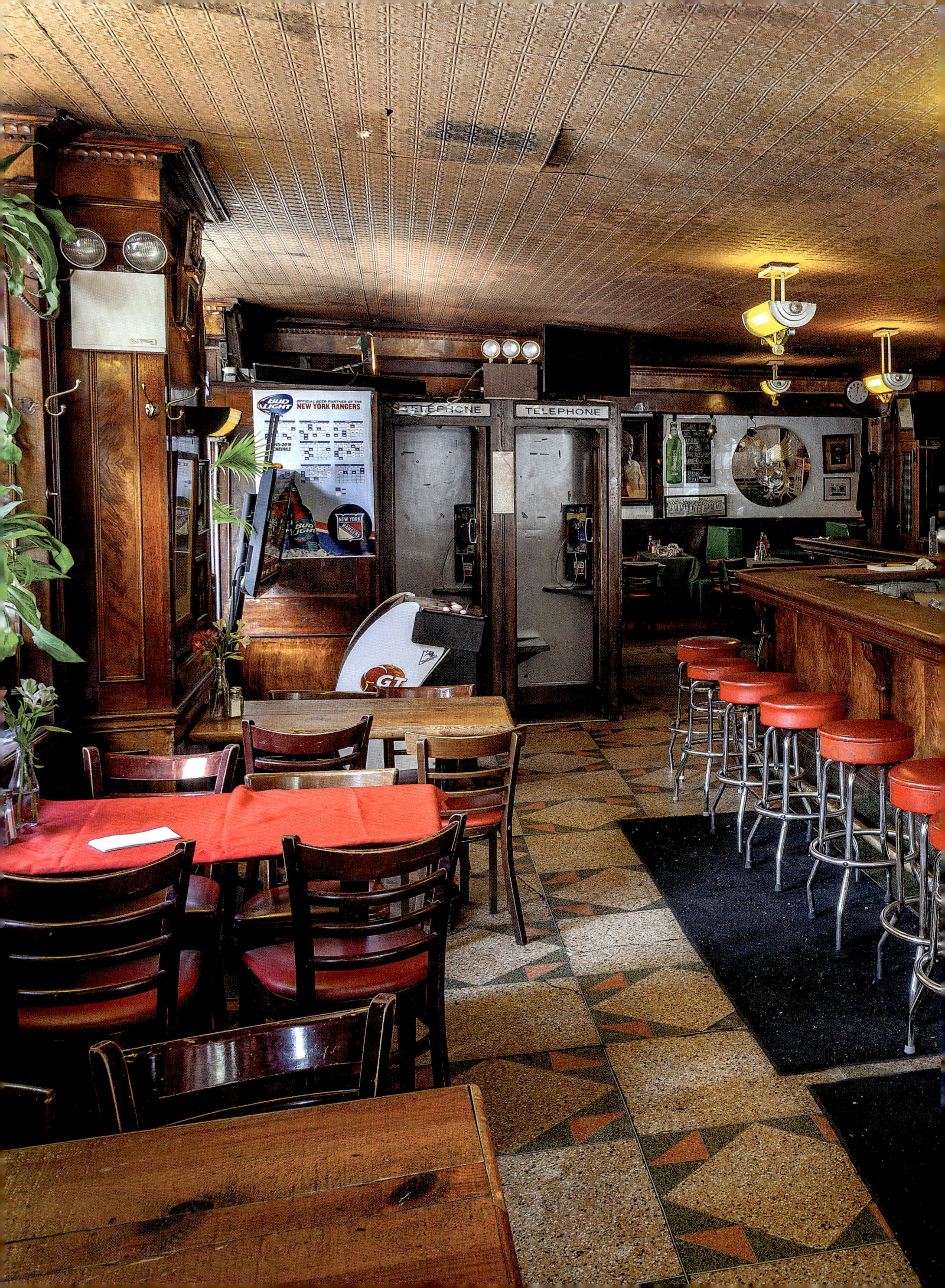
TELEPHONE
TELEPHONE
BUD LIGHT
OFFICIAL BEER PARTNER OF THE
NEW YORK RANGERS
2015-2016
SCHEDULE
GT

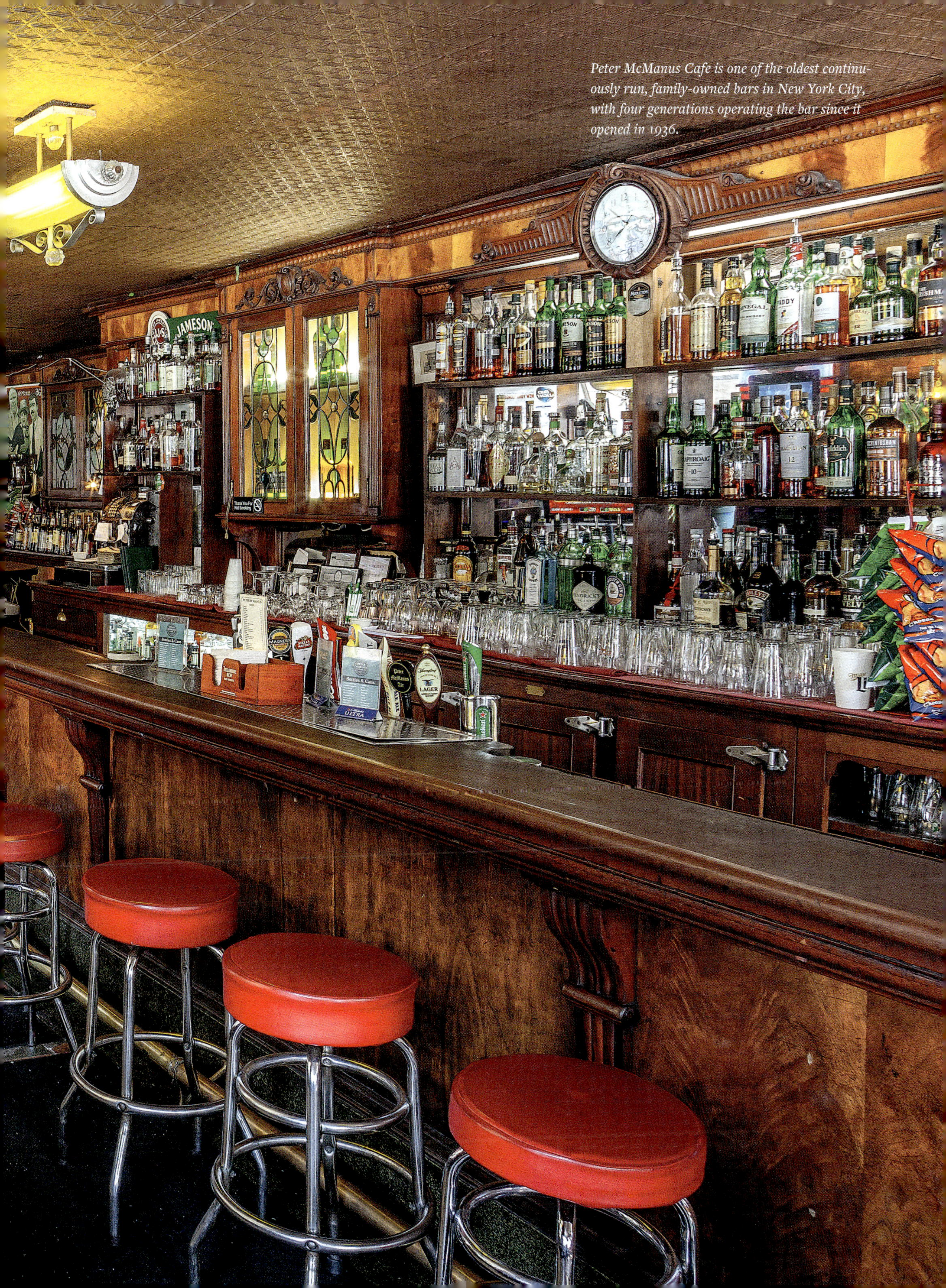

Peter McManus Cafe is one of the oldest continuously run, family-owned bars in New York City, with four generations operating the bar since it opened in 1936.

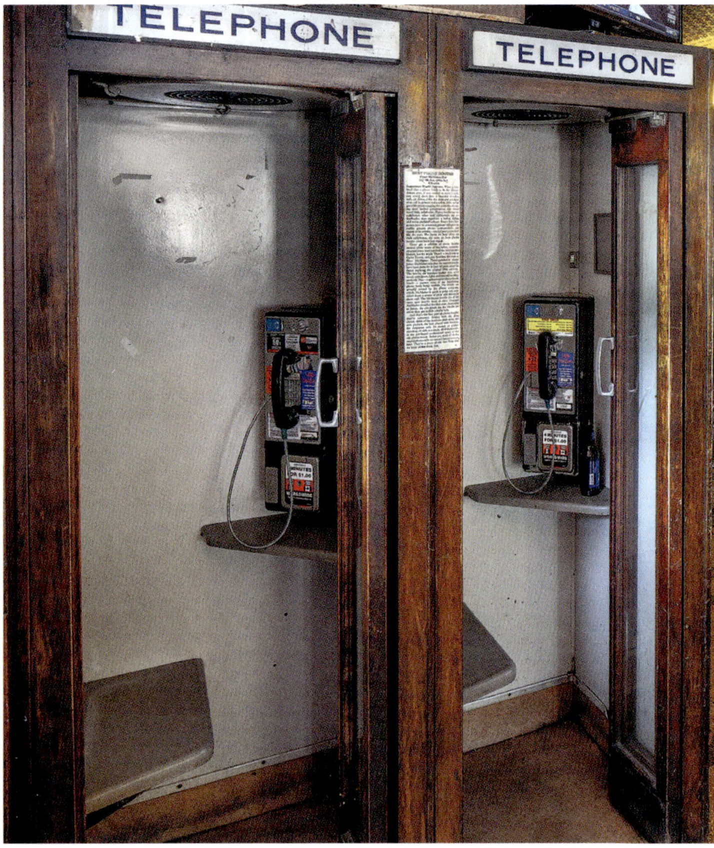

GREAT BARS OF NEW YORK CITY

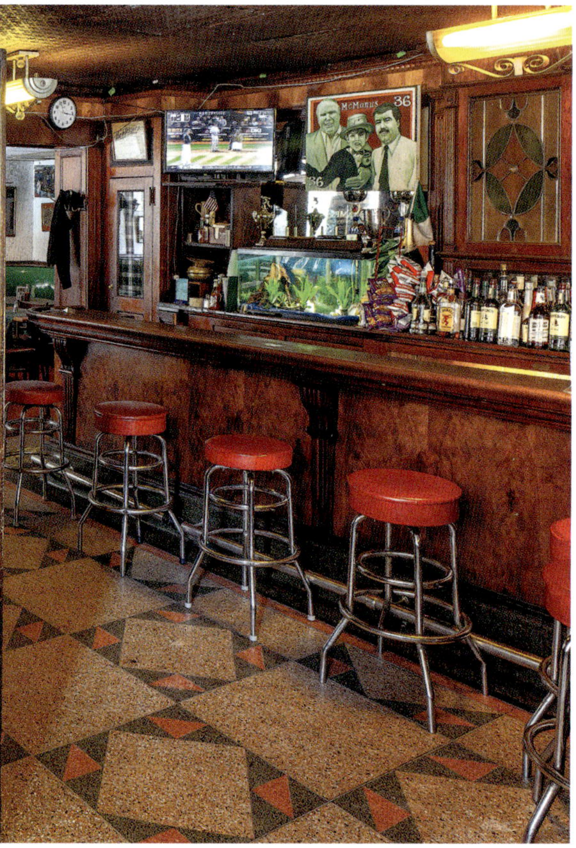

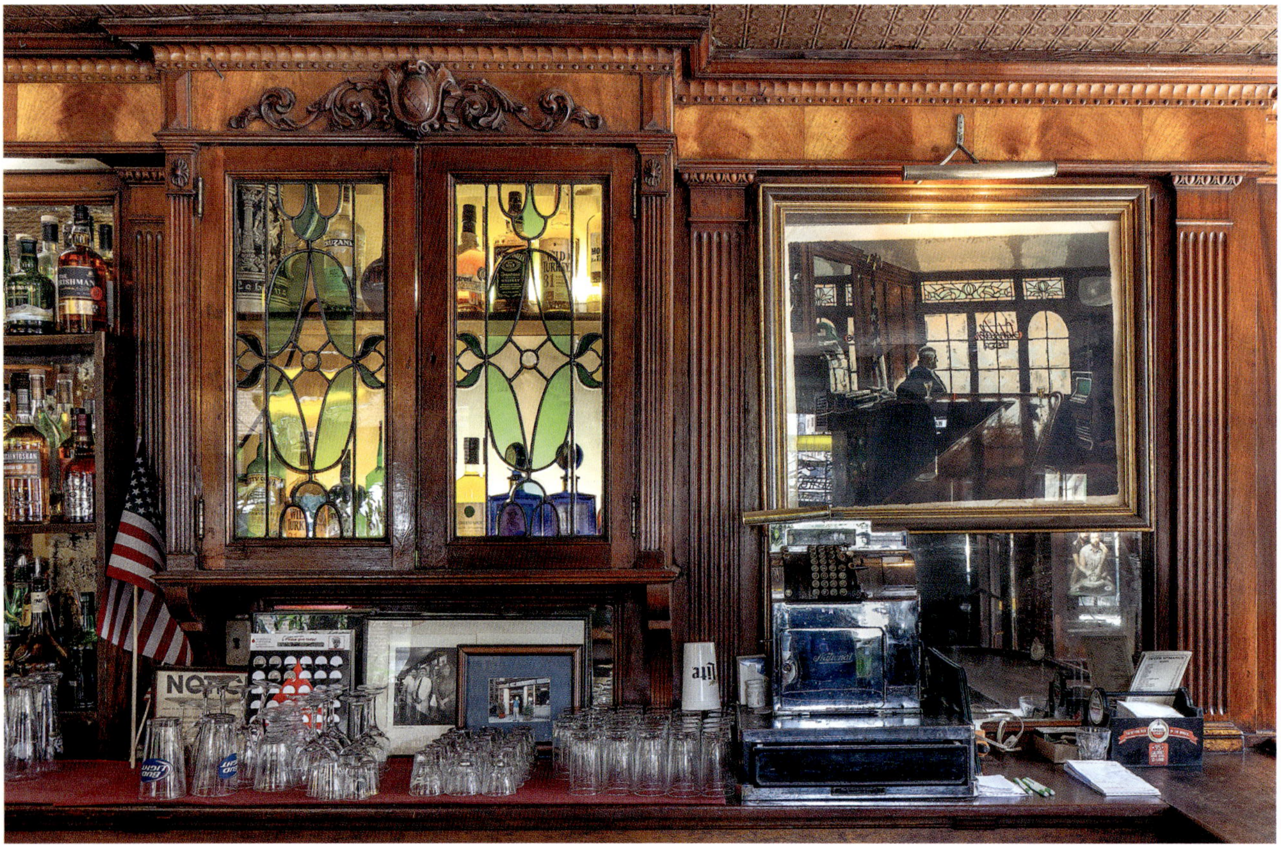

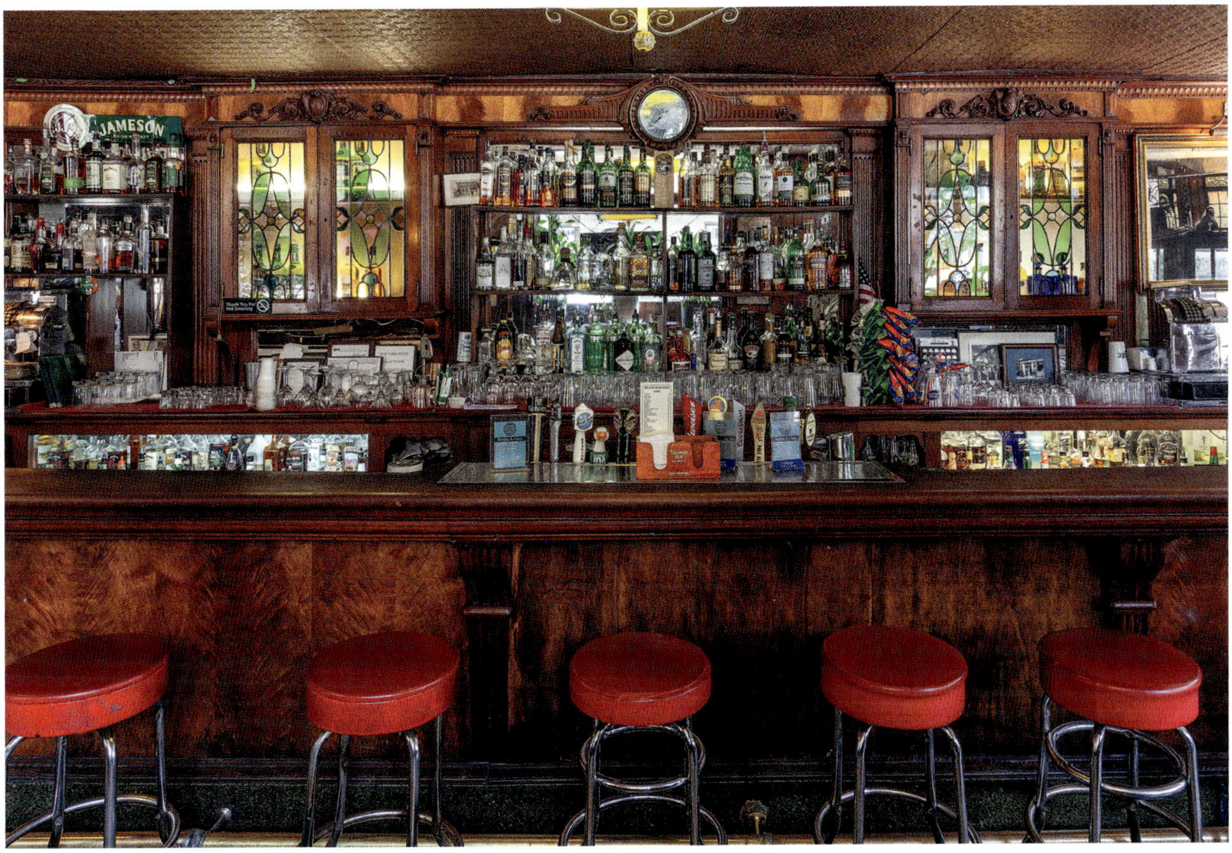

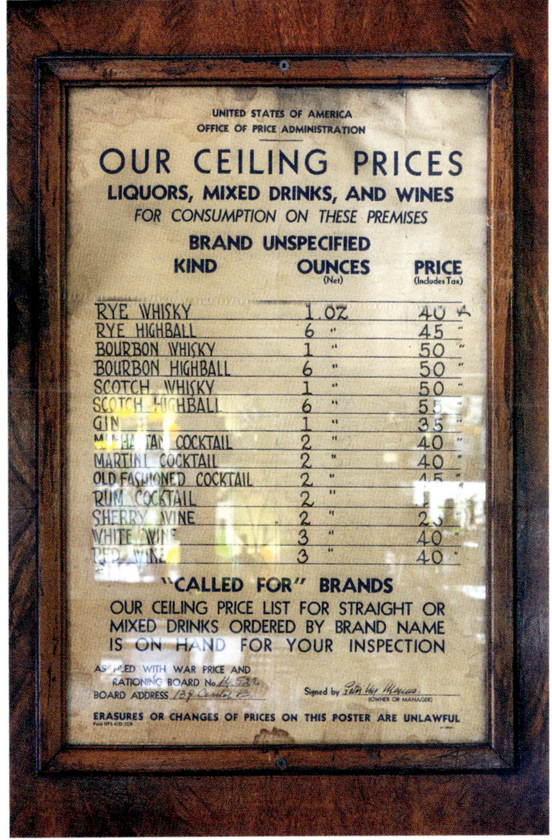

KIND	OUNCES (Net)	PRICE (Includes Tax)
RYE WHISKY	1 OZ	40 ¢
RYE HIGHBALL	6 "	45 "
BOURBON WHISKY	1 "	50 "
BOURBON HIGHBALL	6 "	50 "
SCOTCH WHISKY	1 "	50 "
SCOTCH HIGHBALL	6 "	55
GIN	1 "	35 "
MANHATTAN COCKTAIL	2 "	40 "
MARTINI COCKTAIL	2 "	40 "
OLD FASHIONED COCKTAIL	2 "	45 "
RUM COCKTAIL	2 "	
SHERRY WINE	2 "	25
WHITE WINE	3 "	40 "
RED WINE	3 "	40 "

OPPOSITE TOP   *It's one of the few bars in the city that still has two original phone booths.*

ABOVE   *The custom-made wooden bar is 75 feet (23 meters) long and and carved from seven different types of wood. The backbar also features Tiffany stained glass.*

RIGHT   *A vintage ceiling price list from the bar's early days hangs on the wall.*

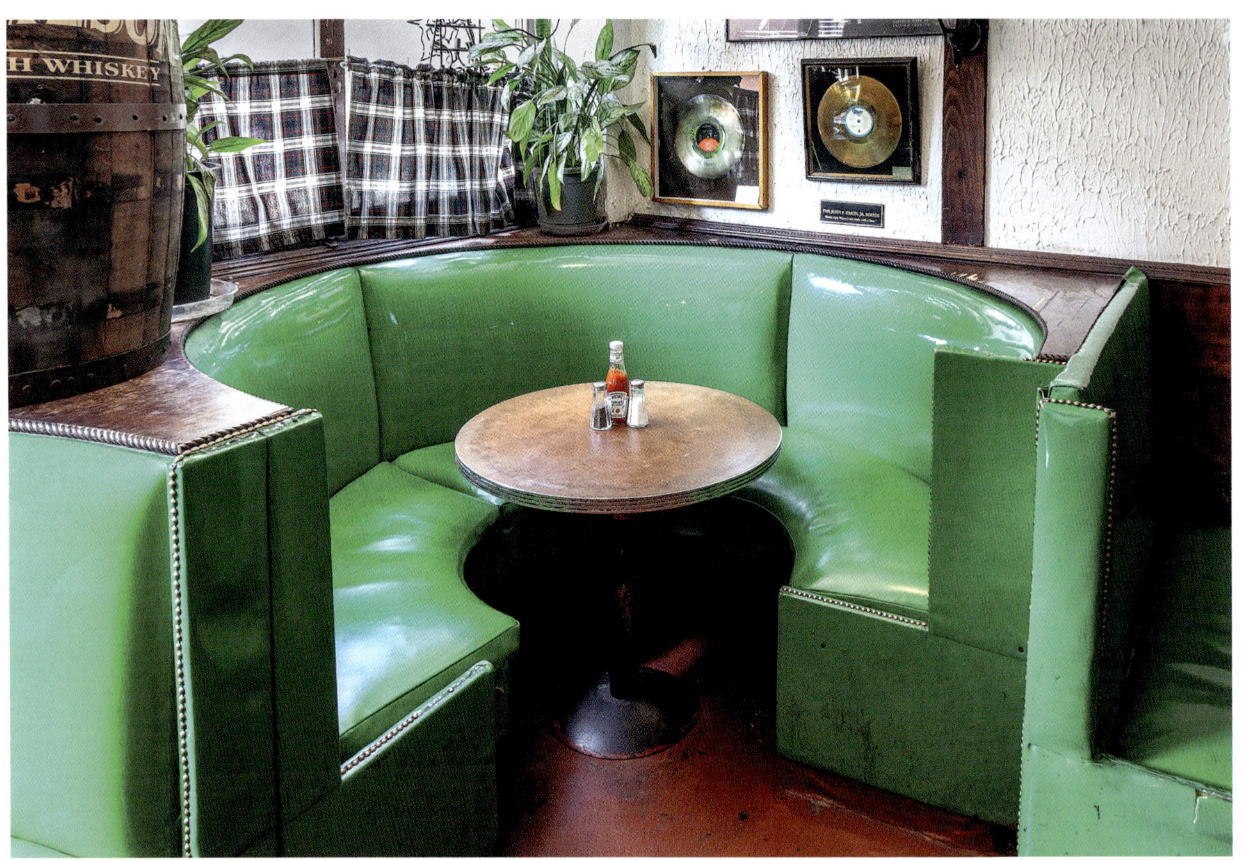

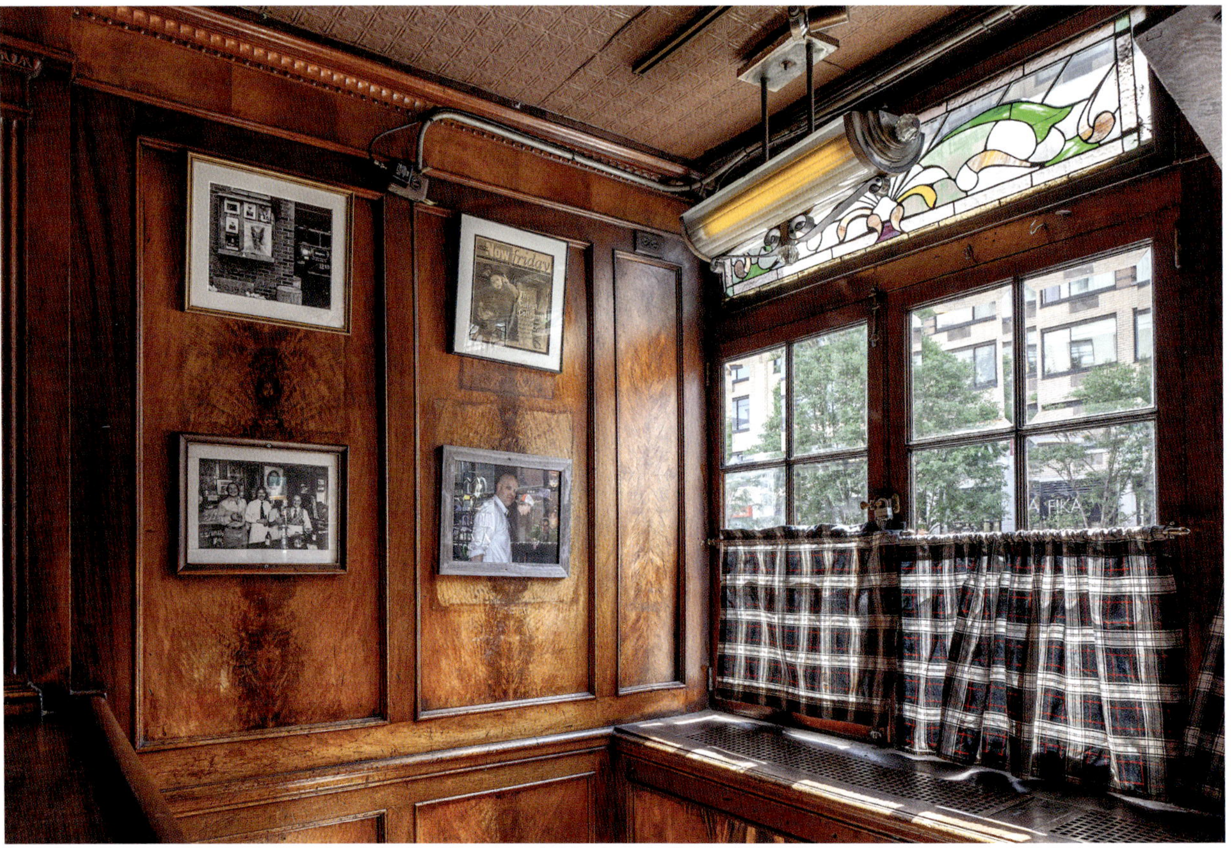

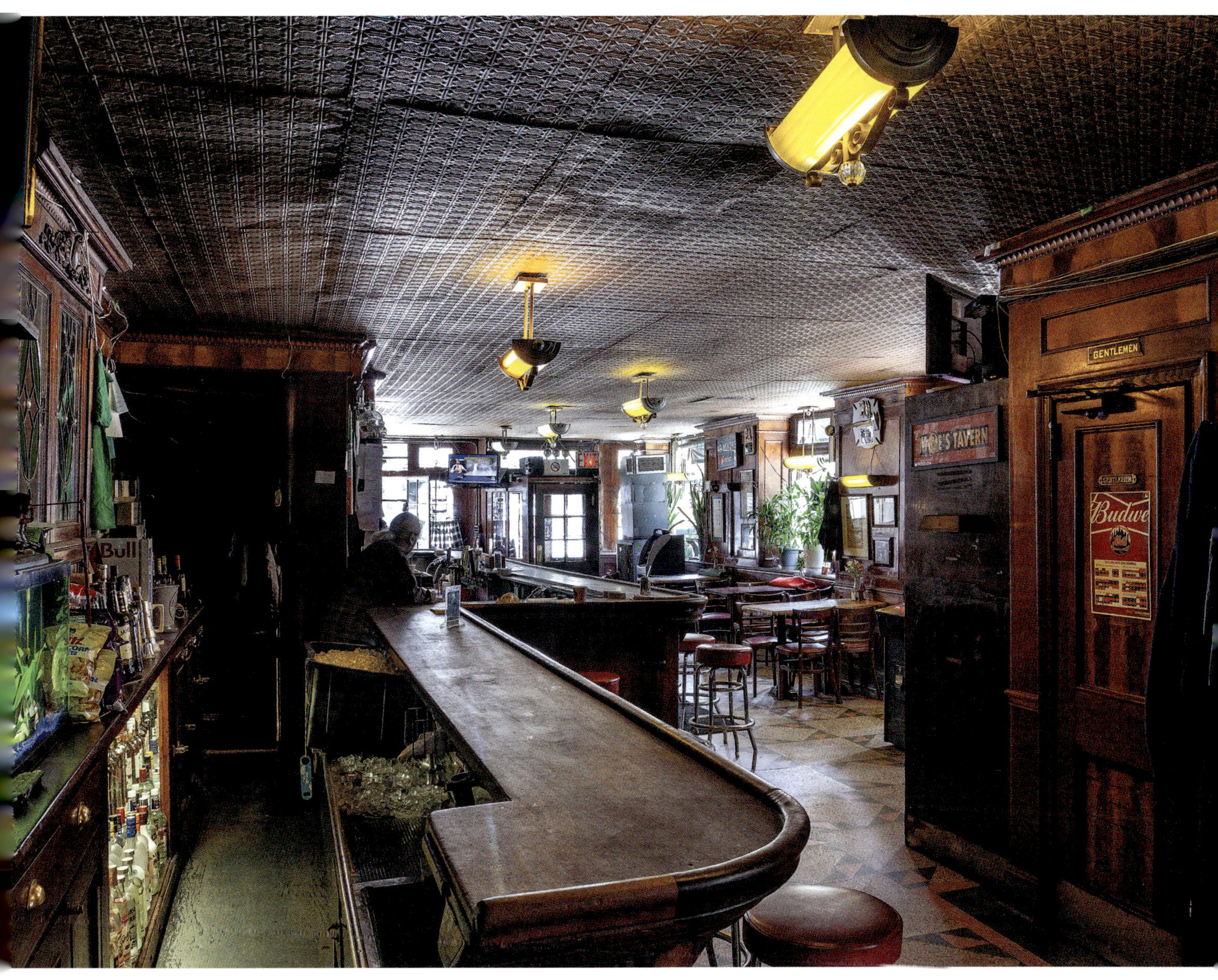

OPPOSITE TOP *The booths in the back room are upholstered in Kelly green, a color named after the common Irish last name and reminiscent of Ireland's lush green landscape.*

OPPOSITE BOTTOM *The stained-glass windows in the facade are original and were made by Tiffany.*

PARKSIDE LOUNGE

317 EAST HOUSTON STREET, LOWER EAST SIDE

From Mafia ties to musical theater, Parkside Lounge's colorful history makes it one of New York City's most mysterious dives that's still beloved by those in the know. Recognizable by its two-piece neon sign from the 1950s, the bar sits at the quiet corner of Houston and Attorney Streets—a sort of middle ground where the East Village meets the Lower East Side.

The building at 318 East Houston Street was constructed as a bar back in 1908, though it didn't take on the name Parkside Lounge until the 1950s, when a different bar, also named Parkside, burned down three blocks away. (That bar had been located next to a park area, hence the name.) Many of the finer details of Parkside Lounge's history have been lost to time, but there is a record that it was once known as the "7-4 Social Club." Its current owner, Christopher Lee, had unearthed from the building's basement a 1940 liquor license given to the Seven to Four Social Club, Inc. by the State of New York.

The space has lived many lives: rumors say it's been a Mafia hangout, an ice house, a discreet place to buy and sell stolen goods, and even a funeral home. In the basement, there's a boarded-up tunnel that goes all the way to the East River, which some believe could have been used for the disposal of bodies...but perhaps it was for drawing water.

Naturally, with all of these urban legends, stories of ghost sightings are frequent. Patrons and staff have reported recurring sightings of an older man as well as a teenage girl. Then there are the unexplained phenomena, like electricity malfunctions and flying objects. Numerous psychics, clairvoyants, and paranormal experts of all kinds have visited the bar to communicate with the spirits.

As the Lower East Side has evolved, so have Parkside Lounge's clientele and offerings, trading its rougher crowd for a more creative one. Since taking over in 2009, Lee has revamped the bar's spacious back room with a new PA system, flat screen TVs, and projector screens. The space is now reserved for live music and entertainment-based events, like stand-up comedy, salsa dancing, and an array of experimental theater works. These include performances from drag queen Christeene as well as Claywoman, a fictional alien alter ego portrayed by actor Michael Cavadias.

Lee, who moved to New York from Louisiana in 1998, first started as a bartender, eventually becoming an operating partner in 2009. One thing led to another, and he ended up on the lease. Living down the street from Parkside, he told the online drinks magazine Punch that he stumbled in one day and was reminded of a bar in New Orleans.

Speaking to the blog Untapped Cities, he said he wanted to channel some of the Gulf Coast flavor he knew into what he calls a "neo-dive bar." According to Punch, this meant adding photos of old Loyola University baseball teams and of the Cane River, a 30-mile (48-kilometer) stretch of Louisiana's Red River. And to deal with the hauntings, he brought in a French Quarter tarot reader to recite prayers, burn sage, and light candles to ward off any potential negative energy.

Fittingly, since 2009, Parkside has become popular with Saints football fans looking to catch a game with the like-minded. That started with the team's Super Bowl run that year but has kept up ever since.

Today, Parkside is a fun and funky neighborhood spot where you never know exactly what you'll find—but the cheap drinks and pool table are always reliable. And if you're ever in search of a late-night standby, it stays open till 4 a.m. every night of the week.

OPPOSITE   *Parkside Lounge has kept its original two-piece neon sign from the 1950s.*

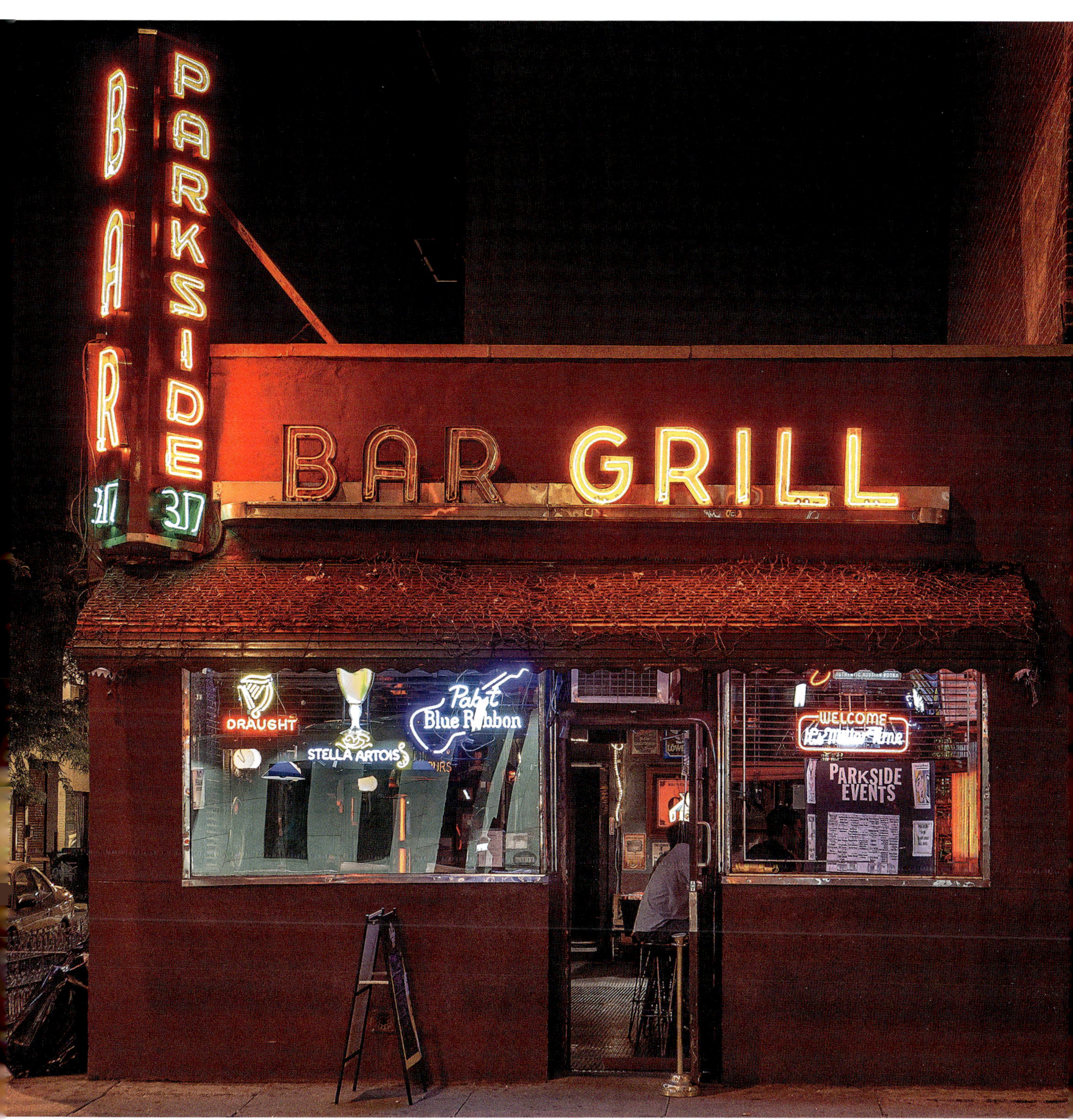

BAR
PARKSIDE
317
317
BAR GRILL
DRAUGHT
STELLA ARTOIS
Pabst
Blue Ribbon
AUTHENTIC RUSSIAN VODKA
WELCOME
PARKSIDE
EVENTS

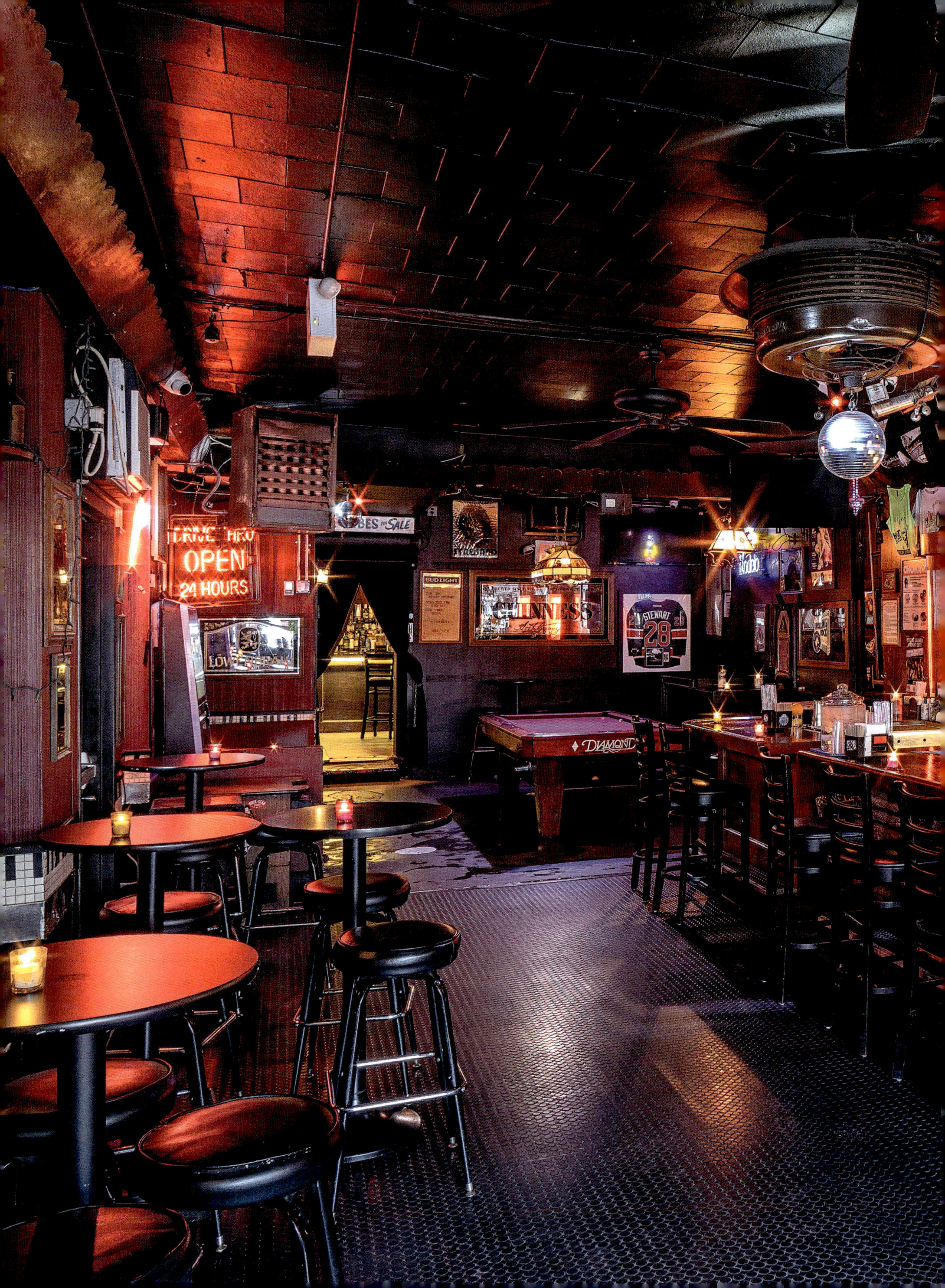
DRIVE THRU
OPEN
24 HOURS
TUBES for SALE
BUD LIGHT
GUINNESS
STEWART
28
DIAMOND

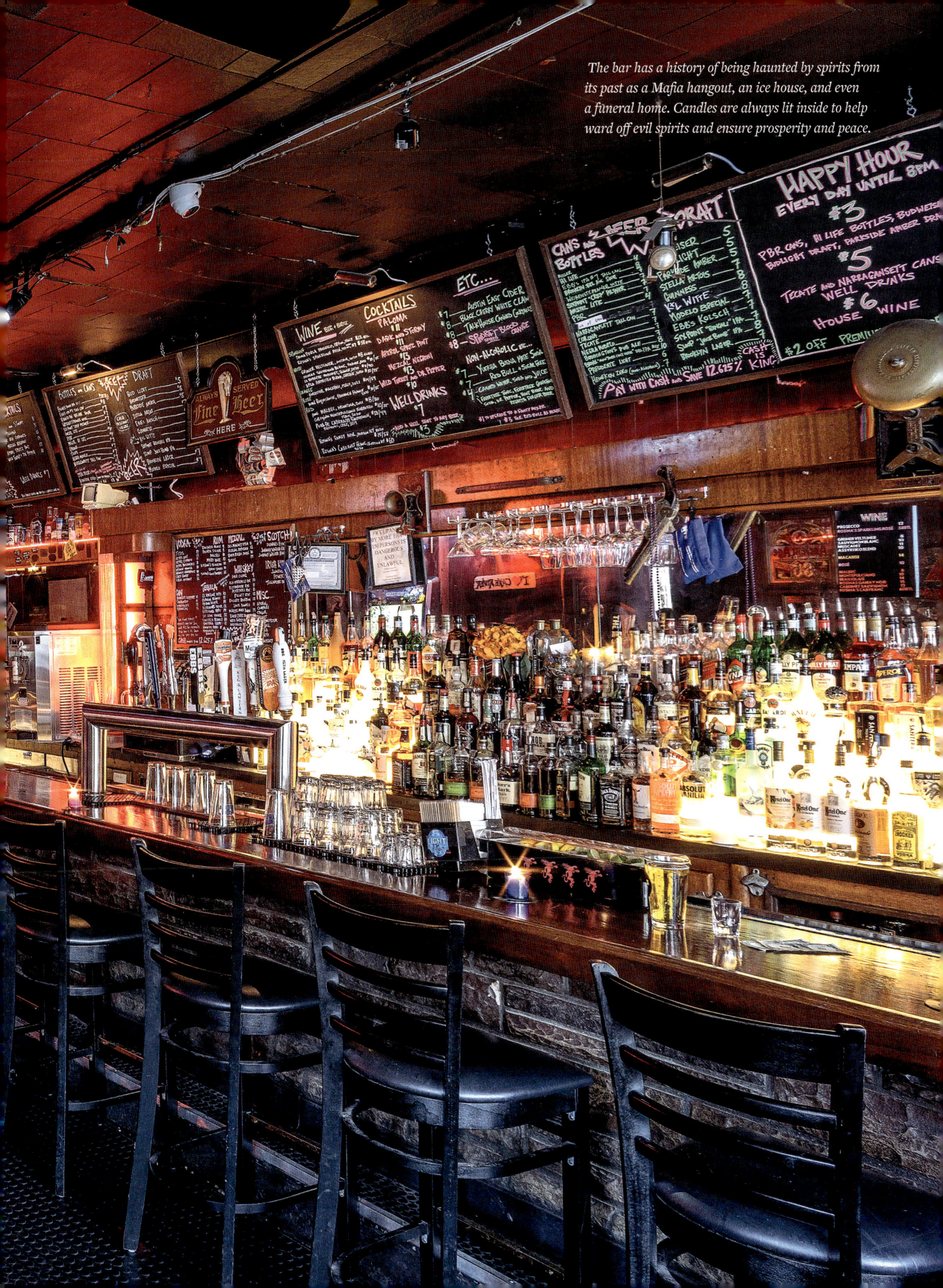

The bar has a history of being haunted by spirits from its past as a Mafia hangout, an ice house, and even a funeral home. Candles are always lit inside to help ward off evil spirits and ensure prosperity and peace.

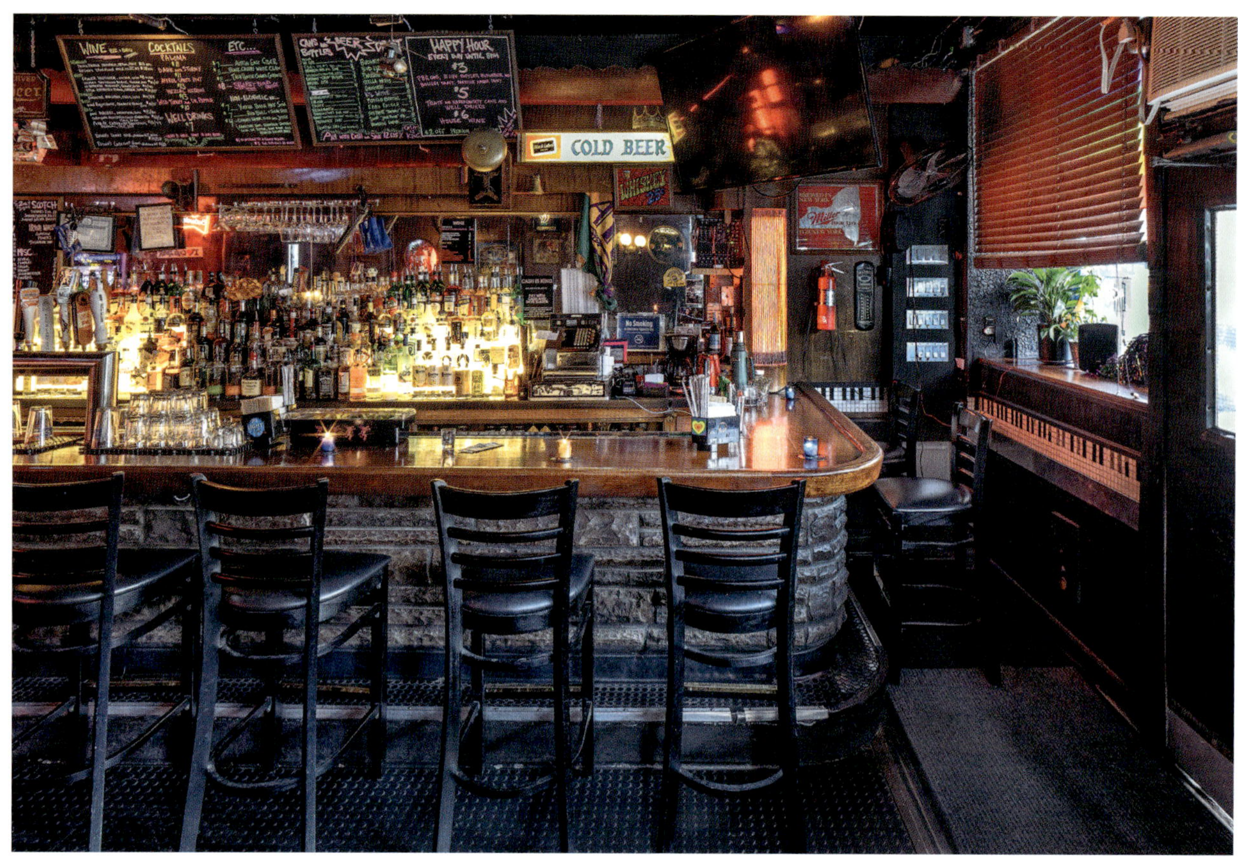

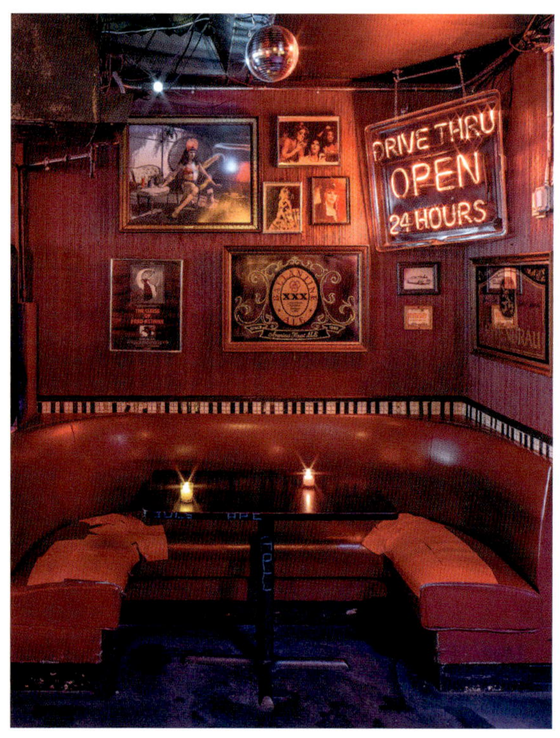

ABOVE *Although the building Parkside Lounge is currently located in has legally housed a bar since the 1940s, it was not named Parkside until 1956.*

OPPOSITE TOP *Parkside Lounge retains its classic dive bar atmosphere, but is now also known as a venue for live music, stand-up comedy, and performance art.*

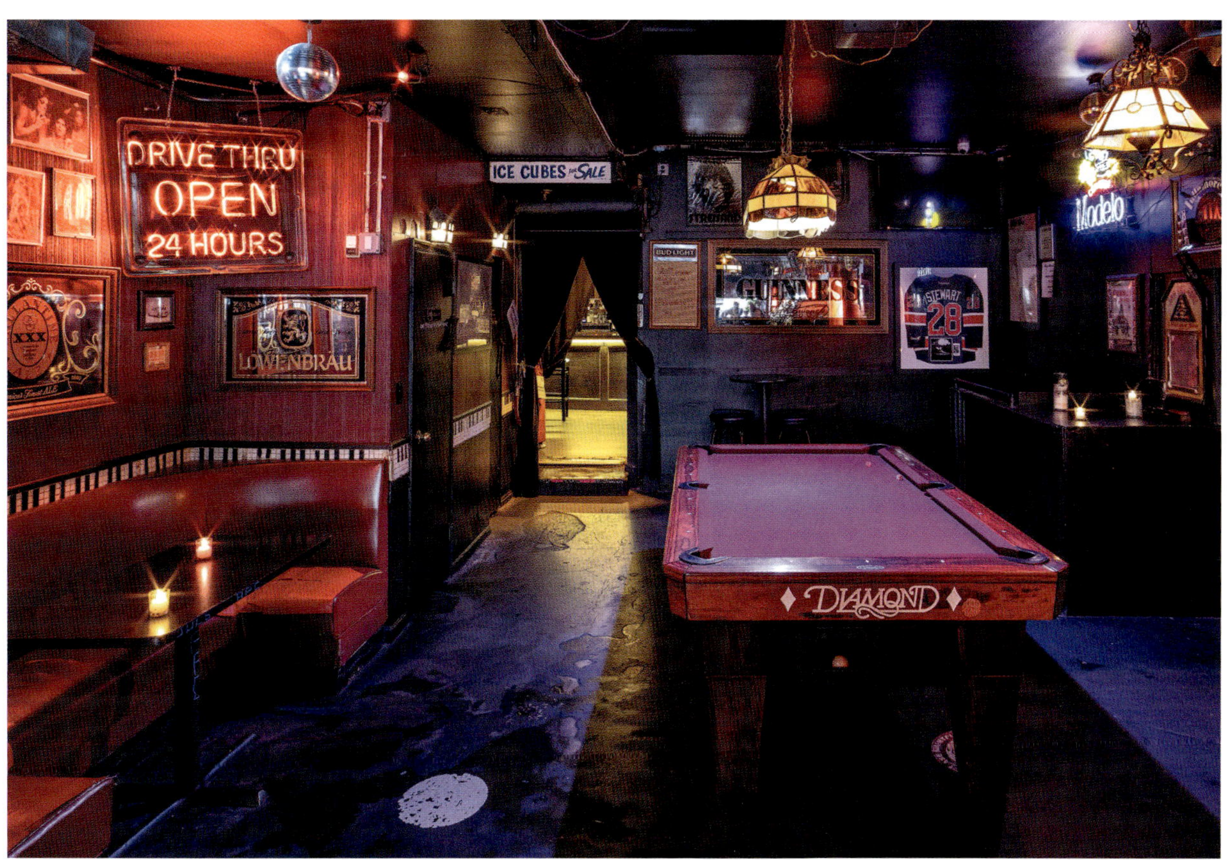
DRIVE THRU OPEN 24 HOURS
LÖWENBRÄU
ICE CUBES FOR SALE
GUINNESS
STEWART 28
Modelo
DIAMOND

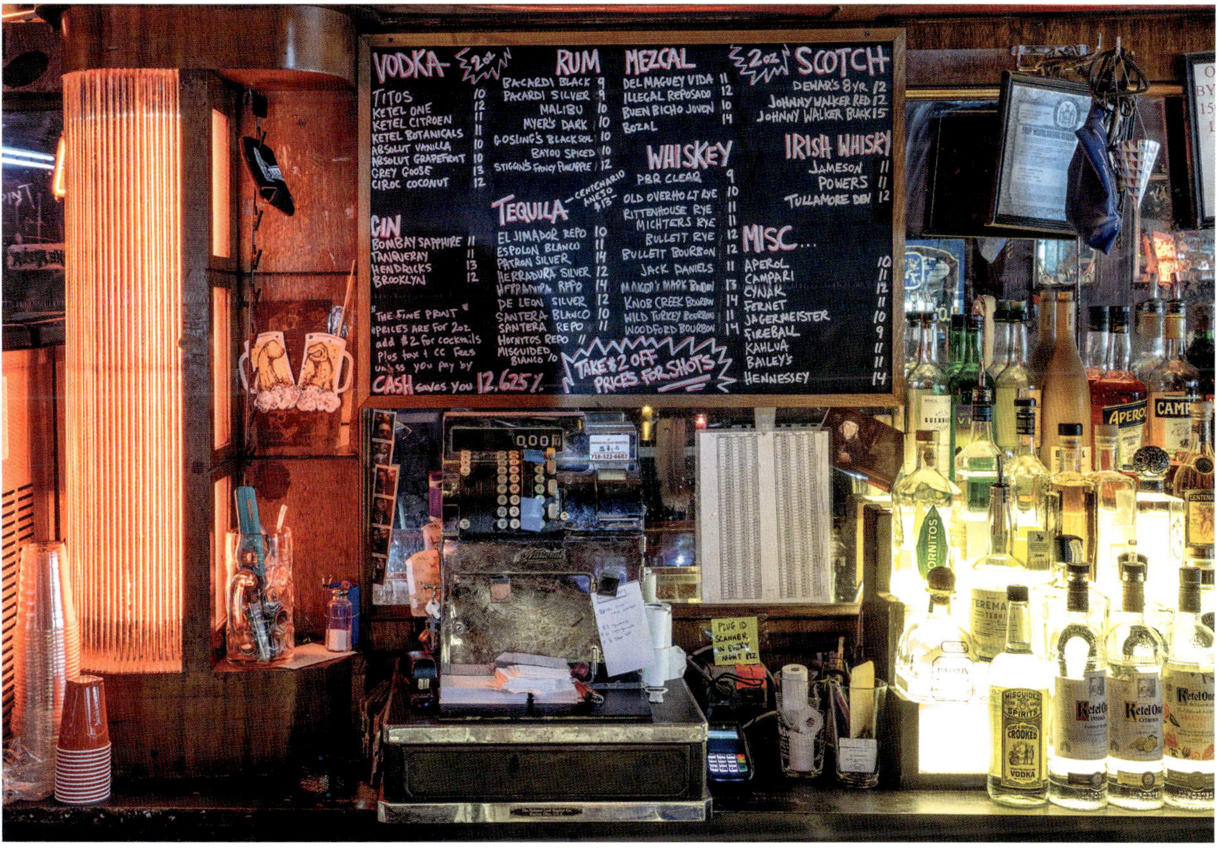
VODKA 2 oz
TITOS 10
KETEL ONE 12
KETEL CITROEN 11
KETEL BOTANICALS 11
ABSOLUT VANILLA 10
ABSOLUT GRAPEFRUIT 10
GREY GOOSE 13
CIROC COCONUT 12

GIN
BOMBAY SAPPHIRE 11
TANQUERAY 11
HENDRICKS 13
BROOKLYN 12

* THE FINE PRINT *
*PRICES ARE FOR 2oz.
add $2 for cocktails
plus tax & CC fees
unless you pay by
CASH saves you 12,625%.

RUM
BACARDI BLACK 9
PACARDI SILVER 9
MALIBU 10
MYER'S DARK 10
GOSLING'S BLACK SEAL 10
BAYOU SPICED 10
STIGGIN'S FANCY PINEAPPLE 12

TEQUILA — CENTENARIO ANEJO $13 —
EL JIMADOR REPO 10
ESPOLON BLANCO 11
PATRON SILVER 14
HERRADURA SILVER 12
HERRADURA REPO 14
DE LEON SILVER 12
SANTERA BLANCO 10
SANTERA REPO 11
HORNITOS REPO 11
MISGUIDED BIANCO 10

TAKE $2 OFF PRICES FOR SHOTS

MEZCAL
DEL MAGUEY VIDA 11
ILLEGAL REPOSADO 12
BUEN BICHO JOVEN 10
BOZAL 14

WHISKEY
PBR CLEAR 9
OLD OVERHOLT RYE 10
RITTENHOUSE RYE 11
MICHTERS RYE 11
BULLEIT RYE 12
BULLEIT BOURBON 12
JACK DANIELS 11
MAKER'S MARK BOURBON 13
KNOB CREEK BOURBON 14
WILD TURKEY BOURBON 11
WOODFORD BOURBON 14

2 oz SCOTCH
DEWAR'S 8 YR 12
JOHNNY WALKER RED 12
JOHNNY WALKER BLACK 15

IRISH WHISKY
JAMESON 11
POWERS 11
TULLAMORE DEW 12

MISC...
APEROL 10
CAMPARI 12
CYNAR 12
FERNET 10
JAGERMEISTER 10
FIREBALL 9
KAHLUA 11
BAILEY'S 11
HENNESSEY 14

DUBLIN HOUSE

225 WEST 79TH STREET, UPPER WEST SIDE

Though it first opened as a speakeasy in 1921, today Dublin House is impossible to miss. Set in a quiet part of the Upper West Side on Seventy-Ninth Street between Broadway and Amsterdam Avenue, the Guinness-pouring pub has been marked by a conspicuous and iconic one-story-tall neon sign depicting a green harp since 1933. In its early days, it was often the first thing to greet sailors docking at the Seventy-Ninth Street Boat Basin.

The origin story of both Dublin House and its signature neon sign are reminders of Prohibition's impact on New York City. In 1921, a year into the ban on booze, Dublin-born Irish immigrant John Caraway rented the townhouse to open a restaurant upstairs and a speakeasy downstairs. (According to the *New York Times*, it was at one point owned by Emily Post, the early-1900s society woman and etiquette writer.)

In 1933, when the ban was lifted, Caraway purchased the building outright, hanging the 12-foot (4-meter) sign outside. Designed by E. G. Clarke Inc., it's now one of the oldest functioning neon signs in existence. The curious long "tails" on the letters *T* and *P* in TAP give away the fact that the sign has been relettered: in its past life, it used to say RESTAURANT. Later, without a need for secrecy, it was able to be advertised as a taproom.

The Caraways would continue to operate Dublin House for decades, with John Caraway's nephew Chris Waters being the last in his family to take charge. In 2006 he sold it to longtime bartender Mike Cormican, who likewise hails from Ireland, specifically Galway, and had been working there since 1993. Cormican continues to run the bar to this day.

Much at Dublin House remains as it was in its early days, from its wood paneling to its two-person booths, large mirror, and original iron gates that still greet drinkers as they enter. However, subtle changes tell of a lengthy history: an old dumbwaiter has long since been replaced by a pay phone booth. There's a vintage Timex wall clock near the entrance. And the long wooden bar bears cigarette-inflicted scars that have been left as symbols of age.

As with many longtime bars in the city, they no longer serve food—though a 1939 guidebook published by the Works Projects Administration revealed Dublin House was once a place to try authentic Irish cuisine. It was perhaps this familiar fare that attracted the likes of famed mobster Mickey Featherstone of the Westies, an Irish American Mafia organization, who was a known patron.

Dublin House's weathered character and unique sense of place made it a coveted destination for producers of the award-winning Amazon show *The Marvelous Mrs. Maisel*, which debuted in 2017. The bar appears in a scene where characters Midge Maisel and Lenny Bruce grab a drink to commiserate their situation.

In 2021, Dublin House celebrated its centennial with three days of festivities. Meanwhile, the harp sign, which had fallen into disrepair, was restored to its former glory in 2022 after Jeff Friedman of the custom neon sign company Let There Be Neon organized a fundraiser, garnering the entire $15,000 needed within twenty-four hours. Cormican was there to flip the switch.

Today the sign remains illuminated whenever the bar is open, which is from 11 a.m. to 4 a.m. daily. Stepping in still feels like walking into the past: the long, narrow room—with its terrazzo floor and low ceilings—is still dark and cozy even when it's light outside. And while several televisions have been added to show sports, there's a back room that is just for parties and darts. And as always, there is Guinness flowing on tap.

"I think people keep coming back over the years because we are a no-nonsense bar—people come to us just for the Guinness," reveals longtime bartender Nicola Cusack. "In the past few years, I've noticed a lot of the younger generation coming here, and it's nice to see the newer crowd mixing with the older generation. It's a great balance."

OPPOSITE *Dublin House's twelve-foot (4-meter), one-story-tall, double-sided neon Irish harp was designed by E. G. Clarke Inc. in 1933 and is visible from blocks away.*

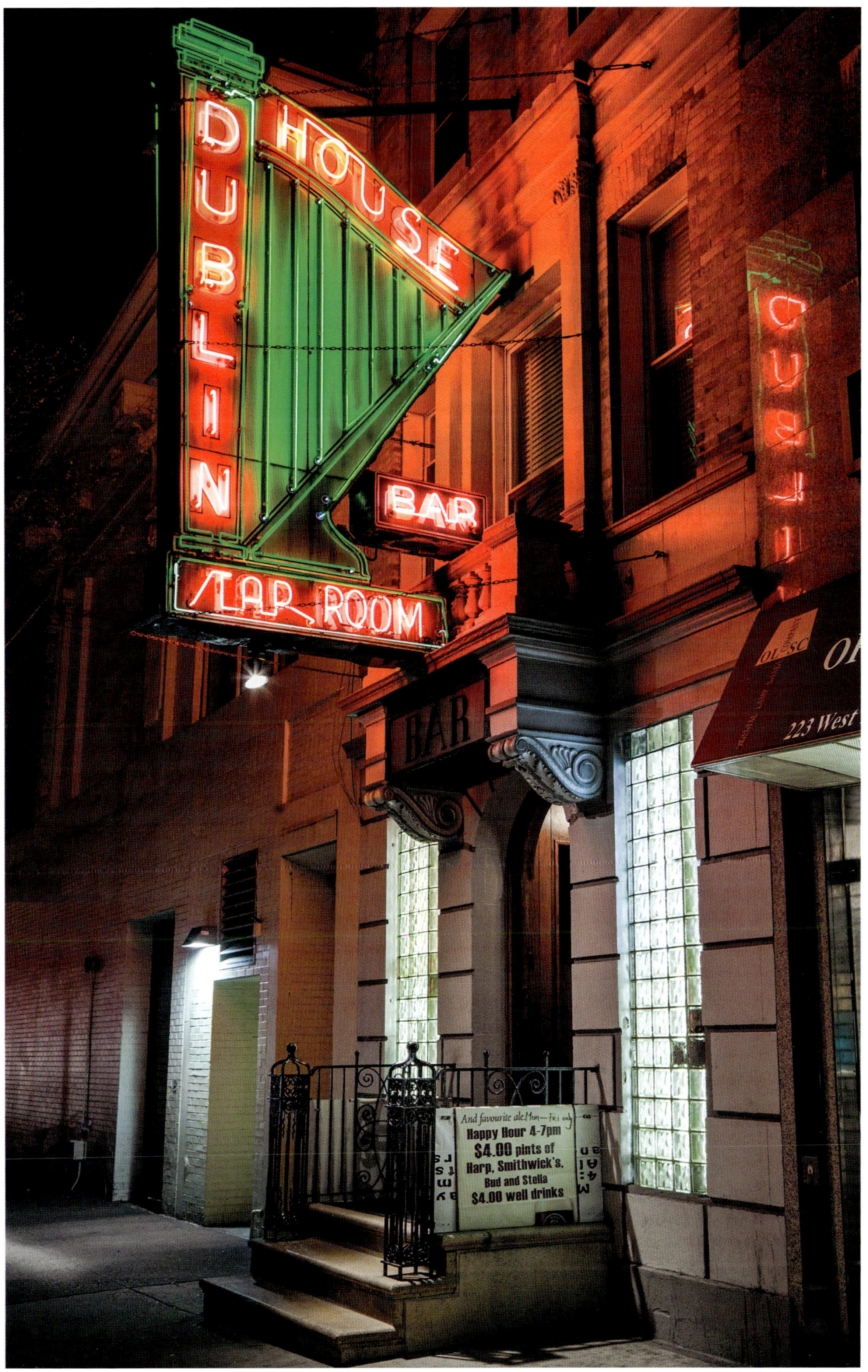

DUBLIN
HOUSE
BAR
TAP ROOM
BAR
And favourite ale Mon—Fri only
Happy Hour 4-7pm
$4.00 pints of
Harp, Smithwick's,
Bud and Stella
$4.00 well drinks
223 West

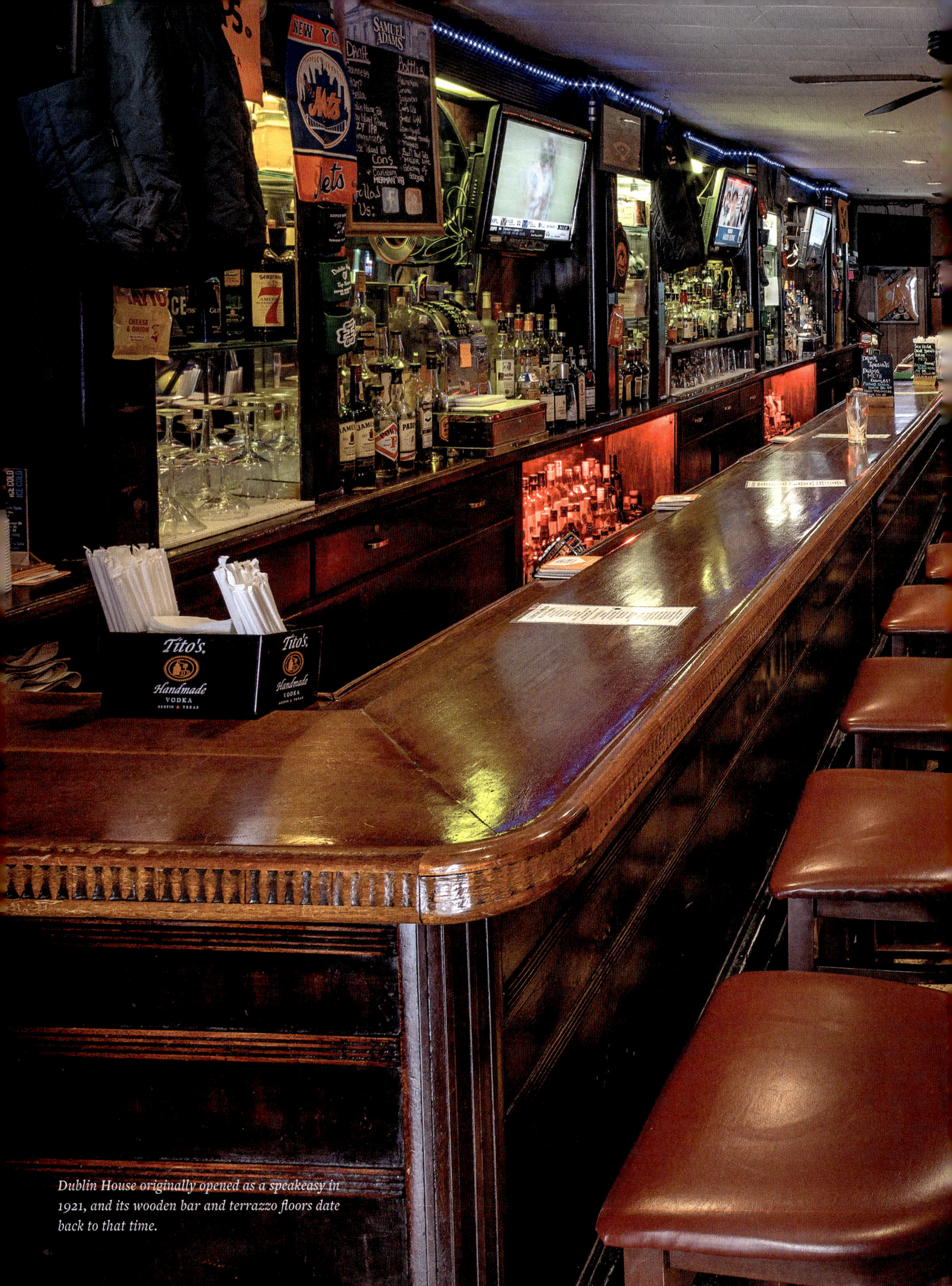

Dublin House originally opened as a speakeasy in 1921, and its wooden bar and terrazzo floors date back to that time.

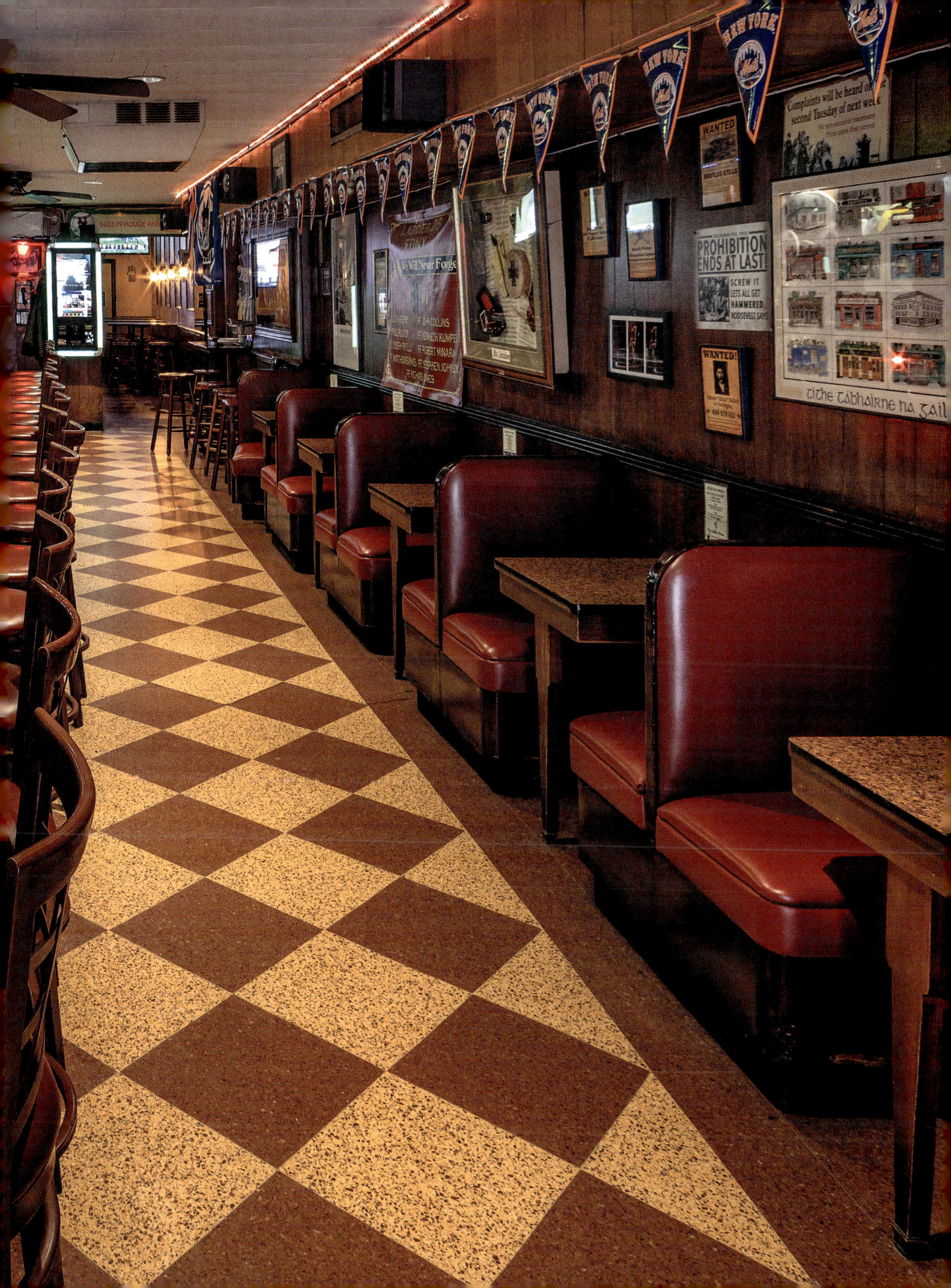

NEW YORK
Complaints will be heard on
second Tuesday of next week
WANTED
BOOTLEG STILLS
PROHIBITION
ENDS AT LAST!
SCREW IT
LETS ALL GET
HAMMERED,
ROOSEVELT SAYS
WANTED

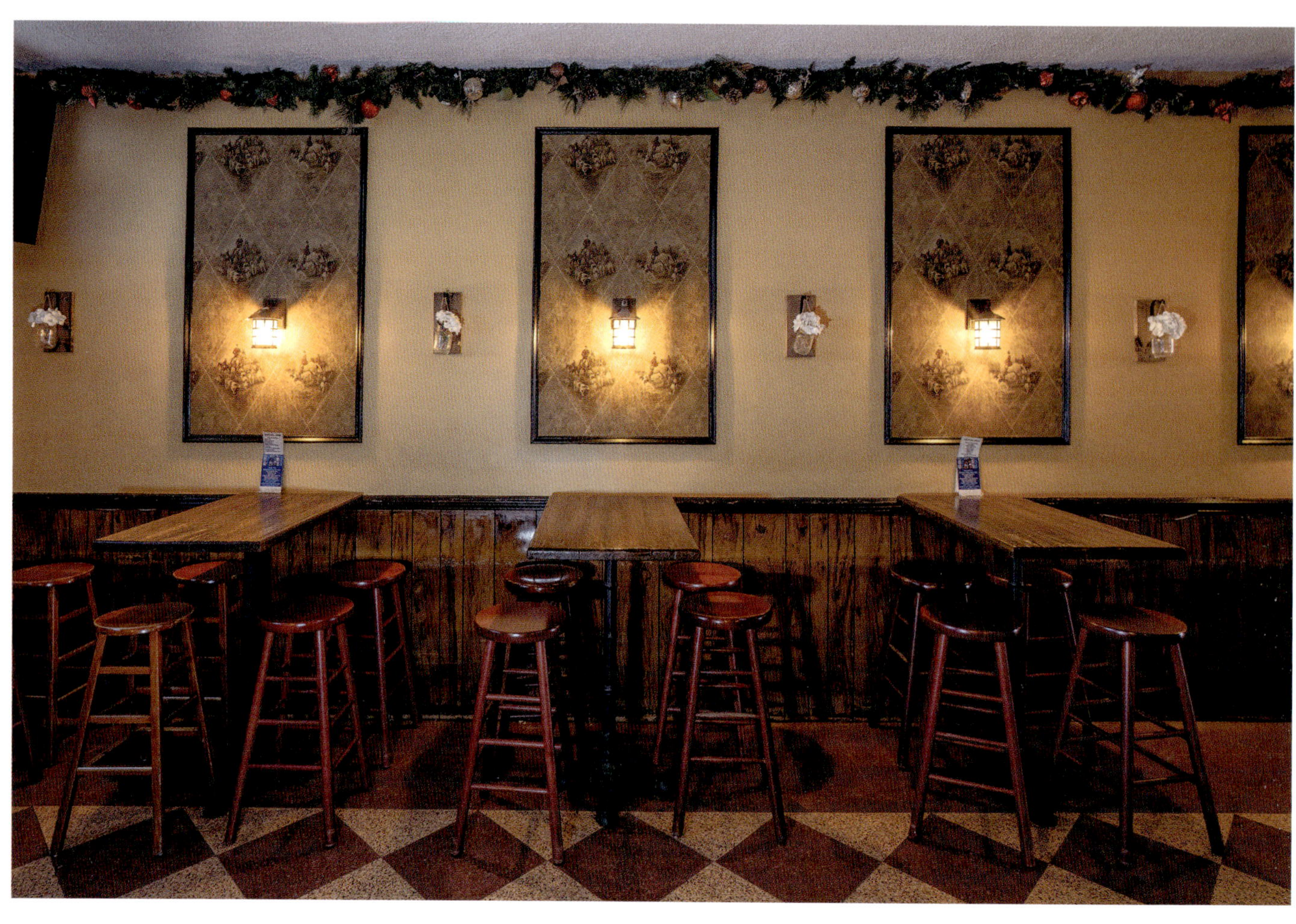

OPPOSITE BOTTOM *A shadow box on the wall proudly displays the elements of "An Seisiún," a gathering of friends to share traditional Irish music and dance.*

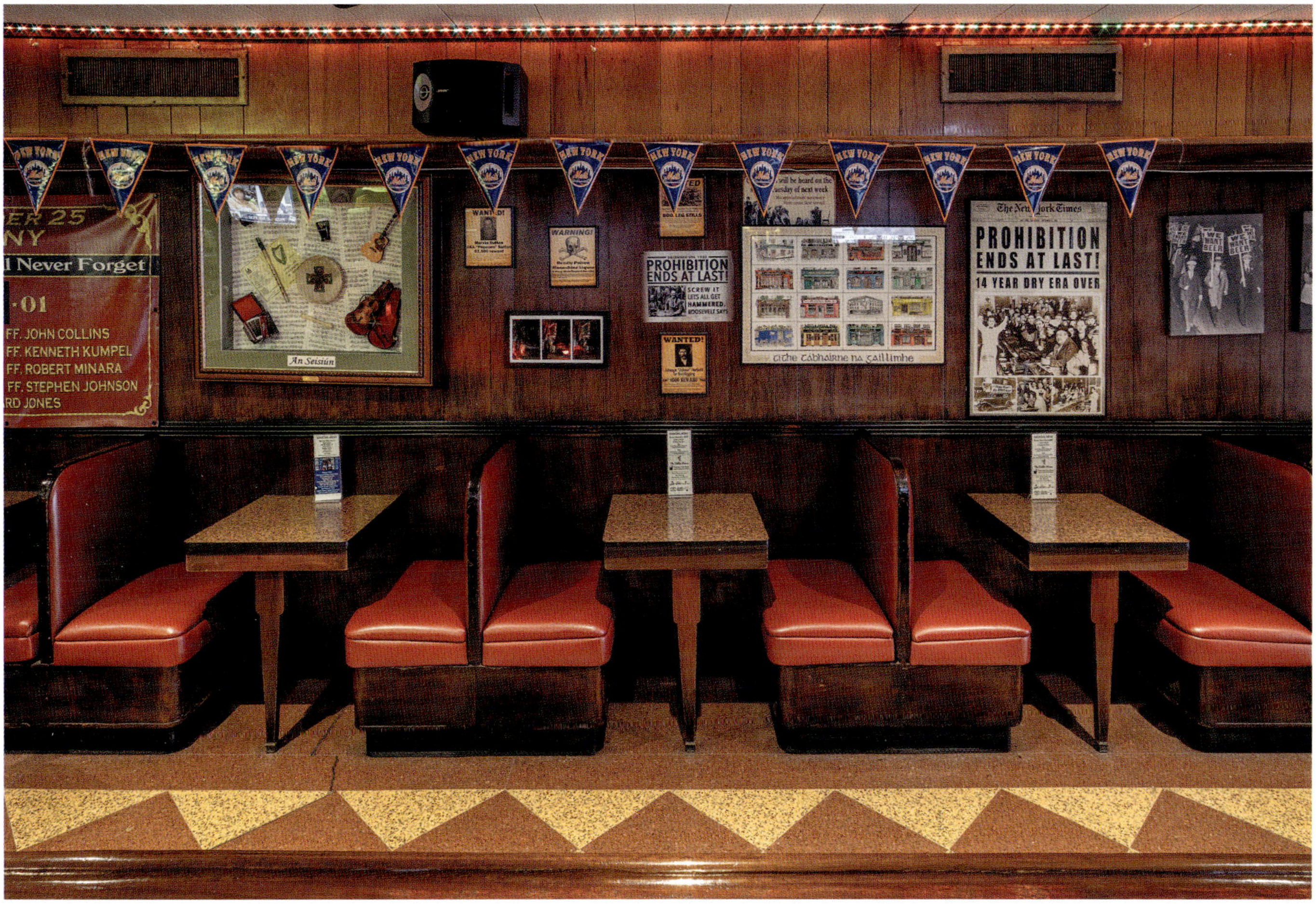

An Seisiún

PROHIBITION ENDS AT LAST!

14 YEAR DRY ERA OVER

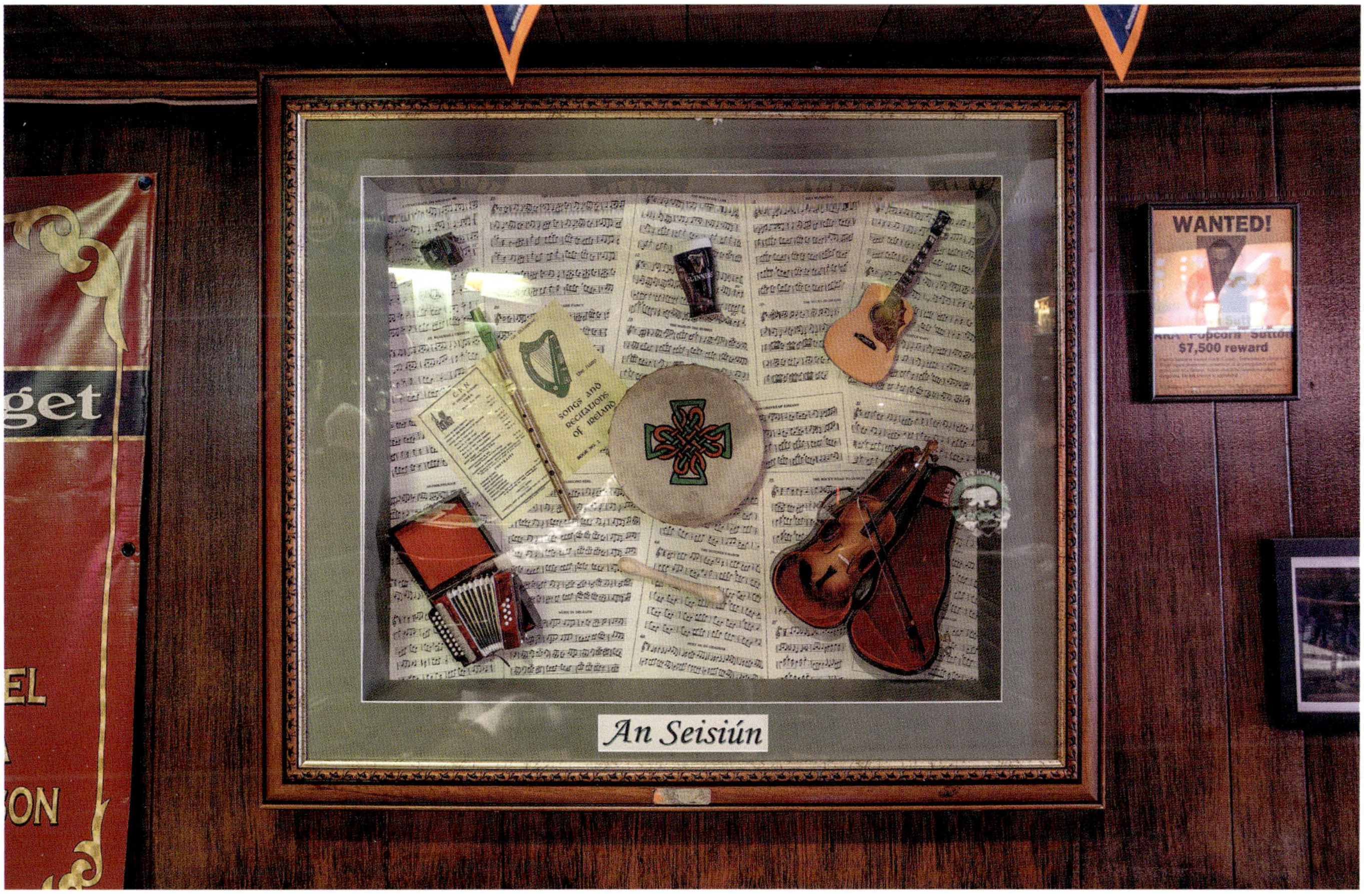

WANTED!

PLEASE DON'T TELL

113 ST. MARKS PLACE, EAST VILLAGE

Though speakeasy-style bars are a dime a dozen in NYC today, it wasn't always so. Indeed, back when Please Don't Tell (or PDT, as it's commonly known) opened in 2007 behind a vintage phone booth within a hot dog shop, it was among the first in a new generation of drinking establishments inspired by the infamous Prohibition era, when bars operated in secret to avoid discovery by busybodies and the law.

Located inside Crif Dogs in Manhattan's East Village, PDT has retained much of its original trimmings: taxidermy-adorned walls, a handful of tables, and fifteen seats at the bar. As the story goes, the owners chose the space based on the fact that Crif Dogs had a liquor license, and the secret entrance to the bar would be inside. But today it's no longer a secret. Ironically it's now one of the most famous bars in the world—and there's even a second location in Hong Kong.

Back when it opened, PDT didn't draw only on the speakeasy aspect of the Prohibition era—it also sought to revive its legendary cocktail culture at a time when people were drinking Cosmos, Amaretto Sours, and Long Island Iced Teas. Though its whimsical, unmarked entry is what drew masses of curious drinkers, it would soon become known globally for its cocktail program, which used fresh ingredients and measured pours to make classic drinks like Old Fashioneds, Manhattans, and Daiquiris.

At the center of this spirited movement was Jim Meehan, an industry icon who co-founded the bar, winning a James Beard Award for his work and creating dozens of cocktails that have since become modern mainstays, like the Mezcal Mule, a spin on the 1940s Moscow Mule that uses the agave spirit along with a house-made ginger beer.

Countless others behind the bar at PDT have contributed to its legacy. The first bartender Meehan hired, David Slape, invented the Paddington, a Hemingway Daiquiri interpretation made with orange marmalade. Another bartender, Don Lee, created PDT's most famous cocktail, the Benton's Old Fashioned—a riff on the Old Fashioned made with bacon-fat-washed bourbon. It's still a bestseller today and appears on the menu in both locations.

These recipes have been printed in numerous publications in addition to Meehan's own expansive cocktail books, including *The PDT Cocktail Book: The Complete Bartender's Guide from the Celebrated Speakeasy*, dubbed by the *New York Times* in 2011 as "the most buzzed-about cocktail guide in the country." In 2017 Meehan also released *Meehan's Bartender Manual*, a more technical guide to mixology that likewise featured over one hundred recipes.

Looking back at the wave of speakeasies that opened in the 2010s, many of which fizzled out long ago, it's hard to remember a time when a hidden door to a bar was still a true novelty. In 2013 Meehan even told the bar industry publication *Class*, "People don't want small, secretive venues anymore."

Yet nowadays PDT remains arguably as popular as it ever was. The beloved taxidermy animals remain, as well as the original method of entry: go into the phone booth and dial 1 on the red rotary phone, which will ring for the host to let you in through a hidden door in the back wall.

The bar's current owner is another lauded bartender, Jeff Bell, who bought it in 2019 following Meehan's departure. Bell had started at PDT nine years prior, working his way up from barback to general manager. He and Meehan are also both involved in the Hong Kong location. "We did a renovation [recently] to replace the physical bar and the hardwood floors—the goal, however, was to use new high-quality materials and still have the bar look the same as before," Bell revealed. "PDT is a special place and a bit of an institution; I didn't want a renovation to render it unrecognizable."

PDT's staying power speaks to the loyalty of its regulars, many of whom became cocktail connoisseurs because of the bar, as well as those who come from far and wide to visit one of the birthplaces of modern cocktail culture. Its location, in the same place for over a decade, stands as a testament to the last era of New York restaurants and bars that opened before the advent of Instagram and TikTok forever altered the city's dining and drinking landscape.

"PDT is hard to get into, so we make sure that once you're inside, it's a special experience," Bell adds. "We are always changing our cocktail menu and constantly searching for new, unique, and rare spirits to populate the backbar so that the product is worth the wait."

OPPOSITE *PDT stands for "Please Don't Tell." It's a speakeasy cocktail bar hidden behind a vintage phone booth inside an East Village hot dog joint, Crif Dogs.*

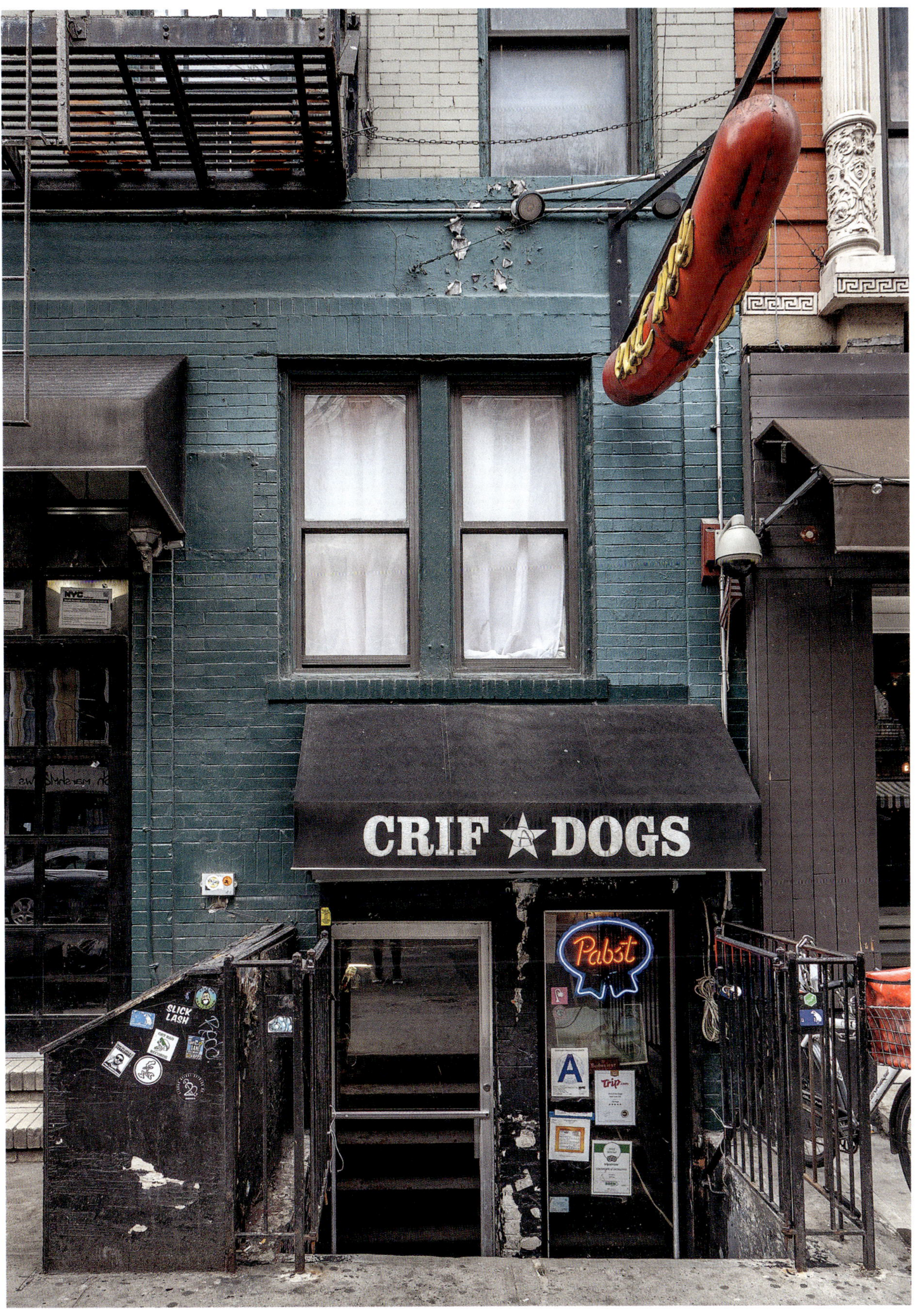

PLEASE DON'T TELL

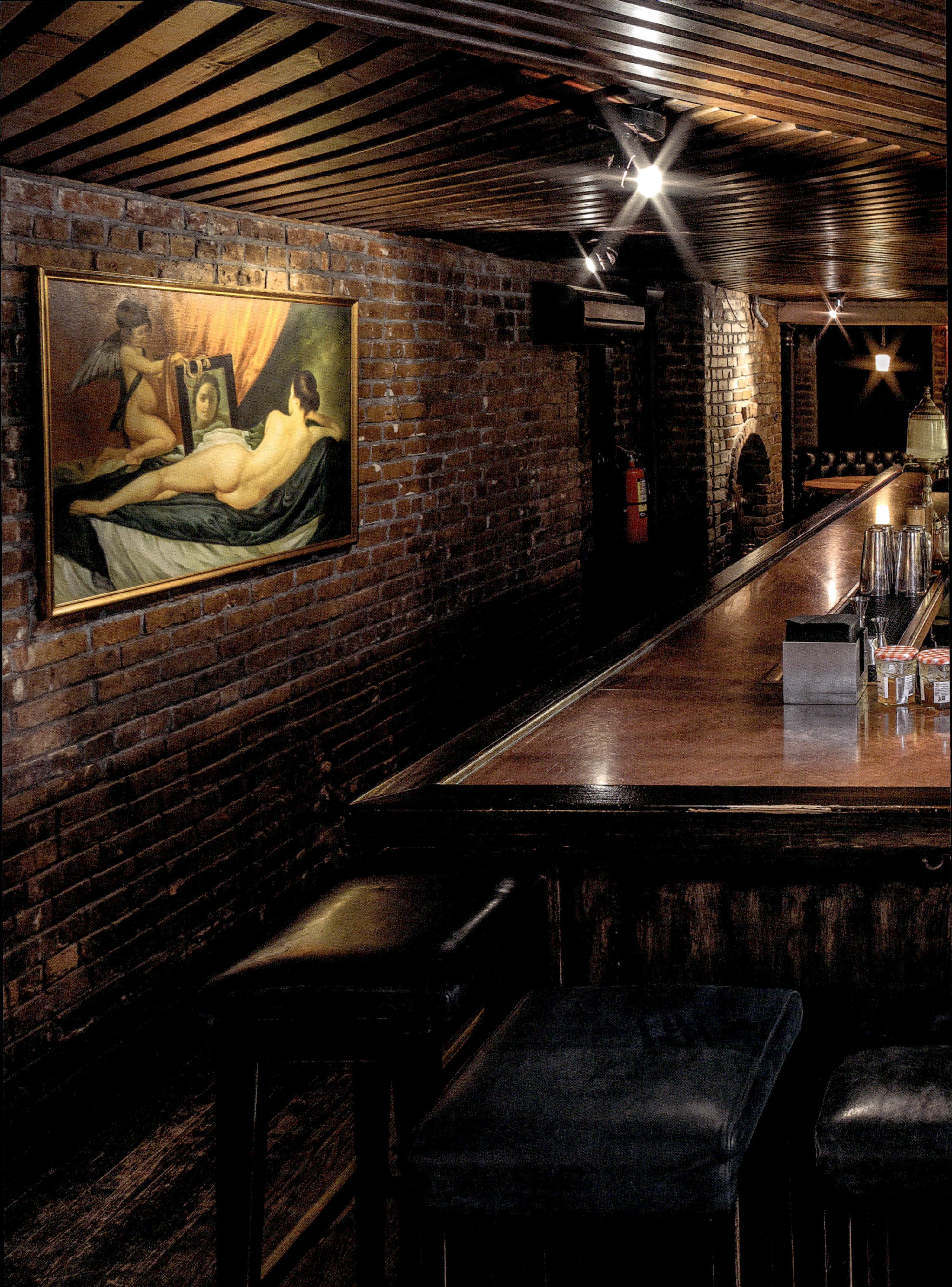

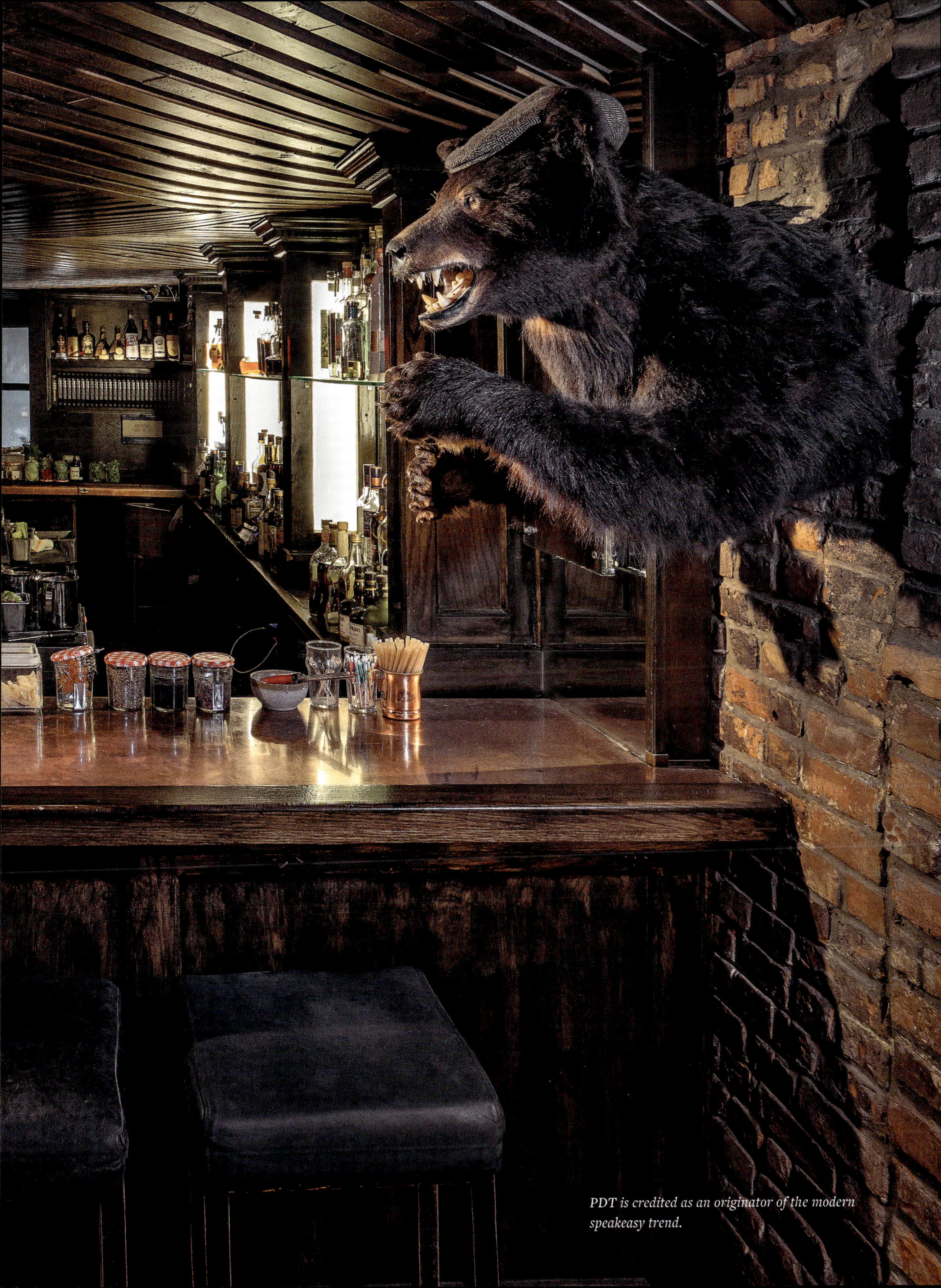

PDT is credited as an originator of the modern speakeasy trend.

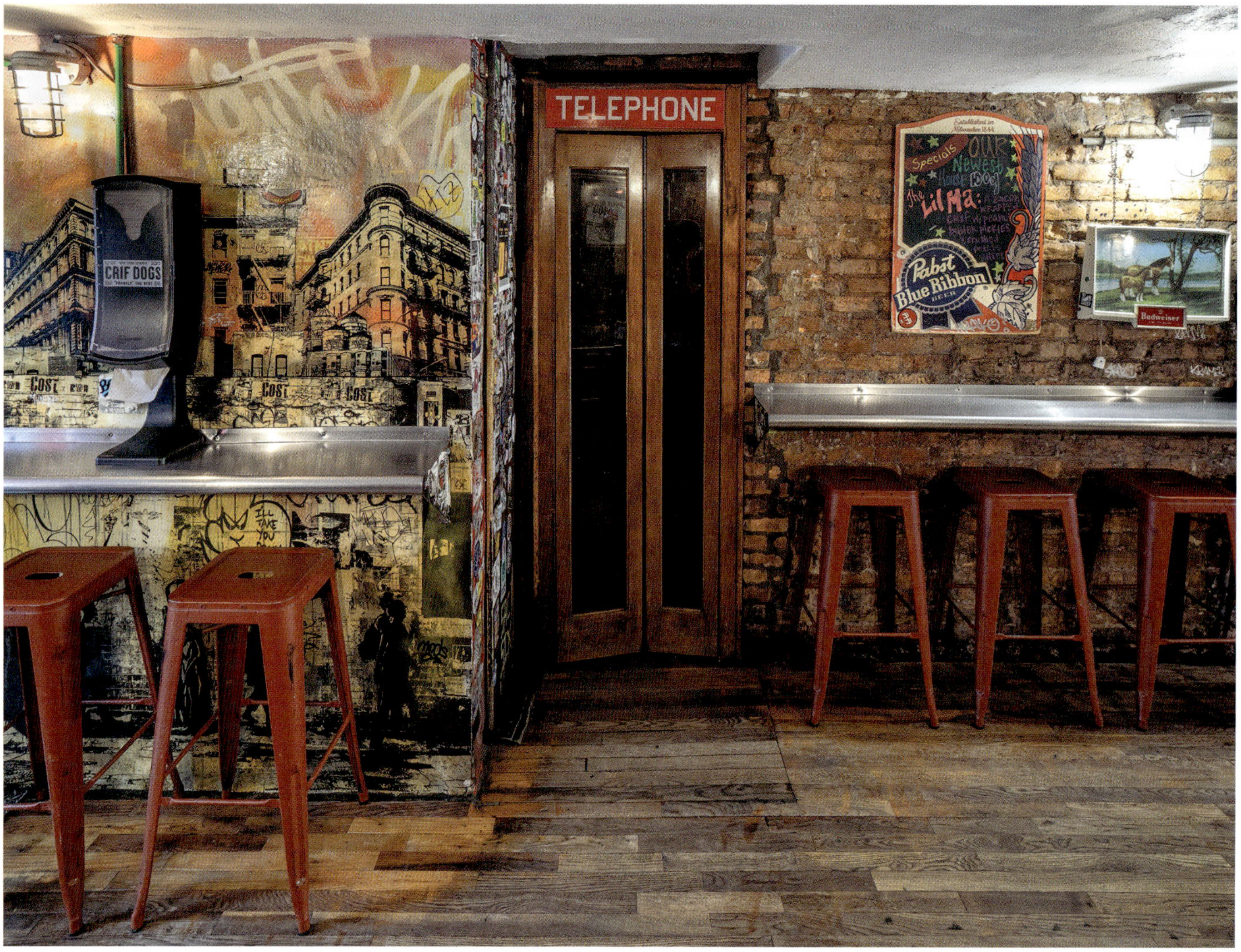

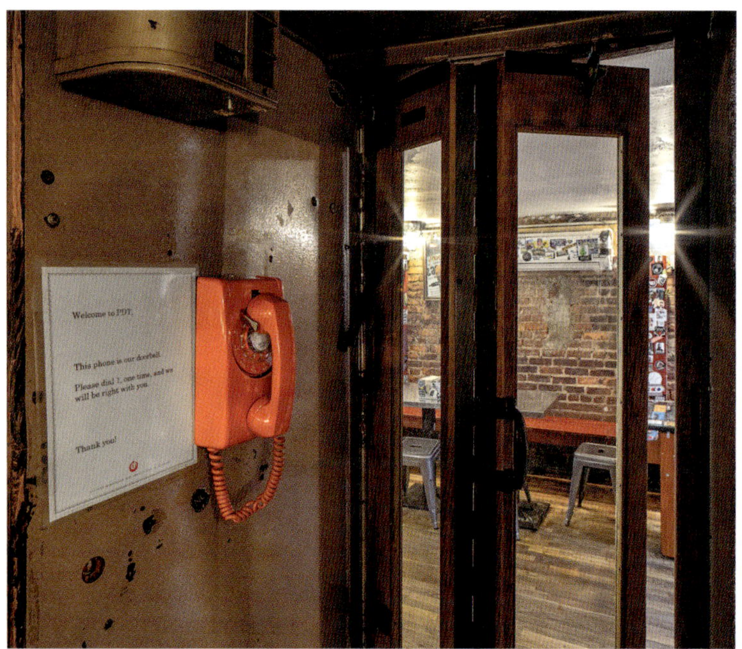

ABOVE   *To gain access, you have to dial 1 from the red rotary phone inside Crif Dogs.*

LEFT   *The phone serves as the doorbell: after the host answers your call, they will let you enter through a hidden door in the back wall of the phone booth.*

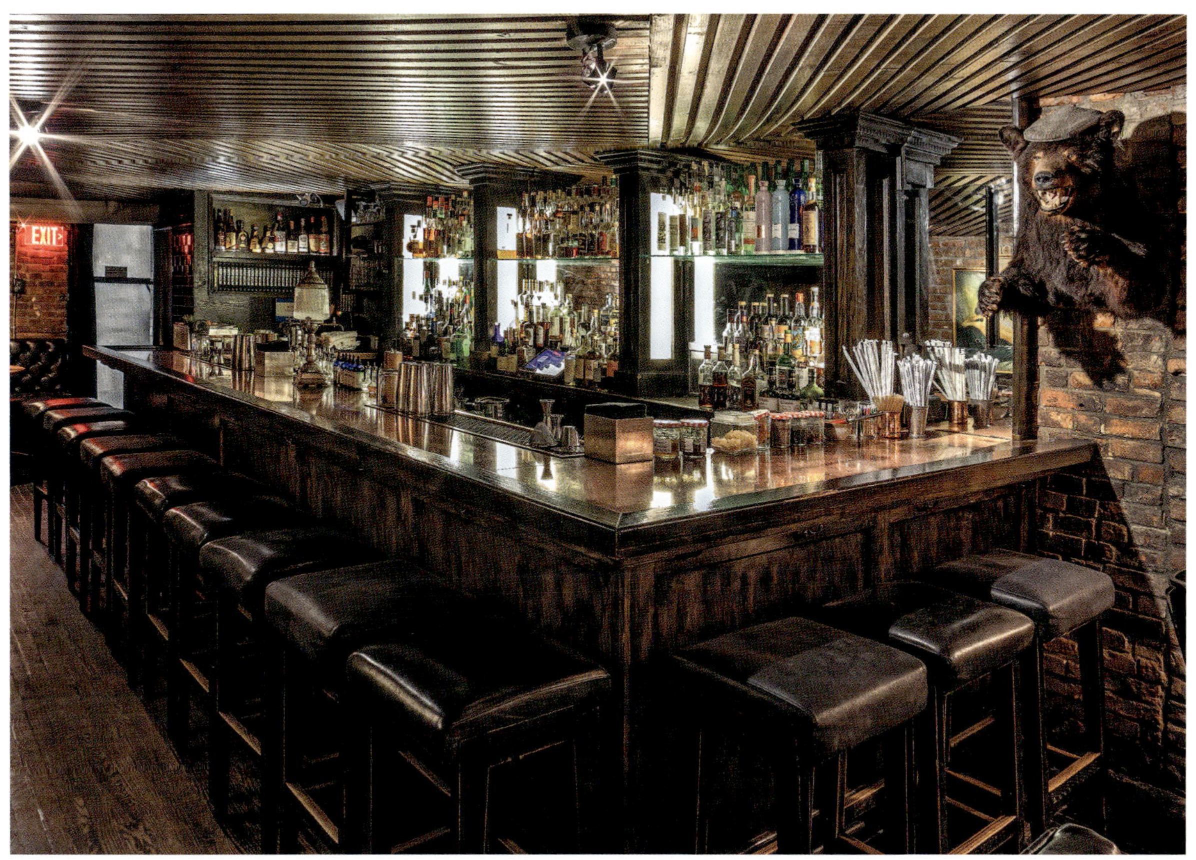

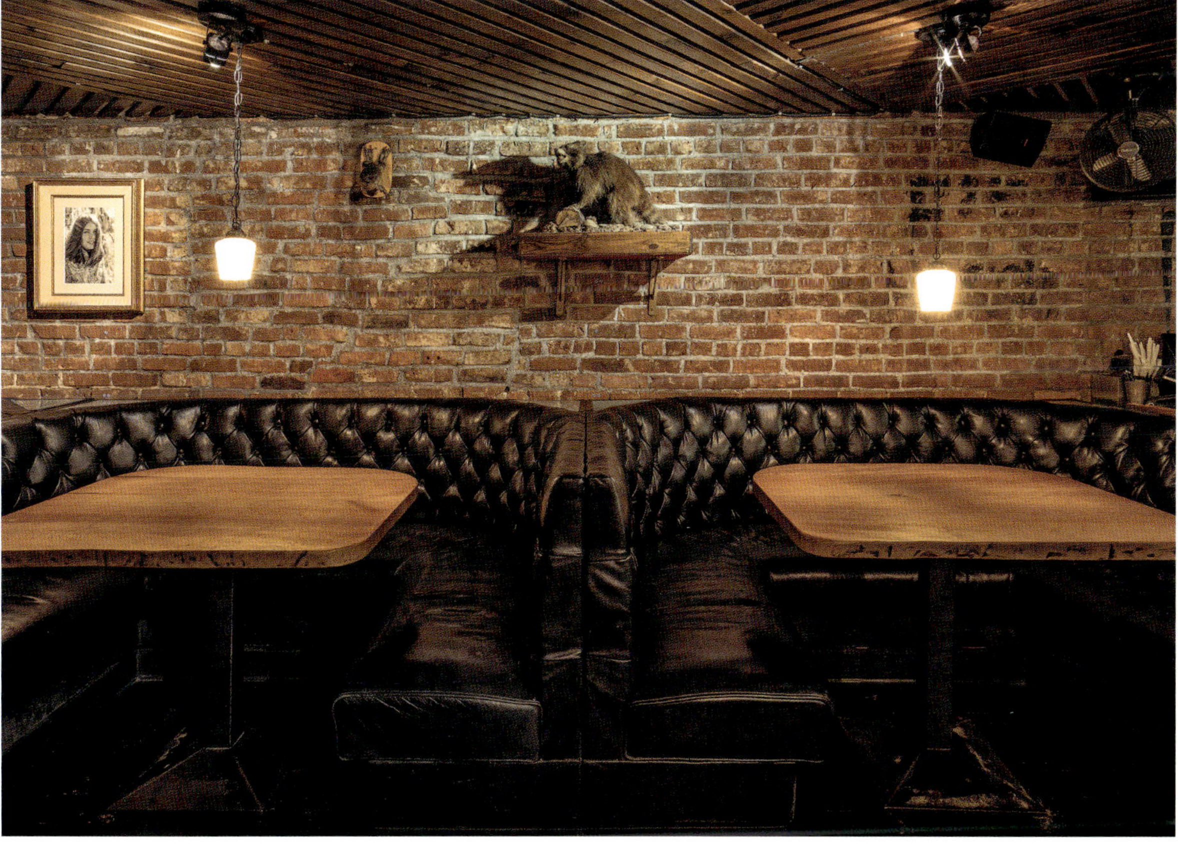

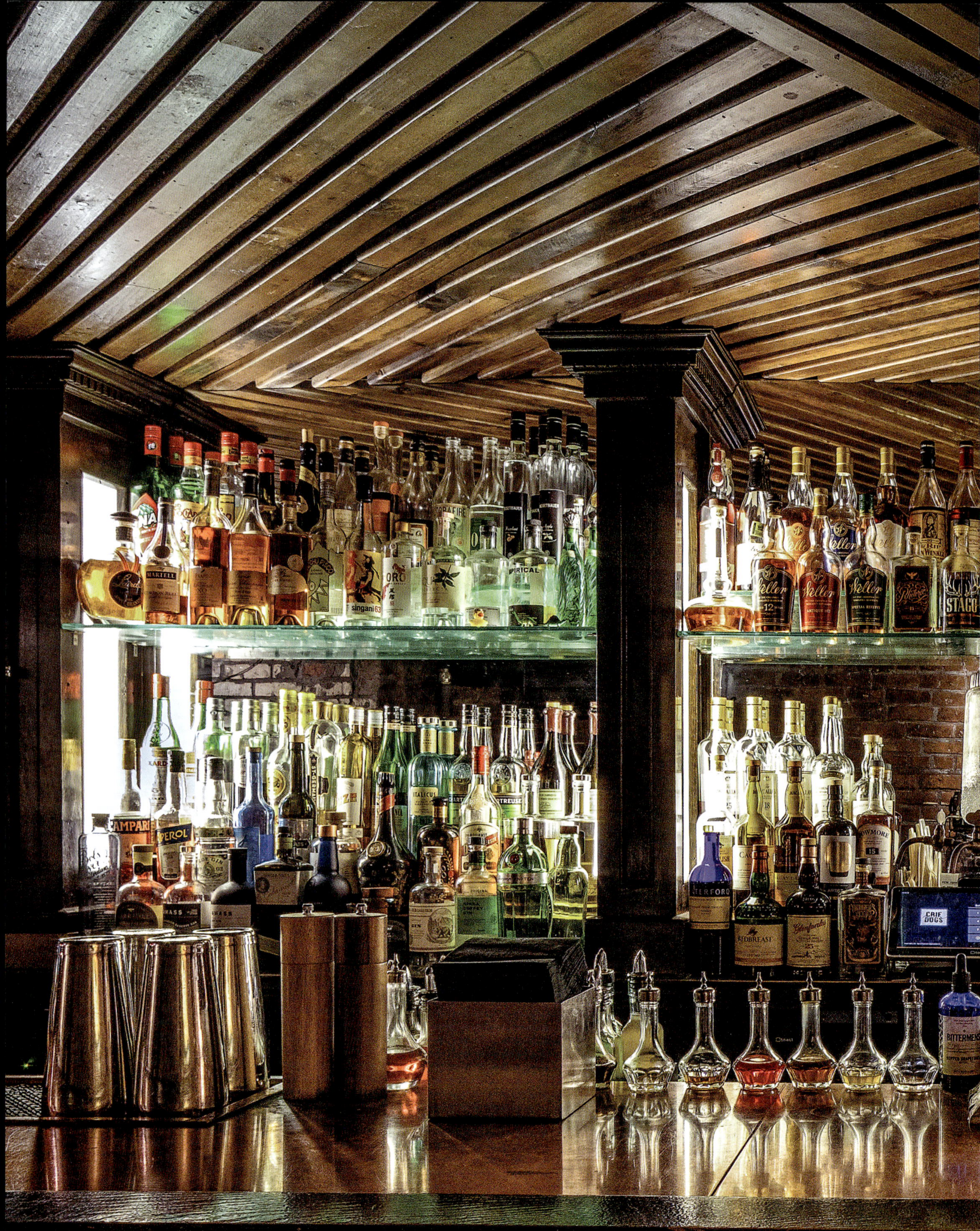

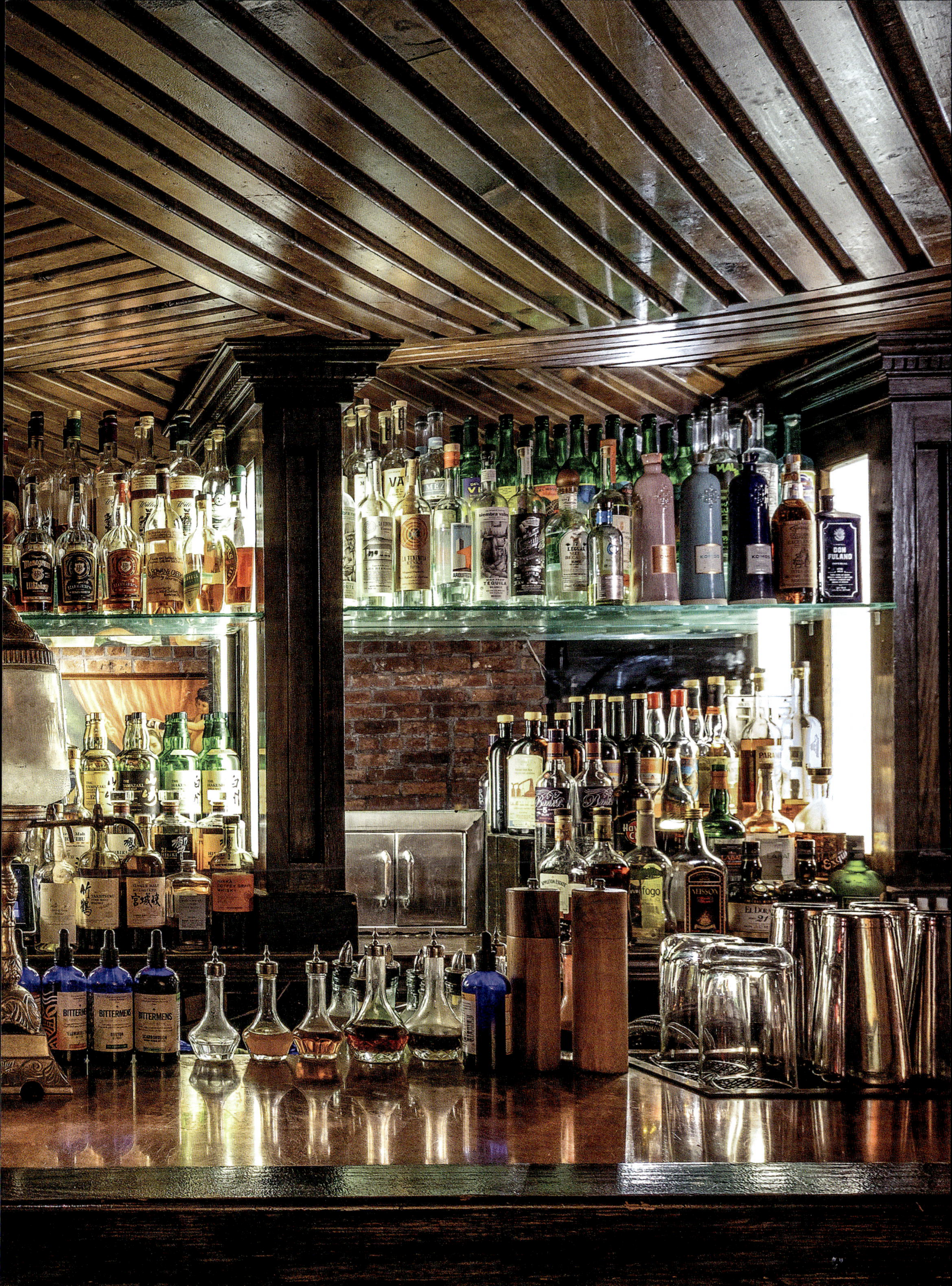

WHITE HORSE TAVERN

567 HUDSON STREET,
WEST VILLAGE

The bar referenced in Gene Raskin's 1968 song "Those Were the Days," The White Horse Tavern, is one of New York's few remaining iconic literary and artistic haunts of the mid-twentieth century. Frequented by everyone from Jack Kerouac to James Baldwin and Hunter S. Thompson, and located in the West Village at Hudson and Eleventh Streets since 1880, it is one of the oldest continuously run tavern in New York City.

At the time the bar opened, taking over the space that was formerly home to James Dean Oyster House, the western side of Greenwich Village was a predominantly working-class Irish neighborhood. Fitted with a 22-foot (7-meter) polished, hand-cut mahogany bar—carved from one piece of wood—it initially catered to longshoremen working the docks at the nearby Hudson River. It takes its name from the once-popular Scotch brand, White Horse Whisky.

During Prohibition, the White Horse Tavern was able to stay open, as it was a favorite of then-Mayor Jimmy Walker. In the 1930s and '40s the bar became a haven for the bohemians and free thinkers who had come to inhabit the neighborhood amid early gentrification. It also attracted communists and union organizers from groups like the National Maritime Union. Around this time, the bar's still-hanging neon sign first went up.

By the 1950s and into the '60s, the bar had gained a reputation with numerous notable writers and Beat poets. Among them were James Baldwin, Anaïs Nin, Norman Mailer, John Ashbery, Frank O'Hara, Allen Ginsberg, Frank McCourt, and Jack Kerouac—who at one point lived nearby and had been thrown out of the bar so many times that someone jotted "Kerouac Go Home" in the men's bathroom.

Journalist and urban planning activist Jane Jacobs lived on the same block as the White Horse; she included the bar in her book *The Death and Life of Great American Cities*. Alternative newspaper the *Village Voice*, a New York institution, is said to have been founded at the White Horse. Beyond writers, the bar also attracted musicians like Bob Dylan and Mary Travers of Peter, Paul, and Mary, who were known regulars. Later on, patrons included Jim Morrison of the Doors and traditional Irish folk artists the Clancy Brothers, who even performed there.

Most famously, while the eccentric Joe Gould ruled nearby at Minetta Tavern (see p. 50), the resident writer of the White Horse was Welsh poet Dylan Thomas—a photo of whom still hangs in the main room, and who in 1953 allegedly had his final drink at the bar before stumbling out, going into a coma, and dying. "I've had eighteen straight whiskies. I think that's the record," he told a companion. Famous last words.

The exterior of the White Horse—now often called the Horse—received a historic landmark designation in 1969. Inside, the bar retains much of its original decor: the largest main room is still decked out in statues and images of white horses. Chandeliers are likewise trimmed with horse heads. The bar's heavy woodwork, tin ceilings, and several fixtures are all original. From the main room you'll find two smaller rooms, each with a pendulum clock. Writers tended to gather in what was once the back room of the bar (it's now the middle room following an expansion in the 1970s).

In 1996 the *New York Times* described the White Horse as "still popular with the young crowds," something that remains true even today. In 2019 Eddie Brennan sold the building housing the bar—contingent upon the leaseholder maintaining the century-old bar as is—to restaurateur Eytan Sugarman, who also owns another historic, former longshoreman's bar: the Paris Cafe in the South Street Seaport district (see p. 122). Sugarman took the history of the space into account when reopening the bar. One thing he did change? They take credit cards now.

Today, step into the White Horse Tavern and travel back to a time when the bohemian spirit inhabited the now-moneyed neighborhood of Greenwich Village. On offer on the bar's reimagined menu: a French dip sandwich, a burger with Roquefort cheese, and a burnt lemon chicken. The bar is crowded nightly with finance bros and students—but stop by during the day to see old-timers reliving the glory days.

OPPOSITE *The White Horse Tavern has been in business since 1880 and is one of the few wood-frame structures still in existence in New York City.*

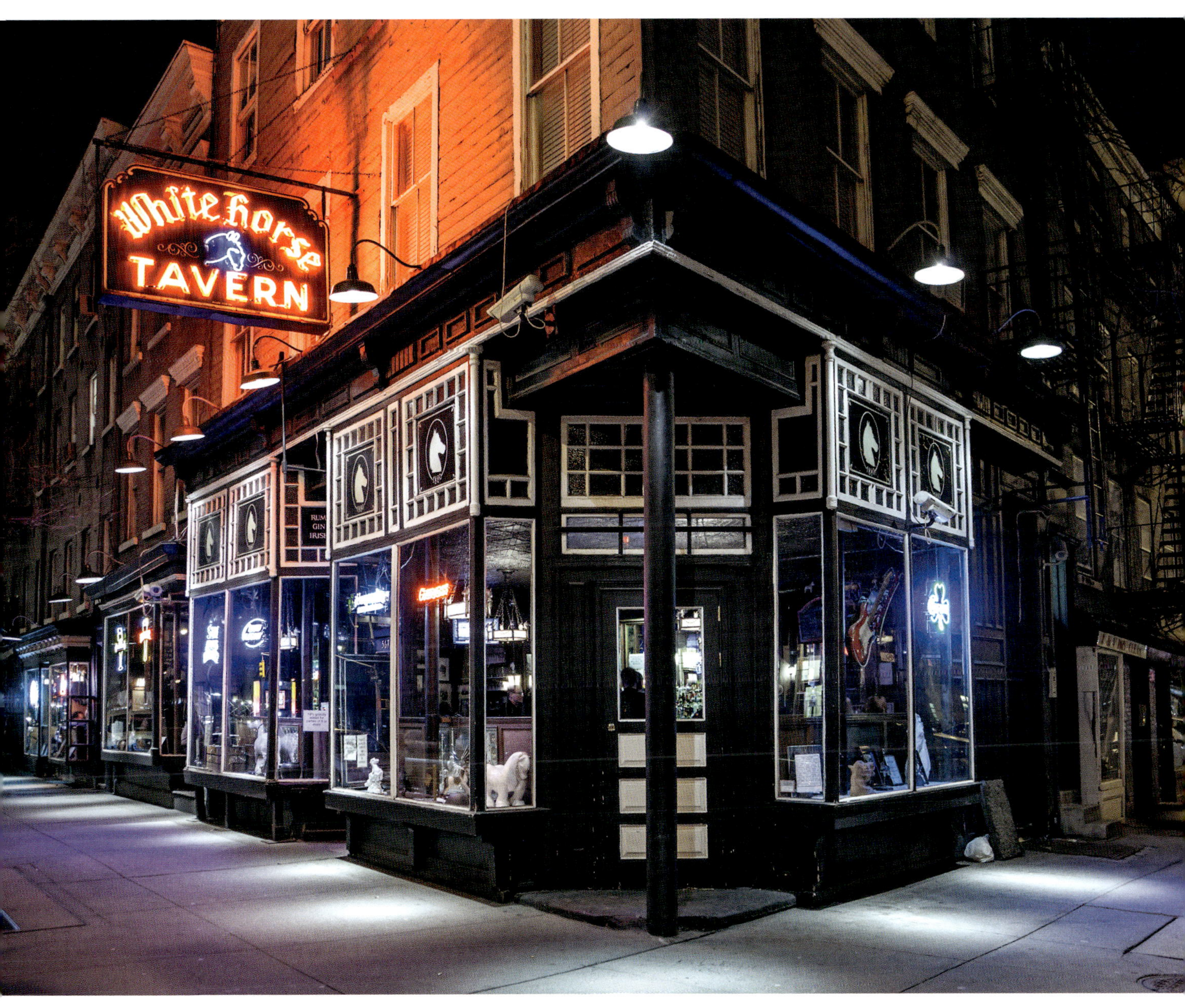

WHITE HORSE TAVERN

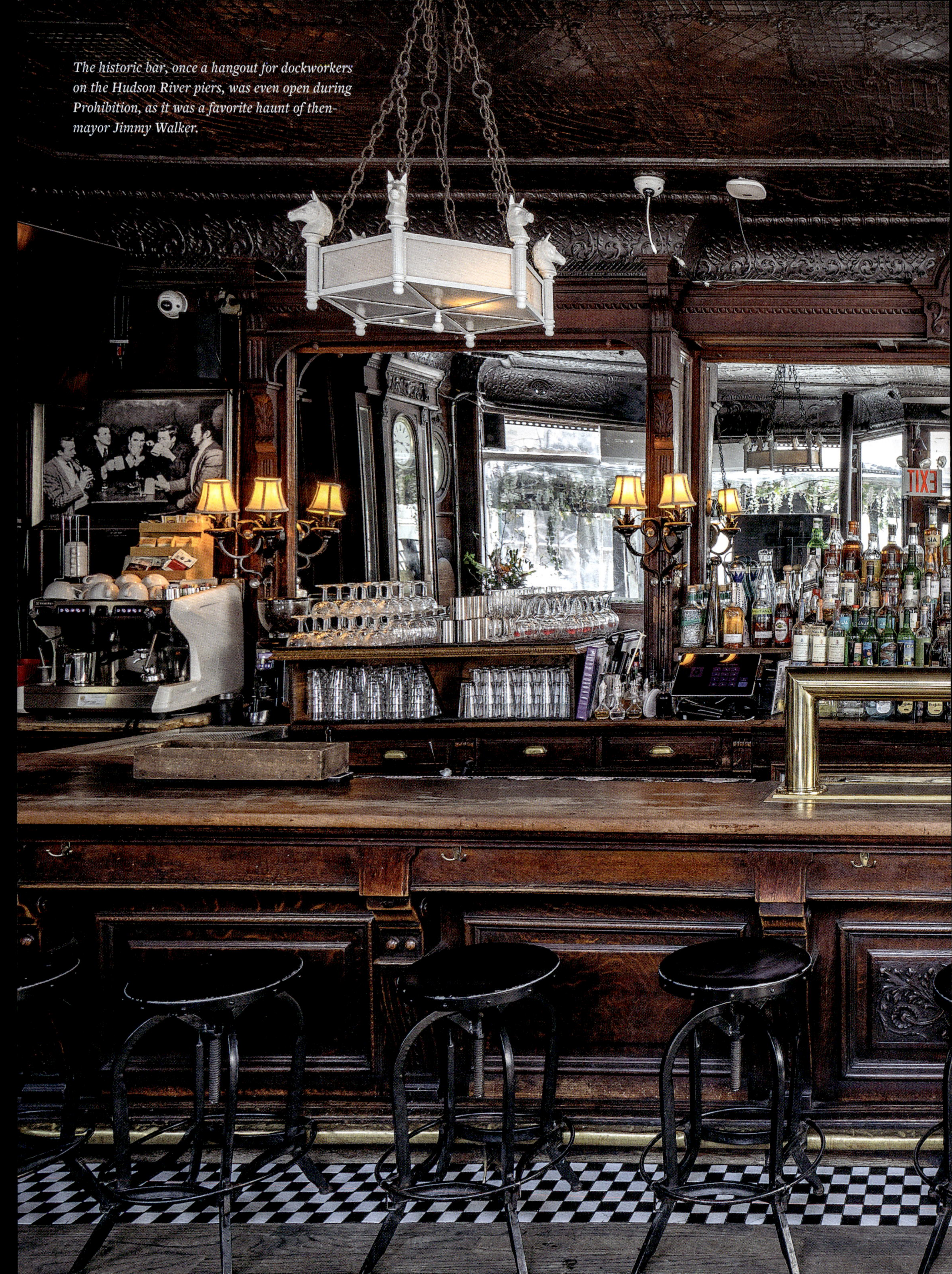

The historic bar, once a hangout for dockworkers on the Hudson River piers, was even open during Prohibition, as it was a favorite haunt of then-mayor Jimmy Walker.

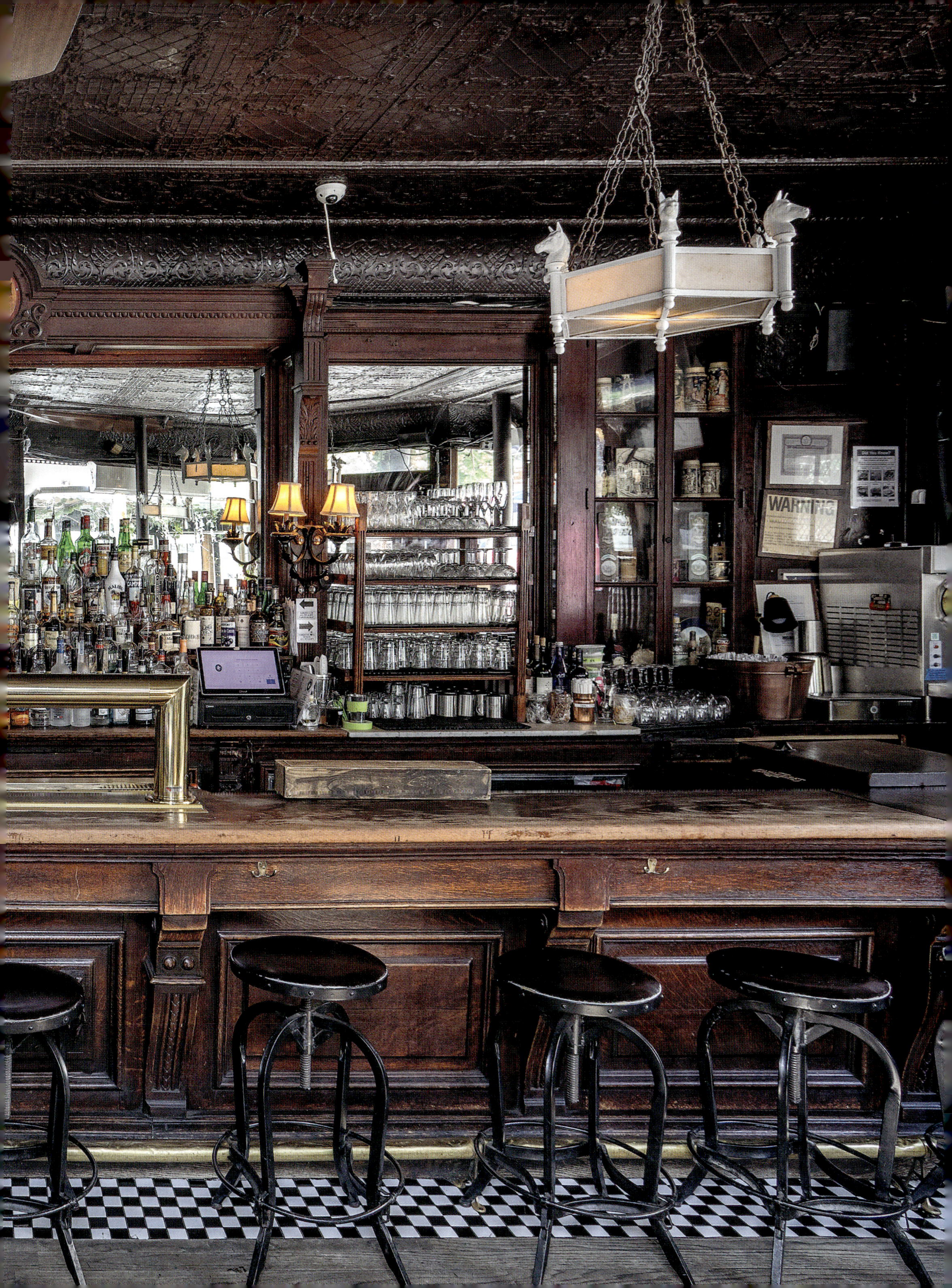

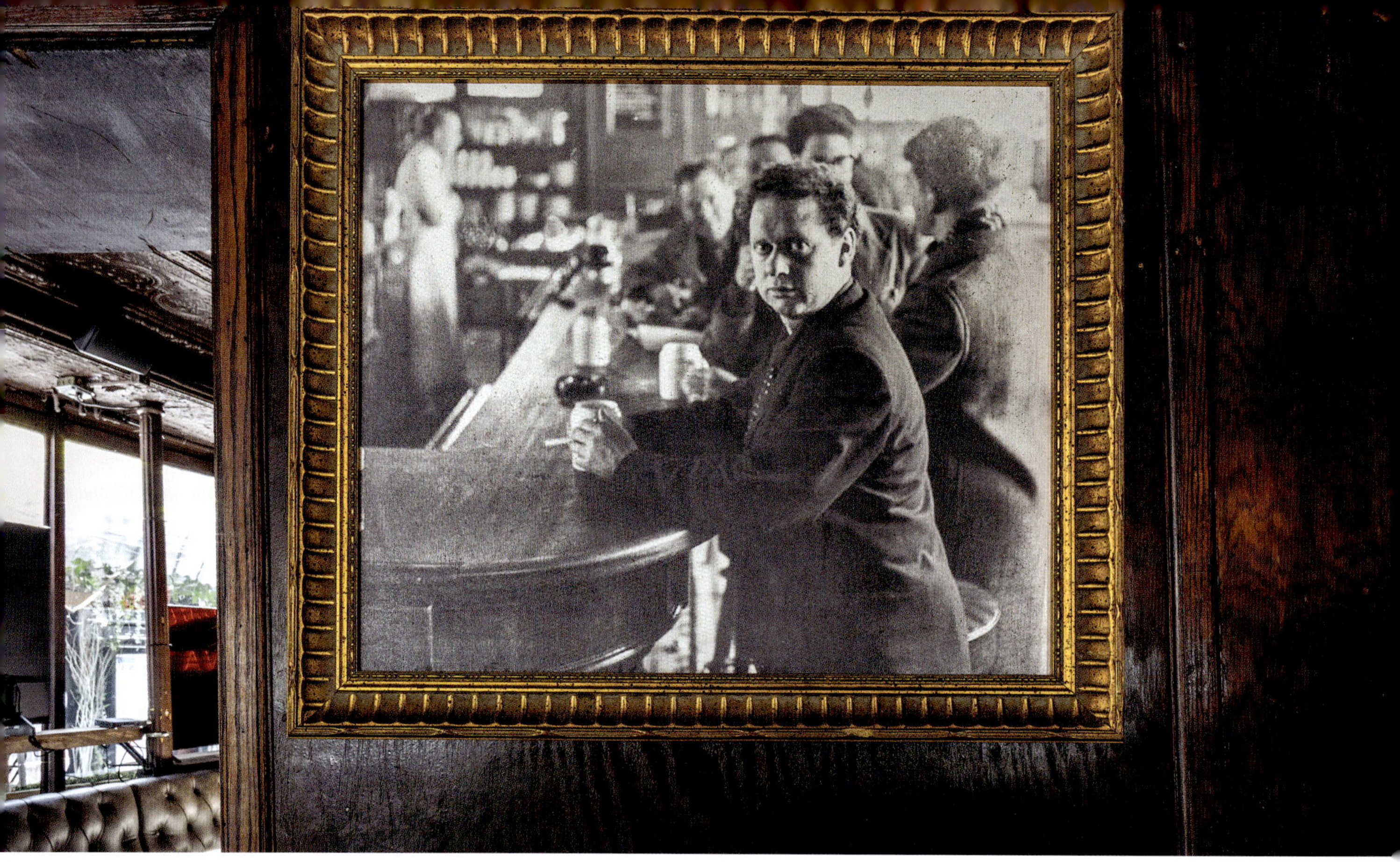

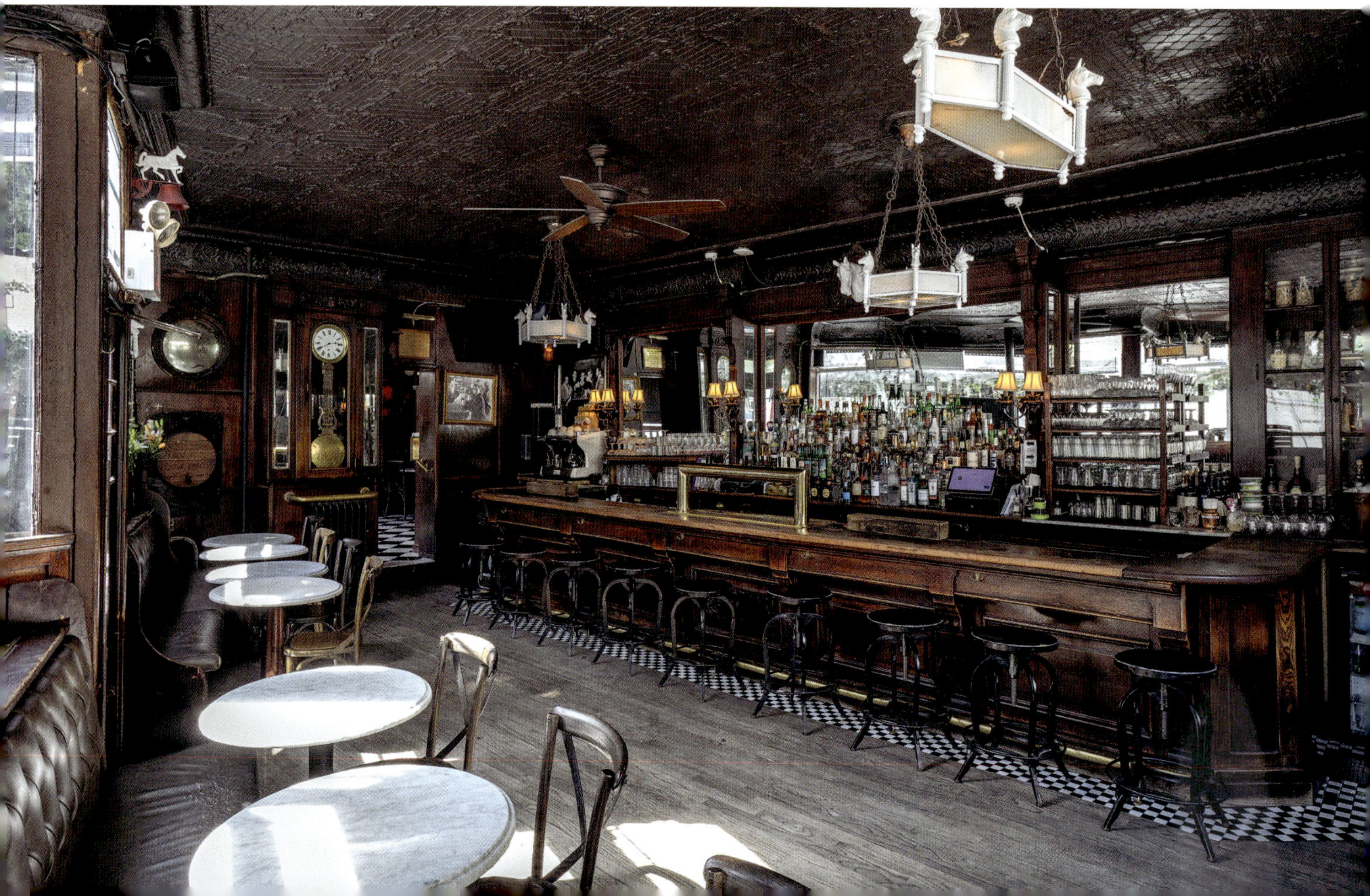

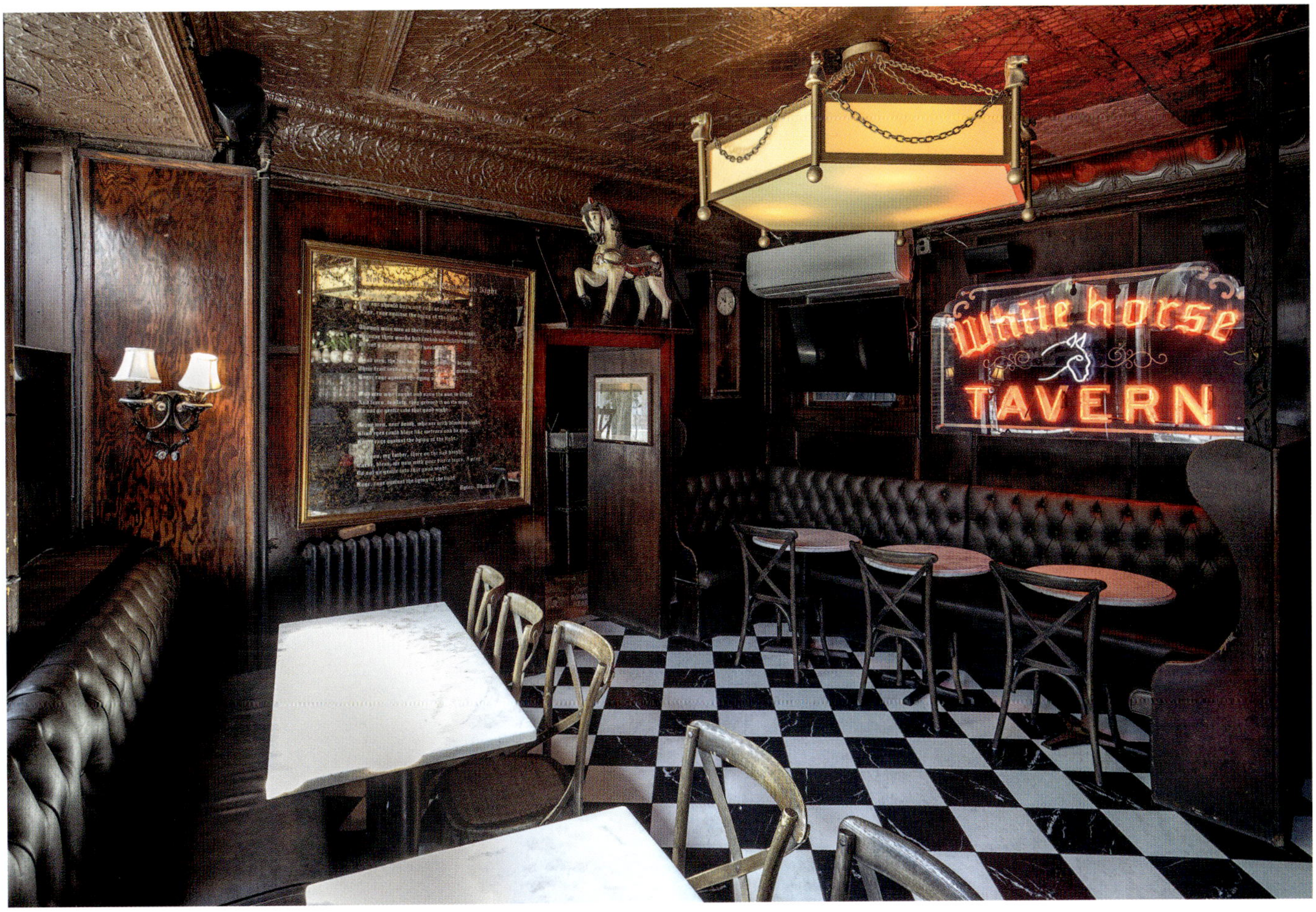

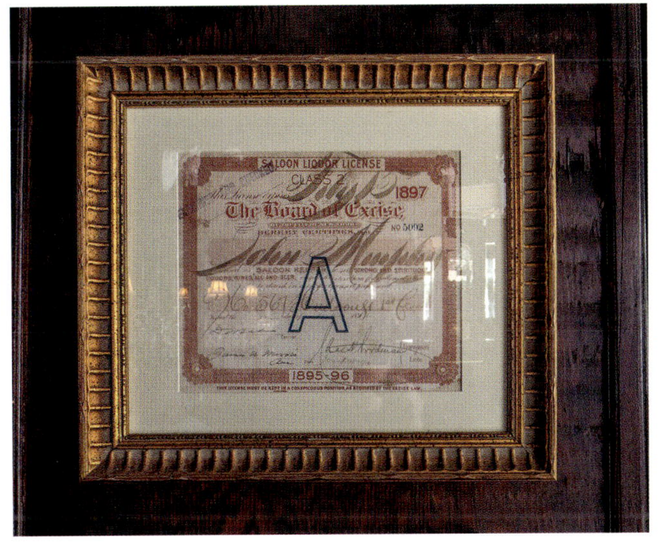

OPPOSITE TOP   *Dylan Thomas was a frequent customer of the bar. Tragically, the White Horse was the last place he drank before becoming ill and dying in 1953. The back room is dedicated in his name.*

OPPOSITE BOTTOM   *The interior of the tavern is original, including the tin ceilings, horse head lamp fixtures, and wooden bar (which is crafted from one solid piece of mahogany, 22 feet (7 meters) long, and hand-cut and polished).*

ABOVE   *In 2019 the entire building was sold, with the sale contingent upon the leaseholder maintaining the century-old bar as is.*

CUBBYHOLE

281 WEST 12TH STREET, WEST VILLAGE

For a long time, Cubbyhole was considered one of New York's last remaining lesbian bars—along with Henrietta Hudson nearby and Ginger's in Park Slope. Since its opening in 1987, the bar has catered to a mix of locals and tourists, offering a safe haven and sense of revelry for the city's LGBTQ+ community.

The story of Cubbyhole starts with its late owner Tanya Saunders, who passed away at the age of eighty-two in 2018. Born in Berlin in 1936, she left Germany with her mother in the wake of the Kristallnacht pogroms, arriving in the United States on the last boat allowed to dock before the government started turning them away. She grew up in Forest Hills, Queens, and worked as a copywriter prior to finding a career in real estate.

But her struggles weren't over. During the 1960s, when it was illegal to sell alcohol to queer people in bars, Saunders became active in the underground scene, participating in speakeasy-style events. When her family refused to accept her sexuality, she and her then-girlfriend married two gay men who lived in their building.

In 1987, while residing in the West Village, Saunders noticed a For Rent sign for a pint-sized, 824-square-foot (77-square-meter) space at the corner of West Twelfth and West Fourth Streets. Partnering with Debbie Fierro, she acquired a liquor license and opened DT's Fat Cat as a piano bar. In 1994, after Fierro left to open another bar, Saunders renamed hers Cubbyhole. The name came from another bar called The Cubby Hole (two words) which had been located at 438 Hudson Street from 1981 to 1990—Saunders bought the name from its owner, her friend Elaine Romagnoli, after it closed. Interestingly, this bar on Hudson Street became another lesbian bar, Henrietta Hudson, which remains open to this day.

Among the many traditions that started during Saunders's era is the practice of hanging souvenirs and tchotchkes on the bar's ceiling. Now an emblematic representation of Cubbyhole, it features a collection of items brought in by regulars from their travels. (Saunders famously kept any hats for herself, making them part of her eclectic fashion sensibilities). The seat covers of the vinyl bar stools, meanwhile, were originally adorned with Looney Tunes characters; comic book characters, including Wonder Woman and other queer icons, were added later.

Saunders continued to frequent Cubbyhole in her older age, even arriving in a wheelchair a week before her passing. She left the bar to Lisa Menichino, who had worked there for twenty-two years, starting as a bartender before becoming a manager. Seeking to preserve the venue's spirit, Menichino renovated the bar in 2022, adding a layer of resin over photos of patrons and other keepsakes.

Over the years, Cubbyhole has weathered various challenges, from the aftermath of the September 11th attacks to power outages during Hurricane Sandy. In 2020, facing a loss of income during the Covid-19 pandemic, the bar closed temporarily, setting up a GoFundMe that raised nearly $80,000 from loyal customers and those who were moved by its story.

Cubbyhole reopened in 2022, inviting returning patrons to enjoy affordable weekday drink specials (plus discounted Margaritas on Tuesdays). Today, you can step inside to catch a glimpse of its iconic ceiling, which now features everything from Japanese paper lanterns and marionette puppets to nylon sea creatures and Barbie dolls. The walls are still a soothing moss green color, and the smooth flagstone floors are original.

As the landscape of LGBTQ+ spaces continues to evolve, Cubbyhole remains a beacon of acceptance, unity, and pride. Its welcoming atmosphere and commitment to inclusivity ensure that it will continue to hold a special place in the hearts of those who seek refuge within its vibrant, ever-changing walls. Even now, it remains cash only.

OPPOSITE *Cubbyhole was founded in 1987 by Tanya Saunders as DT's Fat Cat, taking the current name in 1994. It is known for its colorful decorations, many of which were given to the owner by regulars.*

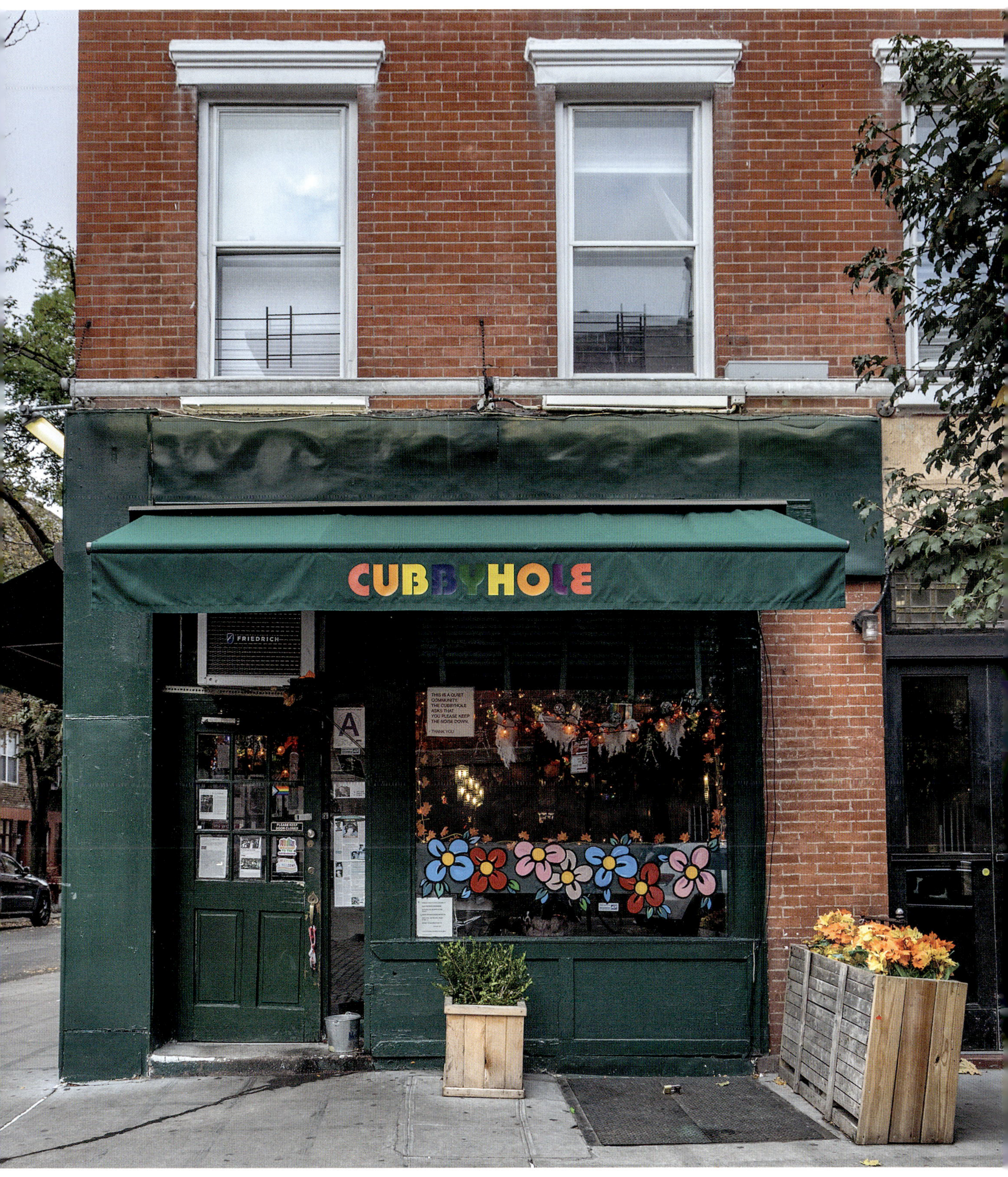

CUBBYHOLE
FRIEDRICH
A
THIS IS A QUIET
COMMUNITY.
THE CUBBYHOLE
ASKS THAT
YOU PLEASE KEEP
THE NOISE DOWN.
THANK YOU!
PLEASE KEEP
DOOR CLOSED

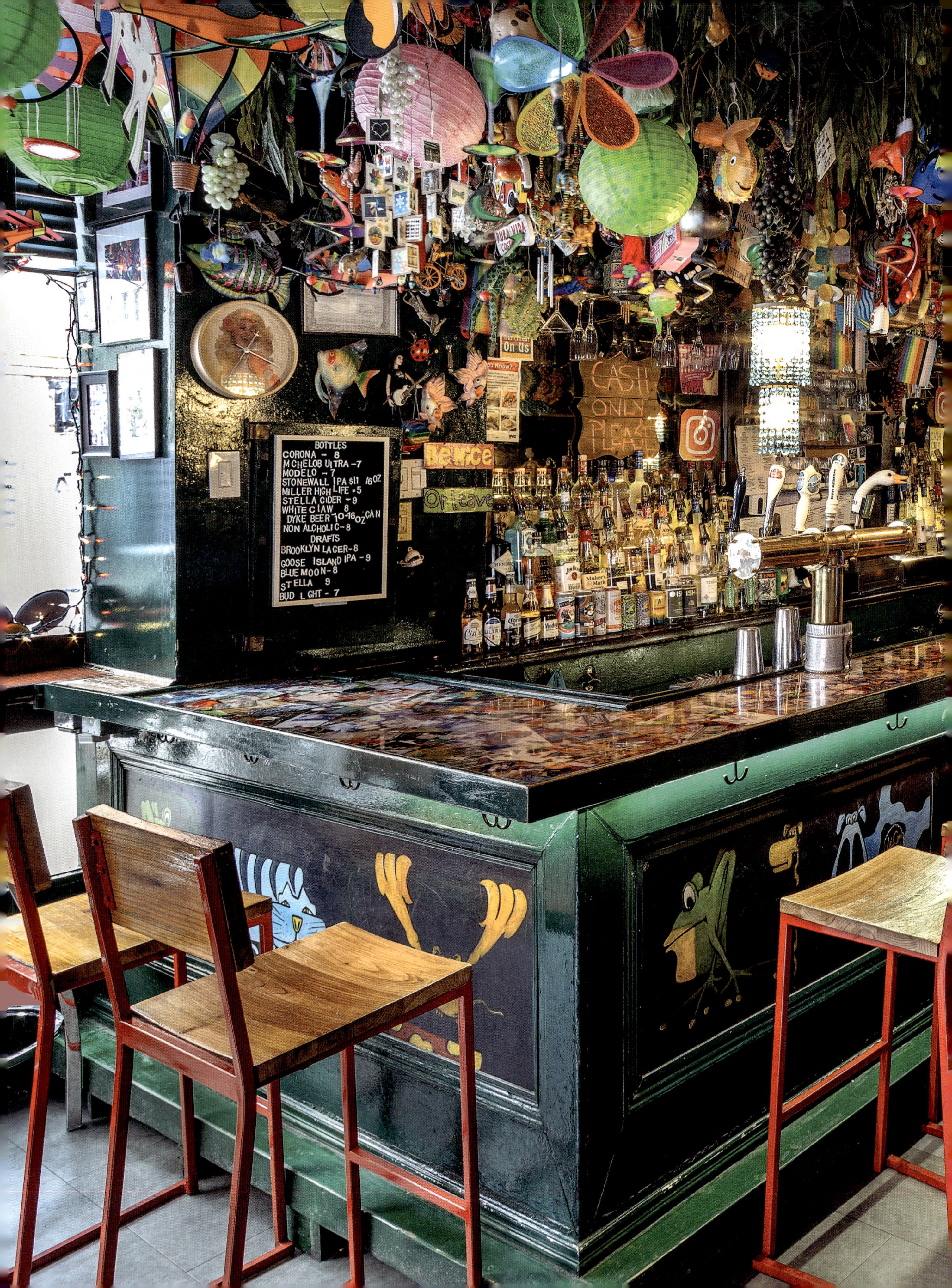

BOTTLES
CORONA - 8
MICHELOB ULTRA -7
MODELO - 7
STONEWALL IPA $11 16 OZ
MILLER HIGH LIFE - 5
STELLA CIDER - 9
WHITE CLAW 8
DYKE BEER 10-16 OZ CAN
NON ALCHOLIC - 8
DRAFTS
BROOKLYN LAGER - 8
GOOSE ISLAND IPA - 9
BLUE MOON - 8
STELLA 9
BUD LIGHT - 7
CASH ONLY PLEASE
BE NICE
OR leave

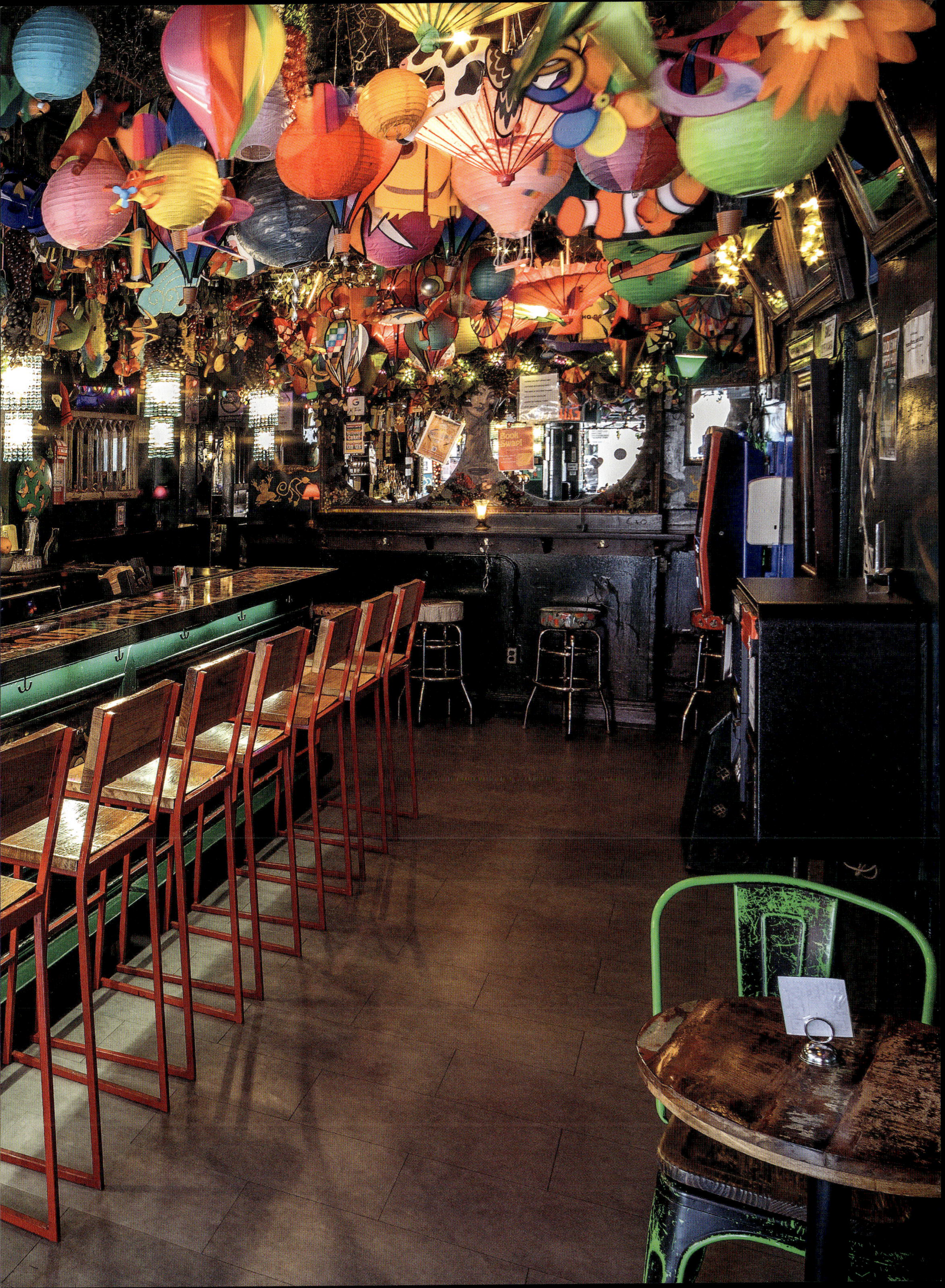

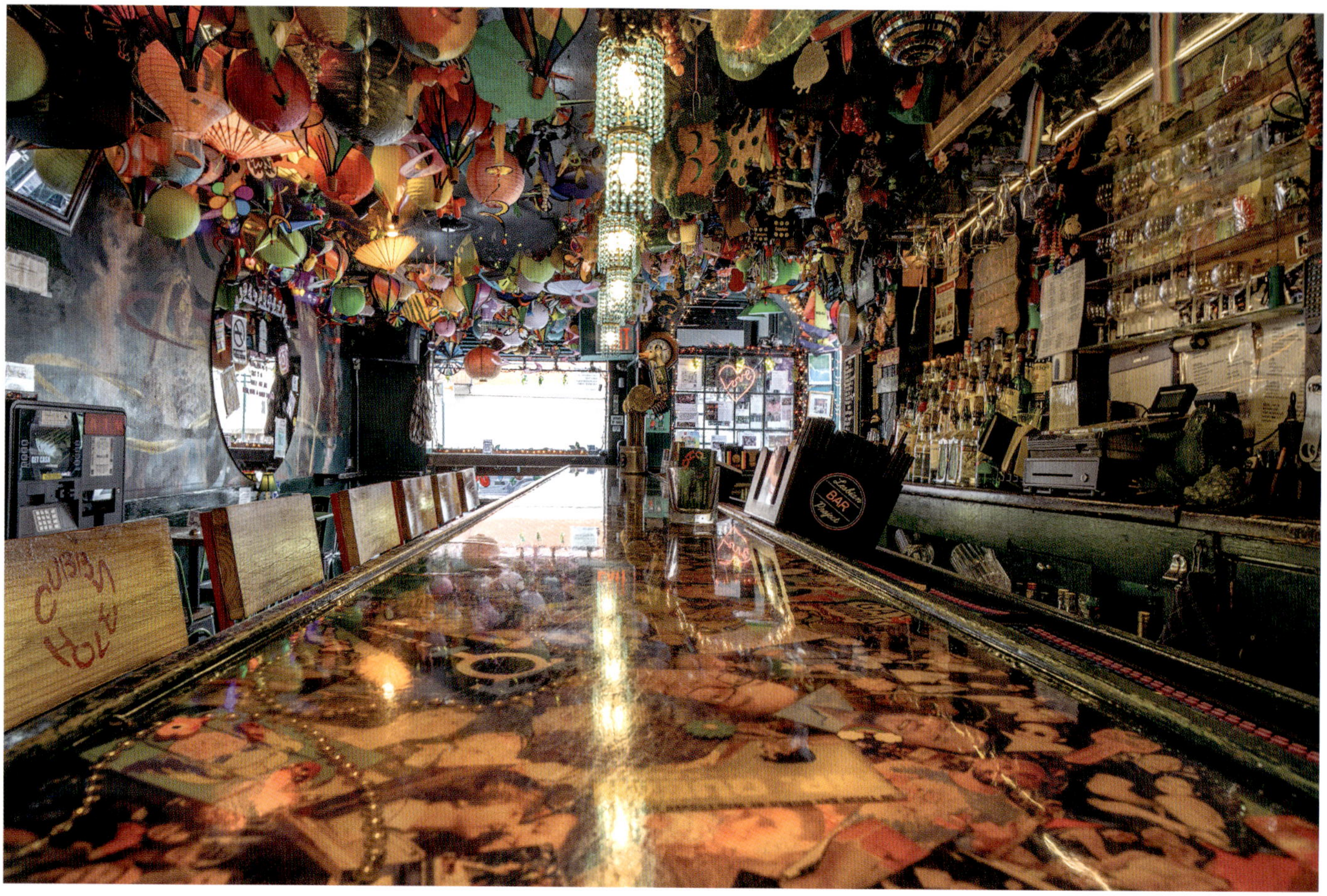

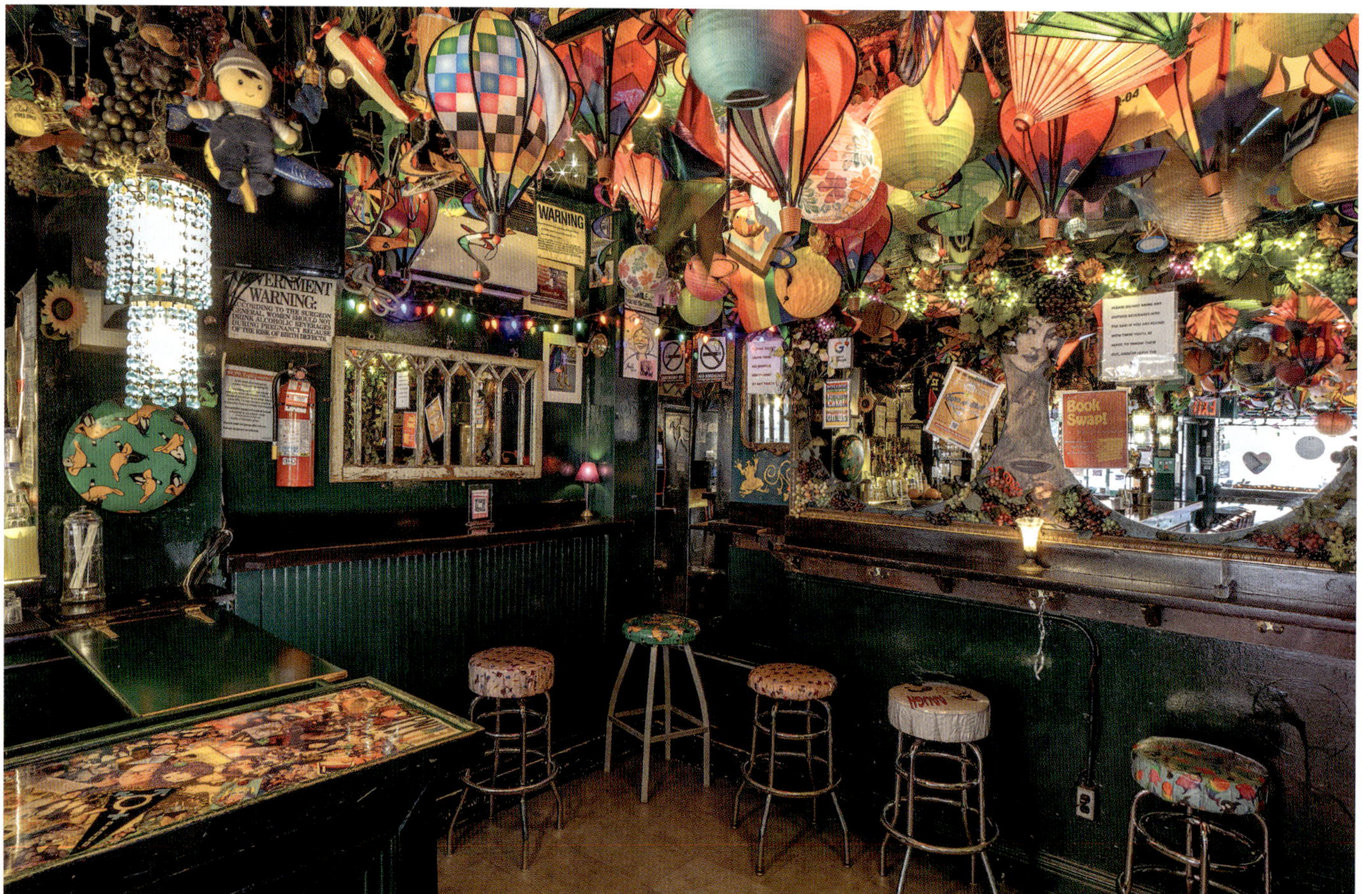

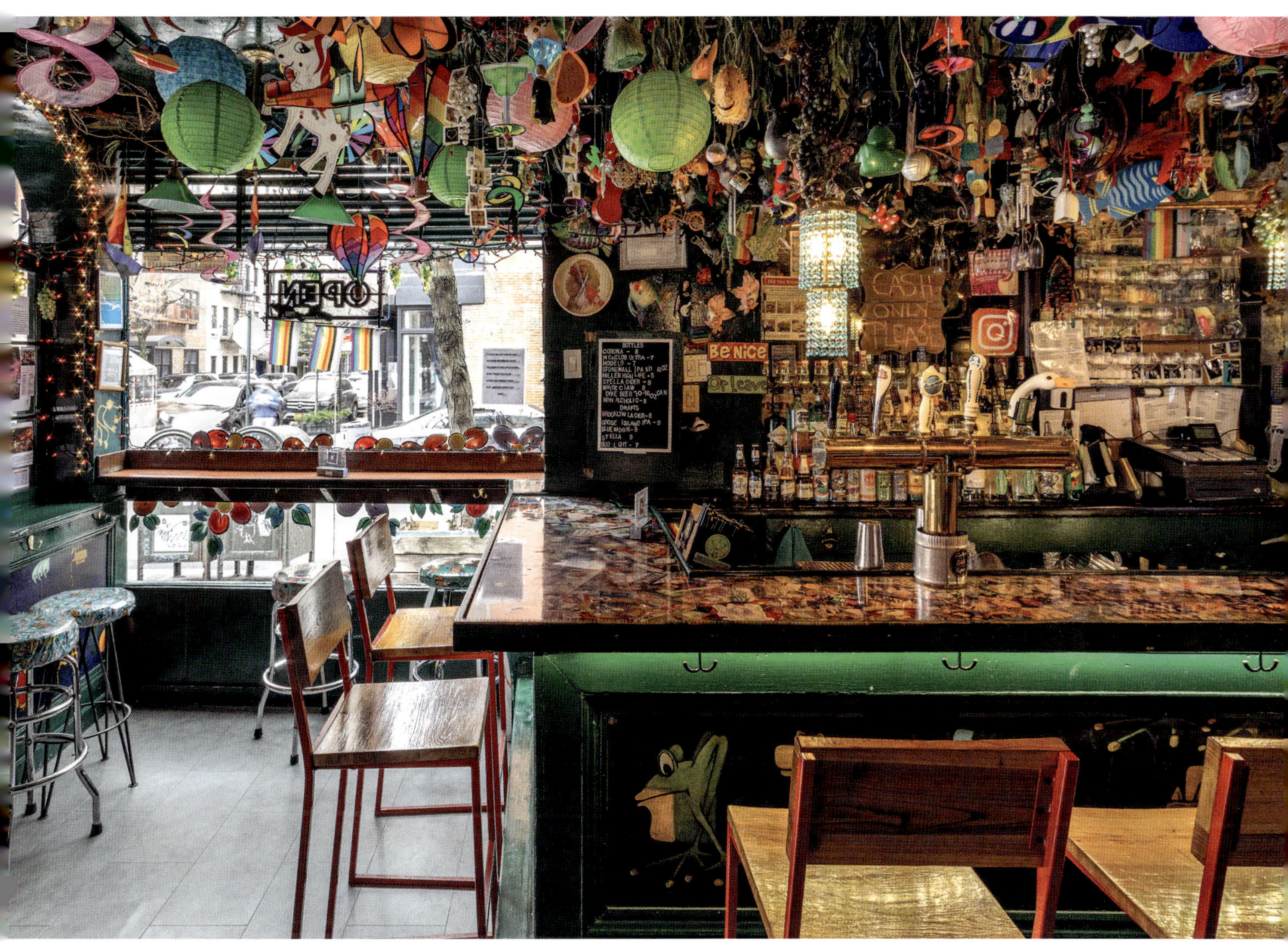

OPPOSITE TOP *Cubbyhole's current owner, Lisa Menichino, renovated the bar top a few years ago, adding a layer of resin over photos of patrons and other keepsakes given to her by customers.*

OPPOSITE BOTTOM *Saunders originally decorated the tops of the stools with Looney Tunes characters. Menichino later added more comic book characters, including Wonder Woman and other queer icons.*

ABOVE *The decorations inside the bar change with the seasons and during the holidays. The items depicted here are spring themed.*

THE EAR INN

Nestled within the historic James Brown House, the Ear Inn stands as one of New York City's most enduring drinking establishments, with a past dating back to the late eighteenth century. In its early days, it was situated just 4 feet (1 meter) from the waters of the Hudson River, where piers docked boats coming and going everywhere from California to China.

Given its great age, much of the Ear Inn's real history has been lost to time. However, if legend is to be believed, the Federal-style wooden house was constructed around 1770 for James Brown, an African American aide to George Washington during the Revolutionary War, who is depicted in artist Emanuel Leutze's famous painting of the Continental Army crossing the Delaware River. Brown, who became wealthy through the tobacco trade, purchased the home down the street from Washington's Richmond Hill estate.

The ramshackle operation that would become the Ear Inn originated in 1817. In the mid-1800s, another proprietor, Thomas Cooke, sold home-brewed beer and corn whiskey to visiting sailors and longshoremen. Over time, the brewery was converted into a full-service restaurant and grew to include a dining room, which supplanted the former backyard and outhouse; during this period, only men were allowed inside. Throughout the ages, the upstairs apartment in the same building has been used as a smuggler's den, brothel, and doctor's office.

During Prohibition, the Ear Inn thrived as a speakeasy, becoming known as the Green Door. After the repeal of the booze ban, it became more publicly known as a watering hole for sailors, offering food, drink, and of course gambling. The Green Door nickname stuck and became known worldwide. One regular, known simply as Mickey the Sailor, is believed to have died after a night of overdrinking in 1920—and now haunts the bar from the afterlife.

It wasn't until the late 1970s, under the reins of current owners Martin Sheridan and Richard "Rip" Hayman, that the establishment received its official name, the Ear Inn. This moniker was created as a way to circumvent the NYC Landmark Commission's protracted review of new signage: instead of replacing the neon BAR sign, they covered part of the letter *B* with spray paint, forming the name EAR. The minor alteration has made the bar even more iconic.

Interestingly, Hayman himself was a shipbuilder and occasional sailor who once worked as an international tour guide. According to a 1998 profile in the *New York Times*, while studying music at Columbia University, he had persuaded the then-owner of the James Brown House to let him live upstairs in the building, eventually buying it for what would today be considered a paltry sum. In the '70s and '80s, he used the space to run a new music journal called *Ear*.

Through Hayman, the Ear Inn bridges its past as a sailor's pub and its present connection to the arts community. In the late 1900s, luminaries such as John Lennon and Allen Ginsberg held court in the bar, with the latter giving poetry readings there. When the *New York Times* revisited the Ear Inn in 2018, it noted the presence of book editors and executives from nearby offices in addition to cocktail fans and tourists from around the world.

Besides hosting famous patrons, the bar has borne witness to key local events throughout its history. Hurricane Sandy's impact in 2012 led to the flooding of the entire basement, resulting in losses of $200,000 worth of equipment and supplies.

Nowadays, after over two hundred years of continuous operation, the neighborhood around the Ear Inn is no longer the gritty sailors' quarter it once was. And the river waters have not danced at its door since 1825, when landfill was used to extend Manhattan island by one block to West Street (though part of the original wooden sidewalk still exists outside the bar).

Catering to new audiences, the Ear Inn is also once again a restaurant, specializing in old-school burgers served with home fries. However, visitors today can still catch a glimpse of its many past lives—from distillery to speakeasy to sailor's clubhouse—in memorabilia adorning the walls, including nautical curios, old beer signs, newspaper clippings, and an array of ear-centric artwork from across the decades.

Further mementos were discovered when construction on the Philip Johnson–designed Urban Glass House next to the Ear Inn began in 2006. Excavation of the tavern's foundation revealed apothecary bottles for elixirs and salves, as well as pieces of the actual original pier on the Hudson River. Today the second floor of the bar has three rooms of gallery space for exhibitions, showcasing relics uncovered during renovations over the years. The James Brown House that is home to the bar was designated a New York City landmark in 1969.

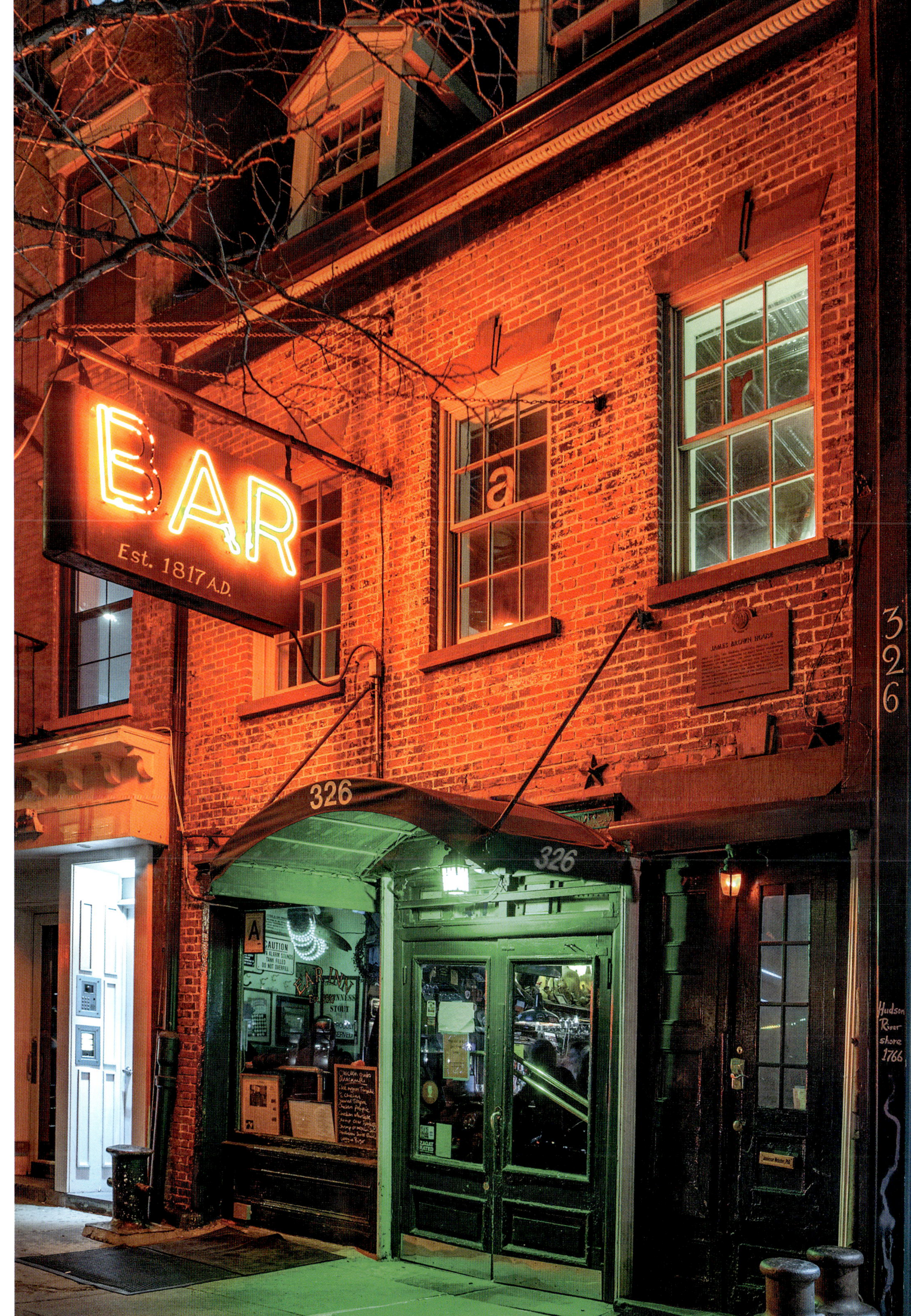

BAR
Est. 1817 A.D.
a
JAMES BROWN HOUSE
326
326
326
Hudson River shore 1766
EAR INN
ORIGINAL GUINNESS STOUT

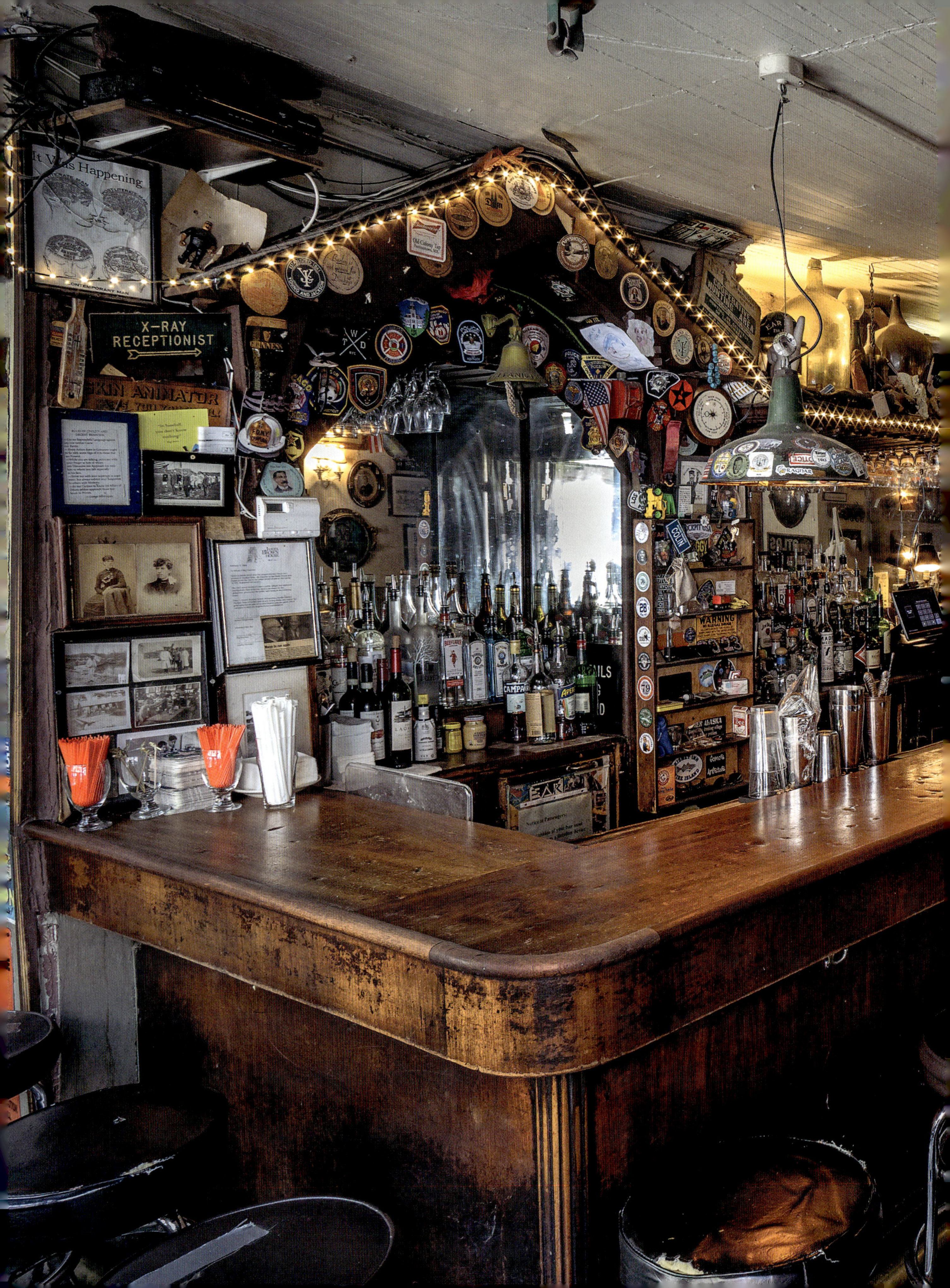

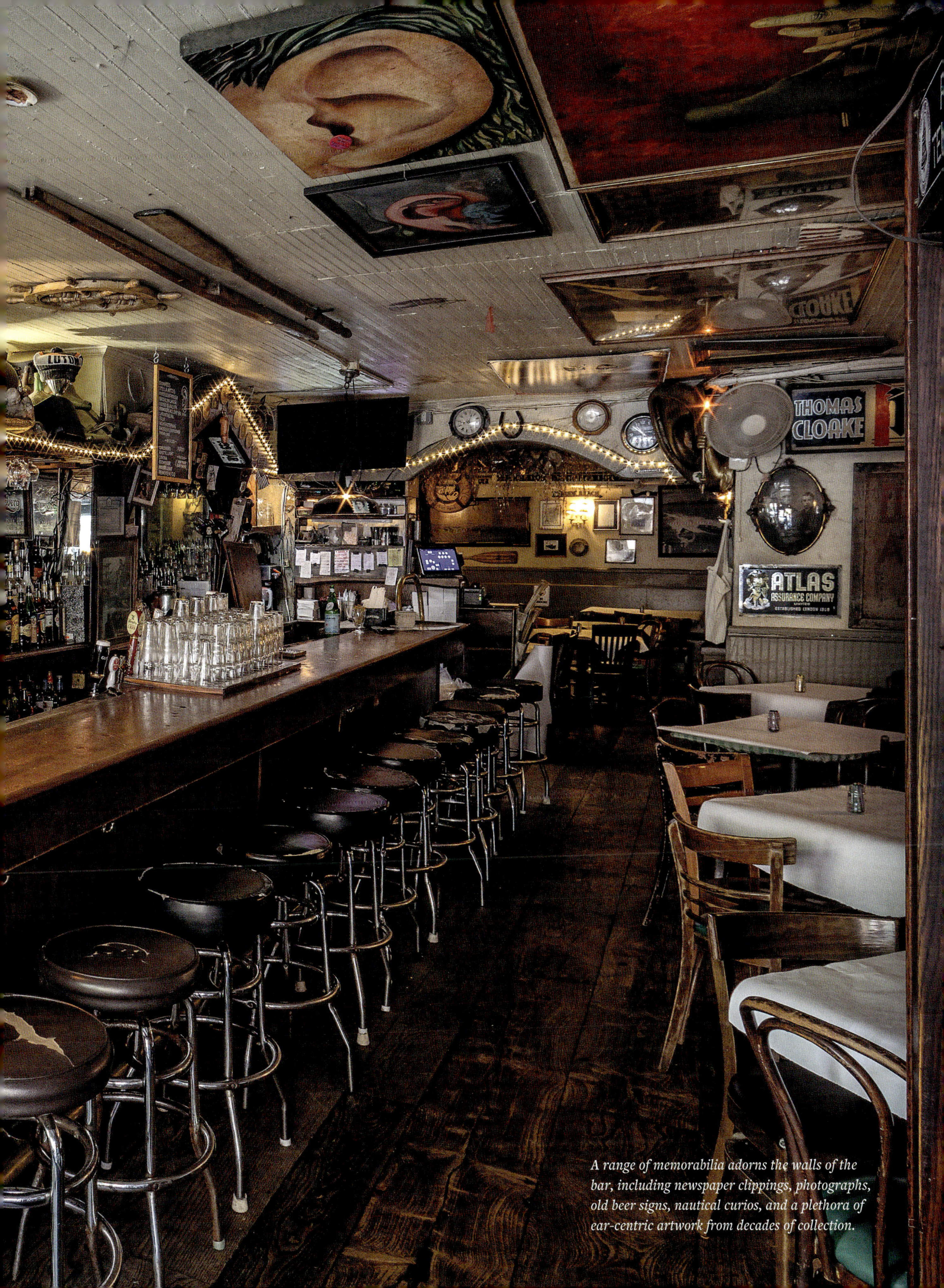

A range of memorabilia adorns the walls of the bar, including newspaper clippings, photographs, old beer signs, nautical curios, and a plethora of ear-centric artwork from decades of collection.

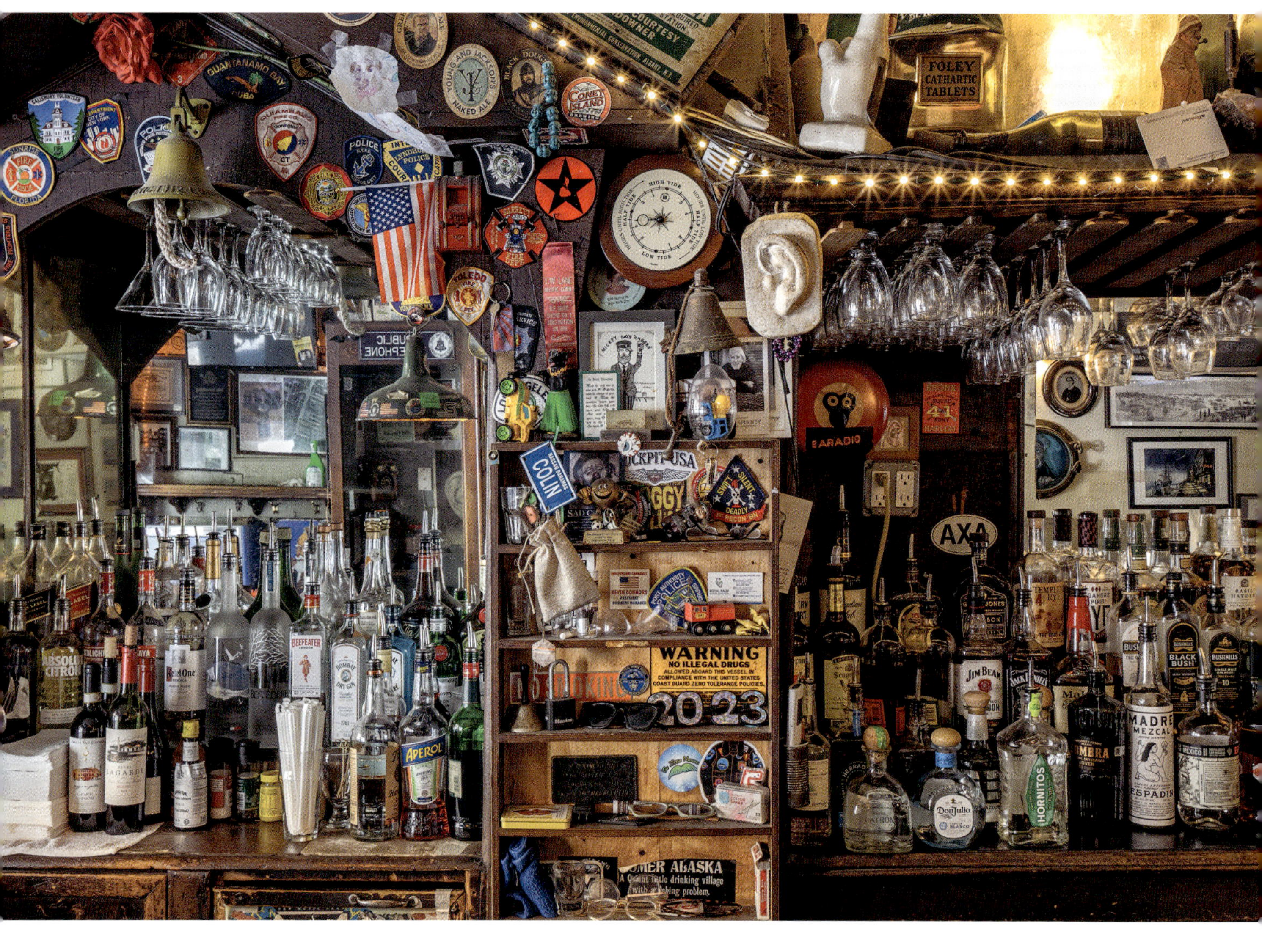

OPPOSITE TOP   *When construction next to the Ear Inn began in 2006, the foundations of the tavern were dug up and stabilized. During this process, excavators found apothecary bottles and pieces of the original pier on the Hudson River.*

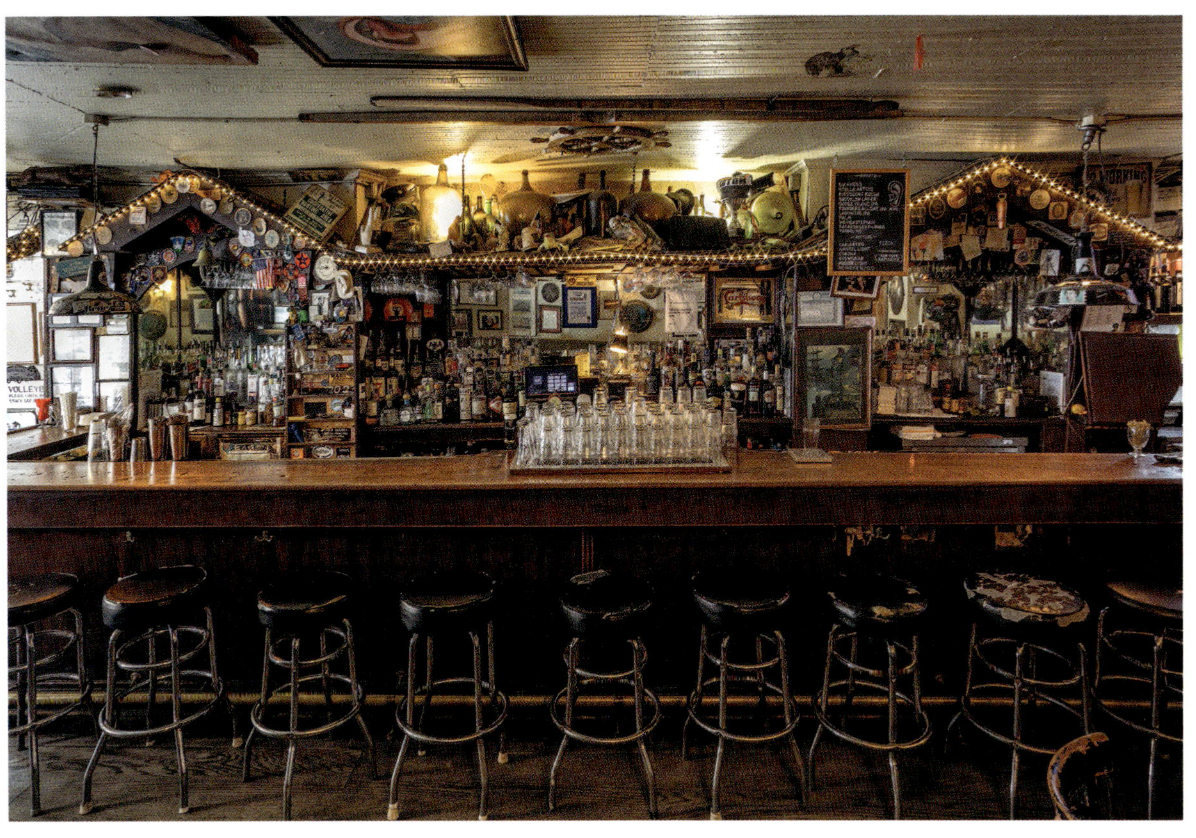

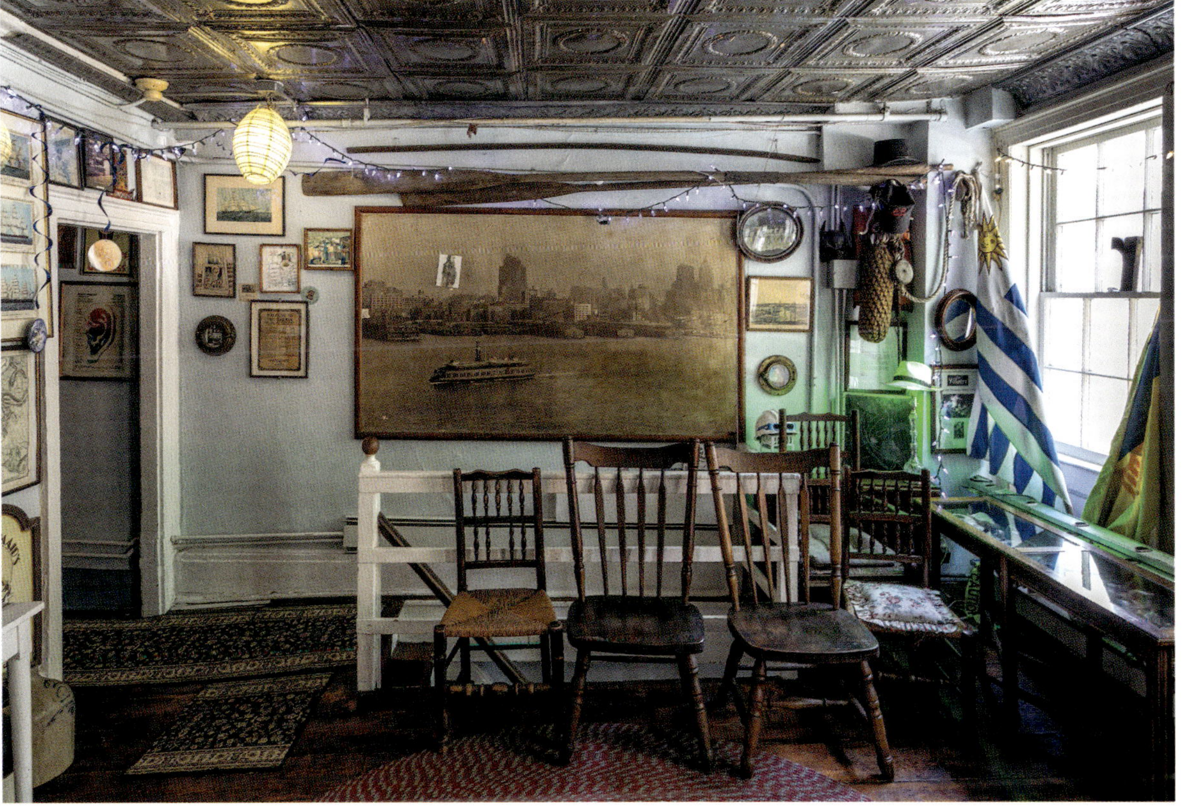

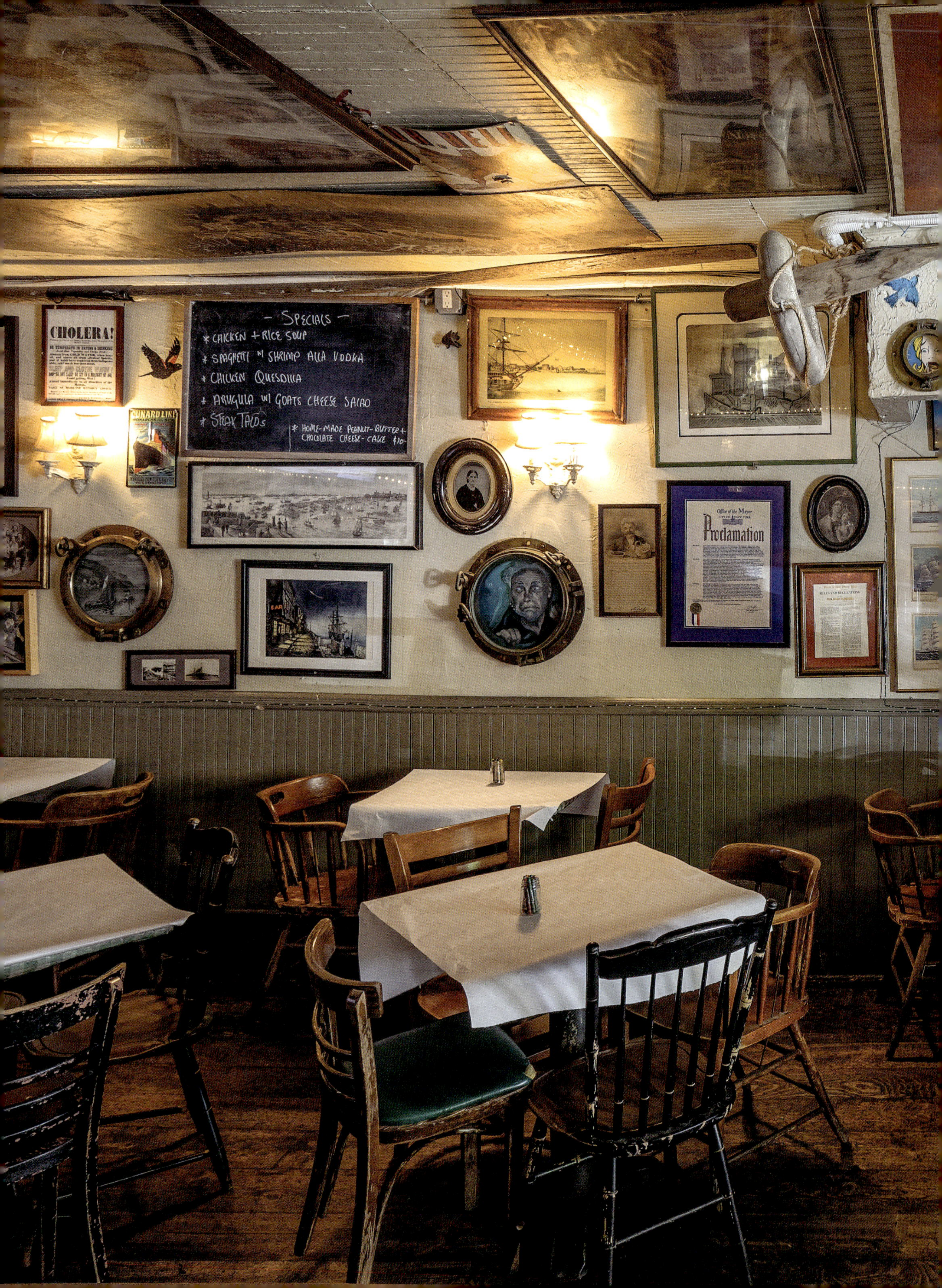
- SPECIALS -
* CHICKEN + RICE SOUP
* SPAGHETTI W SHRIMP ALLA VODKA
* CHICKEN QUESDILLA
* ARUGULA W/ GOATS CHEESE SALAD
* STEAK TACOs
* HOME-MADE PEANUT-BUTTER + CHOCOLATE CHEESE-CAKE $10-
CHOLERA!
BE TEMPERATE IN EATING & DRINKING
SLEEP AND CLOTHE WARM
PROCLAMATION

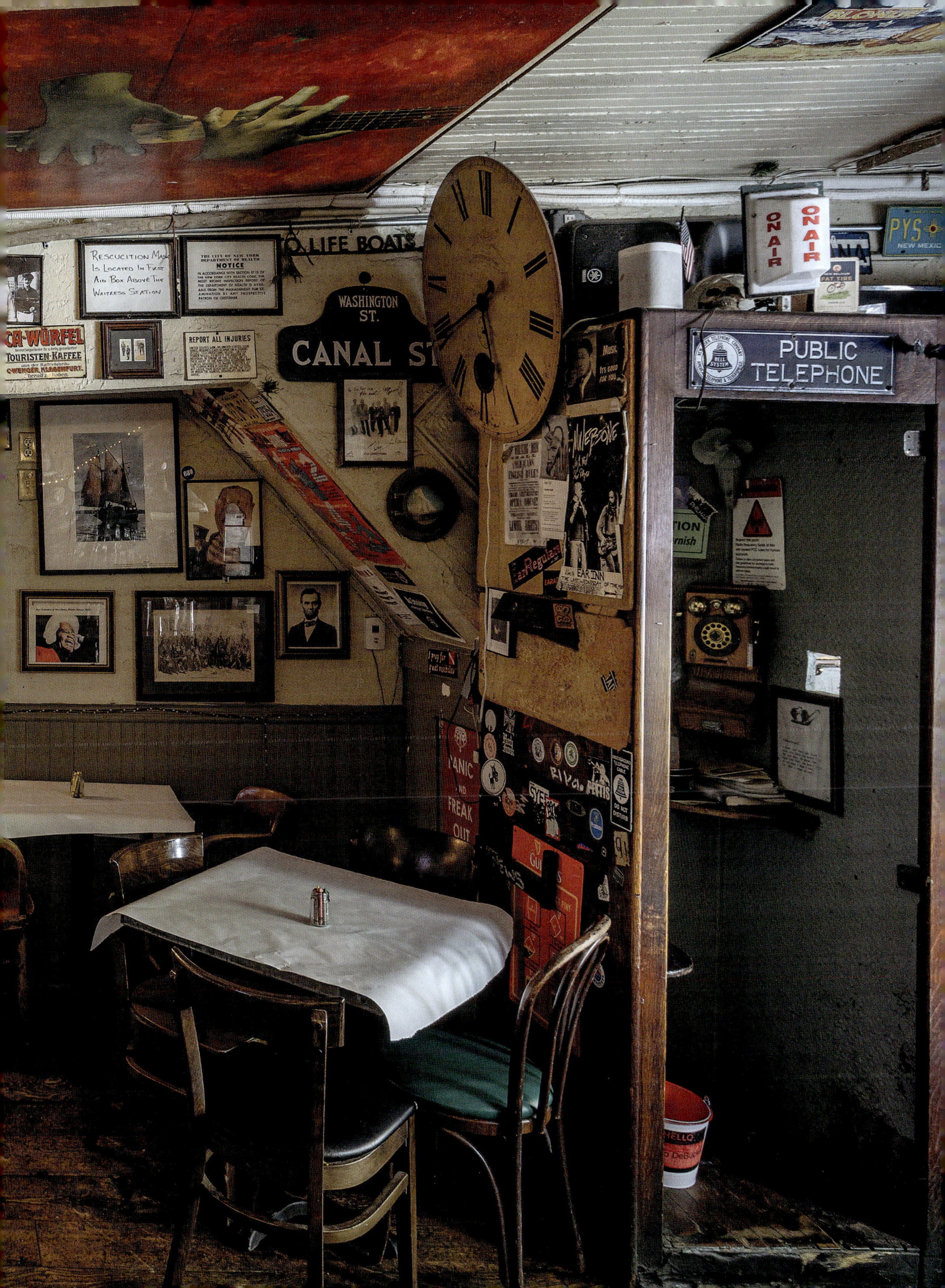

ON AIR
ON AIR
PYS-
NEW MEXICO
PUBLIC
TELEPHONE
RESCUCITION MASK
IS LOCATED IN FIRST
AID BOX ABOVE THE
WAITRESS STATION
THE CITY OF NEW YORK
DEPARTMENT OF HEALTH
NOTICE
TO LIFE BOATS
WASHINGTON
ST.
CANAL ST
REPORT ALL INJURIES
CA-WÜRFEL
TOURISTEN-KAFFEE
Music
It's good
for you
EAR Inn
PANIC
AND
FREAK
OUT
GYPSY
RIV OLD PERTIS
HELLO

THE LANDMARK TAVERN

626 11TH AVENUE, HELL'S KITCHEN

Sitting a stone's throw from the Hudson River on Eleventh Avenue in Hell's Kitchen, the Landmark Tavern holds a rich history, dating back to its founding in 1868 by Patrick Henry Carley. Originally established as a waterfront saloon, it catered primarily to the needs of dockworkers and merchant seamen during a time when the area was densely populated by Irish immigrants.

Interestingly, Carley and his wife designed the space to house a family home within the same building, and the second and third floors served as their residence with their children. This arrangement would remain in place until Prohibition prompted the Carleys to turn their third floor into a secret speakeasy to circumvent the ban on alcohol.

Notably, the tavern is steeped in reports of hauntings; it's rumored that the spirits of the past still roam within its walls. One ghostly presence is said to be that of original *Scarface* star and erstwhile Landmark regular George Raft, who lingers within the bar. Others include a Confederate Civil War veteran who was knifed in a fight and died in the second-floor bathtub (which is still there), and a nineteenth-century child who died in her bed on the third floor.

Yet despite its reputation for paranormal activity, the Landmark Tavern has also been renowned as a standout Irish restaurant for much of its history. When the *New York Times* visited in 1973, it praised the venue's takes on Irish classics like fresh-baked soda bread, braised chicken in sherry, and flaky apple pie. It also cited then–newly renovated decor, like wood-burning potbelly iron stoves, pressed-glass lampshades, and swinging saloon doors meant to evoke the turn of the century.

By the late 1970s the Landmark was a favorite hangout of the Mafia-affiliated Irish American gang the Westies. In 1978 the bar even played host to a meeting between Westies leadership and local labor leaders.

In the years since it first opened, the Landmark Tavern has retained much of its initial charm. Surrounded today by warehouses and offices, the three-story building remains a stand-alone structure. Inside, the mahogany bar, carved from a single hunk of wood, remains a centerpiece. Alongside this, the establishment still shows off an antique cash register and backbar. The likewise original tin ceilings and tile floor were uncovered and restored in the early 2000s. However, there have also been some changes: the Landmark Tavern no longer sits near the water, as it saw an inland shift when landfill was used to extend the island of Manhattan a bit further to create what is now Twelfth Avenue.

As the bar's old-school ambiance endures, so do its menu offerings. It continues to serve a selection of classic Irish brews on tap, ranging from Guinness and Smithwick's to the bar's own namesake lager and IPA. On the food front, you'll find comfort classics like beer-battered fish and chips, shepherd's pie, and Irish bangers and mash.

When the *New York Times* returned in 1995, it noted, "The Landmark has Bass, Murphy's Stout, Saranac, and McSorley's on tap, along with a long list of single-malt whiskies and single-barrel bourbons. It does not court a trendy crowd. It does not get one. Everyone is happy. You will be, too."

Clearly not much has changed. Today the bar is owned by Donnchadh O'Sullivan and Michael Young, who have lovingly maintained its historic interior.

OPPOSITE   *The Landmark Tavern was opened in 1868 as an Irish waterfront saloon on the shores of the Hudson River to serve the longshoremen and workers along the neighboring docks and piers.*

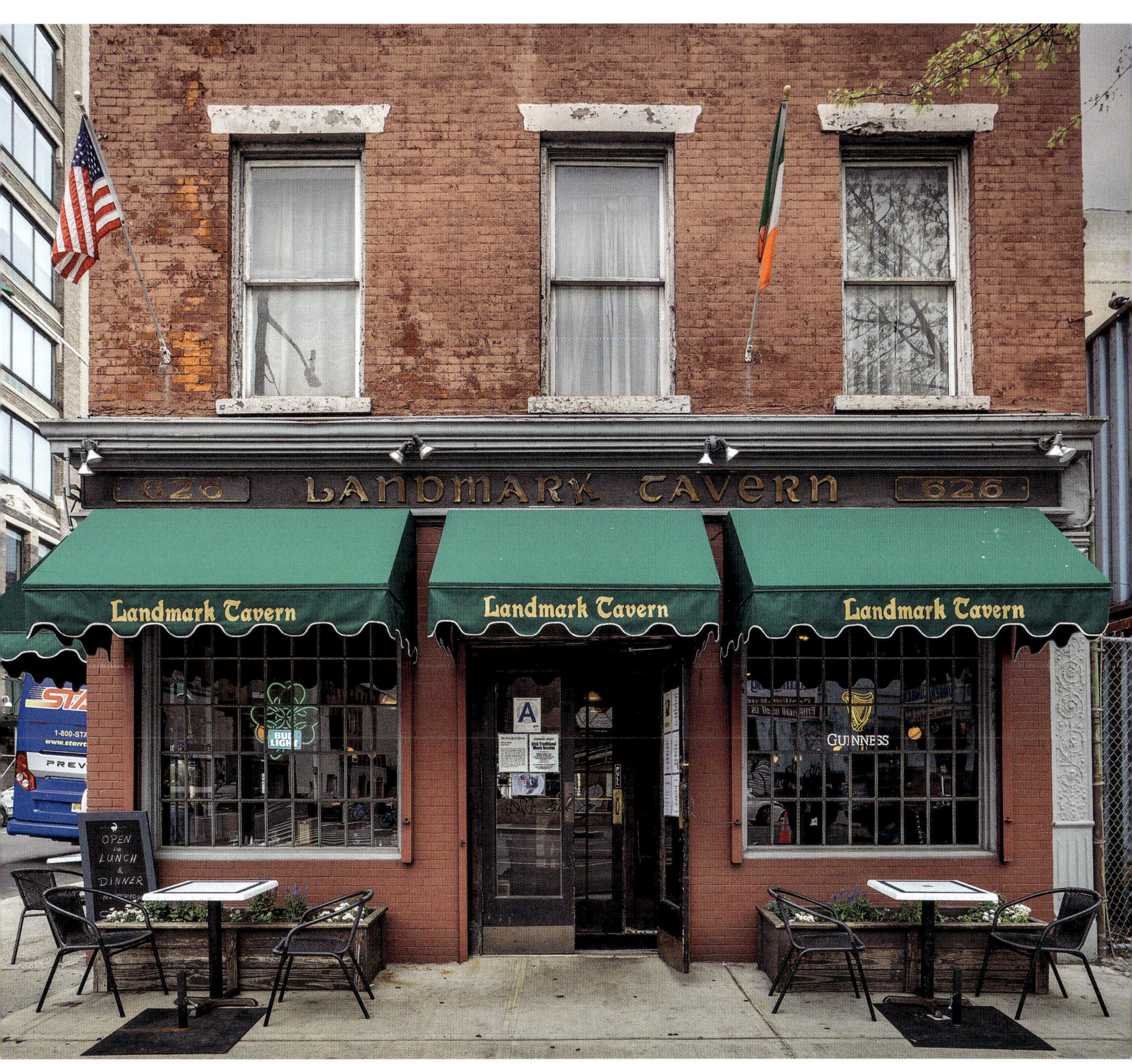

THE LANDMARK TAVERN

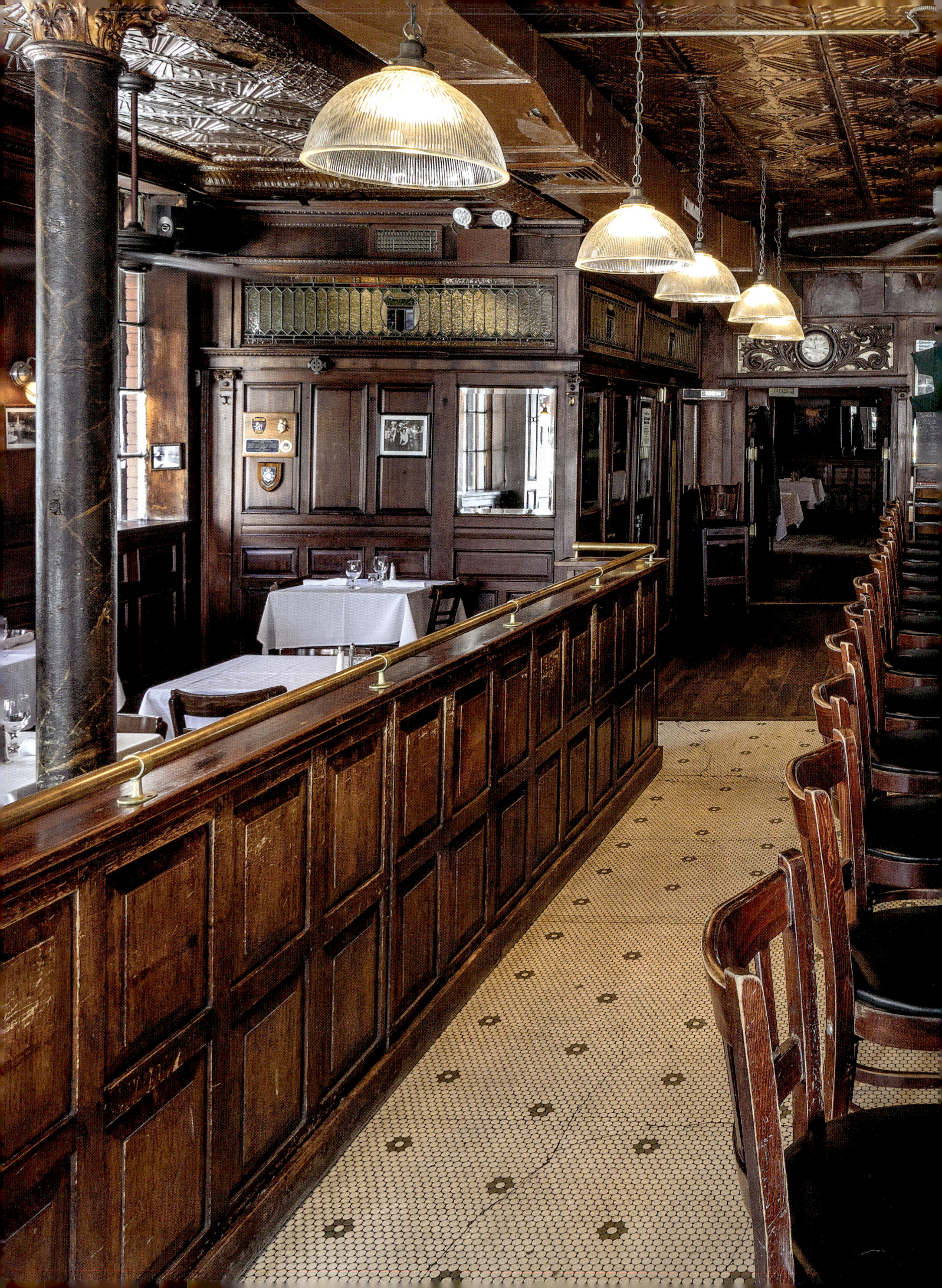

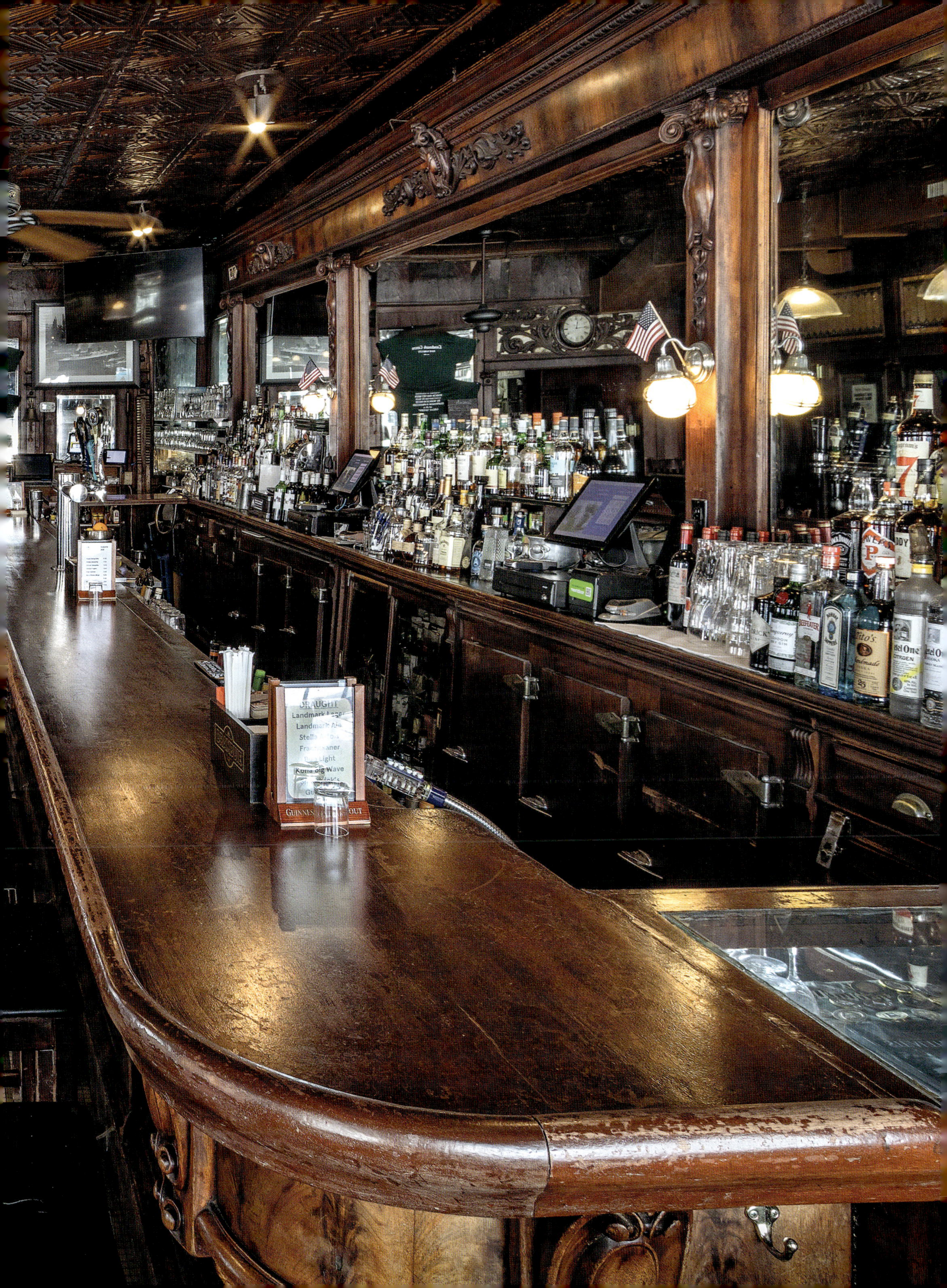

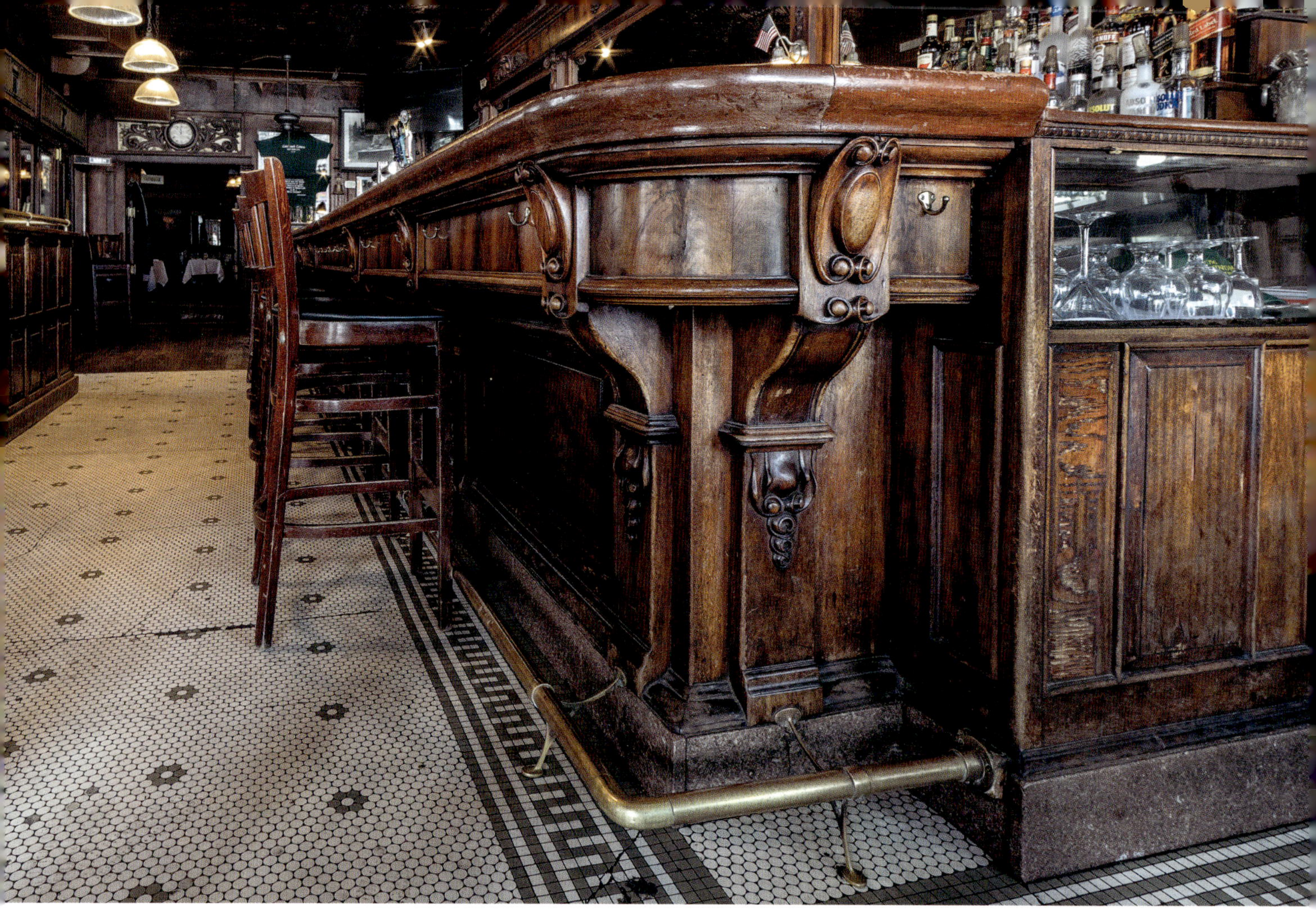

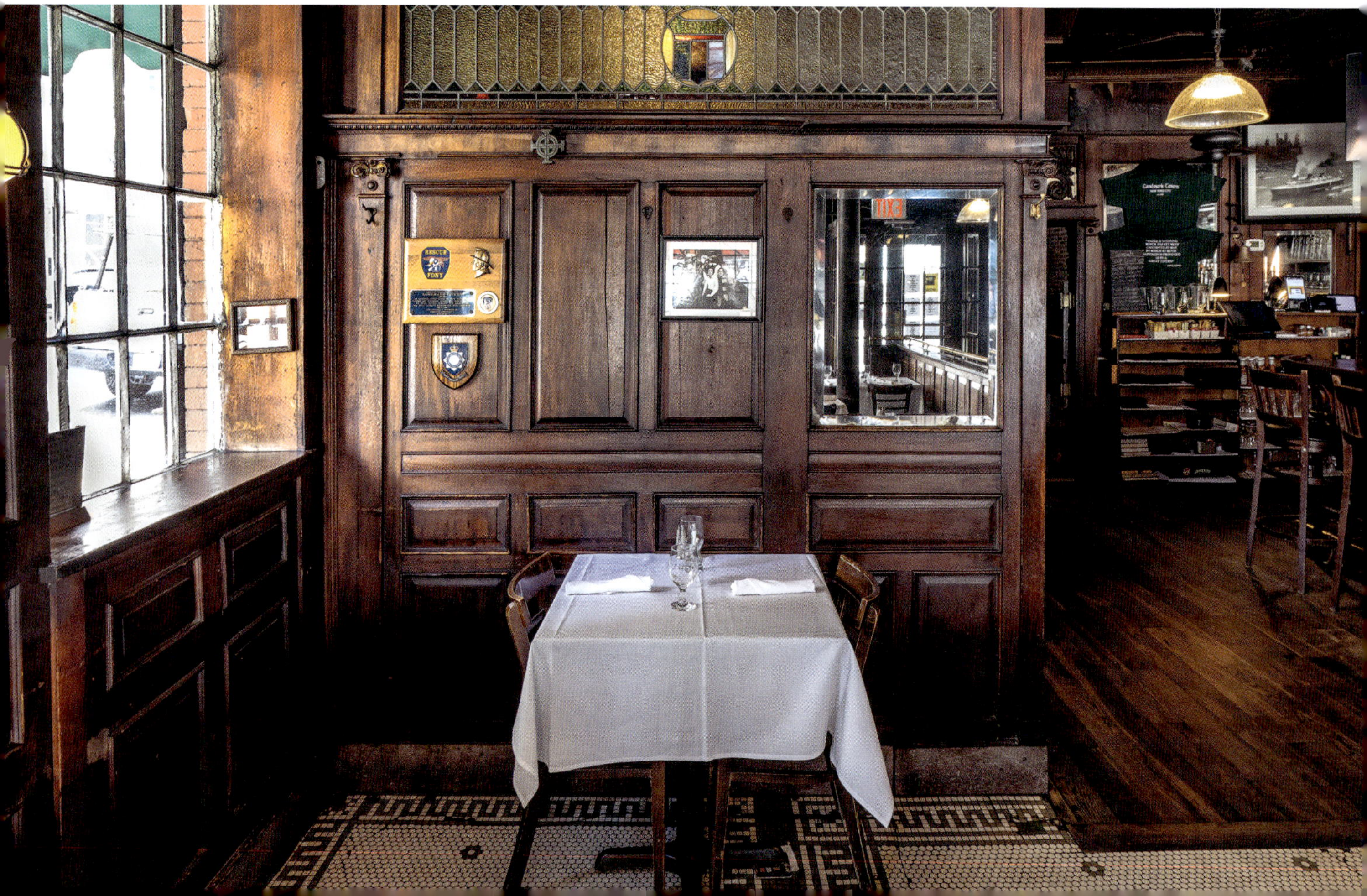

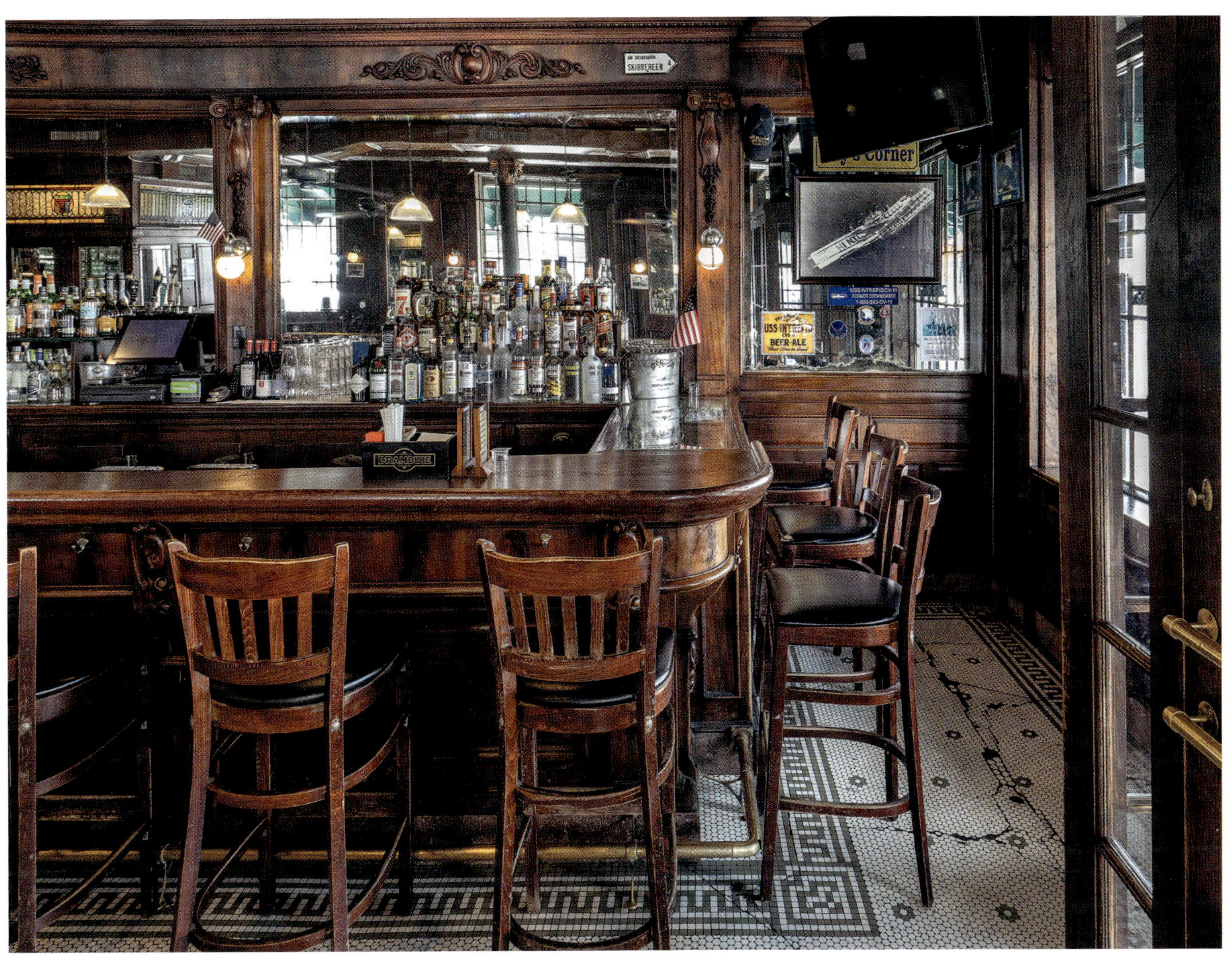

OPPOSITE TOP   *The Landmark is one of the oldest continuously operating drinking establishments in New York City and retains much of its original interior, including its bar, which was carved from a single hunk of mahogany wood.*

ABOVE   *In addition to the mahogany bar and backbar, the tile floors and tin ceiling are also original and were uncovered and restored in the early 2000s.*

BEAUTY BAR

231 EAST 14TH STREET,
EAST VILLAGE

You would be forgiven for thinking that Beauty Bar, a salon-turned-saloon, is much older than it actually is. Though it opened in 1995 in Manhattan's East Village, it retains some of the original furnishings from its past life as a salon, including barbershop chairs and helmet-style chrome-domed hairdryers from the 1950s and 1960s. Meanwhile, vintage perfumes from as early as the 1920s, as well as canisters of Aqua Net, the aerosol hair spray developed in the '60s, line its shelves.

Located on East Fourteenth Street near Union Square, Beauty Bar was the brainchild of nightlife veteran Deb Parker and her business partner Paul Devitt. A Scarsdale native, Parker had studied sculpture at the School of Visual Arts, where she befriended the likes of artists Keith Haring and Kenny Scharf, frequenting renowned downtown clubs like CBGB and the Mudd Club. Through the '80s and '90s, she worked as a dominatrix (briefly), promoter, and bartender at numerous NYC bars and clubs, plus opened some of her own spots along the way. Notable on her resume were a series of now-shuttered, campy themed bars, including Alphabet City's Babyland, which featured kiddy furniture and cocktails sipped from sippy cups, and the nearby Barmacy, set in a pharmacy. Still open today is Parker's tiki bar, Otto's Shrunken Head.

Meanwhile, Devitt had founded the legendary Silk City diner, an eatery and music venue in Philadelphia. While living in Philly, he saw a vintage salon interior for sale, which inspired the concept of Beauty Bar.

With this proven knack for executing a theme, Parker and Devitt devised their most famous venue, Beauty Bar, as a space that allowed guests to get their nails done while enjoying cocktails. The front of the bar still feels like an old-time salon (it was built in the former Thomas Beauty Salon), while the back opens up for events and congregating with drinks. Nearly three decades later, "Martinis and Manicures" remains a beloved staple.

Michael Stewart, the current operating owner, joined the bar as its doorman on opening weekend. He quickly transitioned to manager when Parker and Devitt were turning their focus to creating Barmacy further down Fourteenth Street. Over the years, he bought shares from investors that decided to sell their stake in the bar. Nowadays, Devitt is still a partner, but Parker is focusing on her life upstate.

As gimmicks come and go, Beauty Bar's unique, theatrical conceit has aged remarkably well through the decades. "It's like *Green Acres* come to life and staffed by the cast of *McHale's Navy*," the erstwhile *Village Voice* nightlife columnist Michael Musto told the *New York Times* back in 1997. "It's kitsch appreciation at its finest."

Meanwhile, in the early 2000s, it added an open-format Blue Rinse Back Room that doubles as a dance floor. It's since become a coveted event space that's hosted comedy nights, DJ sets, burlesque shows, and New York Fashion Week afterparties.

Beauty Bar's status as a bona fide downtown institution has likewise made it a stomping ground for the pretty young thing cohorts across the ages. At the height of the hipster era in the late aughts, it was popular with club-kid icons like the Misshapes. Fast forward to 2023: the bar aptly hosted the launch of media company Highsnobiety's beauty vertical, complete with contemporary celebrities like TikTok model Noen Eubanks and *Gossip Girl* 2.0 star Evan Mock.

Additionally, the bar has held afterparties for numerous bands and has been the location for many photoshoots and music videos, including the Roots' "Rising Up" video. Fans of *Sex and the City* may also recognize Beauty Bar as the backdrop for the episode "They Shoot Single People, Don't They?"

For a glimpse into the past life of New York City, you'll have to stop by and dance the night away under the bar's Liberace-esque chandeliers (or the disco ball in the back). Don't miss a visit to the on-site manicurist, either.

OPPOSITE *Beauty Bar, which has been in business since 1995, was built in an old beauty parlor.*

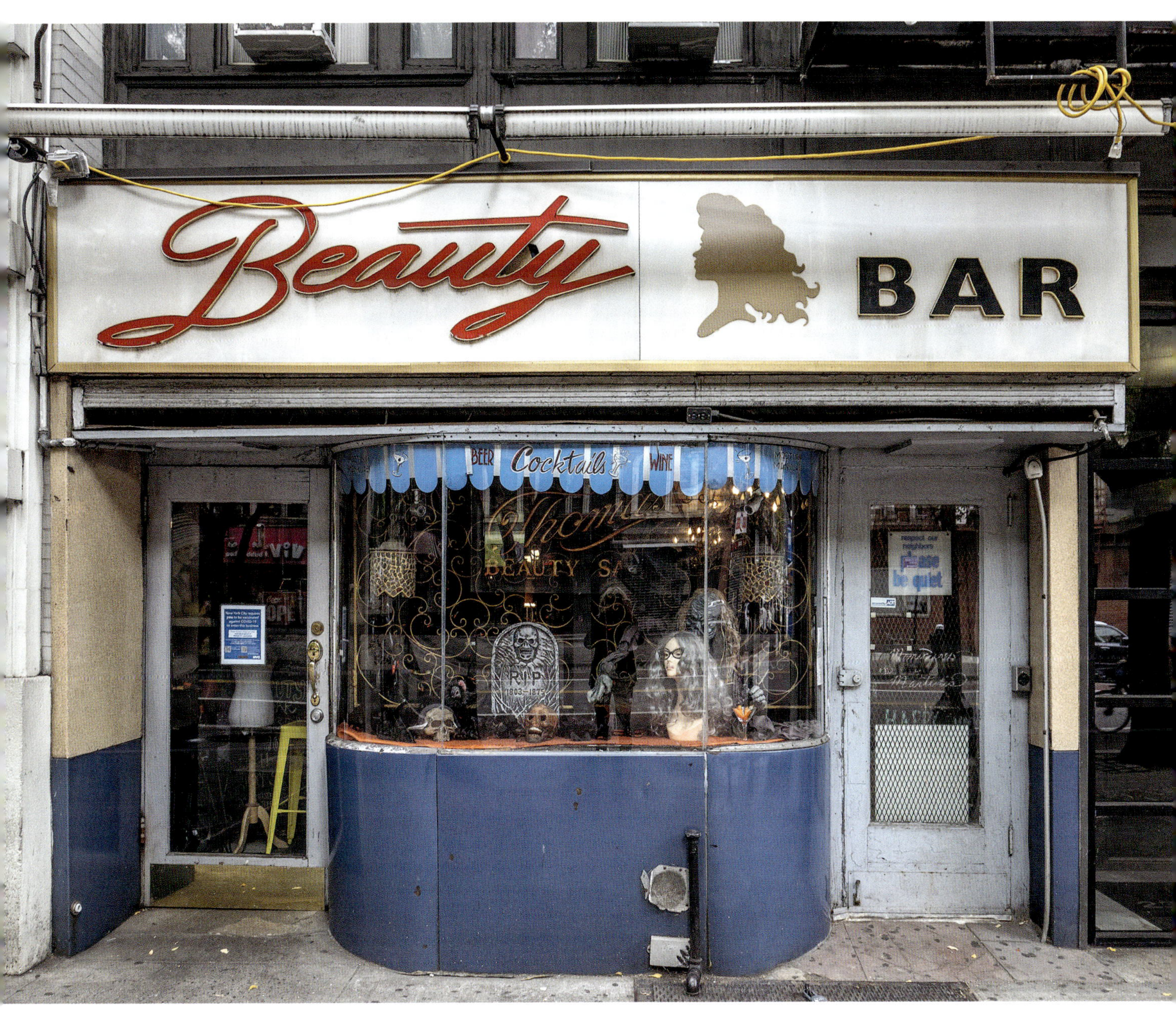

Beauty
BAR
BEER Cocktails WINE
RIP

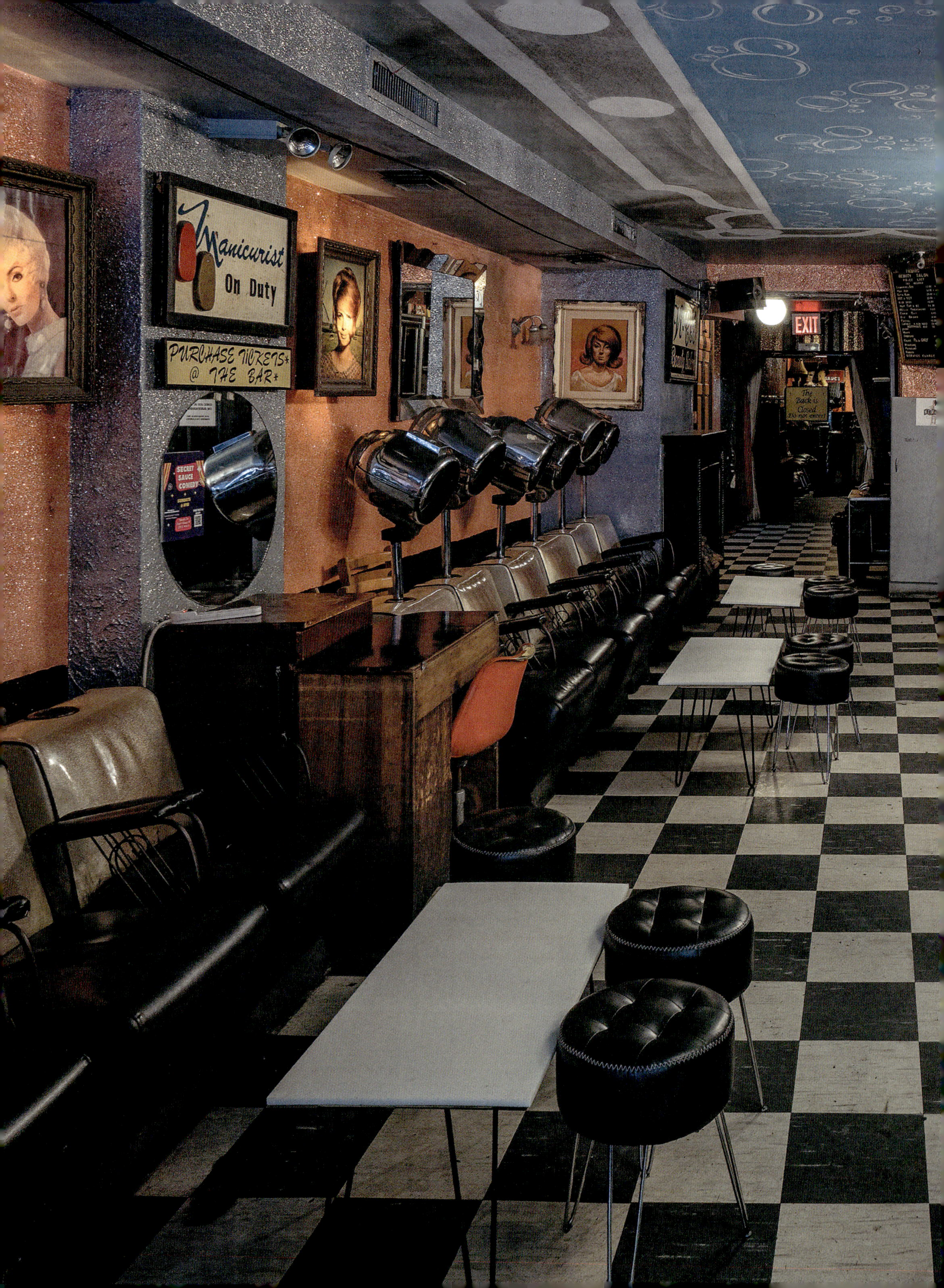
Manicurist
On Duty
PURCHASE TICKETS
@ THE BAR
EXIT
The Back is
Closed
Do not enter

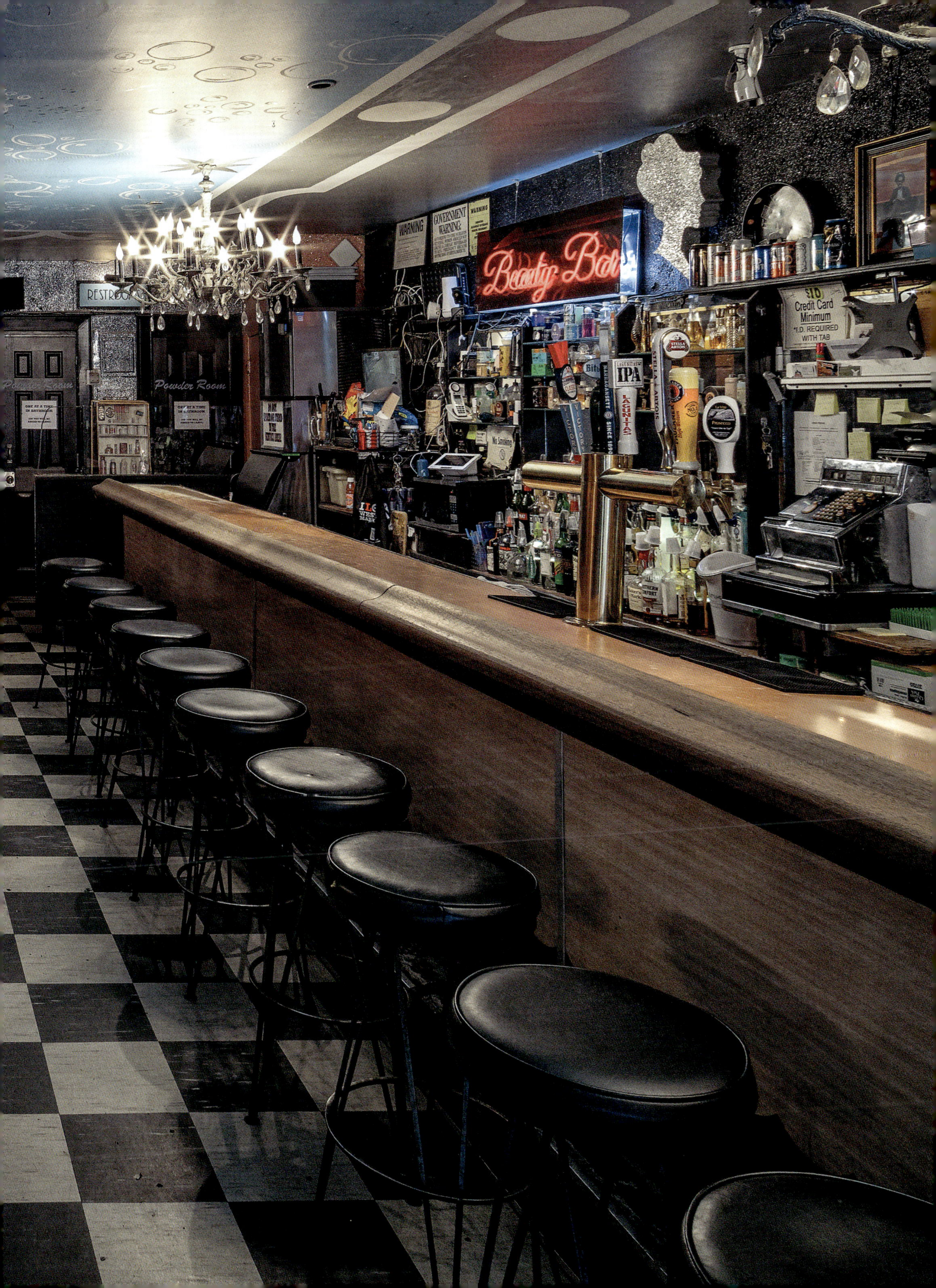
RESTROOM
Powder Room
Beauty Bar
WARNING
GOVERNMENT WARNING
No Smoking
$10
Credit Card
Minimum
*I.D. REQUIRED
WITH TAB

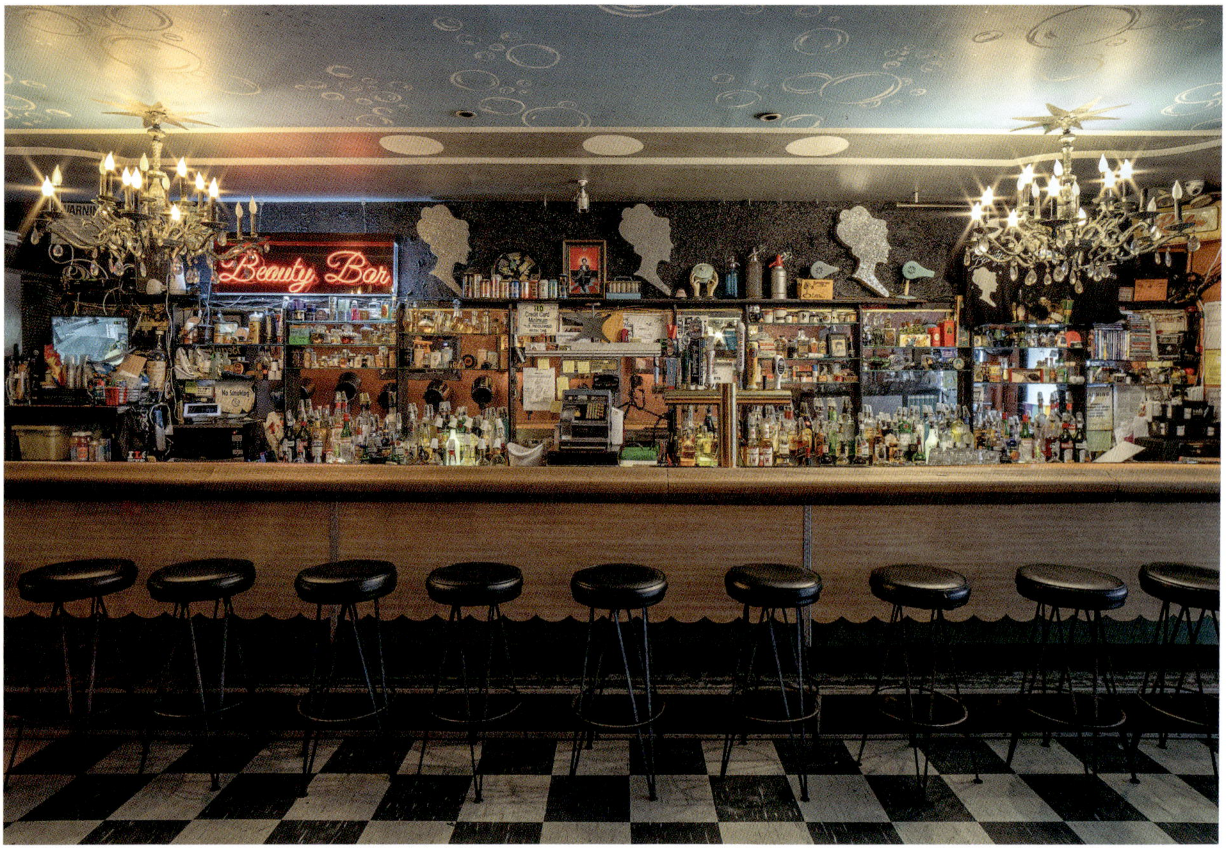

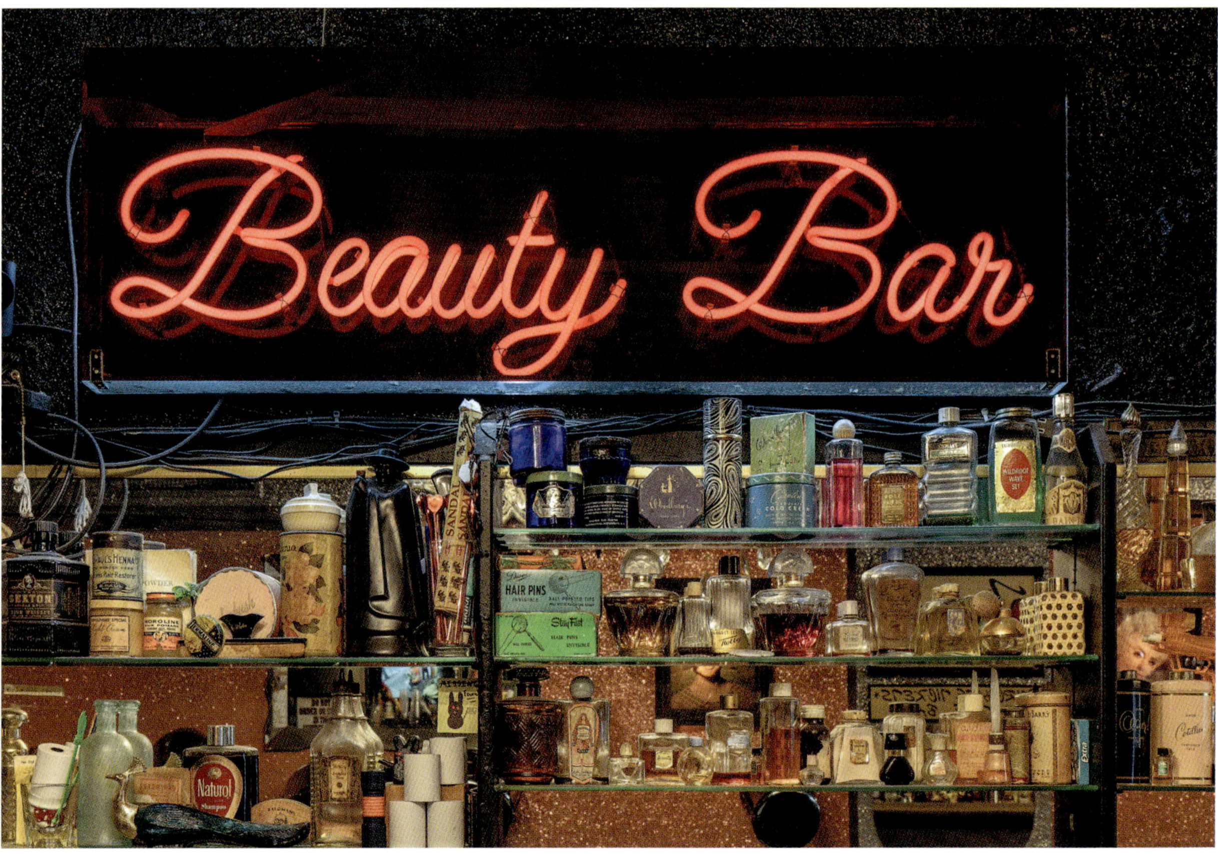

Beauty Bar

Manicurist
On Duty
HASE TICKETS
THE BAR
STERILIZER
STERILIZER
STERILIZER

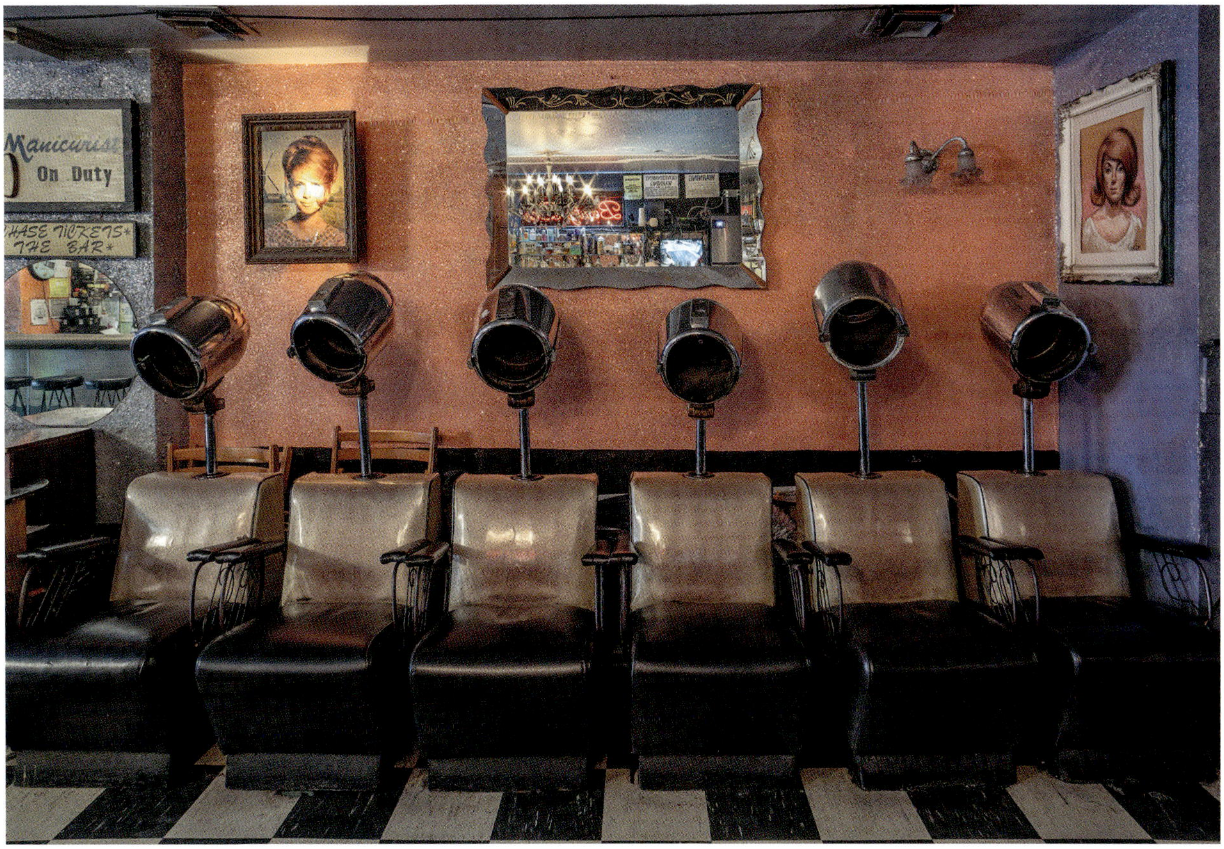

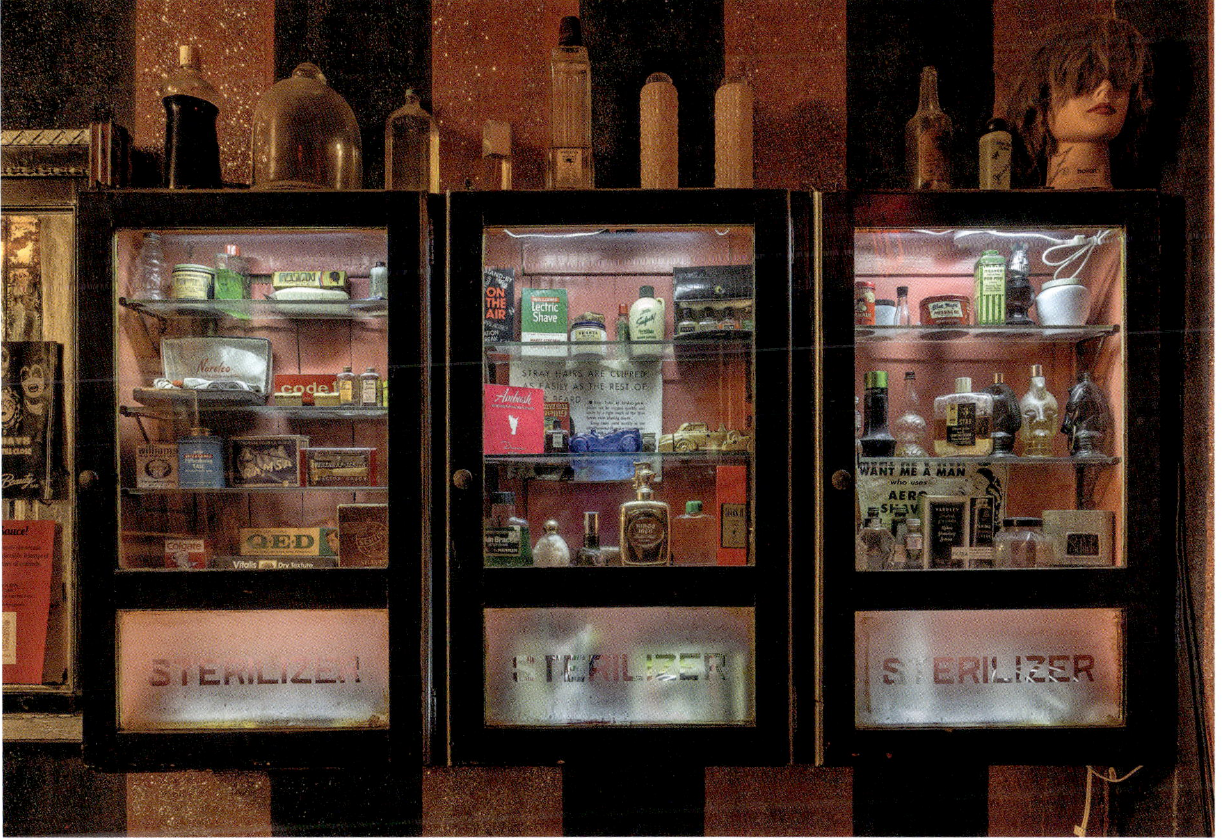

BEAUTY BAR

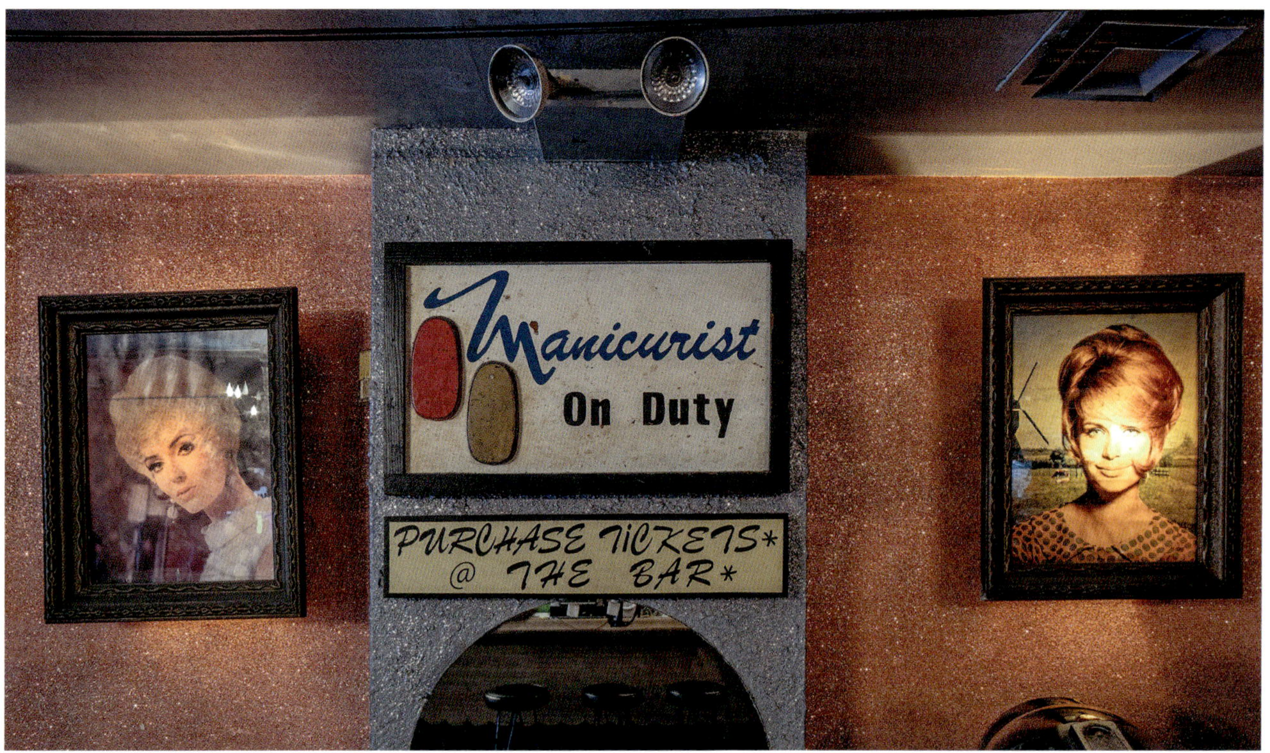

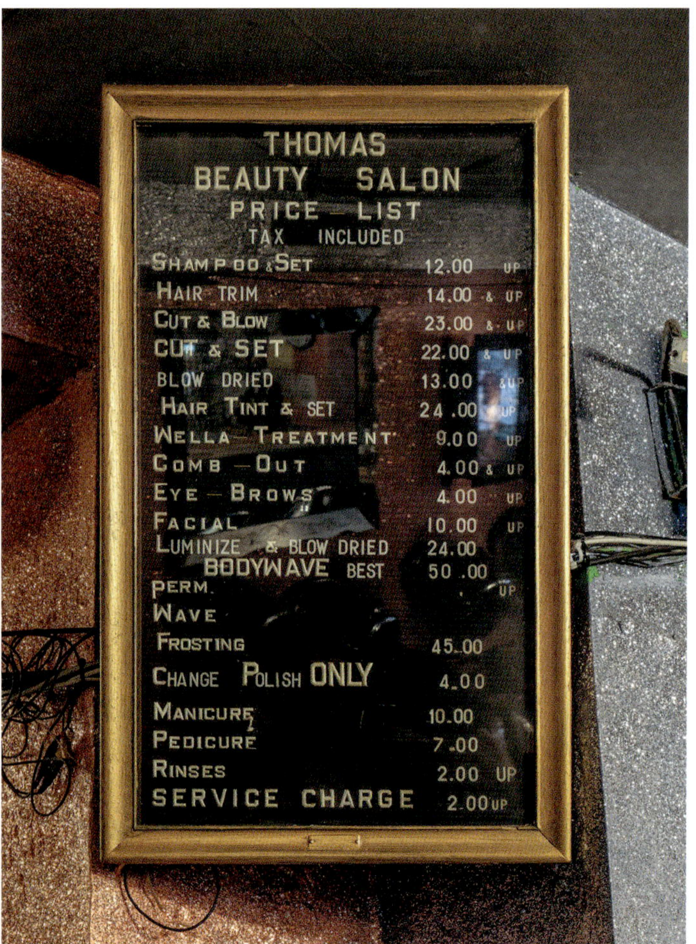

PREVIOUS SPREAD, BOTTOM LEFT
Lining the back wall of the main bar are many vintage beauty salon products.

PREVIOUS SPREAD, TOP RIGHT
The bar kept much of the original interior of the salon, including its vintage chrome-domed hairdryers.

ABOVE *Unique to Beauty Bar, their menu includes a special nails and cocktail offering of a manicure with a Martini.*

LEFT *The price list from its days as a beauty salon still hangs on the wall.*

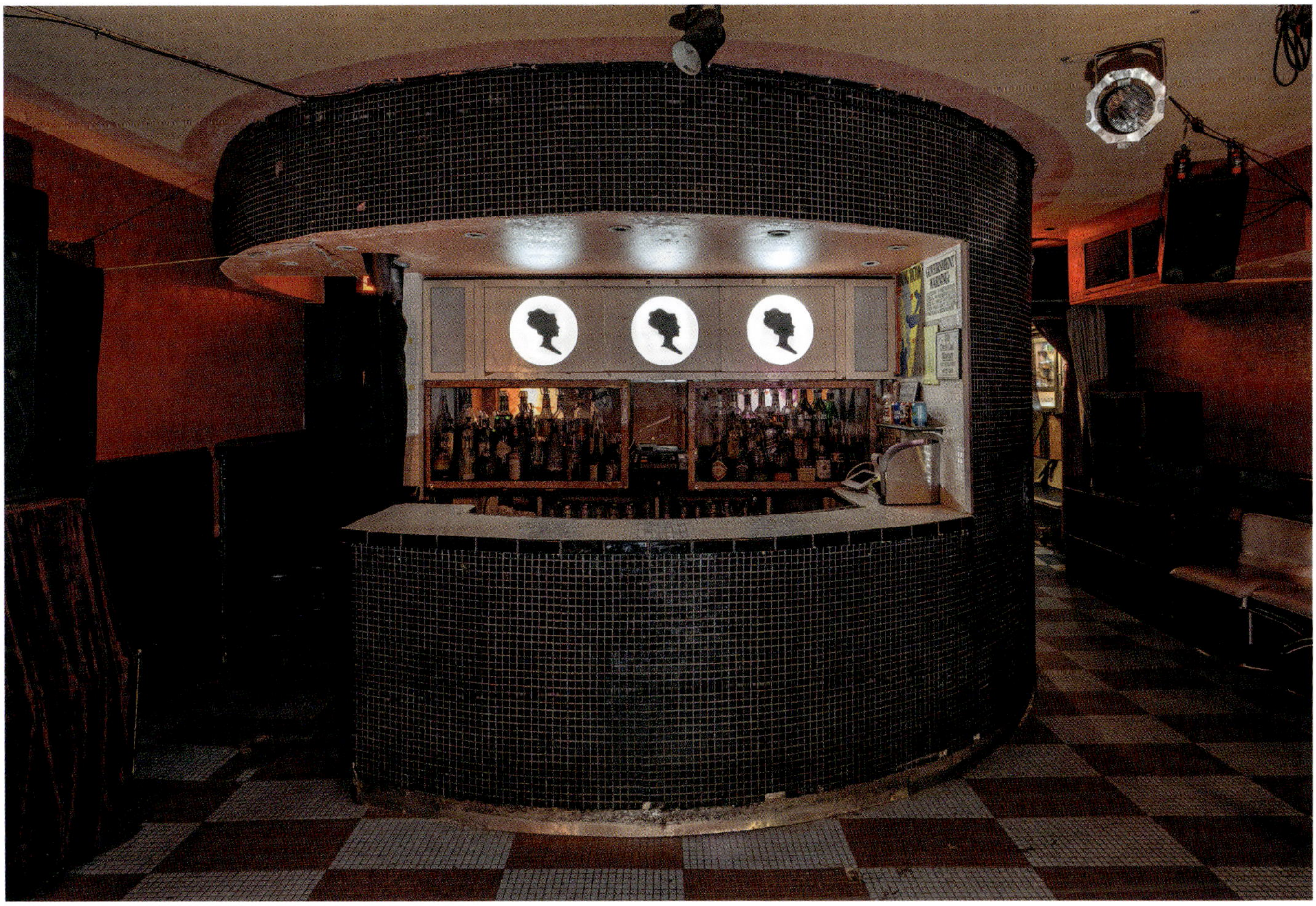

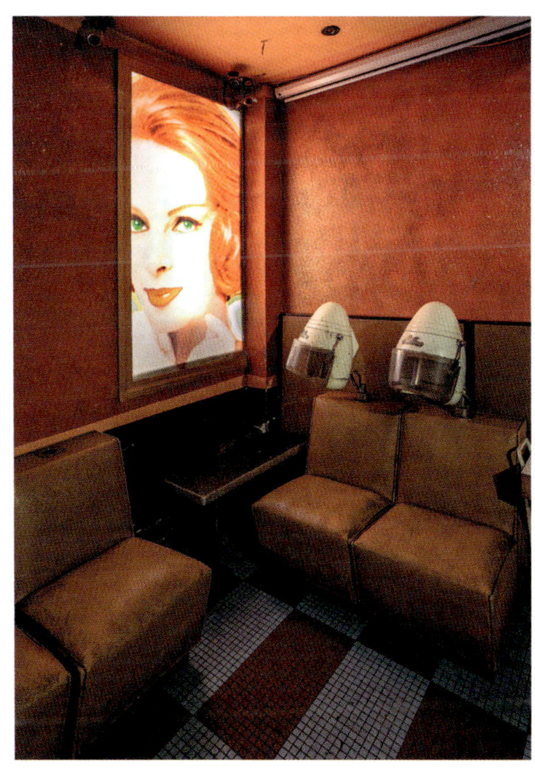

P. J. CLARKE'S

915 THIRD AVENUE,
MIDTOWN EAST

P. J. Clarke's just might be New York City's most iconic burger-slinging saloon. Virtually unchanged since 1884, the Midtown East bar has catered to stars both real—including Frank Sinatra, Jackie Kennedy Onassis, and Nat King Cole—and fictional: it appears often in AMC's '60s-era show *Mad Men* as a favorite haunt of the advertising firm Sterling Cooper.

The original P. J. Clarke's is set in a two-story red-brick Victorian building erected in 1868. A publican named Mr. Jennings (whose first name is unknown) opened it as a bar in 1884, catering to Irish laborers working in the nearby tanneries, breweries, slaughterhouses, and construction sites. In 1902 an Irish immigrant from County Leitrim by the name of Patrick Joseph "Paddy" Clarke started tending bar there. Within ten years he'd save enough to buy the bar and give it his name.

P. J. Clarke's defiantly stayed open through Prohibition, with Clarke quoted as saying the Volstead Act was "like a bad cold—it will go away." During this time the curtains were drawn to conceal imbibers, and the police were paid to look the other way. Beers were served alongside bathtub gin that Clarke distilled himself and Scotch he bootlegged from Canada.

In 1942 the Lavezzo family from Italy, who dealt in antiques and furniture restoration, purchased the building from the Clarke family. The original P. J. Clarke passed away in 1948, and the bar went to the Lavezzos, who added a dining room in the back. Amid the post–World War II building boom, the neighborhood was changing: residential tenements and the nearby Doelger's brewery were all sold to developers to build apartments now on Sutton Place. However, one member of the Clarke family, Charles, who was born upstairs above the bar, continued working there until the 1990s.

Through the 1940s, P. J. Clarke's became synonymous with New York celebrity culture. Frank Sinatra, after a night on the town, would often end up at table 20 (his photo now hangs above it). Meanwhile, after ringing in the New Year with America at Times Square, Dick Clark made the saloon his annual post-broadcast destination, with his first meal of every new year being one of their famed burgers.

On one occasion, singer-songwriter Johnny Mercer is believed to have written his 1943 song "One for My Baby (and One More for the Road)" on a napkin while seated at the mahogany bar—installed at the turn of the twentieth century by George Ehret, America's first great brewer. On another occasion, in 1958 jazz legend Nat King Cole declared his bacon cheeseburger to be "the Cadillac of burgers." The same year, Buddy Holly proposed to receptionist Maria Elena Santiago at table 53. He had met her just five hours earlier at the offices of Peer-Southern Records before inviting her to the bar. "Do you want to marry me now or after dinner?" she responded.

By the 1970s, Jackie Kennedy Onassis was a regular at P. J. Clarke's, often bringing in John Jr. and Caroline for lunch on Saturdays and sitting at a corner table in the back room. Other members of the Kennedy family, including Bobby and Ted, also visited. The latter reportedly beelined for the restaurant after conceding to incumbent President Carter in the 1980 Democratic primary (and allegedly did not tip). And a portrait of John F. Kennedy sits behind the bar, alongside one of Abraham Lincoln.

In 2002 the bar changed hands for just the second time ever when veteran restaurateur Philip Scotti, Arnold Penner, and a group of patrons and investors—including former Yankees owner George Steinbrenner and actor Timothy Hutton—purchased P. J. Clarke's from Daniel H. Lavezzo III. It closed for a year of much-needed structural renovations, reopening in 2003, with extreme care given to return every tile on the floor, every photo hanging on the wall, and every other detail of the bar to its exact position.

Today, the building still stands out on the corner of Third Avenue and Fifty-Fifth Street—a lone holdout against the encroaching wall of concrete and glass. The red-and-white checked tablecloths remain, as does an old jukebox and two human leg bones hanging from the ceiling (an Irish American good luck charm) in the main bar room over the doorway leading to the back room. Black-and-white photos of sports figures and celebrities, along with letters (including one from actress Joan Crawford), adorn the wood-paneled walls. And that's not to mention the oversized porcelain urinals, which Frank Sinatra once joked were so big that then-Mayor Abe Beame could fit inside "with room to spare."

Over one and a half centuries into the business, the reputation of P. J. Clarke's has allowed the brand to expand from its original flagship to five locations, including outposts in Philadelphia and Washington, DC. There's even one in Brazil. However, the location at 915 Third Avenue is still worth the pilgrimage for a stellar burger and pint of beer.

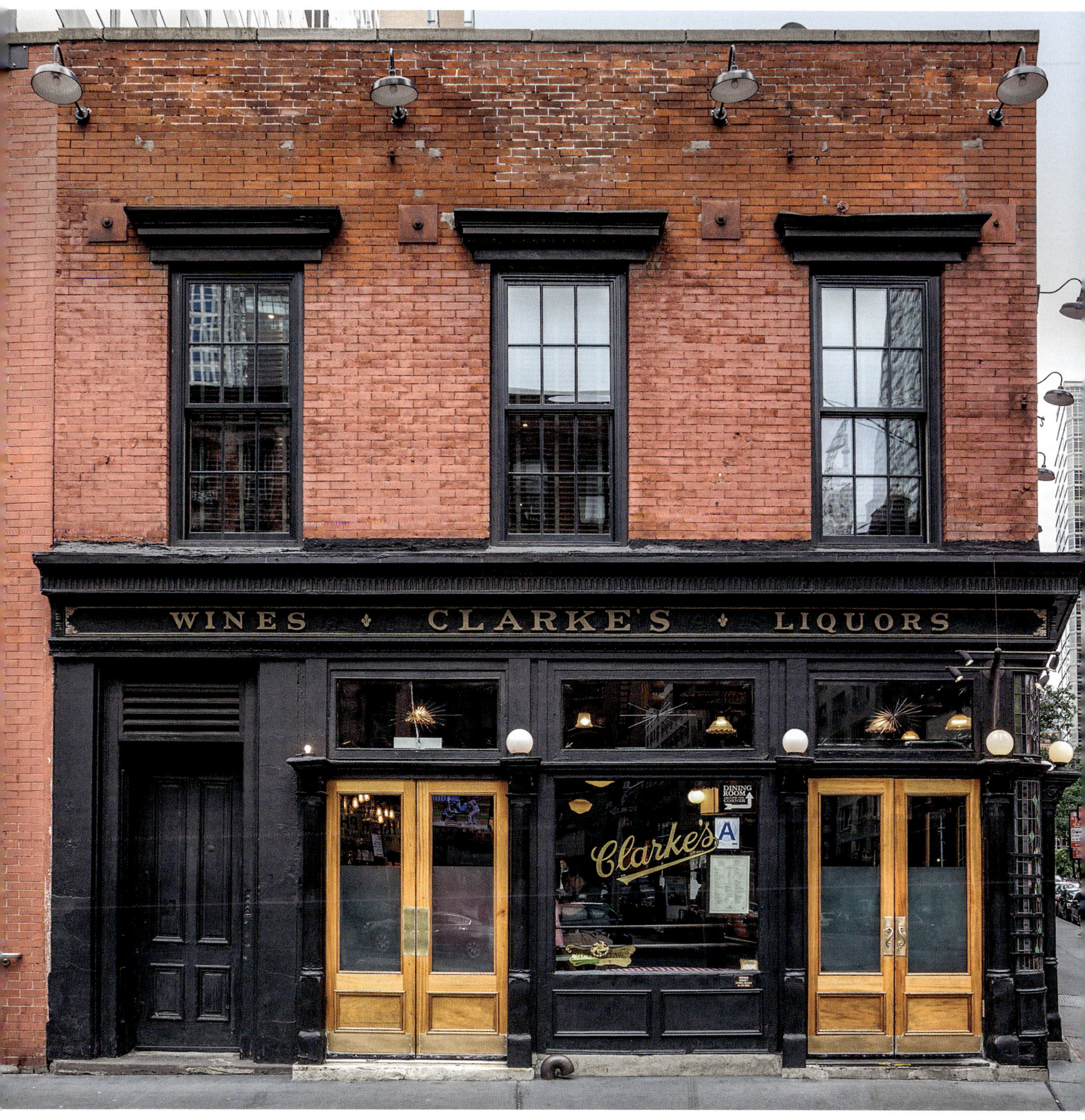

WINES ✦ CLARKE'S ✦ LIQUORS
Clarke's
A
DINING ROOM CORNER

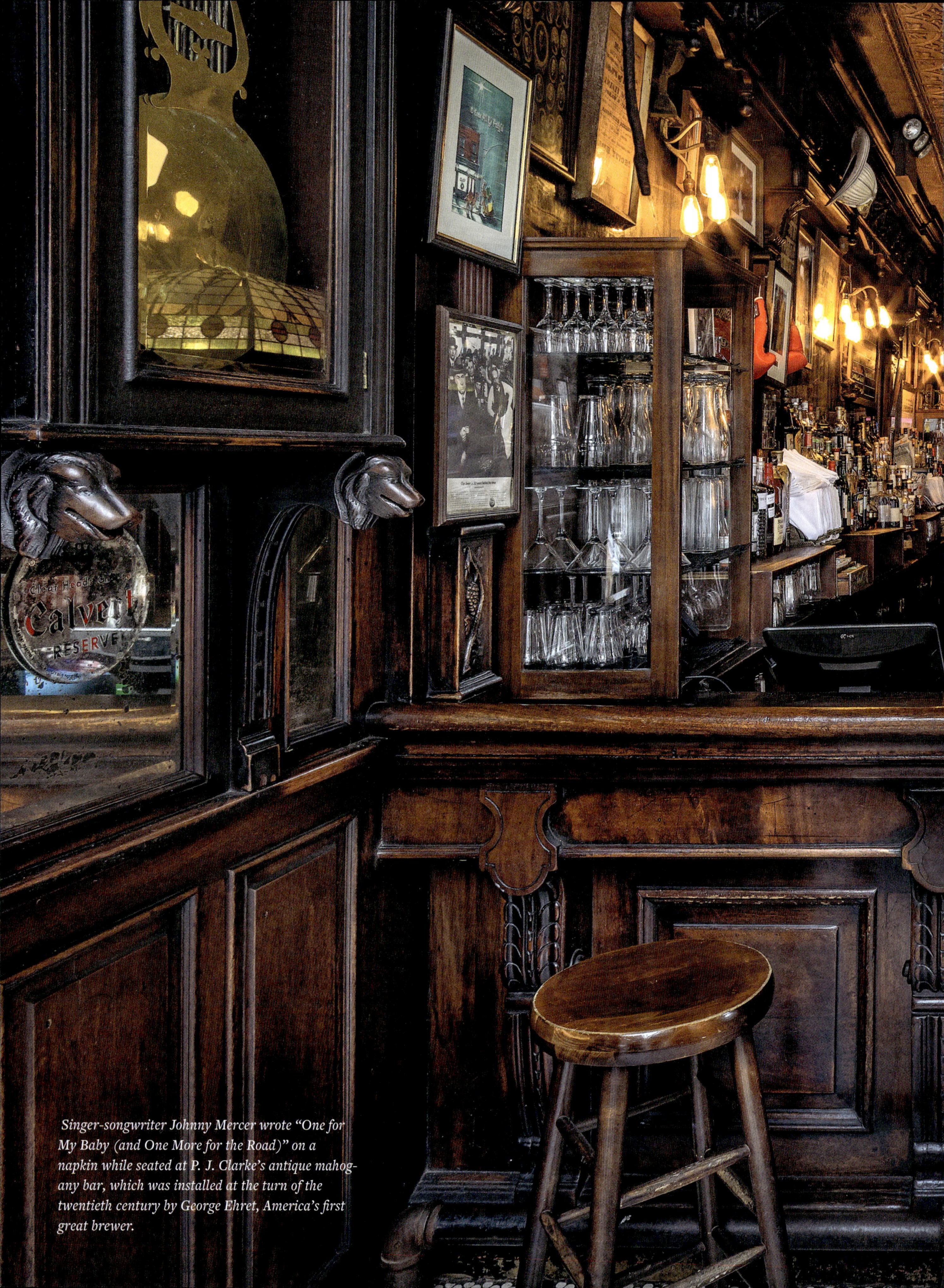

Singer-songwriter Johnny Mercer wrote "One for My Baby (and One More for the Road)" on a napkin while seated at P. J. Clarke's antique mahogany bar, which was installed at the turn of the twentieth century by George Ehret, America's first great brewer.

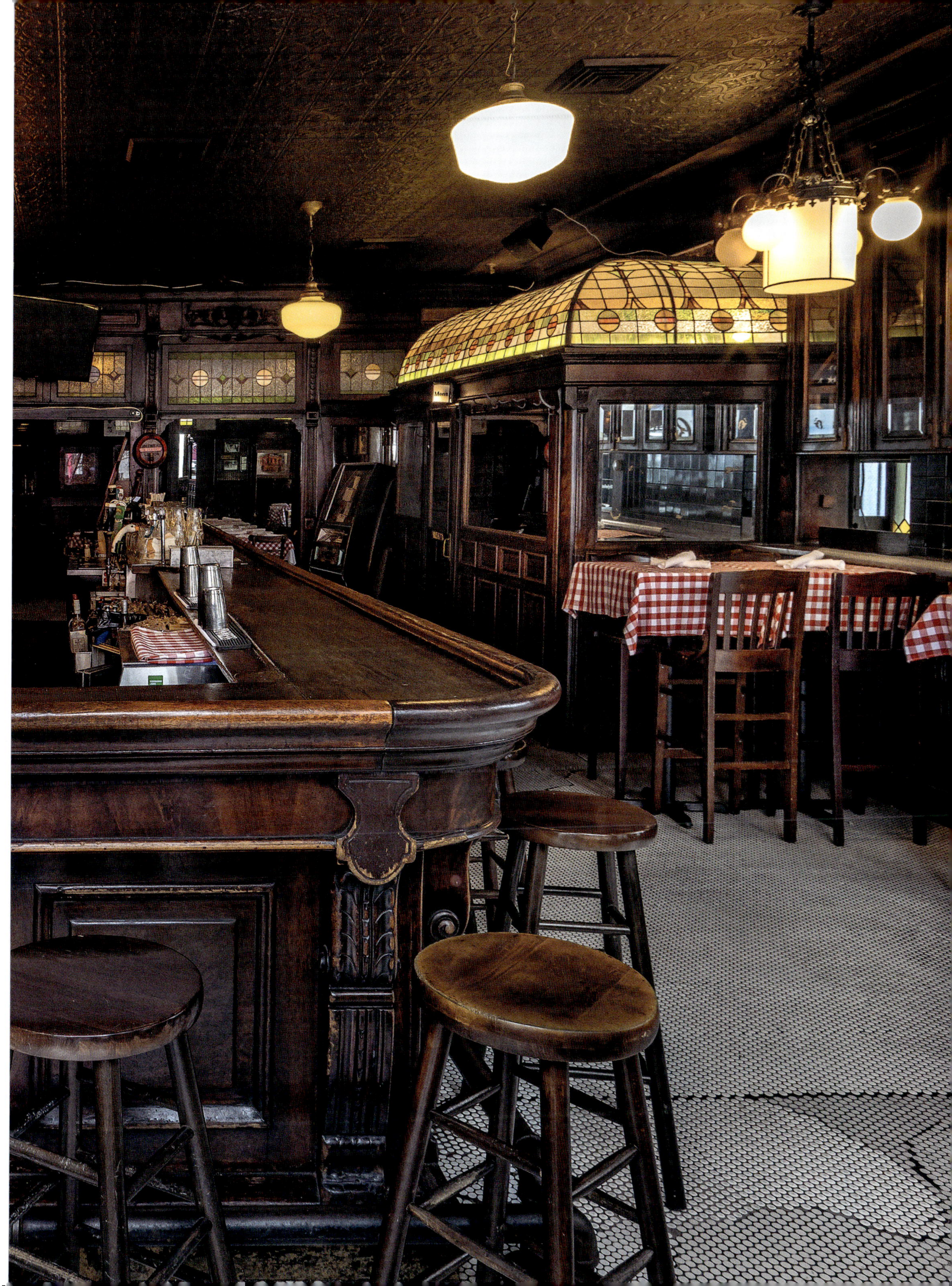

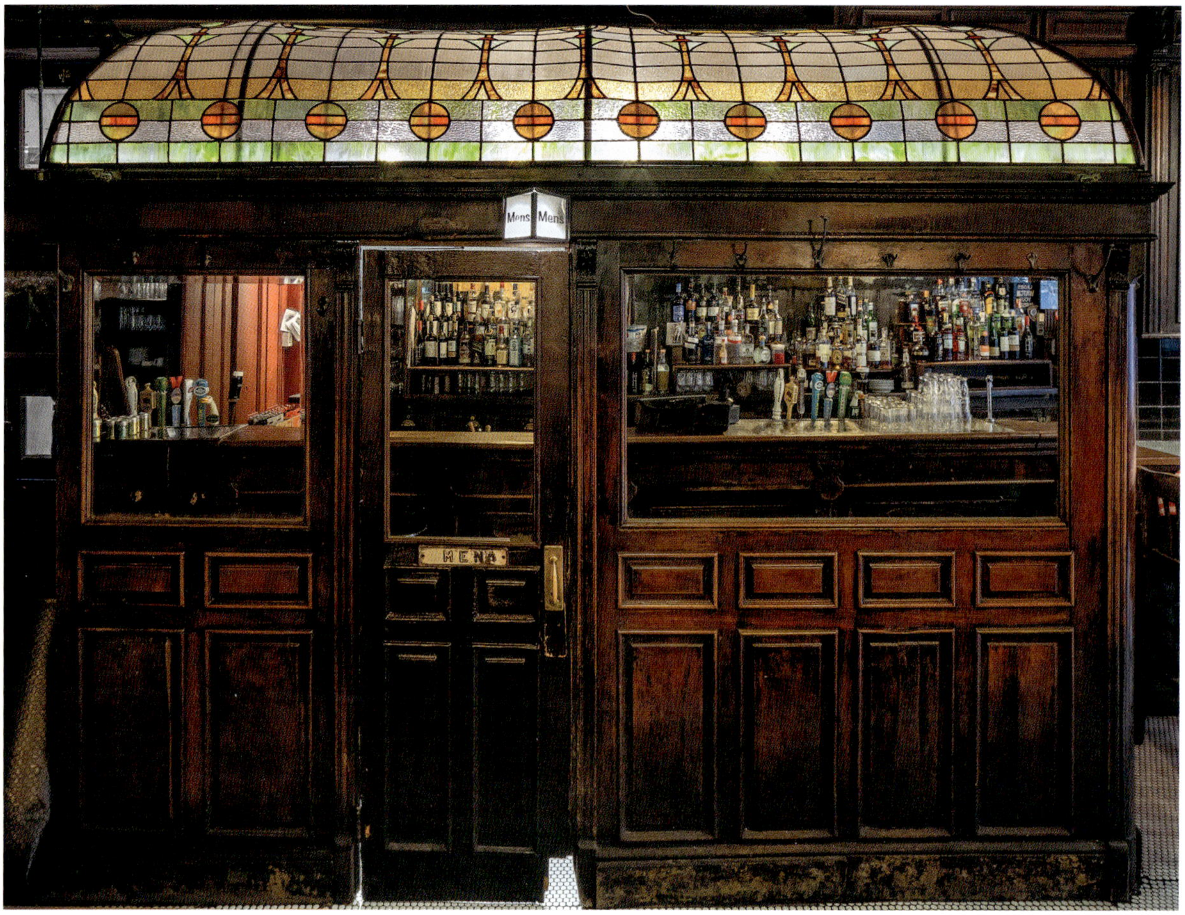

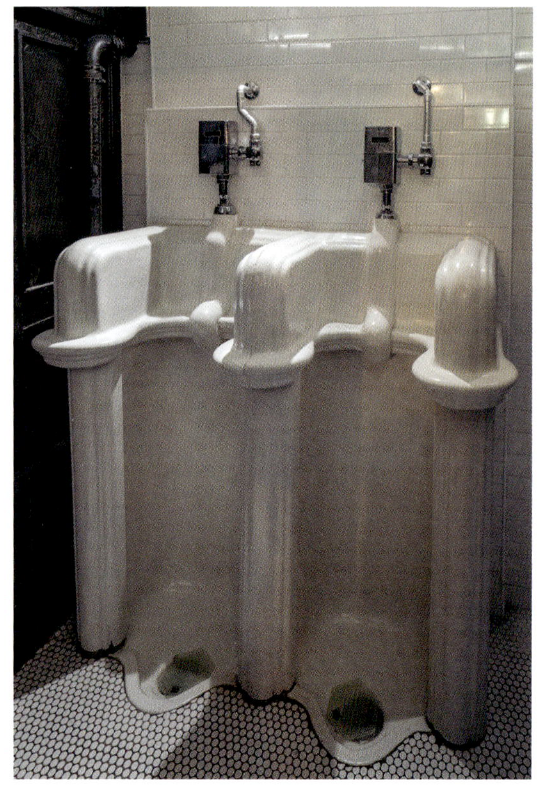

Mens Mens
MENA

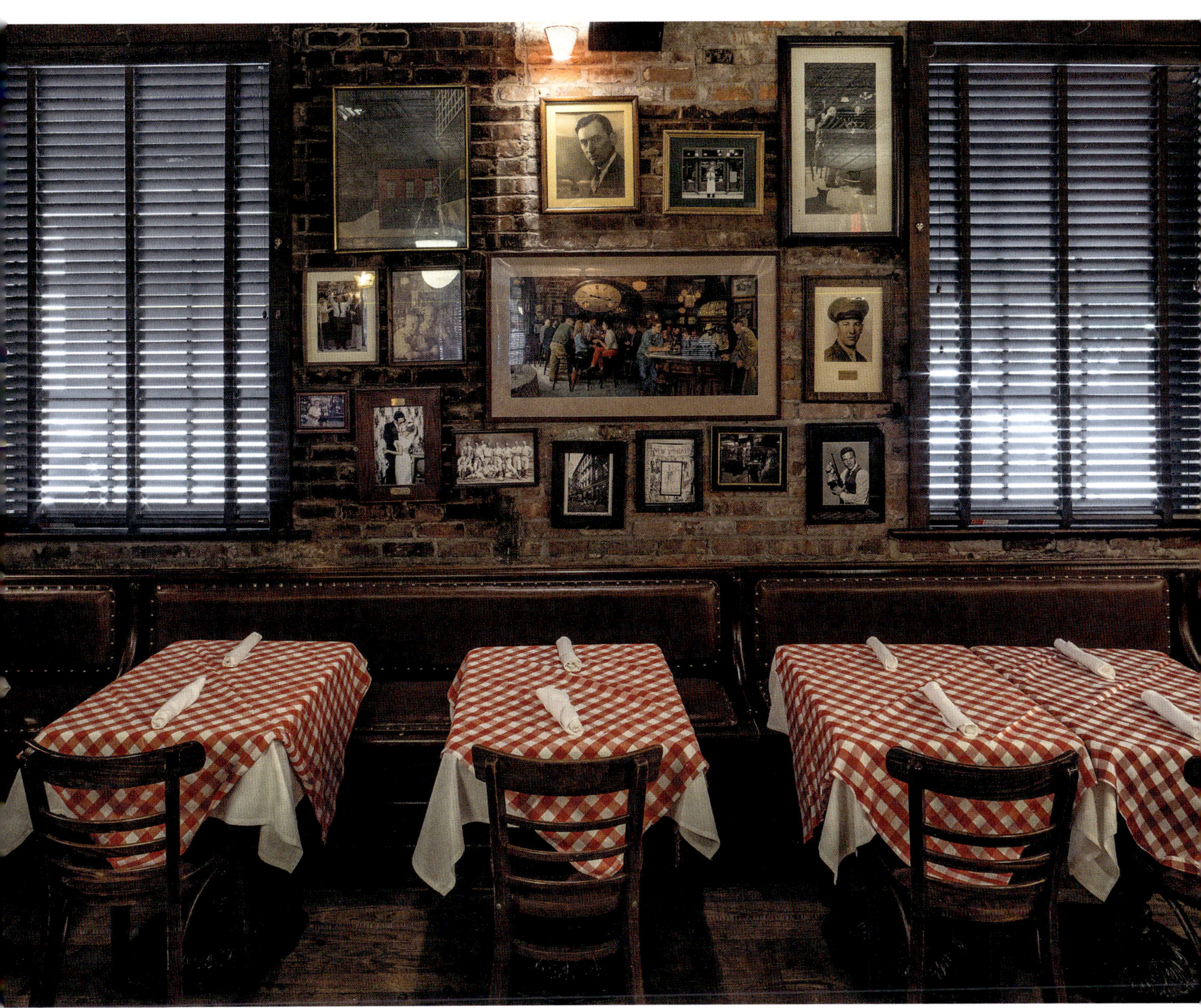

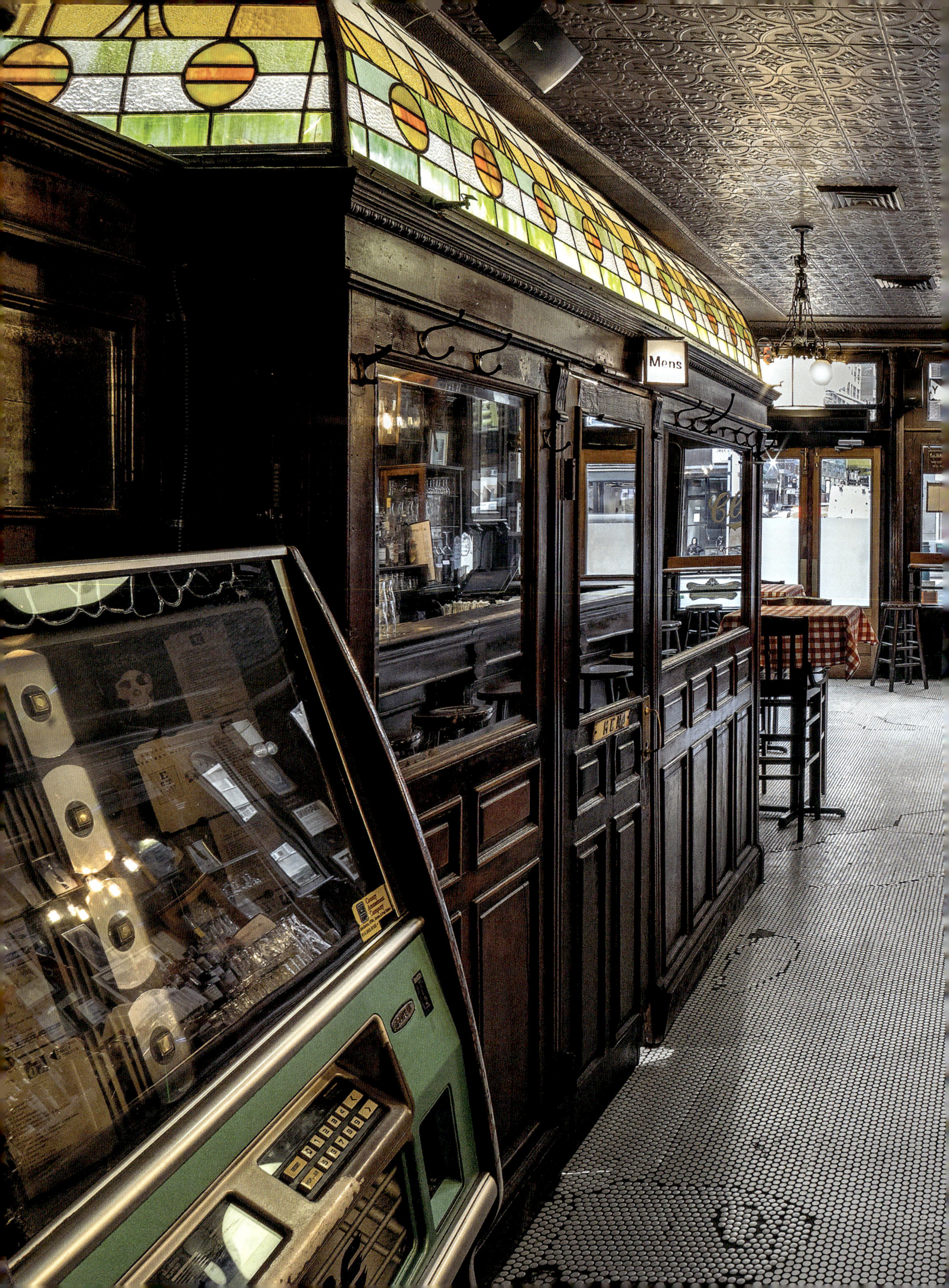

Mens

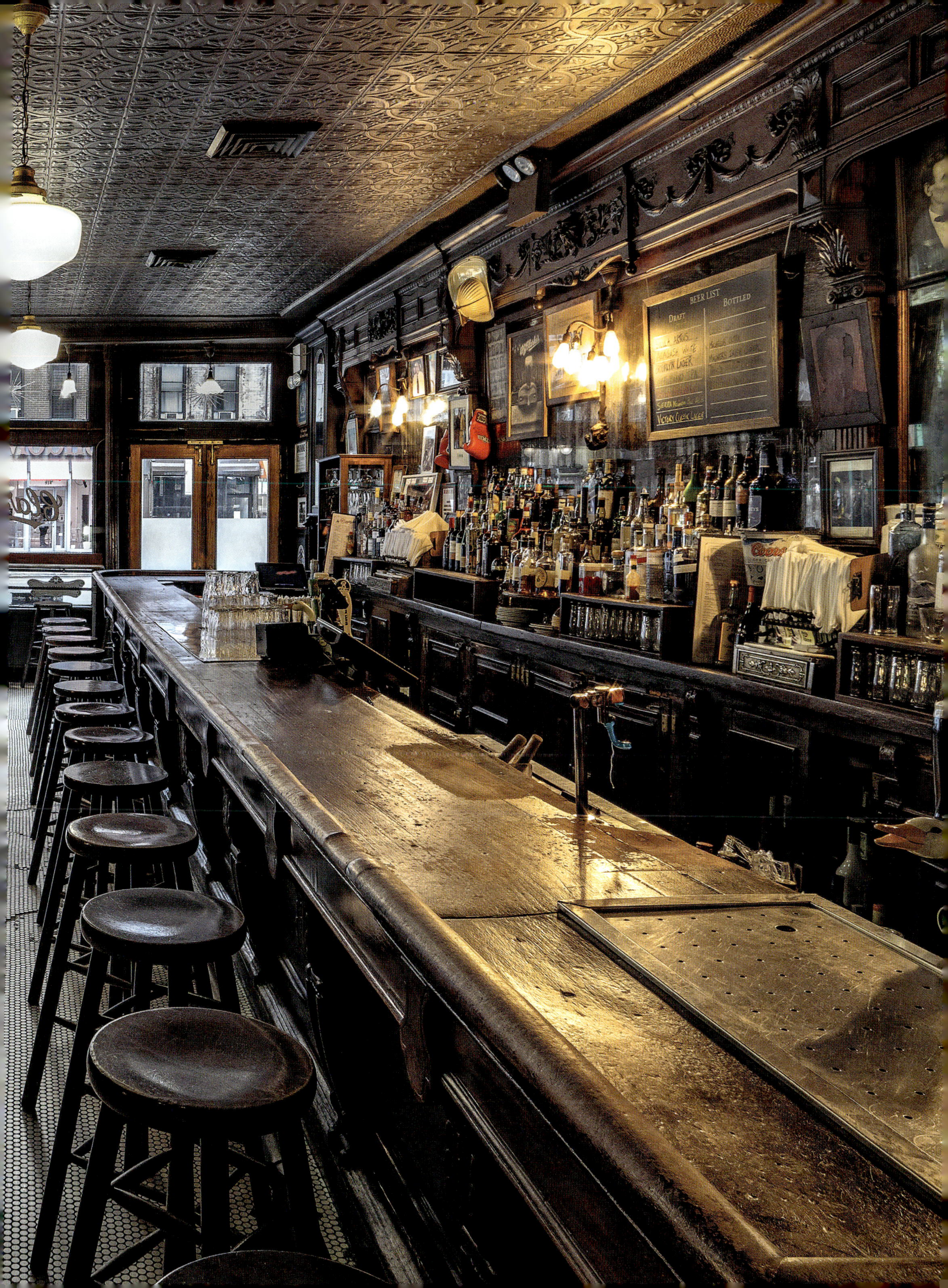
BEER LIST
DRAFT
BOTTLED
STELLA ARTOIS
IRISH ALE
BROOKLYN LAGER
SIERRA NEVADA PALE ALE
VICTORY CASK LAGER

BAILEY'S CORNER PUB

1607 YORK AVENUE, UPPER EAST SIDE

Bailey's Corner Pub is a humble neighborhood watering hole that has faithfully served the Upper East Side's Yorkville area since the early 1950s. Though the bar's name and ownership have changed several times throughout its history, it's maintained its identity as a local institution—especially for sports fans—over the years.

In its first few decades, Bailey's went by numerous different names, including Loftus Tavern, Jack Loftus, Tiernan's, and Nash's Cash Box. It wouldn't officially become Bailey's Corner Pub until 1989.

The history of the bar coincides with a period of great change within the Yorkville neighborhood, which had been, since the early twentieth century, a notable enclave for German refugees moving up from crowded tenements on the Lower East Side. In the '50s, when the Third Avenue elevated train line was demolished, so were the surrounding brownstones, sending many Central and Eastern European residents to the suburbs. By the late twentieth century, the area was also home to many Irish immigrants and was the ending point of New York's sizable St. Patrick's Day Parade.

According to Thomas R. Pryor, a homegrown historian of the Yorkville neighborhood, the bar—known to him in his childhood as Loftus Tavern—was his father's regular haunt, where the young Pryor would often join and enjoy a Coke with maraschino cherries. In his now-defunct *New York Times*–recognized blog Yorkville: Stoop to Nuts, Pryor wrote fondly of his memories in the bar, its sports-loving regulars, and his relationship with proprietor Jack Loftus, who lived above the bar and loved the Giants and Johnny Cash.

"In 1961, on a Lord's Sabbath, my whole family was in Loftus Tavern from noon to midnight," Pryor wrote. "That day, syndicated cartoonist of *The Neighbors*, George Clark, doodled in a front booth nursing a whiskey and drew sketches of Mom and Rory. That night, I spent countless dimes playing 'Walk the Line' on the Wurlitzer jukebox."

While the atmosphere at Bailey's now may be unrecognizable to those who knew it in its earliest days, later proprietors, including current owner Sean Cushing, have preserved some of its key architectural and design elements—including the original tin ceilings, an old cash register, and an antique wooden backbar that predates the venue itself.

Though specific details about the backbar have been lost to time, it's believed to have been constructed in the early 1900s when Yorkville was home to many breweries, including Jacob Ruppert & Company, founded by then–New York Yankees owner Colonel Jacob Ruppert. At the time, many of these breweries would attract business with bars by handling the woodwork and furnishing of their backbars.

Equally muddled is the history of how the backbar came to be at Bailey's. According to an old WordPress blog maintained by the owners of the bar (as well as the bartenders working there), it may have originally sat in a restaurant that was housed within a brownstone at 500 East Eighty-Fifth Street, across the street from Bailey's. When this building was torn down to make way for the high-rise apartments that now sit at the address, the backbar was transported across York Avenue to its current home.

Through the years, Bailey's has been known as one of New York City's best bars for watching and enjoying sports. According to Pryor's blog, the cash register that still stands today used to hide five sets of season tickets for the New York Giants.

Now, on any given day, it's common to find both NFL fans and collegiate alumni enjoying their pints while catching a game on TV. The bar is particularly noted for its following among fans of the Detroit Lions as well as varsity teams like Michigan and Notre Dame.

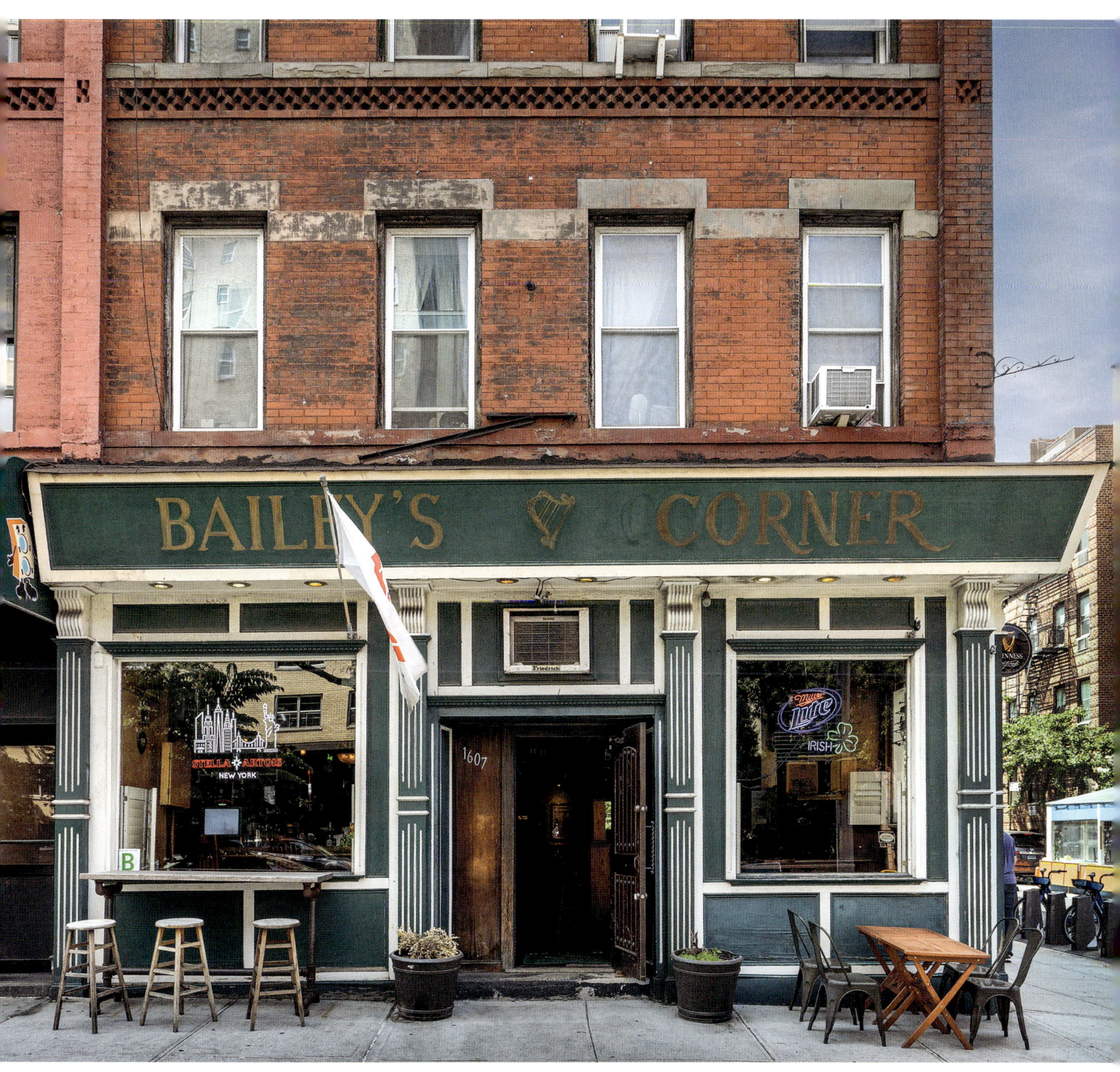

BAILEY'S CORNER PUB

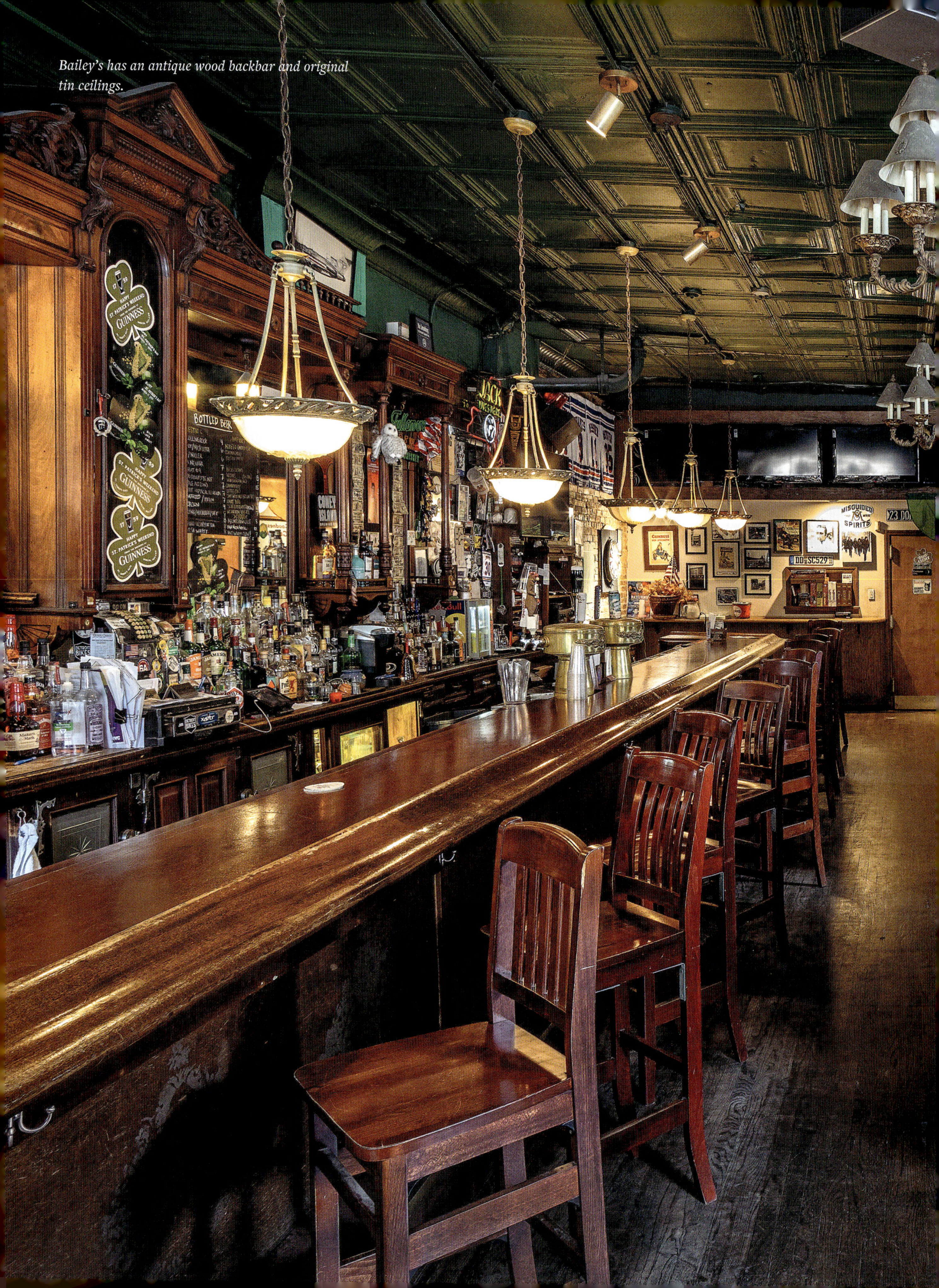

Bailey's has an antique wood backbar and original tin ceilings.

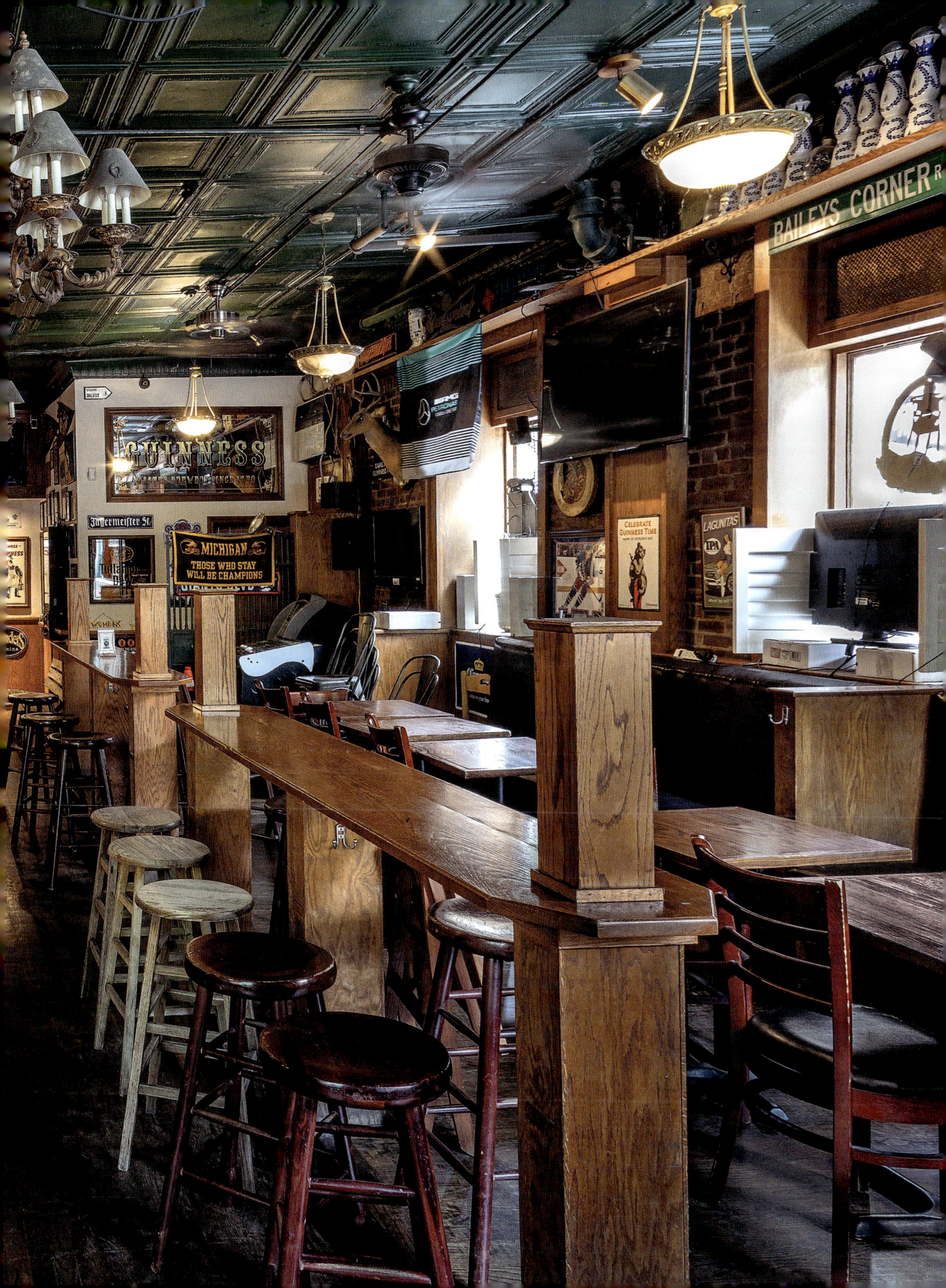
BAILEYS CORNER Rd
GUINNESS
Jägermeiſter St.
MICHIGAN
THOSE WHO STAY
WILL BE CHAMPIONS
WOMEN
CELEBRATE
GUINNESS TIME
LAGUNITAS
IPA

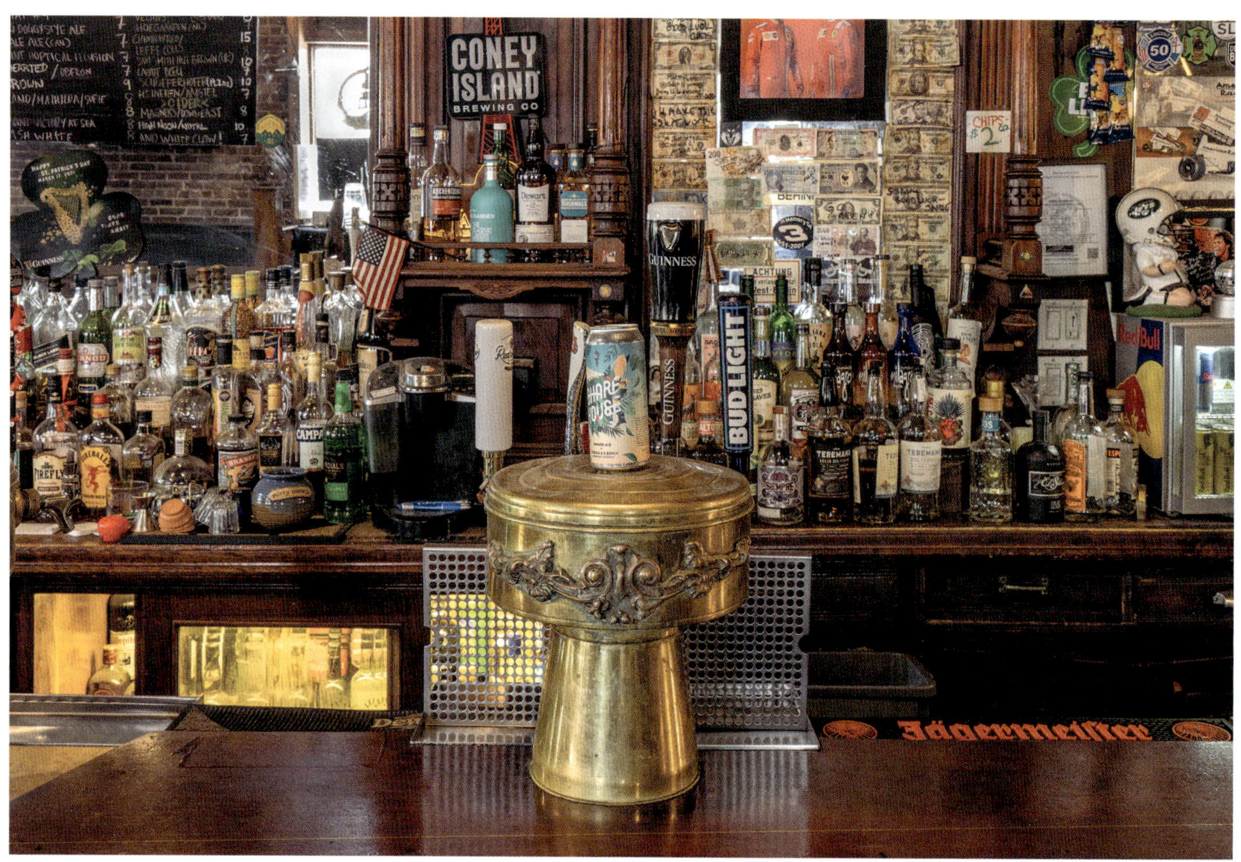

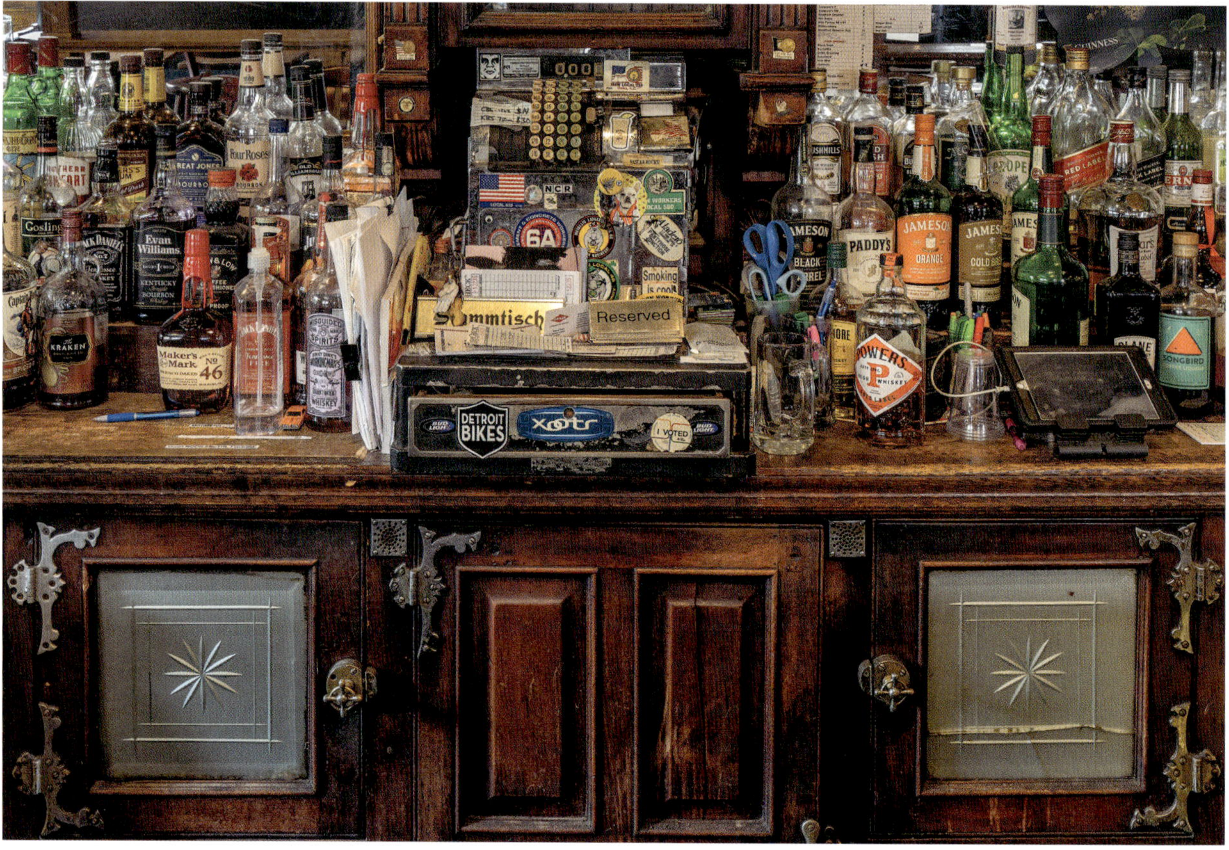

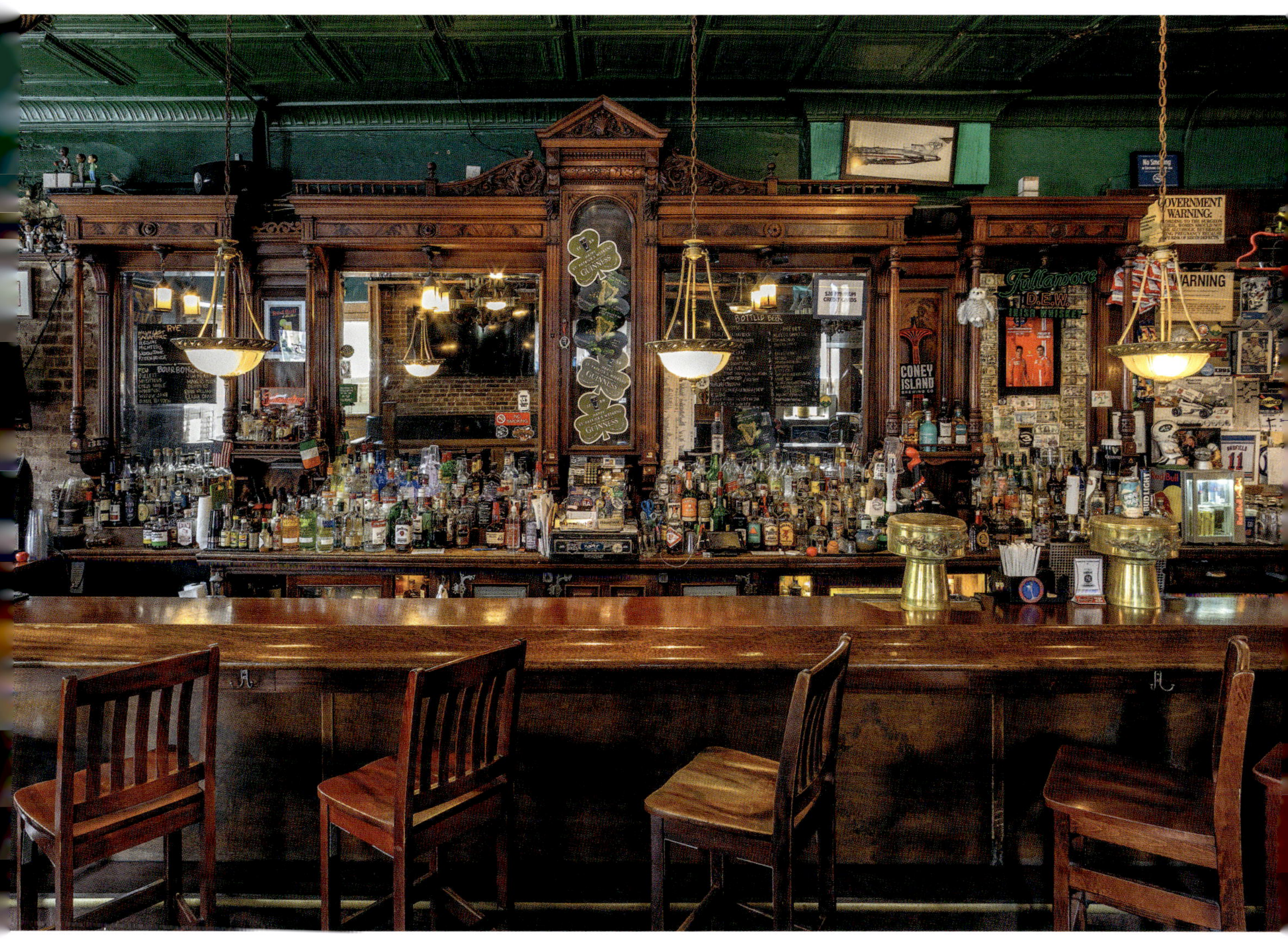

OPPOSITE BOTTOM   *The backbar is believed to have been made in the early 1900s when the Yorkville area was home to many breweries, including Jacob Ruppert & Company.*

ABOVE   *The backbar found its way across York Avenue to Bailey's when the brownstone building across the street at 500 East Eighty-Fifth Street, which housed a restaurant, was torn down.*

HOLIDAY COCKTAIL LOUNGE

75 ST. MARKS PLACE, EAST VILLAGE

I'm staying here | Where I can get a song free with my drink to smooth things along, sings the punk band Bouncing Souls in their 1997 track, "Holiday Cocktail Lounge," named after the St. Marks Place watering hole that its members frequented throughout the 1990s.

Though they're the only band (so far) to have immortalized Holiday Cocktail Lounge in song, the Bouncing Souls aren't the only artists, writers, and musicians who've graced its storied, semisubterranean stools in its many years of history. Indeed, the bar holds space in the rich identity of the East Village, which for decades was the epicenter of the counterculture movement in New York City.

In the 1960s, the humble dive bar played host to entertainment industry titans like singer Frank Sinatra and actress Shelley Winters. The '70s brought poets like Allen Ginsberg and W. H. Auden, as well as David Godlis (later known as Godlis), the artist-photographer known for his work documenting the city's punk culture. And the '80s saw icons like Madonna, Iggy Pop, Keith Richards, Sean Penn, Matt Dillon, and the Ramones enjoying pints and cocktails in the space.

Despite its relevance in recent decades to pop culture, the history of Holiday Cocktail Lounge dates back a bit further to its founding in the year 1950. (It's said to have opened earlier under several names, but records were destroyed by the New York State Liquor Authority, with the earliest records dating to 1933). The bar took over the space previously home to Ali Baba Burlesque—which originally opened in the 1920s as a speakeasy hidden within a salon called Ann's Beauty Shop—before entertaining guests as a popular cabaret through the '40s.

This Prohibition-era predecessor had a similarly notable history: it's believed to have once hosted visiting Russian revolutionary Leon Trotsky and was the city's fiftieth bar to receive a license when booze bans were repealed in 1933. The building that houses it, meanwhile, dates back to 1835.

In 2012, amid a mass shuttering of dive bars across the city, Holiday Cocktail Lounge closed its dented metal doors—seemingly for good. But a rebirth was on the horizon, thanks to a partnership between Robert Ehrlich, the snack king who created Pirate's Booty popcorn, and chef Barbara Sibley, a restaurateur who lived above the venue and owned the long-standing La Palapa Cocina Mexicana next door.

Upon buying the bar, Ehrlich and Sibley sought to modernize its offerings. After all, the 2010s had ushered in the height of the craft cocktail revolution, and $16 drinks were becoming the new normal across the neighborhood. In order to meet this moment, the owners tapped veteran bartender Michael Neff to rejigger the bar program with classic and modern cocktails in mind.

"When Rob bought the bar, he was prepared for a turnkey operation," Sibley recalls. "But it turns out that sometime in the bar's 100-year history a chimney had been eliminated without resupporting the beams. A turnkey operation turned into a four-year renovation. It was an exercise in Zen and archaeology as we tried to balance the historical integrity with the structural integrity of a building built in the 1800s. Truly it was Rob's dedication that saved the bar."

In the years since, this spirited reincarnation has earned Holiday Cocktail Lounge a reputation not just as one of the best dive bars but also one of the best cocktail bars in New York City. However, cheeky offerings, like thoughtfully curated, affordable beer-and-shot combinations (or Boilermakers), nod to its everyman past with a contemporary twist. Today the bar proudly touts its interpretation of "dive elegance."

Well-preserved holdovers from its earlier days as Ali Baba can still be found in the Holiday Cocktail Lounge of today. These include the mahogany horseshoe bar as well as a restored hand-painted mural of a harem girl that was discovered behind a mirror during the renovation. The bar's wooden phone booth, one of the few remaining in the city, stands in its original place and retains its original phone number.

It's not just the furniture that stays true to the past. Despite the fact the world around it has changed so drastically, if you're lucky, a night spent at Holiday Cocktail Lounge can still offer some of the weirdness and spontaneity that made the East Village the iconic, beloved neighborhood it is today.

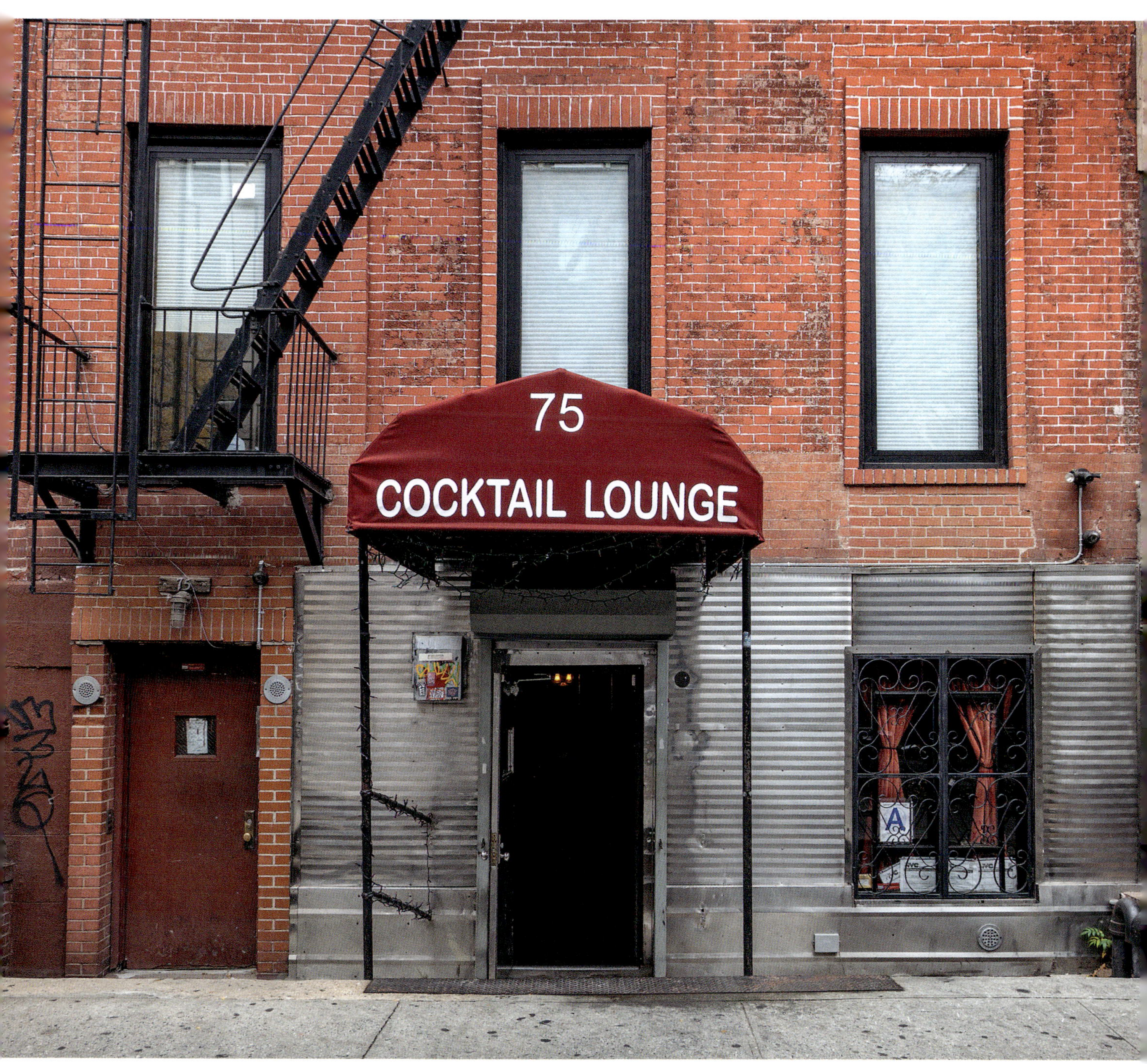
75
COCKTAIL LOUNGE

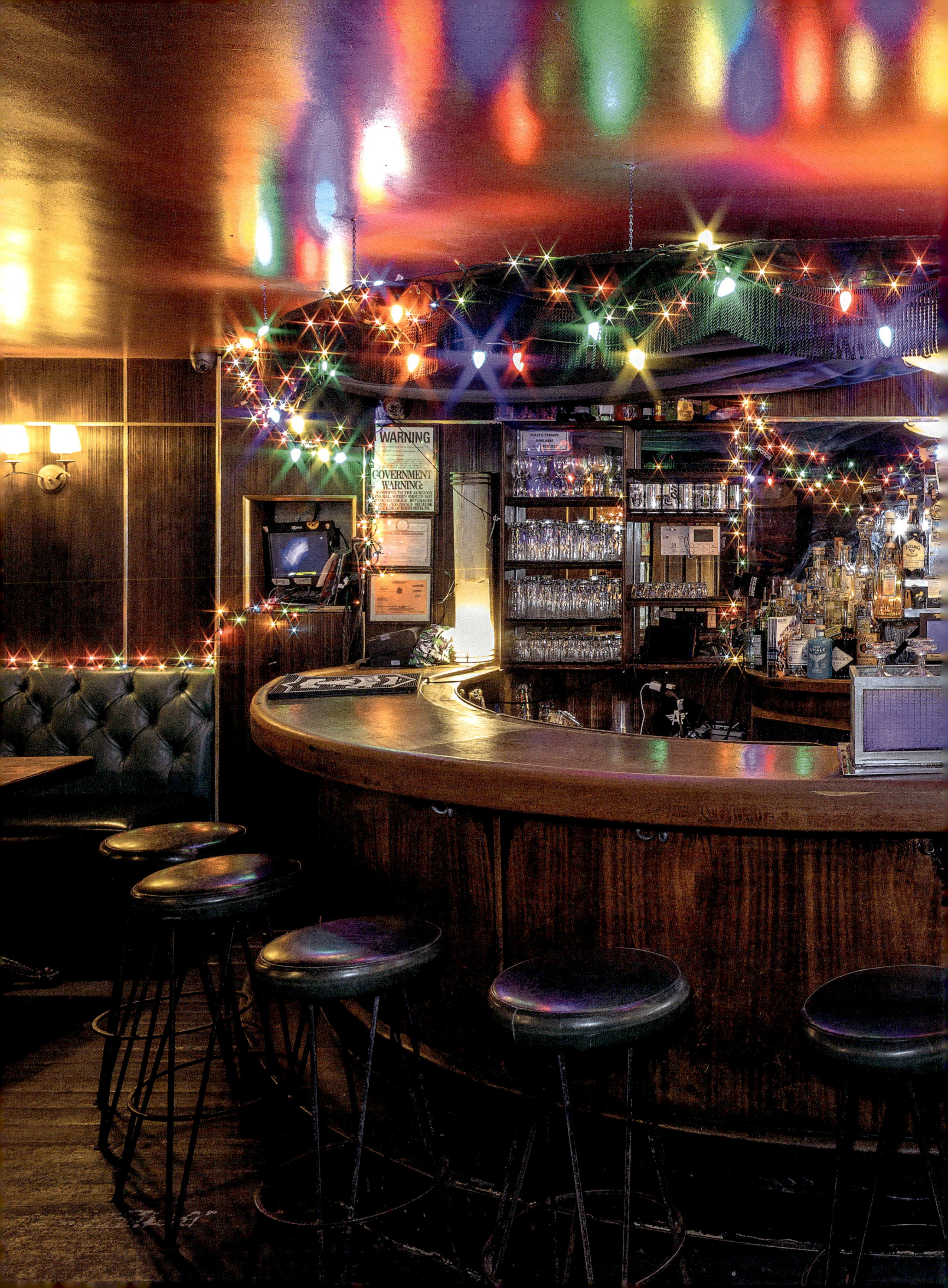

WARNING
GOVERNMENT WARNING:
ACCORDING TO THE SURGEON GENERAL, WOMEN SHOULD NOT DRINK ALCOHOLIC BEVERAGES DURING PREGNANCY BECAUSE OF THE RISK OF BIRTH DEFECTS.
PLASTIC STRAWS AVAILABLE UPON REQUEST

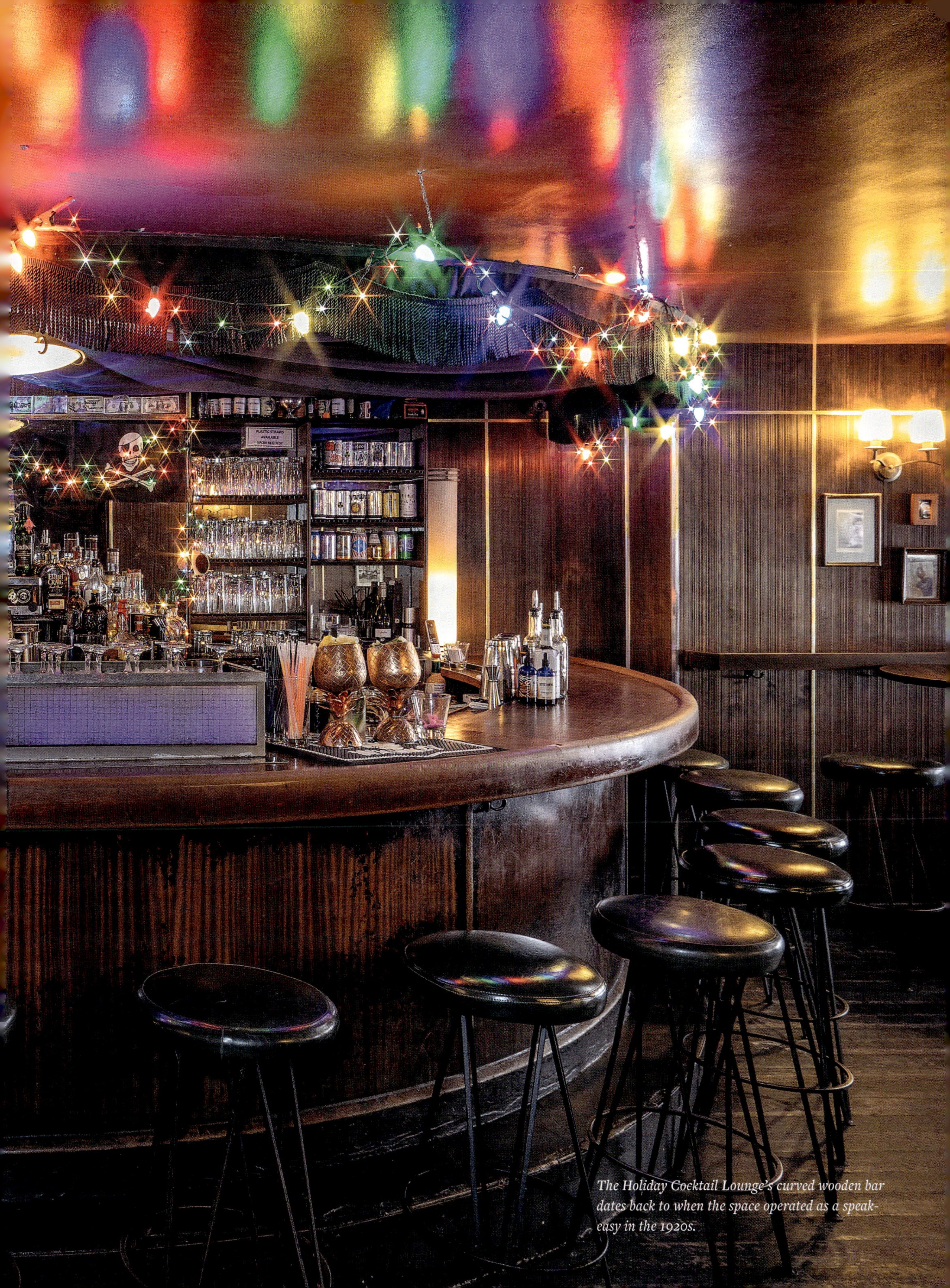

The Holiday Cocktail Lounge's curved wooden bar dates back to when the space operated as a speakeasy in the 1920s.

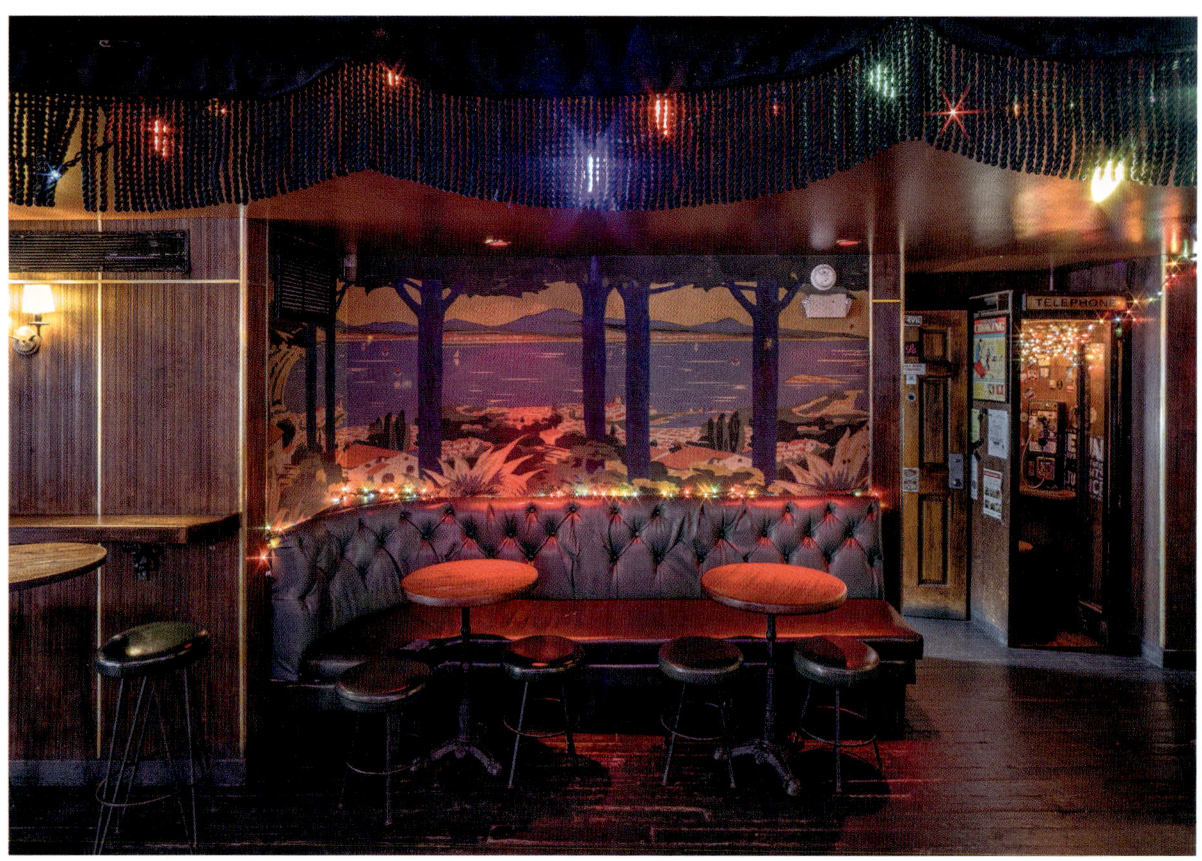

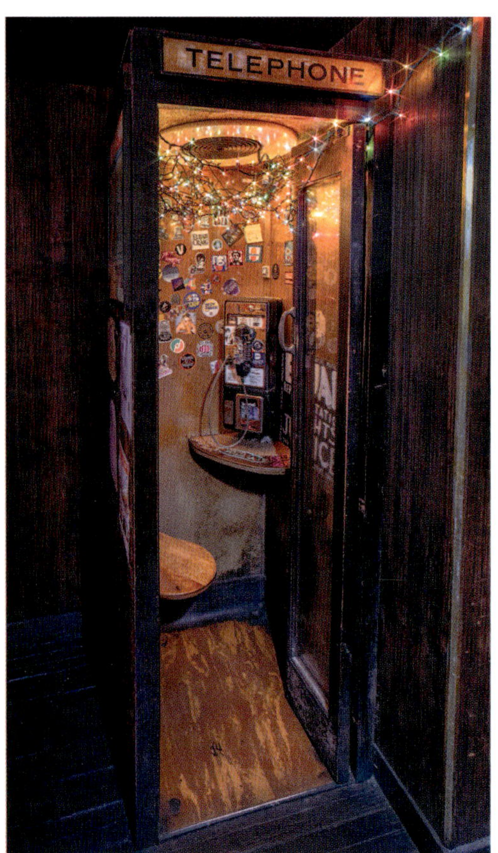

LEFT *The bar still has its original wooden phone booth.*

OPPOSITE TOP *This harem scene mural was hidden behind paneling but was uncovered during renovation before the bar reopened in 2015.*

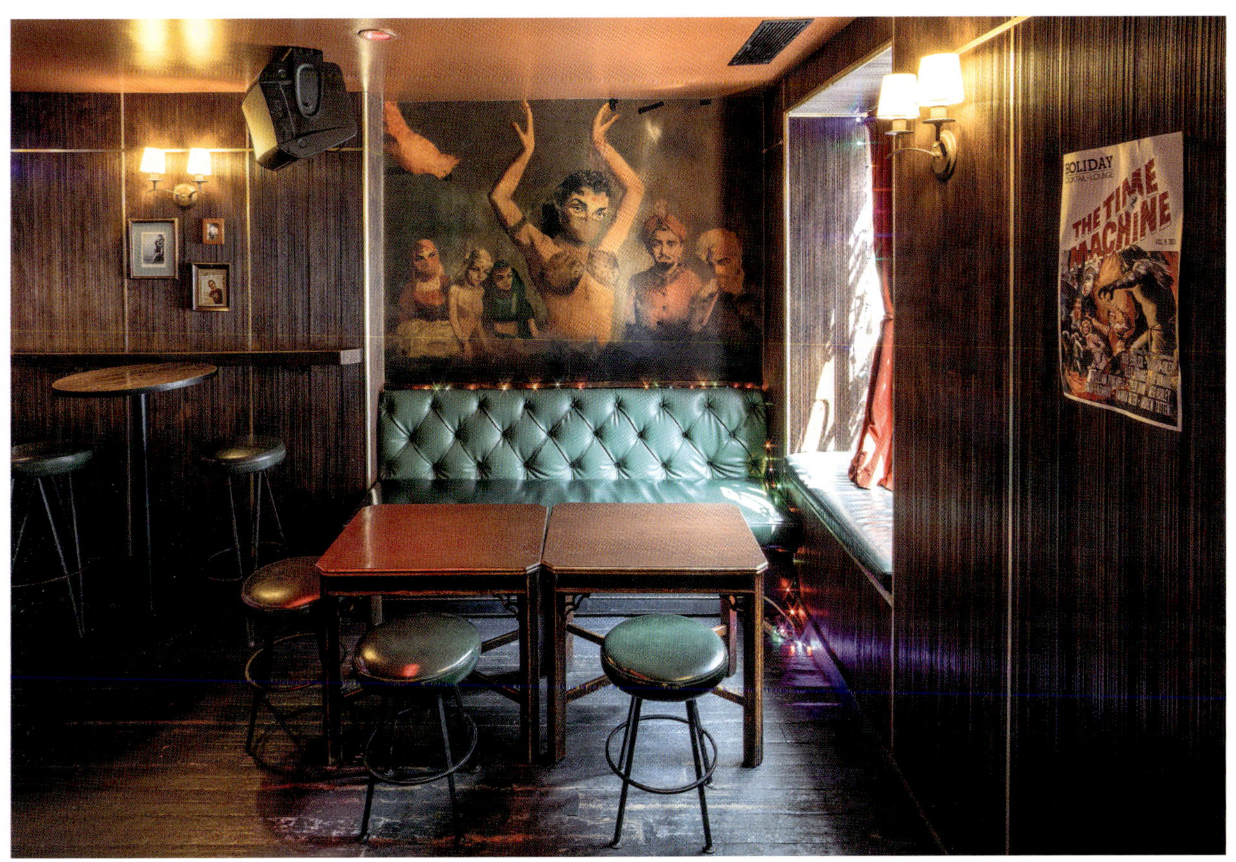

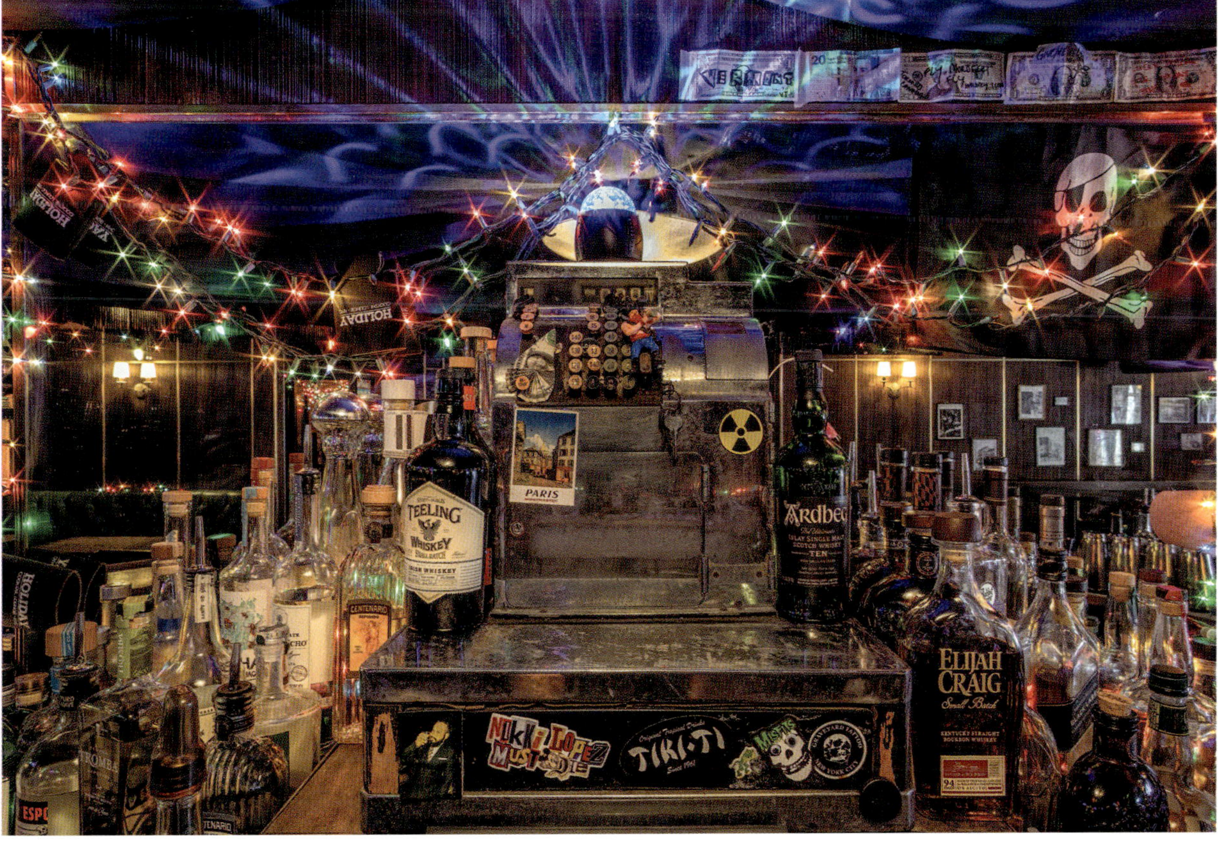

PARIS
TEELING WHISKEY
Ardbeg
ELIJAH CRAIG

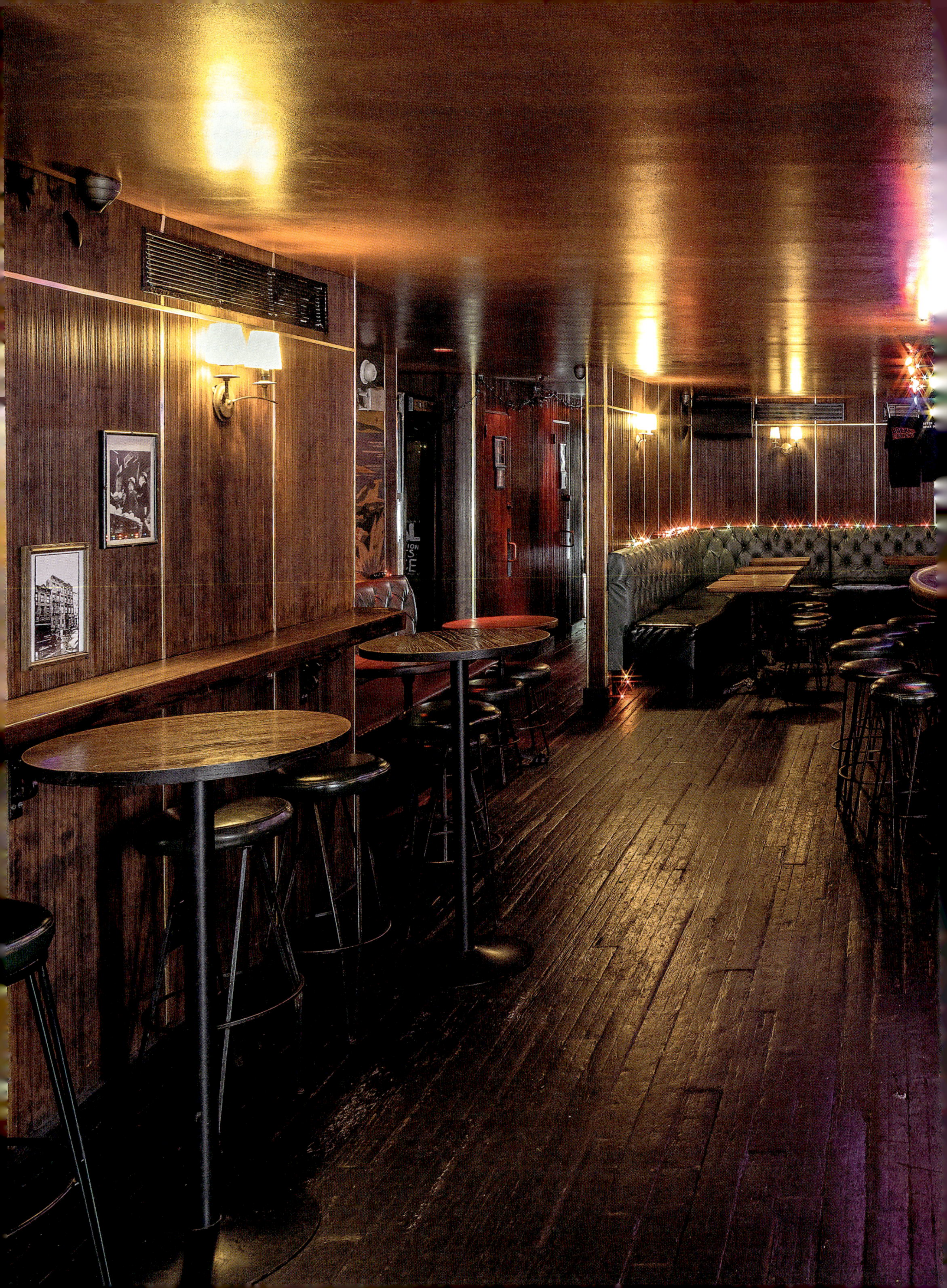

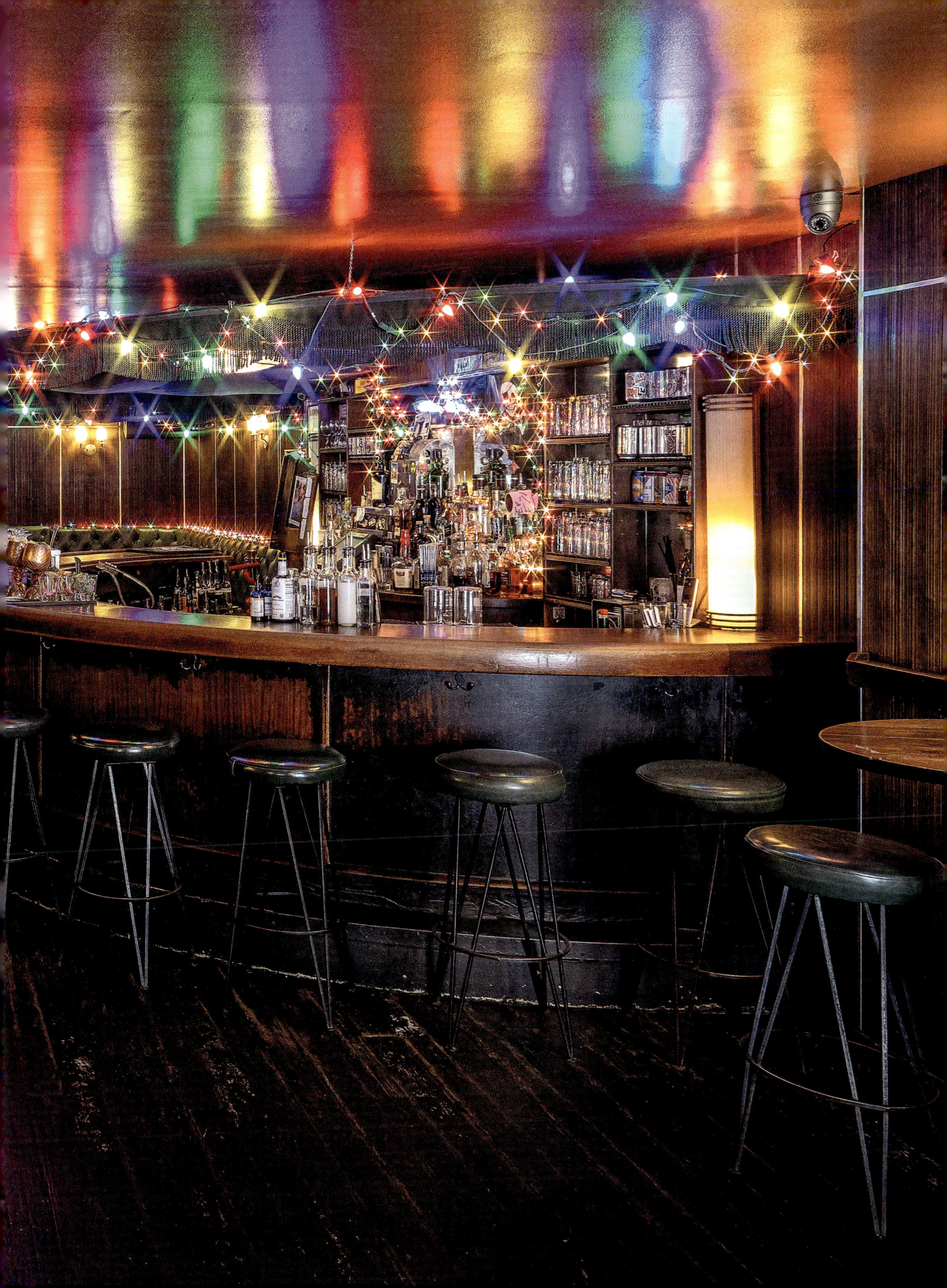

MAP

1 7B HORSESHOE BAR
108 Avenue B, East Village

2 BAILEY'S CORNER PUB
1607 York Avenue, Upper East Side

3 BEAUTY BAR
231 East 14th Street, East Village

4 THE CAMPBELL
Grand Central Terminal,
15 Vanderbilt Avenue, Midtown East

5 CUBBYHOLE
281 West 12th Street, West Village

6 DANTE
79–81 MacDougal Street, Greenwich Village

7 DUBLIN HOUSE
225 West 79th Street, Upper West Side

8 THE EAR INN
326 Spring Street, Hudson Square

9 FANELLI CAFÉ
94 Prince Street, SoHo

10 FRAUNCES TAVERN
54 Pearl Street, Financial District

11 HOLIDAY COCKTAIL LOUNGE
75 St. Marks Place, East Village

12 JIMMY'S CORNER
140 West 44th Street, Times Square

13 JULIUS'
159 West 10th Street, West Village

14 KING COLE BAR
The St. Regis New York, 2 East 55th Street,
Midtown East

15 THE LANDMARK TAVERN
626 11th Avenue, Hell's Kitchen

16 McSORLEY'S OLD ALE HOUSE
15 East 7th Street, East Village

17 MILANO'S BAR
51 East Houston Street, NoLIta

18 MINETTA TAVERN
113 MacDougal Street, Greenwich Village

19 OLD TOWN BAR AND RESTAURANT
45 East 18th Street, Union Square

20 THE PARIS CAFE
119 South Street, South Street Seaport

21 PARKSIDE LOUNGE
317 East Houston Street, Lower East Side

22 PLEASE DON'T TELL
113 St. Marks Place, East Village

23 PETE'S TAVERN
129 East 18th Street, Gramercy Park

24 PETER MCMANUS CAFE
152 Seventh Avenue, Chelsea

25 P. J. CLARKE'S
915 Third Avenue, Midtown East

26 RUDY'S BAR & GRILL
627 Ninth Avenue, Hell's Kitchen

27 SOPHIE'S
507 East 5th Street, East Village

28 SPRING LOUNGE
48 Spring Street, NoLIta

29 THE STONEWALL INN
53 Christopher Street, West Village

30 WHITE HORSE TAVERN
567 Hudson Street, West Village

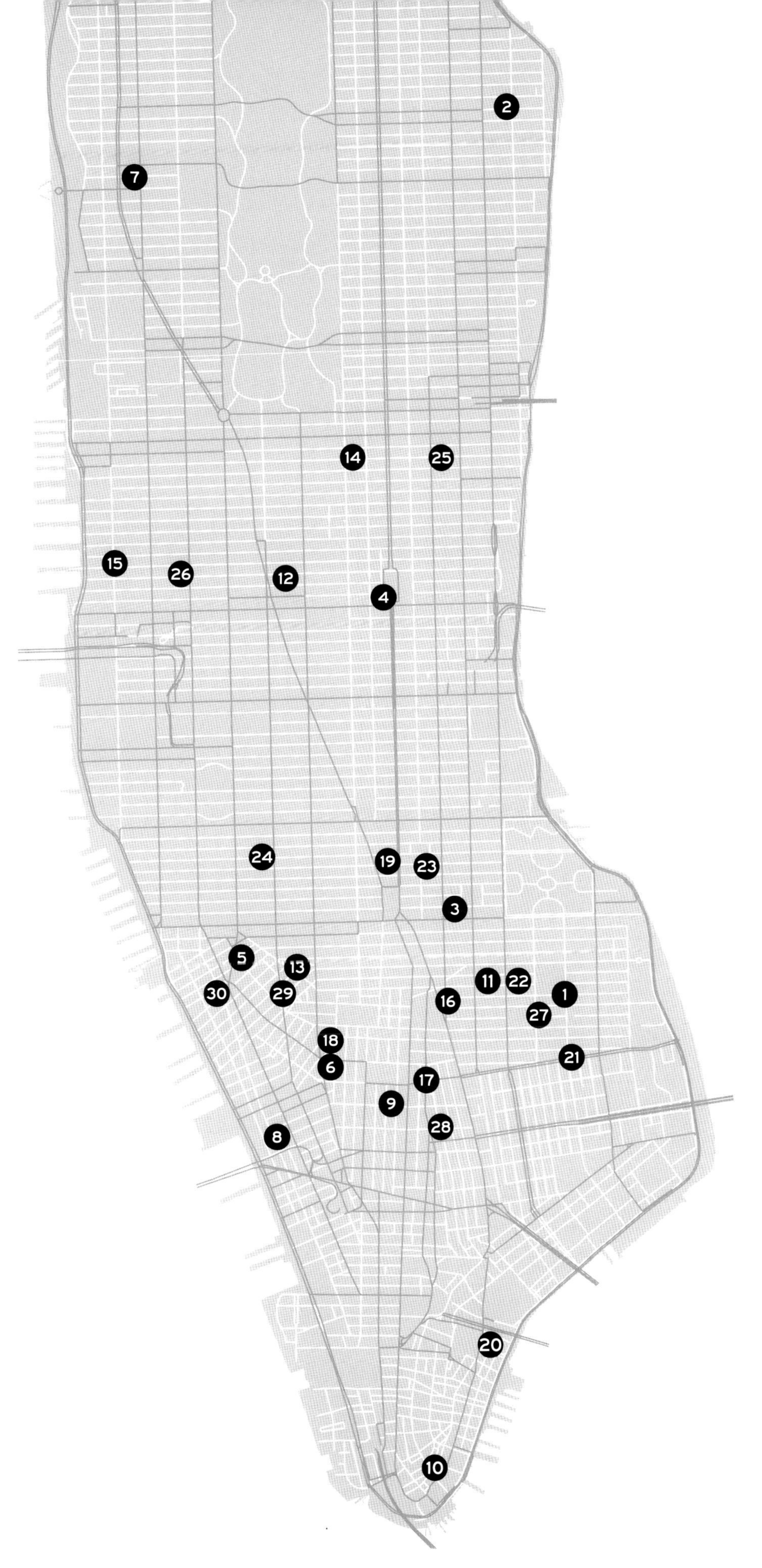

BIOGRAPHIES

JAMES T. & KARLA L. MURRAY are husband-and-wife architectural and interior photographers and videographers based in New York City. Since 1997 they have focused their lens on the streetscape through portraits of store fronts and shop owners, seeking to capture the spirit, energy, and cultural diversity of individual neighborhoods through their work.

James and Karla's critically acclaimed books include *Store Front NYC: Photographs of the City's Independent Shops, Past and Present*, *Store Front: The Disappearing Face of New York*, *New York Nights*, *Store Front II: A History Preserved*, and *Broken Windows: Graffiti NYC*. Their work has been widely exhibited around the world, including in solo exhibitions at the Brooklyn Historical Society, Clic Gallery, the Storefront Project Gallery in New York City, and Fotogalerie im Blauen Haus in Munich, as well as group shows at the New York Historical Society and the Museum of Neon Art in Glendale, California. Their photographs are part of the permanent collections of major institutions, including the Smithsonian Center for Folklife and Cultural Heritage in Washington, DC, the New York Public Library, and NYU Langone Medical Center.

Their photography has appeared in numerous publications, including the *New York Times*, the *London Telegraph*, the *Wall Street Journal*, the *New York Post*, *New York* magazine, and the *New Yorker*. James and Karla were awarded the 2015 Regina Kellerman Award by the Greenwich Village Society for Historic Preservation (GVSHP) in recognition of their significant contribution to the quality of life in Greenwich Village, the East Village, and NoHo. In 2017 through 2020, they were awarded Creative Engagement Manhattan Arts Grants by the New York State Council on the Arts and administered by the Lower Manhattan Cultural Council. They received the prestigious Art in the Parks: UNIQLO Park Expressions Grant in 2018 for their public art installation, *Mom-and-Pops of the L.E.S.*

James and Karla live in the East Village of Manhattan with their rescue dog, Hudson. Their work can be viewed at jamesandkarlamurray.com, and on their Instagram and YouTube accounts @jamesandkarla.

DAN Q. DAO is a culture writer whose work has appeared in the *New York Times*, *Condé Nast Traveler*, *Vice*, *GQ*, *Food & Wine*, and many more publications. He has also worked with leading brands like Suntory and Aman Resorts. He got his start as an editor covering NYC bars at *TimeOut New York*, and has since held staff roles at *Saveur* and *Paper*. During his twelve years living in New York City, he had the privilege to tend bar at the late Sasha Petraske's bars Middle Branch and Seaborne. At the time of writing, he is based in Vietnam, but he will one day find his way back to New York, as well as his hometown, Houston. Besides writing, he runs his own food and drink consultancy, District One Studios.

 James, Karla, and their dog Hudson hang out under the vintage hair dryers at Beauty Bar.

 Dan sits by some of the artwork decorating Sophie's Bar.

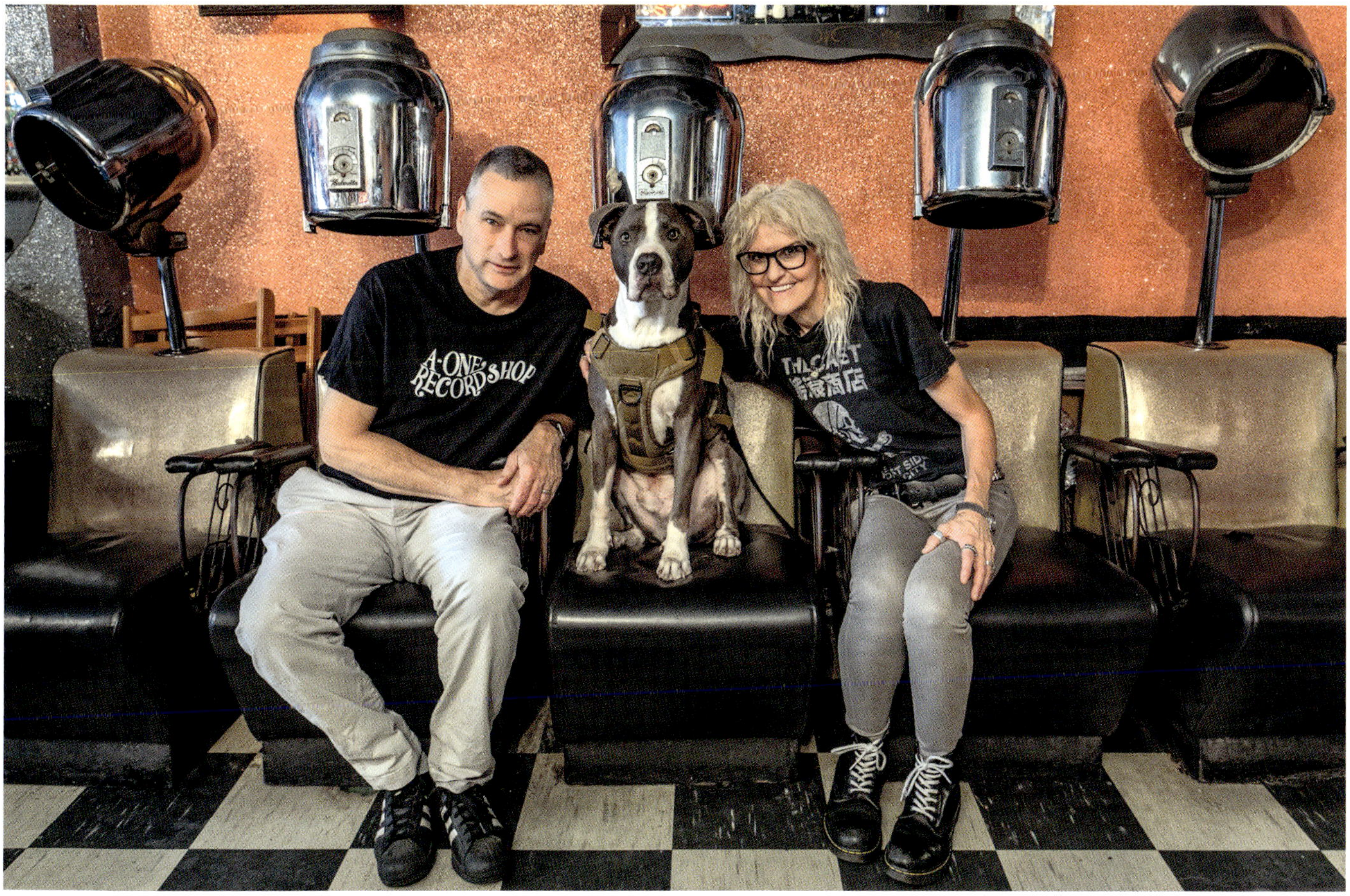

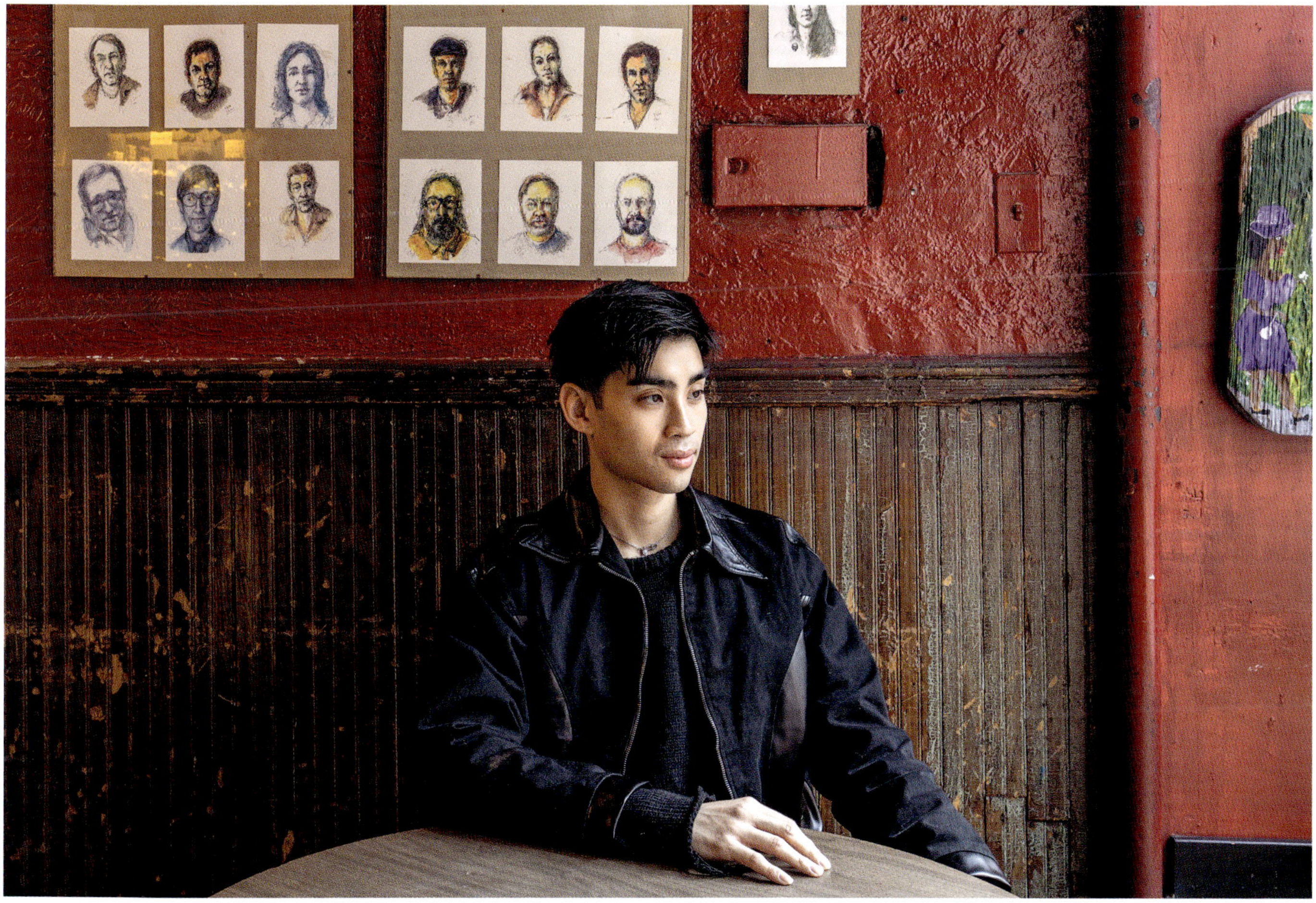